A history of English prison administration

A history of English prison administration

Volume I 1750-1877

Seán McConville

Routledge & Kegan Paul
London, Boston and Henley

First published in 1981
by Routledge & Kegan Paul Ltd
39 Store Street, London WC1E 7DD,
9 Park Street, Boston, Mass. 02108, USA, and
Broadway House, Newtown Road,
Henley-on-Thames, Oxon RG9 1EN
Set in IBM Press Roman 10pt
and printed in Great Britain by
Biddles Ltd, Guildford

British Library Cataloguing in Publication Data

McConville, Seán

A history of English prison administration.
Vol. 1: 1750-1877
1. Prison administration – England – History
I. Title
365'.068   HV9644   80-41987

ISBN 0-7100-0694-2

To the memory of
Dan and Margaret McConville

Contents

Tables

Preface

This is the first of a series of publications that draw upon material gathered in the course of research into the shaping of the prison system during the period from the middle of the eighteenth century until recent times. As a starting date, the year 1750 stands simply for mid-century, and does not allude to any particular event. During the course of the research the starting point was repeatedly pushed backwards in order better to understand the circumstances, events and institutions which are the main subject of this volume. The first three chapters are based on secondary material thus collected, and are included for the reason that they were embarked upon: a necessary background to the state of prison administration which existed in England during the latter part of the eighteenth century. In 1877 an Act was passed to nationalise the local prisons; an event of such importance in English penal history that it is appropriate to end the first volume at this point.

Originally it was intended to concentrate the research on staffing issues in the history of English prisons, but it soon became clear that such a theme could not be treated in isolation. It is impossible satisfactorily to discuss the recruitment, roles and work of staff without paying due attention to the institutions within which they were employed, and to the nature of the duties which they performed. These considerations necessitate an analysis of several aspects of penal policy and administration. One must, for example, examine not only the penal régimes of the various establishments, but also the penal, social and administrative thought upon which the régimes were based. Similarly, one cannot enter into an historical analysis of the administration of prisons without collecting information on certain other public institutions. The practice of fee-taking and the entrepreneurial basis of prison management can only properly be evaluated in the context of the system of public administration then prevailing, which was substantially maintained by fee income. The widespread squalor, starvation and disease of eighteenth-century prisons demand consideration of the dominant penal ideology of maximum general deterrence, and the constitutional doctrine which established a high level of autonomy in local government, and the virtual exclusion of central government from social and penal policy making. It must be acknowledged that by modern standards certain sensibilities were markedly absent in the eighteenth century, but one must go to beyond such an obvious statement, to discover why penal objectives and methods, now so widely considered barbarous and degrading, were viewed with equanimity or even hearty approval by men and women, many of whose other opinions were framed in accordance with high ethical and humanitarian values. But the desire to provide as full an account as possible of the philosophical and institutional context of prison history should not allow the subject of staffing to be neglected, or to be considered unfruitful. It is remarkable how many works dealing with penal and social policy confine themselves to the philosophy, crises and compromises behind new legislation or administrative change, and pass over, with only the most cursory examination, the capacities and reaction of those whose duty it is to apply the new dispensation; despite the fact that time and again instances emerge where the practical problems of management and the exigencies of staffing have substantially altered policy.

There is, therefore, no single theme to this study. Rather, it is an attempt to substantiate the contention that a proper approach to the history of imprisonment in England requires close examination of the various reciprocal relationships between government, criminal and penal policy, prison administration and staffing. Clearly, changes in penal thought and policy had an effect upon administrative structures, management and staff, but the full story of those changes was never simple nor one-sided. Innovations in policy and administration, in the course of solving problems and removing what had come to be unacceptable conditions or abuses, or of achieving new objectives, frequently created or brought to light fresh difficulties, which demanded reconsideration, and not infrequently introduced different categories and types of people into the administration, management and staff of prisons. The fresh interests, values and expectations thus circulating often modified penal ideas and their practical application. Hence the special attention paid here to the duties, standing and influence of gaolers, keepers, governors and higher administrative officials, reflects the key part they played in the changing position of prisons in the life of the country.

It has been claimed that 'what we *don't* know about British penal history is even now much more impressive than what we do know — there are, indeed, few more under-researched aspects of modern British social history . . .'.[1] Recent publications have given cause to revise this statement[2] but it still remains true that the English penal histories so far written have been poorly stocked with material on which to base more specialised studies. Had general prison histories paying greater attention to detail been available, this study could have extended over a greater span of time, and might have been organised differently. Such ambitions have been constrained, however, by the need to discover the facts about many important issues and institutions.

The unsatisfactory state of English penal history is a matter not only of scope, but of the writer's attitude. It is understandable, but somewhat unfortunate, that so much of the history of the penal system in general, and prisons in particular, has been written by those engaged in administration or in campaigns of reform. Thus, although the Webbs' contribution to the history of English prisons is pre-eminent in its range, thoroughness and succinctness, the moving spirit of their labour was a zeal for reform which absorbed them to the exclusion of many other important matters. The role of religious and political ideas in the development of policy, and the changing relationships between the penal system and its broader setting, receive a disproportionately small amount of attention and, somewhat surprisingly in a work so devoted to the analysis of administration, the subject of staffing is also rather neglected. Almost invariably, administrators and reformers as historians are compelled by their interest and objectives to adopt a 'progressive' perspective. Butterfield's well-known remarks on the whig interpretation of history are particularly appropriate to most historical studies of the English penal systems,[3] and Kitson Clark's label, 'history without background' may not unfairly be applied to many studies with a penal theme. Administrators and reformers adopt the simplifying whig

---

1 Noel McLachlan, 'Penal Reform and Penal History', in Louis Blom-Cooper (ed.), *Progress in Penal Reform*, p. 2.
2 Some excellent studies of local prisons have been published and work on various national developments is now being undertaken. Michael Ignatieff's book on the early English penitentiaries, *A Just Measure of Pain*, deserves special mention.
3 'The theory that is behind the whig interpretation – the theory that we study the past for the sake of the present – is one that is really introduced for the purpose of facilitating the abridgement of history; and its effect is to provide us with a handy rule of thumb by which we can easily discover what is important 'from our point of view'. . . . The theory is important because it provides us in the long run with a path through the complexity of history; it really gives us a short cut through the maze of interactions by which the past was turned into the present; it helps us to circumvent the real problem of historical study. If we can exclude certain things on the ground that they have no direct bearing on the present, we have removed the most troublesome elements in the complexity and the crooked is made straight' (Herbert Butterfield, *The Whig Interpretation of History*, pp. 25-6).

perspective because they wish to establish origins, trace policy campaigns and construct hagiographies, in their endeavours to formulate new ideas and relate existing practices and structures to what has gone before. Moreover, penal history is prone to oversimplification and demands cautious handling for another reason, namely that a strong political or emotional charge attaches to any consideration of crime and punishment and,

> Historians with strong feelings often tend to forget that the people they dislike were possibly victims of incapacity and ignorance and ascribe their actions too consistently to simple inhumanity and greed. Accusations on such counts are of course not easy to answer when little direct evidence survives about a man's thoughts, which therefore must be supplied by supposition.[4]

Since much use has been made of official publications, particularly the reports of Parliamentary Committees and Royal Commissions, and various annual reports, some observations on the nature of this material may not be out of place. The Webbs, greatly experienced in the workings of committees of inquiry and in the use to be made of their findings, were outspoken in their judgment of the unreliability of much oral evidence, and were very sceptical about the soundness and representativeness of a great deal of the information so gathered.[5]

Yet there are good reasons for drawing upon the work of such inquiries. First, as the Webbs themselves acknowledge, these committees brought together a plentiful supply of interesting contemporary documents.[6] Second, many scholars would discount some of the stress that the Webbs place on 'the truth' and 'facts'; 'fact' and 'truth' as

---

4   G. Kitson Clark, *The Making of Victorian England*, p. 12.
5   'All the conditions usually present in the taking of evidence by official committees and commissions of enquiry are adverse to the extraction of the truth. The majority of the members of these bodies are neither expert lawyers acquainted with the laws of evidence nor practised social investigators versed in the difficult art of interviewing. . . . The selection of witnesses leaves much to be desired, as this is usually decided by the chairman and secretary, neither of them trained for the task, supplemented by stray suggestions from such members as are interested in bringing forward a particular set of facts or point of view. . . . There . . . is no verification . . . the great mass of oral 'evidence' given before committees of enquiry relates to opinions on general questions, and not to actual occurrences, whilst even the modicum of fact given in evidence is not checked or verified by other enquiries' (S. and B. Webb, *Methods of Social Study*, pp. 152-5, *passim*).
6   'Perhaps the most useful of all the services rendered to sociology by these official enquiries is the collection of contemporary documents that they usually make, and sometimes publish, of contemporary documents not otherwise accessible, to the student. Taken as a whole the massive array of British blue-books stands pre-eminent as a source of information about contemporary public opinion . . .' (*ibid.*, p. 156).

applied to social life and institutions are relative terms, modified by the perceptions of observers and methods of collection and presentation of information. Eighteenth- and nineteenth-century committees of inquiry may nowadays seem to be naïve and misguided in their methods of data collection, yet sophistication of technique, it may be argued, has complicated evaluation without advancing us closer to the Webbs' goal of absolutely objective knowledge. As regards the present study, reports and minutes of evidence have been used to investigate attitudes and values as well as to ascertain 'facts', and statements of 'fact' have been checked wherever possible against information in other documents and publications.

The veracity of officially published annual reports may similarly be questioned, since most of them have been subjected to judicious editing, and manuscripts have occasionally revealed instances of explicit agreement between committee members or other officials to omit from publication references to sensitive or politically embarrassing issues. Deliberate omissions are often highly significant and it has fortunately been possible in this way to pinpoint the exact nature of some censored material.

With the intention of providing some balance to the views and concerns of those engaged in central government affairs, several local authority archives were searched. These were selected mainly because of their connections with important aspects of prison history, but also, in some cases, in order to secure a measure of geographical representativeness. Since interest in this material arose from, and has generally been restricted to its significance for the national picture, no attempt has been made to provide an account of the frequently important part that these prisons have played in local affairs; this is left as being more appropriate to the many essays and books dealing with their individual histories.

Acknowledgments

During the writing of the doctoral dissertation upon which a major portion of this volume is based I was supervised most ably and sympathetically by Dr R.G. Hood, whose close reading and frank criticisms of my work were of inestimable value. He has continued to give greatly valued advice, encouragement and friendship, and I happily acknowledge my considerable debt to him. I am grateful to others who were kind enough to comment upon various drafts of the work, including Miss C.B.A. Behrens, Professor Nigel Walker, Professor Sir Rupert Cross and Dr Louis Blom-Cooper. Miss Isobel Gawler, now of Edinburgh University's Department of Criminology, took endless pains in helping me to avoid obscurities, inaccuracies and poor taste in my style of presentation. I hope that she will add my sincere thanks to those she has received from so many scholars over the years. All errors and defects which may be found in the work are entirely my responsibility, and are the more to be regretted because of the expert advice and assistance I have been given.

As the research was nearing completion I was assisted in abstracting, tracing sources, compiling tables and many other tedious but vital tasks by Mr R.H. Sang, Miss L. Gelsthorpe and Miss J. Draper. A number of librarians have been particularly helpful, including Mr M. Wright and Miss R. Perry (past librarians of the Radzinowicz Library at Cambridge), Miss C. Horwill of the University of Sussex Library, and the staff of the Home Office and Prison Staff College libraries.

A substantial part of the work was supported by a Social Science Research Council Studentship. More recently, I have received financial and other assistance from the University of Sussex, where I am particularly indebted to Mr A. McAllister and his colleagues in the Administration, and to Mr J.E. Simmonds. My interest in penology and organisational and staffing matters was kindled by members of the University of Bath, notably Mrs K. Lyon, Professor S. Cotgrove, Mrs

N. Burton, Mr T. Nichols, and Dr L. Palmier. Although the focus and style of my research have changed greatly with time, I shall always consider myself fortunate to have embarked upon an academic career under the guidance of such sympathetic and enthusiastic teachers. From Professor N. Jepson of the University of Leeds I have received over the years that kindness of manner and generosity with ideas that have made him widely and affectionately known to those who study the English prison system, and who work in it.

My difficulties, especially in the first years, were substantially eased by the superb facilities of the University of Cambridge Institute of Criminology. With countless other students of criminology and penal policy I owe much to the vision and energy of the Institute's founder, Professor Sir Leon Radzinowicz. My time at Cambridge was enriched by membership of Clare Hall and by the friendly support of the President, Sir Brian Pippard, and many Fellows of the College.

Permission to cite from items in their archives has kindly been given by the following repositories: Bedfordshire County Record Office, the Bodleian Library, the British Library, the British Library of Political and Economic Science, Cambridgeshire County Record Office, the University of Durham Library, East Sussex County Record Office, Essex Record Office, Gloucestershire Record Office, Hertfordshire Record Office, and the Public Record Office. Sir John Ruggles-Brise, Lady Alastair Graham, Mr A.W. Pullan and the late Lady Frances Paterson gave me family information and papers which helped greatly to improve my understanding of the history of English prisons. I have also been assisted with material and ideas by several past and present members of the staff of the Prison Department and Home Office, including Colonel J.S. Haywood, Mr D. Fairn, Mr A. Roberton and the late Mr R.C. Bradley.

For their excellent typing, and much tested patience with my innumerable textual changes, I am grateful to Miss M. Guy, Miss J. Annis, Miss V. Annis and Miss M. Cooper. Miss J. Greenfield typed the whole of the final draft with intelligence and fortitude, and to an excellent standard.

This work has been in progress for almost ten years, during which time I have received all kinds of assistance from many more people than I am able to list in a short acknowledgment. My gratitude to them is not a whit the less sincere because they go unnamed.

Seán McConville
University of Sussex

Abbreviations

DNB   Dictionary of National Biography
JHC   Journals of the House of Commons
PP   Parliamentary Papers
PRO   Public Record Office
RC   Royal Commission
RCGP   Report of the Committee of the General Penitentiary
RDCP   Report of the directors of convict prisons
RR   Rules and regulations
RRGP   Rules and regulations for the government of convict prisons
SC   Select committee

1 Imprisonment prior to the eighteenth century: the gaols

The use of imprisonment

According to Finberg, gaols were part of the systems of criminal justice in England as early as the ninth century.[1] Pugh notes that by the accession of Henry III there were only five counties for which no gaol is known to have existed.[2] Some of these gaols were purpose-built (such as the Fleet) but more often they were to be found within the protective walls of castles and towns.[3] Various social and legal changes increased the number of prisons and their importance as a means of maintaining order.[4]

Pugh argues that in medieval England imprisonment had three main uses: it provided for the safe custody of suspects or those awaiting sentence or execution of sentence; it provided for the coercion of debtors or the contumacious; and it was a punishment in itself. These he calls the custodial, coercive and penal aspects of medieval imprisonment.

Two of these functions are uncontroversial. All students of penal history agree that imprisonment was used custodially and coercively. The latter function was greatly expanded in the mid-fourteenth century when a statute (25 Edw. III, St. V, c. 17) placed all creditors on the same footing as the Crown, by enabling them to use imprisonment to secure payment of debts.[5]

---

1 H.P.R. Finberg, *The Formation of England*, p. 139.
2 R.B. Pugh, *Imprisonment in Medieval England*, pp. 59, 385.
3 Leslie Fairweather, 'The Evolution of the Prison', in United Nations Social Defence Research Institute, *Prison Architecture*, p. 14.
4 By the later Middle Ages, says Bellamy, prisons were 'an important instrument in the maintenance of public order'. (See J. Bellamy, *Crime and Public Order in England in the Later Middle Ages*, pp. 162-4, *passim*.)

5   From this statute sprang all the imprisonings for debt, all the prisons or debtors' wards, and all the lamentations which they brought in their train....

Some commentators, however, have been reluctant to accept that imprisonment was used punitively in medieval times,[6] but there is now abundant confirming evidence and it is clear that this type of imprisonment increased greatly from the thirteenth century. Pugh shows that even before the Conquest prisons were being used as a form of punishment, and that in later times they were so employed for a wide range of non-felonious offences.[7] Margery Bassett found instances of punitive imprisonment scattered through the City records 'too numerous to cite', including cases where this penalty had been imposed for stealing, striking a public official and molesting foreigners.[8] She argued that whilst the primary objectives of medieval prisons were custodial or coercive

> the opportunity of using them as places of punishment was not overlooked entirely. Breaches of the peace, disregard for the many ordinances governing life and trade within the city, petty crimes,

---

No piece of fourteenth-century legislation . . . played a more important part in the history of imprisonment. . . (Pugh, *op. cit.*, p. 46).

6 See Lionel Fox's *The English Prison and Borstal Systems*. Clifford Dobb (thesis: 'Life and Conditions in London Prisons, 1553-1643', p. 7) seems to share Fox's view that punitive imprisonment is mainly a modern practice. He repeats this elsewhere:

> Men and women were imprisoned for many reasons of which criminal charges covered only a part of the whole. In very few cases are there any signs that a term of imprisonment was regarded as a punishment as in later times. Prisons were thought of simply as places where persons were kept in safe custody because it was considered too dangerous to leave them at large (Clifford Dobb, 'London's Prisons', in A. Nicoll (ed.), *Shakespeare in His Own Age*, p. 90).

Judges is more dogmatic:

> Prisons were absolutely necessary for the safe custody of accused persons awaiting trial. For the fulfilment of any other purpose they could only be regarded as expensive luxuries. A man or woman once convicted of crime was either unfitted to live or fit to be at large. Why institute penal servitude when the county jails were already full to overcrowding and, moreover, ravaged with pestilence? And so . . . we find imprisonment rarely mentioned as a punishment until quite modern times. It was too exotic and gruesomely a torment even for the hardened stomach of the Elizabethan Age to tolerate (A.V. Judges, *The Elizabethan Underworld*, p. lxii).

7 There was . . . a great deal of penal imprisonment for every type of fraud, contempt, disobedience to authority, failure in public duty, and petty crime . . . and from Edward I's opening years imprisonment of whatever type came increasingly to rest upon statute or municipal regulation (Pugh, *op. cit.*, p. 386).

See also A.D. Smith, *Women in Prison*, p. 58, and E.J. Burford, *In the Clink*, pp. 28-9.

8 Margery Bassett, 'Newgate Prison in the Middle Ages', p. 233, n. 3.

2

and disrespect for the governing body were among the misdeeds sometimes punished by imprisonment. The terms ranged from a few days to a year and a day.[9]

Because of the spread of municipal imprisonment,[10] specific statute provision, the greater use of the action of trespass and the extension of 'benefit of clergy' in cases of felony,[11] numerous offenders were imprisoned as a punishment — sometimes with a fine or a flogging added for good measure.

But although it is analytically helpful to draw distinctions between the three types of imprisonment it is probable that the practical administrative consequences of the use of prisons for these different purposes were trifling. It is true that in some of the larger prisons, from at least the fifteenth century, efforts were made to separate the felonious — charged and convicted — from other prisoners,[12] but classification was generally non-penal in nature.[13] Persons punitively

9 *Ibid.*, p. 233.
10 The London Tun (a lockup) was used for vagrants, curfew violaters, the disorderly and morally defective — pimps, whores and adulterers.

> It was no doubt mainly to accommodate such minor delinquents that urban prisons multiplied and the crown gave the towns themselves the right to keep prisons not only for the 'custody' but for the 'correction' or punishment of such persons (Pugh, *op. cit.*, pp. 42-4, *passim*).

11 'Benefit of clergy' was the means whereby 'clerks' (originally those in holy orders) could avoid the mandatory death sentence for felony. By reading the 'neck verse' (the first verse of the fifty-first Psalm: 'Have mercy on me, O God, According to Thy steadfast love; according to Thy abundant mercy blot out my transgressions'), the prisoner established his clerical status. Then 'The successful "cleric" was branded on his hand to prevent his enjoying the privilege twice, and he might be gaoled for one year. . . ' (E.W. Ives, 'The Law and the Lawyers', in A. Nicoll, *op. cit.*, p. 82). By Tudor times the whole procedure was reduced to farce by prior coaching and memorisation of the relevant verse. I have been unable to discover if the loophole was as widely used before the introduction of the vernacular Bible (see Judges, *op. cit.*, p. 160, n. 15). But any difficulties posed by the Latin Bible in pre-Reformation England were probably counterbalanced by the great number of genuine clerics (those in holy orders ranging from the minor to the highest). These included one of the most undisciplined sections of medieval society — what Trevelyan has described as 'The army of unbeneficed priests, deacons and clerks in holy orders who were scattered about the country in every variety of employment . . . many drifted about from one job to another, forming lazy and criminal habits that made them in the end "unemployable" for any good purpose' (G.M. Trevelyan, *English Social History*, p. 51; see also S.T. Bindoff, *Tudor England*, p. 77). For different reasons, then, extensive use was made of 'benefit of clergy' prior to and after the Reformation, with a consequent recourse to sentences of punitive imprisonment.

12 Bassett, *op. cit.*, p. 240.
13 Thus Babington notes that 'During the forty-five year reign of Elizabeth I Newgate was used increasingly as a state prison. Felons and debtors were still

3

imprisoned could expect the same experience as those from similar social backgrounds held for custodial or coercive reasons. As punishment, secular imprisonment was retributive and deterrent – and it is in this sense alone that it should be understood. When imposing this penalty the sentencer knew that he was sending the wrongdoer to an unpleasant, expensive and dangerous place. A theory of reformative punishment requires the formulation of ideas about the causes of crime and other transgressions. This did not occur in medieval thought.[14] Even to the Church, with its total concern with man's spiritual life, crime was not a phenomenon requiring explanation: it was an inevitable feature of man's fallen and sinful state – of his very humanity. The retributive and deterrent approach to imprisonment persisted with respect to gaols through the seventeenth century and beyond. Babington observes of the mid-seventeenth century that 'The only penological principle . . . seems to have been that the criminal should be encouraged to feel a proper sense of repentance for his crime and a stoical resignation regarding his punishment'.[15]

Viewed simply as instruments of a retributive or deterrent policy, pre-eighteenth-century gaols have far fewer defects than many reformatory and 'progressive' penal historians and commentators would have us believe. Expense, exposure to epidemic disease and other ill-health, and the general social and economic inconvenience of the gaols were hardships of a kind to drive home the lesson and hence, to a certain extent, were desirable.[16]

Not only were conditions suited to the several objectives the gaols served, but when consideration is given to the standard of living in pre-industrial society – never far from a state of bare subsistence and incipient personal disaster for the mass of the population – the virtual

---

sent there, but they shared the gaol with those imprisoned for their religious or political beliefs, or for their alleged treasonable activities (*The English Bastille*, p. 43).

---

14 Bellamy argues that 'Medieval man had little curiosity about causation of crime, although he was aware of the importance of opportunity. Revenge was understood, but not much else' (*op. cit.*, p. 31).

15 Babington, *op. cit.*, p. 53.

16 'In some cases, when a person was sentenced to only a few days' imprisonment, it seems likely that the chief penalty involved was the payment of numerous fees and charges. . . . On Friday 16th March 1593, the Privy Council committed one John Ward to the Fleet, "till Sondaie next in the mornynge before prayers," and one Richard Ironside to the Marshalsea "Till Mondaie next in the morning" ' (Dobb, 'Life and Conditions', p. 14).

The overlapping in functions and the basic usefulness of confinement as duress was also apparent in the case of State prisoners. Families of imprisoned gentry or nobles who had to bear the heavy expense of gaolers' carefully graduated charges were thereby kept in financial subjugation during the period of the imprisonment (*ibid.*).

impossibility of using these prisons in any other way becomes apparent.

The criterion for success in gaol management was not, therefore, the reform of criminal offenders, or even the financial sobering of reckless debtors. It was, quite simply, the ability of the gaol to prevent escapes: to hold suspects and those on remand until the courts required them; to hold debtors and rebels until they paid up or purged their offence, and those under punishment until the sentence of the court expired. One medieval statute ordained that the act of breaking prison was in itself a felony, whilst the keeper of a prison who had neglected or corruptly overlooked this most fundamental duty incurred penalties ranging from fining and dismissal from office to a felon's death.[17] The regulation of prisons consisted, therefore, in one essential: ensuring that the keeper and his staff devoted themselves to the maintenance of custody. From time to time, as will be seen, there were attempts to stiffen control; to prevent, for example, 'excessive' brutality, corruption or extortion. But the *sine qua non* of success for a gaoler was security of bolts and bars.

Administration

Pre-eighteenth-century gaols were administered by several different types of authority, the two most important (numerically) being the counties and municipalities. There were in addition, however, franchise gaols, national prisons and ecclesiastical and other special prisons. Each of these types had its distinctive form of ownership and control.

County gaols

These were normally in the charge of the sheriff, and at Clarendon in 1166 it was enacted that sheriffs should provide gaols for counties hitherto without them. The subsequent administrative history of these prisons, until relatively recent times, is marked by an erosion of the powers of the sheriffs and their assumption by the justices of the peace.

The forerunner of the justice of the peace was an official first appointed during the Civil War of 1263-5, with the title of conservator

17 See Pugh, *op. cit.*, Chapter 11 generally. Moreover, 'If corruption entered in and the "keeper" was found to have connived at the escape, he was to be indicted for felony and if convicted was to suffer a felon's death' (p. 233). This thirteenth-century severity appears to have lapsed, however. In 1696 the then keeper of Newgate, one James Fell, was convicted under precisely such circumstances and, as Babington reports, 'The offence does not seem to have been considered as especially grave for the sentence of the court was postponed indefinitely and Fell was allowed to retain the keepership' (*ibid.*, p. 65). Although, as far as I have been able to trace, no such instances of the death penalty appear in the literature, there are numerous examples of fining, dismissal from office and imprisonment.

or keeper of the peace. Until 1329 the conservators had powers only to record breaches of the peace, but from that date — at first intermittently, and then regularly — they and their successors, the justices of the peace, were empowered to try felonies and trespasses.[18] They were appointed and held office entirely at the pleasure of the Crown; and their duties and authority expanded from the purely legal province at their innovation in the fourteenth century, to an extensive policing and administrative role in local government,[19] as they 'successfully grasped at every shred of power let slip by the sheriff'.[20]

An Act of Henry VIII extended the duties of the justices to the gaols[21] and provided that in most counties justices were to levy a rate out of which to construct new gaols; this task completed, gaol administration would be carried on by the sheriffs. This Act was renewed several times, finally lapsing after about fifty years. Pugh thinks that this period of administrative intervention by the justices and subsequent lapsing of the legislation created great uncertainty about the division of administrative responsibilities;[22] by the seventeenth century, however, the justices had generally taken the responsibility for gaol maintenance out of the sheriffs' hands, the shift in arrangements being probably due to the instructions of the Privy Council which, under the Tudors and Stuarts, placed the greater part of the burden of local government firmly on the justices.[23]

Municipal prisons

By the reign of Henry VIII most municipalities had provided themselves with gaols and lockups to serve their own courts. Prisons were often a part of the town charter, but were also established without this authority.[24]

---

18 Bellamy, *op. cit.*, pp. 94-5.
19 W. Eric Jackson, *Local Government in England and Wales*, p. 29.
20 William O. Hart and J.F. Garner, *Hart's Introduction to the Law of Local Government*, pp. 13-14.
21 23 Hen. VIII, c.2.
22 Pugh, *op. cit.*, p. 346.
23 'In all the social experiments of the Tudors and early Stuarts it was the justices who bore the burden and heat of the day. Two hundred and ninety-three statutes were passed previous to 1603 bearing upon the duties of these humble magistrates, and the parliament of Elizabeth had contributed a total of seventy-eight . . .' (Judges, *op. cit.*, p. xiiv).
   Trevelyan describes the JPs of the time as 'Elizabeth's maids of all work', and points out that if they slacked in the performance of their manifold duties 'the vigilant eye of the Privy Council was upon them, and its long arm was soon extended'. 'The judicial, political, economic and administrative powers of the Justices of the Peace were so various', he concludes, 'and taken together so important that the J.P.s became the most influential class of men in England' (*op. cit.*, pp. 170-1, *passim*).
24 Pugh, *op. cit.*, pp. 98-100.

Within the towns the exact division of labour in the running of the gaols between the mayor, corporation, town justices and sheriffs varied greatly. In London, for instance, the sheriffs bore the primary responsibility under the supervision of the Court of Aldermen, who were, in turn, accountable to the Common Council — the highest legislative body of the City.[25] In early years the London sheriffs had great latitude in the discharge of their custodial duties and were apparently free to decide whether they kept prisoners in their own houses, in their compters or in the common gaol.[26]

Franchise and other prisons

Franchise prisons were held by ecclesiastical and secular lords and served a group of estates, a hundred, a manor or even a soke or liberty within a town, and varied in capacity from a single room in a manor house to a specially constructed part of a monastery. Whereas in medieval England they were so numerous as to be familiar to everyone, ownership came to be restricted to those who had a royal grant or who allowed their periodical delivery.[27] So naturally accepted was this form of gaol-holding that a number of these prisons persisted into the second half of the nineteenth century.

In medieval times there was not what today would be called a national prison system — a group of prisons financed and administered directly by a department of state. Several establishments, however, were used for national purposes by government and the higher judiciary; of these, Newgate was recognised as the leading criminal prison in the kingdom and, although the property of the City, on the instructions of the Crown, Privy Council or superior courts, it accommodated prisoners from different parts of the country, including state prisoners, religious prisoners and notorious criminals and debtors.[28] The Fleet, probably the oldest prison in the country, originally held prisoners of all kinds, but with the increased usage of Newgate and the Marshalsea it latterly became the 'recognized prison for the court of common pleas, the chancery, the star chamber, and for those held by the exchequer for debts to the King'.[29] The Marshalsea and the Tower were even more closely connected with the Crown. Although the latter was used in

---

25 Babington, *op. cit.*, p. 17.
26 Bassett, *op. cit.*, p. 234.
27 Pugh, *op. cit.*, p. 97.
28 Babington, *op. cit.*, p. 43.
29 Bassett, 'The Fleet Prison in the Middle Ages', p. 383. The Fleet had a special relationship with the Crown because it was 'the King's owne proper prison next in trust to his Tower of London, and as that in his fort in the East, soe was this one in the west of the citty and chamber of his kingdome' (The Camden Society, *Economy of the Fleet*, p. 23).

later times almost exclusively for state prisoners, in the thirteenth century it was used also for common felons.[30] The Clink, originally the bishop of Winchester's prison for petty offenders, whores and their associates, was used in Elizabeth's reign to accommodate recusants.[31] The King's Bench seems to have originated as a form of custody and acquired an identity and physical location separate from the Marshalsea of the Royal Household only from the fifteenth century. Appointments to the administration of the Fleet, Marshalsea and Tower were made either directly or indirectly by the Crown.

Certain forest and mining areas had special courts served by their own prisons. The stannaries (tin-mining districts), for example, were granted prison charters in the early fourteenth century.[32]

In addition to these secular prisons the Church in maintaining her own system of justice owned prisons that came under the authority of bishops and episcopal abbots. They might be separate establishments, or accommodated in part of a secular franchise prison held by the bishop or abbot in his lay capacity. The use of the plea 'benefit of clergy' increased the demand for this type of prison which continued to exist until the readjustments between secular and sacred authority of the sixteenth century.[33] Special prisons for academic clerks were provided in the two university towns and maintained at the expense of the lay authorities for university use.[34]

Finance

Expenditure on prisons was in keeping with their limited custodial purposes and what was general practice in public administration until fairly recent times. Apart from the provision of buildings and intermittent structural maintenance, prisons were expected to be self-supporting, just as sheriffs, coroners and justices and their various clerks and subordinate officials were expected to obtain their incomes from fees.[35] As the number of office-holders in medieval and Tudor society was great,[36] and little or no means existed of paying them from centrally gathered revenues, there can be no grounds for branding

---

30 Pugh, *op. cit.*, p. 123.
31 Burford, *op. cit.*, Ch. 8.
32 Pugh, *op. cit.*, pp. 132-3.
33 *Ibid.*, pp. 136-7.
34 *Ibid.*, pp. 137-9.
35 Bellamy is uncertain whether the justices were initially paid by the Crown, but thinks that from the outset they were allowed to retain a proportion of any fines levied. In the reign of Richard II regular payment of 4s. per day was made, up to a maximum of twelve days each year (*op. cit.*, p. 97).
36 Even into the reign of the early Stuarts English counties and villages retained elements of communal self-government, and under the control of squire and justice there existed a wide range of offices. Freeholders took part in the

prison finance as any more 'corrupt' than that of other public institutions of the time.

Pugh has been able to identify some prisons where gaolers were paid a weekly wage, though he feels that this method was not a means of providing gaolers with a livelihood: 'Much more important sources of revenue than payments at the Exchequer or by the hands of sheriffs were the various fees which gaolers collected from their prisoners.'[37] According to Margery Bassett, the Fleet warden was paid a shilling a day, had use of two houses and received certain rents; but this author was unable to discover any reference to the Newgate keeper's salary at all. At both prisons the warden and keeper could be expected to obtain a substantial income from fees and other perquisites.[38]

Fees were levied on entrance and on discharge and on every possible turn of event between. In the Fleet, the most expensive prison in the kingdom, charges from the mid to the late sixteenth century were on a sliding scale, applied according to the social rank of the prisoner, and ranging from a £10 entry fee for an archbishop, duke or duchess down to 13s. 4d. for a yeoman and nothing for a poor man; discharge fees were more moderate, at most £3 5s., at least 7s. 4d. In addition there was a host of underlings — clerks, porters, turnkeys and chamberlains — with their own demands for services rendered; these were also graduated in scale.[39] Fees at City prisons were not as high as those at the Fleet: taken together the fees payable for committal to one of the Counters amounted to about 10s.[40]

Gaolers also charged to ease custody, a procedure which they justified by arguing that an easement increased the possibility of escape

---

proceedings of the county court; the manorial court leet was attended by the peasantry who participated fully. And, as Trevelyan notes,

> in every English village there were various humble offices — such as constable, overseer of the poor, headborough, ale-conner, road-repairer, churchwarden, sidesman and innumerable other small public posts — which the common people filled, either by election or rotation (op. cit., p. 214).

---

37 Pugh, op. cit., p. 166. And from the late thirteenth century, he says, 'examples of fee paying are too common to be worth enumerating. Indeed the system of fee paying expanded, rather than contracted, and remained in full vigour until in the late eighteenth century it came under the censure of Howard'. The payment of fees by prisoners can be traced back as far as the Mercian Kingdom (AD c.650-800) (Burford, op. cit., p. 48).

38 Bassett, 'The Fleet Prison in the Middle Ages', p. 384, and 'Newgate Prison in the Middle Ages', p. 246. See also C.T. Clay, 'The Keepership of the Old Palace of Westminster', pp. 5 and 14.

39 Dobb, 'London's Prisons', p. 94. Bassett gives slightly different figures which ranged from £13.5s.0d. to 19s. for entrance fees ('The Fleet Prison in the Middle Ages', p. 395). In the early fourteenth century a uniform admission fee of 2s. 4d. was levied (Clay, op. cit., p. 14).

40 Dobb, 'London's Prisons', p. 95.

and, therefore, exposed them to monetary and other risks as gaolers. Exemption from, or lighter, fetters or irons could be purchased,[41] as could removal from a close to a more spacious part of the prison. At the Fleet, Ludgate, the Counters, and some other prisons, easement of custody went as far as 'going abroad' — a privilege accorded to debtors at a price of 4*d*. per half day; an extra 6*d*. bought the services of the accompanying *baston*.[42] So attractive was this privilege that, despite its very high charges, some prisoners had themselves removed to the Fleet on the pretext that they were Crown debtors.

These expenses overlapped with another type — the purchase of goods and services from the keeper. At the Fleet rent had to be paid according to rank: gentry had separate rooms by paying 2*s*. 4*d*. weekly, which included the use of a parlour; prisoners of lower degree used the common hall and paid 1*s*. 2*d*. weekly to share a bed in one of the wards; the destitute received nothing but the barest of accommodation.[43] Board at Fleet varied in a similar manner from £3. 6*s*. 8*d*. to 6*s*. But in City prisons charges were much more modest; board and lodgings together cost gentlemen only 3*s*. a week and yeomen 2*s*.[44] Alehouses on the premises run by the keepers provided prisoners with all daily necessities, bedding, fuel, cooking utensils, food and even, sometimes, water, as well as goods for recreation and pleasure. In fact, prisons were profit-making concerns, and the prisoners were the 'customers' who had to yield a steady living to those who risked capital and life within the walls. By Shakespeare's time there was a small army of fee-charging officials making substantial profits as agents in the various sectors of civil and criminal justice. From writ-serving and arrest to final release, few opportunities were missed to impose a charge or extract a gratuity. Generous, but carefully calculated credit was granted, for there could be no departure until all charges were paid — even, it was said, on behalf of the dead.[45]

In all prisons of the medieval and Tudor period there were excellent

---

41 Dobb says that except at Newgate this was a formality in the London prisons. Ironing fees were therefore based on a fiction. Many keepers blamed the ruinous state of the prison buildings for the use or threatened use of irons.

42 Bassett, 'The Fleet Prison in the Middle Ages', p. 397.

43 *Ibid*., p. 395.

44 *Ibid*., p. 396.

45 William Fennor, who had been imprisoned in the Counters, left a bitter account of his squeezing and grasping gaolers. They went so far, he said, as to take fees from the dead and 'scarce let the coffin go out of their gates before his friends hath paid his fees'. But this may have been an apocryphal story, for he goes on, 'Therefore, if these reports be true, it is most abominable for them to act, and most lamentable to hear' (William Fennor, *The Counters' Commonwealth*, 1617, republished in Judges, *op. cit*., p. 477). Sheehan, however, writes of 'several instances' of keepers hiding corpses to force relatives or friends to settle the account of the deceased (Wayne Joseph Sheehan, thesis: 'The London Prison System, 1666-1795', p. 345).

opportunities for extortion. Ironing, for example, need not have actually been undertaken; prisoners would pay almost as willingly upon the threat and sight of some monstrous device. Similarly with accommodation, there are several accounts of prisoners being shown into dank, repulsive dungeons as a prelude to their being offered and paying for more acceptable lodging. Even the highly born were to a large extent at the mercy of their captors; if they were being held for political or religious reasons, they would have already lost some influence and were unlikely to receive the sympathy of the powerful who had placed them in such irksome captivity. All students of penal history agree that complaints of extortion and immoderate charges were ubiquitous and persistent.[46] Moreover, the boundary between customary and extortionate practice would have been difficult to draw. There were, unfortunately, cases of flagrant brutality and torture, but gaolers did not need thus to expose themselves to public censure in order to wring optimum revenue from their captives.

So necessary was a good and constant flow of prisoners that some gaolers felt it improvident to trust in the normal workings of the law. Instead, they had themselves placed on commissions of the peace and indicted quite innocent parties who between committal and release paid numerous fees and charges. Other gaolers compelled prisoners to approve (i.e. accuse) innocent and honest prisoners.[47] So widespread was this practice that it was necessary for an Act to be introduced in 1327 directing the King's justices to discover which sheriffs and gaolers had compelled prisoners to become approvers.[48]

Staffing

In theory all gaols were the King's but in practice, of course, the gaol-holder appointed staff. The county gaols were in the charge of the sheriffs, who bore ultimate custodial responsibility. The Crown could impose a penalty on them in the event of escapes, and creditors could

46 Bassett, 'Newgate Prison in the Middle Ages', p. 246; Babington, *op. cit.*, p. 53; Pugh, *op. cit.*, p. 177.
47 'Gaolers, it seems, were less interested in the maintenance of law and order than in extorting money from those whom the approvers desperately, yet often falsely, appealed. Approvers frequently got the names of their appellees and details of their crimes from gossip in gaol' (Bellamy, *op. cit.*, p. 129).
48 *Statutes of the Realm* (1810 edn), 1, p. 233 (s. 26). See also 13 Edw. I, c.13. Similar extortion was practised by means of the Church courts. An allegation of adultery would bring the accused before these bodies, with consequent loss of time and money and the possibility of excommunication. A threat to inform could therefore extort a heavy bribe and, as Judges notes, 'It was alleged that apparitors carried about with them blank processes *Quorum nomina*, signed or unsigned, with a place ready for the victim's name' (*op. cit.*, p. 140, n. 14). Extortion seems to have been inseparable from many parts of the machinery of justice.

sue for the outstanding debts of an escaped debtor. The sheriffs or their equivalents in franchise, ecclesiastical, national or special prisons appointed working gaolers upon whose efficiency they thereby became dependent. As a result bonds of indemnification were often required from gaolers, which protected gaol-holders from the consequences of an escape.[49]

As prisons were profit-making concerns, usually requiring an initial investment, the office of keeper was usually transferable and often inheritable. In Shakespeare's time the keeperships of Ludgate, Newgate and the two Sheriffs' Counters were (like all public offices of the City) offered for sale by the incumbent or formal holder of the custody and speculatively purchased.[50] The Fleet prison was the classic example both of inheritance and transfer on purchase, being held by one family and their collaterals throughout the middle ages, for at least 428 years.[51] In 1490 the wardenship of the prison was leased at £40 a year, and in 1559 the serjeanty was sold by the last hereditary office-holder for the vast sum of £4,000, and was then leased out at £80 per annum.[52] The warden was expected to provide his own subordinate staff out of prison income, but it is probably safe to assume that even the subordinate offices were self-financing. In 1558, for example, the warden leased for a number of years a portership — a very lowly office indeed — for £20.[53]

Men paying for office naturally expected a good return. This was recognised by the municipal authorities, who sought to mitigate possible excesses of exploitation. The sheriffs, who had the authority to appoint to the City's prisons, were bound on oath not to sell keeperships as 'Gaylors buying theire offices will deal hardly with the pitifull prisoners'.[54] It was decreed, in the mid-fourteenth century, that only men of good character were to be appointed to the keepership of Newgate. The keeper himself had to swear on oath that he would not extort money from the prisoners. Repeated attempts throughout the

---

49 Bassett, 'Newgate Prison in the Middle Ages', p. 234.
50 Dobb, 'London's Prisons', p. 94. Keeperships were also sold as reversions (i.e. to be held after a certain time, or when the office next fell vacant). Sometimes several different grants were sold for the same office, and the purchasers had to wait for the necessary time until their grant matured (Wayne Joseph Sheehan, thesis: 'The London Prison System, 1666-1795', pp. 25-6).
51 Clay, *op. cit.*, p. 15.
52 Bassett, 'The Fleet Prison in the Middle Ages', p. 386. Even as late as the eighteenth and nineteenth centuries examples may be found of family connections with prisons. Eric Stockdale gives the example of the Richardson family, who for seventy years between 1711 and 1814 held the gaolership of Bedford County Gaol. Most appropriately (and profitably) the family were also keepers of the Chequers public house, which stood next door to the prison (*A Study of Bedford Prison, 1660-1877*, pp. 31-2).
53 *Ibid.*, p. 385, n. 14.
54 *Cit.* Bassett, 'Newgate Prison in the Middle Ages', p. 234.

middle ages to stop Newgate keeperships being sold show the lightness of the keepers' oaths and the difficulty of enforcing such an ordinance in self-financing prisons.[55]

Such lucrative offices were valuable patronage, and the sheriffs were often challenged by City authorities or by the Crown over the privilege of appointment. The Crown sought gaol patronage in the fourteenth and fifteenth centuries chiefly, it seems, to provide rewards or pensions for retainers. The sheriffs fought tenaciously to keep their patronage and succeeded in securing it by statute.[56] In provincial municipalities gaol patronage was contested by sheriffs, mayors and aldermen.[57]

Gaolers, in their turn, employed subordinates. These included turnkeys, porters and clerks. Turnkeys appear only as background figures in records and literature, but from all that is known it is evident that they, too, drew their income from various fees and perquisites. Their duties were locking and unlocking the various parts of the prison throughout the day, counting the prisoners at locking and unlocking, and generally being on hand to suppress fighting and riot.[58] Many subordinate staff appear to have lived on the premises (a condition of office even for the keepers of the London prisons, and their deputies).[59] In the Fleet there were special staff to accompany prisoners who had the privilege of going abroad.[60] Around 1620 the warden of the Fleet complained of the need to provide about twenty servants 'for that service onely', and that the £80 or so a year that prisoners paid him for the privilege did not cover his costs.[61] Turnkeys and other subordinates were also needed for court duties[62] and to produce prisoners for various examinations (as, quite wisely, judges and other high officials minimised for themselves the dangers attendant on prison visiting).[63]

---

55 The 'no-farming' proviso was promulgated in 1356 and again in 1421 when it was extended to all the City prisons. In 1431, in order to establish a greater degree of control and supervision, the aldermen directed that keepers were to be appointed annually — even though a suitable incumbent might be reappointed.

56 19 Hen. VII, c.10.

57 Babington, *op. cit.*, pp. 18-19.

58 There are numerous records of riots, fires and mass breakouts in medieval prisons. See, for example, Babington, *op. cit.*, pp. 55-6.

59 Dobb, 'London's Prisons', p. 93. In 1595 and 1636 Newgate keepers were dismissed for failing to live in the prison.

60 Bassett, 'The Fleet Prison in the Middle Ages', p. 397.

61 Dobb, 'London's Prisons', p. 99.

62 An enactment of 1328 provided for gaol delivery at least three times a year.

63 Before the Old Bailey was built, in 1539, the City sheriffs hired a hall for the gaol deliveries. Judges were reluctant to enter or transact business in Newgate because 'commonly prysons were theefes and other malefactours be deteigned for there offences be many tymes vysyted with syknes and by reason thereof the place ys infected and moche peryll and damygys hath chauncyd to the Justyces' (*cit*. Bassett, 'Newgate Prison in the Middle Ages', p. 344).

Clerks were a necessary part of the management of medieval prisons and kept tallies of the expenses incurred by inmates.[64] They read and recorded committal warrants and judicial and royal instructions – an important safeguard against suits for wrongful imprisonment. The gaoler, it is true, would be in court to hear sentence or other disposal or might know prisoners' escorts, but proof of the committal or release authority was most important in case of dispute, and doubtless the use of documents increased as the volume of prison business outgrew the possibilities of personal verification. Civil-law prisoners presented similar problems, as premature release could lead to an aggrieved creditor suing the gaoler; indeed, the documentation for them, especially if several creditors were involved, was probably far more complicated than for criminal or political prisoners. For these various reasons any gaol which had a substantial committal rate would need a full complement of clerks.

Religious services were provided in medieval prisons. The Church insisted on regular attendance at mass and receipt of the Sacrament, and this requirement could not easily be obstructed by the lay authorities. Priestly visits, certainly to prisoners of standing, must have been frequent. Prison chapels were provided at York in 1237, at Newgate in 1431 and at Bury in 1492. The first appointment of a prison clergyman at Newgate was in 1544, when it was provided that one of the four chaplains of St Bartholomew's Hospital would visit 'all the poor and miserable captives within the prison of Newgate, and minister unto them such ordinary service at times convenient, as is appointed by the King's Majesty's book for ordinary prayer'. The chaplain (initially called the 'Visitor of Newgate') was instructed to persuade the prisoners to return stolen property and to 'disclose all such other persons as they know living, which by robbery or murder may hurt a common weal'. 'And in all their extremes and sicknesses', his instructions continued, 'ye shall be diligent and ready to comfort them with the utmost pithy and fruitful sentences of God's holy word.'[65] When, in 1620, a full-time chaplain or 'Ordinary' was appointed, there was initiated one of the most ill-famed prison posts of all times, which gained especial notoriety from the duty of preaching the 'condemned sermon' and accompanying the condemned to execution.[66]

64 Pugh, *op. cit.*, p. 162.
65 Babington, *op. cit.*, p. 45.
66 Indeed, the following description of the condemned sermon and Ordinary by Luke Hatton (1596) shows that even the part-time Ordinary was the focus of curiosity in earlier days:

'See. In yon hall are divers sorts of men
Some weep, some wail, some mourn, some wring their hands,

However, a number of considerations militated against widespread employment of full-time prison chaplains. Expense was one factor, as payment had to be made from public funds. There was also the difficulty of finding reasonably reputable clergymen willing to undertake such hazardous visits. But it should also be noted that the first appointment was apparently in Protestant London at the height of one of the first storms of the Reformation. In its acceptance of the ministry of preaching, as distinct from merely officiating at the Sacraments, London was exceptional, and preaching, from the outset, was particularly compatible with prison visiting.

It was not until the late seventeenth century that a medical practitioner was appointed to Newgate. This innovation was due to the recurrent outbreaks of gaol fever which did not particularly discriminate between unworthy prisoners and honourable judges, aldermen and others connected with the administration of justice. So in 1692 a surgeon from St Bartholomew's began to visit the gaol. This was probably the first appointment of a medical officer to a gaol in Britain.[67]

Prison conditions

The social and organisational consequences of medieval and Tudor penal ideology and administration are fairly predictable and some have been mentioned. Prisons, however, were very individual establishments, and staffing and living conditions consequently varied a great deal. Size of population was an important consideration, but unfortunately there are no surveys comparable with those carried out by Howard and his followers in the late eighteenth century. Because of the very large number of purely custodial commitments, however, all populations would have fluctuated greatly in accordance with the frequency of gaol deliveries. London was exceptional in having so many prisons and such a great degree of specialisation based, in the early seventeenth century,

---

Some curse, some swear, and some blaspheming.' Then
My heart did faint, my head-hair upright stands,
'O Lord', thought I, 'this house will rend in sunder.
Or else there can be no hell this hell under'.

Thus wondering, I on sudden did espy
One all in black came stumbling up the stairs.
'Who's yon?' I asked. And thus he made reply:
'Yon is the man doth mitigate our cares.
He preacheth Christ, and doth God's word deliver
To all distressed, to comfort men for ever'.
    (The Black Dog of Newgate, cit. Judges, op. cit., p. 274)

---

67 Babington, op. cit., p. 64. But Bridewell – which was a house of correction, not a gaol – had a surgeon from its earliest days; see p. 38 below.

on the use of ten important prisons.[68] Physical conditions of prisons —
dependent as they were on local initiative and revenue — also varied,
although there are fairly uniform complaints of decaying fabrics. This
neglect was due partly to the legislative muddling of the responsibilities
of justices and sheriffs already mentioned, but was also an outcome of
local parsimony. Even in the wealthy City, after all, it was not until
Richard Whittington's bequest that the original gatehouse of Newgate
was replaced in 1423.[69]

As safe custody was the only necessary reason for limitations being
imposed on prisoners they could, depending upon their wealth and
social standing, organise their lives very much as they wished. True,
there were some elementary forms of classification: where possible,
felons were kept apart from civil prisoners and misdemeanants, and in
some prisons women were segregated from men and natives from
foreigners. A few — mainly state prisoners — were kept in close confinement, but this was not a form of punishment recognised by common
law and was always imposed by royal prerogative — exercised directly
or through the instructions of a commission.[70]

Prisoners could introduce their servants, spouses and families, either
to visit or to reside; this facility seems particularly to have been used in
the civil prisons.[71] Certain prisons in themselves seem to have posed
little threat of discomfort for certain categories of offenders with
material resources, and one of the scandals of medieval and Tudor
times was the use of imprisonment by 'politic debtors' to their own
advantage. This arose from the inadequacy of the law respecting credit.
Once a creditor had obtained a court order and the committal of his

---

68 In the City and the immediate area, according to John Taylor, there were sixty
   whipping-posts and stocks and cages, and eighteen prisons ('The Praise and
   Vertue of a Jayle and Jaylers', in *All the Works of John Taylor the Water-
   Poet*, p. 131). Besides Newgate there was Ludgate for City freemen and
   freewomen committed for any cause except treason and felony — in practice
   it was almost exclusively a debtors' prison. Then there were the two Counters
   for offenders against City ordinances; Fleet and Marshalsea, both closely
   connected with administration of royal justice and used for all offences
   except treason; Clink (in Southwark) for peace-breakers and religious
   offenders; King's Bench for state prisoners and debtors and Westminster
   Gatehouse mainly for state prisoners. Bridewell (which is discussed in the next
   chapter) should be added to this list, making a total of ten, for though it dealt
   almost entirely with minor offenders it occupied an important place in the
   criminal justice system of London.
69 It had then been in use for about 300 years (Bassett, 'Newgate Prison in the
   Middle Ages', p. 239).
70 Dobb, 'Life and Conditions', p. 29.
71 That imprisonment was not expected greatly to restrict can be seen from the
   description that John Paston gave in a letter to his wife in 1472: 'The Flet
   is a fayir preson, but ye had but smale lyberte therin, for ye must nedys aper
   when ye war callyd' (*Paston Letters*, III, 41-2, *cit*. Bassett, 'The Fleet Prison
   in the Middle Ages', p. 398).

debtor no further action to compel payment was available. 'Politic debtors' were persons who took advantage of the law to obtain large sums of money, feign bankruptcy and when arrested live comfortably in prison, forcing their creditors eventually to settle for a percentage of the amount owed.[72] John Taylor the Water-Poet thus described the two types of debtor in his 'Praise and Vertue of a Jayle and Jaylers':

So Rorers, Rascals, Banquerouts politicke,
With money, or with friends will find a tricke,
Their Jaylor to corrupt, and at their will
They walke abroad, and take their pleasure still:
Whilst naked vertue, beggerly, despis'd,
Beleaguered round, with miseries surpris'd,
Of hope of any liberty defeated,
For passing of his word is merely cheated:
And dungeond up, may tell the wals his mones,
And make relation to the senseless stones,
Where sighs and grones, and teares may be his feast,
Whilst man to man is worse than beast to beast.
Till death he there must take his sad abode,
Whilst craft and coozenage walke at will abroad.[73]

For the involuntary debtor and criminal prisoner without resources imprisonment could be a virtual death sentence.[74] Besides the ever-present risk of disease, many must have starved to death as, whatever may have been the previous position, by the thirteenth century prisoners were expected to find their own keep.[75]

Some prisoners were able to support themselves by continuing their trades in prison, particularly if they practised the easily portable

72 Dobb, 'Life and Conditions', pp. 19-21, *passim*. Another type of debtor chose to remain in prison in order to preserve his possessions for family and heirs. Debts were personal and were cancelled on death. See also Fennor, *op. cit.*, pp. 466-7, and Gamini Salgado, *The Elizabethan Underworld*, pp. 174-5.

73 *All the Workes of John Taylor the Water-Poet*, p. 131. And it was not just the spendthrift who made use of the prisons. Aydelotte notes that 'it is a curious fact that even the jails served now and then as a refuge for Elizabethan rogues and as a basis for their operations. We hear of fellows who lived in jail and would not be persuaded to leave, who kept themselves loaded with suits for debt to cover their other knaveries' (*Elizabethan Rogues and Vagabonds*, p. 83). Prisons were thus used as alternatives to the sanctuaries.

74 Or worse, if Thomas Dekker is to be believed:

Art thou poor and in prison? Then thou art buried before thou art dead. Thou carriest thy winding-sheet on thy back and down the house. Thou liest upon thy bier and treadest upon thy grave at every step. If there be any hell on earth, here thou especially shalt be sure to find it: If there be degrees of torments in hell, here shalt thou taste them (*cit.* Salgado, *op. cit.*, p. 169).

75 Pugh, *op. cit.*, p. 319.

occupations such as cobbling, saddle-making or tailoring. Charity for the destitute might be provided by legacy, or prisoners could beg through a grating into the streets, or even appoint some of their number to walk abroad soliciting food and money. The 1572 Poor Law[76] provided a county allowance for poor prisoners, but there is abundant evidence that its provisions were unevenly and sparsely implemented. Municipalities often arranged that food and other supplies confiscated by way of penalty for violations of the trade laws, would be assigned to the prisons. Upon all these forms of private or governmental generosity the gaoler and his assistants could, of course, be expected to levy a toll.

How did prisons stand in the eyes of the broader community? Pugh argues that 'The law, the church, and what passed for public opinion were opposed to the exploitation of prisoners and the practice of cruelty towards them . . .'.[77] The City authorities promulgated regulations for Newgate, and their other prisons, in the early fourteenth century. These included provisions for some classification and segregation, a scale of permissible fees and charges and new arrangements for the distribution of charities.[78] Between 1443 and 1681 attempts (which met with various degrees of success) were made to ensure regular inspection of Newgate.[79] In the latter year it was provided that prison visitors were henceforth to be elected annually:

> every September two curates and two commoners were to be chosen to inspect the prisons in order to hear prisoners' complaints, to find out why each was being detained, to enquire whether the ordinances were being observed, to determine whether alms were being dispensed fairly, and to inspect the water supply.[80]

Shortly afterwards fines and suspensions were introduced as penalties for prison staff who broke regulations.[81] Attempts to regulate the City prisons became more wide-ranging and persistent as the Common Council and aldermen came increasingly under the influence of Puritanism.[82] In other municipalities similar attempts were made from

76 14 Eliz., c.5.
77 Pugh, *op. cit.*, p. 387.
78 Bassett, 'Newgate Prison in the Middle Ages', p. 241.
79 Sheehan, *op. cit.*, p. 20, n. 4, and p. 21.
80 Bassett, 'Newgate Prison in the Middle Ages', p. 242.
81 *Ibid*.
82   The City government, increasingly as it became more Puritan, tried to do something for the prisoners, legislating against the admission of unauthorised female visitors, irregular behaviour in divine services, gambling and excessive drinking. They tried particularly hard to prevent the sale of the strongest beer and ale to them (Dobb, 'London's Prisons', p. 98).

   Dobb here refers to the period 1600-30.

the fourteenth and fifteenth centuries onward, whilst the Crown sought to control fees in the national prisons that came more directly under its control.[83]

Babington shows that the Court of Aldermen were well informed about the defects and oppressions in their prisons. 'Indeed', he says, 'the repertories disclose a constant preoccupation with the excesses and disobedience of the gaolers; this is apparent even in the initial volumes covering the period between 1495 and 1560.'[84] None the less, standards of inspection, even in London, suffered from long periods of neglect which, given the unpleasant nature of the prisons, and the hazards involved in even stepping over their thresholds, is hardly surprising. In remote county prisons, inspection must have been an extremely rare occurrence.

Prison staff were subject to much social condemnation and suspicion. In a sometimes harsh society their means of livelihood was set apart by the inordinate degree of its harshness.[85] They often wrung their money from misery, and penal history is plentifully punctuated with complaints against them. The strong and vivid literature of the sixteenth and seventeenth centuries contains several such pithy attacks. Taylor seems to be voicing a general feeling of despair and resignation when he writes in the early 1600s:

> That jailes should be, there is law, sense and reason,
> To punish bawdry, cheating, theft and treason,
> Though some against them have invective bin,
> and call'd a Jaile a magazin of sin,
> An Universitie of villany,
> An Academy of foule blasphemy,
> A sinke of drunkenesse, a den of Thieves,
> A treasury for Sergeants and for Shrieves,
> A mint for Baylifes, Marshals men and Jailers,
> Who live by losses of captiv'd bewailers:
> A nurse of Roguery, and an earthly hell,
> Where Dev'ls or Jaylers in mens shapes doe dwell. . . .[86]

Mynshul also developed the theme of gaol as hell:

> As soon as thou commest before the gate of the prison, doe but thinke thou art entring into Hell, and it will extenuate somewhat

83 Pugh, *op. cit.*, pp. 170-1.
84 Babington, *op. cit.*, p. 39.
85 'It must be said . . . that charges of misconduct against prison-keepers, whether those keepers were sheriffs or other "principals", or common gaolers or other "agents", are extremely common and derive from all periods' (Pugh, *op. cit.*, p. 177).
86 Taylor, *op. cit.*, p. 128.

of thy misery, for thou shalt be sure not only to find Hell, but
fiends and ugly monsters, which with continuall torments will
afflict thee. . . .[87]

Fennor, also writing from bitter experience, described gaolers as:

men that, having run through their trades as they have their estates,
at last are forced to take upon them this most base and odious kind
of life; which they no sooner have obtained but are as proud of it as
a lousy prisoner of a fresh suit, or a beggarly rhymer of twelvepenny
dole when he oweth ninepence for ale. They are men that have no
quality in them but one, and that is to ask money, and, like lawyers,
without their fees they will do nothing. They imitate ravens, kites
and crows that feed upon the corruption, stinking garbage, and guts
of any carrion lying in the fields and leave that part that is most
wholesome untouched; so these feed upon the follies and vices of
the age, and have nothing to do with anything that is good. . . .[88]

Contemporaries knew only too well that the system of prison
finance and administration was as much to blame for the gaolers'
unscrupulous methods as were any vicious qualities in the men themselves. This is shown by a pamphleteer of the late seventeenth century:

How commonly do under-officers, gaolers, etc. excuse their
barbarity and unreasonable exactions by alleging that they have no
other way to make up the interest on their purchase-money? . . . It
is this alone that steels and case-hardens a gaoler's conscience against
all pity and remorse, giving him the confidence to demand
extraordinary fees and racked chamber-rent from his prisoners, or
else to crowd them into holes, dungeons and common sides,
designedly made more nasty to terrify the prisoner who, for the
preservation of his life, is thereby forced to part with his money or
is devoured by famine and diseases. This makes him let out his
tap-houses at such prodigious rates that, where poor people should
have the best and cheapest, they have the worst in quality and the
smallest in quantity at excessive prices. Also he farms out his beds
to mere harpies.[89]

Many of the defects and unnecessary oppressions in medieval and
Tudor prisons were recognised and attempts made to legislate against

---

87 G. Mynshul, *Essayes and Characters of a Prison and Prisoners*, pp. 49-52.
Mynshul was a Gray's Inn lawyer who was imprisoned in the King's Bench
prison for debt. The *Essayes* were written during his incarceration. (Aydelotte,
op. cit., pp. 132-3, claims that Mynshul largely cribs his descriptions of prison
life from the 1616 edition of Thomas Dekker's *Villanies Discourred*.)
88 Fennor, *op. cit.*, p. 469.
89 *England's Calamities Discovered* (1696), *cit.* Babington, *op. cit.*, pp. 66-7.

them. But with one significant exception which I shall discuss in the next chapter, the reformation and control of prisons was not seen as a prelude to the reformation of offenders; it was not intended, by seeking to cure the excesses of gaolers and other prison staff, to make prisoners better people, but rather to make custody less productive of evil and more in keeping with Christian morality.

2 Imprisonment prior to the eighteenth century: the houses of correction

Bridewell unto my memory comes next;
Where idlenesse and lechery is vext;
This is a royall house, of state and port,
Which the eighth King Henry built, and there kept Court,
King Edward somewhat ere his timelesse fall,
Gave it away to be an Hospitall:
Which use the City puts it well unto,
And many pious deeds they there doe doo:
But yet for Vagabonds and Runnagates,
For Whores, and idle Knaves, and suchlike mates,
'Tis little better than a Jayle to those,
Where they chop chalke, for meat and drinke and blows.
In this house those that 'gainst their wils doe dwell,
Love well a Bride (perhaps) but not Bridewell. . . .[1]

Thus, within seventy years of its foundation, Bridewell, one of the most momentous social innovations of the Tudor period, was sufficiently notorious and established to be celebrated in the doggerel of John Taylor. Bridewell was an attempt to entrust imprisonment with reformatory and punitive objectives, which were to be secured by a closely regulated régime. This use of prison was a radical departure from existing practice where, as has been shown, if imprisonment was imposed for penal reasons the goal was thought to be achieved purely and simply by the deterrent and retributive loss of liberty, and the pressure on the prisoner of the expense and danger entailed. Against this background Bridewell can truly be treated as the first example of modern imprisonment — certainly in Britain and probably in

1 John Taylor, 'The Praise and Vertue of a Jayle and Jaylers', in *All the Workes of John Taylor the Water-Poet*, p. 131.

Europe.[2] Bridewell and the system of houses of correction to which it gave rise have a central place in the history of English penal philosophy and administration.

In his study of the history of penitentiary imprisonment in America, David Rothman observes that, with few exceptions, historians have described the advent of 'deviant-processing' institutions as a 'reform'. But this, he goes on to suggest, raises the wrong questions:

> The volumes that follow this tradition do not ask why the society adopted this particular measure rather than another. By describing the innovation as a reform, they assume that the asylum was an inevitable and sure step in the progress of humanity. Ostensibly it was an obvious improvement not only over existing conditions, but over *other possible alternatives*. It was exactly the type of device that well-meaning and wise citizens should have supported. But such a perspective is bad logic and bad history. There was nothing inevitable about the asylum form, no self-evident reason why philanthropists should have chosen it.[3]

That being a sensible point, this chapter will attempt to raise some of the right questions: in particular, why Bridewell and the houses of correction were established; what particular assumptions about society and human nature their philosophy and administrative policy rested upon; and why, within a relatively short space of time, their functions, administration and staffing largely became assimilated to those of the common gaols.

Social policy

As with most seemingly radical innovations, closer examination reveals a number of continuities — extensions of, rather than breaks with, existing practices. Moreover, Bridewell and the other houses of correction arose from, and were an integral part of, broader Tudor social policy; and this policy, as several writers have pointed out, was conservative. George Unwin puts this point well when he notes that in almost all social legislation of the period 'we may see the England of

---

2 Mannheim goes no further than to recognise that modern methods of imprisonment came into being in the sixteenth century and that there is dispute about which country has best claim to be the originator: Holland, Italy and England all having their claims (Hermann Mannheim, *The Dilemma of Penal Reform*, p. 49). Austin Van der Slice ('Elizabethan Houses of Correction', p. 47), however, thinks it likely that the English Bridewell was the model for the Rasp Huis of Amsterdam, founded in 1596, and thus probably for subsequent foundations in other countries. Max Grünhut holds that because of the 'striking similarity between English Bridewells and Dutch Houses of Correction, English influence is not improbable' (*Penal Reform*, p. 17).

3 David J. Rothman, *The Discovery of the Asylum*, p. xiv.

the past erecting vain barriers against the England of the future'.[4]
Tawney uses the term 'conservative reconstruction' and observes that
the Privy Councils of the time pursued the ideal of stability rather than
progress:

> Their enemies were disorder, and the restless appetites which, since
> they led to encroachment of class on class, were thought to provoke
> it ... their aim was to crystallize existing class relationships by
> submitting them to the pressure, at once restrictive and protective,
> of a paternal government, vigilant to detect all movements which
> menaced the established order, and alert to suppress them.[5]

This search for stability engendered wide-ranging social and
economic legislation, extending from the regulation of prices and
labour to the relief of distress, and the suppression and reform of the
idle and dissolute. This was a corporatist society: there was little social
anonymity; everyone had a place and a duty to which, for the common
good, the powers, secular and sacred, strove to keep them.

There is disagreement about the causes of increased vagrancy and
destitution in Tudor times. Some analyses stress the effects of the
dissolution of the monasteries, which were the traditional sources of
poor relief; others contend that whilst relief was thereby made more
difficult, the dissolution did not in itself cause the increase.[6] Commentators, however, are agreed that the Tudors and early Stuarts were
plagued with beggars and social unrest: 'All accounts affirm that the
number of beggars was prodigious; thieves abounded everywhere; and
in the unruly north their bands were still a menace to the villages after
the borderline had ceased to be a frontier.'[7] Although society had
always had its poor, its displaced and its idle, the sixteenth century
produced new twists to the old problems. There was, for example, a
concentration of paupers in the large towns, drawn thither by industry;
seasonal unemployment replaced the under-employment of the medieval
peasant; and altogether there was a greater probability that those who
survived into old age would have no land to support them.[8]

Various means were adopted to relieve the poor, but the increase in
their numbers and the necessity for their relief did not immediately
present problems for the established social philosophy of pre-
Reformation England. Religious and social thought was then much

4 George Unwin, *Studies in Economic History*, p. 315.
5 R.H. Tawney, *Religion and the Rise of Capitalism*, p. 170.
6 See, for example, Christopher Hill's *Society and Puritanism in Pre-
revolutionary England*, p. 255, for a statement of this latter view, whilst Frank
Aydelotte argues that both before and after their dissolution the monasteries
increased the beggar class (*Elizabethan Rogues and Vagabonds*, p. 16).
7 A.V. Judges, *The Elizabethan Underworld*, p. xv.
8 Hill, *op. cit.*, p. 267.

more concerned with the state of mind and benefits accruing to the giver than it was with the moral worth of the receiver:

> Now and again, it is true, one of the Fathers of the Church would instruct the faithful that they should not encourage idleness and fraud by their gifts. . . . But the overwhelming tendency of regarding alms as an act of piety, like fasting and prayer, principally from the standpoint of the state of mind of the giver, was in the direction of dismissing all considerations with regard to the character of the recipient.[9]

But one group of the poor seem always to have been unfavourably regarded: vagabonds, in a settled, mainly rural society, were condemned as lacking place, responsibility and moral links with the community. Repeatedly from the reign of Richard II repressive statutes had been enacted against them.[10] Vagabonds posed a demoralising example, threatening political and social order, and their ranks were a breeding ground for crime. Their very appearance in public, for this reason, attracted as much disapproval from the authorities as did their dissolute moral characters. Despite the licensing of special categories – mendicant friars and returning soldiers and seamen – open solicitation for alms was taken as an insult to and subversion of the industry and social order of the commonwealth. Injunctions against public begging were promulgated by several statutes of Henry VIII and Edward VI, for example, 27 Hen. VIII, c.25, and 5 and 6 Edw. VI, c.2; the former seemed to choose the lesser evil in charging the various local authorities to provide relief so that beggars should not be compelled 'to wander idle and openly ask alms'.

Measures against pauperism and vagrancy were promoted with even greater political urgency as the Tudor commonwealth became increasingly Protestant. According to Bindoff, Tudor England was a society 'which ranked, not cleanliness . . . but industry, next to godliness and loyalty, and which condemned idleness as both a sin against God and a crime against the commonweal'.[11] In the social programme drafted by Bucer, Professor of Divinity and Edward VI's Cambridge tutor, was included the declaration that 'wilful idlers are to be excommunicated by the Church and punished by the State'.[12] Thus whilst the number of poor and vagrant subjects was increasing dramatically, political, religious and social attitudes were changing. The tension between these two forces concentrated social policy and administration on the problem of classifying the poor. Otherwise how could the different

9 S. and B. Webb, *English Poor Law History: The Old Poor Law*, p. 5.
10 Van der Slice, *op. cit.*, p. 48. For a comprehensive list of such poor-law legislation see Sir Frederick Eden's *The State of the Poor*, III, Appendix LX.
11 S.T. Bindoff, *Tudor England*, p. 293.
12 Tawney, *op. cit.*, p. 147.

needs of the worthy poor be met and the wilfully idle poor be punished and set to work?

The fact that many forms of minor misdemeanour were condemned more as indications of a wanton, shameless, idle and unproductive life than as misdeeds in themselves, gives Tudor social policy a particular relevance for penal history, as in its administration delinquents were associated with broad categories of the poor. That apparent idleness was the criterion that fused a number of otherwise disparate groups can be seen from the way in which 'vagabond' was defined in 14 Eliz., c.5. It embraced proctors and procurators and persons 'using subtyll craftye unlawful Games'; those 'fayninge themselves to have knowledge in Phisnomye, Palmestrye, and other abused Scyences'; all those able-bodied landless and masterless persons unable to account for the means by which they earned their livelihood; all 'fencers, Bearwardes; Comon Players in Enterludes and minstrels' not attached to a nobleman; 'Juglers, Pedlars, Tynkers and Petye Chapmen' (small traders) unless licensed by two JPs; common labourers, able but refusing to work for customary wages; all makers and users of counterfeit passes (used to pass poor people from one parish to another, *en route* to their place of settlement); all Oxford and Cambridge scholars begging without chancellor's or vice-chancellor's licence; and shipmen and liberated prisoners without proper licences. The term 'vagabond' included, therefore, the socially unworthy nuisances, the disreputable and the suspected: all those who could not establish to the satisfaction of the authorities their place in the social order and productive processes of the commonwealth.

Bridewell

Whipping, branding, enslavement and hanging all had been employed in various attempts to curb the rising tide of vagrancy. None proved effective. Mid-sixteenth-century London resolved upon other remedies. In the first place these involved the organised use of public resources to relieve poverty in the community. It was, as Judges writes, 'A new chapter in administrative history' which

> opened with the decision of the Common Council of London that from Michaelmas 1547 'citizens and inhabitants of the said City shall forthwith contribute and pay towards the sustenation, maintaining and finding of the said poor personages by the space of one whole year next ensuing the moiety . . . of one whole fifteen[th] , and that weekly church collections should be discontinued'.[13]

13 Judges, *op. cit.*, p. xxix. This was probably the first poor-rate ever levied.

In general terms, the City leaders were moving between two distinct modes of social thought: Catholic and Protestant, medieval and modern.[14] They sought to relieve the poor, but by means which would, at the same time, discipline and coerce them. This policy rested on the practical drawing of distinctions among the poor and the application of measures appropriate to the different types.

In seeking an administrative solution to the problem of sorting and differentially dealing with the poor the City turned to a familiar model – the hospitals. In Tudor times the 'hospital' served a far greater range of purposes than its modern equivalent:

> The term hospital was by no means confined to institutions for relieving the sick, but almshouses, orphanages and training homes were often called by this name. St. Thomas's Hospital may be taken as a typical institution of this kind . . . [it] consisted of Master, brethren . . . sisters . . . and nurses. . . . It was founded for the relief and cure of poor people, and in 1535 there were forty beds for the poor, and food and firing was provided for them.[15]

O'Donoghue amplifies the point: 'the word "hospital" originally signified a house which received guests and gave hospitality to sick people, poor people, old people and children. We speak in these days of an almshouse, a workhouse, a hostel or a school'.[16]

Pre-Reformation London had been well supplied with these institutions: in 1536 there were fifteen of them, and four lazar houses. To Henry VIII, who suppressed them, many seemed to fulfil no useful function, or they possessed estates that the Crown could better use. The City, however, sought to preserve some of them. As a result of refounding or new grants there were four royal hospitals functioning by 1552-3. Each served a particular section of the poor: St Bartholomew's, the sick; Christ's, fatherless children; and St Thomas's, the aged sick. Bethlehem, founded in 1274 by Simon Fitzmary and given to the City by Henry VIII, was for lunatics who had no others to care for them. But for one key group there remained no provision – the able poor. In the early 1550s the City's leading secular and religious figures gave urgent thought to the correction of this deficiency.

The unsatisfactory state of existing social policy was the theme taken by Lever in a sermon preached before Edward VI in 1550. His exposition shows to what extent relief and suppression, distress and

---

14 The constructive protestant alternative to indiscriminate charity was to set the poor on work to stimulate self-help. . . . Hard and productive work is of advantage both to the individual and to the community, of which he is a member. Interest and duty here coincide (Hill, *op. cit.*, p. 268).

15 E.M. Leonard, *The Early History of Poor Relief*, p. 19.

16 E.G. O'Donoghue, *Bridewell Hospital*, II, p. 2.

misdemeanour were compounded in the minds of those groping towards the foundation of a new institution for the able-bodied poor.

> Nowe speakinge in the behalfe of these vile baggars . . . I wyle tell the[e] that art a noble man, a worshipful man, an honest welthye man, especially if thou be Maire, Sherif, Alderman, baily, constable or any such officer, it is to thy great shame afore the worlde, and to thy utter damnation afore God, to se these begging as thei use to do in the streates. For there is never a one of these but he lacketh eyther thy charitable almes to relieve his neede, orels thy due correction to punysh his faute. . . . These sely sols have been neglected throughout al England and especially in London and Westminster. . . .[17]

Of the many leading citizens who debated policy at this time Richard Grafton probably played the most important part. It was he, O'Donoghue thinks, 'who pointed out how the poor could be effectively relieved, or reclaimed, by discriminating between the deserving and the undeserving, and by giving a pension or offering work according to circumstances'.[18] Grafton and others sought and secured the aid of Nicholas Ridley, bishop of London, in their attempts to obtain a place in which the worthy and unworthy poor might be distinguished by the test of offering work. They had in mind Henry VIII's palace of Bridewell, part of which was used as the Imperial and Spanish Embassy.

In 1552 Ridley, pursuing this project, wrote to Cecil, in the curiously moving, supplicatory language of the day:

> Good Mr. Cecil. I must be a suitor unto you in our good Master Christ's cause; I beseech you be good to him. The matter is, Sir, alass! he hath lain too long abroad (as you do know) without lodging

17 *Cit.* Leonard, *op. cit.*, p. 30.

18 O'Donoghue, *op. cit.*, I, p. 135. Other European countries were at the time facing similar social problems, and shedding medieval values in their approach to poverty. It seems likely, therefore, that the pioneering ideas of men such as Juan Luis Vives were familiar to Grafton and his colleagues. Vives, an international scholar and courtier, had written a pamphlet on the relief of the poor when he was attached to the court of Henry VIII as tutor to Mary. Very similar suggestions reappeared in a policy paper circulated by the City authorities in 1552. In particular, social policy (in line with Tudor thinking) was presented as a keystone in the bridge between rich and poor. Action to relieve poverty, it argued, should begin with a census of the town's poor – in hospitals, in their own houses and those who were beggars. Then, says O'Donoghue, summarising the document,

> Begging should be absolutely prohibited and . . . all applicants for alms should be made to labour if they are fit to work. Educate the children of the poor (for education may save them from becoming paupers), and send the sick and maimed into hospitals. . . . Relief to be given to the poor in exchange for work, and poor-relief to be administered by the local authorities (*op. cit.*, p. 195).

in the Streets of London, both hungry, naked and cold. Now, thanks
be to Almighty God! the citizens are willing to refresh him, and to
give him both meat, drink, cloathing and firing: but alass! Sir, they
lack lodging for him. . . . Sir, there is a wide, large, empty house of
the King's Majesty's called Bridewell, that would wonderfully well
serve to lodge Christ in, if he might find such good friends in the
court to procure in his cause. Surely I have such a good opinion of
the King's Majesty, that if Christ had such faithful and hearty friends
who would heartily speak for him, he should undoubtedly speed at
the King's Majesty's hands. Sir, I have promised my brethren the
citizens to move you, because I do take you for one that feareth
God, and would that Christ should lie no more abroad in the
streets.[19]

Ridley preached the case before the king who, moved, invited the
citizens to petition the Privy Council. This, after consultation, they did
in 1553. From the wording of the petition it is apparent that Ridley's
initially vague and general charitable request had been considerably
refined and elaborated. The petitioners first pointed out that thievery
and beggary abounded, despite all the various preventative and punitive
enactments. They had come to the conclusion that the reason for the
misery and beggary was idleness and that 'the mean and remedy to cure
the same must be by its contrary, which is labour'. Among the poor
they distinguished three classes for which appropriate provision had to
be made: the succourless poor child, the sick and the impotent, and the
sturdy vagabond, or idle person. Relief was already being given to the
first two categories, which left the able-bodied poor.

Now resteth for the third sort, an house of occupations, to be erected;
wherein as well the child, when he is brought up and grown to years,
and found unapt to learning, neither any honest person desireth or
would have his service, may there be exercised and occupied; as also
the sore and sick when they be cured; who shall not be suffered to
wander as vagabonds in the commonwealth, as they have been
accustomed, but shall there be exercised. And unto this shall be
brought the sturdy and idle: and likewise such prisoners as are quit
at the sessions, that they there may be set to labour. And for that
the number will be great the place where they shall be exercised must
also be great. And this, being (as it were) the perfection of our whole
former travail, is yet undone, and moveth us now to sue for the King's
majesty's house of Bridewell; for that the situation and largeness
thereof seemeth most meet and convenient for this purpose.[20]

19 *Cit*. Thomas Bowen, *Extracts from the Records and Court Books of Bridewell
Hospital*, pp. 3, 4.
20 *Cit*. R.H. Tawney and E. Power, *Tudor Economic Documents*, II, pp. 307-8.

The Privy Council responded favourably and in April 1553 the king acceded to the request. Legal formalities were not completed until 20 June of the same year and, as Edward was already on his deathbed (he died on 6 July), this grant was among the last of his reign.

The religious reformation had deepened and taken a new turn during Edward's reign. Mary's attempts to reverse these changes might, in time, have resulted in the revocation of the grant of Bridewell, as there is some evidence that she was unsympathetic to the project.[21] In any event, there was a delay of some three years before it was handed over, and the City did not take possession until February 1556. A levy upon the City companies defrayed the expenses on equipment and furniture, and in December 1556 Bridewell received its first prisoners.[22]

Although by this time the place of Bridewell in the City's system of poor relief appears to be reasonably well defined, closer examination shows that the new hospital in some respects acted as a stopgap and in others was made to fulfil a combination of tasks, strange even according to the thinking of the day. It was required to provide simultaneously shelter for the wilful and the hapless poor; succour for misfit children and destitute discharged prisoners; punishment and a reformatory stimulus for a motley lot of rogues, rascals, swindlers, petty criminals and drones. Bridewell was also a kind of social lazar house: it kept in limbo various petty offenders, and by keeping them apart from society – in a way in which whipping, stocks or pillory did not do – reduced, for the time of their confinement, scandal to the commonwealth and subversion of its moral solidarity.[23] And to add to these various advantages the inmates were to maintain themselves, at least in part, by the fruits of their labours.

The factor which linked these different categories of social miscreants was, in theory, the beneficial effects of their being taught, exposed to and compelled to labour. Bridewell was at once conceived as a place where inmates were made better, and as a work-offering

21 O'Donoghue, *op. cit.*, I, pp. 258-9. G. Salgado (*The Elizabethan Underworld*, pp. 187-8) notes that one contemporary suggestion for Mary's hostility was that the whores, under examination, would disclose too many scandals involving Roman Catholic priests. There probably were broader differences in policy, however, since an Act of Mary (2 & 3 Ph. & M., c.5) provided for the licensing of beggars – a direct reversal of the previous policy of prohibition.

22 Leonard and the Webbs are vague about the commencing date. The former is only able to put it before 1557 and the latter sometime between 1552 and 1557. O'Donoghue (*op. cit.*, I, pp. 119-30, *passim*) using detailed documentary evidence can pinpoint dates more exactly.

23 Little attention has been paid to the usefulness seen in such social segregation by Bridewell's innovators. The abhorrence with which public begging and social displacement generally was viewed was surely in large part stimulated by the moral and political threat thereby offered to the community. 'Out of sight, out of the public mind' should perhaps have been engraved over the gates of Bridewell.

touchstone which could distinguish the truly delinquent from the unfortunate, the evil-doer from the casualty.[24] Bridewell contained, tested, punished, trained and relieved, all in one go — or so its founders hoped.

Régime

How, then, were these diverse objectives to be achieved? Only one form of reformatory imprisonment had previously been tried — the penitential confinement of the monasteries. Rules of various monastic orders provided this penalty for grave offenders within the cloistered community. Monastic prisons isolated the malefactor, partly as duress and punishment, partly in order to reduce moral contagion, but also with the intention of curing the offender's physical and spiritual defects. Such prisoners were kept in silence, subjected to a special diet, and allowed only the distraction of approved books and conversation with their abbot or some designated elder brother.[25] These methods were to be revived for secular use in the late eighteenth century. As the Elizabethans were familiar with monastic practices, why did they not turn to this form of imprisonment for guidance in their attempts to design a reformatory régime?

Reflection shows this to be an unsubstantial question. Whatever elaboration of a Protestant view of poverty was still to take place, there was a strong antipathy towards popery in the Edwardian, Marian and Elizabethan City. Bridewell, after all, was founded at the height of the Edwardian Reformation and in the very powerhouse of that movement. It would have been inconceivable for London's Common Council to model their hospital upon institutions which had recently, with self-righteous zeal, been suppressed for waste and idleness and aggravation of the problem of poverty. The Protestant connection of monasteries with waste is emphasised by Hill:

> The reformers justified the dissolution of the monasteries because their inmates were idle and unproductive. Luther attacked monks, friars and beggars in the same breath; part of his original case

---

24 Describing the design of the nineteenth-century New Poor Law, the Webbs drew attention to the similarities between its 'workhouse test' and the testing function of Bridewell (S. and B. Webb, *English Prisons Under Local Government*, p. 13). Leonard makes a similar point: 'Bridewell as a place of punishment for idlers was the necessary counterpart of the new schemes for universal relief. You could not relieve and find work for everyone unless you had some means for coercing and punishing the "sturdy vagabond" ' (*op. cit.*, p. 39).

25 For a fuller discussion of monastic imprisonment see Ralph B. Pugh, *Imprisonment in Medieval England*, Ch. 18.

against indulgences had been that they led to the squandering of men's substance.[26]

Monasteries epitomised so many of the evils that Bridewell was intended to eradicate that had they been used at all it would have been as a negative rather than a positive example.

But what need to look for inspiration further afield than the City, where men were made rich, contented and good by their honest endeavours? And, indeed, from the outset it was intended that there should be the closest links between the productive life of the community and the activities of Bridewell. The petition to Edward promised that cap-making would be carried on, together with the manufacture of feather mattresses and 'wool-cards, drawing of wire, spinning, carding, knitting, and winding of silk, and other profitable devices: and the stubborn, and fouler sort, shall be exercised in making of nails and other iron-work'. Furthermore

certain godly and honest citizens will deliver matter in stock, whereof the idle shall be set on work; as wool, yarn, flax, wire, leather, etc. And when the same shall be wrought, to receive the same wrought wares in satisfaction of the stock, allowing for the workmanship thereof; and always as the wares are wrought to renew the stock. And thus shall there never lack matter whereon the idle shall be occupied.[27]

By 1579 twenty-five trades were carried on there.[28] A considerable number of apprentices were trained; orphaned sons of City freemen were received at Bridewell; parish overseers sent children, and yet other children were taken up by Bridewell beadles from the streets. By 1631 there were sixteen tradesmen teaching their various crafts to a total of 106 apprentices.[29]

But labour at Bridewell was not exclusively productive; some activities were undertaken specifically for their penal value. Male prisoners deserving of punishment were set to clean the city ditches (a loathsome task, as ditch and sewer were one); females picked rags and waste paper for the government monopolist, or were set to beat hemp.[30] In 1591 the daily task to be completed by prisoners in the hemp-house

---

26 Hill, *op. cit.*, p. 263. Hill also cites a seventeenth-century condemnation of popery which asserts, *inter alia*, 'monks, nuns and friars live in idleness, making no contribution to national production . . . friars and other mendicants live especially on the alms of the poor, and so the latter can never rise above a mean condition' (*ibid.*, pp. 128-9).
27 *Cit.* Tawney and Power, *op. cit.*, pp. 308-9, *passim*.
28 Van der Slice, *op. cit.*, p. 51.
29 Leonard, *op. cit.*, pp. 217, 354-5.
30 O'Donoghue, *op. cit.*, II, p. 12.

on pain of restrictions on their diet was twenty-five pounds.[31] By Stuart times escorted parties of prisoners were being sent out to sweep the streets.[32] Treadmills were in use from the earliest days and a special hand and foot mill was invented (by a certain Payne!) so that vagrants who had lost a hand or foot should not thereby evade labour.[33] Idleness was discouraged by torture and whipping, besides dietary punishment.[34]

The penal side of Bridewell was further emphasised by the preliminary flogging of certain categories of new prisoners — chiefly prostitutes and vagrants. This punishment was inflicted in public — either at a cart's tail or in Bridewell's whipping-room. Only after this induction did these prisoners pass on to the industrial parts of the prison. Retributive and reformative ends were thus jointly served.

Sentences were generally of short duration, probably averaging about a month. There were many instances, however, in which sentences of several years, or even life, were imposed, particularly for religious offences or incendiarist libels.[35]

Administration

Administration combined both existing and new practices in line with the way in which the system as a whole had been constructed.[36] Two principles were fundamental: there was to be a radical break with the profit-based financial system of the gaols, and a detailed code of regulations was to be drawn up and enforced by regular independent inspection. As has been pointed out, the *raison d'être* of gaols was purely custodial; and provided that security was maintained the gaolers needed no further regulation. With so much latitude allowed, gaolers

31 *Ibid.*, I, p. 221.
32 *Ibid.*, II, pp. 21-2.
33 *Ibid.*, I, p. 239. The mills ground corn, and could be used for up to eighteen vagrants at a time (Judges, *op. cit.*, p. lxii).
34 Prisoners might, for example, be placed in 'Little Ease', a cell so designed that both standing and sitting were impossible. Alternatively they might be subjected to the 'scavenger's daughter' — a set of rod-mounted manacles that bent and compressed the body causing excruciating pain. Prisoners were also suspended by their hands (O'Donoghue, *op. cit.*, pp. 222-3).
35 O'Donoghue, *op. cit.*, II, pp. 29, 40. The prison accommodated about two hundred inmates and had an annual turnover of about two thousand.
36 Leonard well expresses this balance between continuity and change in her general comment that

> There was no sudden break with the older system. St Thomas's, St Bartholomew's and Bedlam (Bethlehem) had all been hospitals for centuries. They had been saved from destruction, improved and enlarged; but essentially the same work was done in the same places. . . . Bridewell was the greatest innovation and the most characteristic institution of the new system (*op. cit.*, pp. 38-9).

engaged in a great variety of relationships and transactions with their prisoners. However, when prisons were given the additional reformatory task, relationships between staff, prisoners and public had to be structured in such a way as to exclude undesirable activities and experiences and inescapably to expose prisoners to other experiences and desirable activities. Hence the need for a system of finance not based on profits. A keeper who drew remuneration solely from the exercise of initiative in dealings with prisoners could not possibly be an agent of the new régime. The reformatory prison was financially and administratively the antithesis of the purely custodial gaol.

The new administration had to be run by an independent, capable body of regulators, whose close engagement in the activities of the prison had no financial incentive and whose loyalties were owed only to the City. To meet these requirements a corporation of governors was established, sixty-six strong, which jointly served London's four royal hospitals. These governors were instructed by the City's 1557 enactments[37] and were subject to biennial elections, whereby only half of the body were elected in any one year, thus ensuring continuity. Fourteen of the total were to be aldermen, the rest 'grave commoners'. Of the highest ranking aldermen two were to be appointed as comptroller and surveyor respectively of all the hospitals. The rest of the governors were distributed equally between the four hospitals, although, despite these specific appointments, all retained authority and responsibility for the hospitals as a whole.[38] Out of the sixteen allocated to each establishment an alderman was to be elected president and a commoner treasurer. Other governors were given departmental responsibilities in keeping with their interest and expertise; the nail-house at Bridewell, for example, was supervised by governors drawn from the Company of Ironmongers. Thus, although amateur administrators, some at least of the governors could be expected substantially and practically to

37 The ordinance stated:

> As the Governors of the other hospitals and Bridewell are all incorporated and made one body, and whosoever is Governor of one of them, is also Governor of them all; and yet, for order sake the said Governors are divided to the several government of the said houses; so in like manner are ye appointed to the government of Bridewell ('Ordinances and Rules . . . for the good government of Bridewell, 1557', cit. William Waddington, *Considerations on the Proper and Original Objects of the Royal Hospital of Bridewell*, pp. 5, 6, 7).

38 Van der Slice, *op. cit.*, p. 51. In theory one should have spoken of the five royal hospitals, but Bridewell and Bethlehem were co-joined for administrative purposes. This 'joint and several' responsibility of the governors further emphasises the fact that together the hospitals were seen as a *system* of relief, with each playing a dependent and important part.

contribute to successful management.[39]

Governors were collectively responsible for payments and accounts and generally were empowered to 'comptroll and rebuke' the employees as they thought fit.[40] In the discharge of their duties they checked and counterchecked each other, as it was ordained that 'Nothing shall be given, paid, nor ordered, but six at least of the said governors shall first give their consent thereunto, and two of the six shall be aldermen'. But, combining this caution with practicality, executive responsibility for finances was given to one person:

> Among those governors, one of the worshipful, and wisest personage, and credible, shall be treasurer for one year and no more. And he to have the charge, as well of the sums of money that are to be received and paid, as also of such stock and wares, as in the said house shall be wrought and unwrought, and to account for the same. . . .[41]

Regular audits and personal inspections were undertaken by the governors to ensure that subordinate staff complied with the regulations and did not corruptly divert any of the considerable flow of revenue and stock of the prison. This was essential if the prison were not to relapse into the ways of the gaols, an especially likely eventuality, as staff could only draw their expectations of institutional life from contemporary practices and these dictated that each public office had particular and immediate rewards.[42] O'Donoghue sardonically notes that 'the officers of the house in the sixteenth century were not always animated with the same sentiments as their absent masters – a jealousy for the good name of Bridewell, and a sense of devotion towards a cause. . . '.[43] That many of the staff were residential only increased, in some respects, the problems of supervision and control. Drunken carousals and other misbehaviour were probably not infrequent. One such incident resulted in orders from the governors placing the offending staff in the 'hole' until the pleasure of the treasurer was known.[44] Despite difficulties of this kind Bridewell does not seem to have had

---

39 It is . . . requisite for the good order of the said house, that the Governors be divided to the oversight of several charges: as some to the oversight of cloth-making; and others to the Smithy and nail-making. And some to the Mill-house and Bakehouse, etc. to the intent that every one of them in their several charges, may shew themselves before God and the honourable City, as worthy and good Governors of the same (*cit.* Waddington, *op. cit.*, p. 57).

40 Leonard, *op. cit.*, p. 37.

41 Tawney and Power, *op. cit.*, pp. 309-10.

42 Even before Bridewell became properly operational, staff and workmen were detected in corruption and theft (Salgado, *op. cit.*, p. 187).

43 O'Donoghue, *op. cit.*, I, pp. 205-6.

44 *Ibid.*

the reputation for staff corruption and extortion acquired later by other houses of correction.

Governors were not confined to duties of administration and management, but also acted as justices in Bridewell's own courtroom. Each day the prison's beadles made their rounds of the wards of the City and arrested offenders.[45] These were brought to Bridewell where any two governors were empowered to admit them. Admission, as has been mentioned, was often followed by a flogging, witnessed and directly controlled by the governors.[46] Altogether the governors played a part in the affairs of the prison that went beyond policy-making and inspection to include close supervision and executive intervention.

From the outset it had been intended that governorships should be honorary. This idea differed radically from prevailing norms of seeking self-interest in the performance of the duties of public office; but it was based on another powerful convention — that worthy citizens should engage in charitable and public activities as a demonstration of their standing. In their petition to the Privy Council the citizens were at some pains to reassure the councillors that their project was wholly altruistic: 'The fees and profits that these governors shall have shall be such as Almighty God hath promised to them that travail in relieving his needy members and none other.'[47] This was brought to the attention of each and every governor when he was ceremonially installed in his office:

---

45 There seems to have been some uncertainty about the legality of this. O'Donoghue notes that during the reign of Elizabeth 'The institution was also vulnerable in the opinion of lawyers, because illegal powers of search, arrest and punishment had been conferred upon it by the charter'. The authority of the governors was consequently frequently challenged (*op. cit.*, I, p. 184). Among those who questioned the powers of the governors in this respect was no less a figure than Sir Francis Bacon (Grünhut, *op. cit.*, p. 17).

46 O'Donoghue gives an account of the whippings, which were carried out

> in a small room, hung with black, situated in the south-west corner of the court-room. . . . When the chairman considered that justice had been well and duly done to the back of the prisoner (male or female), he brought down his gavel smartly on the table . . . (*op. cit.*, II, p. 12).

Prisoners when being so whipped in the presence of Sir Thomas Middleton (lord mayor, 1613-14, and president of Bridewell for eighteen years), by all accounts a man of stern disposition towards prisoners, used to cry, 'Knock, Sir Thomas, knock.' So notorious did this cry become that it was shouted after him in the streets by prostitutes and other denizens of the *demi-monde*.

Bridewell whippings became one of the sights of the capital and 'the court was often incommoded by the jostling, cynical crowds, which flocked on a Wednesday or Friday morning to the performance'. Accordingly 'on February 9th 1677, it was ordered that a balustraded gallery should be put up in the court-room for the public' (*ibid.*, p. 156).

47 *Cit.* Tawney and Power, *op. cit.*, p. 309.

and, forasmuch as ye are wise men and good men and have the perfect and true knowledge of the usage of the said faculty — to the benefit and profit of this House, we do therefore put our whole trust and confidence in you, and *pray* you, and yet nevertheless charge you, (as we are all charged) and as ye tender the furtherance of this acceptable work of God, which is the overthrow of idleness, the begetter of all sin and mischief; — that ye will with all diligence, so endeavour yourselves to the oversight, and governance of this work. As the stock appointed to the same do not decay, nor diminish, but rather be advanced and increased. And this is your charge, wherein if ye travail diligently, and *chiefly now at the first*, for good order sake; . . . Good men will commend you, — all the worthy Governors will love you, — and God Almighty will bless you here with worship, and reward you in heaven with the crown of glory everlasting; prepared for you and all them that fear his name and walk in his ways. Amen.[48]

Almost all lord mayors seem to have become governors and, in a not inconsiderable display of public service, over the years large numbers of successful City figures undertook the office.[49] The scale of devotion to this new duty is all the more significant when compared with the 'neglect' of gaol administration, for which the same circles had responsibility.

Finance and staffing

Bridewell was maintained by an income drawn from endowments, regular levies imposed by the City, gifts of money and stock, and the labour of inmates. The last yielded only a small proportion of the institution's income and, indeed, was almost matched by the fees that employers paid for the upkeep of unruly apprentices whom they had had committed to the prison.[50] By 1630 annual outgoings were

48 *Cit*. Waddington, *op. cit.*, pp. 57-8.
49 Including, in the late seventeenth century, Samuel Pepys, who assumed office in June 1675 (O'Donoghue, *op. cit.*, II, p. 162).
50 In 1630 labour (at the rate of 4*d*. per day for every man and 2*d*. for every woman and boy) accounted for only £40; fees paid for unruly apprentices and others amounted to £36. In the same year rents brought in £1,025.2*s*.2*d*., and gifts £120 (Leonard, *op. cit.*, Appendix XII, pp. 352-3). Bridewell lost some of its original endowment in 1562 when the City transferred the Savoy lands and tenements to St Thomas's. O'Donoghue maintains that, despite the funds raised by levy on the wealthier of the City companies and poor rate levied under the law of 1572 (14 Eliz., c.5), 'throughout the sixteenth century Bridewell had to earn a large part of its income by the profits of prison labour, in the mills, in the lighters, by the collection of rags and bones, and by the manufacture of various articles'. He also says that there were financial difficulties and maladministration during this period and that legacies were few and small. He does not, however, make it clear upon which figures he based his assessment.

over £1,100.[51]

Staff were paid 'a convenient stipend' and were expected to be 'such honest persons as are experts in such sciences and occupations as there shall be exercised'. Taskmasters and taskmistresses were appointed to 'take the charge of every man's task and proportion of work that shall be daily limited and appointed for them to do'. They were authorised to 'correct and punish such as are under their task, if they loiter and be found negligent'. Supporting staff were also provided in the way of 'porters, cooks, stewards, etc., to whom likewise shall be given convenient stipends'.[52]

By the beginning of the seventeenth century the establishment of staff had so increased in size and complexity that the sixteen craftsmen — linen, silk and ribbon weavers, pin and ribbon makers, glovers, hemp-dressers and a carpenter — between them trained 106 apprentices at any one time, while hemp-dressers also kept forty-eight men and women at the punitive labour of beating hemp. Other staff consisted of a preacher, a surgeon, a steward, a matron, porters, beadles, marshal's men, a raker and a nightman.[53] Since 1577 a clerk had been employed on a full-time basis.[54] Annual wages varied from £26. 16s. 8d. (plus rent allowance) for the preacher to £1 for the raker (who removed the night-soil); and in 1630 the total amount was £192. 14s. 0d. for the year. The wages of the steward, the porter and the matron included allowances for their immediate subordinates — a man and maid for each. Considering the general state of medical provision for the poor, the addition of a surgeon to the staff was a great novelty. His duties were 'to view the bodies of such as are brought in diseased or lame within the house and to cure such as be suddenly hurt'.[55] It is worthy of note that because of the close involvement of the governors in management it was possible to do without appointing a keeper or his equivalent to take overall charge of the institution. Among other factors this undoubtedly reflected the mercenary and conniving reputation of the gaoler class and the determination of the governors to avoid such misconduct at Bridewell.

The houses of correction

London's social problems were to be found in other towns as were London's attitude to poverty and willingness to experiment. Several other towns soon followed suit and established houses of correction along Bridewell lines. These included Oxford (1562), Salisbury (1564),

51 Leonard, *op. cit.*, p. 356.
52 Tawney and Power, *op. cit.*, p. 310.
53 Leonard, *op. cit.*, Appendix XII.
54 O'Donoghue, *op. cit.*, I, p. 239.
55 Leonard, *op. cit.*, Appendix XII.

Norwich (1565), Gloucester (before 1569) and Ipswich (1569).[56] None was as large as Bridewell, of course, but financial and administrative structures were similar because the same practical issues of régime presented themselves. Norwich bridewell, for example, could hold twelve incorrigible idlers who were to be kept, according to its regulations,

> for the space of twentie and one days at the leaste and longer yf cause serve and they shall not eat but as they can earne (except som freinde wyll be bownde for them) that the Citie shall nomore be troubled with them with this proviso that such parsons as shall be thether comytted shall be suche as be hable to worke and daielie notwithstanding wyll not worke but rather begge, or be without master or husbande, or ellis be vacabowndes or loyterers.[57]

Offenders were to be received into the prison on a warrant from the mayor (who was *ex officio* master of bridewell) or his deputies. Inmates who refused to work were to be whipped.

The code of regulations set out the hours of work and other conditions for the inmates and the duties of the resident paid 'bailie' (keeper), which included the enforcement and assessment of labour (mainly malt-grinding) and the allowance to the inmates of food and fuel according to the amount of work performed. He was also responsible for receiving and checking all materials and seeing to their proper use. An elaborate administrative system was thought unnecessary, probably because the institution was so small and the paid keeper relatively easy to supervise. Accordingly the bailie was simply paid £30 a year by the city council from which he was instructed to provide supplies and such servants as were necessary to run the establishment in his absence and to perform 'the howse busyness . . . washinge, makynge of beddes, bakings', and who had also to be 'experts in spynne, cards, etc.'. He had in his employ a 'surveyor' — a beadle who carried out daily patrols of the wards and arrested 'whome that is apte for brydwell and brynge them to master maior or to anie of the committies be commaunded thether'.[58]

Norwich bridewell, although firmly based on labour, was more punitive than London's. It catered only for the most hardened adult idlers. Different means were used for dealing with other sections of the able-bodied poor. 'Selecte women' were appointed to take women, maidens and children into their own houses. They were directed to drive their charges

> to worke and lerne, by the howers appoynted in bridewell and with such corrections, tyll their hands be browght into such use and their

56 Van der Slice, *op. cit.*, p. 32.
57 *Cit.* Leonard, *op. cit.*, Appendix III, p. 311.
58 *Ibid.*, p. 313.

bodies to such paynes as labore and learninge shall be easier to them than idleness and as they shall of themselves be hable to lyve of their own workes with their famelies as others do.[59]

The Ipswich institution was called Christ's Hospital and was organised along broadly similar lines. A board of governors met weekly and a paid 'guider' undertook the day-to-day duties. However, there were some differences in detail. Children, the disabled and others in need were received, in addition to the able-bodied idler. The 'guider' was paid by the authorities on a *per capita* basis: 4*d.* per week for inmates undergoing correction, 1*s.* per week for the able-bodied destitute and 8*d.* for those unable to work. A special clothing allowance was given for children and the 'guider' additionally had the value of the inmates' labour.[60]

Bury St Edmunds called its bridewell the House of Correction, and used it for adult vagabonds, following almost exactly the definition provided in 14 Eliz., c.5, with the addition of the Irish. When new regulations were drawn up in 1588, those who committed troublesome offences against the new enclosures but could not be indicted for felony also served sentence there.[61] These regulations are particularly interesting because of their claim that in such cases either the gaol or the house of correction might be used, at the discretion of the magistrate. Administration followed what, by now, was an established pattern in the hands of lay unpaid wardens (equivalents of the London governors), a paid keeper and a 'forren officer' (arresting beadle). The institution was financed by a local tax, raised by the justices. At quarter sessions, decisions on inspection and control could be made in support of regulations stipulating the work and daily routine of prison life and

---

59 *Ibid.*, pp. 313-14. Ann Smith reports that at Winchester women were detained for five years in the house of correction: for three years they were taught a trade, and for two years they worked to repay the expenses of their upkeep (*Women in Prison*, p. 74).

60 *Cit.* Leonard, *op. cit.*, p. 113.

61 'It is ordered, (that forasmuch as there is great complaints in many places, that throughe the idleness and lewdenes of some, and badd disposition of othersome, many hedges are broken, and the wood carried awaie; and sondrie tymes hens, capons, turkeis, geese, ducks, piggs, frute in orcheards, and such smale trifles taken and carried awaie;) and yet the same in sondrie cases neyther felloney nor pety larceny; that therefore all such persons being above the age of xii yeares, which shall in the night or daie tyme committ any of the said offences, (viz.) by breakinge or carrienge awaie of any man's hedge, or cuttinge downe any wood which he cannot justifie to do, or by takinge geese, ducks, turkeis, capons, hennes, piggs, frute, or such like, not amounting to the some or valewe of xiid. being fyrst apprehended and carried before one of her Majestie's Justices of the Peace, shal be sente by hym to the gaile or house of correction, as to the same Justice uppon the examination of the cause shal be thought fitt and convenient' (*cit.* Eden, *op. cit.*, Appendix VII, p. cxli).

the various punishments (and instruments of punishment) that were to be imposed upon the disobedient.[62]

Government concern about the problem of vagrancy and vagabondage remained acute, and by the end of the century a series of legislative enactments had commended the experimental approach of the pioneering towns to the country as a whole.

By a statute of 1576 (18 Eliz., c.3) mayors and justices were authorised to provide stocks of wool, flax, hemp, iron and other materials so that

> Yowthe may be accustomed and brought up to Laboure and Worcke, and then not lyke to growe to bee ydle Roges and to the Entente also that suche as been alredye growen up in ydlenes and so Roges at this present maye not have any juste excuse in saying they cannot get any Service or Worcke . . . and that other poore and needye persons being willinge to worcke mae bee set on worcke.[63]

To buttress this provision the Act also allowed for houses of correction to be built in every county, to which those who refused the offer of work could be sent. These prisons were to be set up by decision of the justices assembled in general sessions, and to be equipped with material and equipment 'for setting on worcke and punishinge' not only the idle able-bodied poor, but also those taken as rogues. The justices were to appoint (also in general sessions) 'censores or Wardens of the Howses of Correction'. The establishment of the house of correction was not made mandatory by this Act, but Van der Slice is probably correct in arguing that it none the less 'stimulated the development of houses of correction throughout England'.[64]

This Act and the related 14 Eliz., c.5 were three times renewed, and remained the basis of English poor law for the next two decades[65] until 1597, when 39 Eliz., c.4 — 'An Acte for the punyshment of Rogues, Vagabonds and Sturdy Beggars' — was passed, repealing all previous legislation. The former authority of the justices to erect one or more houses of correction by means of local rates was, however, reaffirmed. Rogues and vagabonds were to be punished by whipping, and were then to be sent to the nearest house of correction, gaol, or to their place of settlement; from thence they were to be placed in service, or, if

---

62 *Ibid.*, Appendix VII, *passim*.

63 *Cit.* Leonard, *op. cit.*, p. 72.

64 Van der Slice, *op. cit.*, p. 56. Aydelotte comments that the two poor-law statutes of the 1570s 'mark the beginning of the end of the old free, merry, vagabond life. The houses of correction and the provision of wool and hemp did what the whips and stocks, and even the gallows, could not do' (*op. cit.*, pp. 69-70).

65 Except that in 1592 the clauses sanctioning death, imprisonment and earboring were repealed by 35 Eliz., c.7 and replaced by others changing the penalty to whippings.

impotent, in an almshouse. Dangerous rogues were to be banished on pain of death. In 1601 the law was slightly modified by 43 Eliz., c.2; this was the statute on which poor relief was to be based until modern times.

Erosion of the distinctive role of the bridewells

The Webbs estimate that altogether there may have been 200 houses of correction.[66] Coke — perhaps extravagantly — argued that for some time after their establishment they achieved the distinctive objectives for which they had been set up 'for ... whilst justices of peace and other officers were diligent and industrious, there was not a rogue to be seen in any part of England'.[67] Yet by the end of the seventeenth century this extensive system of reformatory prisons lost much of its distinctive identity, and in function and administration the bridewells largely merged with the gaols. How did this come about?

Coke simply says that 'when justices and other officers became *tepidi* or *trepidi* rogues, etc., swarmed again'.[68] The Webbs also throw the blame on the justices:

> Once the master appointed, and his salary fixed, on the understanding that there was to be no other expense thrown on the rates, the Justices, at any rate after the Restoration, seem usually to have given no more thought or attention to the House of Correction than they did to the county gaol. Both institutions were, in effect, run as private ventures of their masters or keepers.[69]

True, they do itemise some factors which may have influenced this change of function, but eventually they concede their perplexity as to the exact course of events.[70]

---

66 S. and B. Webb, *English Prisons Under Local Government*, p. 12.
67 Edward Coke, *Institutes of the Laws of England*, Part II, p. 728.
68 *Ibid*.
69 S. and B. Webb, *English Prisons Under Local Government*, pp. 14-15.
70 They mention the settlement laws and the practice of 'passing' vagrants rather than retaining them for punishment; the contracting out of the poor to an individual who then established his own workhouse — thus keeping a section of the poor out of the houses of correction; and the growing use by the justices of the houses of correction as places to which minor offenders were sent, supposedly to be set to work, rather than to the gaols where they did not work. Elsewhere they say,

> Whether by reason of the very nature of their administration as 'mixed' institutions, or from some other cause, we see them [the bridewells] insensibly becoming, as regards regimen and severity, and apparently as regards the character of their inmates, practically indistinguishable from the gaols of the time (*English Poor Law History: The Old Poor Law*, p. 86).

That administrative factors were important there can be no doubt. The houses of correction were such a novel administrative form that it is almost sufficient explanation to suggest that the forces of conservatism, greed and sloth were only having their natural effect upon society with a compulsion to return to more usual and acceptable customs and norms. Less than fifty years after the establishment of Bridewell, for example, the City authorities briefly attempted to farm it out, only to have to retrieve it within a few months from the lessees amidst scandal and recrimination.[71]

In some respects, even in its early days, Bridewell was not entirely free from some of the administrative features and practices of the gaols. Fees were charged; O'Donoghue argues with fair reason that these authorised charges 'do not appear to have been excessive, and the destitute were not charged at all', but he seems to miss the point. What justification could there be for fee-charging in a reformatory or relieving establishment? Such a practice led to the purchase of other favours from the staff and was an encouragement to extortion similar to that of the gaols.[72]

Bridewell was also from time to time used as an ordinary gaol by the government; on these occasions prisoners were sent there, not for reformation, for that would have been inappropriate, but simply for safe custody. During the reign of Elizabeth, for example, Bridewell served as a state prison for Puritans and Roman Catholics and for Spanish prisoners of war.[73] It was also used, now and again, by the Privy Council for 'men and women who had libelled king, queen or courtier, who were suspected of stealing plate from Whitehall palace or of carrying letters from a suitor to a wealthy ward of the King'.[74] According to Judges, 'As early as 1591, if not before, it was also used

---

71 This was in 1602. The prison was leased for ten years at £300 per annum, and the promoters bound themselves to set the 'idle people and ruffians' to work, and not to use the work-rooms for any other purposes. Within a few months rumours of abuses resulted in an investigation. It was then discovered that only sixty-three prisoners were being held. Of thirty-eight females only eighteen of the poorest sort were at work, and the rest were living a life of vice and ease.

'To reduce the daily number from two-hundred – the average number – to sixty persons the lessees had not hesitated to make wholesale discharges of the vagrants without any reference to the governors, whose authority they flouted', reports O'Donoghue. The contractors accused each other of immorality with the prostitutes (*op. cit.*, I, p. 192. See also Judges, *op. cit.*, p. lxiii).

72 O'Donoghue, *op. cit.*, I, p. 238: in 1599 the matron received 1*d*. per night from those who slept in beds provided by the institution, and 2*d*. per night from those who had their own beds. The porter received 2*d*. per night from every male prisoner and the steward received 2*d*. discharge fee from every prisoner able to pay.

73 *Ibid.*, p. 185.

74 *Ibid.*, II, p. 26.

as a prison of arrest for miscellaneous criminal charges. After the turn of the century it was employed regularly as a common jail for prisoners arrested in the neighbourhood'.[75] Later, during the Civil War, Cavalier captives were consigned to Bridewell.[76] But the presence of these special consignments did not interfere with the usual activities of the prison. However, these were not the uses for which Bridewell had been established, and they can only have created inconvenient precedents in régime and administration and weakened its claim for consideration as a prison of a distinct type.

Legislation and the pressures of the Privy Council also, in a paradoxical way, undermined the separate standing of the houses of correction nationally. In the first decade of the seventeenth century, as the Webbs noted, the house of correction 'was repeatedly pressed on the attention of Quarter Sessions as an indispensable instrument in the struggle against vagrancy. James the First urged the county gentlemen in a Speech from the Throne, to "Look to the Houses of Correction" '.[77] Whereas under the various enactments of Elizabeth the provision of bridewells had been permissive, under James it became mandatory. In 1609, 7 Jac. I, c.4 ordered the counties to provide one or more houses of correction, which were to be equipped with 'mills, turns, cards, and suchlike necessary implements, to get rogues, vagabonds, sturdy beggars or other idle vagrant and disorderly persons on work'.[78] No mention was made in this Act of the relieving function of the houses of correction and Leonard observes that this 'probably marks the time when Houses of Correction ceased to be half workhouses and became very much more like gaols'.[79] So, while this Act ensured that bridewells would come into use throughout the country, its penal emphasis helped to confuse and merge their functions with those of the gaols.

From the 1530s Tudor monarchs had been able to rely on an increasingly effective Privy Council as an instrument of government.[80] In fact, from 1590 to 1640 the Privy Council was probably of greater importance than legislation in 'The establishment of an administrative hierarchy, by which it was sought to get the laws relating to the economic conditions of the poor systematically put in operation all over the kingdom'.[81] The vigilant Privy Council harassed the justices and the mayors into obedience both to the letter and the spirit of the legislation, and by 1635 reports from the justices indicate that houses

---

75 Judges, *op. cit.*, p. 139, n. 10.
76 Leonard, *op. cit.*, Appendix XIV, p. 370.
77 S. and B. Webb, *English Poor Law History: The Old Poor Law*, p. 83.
78 *Ibid.*
79 Leonard, *op. cit.*, p. 137.
80 G.R. Elton, *The Tudor Revolution in Government*, p. 424.
81 S. and B. Webb, *English Poor Law History: The Old Poor Law*, p. 60.

of correction had been established in most places.[82] But these followed the model set forth in 7 Jac. I, c.4, instead of the more complex example of London Bridewell and some others financed by endowment as well as public funds. That this was the intention of the Privy Council's policy is clearly expressed in the January 1630 Book of Orders which directed that houses of correction in all counties should be established next to the gaol.[83] The long-term possibilities of this order are clear: savings in management and maintenance costs could be made if the two physically close establishments were functionally and administratively united. Despite a few exceptions the penal character of the bridewells grew more pronounced and accepted at this time.[84]

But the statutes and Orders in Council only inform us as to the fact that changes were taking place in the function and administration of the houses of correction; for a fuller explanation of the reasons we must look closely at the rearrangements which were taking place in broader social, economic and ideological forces, which can only be discussed here in the most general terms.

Elizabethan social policy was essentially conservative in nature.[85] It emphasised stability and integration, and saw the bridewells as an instrument to that end. Stuart social policy shared many of these characteristics, but was also influenced by the more puritan strains of Protestantism which had developed, and which led people to regard the poor in a different light in their formulation of a theory of social integration. Tawney may well be pointing to the source of that difference when he notes that 'The moral self-sufficiency of the Puritan nerved his will, but it corroded his sense of social solidarity. For, if each individual's destiny hangs on a private transaction between himself and his Maker, what room is left for human intervention?' And:

---

82 Leonard, *op. cit.*, pp. 227-8. Aydelotte argues that 'The task of instructing the Justices of the Peace and Overseers of the Poor in their duties and of making them feel a responsibility to the Privy Council for performing them was not adequately performed until 1630-1' (*op. cit.*, p. 72).

83 Leonard, *op. cit.*, p. 158.

84 The Webbs list a number of houses of correction which could be fitted more easily within the framework of poor relief than the penal system: Richmond House of Correction in Yorkshire, founded in the 1620s, so strongly emphasised the provision of work for the poor that it paid inmates the statutory wage for their labour; Tothill Fields, the Westminster bridewell founded in 1615, also in its early days stressed its relief function by providing non-penal work. During this period the Yorkshire justices proposed the building of a house of correction at Whitby to relieve the victims of the seasonal fluctuations in the fishing trade; furthermore, at Thame (Oxfordshire), Wrexham (Denbighshire), Warrington (Cheshire) and the city of Poole, 'we find, at a later date, the House of Correction and the parish poorhouse existing on the same site and sometimes in the same building' (S. and B. Webb, *English Poor Law History: The Old Poor Law*, pp. 84-5).

85 See above, pp. 23-4.

Convinced that character is all and circumstances nothing, he sees in the poverty of those who fall by the way, not a misfortune to be pitied and relieved, but a moral failing to be condemned, and in riches, not an object of suspicion . . . but the blessing which rewards the triumph of energy and will.[86]

What is suggested is that the always uneasy dividing line between relief and suppression in social policy was generally breached by the maturing of initially ambivalent puritan attitudes towards the poor. It would be unwise to put this forward in other than tentative terms as an explanation for the changes in use and administration of the houses of correction; but it offers a plausible reason why the novel and fledgling identity of the reformatory houses of correction could not be sustained against the familiar utility of the custodial gaols. The able-bodied poor were increasingly treated as criminals and to herd them with vagabonds, vagrants, the morally dissolute and other minor misdemeanants, presented fewer and fewer conceptual problems: such people deserved whipping and punitive imprisonment and both punishments could be inflicted in the penal bridewells. Christopher Hill cites a puritan condemnation of vagabonds which makes clear the extent to which poverty without the will to work was seen as a crime against society. It is possibly an exaggerated statement of the opinion, but it surely illustrates the tendency:

First for rogues and runagates who, being strong and lusty, make begging and wandering their trade of life; that they be severely punished and set to work; that no maintenance or allowance be given unto them (without punishment, unless they settle themselves to labour): for so the Apostle speaketh, *He that will not work, let him not eat*. And what more dishonest thing can be in a Christian commonweal that such men should be permitted? which fill the land with sin, making their life nothing else but a continual practice of filthiness, theft and idleness (which are sins of Sodom), that live without a calling, without magistracy, without ministry, without God in the world; that neither glorify God, nor serve the prince, nor profit the commonweal; but are an unprofitable burthen to the earth or blot to the state, and (as drones) live on other men's labours, and on the sweat of other men's brows. These filthy persons and unprofitable generation, this refuse and off-scouring of the world, must be purged away by the hand of the magistrate, in whose hand there is power, and to whom God hath for this intent committed the sword . . . for the best mercy to such is to help them

86 Tawney, *op. cit.*, pp. 229-30.

out of their sin, by giving them [employment or] due correction, till they do content to labour and eat their own bread.[87]

Administrative and ideological factors were combined with especial force by the Civil War and its aftermath. At one level there was immediate political and administrative upset and shortage of funds:

It was inevitable that, in the anarchy of the Civil War, both private charity and public relief should fall on evil days. In London charitable endowments seem to have suffered from more than ordinary malversation, and there were complaints that the income both of Bridewell and the Hospitals was seriously reduced. In the country, the records of Quarter Sessions paint a picture of confusion, in which the machinery of presentment by constables to justices has broken down, and a long wail arises, that thieves are multiplied, the poor are neglected, and vagrants wander to and fro at their will.[88]

But the Civil War was more than a temporary upset, to be followed by 'business as usual'. It was, rather, the political and administrative culmination of a series of profound social and economic changes, and when the dust had settled it was apparent that the advance to the 'England of the future', against which Elizabethan social policy had striven, had largely been achieved. The power of the Privy Council — a key factor in the outbreak of the Civil War — was shattered, and it had been the Privy Council that had kept the magistrates and town officials diligent in the performance of their duties in the social sphere.[89] The system of poor relief suffered particularly, and the clauses of the 1601 Act relating to the provision of work became a dead letter: Tawney remarks that since these duties had always been unpopular with the local authorities

---

87 John Dod and Robert Cleaver, *The Ten Commandments*, 1607, *cit*. Hill, *op. cit*., p. 275. The change in attitude towards the poor among those responsible for policy and administration is discussed in D.M. Loades's *Politics and the Nation 1450-1660*. He observes that James's council made only feeble attempts to enforce the Poor Law of 1601. The justices, he says,

> had always been inclined to drag their feet over the provision of relief, and this reluctance was so intensified by the spread of what was basically a puritan attitude to poverty among the well-to-do. The poor were seen, rightly enough, as improvident, but instead of regarding improvidence as the consequence of poverty, it was interpreted as the cause. To be poor thus acquired a stigma, and the 'idleness' and 'luxury' of the lower classes became a favourite topic of conversation (pp. 347-8).

88 Tawney, *op. cit*., p. 261.
89 Hill (*op. cit*., p. 224) argues that 'the abolition of the Star Chamber led to the dictatorship of J.P.s in local government'.

whom they involved in considerable expense, it is not surprising that, with the cessation of pressure by the Central Government, they should, except here and there, have been neglected. What is more significant, however, than the practical deficiencies in the administration of relief, was the rise of a new school of opinion, which regarded with repugnance the whole body of social theory of which both private charity and public relief had been the expression.[90]

The houses of correction had their origin in the broad conservative concerns of Tudor social policy, and flourished as an integral part of Elizabethan and Jacobean poor relief and social control. The Webbs and other commentators speak of the decline of the bridewells; that is only one way of viewing the change that they underwent in the seventeenth century. They were no longer required for many of the purposes for which they had originally been intended and were simply permitted to be appropriated to the cheap custodial punishment of minor offenders, and financed and administered accordingly.

90 Tawney, *op. cit.*, p. 261. This view is shared by Hill who notes that after 1660 even the pretence of state regulation had been abandoned, and each parish went its own way. J.P.s were no longer supervised by the Privy Council. With no Privy Council interference, serious attempts to set the poor on work were also abandoned: state policy now concentrated on restricting the mobility of labour (*op. cit.*, p. 285).

3   Prisons in the eighteenth century

The physical condition and haphazard administration of prisons in the eighteenth century are probably the aspects of English penal history most familiar to the general student. The work of Oglethorpe, Fielding, Smith and John Howard has been extensively drawn upon by modern writers to substantiate an account of unrelieved misery, sexual promiscuity, disease, squalor and extortion. Light begins to be shed in the last quarter of the century (if their account is accepted) and from then on penal history is represented as progress — however slow and hard fought. Superficially this is an accurate enough picture, but if history is concerned with explaining the reasons as well as stating the facts, then this outline is not very helpful. Ultimately it leads the student to a series of solecisms, to a characterisation of the legal, religious and intellectual principles of the eighteenth century as callous, barbaric and retrogressive, and to an explanation of improving changes that consists in claiming that society became more caring, civilised and progressive; analysis is then confined to the ingredients of the moral improvement. Such a deterministic approach places policy and policy-makers on a narrow stage of modern design and attributes to them only the aspirations, feelings and choices of the modern commentator.

This chapter will, therefore, examine the social, ideological and constitutional elements in prison policy and administration in the eighteenth century, so as to provide a background against which, in the next chapter, various changes in policy and administration will be considered.

Prisons and their social setting

It would be pointless to repeat here the ample descriptions of the physical and moral state of the eighteenth-century prisons so luminously portrayed in the works of Howard, Neild and the Webbs. A few matters need to be stressed or recalled, however, and it is probably as well to start with the physical quality of these prisons.

The most commonly predominating feature of the prisons was probably their stinking filthiness. The stench of Newgate nauseated even longtime inhabitants of malodorous London:

> The foul and constant smell polluted what little food and water the prisoners could get hold of and impregnated their clothes and clung to their hair. It was everywhere and it was inescapable; revolting their nostrils and clogging their lungs, pervading their whole existence.[1]

Traders living in the neighbourhood protested and petitioned the Common Council for relief because the smell of the prison badly affected business.[2] Reluctance to visit the neighbourhood of Newgate was based on more than delicate sensibilities: the miasmatic theory of disease transmission made even the district appear dangerous. Confirmation was constantly being found for this fear: in 1750, for example, after a new ventilation system had been provided at Newgate, seven of the eleven workmen who installed the machinery contracted gaol fever, as did some of their relatives.[3]

The prison buildings were usually defective in several respects, being sometimes poorly adapted to their purpose or shoddily built. Sewers were overcharged and easily blocked, spilling their contents into the prison. The numbers of inmates rose and fell in accordance with the gaol deliveries, but a state of overcrowding was commonest. Lack of cleaning materials and the apathy towards maintenance of hygiene meant that squalor remained undisturbed.[4] The unregulated, frequently packed, assemblage of unwashed, verminous, often starving and diseased prisoners in ill-ventilated and badly sewered rooms, was a spontaneous breeding ground of typhus.[5] The prisons were such charnel houses that

1 Christopher Hibbert, *The Road to Tyburn*, pp. 86-7.
2 Anthony Babington, *The English Bastille*, p. 99.
3 *Ibid*., pp. 97-9, *passim*.
4 Wayne Joseph Sheehan, thesis: 'The London Prison System, 1666-1795', pp. 84-95, *passim*.
5 Dr William Smith, who visited the London prisons in the 1770s, shortly before Howard, described some of the prisoners whom he saw. They included

> Vagrants and disorderly women of the very lowest and most wretched class of human beings, almost naked, with only a few filthy rags almost alive and in motion with vermin, their bodies rotting with the bad distemper, and covered in itch, scorbutic and venereal ulcers. . . .

At Clerkenwell and at Tothill Fields bridewells 'Thirty, and sometimes near forty of these unhappy wretches are crowded or crammed together in one ward, where in the dark they bruise and beat one another in the most shocking manner' (*State of the Gaols in London, Westminster and Borough of Southwark*, pp. 9-10).

even gaolers and turnkeys were afraid to enter some wards. Outbreaks of gaol diseases were often fatal to witnesses, counsel and judges, besides prisoners and prison staff. In court towns these incidents provoked public panics and heightened the horror of prisons as extremely dangerous places.[6]

But prison conditions in provincial towns were no better. The archbishop of York wrote in 1746 of York prison:

> The prisoners die and the Recorder told me yesterday when the turnkey opens the cells in the morning, the steam and stench is intolerable and scarce credible. The very walls are covered with lice in the room over which the grand jury sit.[7]

Prison hygiene did not alter greatly in the course of years. When Howard made his extensive visitations in the 1770s he was obliged to travel on horseback because the smell given off by his clothes, just from a few hours' contact, did not permit of coach travel. Even his notebook had to be spread open before a fire and disinfected before he could use it.[8] The main variation in the risks run by prisoners and staff seems to have arisen from the dimensions of the establishment: fever was probably a characteristic of the larger prisons; perishing from neglect and heavy fettering a likelier fate in the smaller ruinous ones.[9]

6 S. and B. Webb, *English Prisons Under Local Government*, p. 20, n. 1; *Gentleman's Magazine* (May 1750), XX, p. 235; (July 1767), XXXVII, p. 340; O'Donoghue, *Bridewell Hospital*, II, p. 171 (outbreaks at Bridewell in the late seventeenth and early eighteenth century); Dorothy Marshall, *The English Poor in the Eighteenth Century*, pp. 249-50.

7 *Cit.* Sir William Holdsworth, *A History of English Law*, X, p. 182, n. 7.

8 J.L. and B. Hammond, 'Poverty, Crime and Philanthropy', in A.S. Turberville (ed.), *Johnson's England*, p. 319.

9 Most prison and town populations were small. In 1776 Howard found that there were 4,084 prisoners in England and Wales; 1,696 of these were in London and 2,437 were debtors. In 1779 he found 4,375 and estimated that almost half were debtors. The prisons varied greatly in size, but small establishments predominated. Only four prisons had more than a hundred inmates (King's Bench, Newgate, the Fleet and Clerkenwell bridewell) whilst 130 had under ten. Because of the still comparatively rare use of sentences of imprisonment numbers continued to rise and fall markedly with the pace of gaol deliveries; between 1756 and 1764 at Newgate, for example, the reported population ranged from a minimum of about 130 to a maximum of about 840. (See S. and B. Webb, *op. cit.*, p. 31, n. 3, and Babington, *op. cit.*, p. 137.)

 By the end of George I's reign many towns and industrial villages had grown substantially, but numbers were still small by modern standards. London reached a population of half a million, Bristol and Norwich 50,000; Manchester, Sheffield, Leeds, Halifax, Birmingham and Coventry expanded without reaching 50,000. By the 1770s 'The great majority even of the more flourishing lesser towns only had from two to four thousand inhabitants' (G.D.H. Cole, 'Town-life in the Provinces', in A.S. Turberville (ed.), *Johnson's England*, p. 203. See also J.H. Plumb, *England in the Eighteenth Century*, p. 11).

Staffing, organisation and finance retained their general medieval and Tudor features. Fee-taking and trading on the part of the gaolers and turnkeys had, if anything, expanded in volume and grown more burdensome in type and degree of extortion employed, and, with the practice of garnish or chummage, was a seemingly ineradicable oppression in prison life.[10]

General social conditions — the mortality rate, public health and hygiene, standards of housing and so forth — are often blamed in accounting for the state of the prisons:

> The great difficulty for a humanitarian in the Britain of that age must have been how to devise any form of punitive confinement which would not have been an improvement on the general standard of living conditions in most of the urban areas. . . . It was not surprising that few authoritative voices spoke up in favour of any radical reforms in the penal system. . . .[11]

The majority of the people, according to this argument, must have lived in such primitive conditions that it required primitive measures, corporal or capital punishment, to be effective: any improvement in the prisons might be a positive encouragement to commit crime. As the prisons dealt mainly with the poor, one could say that the state of the gaols and houses of correction was on a level with their standards and expectations.

> The lower strata of the population of the capital, the dockers and unskilled labour of a great mart and port, lived under the most filthy conditions of overcrowding, without sanitation, police or

10 Garnish or chummage were the names given to the demands for money, food or goods frequently made upon threat of violence by ensconced prisoners upon those who were newly-arrived. The spoils were variously shared among the inmates of a ward or section. Sheehan (*op. cit.*, p. 190) says that in London these practices reached a peak during the years 1690-1732, being curbed thereafter by the city authorities. The fee-takers at Bridewell were as determinedly rapacious as any gaol keeper. Ned Ward, who visited Bridewell in 1700, found there a prisoner who had been acquitted of all charges against him, but who was being held because he could not pay the fees. Ward exclaimed:

> Thought I, what a Rigorous Uncharitable Thing is this, that so Noble a Gift, intended, when first given, to so Good an End, should be thus perverted. And what was design'd to prevent People's falling into Misery, Thro' *Laziness* or *Ill-Courses*, should now be so corrupted by such *Unchristian Confinement* as to Starve a Poor Wretch, because he wants Money to satisfie the demands of a *Mercenary Cerberus*, when discharg'd of the Prison by the Court! Such Severe, nay Barbarous Usage, is a Shame to our *Laws* and Unhappiness to our *Nation*, and a scandal to *Christianity* (*The London Spy*, pp. 138-9).

11 Babington, *op. cit.*, p. 93.

doctors, and far beyond the range of philanthropy, education and religion. . . . The death-rate among them was appalling, and was still going up because they were learning to drink spirits instead of ale.[12]

Housing and community conditions, indeed, closely resembled prison life in the poorer areas. Here people lived in overcrowded tenement slums, in close proximity to gin-shops, brothels and 'filthy doss-houses into which for a penny a night were admitted beggars, prostitutes, children and drunken labourers to sleep, regardless of age or sex, and as many as twenty in a small room, on the lousy rat-ridden straw'.[13] 'They know no better, anyway' would have been a ready and complacent argument for querulous or oversensitive ratepayers.[14] Principles of social equity were satisfied in the case of the better-off, and more squeamish, prisoners since they could by purchase do much to improve their conditions. So thoroughly was this line of reasoning accepted that no exception was made for prisons in the application of the window-tax, with the inevitable consequence that gaolers, with an eye to their profits, blocked up many windows, causing further deterioration in

12 G.M. Trevelyan, *English Social History*, p. 331. Cole and Postgate noted that by mid-century it was said that three-quarters of London's children died before reaching the age of five (*The Common People*, p. 60).

13 Christopher Hibbert, *op. cit.*, p. 24. Urban sanitary conditions were generally minimal:

> There was no sanitary system; an open cesspool in the court often served the richer inhabitants; the poor . . . made a public convenience of every nook and cranny. . . . All tradesmen and craftsmen used the street as their dustbin, including butchers who threw out the refuse of their shambles to decay and moulder in the streets. . . . All houses and cellars were desperately overcrowded – ten to a room was common in Manchester. It was reported that often the rooms were without furniture and lacking even beds; the occupants slept close together on shavings for warmth. Disease was rampant and unchecked, smallpox, typhus, typhoid, and dysentery made death a common-place (Plumb, *op. cit.*, p. 12).

There was thus no great contrast between life in such circumstances and life in prison. This point is confirmed by the fact that, according to Sheehan, 'There is scattered evidence that these gaols [the Compters] frequently served a charitable purpose as a refuge for the poor, sick, and helpless of the City' (*op. cit.*, p. 118).

14 Trevelyan observes that, in contrast to poor-law administration, provision for police and prisons was more likely to be viewed parsimoniously by the ratepayers:

> it was legally obligatory to raise a poor rate in every parish to deal with its poor, whereas the ratepayers regarded it as an unusual hardship if the magistrates raised any rate to pay for roads, prisons, sanitation or police (*op. cit.*, p. 352).

And as the Webbs, Dorothy Marshall, and many others have shown, the poor law was administered with minimal regard for efficiency, honesty and hygiene.

living conditions.[15]

Although from time to time there were expressions of public unease and political and legal rumblings, the state of its prisons brought little sustained concern to the community for at least three-quarters of the eighteenth century. Yet these very same prisons and conditions were later condemned as outrageous and unacceptable. It is necessary, therefore, to describe the ideological opinions and constitutional arrangements which allowed this prison policy to prevail.

Philanthropy and contemporary philosophies of crime and punishment

The difficulty with a completely relativist interpretation of prison policy is that it takes too much for granted. It assumes that institutions are uniformly an index to the development of their societies — legal, organisational, educational and so forth. But this view ignores the fact that institutions develop unevenly within the life of the nation, being subject to different social priorities and techniques. The eighteenth century was, for example, the century of large private houses with their associated culture, and substantial developments in music and the arts. Great libraries and museums were founded; naval, agricultural and mechanical sciences brought forth many notable discoveries and new techniques. There was even considerable innovation in lines of thought and modes of endowment and organisation which affected some public institutions, such as hospitals. In other words, prisons — in a seemingly inert (or deteriorating) state — did not reflect the other achievements or the moral and material potential of their society. The relativist view, moreover, implies a high degree of consensus; yet both Anglicans and Dissenters, working together in the three great evangelical and educational societies,[16] held extremely critical views of social and moral conditions and the place of prisons and numerous other institutions in society. Whether viewed as intolerant and bigoted or not, the ideas and activities of such groups alone would make it impossible to argue that there was tacit or active agreement on social and penal policy and moral attitudes.[17] Moreover, several inquiries into prison conditions were

15 Window-tax was first introduced in 1696 and not finally abolished until 1851. It was mentioned by Howard and others as an important factor in the stifling and unhealthy atmosphere of prisons.
16 The Society for the Promotion of Christian Knowledge, the Society for the Propagation of the Gospel in Foreign Parts, and the Society for the Reformation of Manners.
17 Although Lecky says that after the mid-1730s the religious societies sank into comparative insignificance, by the middle of the century the Society for the Reformation of Manners had become extinct (W.E.H. Lecky, *A History of England in the Eighteenth Century*, III, p. 34).

undertaken or demanded by such individuals and groups. Dr Thomas Bray headed a committee of the SPCK (Society for the Promotion of Christian Knowledge) set up by Bishop Compton, which visited Newgate and Marshalsea prisons in 1702; but their report went 'quite unheeded'.[18] A committee of the House of Commons, proposed by John Pocklington in November 1696 to inquire into the Fleet prison, also documented conditions in some detail, but similarly had no perceptible effect on prison policy or administration.[19] Even the famous 1729 committee under Oglethorpe (who had become friendly with Dr Bray) which exposed the tortures and appalling cruelties practised by Huggins, Bambridge, Acton, Barnes and others of the staff in the Fleet and Marshalsea prisons had little practical impact on the condition of the gaols.[20] In the 1730s William Hay 'introduced Bill after Bill for the erection of new local prisons and their supervision by inspectors appointed by the Lord Chancellor'.[21] In 1753 the veteran Oglethorpe (by then a national hero) headed another committee, this time reporting upon the King's Bench. Apart from confirming that prison conditions had changed little, if at all, this inquiry also had little effect.[22]

The appalling visions of horror incidentally given in the plays and novels of Gay and Smollett and Fielding, like the revelations before the House of Commons Committee in 1729, seem to have been taken by contemporaries as matter of course. Even to such exceptional citizens as John Wesley and Samuel Johnson — even to an active-minded, reforming administrator like Henry Fielding — the state of the prisons seemed an evil for which there was no remedy.[23]

18 S. and B. Webb, *op. cit.*, p. 26. The report was entitled 'An Essay towards the Reformation of Newgate and the Other Prisons in and about London'. It was not published for more than 150 years, and first printed in W. Hepworth Dixon's biography of Howard. R.S.E. Hinde (*The British Penal System 1773-1950*, pp. 21-6) reproduces the document in full.

19 *Journal of the House of Commons*, XI, pp. 585, 642-4.

20 Oglethorpe's indignation had been fired by the ill-treatment of his friend, Robert Castell, who was committed to the Fleet for debt. Not even the principal culprits uncovered by this investigation, whose report was described by the Webbs as 'one of the most horrifying of prison documents', were punished. Huggins, Bambridge and their several underlings were prosecuted, but their trials miscarried because the juries were sympathetic (no doubt because a lot of money was involved). Bambridge and Huggins were portrayed in Hogarth's plate of the Oglethorpe Committee's visit to the Fleet, but apparently the whole incident provoked much less popular indignation than that felt by committee members. Huggins 'afterwards lived in comfort to the age of ninety' (Hibbert, *op. cit.*, p. 92).

21 S. and B. Webb, *op. cit.*, p. 27.

22 There was an Act reinvesting in the Crown the appointing patronage of the Marshal of King's Bench, and providing for the rebuilding of that prison: but there were no general consequences for prison administration.

23 S. and B. Webb, *op. cit.*, p. 31.

One can well understand the ring of perplexity in William Guy's observation that between 1729 and 1773 prison reform 'seems to have fallen asleep'.[24] But why should this have been so? It is necessary to take note of the predominant ideology of imprisonment: as has been argued, there was no *necessarily* direct causal relationship between social conditions and institutional priorities.

It is relevant to draw attention to the channels into which humanitarian feeling flowed in the early part of the century. Whilst it inspired private initiative,[25] 'it had as yet little effect on executive, municipal or legislative action'.[26]

> It was not indeed that men of goodwill and capacity were deficient in the England of the first two Georges. . . . But theirs were at best individual efforts; and, owing largely to the political theories of the time, there was no systematic and continued attempt to deal with such problems of local government as the prevention of crime and of dire distress.[27]

That is true enough, but criminological and penological theories might have been added to political theories, for it is notable that such nationally ordered ameliorations of prison conditions as there were in the first part of the century affected only debtors,[28] and it seems likely

24 William A. Guy, 'Address on John Howard', *Journal of the Statistical Society* (1875), XXXVIII, p. 438.

25 The Hammonds note, for example, that 'poor debtors were a favourite object of compassion and the charitable often left them legacies' (*op. cit.*, p. 325).

26 Trevelyan, *op. cit.*, p. 347.

27 Basil Williams, *The Whig Supremacy, 1714-1760*, pp. 138-9.

28 There were, for example, relatively frequent Insolvency Acts (thirty-seven between 1670 and 1800) allowing the release of all debtors in prison on a certain day — a practice which showed that although feelings were aroused they were not translated into movements for institutional change. There was also the Act which followed Oglethorpe's first inquiry, 2 Geo. II, c.22. This prohibited the involuntary detention in bailiffs' 'spunging houses', permitted debtors freely to order food, bedding, etc., forbade the taking of any but lawful fees and ordered a table of such fees to be displayed in every gaol. It also provided that creditors should pay 2s. 4d. weekly to their imprisoned debtors. The maximum fine for violation by the sheriff, under-sheriff, etc., was £50 with treble costs, but despite such penalties violations were difficult to suppress. In 1808, Sir Richard Phillips recorded that there were no fewer than thirteen spunging houses in Middlesex and two in the City. An arrested debtor could go to whichever one of these he preferred (*A Letter to the Livery of London*, p. 179). As late as the 1840s spunging houses were still in use — one well-known establishment was Sloman's, very conveniently situated near Chancery Lane (Montague Williams, *Leaves of a Life*, p. 4).
  The Act which followed Oglethorpe's second inquiry, 32 Geo. II, c.28, was largely directed against 'politic bankrupts', forcing them, after a certain time in prison, to disclose and deliver their assets for their creditors' benefit. The Act repeated earlier provisions allowing (by cumbersome legal process)

that the energies of 'men of goodwill and capacity' were differently directed. But this should not be overemphasised for, in any event, there was, in the reigns of George I and George II, less parliamentary initiative and legislation than in any other period.[29]

To modern observers national inaction on police and prisons seems odd. Reliable statistical evidence is sparse and extremely hard to light upon,[30] but there can be no doubt that many contemporaries thought that disorder had grown to epidemic and intolerable proportions in the first part of the century. In 1731 a writer in the *London Journal* lamented the increase in danger faced by the pedestrian after nightfall in London,[31] but the position was to deteriorate further. Bishop Benson wrote from London, just after the middle of the century: 'There is not only no safety of living in this town, but scarcely any in the country now robbery and murther are grown so frequent. Our people are now become what they never before were, cruel and inhuman.'[32] Indeed, Horace Walpole claimed (at about the same time) that 'One is forced to travel even at noon as if one were going into battle'. Police power, based on the watch system, and extensive use of spies and rewards (and pardons for informers), was quite inadequate to control the levels of crime and, especially, mob violence.[33]

4*d*. a day to imprisoned debtors from their creditors. Section 6 of this Act gave potentially extensive powers of administration to the justices. See below, p. 66.

29 Williams, *op. cit.*, pp. 8-9.
30 But see J.M. Beattie's 'The Pattern of Crime in England 1660-1800' (p. 68). This essay uses archive material which clearly shows a substantial increase in indictments for crimes of violence in the 1730s in the London parishes of Surrey.
31 Norma Myra Macdonald, thesis: 'The Presentation of Oppression in the English Novel from Godwin to Dickens', p. 33.
32 *Cit*. Lecky, *op. cit*., II, p. 103. Benson blamed gin-drinking for this change in character. Excessive gin-drinking — especially noticeable because of the alarming mortality rates — was substantially curbed by the Act of 1751 (24 Geo. II, c.40). Radzinowicz points out that widespread gambling, alcoholism and gin-drinking were only some of the factors contributing to feelings of especial insecurity about the middle of the century. The '45 Rebellion had only recently been crushed and there existed in London a large and unruly mob:

These circumstances were propitious to the formation of a veritable 'classe dangereuse', composed of robbers, thieves, receivers of stolen property, astute vagrants, beggars and prostitutes. An utterly inadequate and often corrupt police, disorganised prisons — even then a public scandal — and the gravely inefficient administration of the Poor Law, all acted as direct or indirect incentives to crime (Leon Radzinowicz, *A History of English Criminal Law*, I, p. 401).

33 The civil power remained right until 1829 (and for years after that in many parts of Britain) an inheritance from medieval England, and at the

When the eighteenth century had far advanced, robbers for whose apprehension large rewards were offered have been known to ride publicly and unmolested, before dusk, in the streets of London, surrounded by their armed adherents, through the midst of a half-terrified, half-curious crowd.[34]

Informed opinion was alarmed by the seeming dissolution of social discipline and the rising tide of disorder. But because of the dominant theories of social control and punishment this alarm did not lead to more action to improve the efficiency of the police or the quality of the prisons. The notion of a large police organisation was anathema in post-Revolution England. Freedom from the coercion of standing armies and the power of the Crown had been one of the planks in the policy of opponents of James II. Owing to this sensitivity and suspicion much reliance was placed on a strategy of spies and rewards, helped by penal laws which, later in the eighteenth century, extended the deterrent of the death penalty to an ever-increasing range of offences.[35] By the end of the reign of George II it has been estimated that no fewer than 160 felonies were punishable with the death penalty. Some

---

root of the system still lay the ancient Saxon principle of involving all men as part-timers in the business of maintaining the peace. . . . The system creaked badly in the seventeenth century and broke down completely in the eighteenth. . . . The total situation by, say, 1760 is thus a very striking one. The nation's first line of defence against disorder was crumbling at the very time when the onset of the Industrial Revolution was bringing the threat of violence nearer (T.A. Critchley, *The Conquest of Violence*, pp. 66-7).

---

34 Lecky, *op. cit.*, II, p. 109; although there appears to have been a decline in at least such flagrant law-breaking. Lecky cites a comment from 1757 to the effect that 'the reigning evil of street robberies has been almost wholly suppressed' and notes that, although London's system of policing (improved by the Fielding brothers) again became quite inefficient, 'the condition of London does not appear to have been at any subsequent period quite as bad as in the first half of the eighteenth century, though the country highways were still infested with robbers' (*ibid.*, p. 112).

35 Leon Radzinowicz points to some of the factors which were associated with this policy:

Liberal criminal procedure, the lack of an adequate police force and the unsatisfactory state of secondary punishments were the most important but not the only factors which favoured the extension of capital punishment (*op. cit.*, I, p. 33).

By 'liberal criminal procedure' he means an application of the processes of the law in such a way as to maximise chances of acquittal: judges overturning cases on a technicality and juries committing 'pious perjury' to avoid returning a guilty verdict on a felony. Wilfred Oldham ('The Administration of the System of Transportation of British Convicts 1763-1793', p. 27) gives several examples of the latter involving the alleged capital or non-capital value of goods and mode of theft, where juries returned perverse but merciful verdicts.

commentators consider even this a low figure, and cite one Act (9 Geo. I, c.22, the so-called Black Act) which, on a strict legalistic interpretation, *by itself* added between 200 and 230 capital felonies to the statute-books.[36]

So alien is this penal policy to modern thought that it is obvious that there are major divergences between today's accepted values and those of the first three-quarters of the eighteenth century. But those divergences should not lead us to overlook the fact that there are similar ones between the early Hanoverian and Tudor and Stuart periods. Mention has been made in the previous chapter of Tawney's view that the individualist strand of puritan social philosophy, as it developed during the seventeenth century, was essentially corrosive of social relations within the community. E.P. Thompson's recent analysis of penal policy carries this speculation convincingly into the early eighteenth century, and provides at least a tentative framework within which the distinctive character of early Hanoverian social and penal philosophy may be understood and appreciated.

> Somewhere between the Puritan gentry and officers of the Commonwealth and the great Whig managers of the 1720s some lapse had taken place. It is a historical problem which demands more serious research than solecisms as to the 'standards of the age'. And 'the age' turns out, on the most cursory inspection of enduring evidence, not to have had any such homogeneous standards.[37]

It is not possible here to go into the issues of political economy and social change which are raised by Thompson's views,[38] but the phenomenon to which they point — what he calls 'The Whig state of mind' — is an essential component of any consideration of the foundations of the predominant values in social and legal thinking during the reigns of

36 E.P. Thompson, *Whigs and Hunters*, p. 23.
37 *Ibid.*, p. 216.
38 Thompson focuses his analysis on the Black Act, which he sees as registering

> The long decline in the effectiveness of old methods of class control and discipline and their replacement by one standard recourse of authority: the example of terror. In place of the whipping-post and the stocks, manorial and corporate controls and the physical harrying of vagabonds, economists advocated the discipline of low wages and starvation, and lawyers the sanction of death. Both indicated an increasing impersonality in the mediation of class relations, and a change, not so much in the 'facts' of crime as in the *category* — 'crime' itself, as it was defined by the propertied. What was now to be punished was not an offence between men . . . but an offence against property. Since property was a thing it became possible to define offences as crimes against things, rather than as injuries to men. This enabled the law to assume . . . the posture of impartiality: it was neutral as between every degree of man, and defended only the inviolability of the ownership of things (*op. cit.*, pp. 206-7).

the first two Georges.

Whether one treats it at face value or as a rationalisation, it is none the less a fact that the extensive recourse to capital sentences entailed by this penal system was regarded as justified on humanitarian grounds. The essence of the system was held to be deterrence, not retribution. Hale's views were probably typical:

> Regularly the true or at least the principal end of punishment is to deter men from the breach of laws, so that they may not offend, *and so that they may not suffer at all*, the inflicting of punishments in most cases is more for example and to prevent evils, than to punish.[39]

Henry Fielding, writing in the 1750s about public order and the administration of criminal law, reiterates this argument. Approvingly he cites another of Hale's observations to the effect that 'Death itself is necessary to be annexed to Laws in many Cases by the Prudence of Lawgivers, though possibly beyond the single Merit of the Office simply considered', and amplifies:

> No man indeed of common Humanity or common Sense can think the Life of a Man and a few Shillings to be of an equal Consideration, or that the Law in punishing Theft with Death proceeds (as perhaps a private Person sometimes may) with any View to Vengeance. The Terror of the Example is the only Thing proposed, and one Man is sacrificed to the Preservation of Thousands.[40]

When faced by an apparently continual rise in crime, the first response of policy-makers who adopted the deterrent strategy was to increase the effectiveness of the central component by calling for more terrifying sanctions. Thus in 1701 the well-known pamphlet *Hanging not Punishment Enough* called for more severe forms of the ultimate sanction, contending that the 'design is not that Man's blood *should* be shed, but that it should *not*'. The penalties proposed would be so much dreaded that 'for Five Men condemned and Executed *now* you would hardly have *one* then'.[41] Some thirty years later George Ollyffe made a similar plea for more blood-curdling forms of execution, including the barbaric punishment of breaking on the wheel. He too asserted

---

39 Holdsworth, *op. cit.*, XI, p. 561 (my emphasis).
40 Henry Fielding, *An Enquiry into the Causes of the Late Increase of Robbers*, p. 92. See also B. de Mandeville (*An Enquiry into the Causes of the Frequent Executions at Tyburn*, p. 37) who commented, in a similar vein: 'The greatest Charity . . . and Compassion we can shew to our Fellow-Creatures, is an extraordinary severity.'
41 *Cit.* Radzinowicz, *op. cit.*, p. 233. Radzinowicz comments that this pamphlet testifies vividly to 'the then firmly entrenched belief in extreme intimidation as the only effective remedy for crime'.

the essential humanity of his proposals: 'Instead of a thousand lives now cut off in the common way of Execution, there may not be near a twentieth part of the Number according to this Scheme.'[42] This doctrine of maximum severity was indeed substantially and influentially upheld as late in the century as 1785 when William Paley published his *Principles of Moral and Political Philosophy*.[43]

It is only against this background of social conditions and penological thinking, *considered together* (and however sketchily represented), that contemporary attitudes to prison policy and administration can be understood. In discussing medieval imprisonment I observed that its three notional functions (adumbrated by Pugh) overlapped in practice. Punishment and coercion were well fulfilled by the conditions of disorder, danger and expense of the prisons, and sentencers had these factors in mind when committing to prison for duress or punishment. Similar considerations supported the use of imprisonment in the eighteenth century. Prison conditions have to be judged primarily by standards of the times. But when such a judgment is made one still finds that prison conditions were thought to be appalling, and prison administration was permeated with what were seen as abuses. Yet taken as a whole, the squalor, danger and extortion of prisons was the outcome of existing penal policy and a means of its practical application. In the 1790s, to many people the close air and squalid condition of a prison were considered as 'its necessary attributes, and even men of respectable judgement have supposed, in the case of Debtors, that the filth of the Prison, *SQUALOR CARCERIS*, was a proper means of compelling them to do justice to their Creditors'.[44] The financial and legal communities, although occasionally perplexed by a conflict in values, continued to believe that debtors should literally rot in prison. If such debtors could not pay, their plight warned others to live within their means, and thus reinforced the systems of credit and commerce. So ignored were the minimal Parliamentary provisions that outside London Howard found only twelve debtors who had obtained their allowance ('groats') under 32 Geo. II, c.28, and what Burke described in 1780 as 'the arbitrary discretion of a private, nay interested, and

---

42 *Cit.* Radzinowicz, *op. cit.*, p. 237.

43   Now that, whatever it may be, which is the cause and end of the punishment, ought undoubtedly to regulate the measure of the severity. But this cause appears to be founded, not in the guilt of the offender, but in the necessity of preventing the repetition of the offence: and hence results the reason, that crimes are not by any government punished in proportion to their guilt, nor in all cases ought to be so, but in proportion to the difficulty and the necessity of preventing them . . . (William Paley, *The Principles of Moral and Political Philosophy*, II, p. 267).

44 A. Wedderburn, *Observations on the State of the English Prisons*, p. 6.

irritated, individual' continued well into the second half of the nineteenth century to use the imprisonment of debtors as exerting not only individual duress but also general deterrence.[45]

For felons and misdemeanants the full rigour of the doctrine of maximum severity and general deterrence applied and it served them right: felons were awaiting execution anyway, and their interim conditions were therefore rather irrelevant; had they been reprieved for transportation, they were alive only as an act of grace and favour. Similar considerations applied in the case of the lesser offender, it being argued that since prison was

> provided for the Miscreant, and for the Miscreant Alone: who, having opposed the *ordinances*, has abandoned *the protection of the Laws*. Leave him to his doom of misery: Let him rot in the vapours of a dungeon; and drag his unwieldy chain, at the mercy of his Keeper.[46]

The sentiments were typical of 'Those gentlemen who, when they are told of the misery which our prisoners suffer, content themselves with saying, *Let them take care to keep out*, prefaced perhaps with an angry prayer. . .'.[47]

Thus was the state of the prisons justified by the theory of general maximum deterrence. For opponents of the sanguinary code this use of imprisonment created a formidable obstacle. They would not wish to represent prisons in the state they were as an acceptable alternative to the death penalty. Towards the end of George II's reign especially, prevailing penal doctrines must have seemed unassailable, and the administration of prisons unobjectionable. 'Where then is the Remedy?' asked Henry Fielding.

> Is it to enforce the Execution of the Law as it now stands, and to reform the present conduct of the several Bridewells? This [latter] would I believe be as difficult a work as the cleansing of the *Augean* Stables of old; and would require as extraordinary a Degree of Political, as that did of Natural Strength, to accomplish it. . . .[48]

Local administration and the prisons

The political ideas of Locke dominated early Hanoverian thinking about public administration.[49] For Locke the state had merely protective

45 This point is underlined by Howard's finding that only about half the counties gave debtors the (discretionary) county bread; felons were *entitled* to this allowance. Without 'groats' or county bread many debtors starved to death or quickly succumbed to gaol fever.
46 *Cit*. James Neild, *The State of the Prisons*, p. liv, n.
47 John Howard, *The State of the Prisons* (3rd edn), p. 12.
48 *Ibid*., p. 50.
49 Williams, *op. cit*., p. 3.

functions; it ensured the conditions under which citizens could enjoy their lives and property with the least possible interference.

Locke was no doubt expressing the whig revulsion from the paternal interference with the lives of the people and their rights of property so dear to James I and his successors. On the other hand his teaching encouraged a whig oligarchy to regard one of the chief objects of government to be the protection of their own rights of property and to adopt an attitude of neglect or indifference to social evils affecting the lower classes of society.[50]

The structure and state of local administration were therefore a reason and a guarantee of continuance for the prevailing doctrines of penal deterrence.

Locke's thinking was in line with the constitutional rearrangements of the Revolution, particularly the fundamental change in relations between central and local government.

The Privy Council no longer, as in Tudor and early Stuart days, kept them [the justices] in awe and guided their action on national principles. The Revolution of 1688, in one of its aspects, had been a revolt of these unpaid local magistrates against the Central Government which had overstrained their loyalty in religion and politics. . . . The Privy Council, by aiming at absolute power in all things, had lost powers which it had formerly exercised for the general good. In the Eighteenth Century the justices of the Peace might rather have been said to control the Central Government through the grand national Quarter Sessions of Parliament, than to be under any central control themselves.[51]

The justices had 'acquired virtual independence as the local oligarchies of the districts' and exercised powers 'over the population which made it possible for them to become the almost irresponsible tyrants of the neighbourhood'.[52] Executive government was notoriously weak in the eighteenth century: it was obliged to introduce Acts covering military, tax and colonial matters,

But the whole field of local government was left very largely to the localities themselves, or to those justices of the peace in the House of Commons who interested themselves in the various problems which arose in that field. . . . And . . . for the most part the initiation

50 *Ibid.*, p. 5.
51 Trevelyan, *op. cit.*, p. 352.
52 Williams, *op. cit*., pp. 50, 53.

of legislation for the purpose of effecting reforms in the law was left to individual peers or members of the House of Commons.[53]

Another authoritative judgment is in complete agreement:

> If we were asked to name a period in English history during which the county possessed the largest measure of self-government, when its local administrators were most effectively free from superior control, either of the National Executive, Parliament or the Law Courts, we should suggest . . . the century that elapsed between the accession of the House of Hanover and the close of the Napoleonic wars.[54]

The municipalities were, if anything, even more actively autonomous: their justices, appointed as they were solely in respect of their municipal office, could not be removed by the Crown.[55] James II's attack on the charters had been another factor in the Revolution, and on this as on other issues, defeat of the Stuart cause had led to a considerable reaction. The hundred years that followed James's defeat have been described as notable for a tendency of a 'legal and conservative character that was carried even to excess. To show a charter was to be above criticism'.[56] Most of the old corporate towns (Bristol, Norwich, Lincoln, Leicester, etc.) during the eighteenth century

> were dominated by families of self-perpetuating oligarchs, utterly uninterested in social administration, who squandered and abused corporate wealth and corporate charities. No matter how

---

53 Holdsworth, *op. cit.*, XI, p. 371. He adds the interesting observation that it is significant 'that many measures passed in this century, and in the first half of the following century, are known by the names of their proposers . . .'

54 S. and B. Webb, *The Parish and the County*, pp. 309-10. In theory (but rarely in practice) it was possible to exercise some control over the magistrates by the issuance of various High Court writs and the pursuit of actions to compel them to fulfil their duties in accordance with the law (see W. Eric Jackson, *Local Government in England and Wales*, pp. 31-2).

In 1789 Lord Loughborough, then Lord Chancellor, and a prominent prison reformer, fined the county of Essex £500 for violation of various prison Acts. The Essex magistrates appealed to the King's Bench and Chief Justice Kenyon ruled that a county could not be fined. Despite their jurisdictive competence it was thus established that the higher courts could exercise no coercive power over the county as represented by the justices (see Robert Alan Cooper, thesis: 'English Prison Reform 1773-1835', p. 104).

As for the sheriffs, they had long since lost the great powers they had possessed as the King's local representatives. By the eighteenth century the office was honorary and subject to annual rotation by election. The main duty was attendance upon the judges on circuit, and the duty of presiding over the county court was usually left to an under-sheriff (Williams, *op. cit.*, p. 49).

55 *Ibid.*, p. 53.

56 Trevelyan, *op. cit.*, p. 365.

obscurantist, incompetent, or corrupt they proved themselves to be, no government in the eighteenth century attempted to modify their powers or limit their privileges.[57]

As for the new, non-corporate towns, they had no resident justices and were 'constitutionally speaking, villages; and ... usually had no more than two parish constables to keep order'.[58]

In Tudor and Stuart times the justices had been the agents – the handmaidens – of social and penal policy-makers; now they were themselves policy-makers. By the middle years of the century they were the butts of Fielding's, Goldsmith's and Smollett's satire exposing their neglect, or corrupt and irresponsible use of power. However, whilst there were many such magistrates – particularly in the urban areas, and especially in Middlesex where they were known as 'trading' or 'basket' justices[59] – the rural magistrates seem to have been less reprehensible: they were

> substantial squires, too rich to be corrupt or mean, proud to do hard public work for no pay, anxious to stand well with their neighbours, but often ignorant and prejudiced without meaning to be unjust, and far too much a law unto themselves.[60]

For the most part, then, policy was made and interpreted by men of substance and integrity, whose neglect of the prisons was none the less disgraceful. There were various enactments which, had the justices chosen, could have been used to regulate the prisons. For the bridewells they had direct and exclusive responsibility (by 7 Jac. I, c.4), but, taking advantage of provisions first made under Henry VIII, they were also entrusted with the responsibility of building and repairing the gaols. By these enactments, it is suggested, the justices 'got control of the

---

57 Plumb, *op. cit.*, p. 37.
58 *Ibid.*, p. 13.
59 Frank Milton describes this type of magistrate who

> often traded in other commodities besides justice, and ... sometimes retailed groceries and legal processes from the same shop. They employed touts or barkers to boost their judicial wares; they would, if ready cash was short, grant warrants on credit to stimulate litigation. They sent out the constables to arrest everyone found on the streets at night, from whom a two-and-fourpenny bail fee could be extracted. They demanded, and received, bribes as a preliminary to licensing public-houses. They levied blackmail and protection-money on prostitutes and brothel-keepers (*The English Magistracy*, p. 16).

> Burke described them as 'the scum of the earth – carpenters, brick-makers, and shoemakers unworthy of any employ whatsoever' (*cit.* J. Steven Watson, *The Reign of George III, 1760-1815*, p. 48).

60 Trevelyan, *op. cit.*, p. 353.

gaols',[61] but it has been argued that they were 'futile Acts, limited in duration, permitting the Justices, for a brief period and under impracticable limitations and conditions to levy a rate for the repair and building of county gaols'.[62] The Acts (11 & 12 Will. III, c.19, and 10 Ann., c.14) were in fact made perpetual by 6 Geo. I, c.19, and powers to build and repair *could* have permitted significant intervention in administration and management.

The justices could also have enforced the available relieving laws in respect of debtors, particularly the Act of 1759 (32 Geo. II, c.28), section 6 of which gave them wide and effective powers of management and control, since it required the quarter sessions to draw up rules and regulations for gaols which, after submission to the judges of assize for approval, could then have been forwarded to the gaoler for display in the gaol. A clause had also been inserted in a general vagrancy Act (17 Geo. II, c.5) ordering quarter sessions to appoint two justices to visit and report on the houses of correction.[63] It is hard to disagree with the view that, though Parliament had given large powers to the justices,

except in a few counties when some justice took the trouble to enforce these statutes, little was done till the legislation of the nineteenth century. It would probably be true to say that no part of the administrative duties of the justices was more neglected than these duties of supervising the gaols.[64]

Prison staffing

Gaolers

From the Civil War until the latter part of the eighteenth century,

---

61 Holdsworth, *op. cit.*, X, p. 181. Somewhat contradictorily he adds, 'But, as yet, they had little or no power to control their management.'

62 S. and B. Webb, *English Prisons Under Local Government*, p. 28.

63 Fielding thought that this statute was too general and vague

to expect any good fruits to come from it. As 'to the true and faithful Account' which they are to yield to the Justices, at the Sessions, of the persons in their Custody, this is at present little more than Matter of Form; nor can it be expected to be any other in the Hurry of a public Sessions, and when the Stench arising from the Prisoners is so intolerable, that it is difficult to get any Gentlemen to attend the Court at that Time (*op. cit.*, p. 50).

64 Holdsworth, *op. cit.*, X, p. 183. The Webbs agree:

The Justices, it is clear, remained unconscious that any direct responsibility rested on them for seeing that the gaols were properly kept, nor can we find that the House of Correction, any more than the gaol, was actually visited and inspected by them (*English Prisons Under Local Government*, p. 29).

members of prison staff[65] seem generally to have been left to their own devices. If the custodial task was fulfilled, then in all but exceptional cases the community at large was disposed to be tolerant enough of the unsavoury commerce and reputation of those who ran the prisons. The strongest general impression of the Georgian gaoler and turnkey that is gained from a perusal of the literature is that of belonging to an untouchable caste: a group of people performing essential but contaminating work.

In the counties the gaolership was part of the patronage of the sheriff and this power was used for both political and financial gain.[66] Elsewhere it was in the gift of municipal officials, the franchise-holder or (especially in the case of the London prisons) the existing office-holder. There was public and government acceptance that the holder of a position should be paid either a lump sum or a proportion of income by his successor.[67] It was not until the end of the century that the

---

65 Gaol and bridewell staff. Very often they were one and the same, but in any case the reformatory task and distinctive identity of the bridewells had been all but lost by the beginning of the century. The Act of 1719 (6 Geo. I, c.19) which made perpetual the powers given to justices to build and repair county gaols, also gave *de jure* acknowledgment to a substantial merging of the two types of prison. Section 2 provided that

> vagrants, and other Criminals, Offenders and Persons charged with small offences are for such Offences, or for want of Sureties, to be committed to the County Gaol, it being adjudged that by Law the Justices of the Peace cannot commit them to any other Prison or safe Custody, which by Experience hath been found to be very prejudicial and expensive: Be it enacted by the Authority aforesaid, That it shall and may be lawful to and for the Justices of the Peace within their respective Jurisdictions to commit such Vagrants and other Criminals, Offenders, Person and Persons, either to the County Gaol or House of Correction, as they in their Judgment shall think proper; any Law, Custom or Usage to the contrary notwithstanding.

Houses of correction thus *officially* became places of custody for all but felons and debtors.

66 According to Plumb, political influence was measured by the number of votes a peer or squire could muster. A large number of votes could be traded for places, pensions and posts for relatives and dependants:

> In a world where there were no appointments by examination or interviewing boards, where every office was in the gift of someone else, it is obvious that an extremely complex system of political bargaining and blackmail must arise. This was true of the eighteenth century and it permeates all the institutions of government (*op. cit.*, p. 38).

67 Despite s.10 of 5 Geo. I, c.15 (1718), which forbade the public sale of gaolerships, this practice seems to have been general:

> During the eighteenth century it was an accepted, although not invariable practice, in the various Public Offices that a person succeeding another in an employment should pay to his predecessor part of his salary, this

justices generally began firmly to establish their control over staff appointments.[68]

Once in office the gaoler's effective independence was guaranteed by his 'self-employed' status, and his drawing of remuneration from fees and more or less unhindered trading. As for the purchase of position (with which it was inseparable), there were a number of justifications for the practice of fee-taking, which went along with the holding of public office throughout the century.[69] The convention fitted well with prevailing Lockeian sentiment, as well and succinctly argued in the following extract:

---

taking the place of a proper pension (Marios Raphael, thesis: 'The Origins of Public Superannuation Schemes in England, 1684-1859', p. 26).

So much was the office of gaoler seen as private property that it was frequently passed on in the family. The history of the keepership of the Fleet has already been mentioned in Chapter 1, and similar arrangements were common enough in the eighteenth century. Richard Akerman the elder, who was keeper of Newgate from 1744 to 1754, resigned in favour of his son, Richard Akerman the younger (Horace Bleakley, *The Hangmen of England*, Appendix I). According to O'Donoghue (*op. cit.*, II, pp. 187-8), 'Employment and residence tended to become hereditary in Bridewell.' Raphael reports that successive assumption of office by relatives also occurred in the customs and excise (*op. cit.*, pp. 46-7). For a general description of recruitment to public office and its payment at this time see Emmeline W. Cohen, *The Growth of the British Civil Service 1780-1939*, Ch. 2.

---

68 24 Geo. III, Sess.2, c.54, s. 7, allowed the appointment of visiting justices to examine the state of the gaol, but did not mention the conduct of the gaoler, though that could be relevant to the condition of the building. s.20 instructed the justices to prevent the selling of liquors by gaolers, and allowed them 'to appoint such Salaries or Allowances to such Gaolers and their Assistants . . . and to vary the same from Time to Time as to them shall seem meet'. The virtual amalgamation of gaols and houses of correction and the establishment of the joint office of keeper and gaoler placed considerable political leverage in the hands of the justices, especially when the tap was forbidden (see 22 Geo. III, c.64). This legislation did not appear until the latter part of the century, but Sheehan (*op. cit.*, p. 190) nevertheless argues that after 1732 'the City authorities finally managed to curb the rapacity of the gaolers'. It is difficult to reconcile this claim with the findings of subsequent inquiries, both public and private.

69 Cohen, *op. cit.*, pp. 27-9. Fee-taking could either be a direct transaction, between the office-holder and his customer, or it could take the form of contracting with the authority involved to perform a service for a fee. This latter method was also widespread and further served to legitimise the former, direct, transaction.

The eighteenth century local governing body, whatever the service which it had to provide, found it easier to avoid the trouble and risk of direct employment, and delighted to put the whole business out to contract for a fixed payment. Whether it was the building of a bridge or the conveyance of vagrants, the transportation of convicts or the lighting of

The idea of public money was not yet fully developed. Hence the eighteenth-century prevalence of the fee-system. Those who took the King's shilling became his men and suffered in the general estimation of their independence. It was preferable to serve the King without depending mainly upon his wages, deriving instead an income from fees for services rendered to individual members of the public. A clerk who charged the public for particular services was earning his living by serving it, and was not a kept man of the Crown. As he met a public need he prospered. Thus in many public offices the official salary was negligible: the emoluments were great. . . . To perform private services in an official position was less degrading than to be a salaried and controlled cog in a machine.[70]

And again the practice was deeply embedded in the culture and economy of the society. Under the name of 'vails' or tips even the domestic servants in a house would levy a toll on guests.[71] Various degrees of pressure could in most cases be brought to bear so as to ensure appropriate payment; and gaolers and their staff had the advantage of a monopoly in this regard. Even in a less disreputable occupation, such as customs and excise, devious methods of extracting fees were practised: 'merchants were often ready to pay excessive fees and gratuities to have their work finished more quickly, while officers were willing to create difficulties for the sake of taking extra money'.[72] Judges, and even officials of the Houses of Parliament, derived substantial income from fees, and the latter protested very loudly whenever legislation seemed likely to affect their emoluments. Holdsworth ironically notes that in the course of the eighteenth century they had little cause for complaint since 'they found no difficulty in increasing their fees, and getting the House to sanction their usurpations'.[73]

Fee-taking was at the heart of public administration and, between the gaoler who bought office in order to squeeze his income from

---

thoroughfares, all difficulties seemed to be solved by asking what contractor would undertake to execute the service for the lowest cash payment. In other cases the right to perform the service was sold, as a privilege, to the highest bidder . . . (S. and B. Webb, *English Poor Law History: The Old Poor Law*, p. 277).

---

70 Watson, *op. cit.*, pp. 61-2.
71   . . . it was commonly reckoned that to dine at the best houses cost anything from ten shillings to a guinea or two, according to the rank of the master. Even the servants of the professional and middle classes took their toll of visitors (Dorothy Marshall, 'Manners, Meals and Domestic Pastimes', in A.S. Turberville (ed.), *Johnson's England*, p. 342).

72 Raphael, *op. cit.*, p. 22.
73 Holdsworth, *op. cit.*, XI, p. 299.

misery and the colonel who paid for the cost of his commission by half-starving or half-dressing his men, there were many more similarities than contemporaries may have wished to realise.[74]

In addition to their current needs, incumbents had to accumulate enough capital to protect them from disgrace and destitution in old age. Revenue for these purposes was extracted from the very poor themselves by the contractors. Thomas Ruggles wrote in 1793 of poor-law administration:

> The general spirit of rigid economy within which the contracting master of the workhouse produces, as well in diet as in clothing, lodging, cleanliness, to scrape from misery, as soon as possible, a property which may enable him to retire from his disagreeable avocation, give propriety to the opinion and expression that a parish workhouse is a parish bugbear, to frighten distress from applying for relief.[75]

As in the case of the prisons, the interests of the polity and of mammon nicely coincided, although the lack of pensioning arrangements caused some keepers to cling to office long after they were disabled by infirmity and old age.[76]

The incomes of keepers and gaolers varied greatly. In many of the small prisons visited by Howard towards the end of the century inmates were few, or, for long periods of time, lacking altogether. The living made by the keepers of these gaols and houses of correction was far from commensurate with the profits enjoyed in the management of large urban and metropolitan prisons: besides the usual fees and mono-polistic trading profit, there were other bonuses. There might, for example, be the godsend of a clutch of wealthy political prisoners, capable of paying very well indeed to minimise their discomfort. 'It was estimated that during three or four months in 1716 William Pitt, the Keeper of Newgate, cleared some £3,000 or £4,000 from his Jacobite prisoners "besides valuable presents given in private".' Moreover, Pitt 'had good reason to believe that by paying a thousand pounds for the keepership he had got a bargain'.[77] The custody of a notorious criminal was another money-maker, as it was a fashionable public diversion to flock to the prison to gawk at and talk to persons such as Jack

---

74 When Pitt lost his commission for political reasons William Pultney, an opposition leader, called it robbery. 'He reasoned thus. Commissions had to be bought with cash; therefore, once bought, the owner had a legal title to them as he might have to a piece of land. Many agreed' (Plumb, *op. cit.*, p. 45).

75 Thomas Ruggles, *The History of the Poor*, p. 285. (Ruggles was an ancestor of Sir Evelyn Ruggles-Brise, chairman of the Commissioners of Prisons in the first decades of this century.)

76 See, for example, Sheehan, *op. cit.*, pp. 234-5.

77 Hibbert, *op. cit.*, p. 88.

Sheppard, Dick Turpin and the highwayman McLean. Three thousand people were said to have visited McLean's cell on the day before his execution in 1750, and the profit made on Sheppard was reputed to have been £200 when he was similarly exhibited.[78] Big urban gaols continued also to benefit from the generous and more regular custom of the 'politic bankrupts': the suppression of the old London sanctuaries of the Mint and the Savoy in 1723[79] must have increased this mutually profitable connivance. When Richard Akerman (probably the best known of the Newgate keepers) died in 1792 he left a fortune of £20,000. He had held office for thirty-eight years and according to one of his obituary notices his wealth had been 'accumulated not parsimoniously, but during a very long possession of a lucrative office'.[80]

Akerman seems to have been unique among the keepers, who despite the wealth that they might hold, were none the less treated as pariahs by respectable society. In his account of the Gordon riots Boswell referred to 'my esteemed friend Mr. Akerman, the Keeper of Newgate, who long discharged a very important trust with a uniform intrepid firmness, and at the same time a tenderness and a liberal charity, which enables him to be recorded with distinguished honour'.[81] Akerman was reported to be very kind to the prisoners under his charge, for which Burke and even Johnson praised him, the latter declaring, 'He who has long had constantly in view the worst of mankind and is yet eminent for the humanity of his disposition, must have had it originally in a great degree and continued to cultivate it very carefully.'[82] His reputation was greatly enhanced by his courageous behaviour during the Gordon riots, when his house and the prison were totally destroyed by the mob. But, despite such praise, it is likely that his position in society was more uncertain and feelings towards him

---

78 Lecky, *op. cit.*, II, p. 135.
79 Lecky, *op. cit.*, II, p. 111. Although there were attempts to amend the old debt law (referred to in Chapter 1) throughout the eighteenth century (by 32 Geo. II, c.28, for example), it still remained substantially true that a debtor who chose to remain in prison could not be compelled to deliver up his property and could spend his money on subsistence. A select committee reported in 1730 that

> the prisoners make large presents to the Marshall [of the King's Bench prison] for the liberty of these Rules; and being under his protection and in his favour, may take houses or lodgings within the Rules, and live in a very easy manner; whilst the poor honest debtor, who hath paid away all his substance, to satisfy his creditor, is a close prisoner within the prison: thus the debtor, who will not pay his creditors, lives at ease; and he who cannot pay suffers (*cit.* Holdsworth, *op. cit.*, XI, p. 600).

80 Bleakley, *op. cit.*, Appendix I.
81 *Boswell's Life of Johnson*, ed. George Birkbeck Hill and L.F. Powell, III, p. 431.
82 *Ibid.*, p. 433.

more equivocal than some writers have been prepared to admit.[83] That he was thought not to be an extortioner by the standards of the day there can be little doubt. Dr William Smith commented on his humane action in keeping Newgate as clean as possible and Howard noted that he 'generously contributed' to the upkeep of some poor prisoners.[84] But Akerman was not *respectable*; respectable society probably felt attracted by Akerman much as aristocratic society found congenial and even courted the prize-fighter and game-cock owner.[85] This impression is confirmed when one notes that Boswell himself had the reputation of seeking out notorious people and that he had what was described as 'a strange propensity for witnessing executions [which] probably brought him into more immediate intercourse with the keeper of Newgate'.[86]

The reason for the general notoriety and disrepute of those who worked in gaols and houses of correction was not altogether the financial arrangements of their trade. Some extortions may occasionally have been viewed extremely unfavourably; but, as has been shown, fee-taking, far from being disreputable, was the recognised financial arrangement for services rendered by those in public office. This was the age in which the principles of political economy taught respect for private property, and when the constitution and legal system were substantially concerned with ensuring the conditions in which the profits of that property purchased, including an office, could be enjoyed. More important in establishing the measure of social standing accorded to prison keepers was the physical and moral pollution that beset their work. There did not then exist the edifying tasks of disciplinarian or therapist to cloak with respectability such daily association with some of the worst dregs and outcasts of society, and constant companionship with the physically diseased. But there was yet another factor. Workers in prisons came, if not from the criminal underworld itself, at least

---

83 Anthony Babington is the most recent writer to accept Akerman's reputation at face value. He describes him as 'a remarkable person and most unlike the majority of his predecessors' (*op. cit.*, p. 119).

84 *Ibid*.

85 The 'drop' was first used at Newgate on 3 December 1783, and was the occasion for the kind of meeting of reputable and disreputable that illustrates this point. As Du Cane records, 'The Governor concluded the proceedings with a breakfast to certain officials and persons of distinction, whose curiosity had led to their being invited to view the proceedings' (Sir Edmund F. Du Cane, *The Punishment and Prevention of Crime*, p. 23).

86 *Cit.* Radzinowicz, *op. cit.*, pp. 177-8, n. 51: editorial notes by J.W. Croker to an 1859 edition of Boswell's *Life of Samuel Johnson*. Horace Bleakley (*op. cit.*) reports that Boswell once rode to Tyburn in the same coach as the condemned man, and that he persuaded Sir Joshua Reynolds to witness an execution.

from the fringes of its economy and culture.[87] While referring to bailiffs, the following description is equally true of gaolers and all those who gleaned a living from the less exalted fringes and processes of the criminal and civil law: they 'lived in an immediately symbiotic relationship to London's criminal society; under cover of their function they had the reputation for engaging in armed robbery and blackmail'.[88] The public were well acquainted with the collusions of the law enforcer and the criminal. In the early part of the century there was the scandal of the notorious 'thief-taker' Jonathan Wild who, whilst pretending to uphold the law, built up a formidable criminal empire. That there were many more like him there could be no doubt. At mid-century, Clerkenwell bridewell, for example, was described as 'a great brothel, kept under the protection of the law for the emolument of its ministers'.[89]

The role of the prisons in the world of crime varied throughout the century, and from prison to prison; whether as brothels, tap-houses, criminal clubs or fraudsmen's roosts they continued to be integral to criminal methods and organisation in the metropolis and probably other big towns. This was well recognised by contemporaries, and was yet another, and probably the conclusive, reason why those who worked in them were well beyond the pale of respectable society.[90]

87 In the poorer areas of London 'Hundreds of people lived entirely upon their earnings as pimps, procuresses, prostitutes' bullies, crimps and male prostitutes. Hundreds more employed in taverns, prisons, brothels and gambling houses earned a living which although perhaps not technically illegal was certainly not honest' (Hibbert, *op. cit*., p. 50). Sheehan (*op. cit*., p. 130, n. 1) mentions the case of John Kirby who fled from Yorkshire to avoid arrest for a £300 debt; he lodged a petition under one of the Debtors' Acts from the Poultry Compter, but was himself keeper of Wood Street between 1766 and 1792, until his promotion to keeper of Newgate, where he remained until 1804.

88 Thompson, *op. cit*., p. 248. In 1707 there were complaints that the deputy keeper of Newgate had rented several rooms to a gang of thieves, who went to and fro several times a day (Sheehan, *op. cit*., p. 254).

89 *Gentleman's Magazine* (June 1757), XXVII, 269.

90 *Hanging not Punishment Enough* refers thus to prisons:

> I have in this paper taken but little notice of the Scandalous Wickedness and Corruption of Prisons, and None of their Keepers; which was not done by omission or ignorance of the mischief that arises from these infamous Places and Men. They are now Known to be the Sanctuaries of Villains, from Whence their Emissaries are dispatch'd and a regular and settled Correspondence is said to be fixed and carried on, through the whole Fraternity of Rogues in *England*. This is a Grievance too great to be spoken of by and by, and under another Head; this requires a Particular Treatise by itself, and this cries aloud for a Regulation and Reformation from the Power and Wisdom of the Parliament, for no less Power and Wisdom than that of a Parliament can Regulate and Reform them (*cit*. Radzinowicz, *op. cit*., p. 235, n.).

Chaplains and surgeons

The chaplains' functions were very limited. A Victorian prison chaplain described his predecessors thus:

> The gaol chaplain of the old school . . . was an official kept for state occasions, then so terribly frequent, and not for the every-day exercise of his ministry amongst the unhappy and guilty persons committed nominally to his spiritual care. . . . His business was not to seek to reform the living . . . but . . . to administer to those appointed to die 'the consolations of religion'. . . .[91]

Chaplains had long since been appointed to Newgate as they had been to the (once) reformatory Bridewell.[92] But apart from these prisons their attendance was at best occasional. A condemned prisoner was thought to be entitled to the services of a priest but, considering the function and place of prisons in society, no other obvious case could be made out for his regular attendance.[93] There is some evidence, indeed, that such charitable visitations provoked the resentment and opposition of the prison authorities. The Wesley brothers commenced regular missions to Newgate as early as 1739, and the sheriffs were still unshaken in their opposition a decade later.[94]

This was a time, in any case, when the clergy stood low in public repute.

> There is little doubt that they were unpopular. Neither before nor since has the clerical order been exposed to such general attack.
> In plays and in novels they were the victims of savage ridicule.
> For much of this contempt they themselves were responsible.[95]

Their unpopularity was in part caused by pluralism and non-residence, which led to many churches being served by rather pitiful curates, hired by the non-resident incumbent. The latter 'makes it a matter of conscience to keep a sober curate on one [of his livings], whom he hires to take care of all the souls in the parish at as cheap a rate as a sober man can be procured'.[96] The rate for a sober man was about £20-£30 a year, though in 1713 Archbishop Tenison spoke of some unfortunates who received only £5 or £6.[97] These curates had no

91 Rev. Joseph Kingsmill, *Chapters on Prisons and Prisoners*, pp. 332-3.
92 Pluralism was forbidden at Newgate in 1746, but not at the other City prisons (Sheehan, *op. cit.*, p. 272).
93 Sheehan draws attention to one Newgate Ordinary who testified in the early nineteenth century that he knew nothing of the state of morals in the prison and that he did not visit the sick or the children 'for it is not in my instructions' (*op. cit.*, p. 269).
94 Hinde, *op. cit.*, p. 19.
95 Gerald R. Cragg, *The Church and the Age of Reason 1648-1789*, p. 127.
96 William Laws, cited by Cragg, *op. cit.*, p. 126.
97 *Ibid*.

security of tenure, and often no fixed abode, and they wandered from parish to parish in search of subsistence. The system of pluralism was made necessary by the low income of many livings. At the beginning of the eighteenth century there were 5,500 livings in which the income did not exceed £50 a year. By the beginning of the nineteenth century (at a time when there had been a fall in the value of money), there were still almost 4,000 benefices with an annual value of under £150.[98] On the other hand a clergyman who managed to secure several livings or even the deanery of a great cathedral might have an income higher than that of many bishops.[99]

In many ways, therefore, the Church resembled other institutions — much income was derived from fee-taking and a form of contracting, and a large proportion of the clergy had low social esteem and status. 'The vast majority of parish priests and curates were not quite gentlemen. They were betwixt and between.'[100] As the century wore on the use of church positions by political patrons, and other changes, began to make it increasingly a more acceptable career for those from higher social classes.[101] For many years, however, the Church, latitudinarian in beliefs and socially and economically enfeebled, made no significant contribution to the administration or staffing of prisons. It is little wonder that it was not until 1773 that the justices were permitted to appoint clergymen to their gaols, and to pay them from the rates.[102]

Prison chaplains (where they were appointed) were 'taken necessarily from the roughest mould. . . . The penitent and impenitent alike received comfort at his hands'.[103] This fits in with what is known of Newgate Ordinaries, who were recruited from the lower fringes of the Church. As late as 1777 they were paid £35 and with other emoluments did not receive more than £100 a year.[104] The authorship and sale of the last speeches and confessions of the condemned were an important source of income, and the opportunities for earnest exhortation which the Ordinaries sometimes had with the condemned on the Tyburn cart were probably used, more often than not, with a mind on collecting material for these mercenary purposes. Sometimes there were disputes over their publication: in February 1745 we find the Ordinary, the Rev. James Guthrie, complaining to the Court of Aldermen that John

98 Rev. N. Sykes, 'The Church', in A.S. Turberville (ed.), *Johnson's England*, p. 26.
99 Plumb, *op. cit.*, p. 43.
100 *Ibid.*, p. 44.
101 Trevelyan, *op. cit.*, pp. 361-2.
102 By 13 Geo. III, c.58.
103 Kingsmill, *op. cit.*, pp. 332-3.
104 The City gave two freedoms a year, which the Ordinary sold for £25 each: there was also a small income from two legacies (Bleakley, *op. cit.*, Appendix II). Sheehan (*op. cit.*, p. 264), by including the Ordinaries' residence, reckons the annual income to have been about £200.

Applebee the printer had infringed his copyright by printing his own versions of speeches and confessions.[105] A droll advertisement from the *Daily Journal*, which was thought to have been inserted by the then Ordinary, well reflects the standing and function of the prison clergyman.

The Time of my Dissolution approaching, and in all probability after my Decease, false accounts of my evil Life and Conversation etc. will be published by some designing Persons for the Lucre of Gain and Profit; I have therefore for the satisfaction of the World, communicated my whole Life and wicked Actions to The Reverend Mr. Wagstaff, in order to be made Publick, to the End all other young Persons may be warn'd from following the like Courses, by my sad and dreadful Example. In the chapel of Newgate this 14th of September 1724. Witness my Hand, John Sheppard.[106]

Regular prison employment of surgeons did not begin until after 1774, when the Gaol Distemper Act permitted magistrates to appoint 'an experienced Surgeon or Apothecary' to attend the prison.[107] Bridewell had a surgeon from an early time, but in this, as in other matters, it was exceptional. Doubtless individual prisoners obtained, and privately paid for, medical assistance from time to time, and physicians were also known to have been employed sometimes to give advice on the prevention of gaol disease.[108] But the social standing of surgeons like that of the clergy was low in the eighteenth century; they were regarded as distinctly inferior to physicians. It was not until 1745 that they ceased to be identified with the barbers in the Company of Barber Surgeons and were granted a company of their own. As late as 1757, 'a majority of judges in the common pleas decided that "a surgeon is an *inferior tradesman*" within the meaning of an act of William and Mary'.[109] But the migration of skilled medical men from Scotland throughout the century did much to raise the corporate efficiency and standing of the profession and the work and discoveries of Sir John Pringle on military hygiene were to exert a great influence on the environment and treatment of the civilian population, including prisoners.[110]

Thus it was that late into the eighteenth century policy-makers and

---

105 Bleakley, *op. cit.*, Appendix II.
106 *Cit.* Hibbert, *op. cit.*, p. 133, n.
107 The authorities do not seem to have acted with much speed in taking advantage of this Act. Dr William Smith's attendance at the London, Southwark and Westminster prisons took place after the passing of the 1774 Act, and was paid for by the Westminster charity (Smith, *op. cit.*, pp. 6-7).
108 E.g. Babington, *op. cit.*, pp. 97-8.
109 Williams, *op. cit.*, p. 389.
110 Trevelyan, *op. cit.*, p. 345.

those entrusted with the management and staffing of prisons were still not seeking any change. *Squalor carceris* well met the requirements of criminal justice as it then stood. The staff entrusted with the running of the gaols and bridewells drew their income from the skilled manipulation of misery. Taking up their dangerous and undesirable occupation as a last resort, consoled by the expectation that the purchase of place would show a good return, they had the very strongest of reasons for opposing change. But if by some chance a gaoler, chaplain or surgeon had sought to modify policy he would have found himself almost totally without influence. It is inconceivable that any parliamentary committee or quarter sessions would have paid serious attention to the views of those tainted by familiar contact with criminality and dishonest money and so conspicuously cut off from the privileges and rights of the reputable.

4   The new prisons

New philosophies

Trevelyan's statement, that 'It is doubly impossible . . . for the English historian to ignore religion, if he would explain other phenomena',[1] is particularly appropriate to any consideration of eighteenth-century penological developments. The century opened with the Church reacting to the travail of the previous century, theologically becalmed, and largely bereft of the invigorating social criticism of Puritanism and other Calvinist traditions; it closed with more and more institutions and spheres of life being brought under the effective assessment and intervention of the Evangelicals. It was not that the prevailing latitudinarianism was indifferent to the world. On the contrary, it

> emphasized the importance of good works of charity and benevolence. The Georgian period was the age of hospitals, alike in London, in the university towns, and in the widespread foundation of county hospitals; and in the rural life of the parish this solicitude found its counterpart.[2]

This benevolent approach was very much in tune with the low-key intellectual and political temper of the reign of the first two Georges, which was not attracted to the polemics of Church government and the demarcation of religious beliefs. Latitudinarianism encouraged individual acts of charity, but did not have the qualities necessary to set in hand a radical re-examination of the key institutions of the times.

Methodism disturbed this calm and was to be responsible, directly or indirectly, for much of the century's philanthropic activity. This movement

1 G.M. Trevelyan, *English Social History*, p. 329.
2 Rev. N. Sykes, 'The Church', in A.S. Turberville (ed.), *Johnson's England*.

was at once Puritan and Middle Class in character; it was even stronger among the laity than the clergy; its devotees were not withdrawn from the business of life but strove to dedicate it to God. 'Conduct, not dogma, stamped the Puritan of the Eighteenth century. . . . He was irresistibly drawn towards the service of man, who through misery or ignorance, or debauchery, deprived God of the glory that was his due. To men of such a mould charity was obligatory'.[3]

Wesley had visited prisons from the earliest days of his ministry, embracing such dangerous charity as an essential part of his spiritual work.[4] His dramatic preaching, in prison as outside it, was of individual salvation,[5] but he (perhaps the most successful organiser of the century) also saw the need for a change in prison conditions and was to be most fulsome in his praise of John Howard, whose work confirmed his own views of the Christian mission. After their only meeting (when both their extensive journeyings intersected in Dublin) Wesley noted in his diary:

> I had the pleasure of a conversation with Mr. Howard, I think one of the greatest men in Europe. Nothing but the mighty power of God can enable him to go through his difficult and dangerous employments. But what can hurt us, if God is on our side?[6]

Philanthropy was tangible witness to the power of God. Only months before Howard's death Wesley reiterated this judgment: 'Mr. Howard is really an extraordinary man, God has raised him up to be a blessing to many nations.'[7] The high regard was reciprocated, Howard recording:

> I saw in him how much a single man might achieve by zeal and perseverance, and I thought, why may I not do as much in my way as Mr. Wesley has done in his, if I am only as assiduous and persevering. And I am determined I would pursue my work with more alacrity than ever.[8]

3 Trevelyan, *op. cit.*, pp. 361-2.
4 Wesley had written of Newgate: 'Of all the seats of woe, on this side hell, few I suppose, exceed, or even equal Newgate' (*Boswell's Life of Johnson*, ed. George Birkbeck Hill and L.F. Powell, III, p. 431, n. 1).
5 W.E.H. Lecky, *A History of England in the Eighteenth Century*, III, p. 80.
6 *The Journal of the Rev. John Wesley, A.M.*, ed. Nehemiah Curnock, VII, p. 295.
7 *Cit*. Eric Stockdale, 'The Bedford Gaol that John Howard Knew', *Bedfordshire Magazine* (Summer 1973).
8 D.L. Howard, *John Howard: Prisoner Reformer*, p. 153. Howard was himself deeply religious. Richard Condon writes eloquently of Howard's motivation:

> Worshipping Calvin's stern judge, he was deeply conscious of his sins and devoted to charity, purity and obedience. He called himself a creature who deserved hell, but trusted that 'where sin has abounded, grace

The fully reciprocated feeling of respect and inspiration that existed between these two men was a harbinger of the outstanding evangelical participation in prison affairs in the century up to 1850. Wesley's influence extended beyond the Methodist movement to revitalise dormant Calvinist elements in the Established Church, emphasising there, too, the need for a vital spiritual religion. This fertilisation of the Church

> produced a revival of religious feeling that . . . incalculably increased the efficiency of almost every religious body in the community. . . . The many great philanthropic efforts which arose, or at least derived their importance, from the Evangelical movement, soon became prominent topics of parliamentary debate; but they were not the peculiar glory of any political party, and they formed a common ground on which many religious denominations should co-operate.[9]

The Utilitarians were the second great philosophical force in the reshaping of the English penal system. Here one tends first to think of Bentham, but Cesare Beccaria anticipated him in several regards — fundamentally, for example, by insisting that the greatest happiness of the greatest number should be the legislator's guiding maxim. He also went ahead of the English philosopher in his psychology, holding that 'pleasure and pain are the only springs of action in beings endowed with sensibility', and in penal thinking by arguing that, since 'it is sufficient that the *evil* which [a punishment] occasions should exceed the *good* expected from a crime', 'All severity beyond this is superfluous, and therefore tyrannical'.[10]

Beccaria's *Dei delitti e delle pene* was first published in 1764. The English translation (*An Essay on Crimes and Punishments*) appeared in 1767. Very favourably received throughout Europe, the work gained a no less influential hold in England, where its popularity was shown by the demand for four further editions which appeared by the turn of the century. One of the reasons why the British took so strongly to Beccaria's penal philosophy was that his political philosophy — the social contract — coincided with that of Locke and the prevailing

---

superabounds' . . . his religious feelings seem to have deepened with age and bereavements. In 1770 . . . he signed a solemn covenant with the Lord, and in 1789 he renewed it. By his prison work he hoped to save the bodies and souls of prisoners, for he believed that only the grace of God had made him less depraved than they, and therefore able to minister to them (Richard Herrick Condon, thesis: 'The Reform of English Prisons, 1773-1816', p. 25).

9 Lecky, *op. cit.*, III, pp. 144-5.
10 Cesare Beccaria, *An Essay on Crimes and Punishments*, p. 96.

post-Revolution orthodoxy.[11] Beccaria's discussion of the legitimacy of punishment testifies most clearly to this:

> Every act of authority of one man over another, for which there is not an absolute necessity, is tyrannical. It is upon this then, that the sovereign's right to punish crimes is founded; that is, upon the necessity of defending the liberty of all entrusted to his care, from the usurpation of individuals; and punishments are just in proportion as the liberty, preserved by the sovereign, is sacred and valuable.[12]

Although this statement sat easily with political convention in England, in the sphere of social philosophy, by linking liberty, justice and parsimony in punishment, it became a critical, intellectual tool and fundamental corrective to the 'whig state of mind' upon which the doctrine of maximum severity had been built. Beccaria took one element in the accepted philosophy of punishment and developed it in such a way that his views could not fail to find a responding echo in the English polity. 'The end of punishment', he wrote,

> is no other, than to prevent the criminal from doing further injury to society, and to prevent others from committing the like offence. Such punishments, therefore, and such a mode of inflicting them, ought to be chosen as will make the strongest and most lasting impression on the minds of others, with the least torment to the body of the criminal.[13]

This predominantly reductionist theory with its rational description of ends and means powerfully challenged the metaphysical approach to criminal law and punishments which, supported by notions of retribution and expiation, justified and multiplied severities in the search for maximum deterrence.

Beccaria's philosophy did not, however, directly call for an enlargement of the part played by imprisonment in the penal process. Noting that this punishment had the peculiar characteristic of preceding conviction, he insisted that 'this difference does not destroy a circumstance which is essential and common to it with all other punishments,

---

11 Michel Foucault, who attempts a much more ambitious political, economic and social analysis of changes in penal philosophy and administration than that given here, makes a similar point:

> It is understandable that the criticism of the public execution should have assumed such importance in penal reform: for it was the form in which, in the most visible way, the unlimited power of the sovereign and the ever-active illegality of the people came together. Humanity in the sentences was the rule given to a system of punishment that must fix their limits on both (*Discipline and Punish*, pp. 88-9).

12 Beccaria, *op. cit.*, p. 7.
13 *Ibid.*, pp. 41-2.

viz. that it should never be inflicted, but when ordained by law'.[14] He thus argued for a closer examination of the circumstances of committal and for administrative changes, so that those accused who were detained were not necessarily and irrevocably stigmatised by their indiscriminate and unavoidable association with the convicted.[15] More radically, his emphasis upon the exemplary element in punishment led him to find imprisonment and transportation unsatisfactory:

> Crimes of less importance are commonly punished, either in the obscurity of a prison, or the criminal is *transported*, to give by his slavery an example to societies which he never offended; an example absolutely useless, because distant from the place where the crime was committed.[16]

Beccaria's views carried to their logical conclusion would inhibit the development of imprisonment in the penal process in another important respect. The Evangelicals placed great importance on the state of mind of the offender, and this was an approach which (as shall be seen) was destined elementally to shape the system of discipline of some influential English prison policy-makers. Beccaria, by contrast, was scornful of such individualisation and held that it was wrong to judge the magnitude of a crime according to the intention of the criminal —

> for this will depend on the actual impression of objects on the senses, and on the previous disposition of the mind; both which will vary in different persons, and even in the same person at different times, according to the succession of ideas, passions and circumstances. Upon that system, it would be necessary to form, not only a particular code for every individual, but a new penal law for every crime.[17]

Beccaria's influence on the use and organisation of imprisonment was, therefore, largely oblique.[18] Yet the broader changes which he urged in law-making, particularly his insistence that certainty of punishment

14 *Ibid.*, p. 115.
15 *Ibid.*, pp. 114-15.
16 *Ibid.*, p. 75.
17 *Ibid.*, p. 25. He added, gnomically, 'Men, often with the best intention, do the greatest injury to society, and with the worst do it the most essential service.'
18 Both on grounds of morality and of deterrent effectiveness Beccaria opposed the death penalty, suggesting instead perpetual slavery as the ultimate penalty. Fining, he thought, tended to swell the numbers of the poor. He favoured corporal punishment for offences against the person, and (as he thought there should be correspondence between offence and punishment) flogging combined with a period of slavery for robbery with violence. His punishment of 'slavery', if we link it with his constant desire to place it in an effective social setting, bears some resemblance to penal public works, as developed later in the English convict establishment and in the Australian penal gangs.

rather than severity was the foundation of efficacy, and that prevention should have priority over punishment, did eventually have a considerable bearing on the changing role and administration of the prisons as instruments in the maintenance of public order.[19] Beccaria's essay

> helped forward the tendency, which had already begun, to reflect upon the deficiencies of the criminal law, and more especially upon its punishments. In fact some of Beccaria's theories had been anticipated, or independently arrived at, by English critics.[20]

His extensive influence on Bentham is clear and was indeed acknowledged,[21] but other prominent members of the campaign to mitigate the penal code also drew inspiration from the essay, including the three key figures of William Eden (later Lord Auckland), Sir William Blackstone and Sir Samuel Romilly.[22]

When consideration was being given to the use of the death penalty a simultaneous assessment of the role and state of the prisons could not be avoided. Eden, for example, wished greatly to restrict the use of the death penalty, and was therefore obliged to search for alternatives. He was critical of the efficacy of transportation for serious offenders and recommended dockyard, mine and other public works in terms which

---

19 Perhaps his most famous observations were

> Crimes are more effectually prevented by the *certainty*, than the *severity* of punishment,

and

> It is better to prevent crimes, than to punish them. This is the fundamental principle of good legislation, which is the art of conducting men to the *maximum* of happiness and to the *minimum* of misery . . . (Beccaria, *op. cit.*, pp. 94 and 155).

20 W. Holdsworth, *A History of English Law*, XI, p. 577. Unease at the immoderate use of the death penalty had long been felt. A correspondent of the *Gentleman's Magazine*, as early as 1750 queried

> Whether the constant and regular assembling to take away so many lives at every session, for crimes not really punishable with death, according either to the Old and New Testament ought to be considered . . . and some corporal punishment to be appointed instead of a capital . . . more criminals are executed at London in a year than has been in all Holland for 20 years (*Gentleman's Magazine* (May 1750), XX, p. 235).

21 Leon Radzinowicz, *A History of English Criminal Law*, I, p. 378.

22 . . . it is impossible to doubt that Blackstone owes much to Beccaria . . . it was Beccaria's book which helped Blackstone to crystallize his ideas and . . . it was Beccaria's influence which helped to give a more critical tone to his treatment of the English criminal law than to his treatment of any other part of English law (Holdsworth, *op. cit.*, XI, p. 578).

closely resembled Beccaria's 'slavery'.[23] Imprisonment, however, he thought injurious: 'It sinks useful subjects into burthens on the community, and has always a bad effect on their morals: nor can it communicate the benefit of example, being in its nature secluded from the eye of the people.'[24]

Eden and other reformers found themselves in some difficulty:

> It is evident that Eden realised the need for devising some system of humane and effective secondary punishments. Yet he does not seem to have grasped the implications of the repeal of the death penalty for a great number of offences simultaneously, and he hardly ever indicates possible alternative penalties. In view of his dislike for general and vague proposals, this may be taken as another indication of how difficult it was then to solve this problem.[25]

Blackstone was better able to translate the element of prevention in Beccaria's philosophy into concrete institutional proposals. With Beccaria he rejected the notion that punishment was undergone as an expiation for past evil; instead he argued that punishment was intended to secure against the repetition of offences.[26] In other words,

> To attain this object it is not enough to impose penalties likely to deter would-be offenders or capable of depriving them of power to commit further mischief. He insists on the reformative function of imprisonment, an emphasis uncommon even among the reformers.[27]

Utilitarians and Evangelicals had prepared a fertile ground for the reception of Howard's investigations and recommendations by the time *The State of the Prisons* first appeared in March 1777. This was why Howard's work was so timely and had such an impact. Earlier exposés,

---

23 He also suggested that the most dangerous offenders be sent to North Africa, there to be exchanged for Christian prisoners; alternatively they might be obliged to participate in dangerous expeditions or to establish new colonies (Radzinowicz, *op. cit.*, I, p. 312).

24 *Ibid*. Eden also favoured public flogging, pillorying and loss of public rights, and thought that a judicious use of fining as an alternative for corporal and capital penalties could help reduce the frequency of their imposition.

25 Radzinowicz, *op. cit.*, I, p. 313.

26
As to the *end*, or final cause of human punishments. This is not by way of atonement or expiation for the crime committed, for that must be left to the just determination of the supreme being: but as a precaution against future offences of the same kind. This is effected three ways: either by the amendment of the offender himself . . . or, by deterring others by the dread of his example from offending in the like way . . . or, lastly, by depriving the party injuring of the power to do further mischief (Sir William Blackstone, *Commentaries on the Laws of England*, IV, p. 11).

27 Radzinowicz, *op. cit.*, p. 346.

such as those of Bray and Oglethorpe, had given rise to concern, but it was ephemeral and short-lived. Throughout the 1780s *The State of the Prisons* was supplemented by information gathered upon further journeys, and revised editions were published in 1780, 1784 and 1792. Howard well understood the local nature of contemporary policy-making and aimed at a wide circulation for his books, subsidising and fixing prices at a low level and distributing free copies to 'all the principal persons in the kingdom, and all his particular friends'.[28]

Howard, a country gentleman, with parliamentary contacts, had a good knowledge of the psychology of the justices and was possessed of a particular ability to record his observations in such a fashion that understatement had galvanic effects. But, besides his skill in presentation and the intellectual receptiveness of the climate, there were other factors at work. He placed very great emphasis, in recording defects and making recommendations, upon the need to prevent the gaol distemper. This disease continued to be a matter of widespread concern and many virulent outbreaks devastated not only court personnel, but the various court towns and the villages into which prisoners or witnesses had returned. Howard was able to blend perceptions and recommendations on this issue with a similar interest in moral pollution and contagion. Just as prisons generated pestilence they increased depravity and crime, with equally deleterious consequences. In a small, mainly settled and rural society likely to connect death with disease and wrongdoing, this repeated association in Howard's work could not fail to have had a considerable psychological impact.[29] The paths of self-interest and altruism coincided in Beccaria's principles of prevention.[30]

28 D.L. Howard, *op. cit.*, p. 54.
29 In the religious sense illness or death was often perceived as a punishment; in a physical sense ex-prisoners were seen as very real dangers to the community. Dorothy Marshall points out that vagrants were greatly feared because

they were suspected of carrying the plague or small-pox from place to place, and so spreading the danger of infection. Small-pox was the terror of the time, and the terrible outbreaks of the plague in London, and all over the country, had increased the habitual terror of these outbreaks of pestilent diseases. . . . One important reason for all kinds of malignant distempers lay in the insanitary condition of the gaols and bridewells, frequent complaint being made that discharged prisoners infected the people among whom they went. . . . Vagrants as a class might have been expected to know more about the insides of Bridewells than most, and many a vagabond who had been imprisoned for a short period and then whipped, and after paying his fees, discharged, must have been turned on the world with the germs of infection in him. . . . Such fear of the vagrants as spreaders of disease was justified, according to many scattered entries alluding to some vagabond who is suffering from the dread infection (*The English Poor in the Eighteenth Century*, pp. 227-8).

30 Howard was himself aware that philanthropy in prison reorganisation was mixed with motives of self-interest and protection, or at least might so be

What began to happen, though not all at once, or even at a rapid pace, was that public reactions to the misery and dangerous pestilences of prisons — which could be accepted as functional and tolerable within a system based on general and maximum deterrence — changed, and these things came to be seen as a threat to the well-being of society.

Even before *The State of the Prisons* was published important reformatory legislation had been secured. In 1773, 13 Geo. III, c.58 was enacted, permitting the justices to appoint clergymen to the county gaols, and to pay them a salary up to £50 from the rates. In February 1773 Alexander Popham, the member for Taunton, attempted to get a bill through the House which would have authorised payment of the gaol fees of acquitted or discharged prisoners from the rates. Though it was this continued detention of 'released' prisoners unable to find their gaoler's fees that first prompted his investigations, promotion of this bill owed nothing to Howard.[31] Popham's measure failed, as the Webbs say, 'like so many others before it ... owing to the apathy or hostility of the members'. Then hearing of Howard's investigations, he had him invited to appear before the House on 4 March 1774, where he made such a very great impression on members that he was given the public honour of a vote of thanks;[32] within the next few months Popham and his supporters (who included two of John Howard's neighbours, John St John and Samuel Whitbread) managed to secure two measures on gaol administration — the Discharged Prisoners Act

---

seen. In his fourth edition (1792) of *The State of the Prisons* he notes the improvements that have taken place since the previous edition and commends 'the liberal and humane spirit which engages the public to alleviate the sufferings of prisoners in general, and particularly, to release many industrious though unfortunate debtors'; but

> the spirit of improvement seems unhappily to stop; scarcely touching upon that still more important subject, the *reformation of morals* in our prisons; it is obvious that, if this be neglected, besides the evil consequences that must result from such a source of wickedness, a suspicion will arise, that what has already been done had proceeded, *chiefly*, from the selfish motives of avoiding danger *to our own health*, in attending courts of judicature.

---

31 Howard did not begin his first tour of inspection until November 1773, too late to have any causative connection with the bill (see William A. Guy, 'Address on John Howard', *Journal of the Statistical Society* (1875), XXXVIII, p. 433). Howard is himself more vague and speaks of Popham's bill miscarrying 'a few years before' 1773, but still making the point that this had been undertaken, in the first instance, quite independently of him (*The State of the Prisons*, 3rd edn, p. 2). R.S.E. Hinde (*The British Penal System 1773-1950*, p. 31) incorrectly assumes that Popham's first bill was inspired by Howard. That others were at the same time also engaged in practical attempts to alter certain aspects of prison administration is a fact of some importance.

32 *Journals of the House of Commons*, XXXIV, p. 535.

(14 Geo. III, c.20) and the Health of Prisoners Act (14 Geo. III, c.59). The latter of these measures empowered the justices to intervene in the running of the gaols in order to secure certain health standards, an innovation in management much more significant than the actual health provisions involved, going far beyond the earlier building and repairing measures, and so broadly drawn that it gave the justices almost unlimited discretion.[33]

The former measure is sometimes represented as abolishing all fees. In fact it did not apply to debtors or to pardoned felons, but provided only for county payment of fees of acquitted or discharged prisoners, who were then to be set free at once in open court; compensation for gaolers was up to a total of 13s. 4d. per prisoner, which did not cover charges for supplies, lodgings, heating and so forth.

Although these Acts further strengthened the position of the justices in gaol administration, their effect under a loosely organised system of public administration and weak executive government could not have been expected to be immediate or wide-reaching. There was a strong sense that the purpose of such legislation was to show the local gentlemen what their duties were, but that it would have been improper thereafter to check on their degree of compliance. Many local authorities would have come to know about the legislation and its purposes from returning members or peers, and one should not totally dismiss the effectiveness of this means of activating legislation even though it lacked any guarantee of uniformity. Howard himself sought to supplement the ordinary means of dissemination, and at his own expense had the two Acts printed and sent to every gaol in the country. During subsequent visits he found that the Acts 'had been strictly obeyed and

---

33 The preamble underlines the point that prisons were increasingly seen as a physical threat to the community:

> whereas the malignant Fever, that is commonly called *The Gaol Distemper*, is found to be owing to a Want of Cleanliness and fresh Air in the several gaols in England and Wales, and the fatal Consequences of that Disorder, of which there has been, of late, too much Experience, might be prevented, if the Justices of the Peace were duly authorised to provide such Accommodation in gaols as may be necessary to answer this salutary Purpose . . . .

The magistrates were empowered to order scraping and whitewashing at least once a year: regular washing and cleaning was to be carried out and ventilation and sick-rooms were to be provided. They were also allowed to appoint 'an experienced Surgeon or Apothecary', paying him from the rates; he was to report on the health of the prisoners. By s.11 quarter sessions might order clothes for prisoners, prevent their being kept underground (when this could be done 'conveniently') and generally make orders for preserving or restoring prisoners' health. The Act was to be displayed on a board in the gaols, and penalties were fixed for disobedient gaolers.

literally carried into effect, in only 15 out of 130 of the prisons that he inspected'.[34]

Local experiment

There were a number of reasons why the 1770s and 1780s were propitious for local prison experiments. First, there had been the general leavening of religious and secular thought,[35] followed, and given a practical direction, by the work and moral example of Howard, who had become a figure of national importance, supported by the king, and lionised by foreign heads of state.[36] The campaign against the sanguinary penal code had achieved notable parliamentary support. Agitation such as was stirred up by the execution of the unfortunate Dr Dodd was both a sympton of new directions in social and penal philosophy, and an event which further strengthened the hand of the reformers.[37] These were decades of radicalism and reform, of the maturing of the various elements of critical thought which had been mounting from the 1760s. Adam Smith questioned the soundness of the economic institutions of the nation, whilst Jeremy Bentham began his formidable clearing of the undergrowth of administration and legislation. Politicians like Fox and Burke adeptly applied these powerful views. Other elements which contributed to the ferment included the dissenting academies, constitutional conflicts such as the Wilkes case, and the shock and self-examination caused by the loss of the American colonies.

Second, there had been changes, too, in the attitudes and effectiveness of the bench and other local bodies. The tradition handed down from the Tudors and early Stuarts 'that they were the eyes and ears of the privy council' had never been quite extinguished among the magistracy. Although the central government was not in a position to direct them in any but a few circumstances, the justices still acted with reasonable efficiency when issues of national security — riots or rebellion — threatened.[38] But on top of this attitude there were new developments. From about the middle of the century the county aristocracy had begun to attend the more important quarter sessions, thus adding a valuable new perspective to their proceedings and weight to their authority.[39] The quarter sessions had improved its general corporate efficiency and become a more flexible administrative body, which meant that it was better able to cope with the running of prisons. 'To a great extent these changes came about gradually, almost imperceptibly,

34 Guy, *op. cit.*, p. 134.
35 See pp. 78-84 above.
36 Lecky, *op. cit.*, III, p. 170.
37 Radzinowicz, *op. cit.*, pp. 1, 468, 473-93, *passim.*
38 Basil Williams, *The Whig Supremacy, 1714-1760*, p. 55.
39 J.H. Plumb, *England in the Eighteenth Century*, p. 85.

over the years, and reflected the increasing momentum of business brought before the Court which made the older haphazard methods no longer practicable'.[40] The contacts between the central and local authorities increased so that, even though initiative still lay with the latter, they amounted to frequent 'co-operation and correspondence between the two, in routine matters as well as in emergencies, and in a purely informal as well as a strictly official way'.[41] In the last quarter of the century it would seem that the extreme autonomy and decentralisation of the early Hanoverian period had waned, in parallel with the decline in classical whig ideology.

The fruits of local initiative in social policy must also have been becoming increasingly obvious. From the early 1760s onward, by means of private Acts of Parliament, various improvement commissions had been set up to provide publicly financed social services such as paving and lighting, sanitation and even policing. Although confined to the moribund municipalities (where they did 'far more to introduce new municipal services than all the Municipal Corporations taken together'),[42] these commissions set a powerful example to the counties.[43] They were 'the most important social development in the second half of the eighteenth century'.[44]

The Sussex prisons

The first local experiment in gaol reform following Popham's Acts took place in Sussex.[45] In 1775, guided by the then radical politician, the Duke of Richmond,[46] the justices in assembly at Michaelmas Sessions

---

40 E.A.L. Moir, thesis: 'Local Government in Gloucestershire, 1775-1800', p. 271.

41 *Ibid.*, pp. 267-8.

42 G.D.H. Cole, 'Town-life in the Provinces', in A.S. Turberville (ed.), *Johnson's England*, pp. 207-8.

43 And from the 1780s the mail coach and other reforms introduced by John Palmer, when comptroller-general, made written communications very much more swift and certain (see H.L. Beales, 'Travel and Communication', in A.S. Turberville (ed.), *Johnson's England*, pp. 154-5).

44 Plumb, *op. cit.*, p. 86.

45 Sussex had been one of the counties singled out by Howard in his 1774 evidence to the House of Commons as having particularly inadequate gaols. The other counties were Cornwall, Monmouthshire, Oxfordshire, Yorkshire, Gloucestershire, Warwickshire and Herefordshire.

46 Charles Lennox (1735-1806), third Duke of Richmond, combined many of the characteristics – radicalism, ability and participation in local and central government – conducive to involvement in reform of prison administration. His family had a tradition of service to the Sussex Bench, his father, the second duke, being described by Fielding as 'one of the worthiest of magistrates as well as the best of men'. The third duke became lord lieutenant of Sussex in 1763. He held office as secretary of state for the Southern Department for several months in 1766. Following Chatham's accession to power he was a constant critic of the government. Subsequently he abandoned

considered the state of the county gaol at Horsham. They agreed that 'the common gaol or prison of the said county was insufficient both as to the Security and Health of the Prisoners' and that a new building was needed and was allowed in accordance with 'the Powers and Directions given and prescribed in and by the several Statutes made and now in force relating to the Building and Repairing [of] gaols'.[47]

The duke himself

> furnished the plan of the prison . . . the gaoler's house, chapel and infirmary. His suggestions respecting a better site, the grounds attached thereto, and the boundary wall, were all adopted; and we find that his attendance and exertions during the whole progress of the works, until their completion in 1779, were assiduous and unremitting.[48]

The new gaol and gaoler's house were handed over to the sheriff at an adjourned meeting of the quarter sessions in August 1779 and John Aldridge, a magistrate, was appointed the gaol's inspector. He was directed to ensure that 'Rules and Orders made at this Sessions for the better Government of the said Gaol . . . be fully and strictly complied with'.[49] The rules were elaborate, extending to thirty-two detailed clauses. Their objective was to secure the good health, order and custody of the inmates, to minimise the contamination between classes of prisoners, and to control relationships between them and the staff. There was no reference to 'reformatory' aims and no provision of work or other penal routine designed to promote reformation. Attention was given to the basic elements in administration and management, namely a paid staff, outside inspection and the provision of all necessities for the upkeep of the prisoners.

The gaoler's salary was £100 a year, with an additional allowance of half a guinea per week for each turnkey he kept, numbering at least two, with a third permitted when the number of criminal prisoners exceeded ten. The gaoler and turnkeys were strictly forbidden to be concerned directly or indirectly in the selling of any goods to the prisoners; fee-taking also was not allowed. A chaplain and a surgeon were also appointed, at salaries of £50 and £5 respectively. The former

his support for reform. (See *Dictionary of National Biography*; Henry Fielding's *An Enquiry into the Causes of the Late Increase in Robbers*, p. 54; Lecky, *op. cit.*, IV, pp. 310-11. Alison Gilbert Olson's *The Radical Duke* deals with the third duke's political career.)

47 West Sussex County Record Office, QAP/4/WE1.
48 *Third Report of the Inspectors of Prisons (Home District)*, PP, 1837-8, XXX, Appendix A, 124.
49 West Sussex Record Office, *op. cit.* All the extracts from the rules which follow are taken from this MS.

was directed to read prayers each morning and to preach a sermon once a week 'at which every person is to attend'; he also had the rather curious duty of examining each prisoner every morning, noting

> his hands and fface and his cell to see that they are clean and to order such Punishment for Neglect as he shall think proper by stopping a proportion or the whole of the Bread Allowance for a time, by confinement to the cell, by putting on Irons or by chaining them Down.

Debtors who breached the regulations were to be punished by confinement to cells. All these punishments were to be 'Subject to the Control of the Inspector'.

Prisoners were kept in separate night cells (measuring 10 feet by 7 feet by 9 feet high) but were allowed to associate in classes of greater or lesser criminals in day-rooms, as arranged under the direction of the inspector, which were located on different floors. Debtors and women were divided off and occupied another part of the building. On entry all prisoners were bathed and de-loused and provided with a uniform, 'of the Cheapest Sort of woolen without plaits or pockets and to be mixed in pieced Green and Yellow'. Food was two pounds of bread a day, but prisoners were allowed, if they could afford it, to supplement this: they could purchase 'Meat, Bread or other Victuals or ... better Bedding but not ... Liquor'. The day-rooms had fires and kettles and half a bushel of coal a day was allowed for each of these rooms during the winter months. Bedding and cleaning materials were provided for each cell, and renewed as necessary. The turnkeys slept in the prison, keeping the inmates under supervision, and no unauthorised or extensive visiting was allowed. None of this amounted to a practical step towards reform, but it seems to have produced an orderly régime.

The county amenities for the prisoners and salaries for the staff were effective means of control, when supported by inspection, and probably carried magisterial intervention as far as could be allowed in the gaols under the existing laws. Most of the provisions could be legitimised as means of safeguarding health in accordance with the Health of Prisoners Act; as for the rest, the gaoler was bound, not by law, but by fear of loss of his position and by a civil contract. In consideration of his salary, house and garden, he was obliged to enter into a bond 'in the penalty of two Hundred Pounds to be fforfeited if he is Convicted to the Satisfaction of the Justices of the Peace' of having traded with the prisoners. Nevertheless the justices felt constrained, in 1787, to secure a private Act which enabled them to dispose of the old gaol site and which gave the force of law to the changes in administration which they had made.[50]

50 William Albery, *A Millennium of Facts in the History of Horsham and Sussex*, p. 397.

Howard thought highly of this new gaol and commended the county's 'noble example', reporting that he had found the prison 'as quiet as a private house'. But this approbation is hardly surprising, since even a cursory examination shows that in the matter of regulations, and even of physical design and location, Howard's suggestions and opinions had been assiduously followed — so closely, indeed, as to make it obvious that the Duke of Richmond must at some stage have consulted Howard directly. The title of the visiting justice ('Inspector'), the recommended diet, separation by classes, hygiene-promoting procedures, emphasis on the importance of a salaried gaoler,[51] building design — all make this as much Howard's prison as that of the duke and his colleagues.[52]

The model upon which Horsham was built and regulated, and Howard's own penological principles, were fundamentally *preventative* rather than reformatory. Horsham was designed with the intention of containing or mitigating the moral and physical pollution and contamination of the gaols. Any reformative hopes were speculative and accidental. This has led one biographer to comment that

> were it not for his intense religious feeling, which led him repeatedly to advocate the appointment of chaplains in all gaols, Howard might be accused of regarding prisoners almost as animals, who had no conception of a future and only needed clean, dry housing and adequate food to reach acquiescence in their confinement. One could imagine his ideal prison as rather like a modern zoo, with well-scrubbed animals, staffed by well-tempered keepers.[53]

But, in a preventative régime, no less than in one which was entrusted with reformatory ambitions, the regulation and control of staff were cardinal necessities. Howard had learned important lessons from penal history, as well as from his own observations. No fee-taking, trading gaoler could be controlled more than nominally in his relations with the prisoners, and therefore (given a sound and well-provided prison) salaries and outside inspection were the foundation upon which all other regulation had to be built.

Petworth house of correction, the next new prison to be built in Sussex, was undertaken with reformatory, in addition to preventative,

---

51 He wrote:

> Gaolers should have salaries proportioned to the trust and trouble; since no office, if *faithfully* and *humanely* administered, better deserves an adequate encouragement; yet not so much as to raise them above attention to their duty, and the *daily* inspection of their gaols (*The State of the Prisons*, 3rd edn, p. 26).

52 See Section III of *The State of the Prisons*, 'Proposed Improvements', pp. 19-43 (3rd edn).

53 D.L. Howard, *op. cit.*, p. 73.

objectives. The old prison had been built in 1625, and at the time of Howard's visitation in 1782 was in a ruinous condition:

> two rooms: one 17 feet by 10, the other 18 by 9, 6 feet high: too small for the general number of prisons. No chimney; no glass or shutters to the windows: no court: no water: no employment. This prison (rented by the county) has caused the death of many poor creatures: but I have now the pleasure to hear that it will soon be discontinued, a new one being under the consideration of the justices.[54]

In the same year Thomas Gilbert, the poor-law campaigner, obtained an Act to improve the administration of houses of correction.[55] It permitted quarter sessions to nominate for each district in which there was a house of correction an inspector, who was obliged to report on the state of the prison to the next Michaelmas Sessions. The Act forbade the keeper the tap and any other trading; remanded felons were to be separated from those sentenced to hard labour; women were to be separated from men. Implements for hard labour were to be provided, but all those not committed to hard labour were to do work 'which is not severe'. The justices were to fix a reasonable salary for the keeper as well as allowing him a portion of the profits of the prisoners' labour; the Act prohibited the appointment of a woman as keeper, and (bringing the houses of correction into line with the gaols) allowed the

---

54 John Howard, *The State of the Prisons*, 3rd edn, p. 272.
55 22 Geo. III, c.64, 'An Act for the amending and rendering more effectual the Laws in being relative to the House of Correction'. A schedule of rules, orders and regulations was annexed. The seven clauses directed that prisoners should be kept to hard labour with employment adapted to strength and ability; males and females should be separated; it prescribed the diet; and it provided for the cellular punishment of the refractory, as entered in a book kept and inspected by the justices. This Act was subsequently amended and further explained by 24 Geo. III, c.55 (1784).

Thomas Gilbert (1720-98) was Lord Gower's land agent, and was an MP from 1763 until 1795. He had an interest in the expansion and improvement of roads and canals, but achieved his reputation mainly as a campaigner for poor-law reform. His Houses of Correction Act was designed to support his other measure, passed in the same session, 22 Geo. III, c.83, the well-known 'Act for the Better Relief and Employment of the Poor'. By this Act Gilbert wished to remove administration of the Poor Law from the unpaid, annually elected overseers. Another important change was that the workhouse was to be only for the impotent poor. As for those able and willing to work, but without employment, the guardian was required to find them paid employment or 'to maintain or cause such person or persons to be properly maintained, lodged and provided for until such employment shall be procured'. Idle and disorderly persons were to be committed to the house of correction, which thus became an essential part (as in Elizabeth's system) of poor relief. Bridewells of necessity had therefore to be reformed in administration and régime.

justices to appoint a Church of England clergyman to officiate at divine service, at a salary not to exceed £20 a year. At the Summer Sessions two Sussex magistrates were elected to inspect the Petworth house of correction in the light of the new legislation.

Their report to the Michaelmas Sessions confirmed Howard's findings:

> from the Nature of this Place it is impossible that the Prisoners can be employed in work. That the said House of Correction is in every Particular improper for the purposes intended and that it would be impossible to make any alteration or additions to the same to answer the good intentions of the said Act.[56]

As applied in Sussex, Gilbert's House of Correction Act makes it clear that although practical distinctions between gaols and bridewells may have diminished in the course of the late seventeenth and the eighteenth century, a theoretical recognition of the particular corrective function of the bridewell survived.[57] The Sussex justices used Gilbert's measure to produce a reformatory, corrective prison which, over fifty years later, the zealot inspectors of prisons, William Crawford and Whitworth Russell, were happy to proclaim an ancestor of their own separate system: 'this prison affords the earliest instance of the complete adoption of the separate system of prison discipline in the kingdom, and, we might add, in the world'.[58]

The Duke of Richmond again played an active part in supervising the building of the new prison. Like Horsham gaol it was built on open arcades (to the plans of James Wyatt), designed to counter escape

56 West Sussex County Record Office, QAP/5/W1.
57 Howard, although entertaining no substantial reformatory hopes for gaols, had somewhat different views about bridewells: 'this prison ought to be quite separate from the gaol: at least not within the same walls: nor should even the court-yard be common to both'. The prisoners

> in *work* . . . ought, most certainly, to be employed. This is indispensably requisite. *Not one* should be idle, that is not sick. . . . The keeper should be a master of some manufacture; a man of activity, prudence and temper. And he should keep his prisoners at work ten hours a day; meal-times included (*The State of the Prisons* (3rd edn), pp. 37-8).

Wedderburn (admittedly writing a decade later) also emphasised the legal difference:

> An House of Correction is destined for the reception of those who are accused, or convicted of small offences, of persons apprehended upon a sudden breach of the Peace, of those who have not given satisfaction to their Parishes, for the support of their illegitimate offspring; of Vagrants, refractory apprentices, Journeymen and Labourers, or Artisans, who have not observed the regulations of their trade, or the conditions of their engagements (*Observations on the State of the English Prisons*, p. 10).

58 *Third Report of the Inspectors of Prisons (Home District)*, *op. cit.*, 43, n.

attempts and to prevent damp. Construction took several years and the building was not occupied until 1789. It consisted of thirty-two cells on two floors; a separate system (stalled) chapel of thirty-two pews; two infirmary rooms, and two turnkeys' rooms.[59] There were four airing yards, in each of which one prisoner at a time was exercised for one hour; for the remaining twenty-three hours of each day they were locked up except for attendance at (daily) divine service. Petworth was the first prison in which building and system of discipline were so closely related, a connection to be repeated in the separate system establishments of the 1840s.

As separation was the dominant idea in the régime any attempts to communicate were punished (by stoppage of part of the daily allowance of two pounds of bread), although it was reported that 'there were very few punishments, scarcely more than one a week'.[60] Sentences were generally short, but some prisoners were kept for two years in separate confinement. The governor's son (himself a turnkey at Petworth for twenty years) stated that he 'never knew any upon whose mind or body this mode of punishment had any prejudicial effect'.[61] The only prisoner permitted easement of the rigid discipline by reason of his holding the position of wardsman, was one 'who had been acquitted on a charge of murder, on the ground of insanity, and who was confined in the House of Correction eighteen years; during the whole of which time, however, he never showed the slightest symptoms of insanity!'[62]

This system of discipline continued for almost forty years, until 1816.[63] Reviewing it twenty years after it had lapsed the inspectors of prisons pass a remark which gives rise to an interesting question:

59 The two Sussex prisons were small by modern standards. Horsham gaol had also been built on two floors: 'On each floor, both on the debtors and felons side, there are ten rooms . . . besides a day-room . . . and a lodging-room for a turnkey' (John Howard, *The State of the Prisons* (3rd edn), p. 271).
60 *Third Report, op. cit.*, 45, n.
61 *Ibid.*, 44, n. This seems hardly believable in the light of subsequent experience at Millbank and Pentonville.
62 *Ibid.*, 45, n.
63 There was then an increase in numbers, which meant that separation could not be maintained. Prisoners subsequently worked in association, were allowed books in their cells and regular visits, not only from the chaplain, but from friends and relations. The arcades were converted into rooms in 1817, to provide extra accommodation. They had been thus used during the separate system, but in a limited fashion, to house vagrants: 'This was done in order to prevent the vagrants from interfering with the criminal prisoners to whom the thirty-two cells . . . were exclusively allocated' (*Third Report, op. cit.*, 44-5, *passim*). It is also likely, however, that impetus was given to the modification of the Petworth system of discipline by the Parliamentary attack made on the prison by Henry Bennet in June 1816. Bennet told the House that for the offence of vagrancy prisoners had been subjected to the rigours

what is very remarkable [is that] ... in scarcely any respect does the system, in this its earliest period, appear to differ from the most improved construction and administration in the present day: it seems to have suddenly started into existence in full maturity and perfection; furnished with nearly every appendage that was calculated to give force and efficacy to its operations.[64]

Gilbert's Houses of Correction Act did not provide for separation, merely segregation of males from females. From whence, then, did the Sussex justices get the notion of a separate system?

Howard has sometimes been said to have supported a reformatory system of discipline based on separation. But his reasons were pragmatic, and rested mainly on security and non-contamination. From his comments on cells can be gathered the gist of his concerns:

I wish to have so many *small rooms* or cabins that each criminal may *sleep alone*. ... If it be difficult to prevent their being together in the day-time; they should by all means be separated at night. Solitude and silence are favourable to reflection; and may possibly lead them to repentance. Privacy and hours of thoughtfulness are necessary for those who must soon leave the world. ... The like provision for such as return to society cannot be less needful. ... The separation I am pleading for, especially at night, would prevent escapes or make them very difficult: for that is the time in which they are generally planned and effected. This also would prevent their robbing one another in the night. Another reason for separation is ... gaolers ... hardly know where to keep criminals admitted to be *evidence* for the King: these would be murdered by their accomplices if put among them. ...[65]

His passing reference to the possibility of repentance in prisoners as one of the effects of separation may be judged a pious speculation rather than a strong conviction.

But there was, in contemporary penological discourse, a much firmer commitment to reformatory separation preached at least as early as 1740 by Bishop Butler:

of separation for as long as thirteen months, that a boy had received three months for destroying a pheasant egg, and that a woman had been driven insane by the separate régime (*Hansard* (First Series), XXXIV, cols 1262-3).

64 *Third Report, op. cit.*, 45.

65 John Howard, *The State of the Prisons* (3rd edn), p. 22. Howard did not favour the total separation of solitary confinement: 'Samuel Whitbread, son of one of Howard's closest friends, retorted to Wilberforce (in a Parliamentary debate) that the reformer "distinctly and without reserve expressed his abhorrence of solitary confinement ... I have heard him say that such a punishment was too severe for human reason to bear ..." ' (*cit*. Condon, *op. cit.*, pp. 32-3).

Then as the only Purposes of Punishments less than capital, are to reform the Offenders themselves and warn the Innocent by their Example, everything which should contribute to make this Kind of Punishment answer these Purposes better than it does, would be a great Improvement. And whether it be not a thing practicable, and what would contribute somewhat towards it, to exclude utterly all sorts of Revel-mirth from Places where Offenders are confined, to separate the Young from the Old, and force them Both, in Solitude, with Labour and low Diet, to make the Experiment, how far their natural Strength of Mind can support them under Guilt and Shame and Poverty; this may deserve Consideration. Then again, some Religious Instruction particularly adapted to their Condition, would as properly accompany those Punishments which are intended to Reform, as it does capital ones . . . it cannot but be even more incumbent on us, to endeavour in all Ways, to reclaim those Offenders, who are to return again into the World, than those who are to be removed out of it: and the only effectual Means of Reclaiming them, is to instil into them a Principle of Religion.[66]

Bishop Butler was one of the authorities to whom Howard referred his readers on the issue of separation; Jonas Hanway was the other. The latter campaigned on a diversity of issues throughout his life and was, in the 1770s, the most vociferous advocate of separation. He wrote,

Everyone has a plan, and a favourite system: mine is solitude in imprisonment, with proper profitable labour and a spare diet, as the most humane and effectual means of bringing malefactors who have forfeited their lives . . . to a right sense of their condition.[67]

So the *idea* of reformatory separate confinement was in circulation for a good part of the eighteenth century, and was taken up and skilfully advocated by one of the country's leading publicists in the 1770s.[68] There were two reasons why it might have attracted the Sussex magistrates. In the first place they were redesigning administration and

---

66 Bishop Joseph Butler, *Sermon Preached Before the Lord Mayor*, pp. 20-1. Howard refers to this sermon, though I think that he mistook the date; he describes it as a *Spital Sermon*, preached on 14 April 1750 (*op. cit.*, p. 22, n. 1).

67 Jonas Hanway, *Solitude in Imprisonment, with Proper Profitable Labour, and a Spare Diet, the Most Humane and Effectual Means of Bringing Malefactors . . . to a Right Sense of their Condition*, p. 4.

68 There were on the Continent various reformatory institutions upon which Howard reported and which could be used as models by those seeking to design a system of reformatory discipline. Howard refers to the house of correction for boys in the Hospice of San Michele (founded in 1702) and to the reformatory prison at Ghent (founded in 1775). Nearer home, many students of penal measures would have known of the *principles* upon which Bridewell and the other houses of correction had been founded.

discipline for a house of correction, the corrective function of which probably had never been totally lost from sight — at least as a legal distinction; Gilbert had revived that function in his Act. So there was a predisposition to look out for means of making correction more effective: thus the interest in separation. In the second place, the Sussex magistrates had already employed separation as a *preventative* device in Horsham gaol, and the remarks of Howard on the subject show how easily, through discourse and speculation, separation for preventative reasons might shade into reformatory hopes: Howard's notion that 'solitude and silence are favourable to reflection; and may possibly lead them to repentance' became almost irresistibly translated into a sure and certain means of reform. If for some magistrates the aim of imprisonment ceased to be merely expiatory with the effect of general deterrence, worked by means of expense, starvation, disease and misery — turning magistrates' neglect and gaolers' spoiling greed into policy — then the converse, i.e. an austere, reflective, sufficient, godly régime of custody, became transmuted into a formula not merely for penal loss of liberty, but for reform. The contrast between the physical *state* of the two kinds of prison was too great for the magistrates to resist the conclusion that if one led to pollution and decay, the other would lead to regeneration and civic rebirth.[69] The two Sussex prisons were not only the forerunners of the contending separate and associated disciplinary systems whose rival claims were to dominate the discussion of penal policy in the next century; they also happen to exemplify, with historical symmetry, the ease with which reform can be born of preventative measures in penal policy.

The Gloucester Penitentiary

In 1779 Howard collaborated with Blackstone and Eden to procure an Act (19 Geo. III, c.74) to establish a national penitentiary.[70] This measure, for a variety of reasons, was never implemented, remaining, save as an example, 'a dead letter'.[71] During the 1780s, however, there was a spate of local prison Acts. These were obtained by various quarter sessions, and allowed the justices to make alterations in the buildings

---

69 Reformist ambitions were made even more attractive for policy-makers because the new buildings involved expenditure of a large sum of public money. It may be that the more elaborate objectives were approved by way of placating considerable civic discontent — as at Petworth.

70 Howard advised; Blackstone and Eden drafted the bill. Although Howard expressed some minor differences of opinion over their draft, the Act embodied his four main principles — secure, roomy and sanitary buildings, salaried gaolers, preventative objectives and régime, and systematic inspection by an outside public body.

71 Henry Grey Bennet, *A Letter to Viscount Sidmouth . . . on the Transportation Laws, the State of the Hulks, and of the Colonies in New South Wales*, p. 4.

and administration of their several gaols and houses of correction. The first and most important of these Acts was that of 1785 permitting the Gloucester magistrates to refurbish all the county prisons and to apply the principles of the Penitentiary Act to Gloucestershire by the erection of a penitentiary prison.[72]

When Howard visited the county gaol in Gloucester castle (which also served as one of the county bridewells) he found it in poor condition. The premises were much too small for the number of prisoners involved: 'The whole prison', he wrote,

> was much out of repair, and had not been white-washed for many years. . . . There is no separation of the women, or of the bridewell prisoners. The licentious intercourse of the sexes is shocking to decency and humanity. Many children have been born in this gaol. There is a small chapel, but all the endeavours of the chaplain to promote reformation among the prisoners must necessarily be defeated, by the inattention of the magistrates, and their neglect of framing and enforcing good regulations. Perhaps this is the reason the chaplain seldom attends.[73]

The Gloucestershire counterpart of the Duke of Richmond as initiator and manager was Sir George Onesiphorus Paul.[74] At the Spring

---

72 The Act was 25 Geo. III, c.10, 'An Act for building a new gaol, a Penitentiary House, and certain new Houses of Correction, for the County of Gloucester and for regulating the same'. The other Acts included 26 Geo. III, c.24 (new gaol and house of correction for Shropshire 'and the several Boroughs, Towns Corporate, Liberties, Franchises and Places within the same'); 26 Geo. III, c.55 (new house of correction for Middlesex); 27 Geo. III, c.58 (disposing of the site and premises of the old Sussex gaol and recognising the legality of the new gaol); 27 Geo. III, c.60 (gaol, debtors' prison and house of correction for Staffordshire); 28 Geo. III, c.82 (rebuilding Chester gaol), and 31 Geo. III, c.22 (new gaol and session house for Surrey).

73 John Howard, *The State of the Prisons*, pp. 362-3. Howard also reported: 'I am happy to hear in October 1783, that this county had determined to build a new gaol, and to reform the bridewells; which is principally owing to the spirited exertions of the chairman of the grand jury *Sir George Onesiphorus Paul*.'

74 Paul (1746-1820) was the son of a Woodchester (Glos.) woollen cloth manufacturer. In 1763 he went to St John's, Oxford, and then spent several years in travelling. In 1780, in striking parallel to Howard, he was elected High Sheriff of Gloucestershire and, says the *Dictionary of National Biography*, 'it was then probably that the state of the county gaol and houses of correction began to attract his attention'. Paul, the *DNB* adds, 'though intimately acquainted with Howard's writings, does not seem to have known him personally'. Condon, however, suggests that Paul met Howard before October 1783, and that Howard then informed him what he planned to say about the old Gloucester prison in the appendix to the 1784 edition of *The State of the Prisons* and mentioned an architect (Blackburn) who would build a new prison (*op. cit.*, p. 99). Robert Alan Cooper (thesis: 'English Prison Reform 1773-1835', p. 91) also suggests that there were discussions between Paul and Howard.

Assizes held at Gloucester in 1783 Paul, as foreman of the grand jury, addressed the jurors on gaol fever, suggesting means of treating and preventing it. His appeal was a vehicle for his views on the purposes of imprisonment:

> I am far from thinking that prisons should be places of *Comfort*. They should be Places of Real Terror, to those whom the Laws would terrify; of Punishment to those whom they would punish; but of mere, though secure Confinement to those, whom, on just grounds of Suspicion, the police thinks fit to confine for further Examination.

The régime should be such 'as will produce Reflection; the Food such as will support Life, and preserve Health, but by no means animate the spirits. Dejection and Solitude are the natural Parents of Reflection'. Even religion was to offer little comfort: 'The Terrors of a future World are Essential to the Reformation of Men, who have learnt to brave the Powers of this.' His intentions were thus reformatory, but (as with Petworth) reformation was to work through harshly punitive experience. Limits to the punishment were fixed according to Beccaria's principles of parsimony which, together with the objective of prevention, provided reasons for rejecting the old standards of imprisonment: 'You can no more add an atom of Punishment to the Sentence of the Law, than you can inflict punishment on one absolutely innocent.' Further, 'whilst the Conduct of Prisons is by the Laws entrusted to our Direction, every Suffering, not warranted by the Spirit as well as Letter of the Law is extrajudicial Punishment, for which we are answerable to injured Humanity'.[75] Paul convinced his colleagues, and at the following Michaelmas Sessions a motion was carried in favour of the building of a new gaol and houses of correction. Paul was appointed chairman of the committee which was to supervise construction and obtained the special Act necessary for the work to go forward. Under its provisions the magistrates were required in the making of rules and regulations

> to have regard to the discipline, provisions and directions of the 19th Geo. III concerning the two National Penitentiary Houses there mentioned, as nearly as shall appear to be consistent with the more limited design of the Penitentiary House for the county of Gloucester.

---

75 Sir G.O. Paul, *A State of Proceedings on the Subject of a Reform of Prisons Within the County of Gloucester*, pp. 10, 22, 37, 23 and 8 respectively. It is obvious, from the concepts, and even terminology, that Paul had been influenced as much by Beccaria's philosophy as by Howard's observations. But his education, rounded off with a 'grand tour', makes a knowledge of Beccaria and attraction to Utilitarianism hardly surprising.

Paul's view of the National Penitentiary Act helps to explain the thinking behind the local Act: 'By this Act was first created a legal system of punishment, by mode of confinement — by labour and a modified seclusion; a system of penal imprisonment, as a substitute (at the will of the Crown) for punishment by death and transportation.'[76] It is this substitution of imprisonment for transportation that gave Gloucester its particular importance. It was more than a reformed custodial gaol or corrective bridewell for minor offenders: Gloucester Penitentiary was intended to cater for pardonable felons, and in this aim it had a direct effect upon the debate on the capital sentence and its alternatives.

The Gloucester Penitentiary received prisoners only indirectly: they were not sent there by sentence of the court; the punishment imposed in the first instance was transportation or death. Then convicts awaiting transportation (including those whose death sentence had been commuted) were closely observed in the period before their intended removal:

> when the transport convicts exhibit a disposition favourable to penitence, we do not solicit an order [from the Secretary of State] for their removal; if they continue to behave well for two, three or four years, according to circumstances, application is made to the Secretary of State . . . who has always been ready to represent the cases to the King for pardon.[77]

The new penitentiary was opened in July 1791, and provided thirty-two cells for males and twelve for females (later increased to fifty-four and eighteen). The regulations[78] enjoined solitude, which was interpreted both in preventative and reformatory terms; prisoners had separate cells both day and night. But solitude was not unbroken: they met their fellows when washing and at chapel, and there was also association at exercise. Moreover, they were taken from their cells (two at a time) to work the treadwheel which raised water. The daily routine was punctuated by visits from the governor, chaplain, taskmaster or instructor, while the surgeon was obliged to see each prisoner at least twice a week.[79] Breakfasts were delivered to the cells by two of the inmates. Bread was doled out at exercise, but eaten in the day-cell.

Insistence on solitude was in furtherance of internal change, a response

---

76 Evidence given to the *Select Committee on Penitentiary Houses (Holford Committee)*, PP, 1810-11, III, 584, 611.

77 *Holford Committee*, 598.

78 Paul told his fellow magistrates at the Michaelmas Session in 1789 that the regulations for the government of the new prisons had been 'hastily drawn up for Mr Howard's perusal previous to his very sudden departure on his forlorn tour of the east' (*Dictionary of National Biography*).

79 *Third Report, op. cit.*, 46.

going deeper than mere external compliance. Paul held that imprisonment should be directed to

> The punishment of the *mind* rather than the body. Their clothing is comfortable, yet humiliating; secluded from the society of their friends they are daily visited by gentlemen attentive to their spiritual and bodily welfare; food is prepared for them sufficient for all the purposes of life and health, whilst the use of money is denied, and by this denial, every means of luxury, of partial indulgence, and of corruption is prevented.[80]

The humiliation of the prisoner was given prominence in the regulations: 'Offenders shall be clothed in a coarse and uniform apparel, with certain obvious marks or badges affixed to the same, as well to humiliate the wearer, as to facilitate discovery in case of escape.'[81] But solitude and shame were not merely punishments; they were the prerequisites of reformation, a benefit to both the prisoner and society:

> It is not sufficient that the manners of a prison should be barely not corrupting, the Public should have Confidence in its full Power of Reformation. Whilst a Prison Contaminates a Man in the Eye of Society, and destroys all future confidence in his Honesty, a Commitment is, in Effect, a Condemnation to the Punishment of those Crimes, his future Necessities may induce him to perpetrate.[82]

Labour had a comparatively small place in the penitentiary régime. In the National Penitentiary Act work had been treated as a means of reducing the resistance of the prisoner, and that designated was of a highly punitive nature.[83] This approach was not fully adopted by Paul

---

80 Sir G.O. Paul, *Address Delivered at a General Meeting . . . held on Monday the 9th July, 1792*, p. 52.

81 'Rules Orders and Regulations as they relate to the Penitentiary House', Rule 26 (*cit. Holford Committee*, Appendix 2).

82 Paul, *A State of Proceedings on the Subject of a Reform of Prisons Within the County of Gloucester*, pp. 50-1. Consistently with this approach, certificates of good conduct were issued to discharged prisoners at Gloucester, and a reward was given to those who were in respectable employment for a year.

83 The Act instructed the governor to keep the prisoner

> so far as may be consistent with his or her Sex, Age, Health and Ability to Labour of the hardest and most servile Kind, in which Drudgery is chiefly required, and where the Work is little liable to be spoiled by Ignorance, Neglect or Obstinacy, and where the Materials or Tools are not easily stolen or embezzled, such as treading in a wheel, or drawing in a Capstern, for turning a Mill or other Machine or Engine, Sawing Stone, polishing Marble, beating Hemp, rasping Logwood, chopping Rags, making Cordage, or any other hard and labourious Service.

Less exacting but equally dull and chastising labour was laid down for those of less health and ability — spinning, net-making and oakum-picking.

who, in concentrating on separation, subordinated all other business to that end, allowed work as a privilege, and it could therefore be of a less onerous nature. The hours of labour were long — 'as many as the season of the year . . . will permit'[84] — but the punishment was its withdrawal, not its imposition.

Religion was important in the penitentiary. It was terror-preaching, and thus deterrent, but it also had a part in the reformatory process. Indeed, one cannot make sense of the Gloucester régime without a full appreciation of the importance placed on the cellular visits and admonitions of the chaplain and governor. Solitude was central to their policy only because it was thought to be a precondition of reflection, a preparation for the beneficent influence of the senior penitentiary officials. Paul's opinion, 'Dejection and solitude are the natural parents of reflection', almost exactly echoes Bishop Butler's.

In a separate system, few difficulties might be expected to arise from refractory inmates. Opportunities for combinations and conspiracies were *a priori* minimal. Staff control was facilitated thanks to the early precaution of selecting inmates on the basis of fairly prolonged observation. Moreover, they had formidable executive powers over the sentence of the court, as the Gloucester Penitentiary prisoners were serving what was, in many respects, an indeterminate sentence. The prisoners were, after all, subject to release at the discretion of the staff and magistrates. In any event, the initial contrast between a long period of transportation — perpetual banishment, in practical terms, for most of them — and a few years in the penitentiary, was so great as to be an inducement to all but the most obdurate and stupid of prisoners.[85]

It is likely that Howard himself first thought of using oakum (which in the nineteenth century became the typification of prison labour) for penal purposes. In a note on the Surrey county bridewell at St George's Fields he lamented that the prisoners were without employment and went on to suggest that

> If the great quantities of old cables and ropes piled up at the Tower were delivered out to the several keepers of bridewells in and about *London* to be wrought for use and prompt payment made for the work, this would prevent the excuses of keepers for not employing their prisoners.

He had seen this practice in Holland where the Admiralty and India Company supplied the ropes and took the oakum when it was ready (*The State of the Prisons* (3rd edn), p. 277, n.).

---

84 19 Geo. III, c.74, s. 34, adopted as Rule 3 for male convicted felons. 'Rules Orders and Regulations, etc.' (*Holford Committee*).

85 Paul was well aware of the importance of these factors as controls. In evidence to the Holford Committee he claimed a high success (low reconviction) rate and said:

> But I beg to add that if the power of transportation had been suspended, and if in consequence of that suspension we had been compelled to retain *all* persons convicted of larceny and other greater crimes, as an alternative

103

With these intimidating sanctions, and a small prison population, mainly of rural origin, the authorities had little need to have recourse to the more direct devices of control — the whip and the dark cell. Only three men were whipped in the first nineteen years of the prison's history, and it was with some obvious satisfaction that Paul was able to tell a parliamentary committee that they had 'not an idea how easily these prisoners are governed'.[86]

Thus, within the space of two decades local initiative, exercised in propitious ideological and political conditions, had provided a new range of prisons which catered for all types of inmate, from debtor and misdemeanant to convicted felon. During this same period the penal responsibilities of central government came under considerable strain and scrutiny. The practical experience of the local innovations in prison policy and administration might well be applied to national problems.

---

punishment for transportation, I think it more than probable that we should not have reformed a man (*Holford Committee*, 599).

Paul stated that during the first sixteen years of its existence, with a total of 704 commitments, the longest sentence served at Gloucester was one of four years.

---

86 *Holford Committee*, 599. Whipping could only be imposed by order of the magistrates.

5 The idea of a national penitentiary

The hulks: the legacy of transportation

Central government became directly involved in the ownership and administration of prisons through its part in carrying out transportation. This punishment, which can be traced back (as banishment) to the twelfth century, was authorised by legislation and by exercise of the prerogative, in conditional pardons.[1] Legislation began in 1593 by providing abjuration of the realm as an alternative to martyrdom for certain religious offenders.[2] In 1597 the justices were empowered to banish or send to the galleys rogues, vagabonds and sturdy beggars (39 Eliz., c.4). Transportation was greatly expanded under the early Stuarts and Commonwealth, and after the Restoration it was regularly attached to conditional pardons. In the course of the eighteenth century, stimulated, at least in part, by rising imperial ambitions, criminal legislators provided transportation as a penalty and it 'became one of the legislature's most favourite forms of punishment'.[3] Most of the transported went to the American colonies of Maryland and Virginia. The revolt of 1775 closed this depository, and stopped the export (then proceeding at a rate of about 960 a year).[4] Central government, faced

---

1 Sir William Holdsworth, *A History of English Law*, XI, p. 569.
2 A.G.L. Shaw prefers to treat the statute of 1585, which substituted banishment in place of martyrdom for Jesuit priests (35 Eliz., c.2), as the start of transportation legislation (*Convicts and the Colonies*, p. 22).
3 Holdsworth, *op. cit.*, XI, p. 574.
4 Shaw, *op. cit.*, p. 34. However, it should be remembered that even prior to this many sentenced to be transported were kept at home:

> There were, no doubt, always a certain number of prisoners who, though sentenced to transportation, did not actually leave the country, and, until the hulks were established, these remained in the local prisons, for there were no others, as did also convicts in the interval between sentence and transportation. The cost of maintaining these was borne partly by a

with the ceaseless outpourings of the courts, had to resort to emergency measures. Their chosen device was to put the convicts to hard labour, holding them in floating prisons, or hulks,[5] moored on the Thames. The hard labour consisted of various public works to improve the navigation of the river.[6] The Act also authorised use of the houses of correction for the serving of sentences of hard labour,[7] but as it simply moved responsibility and expense from central to local government it is hardly surprising that this part of the Act came to nought.

When the hulks came to be put in charge of an overseer by appointment of the Middlesex justices, Duncan Campbell, an experienced transportation contractor, was chosen. Under the Act the overseer was obliged to keep his charges at hard labour 'in raising Sand, Soil and Gravel from, and cleansing the *Thames*, or in any other laborious Service for the Benefit of the Navigation of the *Thames*',[8] but in no other kind of work. His authority extended to punishment by whipping and to commendation for a shortening of sentence. He was obliged to make returns, on oath, to the Court of King's Bench on the first day of every law term; but, apart from this last, Campbell (who also was contractor for the custody and maintenance of the prisoners) was subject to no control after his appointment. He immediately had two ships – the *Justitia* (which he had used for transportation) and the *Censor* – fitted out and moored on the river, and received his first prisoners in the summer of 1776.[9] The Hard Labour Act was continued by 18 Geo. III, c.62, and 19 Geo. III, c.54.

A number of mutinies and spectacular escape attempts led to

---

county allowance and partly by a King's allowance of half-a-crown a week, which the Sheriff charged for every transferred 'Assize convict' in his 'bill of cravings' (*Report from the Departmental Committee on Prisons*, 1895 (Gladstone Committee), Minutes of Evidence, 459).

Shortly after the American wars the British government rather ingenuously attempted to revive transportation to that country along former lines (Wilfred Oldham, thesis: 'The Administration of the System of Transportation of British Convicts 1763-1793', Ch. 4).

---

5 Government already had experience of this type of custody, which had been used for prisoners of war for many years (Francis Abell, *Prisoners of War in Britain*, Chs 3-6).
6 See 16 Geo. III, c.43, 'An Act to authorise, for a limited Time, the Punishment by Hard Labour of Offenders who, for certain Crimes, are or shall become liable to be transported to any of his Majesty's Colonies and Plantations'.
7 ss. X, XI, XII and XIII. s. XVIII provided that where houses of correction were so used the convicts for transportation were to be kept apart from the other prisoners 'confined for any offence under the Degree of Petit Larceny, or other Crime not . . . subject to a Sentence of Transportation'.
8 s.V.
9 Wilfred Oldham (*op. cit.*) provides a useful and detailed description of the hulk administration; see especially pp. 123-38.

considerable public discontent within the first few years, heightened by Howard's report of his visit. In 1778 advantage was taken of the annual renewal of the Act to obtain a committee of inquiry, headed by Sir Charles Bunbury, which revealed 'that from August 1776, when the convicts were first put on board the Justitia, to March 26, 1778, out of six hundred and thirty-two prisoners who had been received, one hundred and seventy-six had died'.[10] Despite these appalling mortality figures the hulk system was continued but with various improvements affecting health and management.[11]

The Penitentiary Acts

The hulks defeated the preventative and reformatory hopes of the penal campaigners who, under the influence of Beccaria, also viewed transportation with great distaste. A growing body of opinion favoured useful, and possibly reformatory, confinement at home as against riddance by exile.[12] It was against this background, and in the midst of moves to mitigate the severity of the penal code, that in 1778, with Howard's close advice, Blackstone and Eden drafted the Hard Labour Bill.

In its original form this bill sought to establish a total of nineteen labour houses in various countries which were to be amalgamated into districts for purposes of finance and administration. These were to be of different capacities, calculated on the basis of past committal figures, ranging from accommodation for about fifty convicts a year in Wales, to that in the district of London (excluding the City) housing almost nine hundred. This ambitious scheme was greatly modified, without altogether sacrificing its penal philosophy, and the bill was enacted as the Penitentiary Act.[13]

This new measure seemed to indicate a firm government commitment to penitentiary imprisonment, and the penal reformers were jubilant. Blackstone wrote:

10 John Howard, *The State of the Prisons* (3rd edn), p. 465. For the full report of the Bunbury Committee, see the *Journals of the House of Commons* (1778), XXXVI, pp. 926-32.

11 On a subsequent visit Howard reported: 'Of late, but few of them have died: this shews that their situation is better with respect to health; but the association of so many criminals is utterly destructive to morals' (*op. cit.*, p. 466).

12 See *Report Respecting Transportation of Offenders*, PP, 1785, XL; and George Holford's *Statements and Observations Concerning the Hulks*. W. Branch Johnson's *The English Prison Hulks* provides a useful general description of some of the contemporary reactions.

13 See Jeremy Bentham, 'A View of the Hard-Labour Bill', in *The Works of Jeremy Bentham*, IV (John Bowring's edn, pp. 6-9, 34-5).

> If the plan be properly executed, there is reason to hope that such a reformation may be effected in the lower classes of mankind, and such a gradual scale of punishment be affixed to all gradations of guilt, as may in time supersede the necessity of punishment, except for very atrocious crimes.[14]

The Act ('to explain and amend the Laws relating to the Transportation, Imprisonment and other Punishment, of certain Offenders') authorised central government to erect two national penitentiaries (one each for males and females), which were to be administered under its direct charge and responsibility. Together with the hulks (to be reserved for 'atrocious and daring offenders') these two prisons would constitute a considerable prison establishment, with an intake of about one thousand a year. In the penitentiaries, it was hoped, a régime of

> solitary Imprisonment, accompanied by well-regulated Labour, and Religious Instruction . . . might be the Means, under Providence, not only of deterring others from the Commission of . . . Crimes, but also of Reforming the Individuals and inuring them to Habits of Industry.[15]

Offenders could be sent to the penitentiaries by conditional pardons, and also by means of direct court sentences.[16]

But the high hopes of Blackstone and the others were not to be fulfilled. The three supervisors who were appointed to take charge of the building of the new prisons could not even agree upon a site. Howard and his friend, Fothergill, favoured Islington; Whately, the other supervisor, Limehouse. Their disagreement went to the High Court for resolution, and three new supervisors were appointed — Sir Gilbert Elliot, Sir Charles Bunbury and Thomas Bowdler.[17] Although the triumvirate speedily found a new site at Battersea Rise, and held an

---

14 *Cit*. Shaw, *op. cit*., p. 44. Despite his hopes for the new Act, Blackstone referred to it as his 'emasculated offspring' and complained in 1779 that 'the Bill is so changed from my first Sketch in 1776, that I hardly know it again, and must desire to have the Justice done me to say that the Bill as at present garbled is none of mine' (*cit*. Robert Alan Cooper, thesis: 'English Prison Reform 1773-1835', pp. 80, 77).

15 s.5.

16 But in limited numbers, specified for each circuit (ss. 25, 27).

17 D.L. Howard, *John Howard: Prison Reformer*, pp. 85-8; Richard Herrick Condon, thesis: 'The Reform of English Prisons, 1773-1816', Ch. 3. Bentham commented sarcastically:

> They quarrelled before the first stone was laid, and before it was agreed where it should be laid: they quarrelled about that very question. But there could not have been a stone laid but what would have been just as capable of raising a quarrel as the first — no, nor a barrel of flour been to be bought, nor a bundle of hemp, not a petticoat, nor a pair of breeches ('Panopticon: Postscript, Part II', *Works*, IV, p. 127).

architectural competition (won by Howard's friend, William Blackburn), they were still no more successful than their predecessors. The Treasury refused their application for the funds necessary to begin building in September 1782, stating that 'new measures were about to be taken with respect to felons which made the hastening of the Penitentiary Houses less necessary'.[18]

In 1784 the Penitentiary Act expired and was replaced by a temporary measure (24 Geo. III, c.12) and then by an Act for the renewal of transportation (24 Geo. III, c.56). This latter was intended to secure 'the effectual transportation of felons and other offenders'. It continued the penitentiary provisions, but took no further steps to implement them. The hulks were also continued, but imprisonment therein, as well as being a substitute for transportation, also became a preliminary to it. Power to transport was thus resumed, but without a specific destination being mentioned. Pitt wrote to Wilberforce in 1786 that 'The multitude of things depending has made the Penitentiary House long in deciding on'.[19] In 1787 the hulk establishment was extended to Portsmouth and in 1788 to Woolwich, making the dockyard labour of the convicts more widely available.[20]

Various alternatives to the American colonies as penal depositories had been put forward; the Gambia was suggested, as was the Cape, Madagascar, Tristan da Cunha and Algiers. There had been abortive trials with transportation to West Africa, the West Indies and South America.[21] Other penal nostrums were suggested, such as employment in the coal mines, in rope-making or in the North Sea herring industry. By the summer of 1786, however, New South Wales had become the focus of serious discussion and the government decided to found a penal colony at Botany Bay.

Besides these practical developments, which reduced the pressures for government action on the penitentiaries, a considerable change was taking place in the philosophical outlook and economic climate of the nation. Penitentiary imprisonment under the direct charge of central government was still a novel and untested idea, and with the death of Howard and the recession of the campaigns for national penal reform it lost much political purchase. Indeed, drastic curtailment was experienced over a much broader front of social debate and experiment due to the effects of the French Revolution and, in February 1793, to the outbreak of war. Energies were directed to far different and more urgent priorities as the war developed in its first years to the point of

18 *Cit.* Cooper, *op. cit.*, p. 83.
19 *Cit.* Shaw, *op. cit.*, p. 44.
20 *Ibid.*, p. 45, n. 3.
21 Wilfred Oldham, *op. cit.*, Chs 3-5.

imminent national collapse.[22]

With instability came reaction to all suggested change:

> with its violent disturbances of economic life, and its mood of
> 'anti-Jacobin' reaction against all proposals for reform and all
> sympathy with the claims and sufferings of the poor — the war
> formed the worst possible environment for the industrial and
> social changes then in rapid progress.[23]

Pitt reversed his attitude towards reform of the criminal law; in the face of the threat posed by the French Revolution he 'made everything subservient to the task of averting it. All reforms were put on one side, till the barometer should rise to a more promising level'.[24] But the reforming zeal of the Utilitarians and the Evangelicals[25] was now working, like yeast, too strongly in the conscience of the nation, and the pace of economic and social change was too far advanced for this period to be more than an interlude. Arrears of work on administrative and social problems rapidly accumulated, and long before the end of the war, but when the peak of national danger had been passed, campaigns on the criminal law and penal system were resumed.

When this happened, the complicated nature of intellectual and political developments during the war period became more apparent:

> The first consequence of the new forces released after 1790 was to
> solidify the surface of the established order. But as widespread

22 The mutinies at the Nore and Spithead in the summer of 1797 occurred at a time of soaring food prices and widespread starvation among the poor. An invasion by the French and their allies was barely averted. Plumb notes that the whole financial structure of the country seemed at that point to be in collapse. So bad was the situation that Pitt attempted to make peace with the French on terms that were all but the acknowledgment of defeat (J.H. Plumb, *England in the Eighteenth Century*, p. 201; G.D.H. Cole and Raymond Postgate, *The Common People*, pp. 166-7).

23 G.M. Trevelyan, *English Social History*, p. 463. Romilly said of this period: 'Among the higher orders it has produced a horror of every kind of innovation; among the lower, a desire to try the boldest political experiments, and a distrust and contempt of all moderate reforms' (*Cit.* Holdsworth, *op. cit.*, X, p. 19, n. 3).

24 Lord Rosebery, quoted by Leon Radzinowicz, *A History of English Criminal Law*, I, pp. 343-4.

25 The Hammonds' somewhat whiggish comment is not inappropriate:

> The positive achievements of these men, and of men like them, may seem inconsiderable and the nation they had begun to educate was thrown back with violence in the panic spread by the French Revolution. But a disparaging view would be a shortsighted view. Few reformers live to see the full triumph of their efforts, and most of them die thinking of their work as wasted. The test comes afterwards. . . . Of these early philanthropists we may say that, if they could not save the eighteenth century by their energy, they helped to save the nineteenth by their example ('Poverty, Crime and Philanthropy', p. 334).

changes proceeded beneath this surface it became brittle. To doubt the virtues of the established order became dangerous. But for the young to do so was almost inevitable. In every department of thought and expression a new passion began to show, the product of uncertainty and conflict.[26]

The new generation of campaigners, therefore, did not take up where the old had left off. Theirs were more fortified arguments, and the circumstances to which they addressed themselves were more palpably sundered from the medieval institutional inheritance. In criminal law and penal administration the leading critic was Sir Samuel Romilly. He argued both for a mitigation in the use of capital measures and for a substantial development of alternative, secondary, punishments.[27] At his urging the House of Commons agreed, in 1810, to reconsider the national penitentiaries, and at the suggestion of the home secretary a select committee was appointed to review the existing laws and provisions.[28] It was headed by George Holford.[29]

Conflicting models for the penitentiary

The Holford Committee's ostensible problem was whether existing prisons could be adapted for purposes of penitentiary imprisonment, or whether a new type of administration and management was necessary. The chief witnesses personified the conflicting views: Sir George

26 J. Steven Watson, *The Reign of George III, 1760-1815*, p. 355.
27 He described the Penitentiary Act as a plan

> which unites the advantages of a charitable with those of a penal institution, and has in view that important end of punishment, which has been overlooked in almost all our other laws — the reformation of the criminal: for, at the same time that it promises to subdue the fiercest and most ungovernable spirits by solitary confinement and continued labour, it would be a kind of asylum to that very large description of offenders, who are rendered such by the defects of education, by pernicious connexions, by indigence, or by despair.

> He could not understand what had delayed implementation of the Act, 'for, though the expense of erecting the penitentiary houses would be considerable, yet that is surely but a trifling object, compared with the benefit which, as it should seem, must necessarily result to the country from such an institution' (*cit*. James Heath, *Eighteenth Century Penal Theory*, pp. 270-1).

28 *Hansard* (First Series), XVII (1810), cols 322-52.
29 Holford (1767-1839) was an MP from 1803 to 1826, and from 1804 to 1810 was secretary of the Board of Control for India. The other members of the committee were Richard Ryder (home secretary), Sir Charles Bunbury, Sir Charles Price, N. Vansittart, Sir Samuel Romilly, C. Bathurst, F. Burton, H. Leycester, Sir Evan Nepean, C. Long, Sturges Bourne, J. Blackburne, W. Mellish, William Wilberforce, J. Fane, W. Dickinson, W. Lygon, William Wynn, J. Abercromby and W. Morton Pitt.

Paul was examined on the Gloucester Penitentiary and the Reverend John Becher on the house of correction at Southwell. The localities were well known to have made great changes in their prisons, and it was considered that they could offer much practical experience. Both men had been commended by Romilly in the debate which had led to the committee,[30] and each was possessed of a desire to influence policy at a national level.[31] As these two men witnessed to the benefits of the new, the keepers of Newgate and the county gaol at Southwark commended the old, and still dominant, practices. There were also two witnesses to the might-have-been: Jeremy Bentham gave evidence in support of his 1794 contract with the government, in which he had undertaken to build and administer a penitentiary prison, his famous Panopticon;[32] the Howard, Blackstone and Eden Act of 1779 (19 Geo.

30 *Cobbett's Parliamentary Register*, XVII, p. 322. Paul and Becher are described by the Webbs as friends of Holford (*English Prisons Under Local Government*, p. 48).

31 Of the two prisons, Gloucester Penitentiary had achieved the greater national renown. The royal family had shown its interest even as the building was being constructed, and King George and Queen Charlotte had visited. Prince William of Gloucester sent a donation of a 'Ten Pound Note for the Use of the Prisoners' (E.A.L. Moir, 'Local Government in Gloucestershire, 1775-1800', p. 199). The local nobility and gentry were no less interested and records of parties of distinguished visitors appear fairly frequently in the officers' journals. On 5 October 1802, for example, the governor recorded the visit of Lord Bathurst, Lord Ducie and a number of other notable visitors, who were accompanied by Sir George Paul (Gloucestershire Records Office, County Gaol, Governor's Journal, ref. Q/GC3/3). Of the Gloucester achievement Paul had said:

> Struck with the vast theory of prison reform which had been directed to the feelings and to the police of mankind, I undertook the task of reducing it to practice on a much broader principle than that of more provincial regulation (*Address Delivered at a General Meeting . . . held on Monday the 9th July, 1792*, p. 52).

On Becher see p. 116, n. 42 below.

32 Bentham's contract had a long and tortuous history. At one point he drafted a letter itemising his negotiations with the Treasury and the Home Office; the 'letter' grew into a document of some several hundred pages! Initially he had considerable difficulties in securing the necessary lands. Meanwhile, the government changed its original specification for a 1,000-inmate prison to one calling for a 2,000-inmate prison, and then a 500-inmate one, haggling all the time about the funds that it would advance. But much of this seems to have been delaying tactics and a camouflage for the scuttling of the scheme: government was committed to the expensive colony in New South Wales, and judged that it could not have that *and* the Panopticon.

In 1800, the then secretary of state, the Duke of Portland, called for an abandonment of the project,

> considering the number of years which have elapsed since the first steps were taken with a view to the adoption of any plan of this kind and the variation of circumstances which have occurred during that period, the

III, c.74) was also considered, both in the evidence of Paul and as influential background against which the committee worked.

As the proceedings unfolded, it became obvious that the actual line of conflict lay, not between the old and the new models of imprisonment, but rather between varieties of the new: the rival merits of the administration proposed by Bentham and that embodied in the 1779 Act, and applied by Paul and Becher. The evidence relating to Newgate and Southwark gaols was significant only as a backdrop.[33] As the different approaches were successively contrasted, a further contraction in the area of dispute became apparent: differences were most intense in relation to the post of governor of the various establishments – his tasks and place in prison administration. But the significance of the concentration upon this one point is fully apparent only in the context of the competing views of criminality, penal policy and administration which were involved.

In contrast to Beccaria, Bentham was subjective in his approach to crime and punishment.[34] Both based their psychology upon the twin springs of pain and pleasure; but, for Bentham, the intensity of pain or pleasure was not necessarily related directly to the strength of their external causes, but was mediated by a number of individual factors. These he called 'circumstances affecting sensibility', which were comprised of a number of variables[35] such as sex, age, strength, bodily

---

improved state of the Colony of New South Wales . . . as well as the various improvements which have since taken place in the different gaols of the Kingdom, and the great increase of terms which Mr. Bentham now proposes. . . .

In 1801, the Treasury Board proposed to Bentham that he should build a 500-inmate prison; he was invited, if he did not wish to go ahead with this revised scheme, to indicate what he considered would be suitable compensation. Bentham thought that a scheme for 500 inmates was too small to be commercially successful; and this effectively brought the undertaking to a close. The Holford Committee agreed with Bentham that although the original contract had not actually been signed, 'public faith had been pledged'. The financial muddle, however, was not cleared up until October 1813. See L.J. Hume, 'Bentham's Panopticon: An Administrative History', *Historical Studies* (October 1973), 61, pp. 703-21, and (April 1974), 62, pp. 36-54, for a detailed account. (The quotation from the Duke of Portland is given on pp. 37-8, April 1974.) See also Major Arthur Griffiths, *Memorials of Millbank*, I, pp. 17-26.

33 The committee explicitly referred to the opposing claims to superiority of the two main approaches and contrasted the relevant Acts, 19 Geo. III, c.74, and 34 Geo. III, c.84, which had been intended to give effect to Bentham's scheme as outlined in *A Proposal for a New and Less Expensive Mode of Employing and Reforming Convicts*.

34 'In its essence Bentham's philosophy is individualistic, and his approach, both to criminal acts and to punishment, consequently primarily subjective' (Radzinowicz, *op. cit.*, I, p. 371).

35 Amounting, with subdivision, to thirty-two in all (*ibid.*).

imperfections, mental state, moral sensibility, usual occupation and financial circumstances. Bentham insisted that the application of such factors led to individualised judgments when the evil of an offence was estimated and when evaluating satisfaction for an injured party, or choosing the most suitable punishment to impose upon an offender.[36]

It is hardly necessary to insist on the penological import of these remarks, emphasising as they do the difference between a nominal and a real punishment, and indicating the various factors which are at the root of these differences.[37]

Bentham's individualistic psychology and penal philosophy led him inevitably to an appreciation of the importance of separate confinement — an immediate method to ensure the differential application of a wide enough variety of penal circumstances to the offender. 'When I had read Mr. Howard's book on Prisons,' wrote Bentham, 'one fruit of it was, a wish still more earnest than what I had been led to entertain from theory, to see some general plan of punishment adopted, in which solitary confinement might be combined with labour.'[38] He saw reformation, however, as only one, and that a subordinate, end of punishment:

General prevention ought to be the chief end of punishment as it is its real justification. If we could consider an offence which has been committed as an isolated fact, the like of which would never recur, punishment would be useless. It would only be adding one evil to another. But when we consider that an unpunished crime leaves the path of crime open not only to the same delinquent, but also to all those who may have the same motives and opportunities for entering

36 Or adopting the laws of another country (*ibid.*, p. 373).
37 *Ibid.*
38 'A View of the Hard-Labour Bill', *op. cit.*, p. 3. Bentham met Howard in the spring of 1778 and wrote eulogistically of him to a friend:

He is, I believe . . . one of the most extra-ordinary men this age can shew. For these 4 or 5 years past he has devoted the whole of his time to this one object. His own private affairs he says suffer for it a little: but this he does not mind. . . . He has a constitution as irony as your own, yet observes a severity of regimen to which happily you have no need to subject yourself. While upon his travels he allows himself every *other* night for sleeping. . . . He fears no contagion: he has been in many a gaol so pestilential, that the Gaoler himself has not set foot in it for months. . . Honest Gaolers receive him with open arms: dishonest ones tremble at his approach. He renders both sorts alike, pliant to his purpose: the one by their hopes, the other by their fears. Practise has made him familiar with all their arts and all their ways: when he has addressed himself to any of them for the first time he has commonly been taken for a brother of the profession (T.L.S. Sprigge (ed.), *Correspondence of Jeremy Bentham*, II, pp. 106-7).

upon it, we perceive that the punishment inflicted upon the individual becomes a source of security to all.[39]

Bentham rejected expiation, therefore, but laid emphasis upon general deterrence,[40] as did those who upheld the sanguinary code. In common with Beccaria, he subjected deterrence to the rule of parsimony.

In the design of a penal régime Bentham insisted that there should be adherence to three principles: firstly, the rule of lenity: 'The ordinary condition of a convict doomed to forced labour for a length of time, ought not to be attended with bodily sufferance, or prejudicial, or dangerous to health or life.' Secondly, the rule of severity:

Saving the regard due to life, health, and bodily ease, the ordinary condition of a convict doomed to a punishment which few or none but individuals of the poorest class are apt to incur, ought not to be made more eligible than that of the poorest class of subjects in a state of innocence and liberty.

Thirdly, the rule of economy:

Saving the regard due to life, health, bodily ease, proper instruction, and future provision, economy ought, in every point of management, to be the prevalent consideration. No public expense ought to be incurred, or profit or saving rejected, for the sake either of punishment or of indulgence.[41]

39 Jeremy Bentham, *The Rationale of Punishment*, pp. 20-1. He goes on:

That punishment which considered in itself, appeared base and repugnant to all generous sentiments, is elevated to the first rank of benefits, when it is regarded not as an act of wrath or of vengeance against a guilty or unfortunate individual who has given way to mischievous inclinations but as an indispensable sacrifice to the common safety.

40 Because of his insistence on the need for an exemplary element he, with Beccaria, opposed transportation. He condemned it as unequal: 'A man who had money might buy off the servitude', and 'nothing can be more unequal than the effect which a change of country has upon men of different habits, attachments, talents and propensities. Some would have been glad to go by choice; others would sooner die'. He also rejected it as unexemplary, wasteful and uncertain in its reformatory powers and ability to prevent the offender doing further mischief ('A View of the Hard-Labour Bill', *op. cit.*, p. 6).

41 'Panopticon: Postscript, Part II', *op. cit.*, pp. 122-3. An unstated but fundamental principle was, of course, the incorporation of an exemplary element. He suggested two alternative mottoes to be engraved over the doors of penitentiary houses: 'Had they been industrious when free, they need not have drudged here like slaves', or 'Violence and Knavery are the Roads to Slavery'. These inscriptions, together with a suitable device, might, he thought, 'contribute to inculcate the justice, to augment the terror, and to spread the notoriety of this plan of punishment' ('A View of the Hard-Labour Bill', *op. cit.*, p. 32).

115

Although they differed sharply on matters of administration, Paul generally shared Bentham's philosophical views. According to Paul, punishment should be exemplary and retributive, but moderated in severity by the principle of parsimony. Reformation was an important part of the Gloucester philosophy, but it was difficult to disentangle from prevention and individual deterrence. With his emphasis on punishment of the mind, Paul was individualistic in his philosophy, but less so than Bentham. Separation was, therefore, a central, but not the supreme, ingredient of the Gloucester system.

Since a different category of prisoner was involved, the philosophy and régime of the Southwell house of correction, about which the Reverend Thomas Becher[42] gave evidence, were shaped by concerns distinct from those which influenced Bentham and Paul. The latter addressed themselves to the handling of felons, but the Southwell inmate was a suspect awaiting trial, a non-capital felon or a disorderly apprentice or other minor misdemeanant. Sentences were short — a few days, weeks or months — and two years at most. This made for a more 'behaviourist' outlook.[43] The Gloucester approach, although

42 John Thomas Becher (1770-1848) is, like Paul, an excellent example of the zealous county magistrate affecting not merely local, but national policy. He attended Westminster and Oxford, and in 1799 was presented to the perpetual curacies of Thurgarton and Hoveringham in Nottinghamshire, in which county he had strong family connections. He became vicar of Rampton, Nottinghamshire, and Midsomer Norton, Somerset, in 1802, and a Prebendary of Southwell in 1818. He was presented to the Rectory of Barnborough, Yorkshire, in 1830. His active intellectual and administrative life rectifies the one-sided picture of an indolent and even dissipated pluralist clergyman.

He became a visiting justice of the bridewell of his division of Nottinghamshire in January 1806 and, as a result of his observations, published in September of the same year *A Report Concerning the House of Correction at Southwell*. As a response to the industrial disorders in Nottinghamshire he published, in 1812, his *Observations on the Punishment of Offenders*, a pamphlet of a legal rather than a penological nature. In 1816 he became chairman of the quarter sessions for the Newark division of Nottinghamshire, and held office for thirty years.

His interest in social policy was greater even than his considerable interest in penal matters. He published books on friendly societies in 1825 and 1826, and in 1828 *The Antipauper System*, an account of the reforms he had been instrumental in securing in the administration of the poor laws at Southwell. His local work on poor-relief and the bridewell achieved national renown. Becher's influence was heightened when the man he had appointed to run his deterrent workhouse, George Nicholls, became a poor-law commissioner and, in 1847, permanent secretary, when the commission was replaced by the Poor Law Board.

For further information on Becher see the *Dictionary of National Biography*; Norman Longmate, *The Workhouse*; and S. and B. Webb, *English Poor Law History: The Old Poor Law*, p. 254, n. 3, and p. 257, n. 2.

43 Ostensibly the rebuilding and administrative restructuring of the Southwell house of correction had been prompted by Gilbert's Houses of Correction

exemplary and deterrent, was deeply concerned with securing and assessing internal change, and was considered inappropriate to Southwell conditions. Becher's prison aimed only to effect a change of life, in contrast with Gloucester's change of heart; compliance as distinct from conversion:

> We treat mankind as constituted of habits, and our principle is to eradicate those which are bad, and to implant others which are better. With this intent, we frequently receive a man filthy, diseased, drunken, idle and profane; and that man in a short time becomes clean, sober, healthy, diligent and to all appearances a good moral man.[44]

All three approaches concentrated upon the use of prisons beyond the merely custodial and exemplary; all sought in various ways to control the experience of imprisonment to secure preventative ends as well as a change in character or behaviour. And in this they differed very considerably from most of the other prisons of the day.

The régimes of the three establishments reflected their different concerns. Bentham's plan (like Petworth house of correction) relied heavily upon the characteristics of his Panopticon.[45] The central feature

---

Act. The minutes of the quarter sessions (27 September 1806) noted receipt of Becher's report which stated that the existing prison was inadequate to carry out the improved system of discipline and to carry into effect the 'general provisions of the Legislature for the Regulation and management of such Prisons' (Nottinghamshire Records Office, ref. QAG5/1A). But from whence did Becher's original interest and administrative ideas develop? There is no firm evidence, but it would seem probable (given his interest in poor-law administration) that he had read Sir Frederick Eden's *State of the Poor* which appeared in 1797; and which, according to Plumb, received great publicity (Plumb, *op. cit.*, p. 154). This work gave a good deal of information on the early (Elizabethan) bridewells, their objectives and administration. It is also possible that Becher became acquainted with the polemic conducted between William Waddington and Thomas Bowen over the origins and objectives of Bridewell hospital. Their respective publications, *Considerations on the Proper and Original Objects of the Royal Hospital of Bridewell* and *Extracts from the Records and Court Books of Bridewell Hospital*, appeared in the January and June of 1798 and contained very extensive extracts from original records. Perhaps, therefore (as an intriguing example of circularity in history), the model for Southwell house of correction was, at least in part, Bridewell and its ancient offspring.

---

44 *Report from the Committee on the Laws Relating to Penitentiary Houses*, PP, 1810-11, III, 606 (Holford Committee). These views have a marked resemblance to some of those of the modern behaviour therapists. Presumably Becher was being unconsciously ironical when he said '*to all appearances* a good moral man'.

45 Robin Evans, 'Prison Design 1750-1842', provides a thorough discussion of the design of the Panopticon and other prisons of the period. Helen Rosenau, *Social Purpose in Architecture*, also interestingly discusses the

of its design was dictated by his own theory of psychopathology. As pain and pleasure were the determinants of action, those who acted without reference to the promptings of felicity must be radically deficient, unable to perceive, or indifferent to, the consequences of their conduct; this made them very odd and dangerous. 'Delinquents', wrote Bentham,

> are a peculiar race of beings, who require unremitted inspection. Their weakness consists in yielding to the seductions of the passing moment. Their minds are weak and disordered, and though their disease is neither so clearly marked nor so incurable as that of ideots [sic] and lunatics, like these they require to be kept under restraints, and they cannot, without danger, be left to themselves.[46]

So the most suitable and logical building was one in which this 'peculiar race of beings' would always be totally visible.

The principle of the Panopticon (or inspection house) was applicable, Bentham claimed, to

> any sort of establishment in which persons of any description are to be kept under inspection; and in particular to Penitentiary Houses, Prisons, Houses of Industry, Work-houses, Poor-houses, Manufactories, Mad-houses, Lazarettes, Hospitals and Schools.[47]

The chief merit of Bentham's building was the ease with which control and containment could be effected. It possessed the 'fundamental advantage' of 'the *apparent omnipresence* of the inspector ... combined with the extreme facility of his *real presence*'. This enabled the governor to supervise alike the activities of prisoners and of subordinate staff:

> On the common plans, what means, what possibility, has the prisoner, of appealing to the humanity of the principal for redress against the neglect or oppression of subordinates in that rigid sphere, but the *few* opportunities which, in a crowded prison, the most conscientious keeper *can* afford — but the none at all which many a keeper *thinks* fit to give them. How different would their lot be upon this plan! ... Were *Newgate* upon this plan, all Newgate might be inspected by a quarter of an hour's visit by Mr. Akerman.[48]

The Panopticon also guaranteed solitude; for the prisoners were 'to the keeper, a *multitude*, though not a *crowd*; to themselves, they are

influence of Bentham and Howard on prison building within the context of a broader discussion of institutional architecture (although she is unfortunately inaccurate on one or two points of detail in relation to prisons).

46 Bentham, *The Rationale of Punishment*, p. 354.
47 'Panopticon', title page.
48 *Ibid.*, p. 45.

solitary and sequestered individuals'.[49]

Neither at Gloucester nor Southwell was design so important, although both had been built as prisons. Gloucester Penitentiary, as has been mentioned, shared premises with the county gaol, but the respective inmates were kept apart and met only in the chapel and the infirmary, and then under close supervision.[50] Southwell house of correction had sole use of the premises which it occupied; its construction followed the windmill design, a central block with three wings, and had been completed in 1807.[51]

The three systems used the effects of labour, seclusion and religion in different ways.[52] Both the Panopticon and Southwell placed considerable stress on profitable and rewarded labour. Bentham proposed that his prisoners should receive one quarter of the profits of their labour: a part to be paid immediately, and a part to be 'convertible, on the expiration of their respective terms of imprisonment, into annuities for their future benefit'.[53] As an inducement he even offered the prospect of marriage between inmates to enhance the effectiveness of his system of material and immediate rewards.[54]

49 *Ibid.*, p. 47.
50 For an account of the design of this prison see Thomas A. Makus, 'Pattern of the Law', *Architectural Review* (October 1954), no. 694, pp. 251-6.
51 At a cost to the county of £6,000 including all fittings. The net annual running cost in 1810 was slightly below £417, which worked out at approximately £16 per annum for each unit of accommodation.
52 These aspects of Gloucester Penitentiary have been described in the previous chapter, and so will not be repeated here.
53 *Holford Committee*, 581. Bentham also saw labour as a means of providing some compensation to the victims of crime: 'It is only in a plan like the Panopticon, in which, by the combination of labour and economy in administration it is possible to obtain a profit sufficiently great to offer at least some portion of indemnity to the parties injured' (*The Rationale of Punishment*, p. 361).
54 'Why should not unmarried prisoners be allowed to inter-marry. It would operate as a powerful spur to those who aimed at attaining this reward, which should only be bestowed on account of orderly conduct and industry' (*The Rationale of Punishment*, p. 356).
   But in his original proposals Bentham had been more daring:

   Must the iron law of divorce maintain throughout the whole of so long a term an unremitted sway? Can the gentle bands of wedlock be in no instance admitted to assuage the gripe of imprisonment and servitude? Might not the faculty of exchanging the first allotted companion, for another far otherwise qualified for alleviating the rigours of seclusion, be conceded, without violation of the terms, or departure from the spirit of the sentence? Might not the prospect of such indulgence be an incentive to good behaviour, superadded to all that punishment can give? These are questions to which a humane manager would surely be glad to find (and why need he despair of finding?) a fit answer on the lenient side ('Panopticon: Postscript, Part II', *op. cit.*, pp. 136-7).

   Presumably the later modification was prompted by political caution.

Becher's 'behaviourism' led him to the use of rewarded labour, which local industrial conditions made comparatively easy to apply at Southwell.[55] Manufacturers provided raw materials for a number of the prisoners who had useful skills and experience, and used the finished products. The system of reward was complicated, but ensured that prisoners received both immediate and deferred benefit. The profits from labour were divided between the county (to defray running costs), the governor (to augment his salary) and the prisoner: a work quota was set, based on an estimate of half of what each prisoner could produce by reasonable exertion, profit from which was divided between the three parties; but profit from a prisoner's production above this — his 'extra-share' — was his own solely and exclusively.[56] Their earnings had a direct bearing on their diet: as the county provided only a basic allowance of one penny and eighteen ounces of bread a day, extra food had to be purchased from earnings, and payment had also to be made for clothing and heating fuel.[57] The unspent balances from earnings were retained by the authorities and given to prisoners on their release; or a prisoner could request that the whole or part of his savings should be sent to his family, 'which is very frequently done'. For a skilled worker both earnings and savings could be relatively high.[58]

Becher saw the system of rewarded labour as the basis of his régime, though he did not claim that it would reform all offenders:

> I know of no means of reforming criminals, excepting those which I have stated; our principle is nothing more than bread and water, and to give all other sustenance in proportion to their personal exertions and good conduct. Although every man is capable of being reformed, yet the propensities of some to crime, are so deeply rooted, and their aversion to labour so invincible that neither the

55 Southwell was a manufacturing district at the time. See James Neild, *The State of the Prisons in England, Scotland and Wales*, pp. 532-6.
56 This method of calculation was intended to curb possible greed and exploitation on the part of the governor, by preventing him 'from having such an interest in the quantity of work done in the prison, as might tempt him to urge individuals to labour beyond their strength' (*Holford Committee*, 587). This was a useful safeguard, given the general desire of many prison administrators to link the governor's salary to the work output of the prisoners, so as to secure economically self-supporting prisons.
57 Prisoners were not allowed to spend more than 3s. per week of their earnings on clothing, fuel and food (*ibid.*, 587). The blind and the sick were given assistance by the justices.
58 Becher gave the example of 'T.B.', a framework knitter serving a two-year sentence. This man's 'extra-share' amounted to 4s. 3d. per week. A craftsman could earn considerably more: 'W.G.', a shoe-maker, also serving a sentence of two years, had an 'extra-share' of 11s. 2d. per week, and had savings amounting to £20 on release.

influence of moral instruction nor of habits, could enable us to let them loose again upon society. . . .[59]

At Gloucester, although Paul had not gone as far in the direction of purely penal work as the 1779 Penitentiary Act provided, there was little place for profitable or rewarded labour.[60] As has been seen, it was mainly used as a means of relieving the tedium of solitude.

By the time of the Holford Committee Bentham had modified his original views on seclusion: 'I assumed solitude as a fundamental principle . . . I have since read a little: I have thought more.'[61] The Panopticon scheme, he argued, could be applied to 'mitigated seclusion', and with equal facility to 'absolute seclusion'. In his mature scheme Bentham favoured the former because 'it clears the punishment of its inconveniences, and gives it the advantages that have been looked for from solitude'. If the Panopticon were used to secure solitude, 'it enables you to screw up the punishment to a degree of barbarous perfection never yet given to it in any English prison, and scarcely to be given to it by any other means'.[62] Absolute seclusion had but one use in penitentiary discipline, he argued, namely,

the breaking the spirit, as the phrase is, and subduing the contumacy of the intractable. In this quality it may be a necessary instrument: none, at any rate, can be more unexceptionable; none can be more certain in its effect. In what instance was it ever known to fail?

But in this quality the demand for it can be but temporary. What it does, if it does anything, it does quickly — better, according to Mr. Howard, in two or three days, than in more. Why, then, an immense expense to set up a perpetual establishment for the sake of so transitory a use?[63]

Instead of absolute separation, therefore, Bentham proposed modified separation. Prisoners would be allowed to associate, but not in classes or wards. His was a smaller group called a 'company'. The companies were to be formed according to two rules: first, 'Put not in the same company, corrupt and uncorrupted'; and second, 'The more corrupt the individuals, the less numerous make the company'. The companies would not be large: 'The choice as to numbers will be in general between

---

59 *Holford Committee*, 609. For this reason Becher favoured the continuation of transportation for some offences.
60 Though his friend William Morton Pitt, who was a member of the Holford Committee, was strongly in favour of rewarded and productive labour in a prison régime. Dorchester Penitentiary, for which Pitt was largely responsible, closely followed the Gloucester model, except in that one respect (Cooper, *op. cit.*, p. 99).
61 'Panopticon: Postscript, Part I', *op. cit.*, p. 71.
62 *Ibid.*
63 *Ibid.*, pp. 71-2.

four, three and two', and his two rules would help to decide which number was chosen.[64] Bentham also sought to make all members of a company to some extent responsible for the behaviour of the group as a whole.

The social determinism in Becher's penology led him to design a régime which permitted association rather than enforced seclusion since, by definition, habits could only be fostered in a social setting. Thus solitude was used at Southwell 'merely as an instrument to bring men to a sense of obedience and duty; the association of prisoners is regulated by this maxim'.[65]

On reception Southwell prisoners were placed in a separate cell for between twelve and twenty-four hours; the governor prolonged this period if he was not satisfied with their manner. If submission was still not secured after further solitude the process was intensified by 'a method of darkening the cell, by a shutter that admits air but excludes light . . .'. But submission was the sole object of this exercise: 'As soon as he becomes tractable and submissive, we permit and endeavour to induce him, to live within the prison, in every respect, as he ought to live in society.'[66]

Association was not unregulated, however. Inmates were divided into six classes, and mixing was allowed only between members of the same class. Each class (none of which exceeded five members) was confined to its own set of rooms, called 'wards', consisting of a day-room, work-room and solitary work-room. Becher argued that there was thus little contamination and emphasised the close supervision and small numbers involved. Indeed, 'in that small circle in which the offender is allowed to move, he may be expected, under proper management to form habits of industry and self-interest, which he will be likely to practise on his return to society'.[67]

The conflict over administration and management

Despite similarities between the penal psychology and régime of Southwell, and that proposed by Bentham, despite the contrasts between Southwell and Gloucester, both local prisons fundamentally diverged from Bentham's model on matters of administration and management.

64 'Panopticon: Postscript, Part II', *op. cit*., pp. 139, 137-44, *passim*.
65 *Holford Committee*, 604.
66 *Ibid*., pp. 604 and 606. Solitude was also used as a punishment for those who misbehaved; they were confined to their separate sleeping cells on Sundays.
67 *Ibid*., p. 588. Such association was, of course, helpful to the system of labour. The classes were: felons for trial, petty offenders for trial, convicted felons and convicted petty offenders. The females were classified simply as felons or petty offenders.

Bentham, as might be expected, generally anticipated the main elements of this conflict. Under the heading 'Management – in what hands, and on what terms', he wrote:

Every thing depends upon the *hands* and upon the *terms*. In what hands, then? Upon what terms? These are the two grand points to be adjusted and that before any thing is said about regulations. Why? Because . . . upon these points depends . . . the demand for regulations. Adopt the contract-plan – regulations in this view are a nuisance: be there ever so few of them, there will be too many. Reject it – be there ever so many of them, they will be too few.[68]

But at Gloucester and Southwell the disciplinary systems were regulated by detailed sets of rules defining the manner in which officials and prisoners interacted, and the penal routine of the latter; and the administration was so framed as to ensure maximum compliance. As they had to anticipate a large number of eventualities, and regulate the performance of a diversity of activities, complex rules were necessary.

Bentham contrasted contract-management with trust-management, the latter being provided in the Penitentiary Act.[69] 'By whom', he asked,

ought a business like this to be carried on? – by one who has an interest in the success of it, or by one who has none? – by one who has a greater interest in it, or by one who has an interest not so great? – by one who takes loss as well as profit, or by one who takes profit without loss? – by one who has no profit but in proportion as he manages well, or by one who, let him manage ever so well or ever so ill, shall have the same emolument secured to him?[70]

He pushed his argument against the trust-management of the Penitentiary Act further:

And whom does the management depend upon, after all? Upon this governor? – upon the man in whose breast this important junction [interest with duty] is to be formed? Oh no: upon a quite different set of people; upon a committee, and who are this committee? A set of trustees, three in number, who would be turned out with infamy, if they were found to have the smallest particle of what is here meant by *interest* in the whole concern. They are the persons

---

68 'Panopticon: Postscript, Part II', *op. cit.*, p. 125.
69 Under the Act a committee of management, consisting of 'three Gentlemen, or other credible and substantial persons', was to be appointed by the Privy Council. These committee members were to be paid a daily attendance allowance. They had extensive powers to hire and dismiss staff, and to inspect prisoners and accounts, and to examine upon oath.
70 'Panopticon: Postscript, Part II', *op. cit.*, p. 125.

to manage, they are the persons to contrive; they are the persons to work: the governor, with his magnificent title, is to be their tool to work with. Upon them everything is to depend; upon his excellency nothing: he is their journeyman; they are to put him in, they are to turn him out, and turn him out when they please.[71]

Bentham rejected the concept of trust-management and administrative control by rules and regulations. He sought instead to construct a physical, economic and moral environment in which control and regulation would be self-imposed; inmates and staff alike would fulfil the objectives of the institution and society whilst pursuing their own self-interest. The selfish impulse was not to be stemmed: administrative channels rather were to be cut to direct it towards institutional goals.

Bentham's administrative safeguards arose directly, and were inseparable, from the system of finance which he adopted in his contract with the government. He was to be paid an annual allowance for one thousand prisoners; that allowance would be maintained, even if inmate numbers fell. Additionally, he was to receive three-quarters of the profits from the prisoners' labour (the remainder going to the prisoners themselves). In return he undertook to feed and clothe the prisoners, provide beds and bedding, maintain a warm and sanitary building and employ staff (including a clergyman, a surgeon, and a number of schoolmasters).[72]

On the basis of these mutual stipulations, Bentham (or his nominee) was to have total authority:

Every arrangement, in regard to the treatment of the prisoners, as well as the determination of the manner in which they should be employed, of the hours of the day or night in which they should labour, and of the classes or numbers which should either work together, or associate at their meals or times of exercise or recreation is entirely left at the discretion or will of the Contractor, while every officer and servant, connected with the establishment, is to be placed there by his appointment and removable at his pleasure.[73]

The contractor's self-interest and the well-being of his prisoners were conjoined mainly by means of financial penalties, supported by almost uninterrupted public inspection. Maltreatment of the prisoners was to be difficult to conceal because the public were to have access to an inspection room from which all prisoners could be seen, and from which, by means of a system of speaking-tubes, conversations could

71 *Ibid.*, p. 126.
72 And still he calculated in 1813 that, had the government gone ahead with the original contract, he would by then have accumulated profits of £689,062 10s. 0d.! (Hume, *op. cit.*, p. 49.)
73 *Holford Committee*, 581.

also be conducted with them. Bentham thought that the inquisitive public would always be on hand, drawn by the novel nature of the prison. He argued:

> Publicity is the effectual preservative against abuse — under the present system, prisons are covered with an impenetrable veil; the Panopticon, on the contrary, would be, so to speak, transparent. Accessible at all hours to properly authorised Magistrates; accessible to everybody, at properly regulated hours, or days. The spectator, introduced into the central lodge, would behold the whole of the interior, and would be a witness to the detention of the prisoners, and a judge of their condition.[74]

But the main check was to be provided by the contractor's financial interest. He was to be obliged to assure the lives of his prisoners:

> A calculation is made of the average number of deaths in the year, among this mixed multitude committed to his care, and a certain sum is allowed to him for each; but at the end of the year, he is required to pay a similar sum for everyone lost by death or escape. He is, therefore, constituted the assurer of the lives and safe custody of his prisoners; but to assure their lives is, at the same time, to secure the multitude of cares and attentions, on which their health and well-being depend.[75]

Indeed his financial interests were almost total in their constraint:

> The more orderly and industrious the prisoners, the greater the amount of his profits. He will, therefore, teach them the most profitable trades, and give them such portion of the profits as shall excite them to labour. He unites in himself the characters of Magistrate, Inspector, Head of Manufactory, and of a family; and is urged on by the strongest motives faithfully to discharge all these duties.[76]

---

74 Bentham, *The Rationale of Punishment*, p. 352. This once more emphasises the importance of the building in Bentham's scheme. The qualities of the Panopticon ensured that all prisoners would be visible at all times, as would all staff; this not only assisted control, but was an embodiment of that exemplary element which was so fundamental to his philosophy of punishment.

75 *Ibid*.

76 *Ibid*., p. 351. Bentham claimed that his attitude was superior to one based merely upon morality:

> Religion and humanity animated the founders of the American Penitentiaries: will these generous principles be less powerful when united with the interests of reputation and fortune? The two grand securities of every public establishment — the only ones upon which a politician can constantly rely — the only ones whose operation is not subject to relaxation — the only ones which, always being in accordance

Bentham further provided that the contractor would be liable to a financial penalty should inmates be reconvicted after their release; he was also required regularly to submit a report, upon oath, to the judges of the King's Bench.

The 'trust-management' at both Gloucester and Southwell rested in the first instance upon the visiting justices appointed by quarter sessions. Gloucester, of course, took its model from the 1779 Penitentiary Act, but gaols were in any event covered in this respect, after 1784, by the provisions of 24 Geo. III, c.54.[77] Southwell, being a house of correction, came under the direct control of the justices, whose powers and duties had been reiterated and supplemented by Gilbert's Houses of Correction Act. Thus Gloucester visiting justices were obliged to examine the state and condition of the prison,

> either together or singly, at least three times in every quarter and oftener if need be, and to make reports at every Quarter Sessions thereupon. But every other justice for the county may visit of his own accord, and report abuses to the Quarter Sessions.[78]

> with virtue, may perform its part, and even replace it when it is wanting (*ibid*., p. 368).

> Bentham's 'Head of Manufactory' metaphor and the fact that he thought the Panopticon principle could be applied to manufactories (pp. 60-1, 'Panopticon') show how impressive was the factory model and how close was the central control task of both, in his mind. Associations between penitentiary prisons and factories seem also to have been made by working people, as J. Steven Watson's observations indicate:

> It was not the long hours or poor pay or physical conditions which made the factory detested. In the domestic system working families worked long hours in hovels for pittances. What was detested in the factory was a feeling of servitude and discipline. In a man's own home he could work twenty hours and be drunk for four; in the factory he worked to a time-table and was not his own master even to sweat himself. Though this organization of labour which goes with factory life was the great hope for future improvement, it was at the start its most unpopular feature (Watson, *op. cit*., p. 524).

> Woodward pointedly confirms this view: 'Factories were not adding to the burden of occupied time, but their discipline and regularity were a greater strain on the workers; the Belfast weavers called factories "lock-ups" ' (*The Age of Reform 1815-1870*, p. 12).

77 'An Act to explain and amend an Act of Will. III enabling justices to build and repair gaols, and for other purposes.' S. VII authorised the quarter sessions to appoint one or more JPs 'to visit and superintend the gaols thereunto belonging' and to report 'the state thereof'. Quarter sessions, as has been mentioned, had also been given considerable powers under the Gaol Distemper Act (14 Geo. III, c.59).

78 *Holford Committee*, 584. Paul found his own supervisory duties 'a terribly demanding chore and . . . claimed that [they] wore out his constitution and a large part of his fortune . . .' (Cooper, *op. cit*., p. 91).

Executive authority at Gloucester was vested in the governor. He appointed and supervised the humbler members of the staff.[79] The remainder were appointed by the quarter sessions, and had a significant and intentional degree of independence from the governor. Salaries for the subordinates came directly from the county, not from a special allowance given to the governor (as had been the case at Horsham and Petworth), emphasising the fact that these were public servants and were not to be seen as the personal employees of the governor.[80]

Paul realised that to a very large degree, however stringent and efficient his methods of control, the prison's success would be determined by the choice of staff, particularly the governor. He told his colleagues that 'The effect of this munificent effort of the county depends on your choice of keeper'.[81] Both Paul and his audience were entirely familiar with the peculation and tyranny of the fee-taking gaolers, and the way in which their intimacy with criminals shaded into abetment. This was the basis of Paul's, no less than Bentham's and Becher's, concern with control and inspection in prison administration. It was likely that Paul had also in mind the positive example of Abel Dagge, the keeper of Newgate in the neighbouring great city of Bristol. Dagge was converted by George Whitfield in 1737 and, setting about the reform of his own prison, achieved results which were widely commended.[82]

---

79 These were a taskmaster and a clerk who were the only officials appointed specifically to the penitentiary (though temporary assistants were employed from time to time). The gaol and penitentiary were jointly served by a gate-porter, relief assistant, matron (for the female prisoners), and a night-guard. A female messenger was employed to take and fetch orders for the debtors and prisoners on remand in the gaol. There was also an assistant employed solely for duties in the gaol. J.R.S. Whiting (*Prison Reform in Gloucestershire 1776-1820*, Ch. 4) gives a detailed and individual account of these officials.

80 By contrast, see the evidence to the Holford Committee of John Newman, keeper of Newgate, and James Ives, keeper of the county gaol at Southwark. Both appointed and remunerated subordinates, whom they described as their servants.

81 *Address to His Majesty's Justices of the Peace for the County of Gloucester, On the Administration and Practical Effects of the System of Prison Regulation Established in that County* (1809).

82 In October 1760 Wesley wrote of Bristol Newgate: 'What a change is in this place since I knew it first?' The *Annual Register* of 1761 was startled: 'The Regulations that have been lately made in that miserable mansion of misery, Newgate in Bristol, must sensibly affect every breast with pleasure that has the least spark of humanity unextinguished in it' (IV, p. 61). Howard wrote: 'The first case must be to find a good man for a gaoler; one that is honest, active and humane. Such was Abel Dagge, who was formerly Keeper of Bristol Newgate. I regretted his death, and revere his memory' (*The State of the Prisons* (3rd edn), p. 25). Johnson's comment upon Dagge was similar to that which he had made about Akerman, the keeper of Newgate:

The governor's duties consisted in various forms of inspection and control of inmates, subordinates and the prison building. He could not absent himself from the prison overnight without the written permission of a visiting justice.[83] He adjudicated on prison offences, and imposed punishments or, where appropriate, passed the case to the magistrates.

There was also an elaborate set of books for which the governor was responsible. These were intended partly as a means of regulating his conduct of the business of the prison, and partly to enable him to control and check upon subordinates. But these books were also an aspect of Gloucester's innovatory régime, which related the proportion of sentence served by the prisoner to his institutional performance. Expansion of such executive authority required that systematic records of prisoners' behaviour and attitudes be available, and introduced an element of judicial assessment into the role of the governor. Doubtless this function was, at first, very little more than noting favourable dispositions and marking infractions of the rules, but it was to expand considerably as part of the authority and responsibility of certain governors.[84]

Virtue is undoubtedly most laudable in that state which makes it most difficult, and therefore the humanity of a gaoler certainly deserves this publick attestation; and the man whose heart has not been hardened by such an employment, may be justly proposed as a pattern of benevolence. If an inscription was once engraved 'to the honest toll-gatherer' less honours ought not to be paid 'to the tender gaoler' (*Boswell's Life of Johnson*, ed. George Birkbeck Hill and L.F. Powell, III, p. 433, n. 1).

---

83 He had to see each prisoner at least once in twenty-four hours, and similarly to inspect the accommodation. He was obliged to report to the magistrates any subordinate who swore, who was drunk or in any other way misbehaved (*Holford Committee*, Appendix 2, clause XXXI). His house (which was provided by the county) was so placed and designed as to enable him easily to view the gaol. His disciplinary duties included the requirement that standards of cleanliness were upheld in the prison. He was responsible for the purchasing, storing and quality of food. This was partly for reasons of health, but also to guard against inmate or staff theft. He himself had to enter into a bond, to be forfeited should he violate his trust, and he was obliged to purchase supplies in the open market. According to Paul this gave public protection against peculation over and above the 'occasional observation of the visitors, the chaplain and the surgeon' (*Holford Committee*, 613). The governor was, of course, forbidden to have any material interest in the supply of any goods or services to the prisoners.

84 There is no actual list of the books kept at Gloucester at this time, but they were probably similar to the Southwell books, which included a punishment book, journal, description-book, calendar, work-book, register and accounts (Southwell Rules and Regulations, reproduced in proceedings of *Holford Committee*, Rules 21-6 and 28).

The governor was carefully chosen, given an adequate salary[85] and made subject to an extensive code of rules and regulations. He was the main agency for ensuring adherence to these provisions, and was himself liable, along with his books and accounts, to the personal inspection of the visiting justices.

But still further elements of control, formal and informal, were built into the administration. These were directed at the governor himself. Besides ecclesiastical and reformatory tasks the Gloucester chaplain was entrusted with the general duty of observing and (if necessary) reporting upon the governor and other staff. Paul was explicit: 'It is made part of the Chaplain's duty frequently to see and confer with the prisoners, without the governor or other officer being present, to enquire into their situation, and to observe the state of their cells.'[86] Indeed, the inspection role of the chaplain was put forward as the main reason why he (and the surgeon) should be appointed and paid directly by the justices; otherwise 'There would be no protection from the ill-treatment of a governor, from the inspection of officers appointed by himself, and removable at his discretion.'[87] Direct appointment and independent responsibility of these senior staff could not of themselves guarantee against collusion, but the attention paid by Paul to internal regulation was yet another indication of his anxiety to avoid the maladministration of his prison by the governor and his subordinates.

Both chaplain and surgeon appear to have taken their duties seriously. The former was in the prison every day to read prayers, and to hold divine service. The prison records show, however, that his attendance far exceeded this minimum, and that his stays in the prison were prolonged; he is recorded, for example, as visiting especially to see dinner served to the prisoners. The surgeon was obliged to see each prisoner at least twice a week, but in fact he, too, visited far more frequently, and altogether a high level of attendance was maintained: in 1802 there were only two days when there was not a visit from either the chaplain or the surgeon; and the same frequency of visiting seems to have been kept up throughout the year. That this was the main means of regulating the prison is apparent from the fact that in August of that year there was only one visit from the visiting justice.[88]

---

85 Paul held that 'A gaoler's salary should be a liberal Independency, he should draw no Emolument from Misery, or from Means that disturb the Regularity of his Household' (Paul, *A State of Proceedings on the Subject of a Reform of Prisons*, p. 37). Following the Penitentiary Act Paul linked at least part of his governor's salary to the output of the prisoners (25 Geo. III, c.10, s.43).

86 *Holford Committee*, 585.

87 *Ibid*.

88 Gloucestershire Records Office, County Gaol, Governor's Journal, ref. Q/GC3/3 (1802). At one point in 1796 the surgeon was directed to confine entries in his journal to medical matters only. Paul agreed with this

The other duties of the chaplain and surgeon were in keeping with the system of discipline. Religion had a superior role in the Gloucester régime: solitude, sparse diet and unrewarded labour were all intended to make the prisoner malleable; religion was the reformatory fixative. Besides his routine of services and visiting, the chaplain was obliged to see any prisoner, sick or well, who desired spiritual advice and instruction. At the expense of the county he was directed to provide 'books of moral and religious instruction' in suitable and deserving cases. That he had great authority within the prison can be confirmed from his successful bid, in the early years, to alter the structure of the régime. A system of discipline progressing in stages had been in operation from the outset and the chaplain had come to object: 'The impressions made upon their mind during their former term of seclusion [the first stage], were immediately obliterated by idle conversation naturally taking place between associates.'[89] He presented his criticism to the justices, who changed the system. The Gloucester chaplain saw himself (and was so seen by the justices) as responsible not only for the individual welfare of the prisoners, but also for the general moral and reformatory climate of the prison. There were, in the very amorphous nature of these wider duties of regulation and comment, the seeds of a conflict with the interests and role of the governor that went far beyond the prevention of the latter's lapsing from integrity of conduct. As shall be seen, this conflict was intensified in the decades that were to come.

The surgeon's duties were more clearly demarcated, and thus contained less potential for conflict with colleagues. He was responsible for assessing the mental and physical health of the prisoners and for administering appropriate medicines or ordering such easement in discipline or supplementation of diet as might be requisite: he had to be particularly on guard against the introduction of lice and contagious diseases. In these matters the governor was obliged to comply with his recommendations, though the surgeon's directions of individual easements in the discipline had to be reported to the justices.[90]

At Southwell arrangements were broadly similar in respect of staffing.[91] The visiting justices, however, seem to have been involved

---

command at the time, but later said that the restriction had been incorrect (Whiting, *op. cit.*, p. 41).

89 *Holford Committee*, 585.

90 *Ibid.*, 595.

91 Becher did not give as full an account of staffing as did Paul, and the Southwell rules only refer to 'the several officers of the prison'. The governor had a deputy and, at the time of the Holford Committee, probably only one other full-time assistant was employed (though there may have been occasional or part-time help to cope with fluctuations in population, escort duties, etc.). Partly because of its size, and partly because of the régime and the close supervision of the justices, the chaplain and surgeon were employed on a part-time basis only.

to a greater extent, and Southwell's rules indicate their style of participation: 'The governor exercises his authority under their superintendence.'[92] The visiting justices commended deserving prisoners to the assize judge for pardons, examined books and accounts, punished prisoners for 'repeated or enormous offences', and could appoint temporary staff. They also decided which traders were to supply the requirements of the prisoners (an important power and safeguard, as the Southwell inmates had a not inconsiderable amount of spending money). The extent to which the justices exercised executive power was in sharp contrast to the limits set at Gloucester where Paul had even complained that his governor was failing fully to act on his own initiative.[93]

The question of the balance of authority and responsibility judged most appropriate for governors was by no means settled at either prison and this, too, was to be an issue in prison administration in the years ahead.[94]

Recommendations of the Holford Committee

The main recommendation of the Holford Committee was, in large measure, a foregone conclusion: the committee was of the opinion that many offenders could be reclaimed by penitentiary imprisonment; by this they meant 'a system of imprisonment not confined to the safe custody of the person, but extending to the reformation and improvement of the mind, and operating by seclusion, employment and religious instruction'.[95] This system of imprisonment should be carried out in a specially constructed building large enough to

---

92 *Holford Committee*, 586.

93 I venture to say that the rules in general have been strictly attended to. The avoiding to act with discretionary authority, has been sometimes carried to an extreme. Mr. Cunningham, the keeper of the gaol, in cases of doubtful interpretation, is disposed to relieve his own responsibility by obtaining special orders from magistrates (*Holford Committee*, 594).

94 A strong hint that this may have been a problem at Southwell from the very earliest days is given by the turnover in governors, with four appointments being made in the first sixteen years. This turnover could not have been due to an inadequate salary as, with allowances, this came to £150, plus fuel and house (£200 after 1822). This was more than could have been expected by an entrepreneur gaoler in an establishment of similar size. At the time of the committee, the same governor had held office at Gloucester for eighteen years. It seems possible that friction, due to the much stronger executive role of the justices at Southwell, may have been responsible for this inability to keep governors (Nottinghamshire Records Office, ref. QAG5/120).

95 *Holford Committee*, 573.

accommodate several hundred prisoners,[96] a recommendation of very great importance. By accepting it central government undertook a novel commitment, and made a fundamental alteration in the pattern of English prison administration. The hulks had been seen as 'temporary expedients', and in any event could be considered as part of the system of transportation. Administration of a central penitentiary involved a large financial outlay, permanent upkeep expense, and an inescapable need for central government to establish its own views on penal discipline and administration. The secondary recommendations of the committee were addressed to the latter requirement and rejected (in Bentham's terms) contract-management in favour of trust-management.

In explaining the grounds of their proposals the committee raised a number of objections to Bentham's scheme. They noted his failure to comply with the clause in his contract which required him to erect the Panopticon; but, from the context and the history of government prevarications on this matter, it is clear that this criticism was used as an excuse, a mask for their other objections.[97] Had Bentham's administrative views been acceptable, the matter of the building could have been resolved. Likewise the committee's claim, that the preservation of

96 They recommended sufficient capacity to accommodate all the females sentenced to transportation within the counties of London and Middlesex, and a large proportion of all males sentenced to seven years' transportation. Females sentenced to fourteen years and to transportation for life should be held on a temporary basis only. The committee felt that an overall limitation had to be placed on inmate numbers because of the expense to the government and because of the danger of a large number of serious offenders being held so near the metropolis.

They did not wish to report at the time on the matter of a more extensive national penitentiary system and on the future use of the hulks. They agreed in principle with the original intentions of Howard, Blackstone and Eden that a penitentiary would be desirable for each circuit, but thought that existing buildings might be used in order to avoid expense, if counties and central government could agree on a financial arrangement.

Both Paul and Becher opposed the scheme for a national penitentiary. Paul had argued on grounds of security, and of the difficulties of adequate inspection and expense. Becher, who preferred the concept of a system of district penitentiary houses, stressed the expense of a national penitentiary and the undesirability of displacing prisoners from their neighbourhood.

The third report of the committee was presented in June 1812 and was concerned with the hulks, for which a number of reforms were suggested. The anticipated further report on a national penitentiary system was not made by this committee.

97 Cooper (*op. cit.*, pp. 158-9) reports that even before Bentham had testified Holford indicated to the home secretary that the committee would probably decide in favour of Paul and Becher. Bentham was told by Romilly of the recommendation against the Panopticon. William Morton Pitt and Sir Charles Bunbury were accused by Bentham of betrayal, who also alleged that Holford had packed the committee in order to destroy the Panopticon scheme and get himself a position (Condon, *op. cit.*, p. 181).

the material interest of the contractor, so essential to Bentham's scheme, was in contravention of Gilbert's Houses of Correction Act, was a contrived technicality. More substantial, perhaps, was their related reason that insufficient attention would be paid to religious instruction and moral improvement under Bentham's scheme,

> Every part of which is to be formed and directed by a person whose interest it must be that the prisoners committed to his charge should do as much work as they were competent to execute, and that most profit would be produced.

In such circumstances, they stated, the chaplain's reformatory work would be impeded. Suggestions as to which prisoners should associate together, or as to changes in régime which might be morally but not economically suitable, would not 'meet with the same encouragement, when addressed to a Governor, whose profits they were calculated to diminish, as if they were communicated to persons having no interest in the produce of the prisoners' labour'. Indeed, 'The experiment of reformation would not be fairly tried'.[98]

But the main force of their argument was directed at Bentham's checks and safeguards and arrangements for inspection and control. The committee were convinced that penitentiary imprisonment required administration of the Gloucester and Southwell (trustee-management) type. The essentials were an independent, vigilant, accountable and authoritative regulatory body; a salaried and materially disinterested governor checked by colleagues with access to and directly responsible to the control body; a code of rules and regulations, and a bookkeeping system. In particular the committee stressed the need for independent supervision within the prison: in the persons of chaplain and surgeon they saw 'the most obvious channel of complaint, if the governor be concerned in the supposed injury . . .'. But to carry out this duty the chaplain and surgeon could not be employees of a contractor, as had been suggested by Bentham. It was the task of the chaplain on the one hand to 'endeavour to reconcile the mind of the offender to the lot which he has brought upon himself by his misconduct, so on the other to prevent any hardship or privations which the law did not intend to impose'. The surgeon's function was similar. But

> to make these officers of real use in this particular they must occasionally confer with the prisoner without the presence of the Governor or his servants; they must neither be under strong obligations to the Governor, or subject to his power; and they must be in habits of communicating with persons armed with

98 *Holford Committee*, 581-2.

sufficient authority to punish or redress the grievances laid before them.[99]

Thus was rejected the very basis of Bentham's conception of the contractor who 'unites in himself the characters of Magistrate, Inspector, Head of a Manufactory; and of a family; and is urged on by the strongest motives faithfully to discharge all these duties'.

Although they had opted for trust-management the committee did not follow the scheme proposed originally in the Penitentiary Act, which provided for a triumvirate committee of management paid on an attendance basis. This was rejected because it created 'new places of profit'. Instead they thought (in terms which irresistibly recall the Bridewell governors) that there should be a body of persons 'whose rank or position in society may induce them to employ a portion of their time for the benefit of the prisoners and the public'.[100] Specifically they envisaged a committee of fifteen to twenty 'Aldermen and Gentlemen'. Appointment was to be renewed annually, to keep up an active membership, and there should be annual reports to both Houses of Parliament.

To implement their proposals the committee suggested the immediate appointment of three supervisors to take charge of the construction of the new prison. To avoid delay they further recommended that the project should be started by means of a short Act, with the more detailed legislation following later.[101]

99 *Holford Committee*, 583. They added that, under Bentham's scheme, there was insufficient opportunity for prisoners to raise grievances: this was of particular importance because 'something of a more strict discipline may be looked for than in ordinary prisons' and therefore 'opportunities for complaint should be frequent and redress near at hand'. In short, 'The proposed system affords no significant protection to the prisoner, upon any point' (*ibid.*, p. 582).

100 *Ibid.*, 589.

101 The report and recommendations of this committee were far more novel and radical than first reading might suggest. Bentham's scheme, with its emphasis on design and gadgetry, does appear far-fetched, but if these aspects of his scheme are disregarded, and only the financial and administrative elements are considered, his contract can be seen to correspond much more closely with contemporary poor-law and penal practice than did the scheme finally recommended by the Holford Committee. Transportation had long been administered on a contractual basis, and Duncan Campbell, the former transportation contractor, uniting in himself the offices of overseer and contractor, was in many ways to the hulks what Bentham's governor would have been to the Panopticon. As overseer he had charge of discipline, and as contractor he was responsible for clothing and feeding the prisoners, and for equipping and manning the ships. Even though this system was modified by 46 Geo. III, c.28, though an inspector appointed, the office of overseer abolished and the role of the contractors limited to provisioning, the Bentham scheme had considerable specific precedent to recommend it — especially if his regulatory devices were accepted as being workable. Essentially he was seeking to bring the entrepreneur gaoler to the service of reformatory imprisonment, and his suggestions were ingenious and well worthy of serious attention.

6   The penitentiary realised

Establishment of the penitentiary[1]

The Holford Committee submitted its first report on 31 May 1811, and just a year later the government appointed a committee of three to supervise the building of the new penitentiary.[2] A national architectural contest was organised at the same time and at the end of June 1812 prizes were awarded to the three best entries.[3] The land originally bought by Bentham as the site of the Panopticon was transferred to the supervisors and construction commenced at the end of 1812.[4] Sufficient progress had been made by February 1816 for the supervisors to request the appointment of a management committee,[5] who were

1 The administrative records of Millbank Penitentiary were destroyed in a fire in the last century (communication from the Prison Department). For sources of information in writing this chapter I have had to rely on manuscript material of outside origin and upon published books and pamphlets.
2 PRO, HO 21, Entry Book, Millbank Penitentiary, p. 3. Holford, Becher and Lord Farnborough were the three supervisors.
3 £400 was distributed. Altogether forty-three designs had been submitted in the well-advertised competition. Work in accordance with the modified winning design was carried out under the supervision of a leading architect (Hardwicke).
4 The site was in Tothill Fields, close to the Mill Bank, from which the prison took its name. The name was spelt in two ways from the earliest mention of the prison. The management committee, from its first to its last report, favoured 'Milbank'. Thomas Fowell Buxton, however, used the 'Millbank' form in his 1818 publication (*An Enquiry Whether Crime and Misery are Produced or Prevented, etc.*), as did Holford in an article of 1830 (*Letter to the Editor of the Quarterly Review on a Misstatement . . . Relative to the Supposed Ill-success of the General Penitentiary at Millbank*). On the other hand, Holford had been provoked to write by an article in which the author had used the 'Milbank' form (*Quarterly Review* (January 1830), XLII, p. 235). The more commonly accepted 'Millbank' form has been adopted for present purposes, except in direct citations.
5 As provided for in the enabling Act, 52 Geo. III, c. 44, Entry Book (*op. cit.*), p. 20.

nominated without delay by the Prince Regent in Council. On 26 June 1816 the cell doors were locked on the first prisoners — a party of forty female convicts from Newgate.[6] Various problems with new buildings, and delays with those still uncompleted (largely due to subsidence), extended construction work until mid-1822, and almost doubled the original estimate of just over a quarter of a million pounds. The final outlay placed Millbank Penitentiary among the most expensive of English public buildings.[7]

The government, in its first venture into penitentiary imprisonment, had acquired a building as spectacular and massive as had been its cost. It was so extensive that

> the outlines of the structure may be traced on any well-drawn plans of London. In form it consists of six pentagonal buildings, surrounding an open courtyard; the whole surrounded by a lofty wall of octagon shape. This wall encloses an area of about sixteen acres, seven of which are covered with the buildings and airing yards; the other nine laid out as gardens. . . . The corridors in which the cells are situated are upwards of three miles in length.[8]

6 *The Times*, 27 June 1816, 3b. The report makes it clear that the opening of the prison aroused considerable public interest. On Tuesday, 25 June,

> several noblemen and ladies of distinction visited this extensive prison, and went over the different cells which were then ready for the reception of female convicts. A deputation of the committee of the House of Commons arrived about half-past three, and inspected every part prepared for the prisoners.

Certain members of the staff (excepting the male turnkeys, who had not yet been appointed) entered into employment at the same time. The convicts were moved in on the morning of the 26th at 3 a.m., presumably to avoid public commotion. The women

> were carried in caravans, chained together, from Newgate to Blackfriars-bridge, there put on board a barge prepared to receive them, and conveyed under a strong guard of police-officers to Millbank. . . . There will be no male prisoners received for some weeks, their cells not being yet ready.

Griffiths (*Memorials of Millbank* (1875), I, p. 48) is thus slightly misleading when he asserts that the first prisoners were received on 27 June. J.E. Thomas (*The English Prison Officer*, pp. 12-13) is himself in error when he says that 'The Gladstone Report is wrong when it states that Millbank was opened in 1816. It was completed in 1821 . . .'. Following the first receptions in 1816 the prison population was gradually built up, and incoming convicts were accommodated in the newly completed parts of the prison. Thomas's error arises from a misreading of Du Cane (*The Punishment and Prevention of Crime*, p. 125).

7 'It may be doubted whether the Taj at Agra, the Cloth Hall at Ypres or the Cathedral at Chartres had cost anything like this sum' (S. and B. Webb, *English Prisons Under Local Government*, p. 49).

8 W. Hepworth Dixon, *The London Prisons*, p. 132. To many in the mid-Victorian era the prison remained daunting, not only in size, but in appearance:

Many even of those who worked there were struck by the unmanageable size and complexity of the buildings. Griffiths illustrates this with one old warder,

> who served for years at Millbank, and rose through all the gaol grades to a position of trust, and who was yet unable, to the last, to find his way about the premises. He carried with him always a piece of chalk, with which he 'blazed' his path as does the American backwoodsman the forest trees.[9]

The design of the buildings was, to the same writer, symbolical of its significance as an important juncture in prison history:

> Angles every twenty yards, winding staircases, dark passages, innumerable doors and gates. . . . Millbank is suggestive of an order that has passed . . . a period when the safe custody of criminals could be compassed, people thought, only by granite blocks and ponderous bolts and bars.[10]

The building had originally been intended for 800 prisoners, but while construction was in progress the designs were altered, extending accommodation to 1,000. Although Millbank Penitentiary was never to be used to its full capacity,[11] it exceeded all provincial prisons in

---

There is a systematic irregularity about the in and out aspect of the buildings, which gives it the appearance of a gigantic puzzle; and altogether the Millbank prison may be said to be one of the most successful realisations, on a large scale, of the ugly in architecture, being an ungainly combination of the mad-house with the fortress style of building, for it has a series of martello-like towers, one at each of its many angles, and was originally surrounded by a moat, after the fashion of Bedlam and St. Luke's (H. Mayhew and J. Binny, *The Criminal Prisons of London*, p. 234).

---

9 Major Arthur Griffiths, *op. cit.* (1875), I, p. 33.

10 *Ibid*. Later administrators enlisted the buildings' complexity as a security aid. In the governor's offices there hung a plan, over which was fitted a draw-curtain. When prisoners were brought to this office the curtain was closed to prevent the layout of the prison from being made known (Major Arthur Griffiths, *Fifty Years of Public Service* (1904), p. 203). Seventy-odd years after its foundation Sir Edmund Du Cane, contrasting the complexity of Millbank with the simplicity of the newly built Wormwood Scrubs, emphasised the cost and administrative problems posed by Millbank (Sir Edmund F. Du Cane, *A Description of the Prison at Wormwood Scrubs with an Account of the Circumstances Attending its Erection*, p. 1).

11 Population fluctuated between 400 and 700. At the end of 1816 only sixty-three (female) prisoners were held (*Report of the Committee of the General Penitentiary at Millbank* (henceforth cited as *RCGP*), PP, 1817, XVI, 329). In December 1832, with the prison well established, the roll total was 519 (*RCGP*, PP, 1833, XXVIII, 659). So accepted was it by this time that the full capacity would not be employed, that amended regulations referred to vacant parts of the prison and the uses to which they should be put. In

population.[12] Those metropolitan prisons which held a large number (notably Cold Bath Fields House of Correction, and Newgate) provided ward-type, rather than cellular, accommodation, and thus had smaller buildings.

Both on a *per capita* basis, and as gross expenditure, running costs were high. In 1820 it cost £35. 0s. 10d. to maintain each prisoner; in 1821 the sum was £25. 11s. 7d.; and in 1829 (when a larger population might have been expected proportionately to reduce expense) upkeep amounted to £30. 3s. 0d.[13] Hopes of savings based on the expectation of profits from the prison's industries notwithstanding, net expense to the government ranged from over £28,000 in 1823, the year of the epidemic, down to about £16,000 in the fairly typical year of 1830.[14]

With this clear evidence of high capital and current costs, it is hard to understand Buxton's description of the prison as 'a grand national experiment', and Bennet's rhetorical gush of praise: 'Why limit this great blessing? Why not extend the reformatory prison system throughout the country? Why stop at Millbank?'[15]

Millbank existed alongside the hulks and transportation, and did not replace more than a fraction of their capacity. It was decided that the penitentiary should have what were considered potentially the most responsive types among the convicts,

> whose misfortunes, more than their moral turpitude or confirmed habits of crime had subjected them to the sentence of the law. Young persons of both sexes, offenders for the first time, the victims to artifice and seduction, and all the various shades of

---

1828 and 1829, however, the population was high: 694 on 31 December 1828, and 627 on 31 December 1829 (*RCGP*, PP, 1830, XXIII, 387).

---

12 See John Howard, *The State of the Prisons*; Neild, *The State of the Prisons*; or *An Account of All the Gaols, Houses of Correction or Penitentiaries in the United Kingdom*, PP, 1819, XVII, p. 371. According to the last, the largest provincial prison was then Liverpool Gaol, which had a maximum capacity of 500.

13 *Accounts, RCGP*, PP, 1830, XXIII, 387. Despite all the inconveniences (provisioning, access, etc.) arising from their being floating prisons, it was considerably cheaper to keep convicts in the hulks, where in 1811 *per capita* upkeep was estimated at £20. 0s. 6d. (*Holford Committee*, 3rd Report, PP, 1812, II, 363). These costs show, incidentally, why the magistrates had refused (some forty years previously) to provide the convict accommodation which central government had requested in exchange for a maintenance allowance of only 2s. 6d. per week (£6. 10s. 0d. per annum). Millbank's committee frequently argued that government's failure fully to utilise the prison's capacity was one of the main reasons for high running costs.

14 *RCGP*, PP, 1831-2, XXXIII, 551; *RCGP*, PP, 1824, IV, 106.

15 Buxton, *op. cit.*, p. 92; and Henry Grey Bennet, *A Letter to Viscount Sidmouth . . . on the Transportation Law, the State of the Hulks, and of the Colonies in New South Wales*, p. 4.

early guilt which the severity of the law punishes with the same sentence as more hardened criminality.[16]

But allocation was a matter of executive discretion:[17] as a contemporary writer pointed out, 'imprisonment in the Penitentiary is a substituted punishment; those who have been capitally convicted are imprisoned for ten years; those who have been sentenced to transportation for seven and five years'.[18] Choice of prisoners was vested in the Home Office, not the prison officials, as had been the case at Gloucester. In the early years there were complaints that selection procedure was not functioning as it should,[19] and authority was eventually given to th~

---

16 *Select Committee on the Penitentiary at Milbank*, PP, 1824, IV, 407, 13. George Holford thought the most suitable type to be 'one whose offence is of such a nature, as to call for a severe punishment, but whose heart has not been hardened or corrupted by a profligate course of life, or a long continuance in other prisons' (*The Convict's Complaint in 1815, and the Thanks of the Convict in 1825 . . .* (1825), p. xiii).

17 Some of the prisoners were mere children, seven years old. See *Letters written by Direction of the Secretary of State for the Home Department to the Committee for the Management of the Penitentiary, with the Report of the Committee in Answer Thereto*, PP, 1837-8, XLII, 317. Matilda Seymour received a seven-year sentence of transportation. The gaoler who sent her to Millbank gave her an age of ten. She said that she was seven. Other children involved in the incident were Anne Crane (seven years' transportation), ten years old, and Harriet Simpson (ten years' transportation), who was said to be ten years old, but who claimed to be eight. The children were released following public objections and the intervention of Middlesex quarter sessions (*The Times*, 23 and 24 February 1838).

18 *Quarterly Review* (January 1824), 30, p. 429; attributed (*Wellesley Index to Victorian Periodicals*, I, p. 703) to George Taylor or J.T. Coleridge. The exercise of executive discretion on such a scale was a substantial modification of the accepted notion and practice of equal penalties for equal crimes. In thus reconciling uniformity and individualisation it was thought possible to uphold the general deterrence of the sentence of the court, whilst allowing for executive consideration of individual circumstances. In 1823 a select committee on Millbank addressed itself, in part, to the means whereby objective and subjective approaches to punishment might be reconciled. It argued that punishment should be so administered as to produce 'terror in evil doers' and should also be 'operative by example in the prevention of crime'. From this the committee reasoned that 'the term of confinement should be sufficiently long to insure a change being effected in the evil habits and opinions of the prisoners; thus uniting the example of the punishment to the reformation of the offender'. They argued that in pursuit of these ends care should be taken to avoid arousing public sympathy, and that sentences should be no longer than was necessary for punishment or reformation. *Select Committee on the Penitentiary at Millbank*, PP, 1823, V, 2 and 12. Bennet, who was chairman of this committee, had argued along exactly these lines some years before (*op. cit.*, pp. 2-3).

19 See evidence of Captain Chapman, then governor of Millbank, to the 1831 select committee, PP, 1831, VII, 559, 17. By the end of the 1830s, the selection of prison lay with the courts.

committee of management (without being much used) to recommend for removal troublesome or unsatisfactory prisoners.[20]

Régime

The Holford Committee, having considered the respective merits of the Gloucester and Southwell systems, had taken the seemingly sensible course of combining the best features of both at the national penitentiary by the application of the progressive stage system first suggested in the Penitentiary Act of 1779.[21] Prisoners in the first class would be subject to a more severe régime of stricter seclusion, akin to that followed at the Gloucester Penitentiary; the Southwell régime would govern the routine of the second class. This product of compromise appeared to be practicable and equitable: the newly arrived prisoner would be purged and punished, buoyed up by the prospect of the privileges of the second stage. But there was fundamental incompatibility in the philosophies and objectives directing the respective régimes of Gloucester Penitentiary and the Southwell house of correction,[22] the depth of which the Holford Committee failed to appreciate. Consequently the rashly devised administration of Millbank could blame its hybrid origin for the incurable stresses that hampered the efforts and contributed to the ultimate failure of the penitentiary.

The actual lengths to which systematic separation of the prisoners was carried varied from time to time: in general, however, just under half the sentence had to be served before association and other benefits were allowed; some flexibility had been introduced by discretionary permission to move between the classes.[23] But even under the strictest rules of the first class separation was less than total. Prisoners were

---

20 By 7 & 8 Geo. IV, c.33.
21 19 Geo. III, c.74, s.38 had provided for a three-class progressive stage system. Prisoners' sentences were to be equally divided into three stages (called classes):

> The confinement and Labour of such Offenders as shall from Time to Time be ranked in the first Class, shall be the most strict and severe, and the Confinement and Labour of the Offenders ranked in the second Class shall be more moderate, and the Confinement and Labour of those ranked in the third Class, shall be still more relaxed. . . .

22 See above, chapter 5.
23 Demotion from the second class was regarded as a heavy punishment, rarely inflicted, and then only with the authority of the committee. See Holford's evidence to the 1823 SC, op. cit., 77-8, and Chapman's evidence to the 1831 SC, op. cit., 10. Chapman indicated that, on a five-year sentence, a prisoner could expect to be promoted to the second class in eighteen months or at most two years. According to him some fifty prisoners had been demoted at their own request, which among other things meant that they then ceased to be eligible for pardon (remission) (ibid., 13).

kept in solitary confinement proper for five days after reception, during which time they were visited by the chaplain and the governor; once this initiation was undergone, there were numerous opportunities for communication. They were permitted to converse with a 'partner' during exercise, and left their cells to attend school and chapel. The cells had an openwork iron inner door and a wooden outer door, which was supposed to ensure seclusion; but to facilitate supervision and task instruction the outer doors were generally left open and, as the staff complained, little could then be done to stop conversation. Second-class prisoners not only worked in association but, because of staff shortages, were unsupervised for long periods.[24] In the later years, for a number of reasons, the Millbank authorities adopted a much more stringent separate system; until then they largely consoled themselves and reassured the public by emphasising the benefits of night-time separation.[25]

Labour served several functions in the Millbank régime: it was of political value inasmuch as the public derived comfort from the fact that convicts were helping to defray the considerable expenses of their own upkeep; it was also a reformatory device, by daily exposure to which a socially desirable habit and source of satisfaction might be established; moreover, it facilitated control. In 1818 the governor told a visitor that it

> was the right hand of police [order] . . . while the prisoners were employed, they were decent in their behaviour and language; but . . . if they were not engaged in work, they would be in mischief; in fact . . . when work ended . . . troubles began.[26]

As the years went by, however, the prison authorities were forced to acknowledge that their industries were unable to make the expected contribution towards defraying maintenance expenses; and also to accept that the promise of labour's reformatory power had not been fulfilled. The formidable handicaps besetting prison employment – a

24 See Holford's evidence to the 1823 *SC, op. cit.*, 77, and Chapman's evidence to the 1831 *SC, op. cit.*, 13. Only one warder attended to a ward of thirty men, divided into seven or eight working cells, and he had several duties in addition to supervision.

25 Holford's observation was typical of this:

> Of all the points to be attended to in a place of confinement, in which any hope of reformation is entertained, that of giving to each person a separate night-cell is the most important. . . . There is nothing so discouraging to the repentant criminal, as the fear of being laughed at by his former colleagues and confederates in vice. . . . Conscience will often lose by day the ground which she has gained during the night; but unless they have separate night-cells, she will probably never gain any ground at all (Holford, *op. cit.* (1825), pp. xi-xiii).

26 Buxton, *op. cit.*, p. 91.

constantly changing labour force, low and variable skills, the need for intensive supervision, and the particularly severe impact of any outside recession in trade — were altogether fatal to profit-making. From six main trades which were taught and practised in the early years the industrial repertoire shrank to one — weaving.[27]

Much importance was attached to religion, the third major element in the régime. In each ward, morning and evening, a monitor, selected from the prisoners, conducted a service and gave instruction in the catechism; and there were the usual Sunday services in the chapel and regular visits to each cell by the chaplain after the hours of labour. As time went on, the place of religion tended to gain in prominence rather than to diminish.

In the early years the most serious penalty that could be inflicted for offences against regulations was confinement (usually accompanied by a restricted diet) in the dark cells. These were underground, measuring only nine by seven feet and reached by a passage of Stygian blackness so narrow that it had to be traversed sideways: 'It's impossible to describe the darkness — it's pitch black; no dungeon was ever so dark as it is.'[28] The only light for the occupant during the entire period of punishment was that brought by the turnkey when he delivered food three times a day. Evidence was given to the 1823 select committee (without provoking adverse comment) that convicts, male and female, had been kept in the cells for as long as three weeks. There was no heating and no removal for exercise; and, as it is known that other parts of the prison achieved afternoon temperatures of only 46° Fahrenheit during the winter of 1822-3, the cold in the punishment cells must have been intense. Physical conditions apart, there is no doubt that the psychological damage caused by prolonged sensory deprivation made this a terrible punishment indeed. That prisoners so confined could not have escaped severe damage to their health, especially as the food was usually only bread and water, was well recognised since as a matter of course they were taken to the infirmary after this ordeal.[29] Yet probably

27 Griffiths, *op. cit*. (1875), I, p. 58.
28 Mayhew and Binny, *op. cit*., p. 258.
29 *Rules and Regulations of the General Penitentiary at Milbank* (henceforth *RR*), PP, 1817, XVI, 333, Pt II, s. 1, 12; 1823 *SC*, *op. cit*., pp. 41, 55, 59; Griffiths, *op. cit*. (1875), p. 120. The authorities did not think that the punishment was sufficiently deterrent, however, and in their report for 1826-7 (PP, XX, 653, 1) the committee complained that it lost effect through repetition. This was one of the arguments put forward in favour of whipping, and was reiterated some forty years later. Giving evidence to the Carnarvon Committee of 1863 Dr W.A. Guy, the medical superintendent of Millbank prison, said:

> My experience of the dark cell is, that we find both men and women going to the dark cell over and over again; the women will often commit offences in order that they may go there; they have a certain morbid

the prison authorities would have argued that chastisement was inflicted only in proportion to the prisoners' contumacy and insubordination: confinement could be shortened if the governor judged that the offender had repented, and release could often be won by an apology and a promise of better behaviour.

For the first eleven years from the opening of the penitentiary, its prisoners could not be whipped. Power to whip was held by the magistrates of every other criminal prison in the country, and was a frequently imposed court sentence. Despite drastic curtailment of the use of capital penalties, popular and judicial opinion favoured corporal chastisement. Women were flogged in public until 1817 and in private until 1820.[30] A certain atmosphere of fiesta still attended execution of the capital sentence, and it was not until 1868 that this ceased to be a public spectacle. Indeed the medieval practice of gibbeting survived well into the middle age of Millbank, not being abolished until 1834.[31] Against this background it is a matter of some surprise that the penitentiary committee so long delayed its call for the introduction of whipping; internal and external pressures to provide this punishment must have been considerable; yet even when eventually given, the power was very infrequently exercised.[32]

Whereas the dark cells, whipping and down-grading in class were severe punishments and apparently effective, others were more moderate. It had been decided, following Southwell, that the convicts should be entitled to a portion of the profits of their earnings,[33] which could be wholly or partly confiscated as a punishment. Later, as the prison's industries contracted, earnings declined to a general level of not more than 1s. 3d. per month. Moreover, as the cash was not available until

---

pleasure in being in the dark cell, and as the cells are side by side . . . they can hear each other shouting and singing and cursing. They take a kind of pleasure in being there, and I do not think that the dark cells are any service to the majority of prisoners who are sent there (PP, 1863, IX, 399).

---

30 Henry S. Salt, *The Flogging Craze*, p. 15.
31 Albert Hartshorne, *Hanging in Chains*, p. 110.
32 Authorisation was given by 7 & 8 Geo. IV, c.33. The first prisoner flogged received 100 strokes of a 150-stroke sentence imposed for assault upon an officer (Griffiths, *op. cit.* (1875), I, p. 169). It is not clear why the Millbank committee were not from the outset given powers to whip. The 1779 Penitentiary Act (s. 47) had allowed its proposed committee to impose 'moderate whipping, or repeated whippings' for 'enormous' or repeated offences.
33 *RR*, Pt. II, s. 6, c.7, divided the profit from prison labour as follows: three-quarters to the establishment, one-eighth to the prisoner, and the remaining eighth between master manufacturer, taskmasters and turnkeys. The linking of staff income to prisoners' output derived from both the Transportation Act (19 Geo. III, c.74, s. 18) and the Houses of Correction Act (22 Geo. III, c.64, s. 9).

release, fining meant little to prisoners who still had several years to serve.[34] During the early years, when a craftsman could accumulate as much as £17 on release, fining appeared to be a more telling sanction. To increase their savings prisoners could even work after hours, but this privilege was specifically forbidden to any prisoner not 'industrious during the regular hours of labour, and generally well-behaved'.[35] The authorities also had power to withhold the discharge grant, which, in cash, clothing and tools, might amount to £3. But neither (in most cases) could this be considered an immediate punishment.[36]

Throughout most of its history the penitentiary had at its disposal perhaps the most convenient and effective of all penal sanctions: executive remission of a portion of sentence. Under the name of pardoning it was, to begin with, little used, then used quite extensively but not fully appreciated, and finally abolished. Before abolition, however, its use had grown from three cases in a population of 223 in 1818, to 178 early releases out of a population of just under 400 in 1836.[37]

Millbank's dietary in comparison with the gaols and houses of correction looked extremely full. Critics, however, did not take into account the much greater lengths of Millbank sentences. Thus, although naval and military physicians had accumulated much relevant knowledge of the danger in such a step, the committee were persuaded at one point to reduce the dietary scale. This decision was a major factor in the scurvy epidemic which followed shortly afterwards, causing at

34 *RR*, Pt III, 12; 1831 *SC, op. cit.*, 18. Buxton argued that an element of immediate benefit (and therefore potential deprivation) should be introduced by reducing diet to a minimum and making all food above that dependent on effort (*op. cit.*, pp. 97-8).

35 *RR*, Pt III, 13.

36 Incentives to good behaviour were also given after release. A person who demonstrated satisfactory conduct could, at the end of his first year of liberty, apply for a gratuity of up to £3. (Yet Chapman reported in his evidence to the 1831 SC that many eligible prisoners did not apply.)

37 *RR*, Pt III, 16, provided that any prisoner in the second class who displayed 'extraordinary diligence or merit' could be recommended for a pardon. The increased use of pardoning was in part a response to the findings of the 1823 select committee that it was a useful addition 'to the stock of rewards and punishments' (*Second Report of the Select Committee*, PP, 1824, IV, 407, 5. See also *RCGP*, PP, 1819, XVII, 333; *RCGP*, PP, 1837, XLVI, 305). Chapman described pardoning procedure to the 1831 select committee:

that power is usually exercised when a prisoner of a seven years' case, I would say, generally has been three and a half years in the Penitentiary, provided he has conducted himself well, that I can give a favourable report to the Committee as to his general conduct, and that the chaplain can also state his moral and religious improvement. The Committee on looking into the matter (which they do very minutely) exercise that power, and submit his name for pardon, for a very well behaved man at the end of three and a half years . . . (PP, 1831, VII, 519, 13).

least thirty deaths. The penitentiary had to be completely abandoned for a time, the female prisoners pardoned, and males transferred to the hulks.[38]

The subsequent inquiry repeatedly grappled with the principle of less-eligibility, and how best it might be applied to the penitentiary.[39] Holford described some of the pressures which had led to a curtailment of the diet. He recalled that to many 'respectable and experienced magistrates'

> the luxury of the Penitentiary was a standing joke. The prison was called 'my fattening house'. I was told that the public economy might be safely [conserved] by parting with many of our officers, as it was unnecessary to keep up an establishment to prevent escape, though it might perhaps be proper to apply for a guard to prevent persons from rushing in. . . . one of the members for Essex . . . termed the dietary 'an insult to honest industry' and 'a violation of common sense'.

There had been attacks by the newspapers, and threats to oppose the annual vote of money when it came before Parliament: 'the charge the

---

38 For an interesting account of the epidemic, including the involvement of Roget, the famous lexicographer, see D.L. Emblem, *Peter Mark Roget*, Ch. 10.

39 Those who administered the poor law of 1834 also had to face this problem. As it was then recognised that physical conditions could not be allowed to deteriorate below those of the poorest freemen, social and psychological conditions were made less eligible. Workhouse inmates were subjected to the deterrent discipline of penal labour and the breaking-up of families (see Norman Longmate, *The Workhouse*, p. 55). A contemporary argued on similar lines in relation to Millbank. He accepted that the penitentiary prisoners had to be provided with clean, well-ventilated cells, clothing and so forth, but argued that 'whatever conduces to health must be conducive to comfort; and if this comfort be unattended with labour, their imprisonment will be more agreeable than their home, and crime will cease to be prevented by any fear of the punishment which is its consequence'. But there was no necessity for a return to the conditions of the common gaols: 'the evil tendency of the comforts of a gaol, as affording encouragement to crime, may most effectually be counter-balanced by a system of labour'. He went on to call for the introduction of the treadwheel for convicted prisoners and trade instruction for the unconvicted (John Headlam, *A Letter to the Rt. Hon. Robert Peel*, pp. 19-21). Holford himself, as a result of the experience of the epidemic, developed a three-fold argument against simple material comparisons in applying the principle of less-eligibility. First, he said, it was a medical problem, and that the prison could not replicate within its walls the conditions of the poor freeman — 'these evils from which it is not in our power to relieve other classes of the community'. Second, he pointed out (following Beccaria and Paul) that the sentence of the law did not include disease and death, and that in any case not all prisoners had had the same standard of living. Finally, he argued that in fixing dietary scales, account must be taken of the extra needs that prisoners had because of the moral and physical conditions of their imprisonment (Holford, *op. cit.* (1830), 15, 16).

public made . . . was that honest labourers out of doors had not so good food as the prisoners found within the walls of the prison'.[40] The reduction of the diet and the consequent epidemic taught a valuable lesson to government and penal administrators alike. However desirable on political and other grounds less eligible conditions might be, they had to be based on methods which did not result in undermining the physical well-being of inmates, entailing fatalities and institutional collapse.

Administration and staffing

At the head of the penitentiary was the committee of management, a body corporate, responsible for the finances of the prison, and obliged to make an annual report to Parliament. Its powers of appointment and dismissal were total. It had to meet at least once a month and, in a now familiar fashion, carried out its task of inspection and regulation chiefly through the appointment of one member as a visitor.

In practice, committee meetings were a great deal more frequent than the monthly minimum; during parliamentary sittings there was a meeting each week. The effect of such frequent proceedings upon the Millbank staff was increased by the high social standing of its members:

> statesmen and high dignitaries, dukes, bishops, and members of parliament were to be found [there] . . . exercising a control that was far from nominal or perfunctory, not disdaining a close consideration of the minutest details, and coming into intimate personal communion with the criminal elements, whom, by praise or admonition they sought to reward or reprove.[41]

Members included such experienced prison administrators as William Morton Pitt and Thomas Becher. If these two were precluded from frequent attendances by their residence in the provinces, their absence was more than compensated for by the assiduous efforts of George Holford who, having been principally responsible for the establishment of the prison, remained closely involved in its administration for twenty-five years.[42]

The visitor inspected the prison between meetings. He was obliged

---

40 1823 *SC*, *op. cit.*, 114, 118. The Essex member in question was Charles Callis Western who made the observations on Millbank's dietary in his *Remarks Upon Prison Discipline*, p. 113. The dietary scale had originally been based on that of the Gloucester Penitentiary, the only comparable prison (in terms of régime and length of sentences served) then existing.

41 Griffiths, *op. cit.* (1875), I, p. 1. The speaker of the House of Commons was among the members of the original committee (Entry Book, *op. cit.*, pp. 24 *et seq.*).

42 He was a member of the committee until his death in 1836.

to report his observations, but was empowered to act in emergencies and to issue occasional orders 'which might be made or given by the Committee if they were sitting'.[43] As much by what it did not say, this statement of the task of the visitor left considerable scope for personal interpretation.

The senior paid official was the governor. His duties and powers were outlined in no less than twenty-nine clauses in the rules and regulations, receiving more attention than was addressed to any other post in the prison, at the same time emphasising to what an extent the desire to control this post influenced the administrative structure. At this point his duties may be stated as the maintenance of the custody and discipline of the prison, chiefly by means of systematic and regular inspection. He had also certain, largely formal, duties in relation to the prison's industries,[44] and was in all matters accountable to the committee.

The governor's powers over prisoners were clear: he could apply a range of authorised punishments for violations of discipline, and refer especially grave offenders to the attention of the committee. But his authority was not so clearly defined in relation to staff. He could suspend, but not dismiss, subordinate staff only; he had no powers of suspension over those designated as 'superior' in the rules, namely the chaplain, surgeon, steward, master manufacturer, secretary and matron, who, in keeping with the original recommendations of the committee, owed their partial protection to their use as internal checks on the governor. Powers of appointment and dismissal were vested exclusively in the committee. The nowhere clearly defined responsibility of the governor for the morale of the prison was traceable to the tacit understanding that he should 'influence' staff as well as issue formal orders.[45]

The governor's own employment was subject to a number of conditions. He could engage in no other occupation, he was only eligible if married and he had to reside, with his family, within the prison. The importance placed upon his continuous presence was shown by the requirement that before absenting himself he had to note the occasion in his journal and formally give charge of the prison to his deputy, the master manufacturer.[46]

43 *RR*, Pt I, 10.
44 *RR*, Pt II, s. 1.
45 The committee placed great emphasis on the governor's influence upon his subordinates. For example, Nihill, who was governor from 1837, was praised by the committee for carrying out his duties 'with intelligence, energy and firmness, blended with a mildness of temper and deportment, which is calculated to diffuse a beneficial influence over the subordinate officers' (*RCGP*, PP, 1837-8, XLII, 311, 2).
46 *RR*, Pt II, 25. The governor's salary was £600 plus accommodation, furniture and heating. He was not allowed a proportion of prisoners' earnings, an emolument which went to other superior staff and to the subordinate

The chaplain's duties comprised the usual ecclesiastical offices, including the ministration of baptism. This latter was based on the likelihood of his receiving into the Church converted convicts, and the infants of the female prisoners; there were also at Millbank the families of prison staff to whom his care extended. His pastoral duties included 'visiting, admonishing and instructing' the prisoners, the distribution of tracts and books and 'constantly visiting the sick, and reading prayers every day in the infirmary, and [being] in constant attendance . . . from morning to night'.[47] Among other miscellaneous duties were arranging tuition for illiterate prisoners, supervising the evening classes, and the censorship of letters. Although in some of these tasks he had the assistance of a schoolmaster, the Millbank chaplaincy was obviously no sinecure.

Several conditions attached to the chaplain's appointment: 'He shall be in Priest's Orders, and approved by the Bishop of the Diocese; shall have no profession, avocation or duty whatsoever; and shall be resident in the prison.' It was required that he should be married at the time of his appointment, and that he should procure a substitute during any absence from the prison. He was further obliged to note any 'accidental' failure to perform his duties in his journal. His salary was £400, with the perquisites of accommodation, furniture, heating and, at a later point, the services of a gardener. This was a not ungenerous reward, as a contemporary writer commented:

> The chaplain is very properly made one of the most responsible and important officers of the prison; his salary is regulated, not extravagantly and, yet liberally, with reference to the number of prisoners; a pension is provided for him in case of sickness, age or infirmity. . . .[48]

The matron was a deputy governor with appropriate duties within the female section of the prison, and kept the governor informed of her sphere of superintendence by regular reports. Her conditions of employment were the same as his 'as far . . . as are applicable'.[49]

---

officials. Nor was he allowed the rations which were distributed to the latter. (A later governor, Captain Chapman, was additionally awarded over £130 in lieu of his army pension, and was provided with a gardener – see Entry Book, *op. cit.*, p. 75.)

---

47 1823 *SC*, *op. cit.*, 301.
48 *Quarterly Review* (February 1824), 30, p. 412.
49 She received a salary of £250, plus one twenty-fourth of the profits from the female convicts. This post declined in importance and remuneration; after some unsettlement with the first occupant it was for several years unfilled. In 1835 the matron was paid only £180, though there was by then an assistant matron with a salary of £100 (*RCGP*, PP, 1833, XXVIII, 659, 3, and *RCGP*, PP, 1835, XLV, 221).

The secretary was the special employee of the committee and attended all meetings, with a general responsibility to report 'any irregularity or other matter requiring their attention which may have fallen under his observation'.[50] He kept minutes, drew up and examined account-books and saw to the committee's correspondence.

The surgeon was a full-time officer, 'competent to discharge the duties of Surgeon, Apothecary and Man-Midwife ... a Member of the Royal College of Surgeons ...'. His medical duties included the care of subordinate officers in addition to the prisoners, and the examination of all newly admitted prisoners, and all those under dietary or cellular punishment. An honorary consultant surgeon and a physician were also available, upon whom the surgeon could call for advice and assistance.[51]

The master manufacturer handled the prison's industries, directing the employment of inmates through the taskmasters and turnkeys, ordering and issuing materials. He also acted as deputy during the governor's absence, and collected the daily and weekly reports of the taskmasters on his behalf, 'noting thereupon such observations as may occur to him'.[52]

The steward, responsible for the domestic provisioning of the prison, issued rations to the kitchens and to his inferiors. In such a large and complex institution at a time when accountancy methods and stock control were not very highly developed, he must have been obliged to keep up a constant campaign against pilferage and wastage.[53]

50 He was not resident and there was no formal restriction on his holding other positions (*RR*, Pt II, 1-4). His salary was £300, increased in 1835 to £400, out of which he had to pay his own clerk. There was then a clerk to the governor, who was paid £132. 10s. 0d. and a clerk of works at £54. 12s. 0d. At various times complaints were made that Millbank did not have enough clerks to maintain its complex system of books (*RCGP*, PP, 1835, XLV, 221).

51 *RR*, Pt II, s. 5. This 'lavish' medical provision was seized upon by critics as yet another example of the pampering of criminals. The authorities seem chiefly to have been concerned, with some good reason as it emerged, with the prevention of epidemics. The surgeon was paid £400 and was provided with accommodation and heating.

52 *RR*, Pt II, s. 6. As deputy he was directed not to 'leave the prison in the absence of the Governor, nor at any time, without apprising the Governor of his intention'. His salary was £200 plus one twenty-fourth of the profits from the male prisoners' labour.

53 He was also resident in the prison and could not leave without notifying the governor or his deputy; his salary was £150 (*RR*, Pt II, s. 7).

Mayhew and Binny met the steward when they visited Millbank in the 1850s. It had then ceased to be a penitentiary, and the duties of steward had incorporated some tasks formerly carried out by the master manufacturer. The steward described his work:

I pay all moneys for the prison ... and take account of clothing, provisions, necessaries of every sort, and pay all the warders too, every

The establishment of subordinate officers fluctuated between sixty and eighty, and it is likely that, had the penitentiary been filled to capacity, a number in excess of one hundred would have been needed.[54] The largest group was made up of the taskmasters, each of whom had charge of a pentagon, and the turnkeys, who took charge of the wards. At a later time an intermediate grade of assistant taskmasters was introduced. The functions in the female section were similar and were performed by taskmistresses and female turnkeys. Nurses, directed by the surgeon and matron, worked in the prison's three infirmaries; and in each of the four male pentagons there was a miller or machine-keeper.

Below the subordinate officers there was a grade of staff called 'servants', consisting of the three gate-porters, a messenger and four 'patroles', the last of whom were mainly in charge of the night-time security of the prison's outer wall. In addition to these servants (but not part of the permanent staff establishment), labourers were employed in the gardens.[55]

---

week. Everything the warders require they must come to me for. They get an order signed by the governor. . . . It's likewise part of my department to take charge of any money the prisoners have earned while in prison, in case of their going away; not that any money passes here, for it's merely a nominal transaction, and placed to their credit against their time being up, when it is paid to them (Mayhew and Binny, *op. cit.*, pp. 254-5).

---

54 A budget was submitted in 1832-3 for seventy inferior officers. (See *Estimate of the Sum that will Probably be Required to Defray the Charge of the Establishment of the Penitentiary at Milbank*, PP, 1831-2, XXVII, 638.) In the 1850s, when Millbank was used as a convict depot and held 1,100 inmates, staff numbers exceeded 120, including 103 subordinate officers (Mayhew and Binny, *op. cit.*, p. 259).

55 *RR*, pp. 3, 4; 1823 *SC*, *op. cit*., Appendix E, No. 8. This latter document is entitled 'Description of some of the Inferior Officers employed in different parts of the Penitentiary, for the care and management of the prisoners', and is the most comprehensive existing description of the duties of the lower officers.

Salaries were £50 and £60, respectively, for turnkeys and taskmasters, plus rations and a share in profits from labour. The 'patroles' were paid £50, and also received daily rations of 1 lb wholemeal bread, ¾ lb 'good Beef or Mutton, exclusive of Bone', 1 lb of 'sound Potatoes' and 'Salt and Pepper, as the Committee shall direct' (*RR*, Pt V). By 1835 these rations were worth £9. 5s. 0d. per annum. See *Estimate of the Sum that will probably be required* . . . , PP, 1836, XXXVIII, 378.

For the sake of comparison it can be pointed out that by 1834 when craftsmen were employed in the prison, a baker was paid £60 plus rations, millers and machine-keepers £50 plus rations, a cutter for the tailors' shop 30s. per week plus rations. The taskmasters' percentage amounted to £21. 9s. 3d. in 1833 and turnkeys' £3. 11s. 6d. On the female side, the parallel figures were only £7. 10s. 11d., and 18s. 11d. Accommodation, furniture and bedding were given in addition to rations to those inferior

Thus, in terms of public investment, running costs, size and organisational complexity, Millbank Penitentiary posed distinctly new administrative problems. At a time when the Home Office was staffed by a handful of clerks, this prison was virtually a new department of state. Many of the administrative difficulties that arose were due to its size and the lack of experience of the administrators. But other problems originated, as has been hinted, in the conflicts inherent from the outset in the prison's goals and methods. The solutions chosen could not but have considerable implications for the development of participation by central government in prison administration, directly and indirectly. It is to those conflicts and their solutions that we now turn.

The recruitment and control of staff

From what has been said in previous chapters it should be obvious that the recruitment of suitable staff was a critical and difficult task for the Millbank committee. Upon the success of their efforts and the securing of an efficient means of staff control, depended the future of the prison. Millbank would otherwise offer rich pickings for the corrupt and, because of its relationship to central government, would be overwhelmed by political protest.

The governor was the central figure. In making this appointment, precedent and the experience of Gloucester and Southwell were no adequate guides. The committee's perplexity was reflected in and increased by the rapid succession of governors in the early years. Their chosen candidates had few characteristics in common beyond the dull, rather unheroic virtue of 'respectability'.

The committee was loath to appoint a person with experience of other prisons. Such a man could not, *ipso facto*, be 'respectable' and would very likely have the ability and inclination to take advantage of his post for private profit. As Holford observed,

we could not expect to find any person in any other prison, whom we could transfer to the Government of the Penitentiary, and accordingly we were obliged to take our chance, among the most eligible persons that offered without experience.[56]

Indeed, by choosing an inexperienced man, the committee's superior knowledge of prison management would redound to its advantage; it

officers who resided in the prison. Taskmasters' and turnkeys' salaries and emoluments were thus on or above the level of prison craftsmen's earnings (*RCGP*, PP, 1835, XLV, 221). It has been estimated that London building labourers were at about this time being paid an average weekly wage of 18*s*.; shipwrights were paid 36*s*. (G.D.H. Cole and Raymond Postgate, *The Common People 1746-1946*, p. 302).

56 1823 *SC*, *op. cit.*, 78.

might be possible to train a new man to the committee's own methods.

The first governor was John Shearman, a solicitor, who had some familiarity with police procedures, and was strongly recommended by the home secretary.[57] Shearman was sent by the committee on a tour of 'several of the principal gaols of the Kingdom' as an induction exercise.[58] Despite this and his high recommendations he held his post for only fourteen months.[59] In the next six years there were three other appointments.[60] None of these false starts involved scandal, but in each case (except the last) it became clear that the committee had failed to identify the necessary qualities for the post, and that mere 'respectability' was not enough.

The appointment of Captain Benjamin Chapman, which terminated this rapid succession of governors, was of particular significance. The select committee of 1823 recognised that in this appointment an important precedent had been set, Chapman being 'a person of education and superior condition in life', and they recommended that 'this office should always in future be held by a person of that description'.[61] Chapman 'had been a captain and paymaster in one of the best regiments in the service', and by holding the post for over fourteen years he demonstrated that both socially and professionally he had the necessary qualities satisfactorily to fulfil the duties of governor.[62]

---

57 *Ibid.*, p. 181; Griffiths, *op. cit.* (1875), I, p. 49.

58 PRO, HO 21, p. 23. The prisons visited were Dorchester, Gloucester, Shrewsbury, Chester, Manchester, Liverpool, Lancaster, Southwell, Lincoln, Wakefield and Preston. The home secretary (Lord Sidmouth) provided a letter of introduction. See Griffiths, *op. cit.* (1875), I, p. 50, for a summary of the governor's report.

59 Holford said that Shearman had resigned because he expected more money and less work (1823 *SC*, *op. cit.*, 78). Shearman himself complained of interference by the committee and the changed tenure of the position from life to dependence on the committee's approval *after* he had taken up the post (*ibid.*, 181). Griffiths (*op. cit.* (1875), I, p. 50) said that the committee had found fault with Shearman's frequent absences from the prison, and that he was apparently attempting concurrently to carry on his previous business as solicitor.

60 John Shearman had charge from 25 March 1816 to 9 May 1817; Henry Ryde from 9 May 1817 to 10 June 1818; John Couch from 10 June 1818 to 29 May 1820. Jordinson White, the master manufacturer, was then acting governor until Couch (who had been ill with a brain disease) resumed his duties from 7 July 1820 to 25 March 1823, when Benjamin Chapman became governor. During this period there had also been three matrons, two master manufacturers and two stewards (1823 *SC*, *op. cit.*, 123). In the spring of 1823 the surgeon, Mr A.C. Hutchinson, was dismissed, because of his alleged drinking habits (*The Times*, 29 May 1823, 3e).

61 *Ibid.*, p. 406.

62 *Ibid.*, p. 120. Besides the solicitor, Shearman, previous governors had included a managing clerk and an army clothier. It is interesting that just a few years later the superintendent of the hulks stated that he did not think military experience and substantial social position suitable qualities in the

Even in a conventional gaol, subordinate staff presented many problems for the gaoler. James Ives, keeper of the county gaol at Southwark, declared that 'There was a wonderful difficulty with servants, [and] ... more difficulty to get servants to do right, than there is to manage the prisoners'.[63] The Millbank committee was always discreet in its references to staffing problems.[64] Nevertheless there is abundant evidence to show that they constituted one of the prison's major administrative difficulties.[65]

Just as the comfortless living conditions of the poor posed the issue of less-eligibility for the Millbank dietary and régime, other social conditions inhibited the recruitment of able and honest subordinate officers. Access to education was restricted and the general state of prisons encouraged expectations of illicit gain among many prospective employees. Nor was the task of the subordinate officers in the penitentiary simple. Ives's difficulties had been with staff whose work was restricted to mere supervision — being on guard against escapes and seeing prisoners through the various routines of the day. Millbank, however, was an institution with declared aims of moral transformation, in which edifying attitudes and demeanours were expected from all staff, including those of the lowest order. So, in addition to the competent discharge of their various supervisory and reporting duties, the subordinate staff were expected 'to enforce ... orders with firmness but ... act with the utmost humanity towards all the prisoners under [their] care'. They had at the same time to keep their social distance and were directed not to be 'familiar with any of the prisoners or converse with them unnecessarily'; they were to 'treat them as persons under ... authority and control and not as ... companions or associates'.[66]

The failure of Millbank's management to inculcate the desired attitudes among its subordinate staff was manifested in the numerous

---

kind of person he employed. He was asked: 'Do you not think that you might probably have persons of a superior description, such as retired lieutenants?' 'I have found that they have not answered my purpose so well as persons trained in the service' (1831 *SC, op. cit.*, 45). The hulks retained many vestiges of the old gaol system, however, and this might well have been the reason why Capper found these 'persons of a superior description' unsuitable. The issue of military versus prison experience is discussed in Chapter 10.

---

63 *Holford Committee, op. cit.*, 657.
64 Year after year the committee's reports obliquely referred to their staffing difficulties by stating that 'in general' or 'on the whole' they were satisfied with their conduct. (See, for example, *RCGP*, PP, 1820, XII, 361 and *RCGP*, PP, 1830, XXIII, 387.)
65 However, Playfair is much too sweeping when he says of the Millbank staff that they were as 'ill-educated as they were poorly paid and as brutal, most of them, as they were corrupt' (Giles Playfair, *The Punitive Obsession*, p. 34).
66 *RR* (1819), *op. cit.*

instances of trafficking and associated scandals which were brought to light from time to time. The most common practice seems to have been the bribing of subordinate officers to supply newspapers, magazines, wines, spirits, food and tobacco: typically, former prisoners would arrange to meet officers at public houses, where they placed orders for their 'clients' and paid over the necessary funds.[67] Even the eventual policy of recruiting subordinate staff mainly from the army and navy provided no solution,[68] and one after another the annual reports continued to refer, though usually in a guarded fashion, to misconduct and dismissals.

In other prisons these offences would doubtless have been viewed as venial: in the penitentiary, which was attempting to enforce a régime intended to restructure the attitudes of prisoners, the transgressions were intolerable, amounting to breaches in the carefully constructed moral embankments of the disciplinary system. The committee had yet another difficulty. The more ably they detected and punished staff for violations of discipline, the greater the damage that was done to the high standing of the penitentiary as a national foundation. In the later years more and more emphasis was placed on better recruitment as the first line of defence. Thus in 1840 the committee noted in its annual report:

> The instances of misconduct which have occurred have been
> properly visited with dismissal, or other suitable punishments; and it
> is to be expected that the firm determination of the Committee to
> persevere in this vigorous course will tend not only to purify the
> general body of officers from unworthy individuals, but to raise the
> moral tone of those who are continued in the establishment.

At the same time it was hoped that recently agreed salary increases would have the effect of 'attracting the services of persons possessing superior qualifications to those which have heretofore been expected in that class of men, but it will obviously require time for this principle to develope [sic] its beneficial operation'.[69] But the following year, whilst the committee was able to announce that the increased salaries had attracted 'several persons of superior qualifications into the service of the establishment', they could only comment, as usual, that staff performance was good 'in general'.[70] The committee wrestled with the situation to the last, and their final report mentioned the introduction

---

67 Griffiths, *op. cit.* (1875), I, pp. 215-16.
68 'Our description of officers are usually well-reommended, non-
    commissioned officers' (1831 *SC*, *op. cit.*, 18).
69 *RCGP*, PP, 1840, XXXVIII, 679. But the new scale of payment did not
    exceed that already being paid in the Middlesex house of correction, the
    committee reported.
70 *RCGP*, PP, 1841, XVIII, 649.

of a new intermediate rank as a possible cure.[71]

The theme of staffing thus runs through the committee reports. In the penitentiary, no less than in the gaols and houses of correction, a strong concentration of administrative and managerial effort was required if the centuries-old pattern of profitable trading and collusion with prisoners was to be ruptured. It would seem that here, despite the striving and innovation, the penitentiary committee were only partly successful. Moreover, it can be shown that in some fundamental respects the organisation of the penitentiary itself aggravated the problems of staff control.

A condition of residence was attached to several senior posts, and no subordinate officers were allowed to sleep out of the prison except in 'unforeseen or unavoidable necessity'. This provision was intended as a precaution against the abuses likely to arise from an absentee staff, and to ensure their presence in case of emergency; it also acted as a measure of control over the off-duty behaviour of officers. On the other hand, some of the rules indicate that numerous difficulties arose from having so many staff in residence: it was necessary, for example, specifically to forbid them to keep poultry, pigeons, rabbits or pigs; and there were explicit conditions of service which would facilitate the dismissal and removal of any unsatisfactory domestic servants of the inferior officers.

The 1823 select committee was informed that there were forty residents in the central block of the prison, the hexagon, namely the senior staff, their wives, families and servants;[72] only a few years later the total had increased to seven senior and fifty-six subordinate resident officers, male and female.[73] A late Victorian administrator describes the consequences, with an almost audible snort:

> The officials, nearly all of them of mature age, having grown up children, young ladies and young gentlemen, always about the place, and that place from its peculiar conditions like a ship at sea, shut off from the public, and concentrated on what was going on within its walls. Gossip of course — probably worse, constant observation of one another, jealousies, quarrels . . . subordinates ever on the look out to make capital of the differences of their betters, and alive to the fact that they were certain of a hearing when they chose to carry any slanderous attack. . . .[74]

Officially encouraged tale-telling flourished in an emotional atmosphere which inevitably undermined morale and discipline. The coming and

---

71 *RCGP*, PP, 1843, XLIII, 491.
72 1823 *SC, op. cit.*, Appendix E, No. 6. Only one inferior officer is mentioned as having a family living in the hexagon; though it is not clear if other subordinate officers had families living elsewhere within the prison.
73 *RCGP*, PP, 1826-7, XX, 653.
74 Griffiths, *op. cit.* (1875), I, pp. 69-70.

going of numerous civilians into all parts of the prison made it practically impossible to control trafficking. If there are added to this the long hours worked by the staff and the fact that no holidays or other sustained breaks were allowed, Griffiths's mild understatement only draws attention to the unfortunate reality: 'Of a truth, the life inside the Penitentiary must have been rather irksome to more people than those confined there against their will.'[75] The evils of its residential population continued to strain the administration of the penitentiary to the last.

Moreover its smooth running was further deranged by friction in the working relationship between the governor and the committee. The latter had aimed from the outset at wielding unobtrusive but effective control over the activities of the governor, no less than of other staff. Indeed, the choice between Bentham's contract-management and the trust-management of Southwell and Gloucester had been made by the Holford Committee on this issue. Against such a background (and with Holford its most active member) it is little wonder that the committee sought to make a success of their supervisory tactics.

But the very composition of the committee stood in the way of their schemes. Here was a body consisting of men of affairs with high social, political and religious status. True, the legality of their regulations was formally subject to the judgment of King's Bench, and as a public committee they were answerable to Parliament for their work as a whole. But over a wide range of day-to-day transactions they were subject to no other authority or supervision. The status, political connections and authority of the individual members had undoubted benefits; it guaranteed a high level of probity and independence. But a price had to be paid for these advantages:

> Millbank was a huge play-thing; a toy for a parcel of philanthropic gentlemen, to keep them busy during their spare hours. It was easy to see . . . that they loved to run in and out of the place and show it off to their friends. . . .[76]

In the early years frequency of visiting for social reasons, or because of the novel interest of the prison, became accelerated by the need for tighter control, especially during, and because of, the quick succession of the first four governors. Holford, rather defensively perhaps, described the committee's concern during that period:

> we were quite aware that it was not likely that different persons brought in to fill situations in a new establishment, of which persons the Committee had in general no previous knowledge, were likely all to suit us, and we knew therefore that we ought to watch

75 *Ibid.*, p. 70.
76 Griffiths, *op. cit.* (1875), I, 59.

vigilantly over their conduct, to keep those who answered our expectations, and to part with those who appeared to be unfit for their situations; neither could we expect to make a complete system of rules and regulations at once . . . these circumstances . . . will explain why different members of the Committee should have been a good deal of time in the prison, and why I myself for a considerable period, did everything but sleep there. . . .[77]

He added that the committee had hoped that once the prison was well established a less rigorous and detailed intervention would be possible.

The committee's inspection was carried on in two ways. Any member could visit at any time, and many did so;[78] but the duty rested mainly with the visitor. As has been pointed out, the rules were so loosely drawn up in relation to the visitor that considerable variation was possible in the way in which a member carried out this task. Visitors differed in their definition of what should be considered an emergency worthy of their intervention; governors also differed in their willingness to act on their own authority or to consult the visitor.[79] Involvement ranged from Holford's very frequent intervention[80] to the rather more constrained style of William Courtney, who saw the visitor as

a Committee man delegated to do the duty of superintendents [sic], which the Committee is in the first instance directed to do. . . . One of the most important duties is . . . to visit the prisoners who might be confined in the solitary cells . . . my habit in visiting the prison was to go into the Penitentiary, and without saying where I was going particularly, if I could, without letting the governor know it, to take one pentagon and walk round it with the officer I might find there.[81]

---

77 1823 *SC, op. cit.,* 297.

78 . . . any Member of the Committee, not being a Visitor, may at his pleasure inspect any part of the prison, and make such enquiries of the several officers and servants of the Establishment as he may think proper, and shall report such matters as may appear to him to require particular attention to the Visitor of the Committee at his discretion (*RR*, PP, 1819, XVIII, 333).

This provision was very similar to the right of visit given to county magistrates in the local establishments. The clause did not appear in the 1817 version of the rules.

79 The governor was directed: 'In cases of emergency, and which are not sufficiently provided for in the Rules and Regulations he shall apply to the Visitor, and conform to his direction' (*ibid.*).

80 It was said of Holford that he was 'the most active gentleman there, and no man had more zeal in the establishment, or the welfare of the establishment more at heart' (Shearman to 1823 *SC, op. cit.,* 181).

81 *Ibid.,* 212.

The governor would therefore find that visitors treated him very differently as they carried out their duties. It would have been all but impossible, for a number of reasons, for a governor to tell a visitor that his intervention was unhelpful, or that he was exceeding his powers. The governor was formally safeguarded, to some extent, by the requirement that any orders issued by the visitor should be entered in a book. However, it emerged in the evidence given to the 1823 select committee that this provision had often been ignored.

The most serious result of the committee's failure to limit the duties and powers of the visitor was the undermining of the position of the governor. It is clear that some committee members regularly undertook an executive instead of an emergency part in the administration of the prison. Shearman, the first governor, gave this as one of the main reasons for his resignation.

> I had conceived that I was the servant of the Committee, and that all the executive part of the duty of the Penitentiary was to be done by my agency . . . visitors did that which I thought was not correct, because they went to the Penitentiary and gave orders and directions for things to be done to the inferior officers, which I thought ought to come through me . . . prisoners were occasionally removed from one ward to another, I knew nothing of it, no communication was made to me, and if the inferior officers had a request they got too much into the habit of reserving it to speak to visitors, that I conceived I was almost a nonentity in the situation. . . .[82]

The governor's position was also weakened by the way in which the committee's information was gathered:

> to make the more sure that nothing should be neglected, and no irregularity overlooked, the Committee encouraged, or at least their most prominent members did, all sorts of talebearing and a system of espionage that must have been destructive of all the good feelings among the inmates of the prison.[83]

It was said by Shearman that there had been

> A very painful system going on in the prison against the officers by that degree of what I might term spyism. I have no doubt at all that it arose from the purest motives, thinking it was the best way to conduct the establishment, setting up one person to look after another.[84]

---

82 *Ibid.*, 179.
83 Griffiths, *op. cit.* (1875), I, p. 68.
84 1823 *SC, op. cit.*, 179.

William Morton Pitt's extensive experience of prison administration led him also to complain about the effects of tale-bearing upon the morale of staff:

> I have frequently received communications from Mr. Holford of information that he had received from prisoners, and from inferior officers, and servants of the establishment, which have much surprized me . . . I thought information of that sort was highly objectionable . . . it was very detrimental to the discipline of the establishment . . . being so ready to lend a willing ear to such communications operated as an encouragement to tale-bearing. The consequences of which, certainly have appeared to me to have been disputes, cabals, or intrigues.

The system tended, he said, 'to insubordination from the inferior to the superior officers and to diminish the respect with which the prisoners would hold their officers in general'.[85]

Holford's defence was that close committee supervision and executive intervention had been necessary in the early years, and that, in any case, much depended on the capacity of the governor actively to assume authority. But experience, and possibly the airing of these difficulties before the 1823 select committee, prompted a greater awareness of the need to sustain the authority of the new governor, and there was no further record of excessive intervention by the committee of management. It seems to have been recognised that, whatever short-term benefits might have arisen from piecemeal decision-making by visitors, the organisation's well-being and long-term gaols could be achieved only through the agency of the governor.[86] No amateur was able to wield the authority and provide the continuous supervision necessary to ensure effective control and an acceptable level of morale.

---

85 *Ibid.*, 165. Henry Ryde, the second governor, also complained of the tale-bearing system: 'during the whole period that I was there, there was a continual complaint, one officer against another, and a system that was quite unpleasant with an establishment of that nature' (*ibid.*, 187).

86 As was clearly recognised in a letter of William Morton Pitt's published in *The Times*:

> The fundamental error seems to have been, that with the exception of the newly appointed Governor, those who have been appointed to that office have never been invested with the powers due to their situation, and necessary to maintain order and subordination, . . . in point of fact the committee have been considered the *governing* instead of the superintending power. Under a Governor, qualified by his rank in life, his habits, and firmness of character, for this station, and duly supported by the Committee, much that we have reason to deplore could scarcely have existed (*The Times*, 29 May 1823, 3e).

Conflict and demise

The difficulties arising from political relationships with the broader community, staff recruitment, and effective control were all affecting the degree of success that the prison could achieve. From the outset, however, a far more intractable obstacle was posed by the contradictions that riddled the penal aims of the establishment. Policy and régime were a mixture of the main elements of the philosophies and methods of Gloucester Penitentiary and the Southwell house of correction, strung together. Yet these goals and methods were radically different. Whilst both aimed to be deterrent, Gloucester sought to secure a basic change in attitude, by means of seclusion and religion, and Southwell wished rather to produce a change in behaviour, depending chiefly for this purpose upon rewarded labour and various disciplinary sanctions. It had been thought that these two different approaches could be amalgamated by means of a progressive stage system. But experience, gained through the clashes in the competing roles of governor and chaplain, was to show how unsound this compromise had been.

There were several potential areas of conflict between the chaplain and the governor. The position of the latter had been weakened in the early years by the series of misfits whose stay was quite brief as well as by the uncertain demarcation of duties between the governor and the committee. But the chaplain also had been explicitly given the role of acting as internal check upon the governor and other staff and, for this reason, allowed direct access to the committee.[87] However, there were some restrictions placed upon his activities, in particular he was directed to 'interfere as little as possible with the work carried on in the prison',[88] but this provision was bound to become increasingly less important as hopes of highly productive and remunerative prison industries faded.

From the outset it was rather naïvely envisaged that the governor and chaplain would be 'each supreme in his own department: the

---

87 The rule stated:

> In the performance of his duties he shall be subject to no control but that of the Committee. He shall represent to the Committee whatever may appear to him to be worthy of their notice; or suggest any thing which he may conceive to be likely to prove beneficial to the prisoners, or tend to their personal reformation (RR, PP, 1819, XVIII, 333, s. III, 6).

> It was also provided that whereas the governor was to be given the decisions and instructions of the committee through the secretary, 'such resolutions of the Committee as relate to the chaplain shall be communicated to himself directly' (RR, 1818 edition, PP, 1818, XVI, 237). This provision was not in the original (1817) edition of the rules.

88 Ibid.

governor as head of the penal, the chaplain of the religious part of the system'.[89] But as the chaplain was to some extent the governor's keeper the latter could not be supreme in his own department. Moreover, as religious interests were so pervasive, the priestly prerogative could be expanded into many activities without effective challenge. Indeed, the chaplain, to perform his duties, had to be involved in penal matters, as an early amendment to the rules noted:

> It being of the utmost importance that the chaplain should be fully informed concerning the moral state and condition of the prison, the governor and matron shall communicate to him, without delay, all breaches of decorum arising within their respective departments, and all such occurrences and circumstances as may appear to render his interpretation by way of advice expedient and that the inferior officers attached to the several Pentagons shall also consider it to be their duty to give the chaplain the earliest information on such subjects when they shall meet him in the parts of the prison to which they respectively belong.[90]

Thus not only was the chaplain given direct access upward to the committee, but he had also direct contact with the inferior officers, which placed him in a very influential position. The chaplain was also able to authorise infirmary visits for prisoners, and it was he who censored their letters. Further, the chaplain's direction of the educational curriculum brought him into close contact with a large number of prisoners for several hours each week. All of these incursions upon the 'penal department' were in addition to the general responsibility, which he held in common with all other officers, to observe and report any breaches of discipline.[91]

The functions of the chaplain and governor in relation to the prisoners

---

89 *Cit.* Griffiths, *op. cit.* (1875), I, p. 203.
90 *RCGP*, PP, 1819, XVIII, 333, s. 11, 12. The governor was also obliged to notify the chaplain of any prisoner placed under punishment.

There were several changes in the rules enhancing the authority of the chaplain in the early successive editions, and the very form in which they were set out showed his increased standing. In the original rules the committee were dealt with under Section I, and the governor in Section II. By 1819, the committee were still the subject of Section I, while the duties of the chaplain occupied Section II, and the governor's were postponed to Section III.

91 A chaplain actually used his classical education to expose a case of malingering. He was suspicious of a prisoner who had been removed to the infirmary, suffering with a bowel complaint:

> I looked into his cell, and I saw in one part of it a quantity of flax. It led me in the evening to look into Pliny's natural history to see what the medical properties of flax were, and I found it would have that effect of producing sickness . . . he acknowledged afterwards to me that he had sucked the flax on purpose (1824 *SC*, PP, 1824, IV, 409, 22-3).

are contrasted in an interesting section of the examination of witnesses by the 1823 select committee. The chaplain was asked: '... have not the greater portion of the prisoners in the Penitentiary confided to you the whole history of their past lives?' 'Yes, one of them made a discovery to me some time ago, by which a gentleman got a great deal of property back that he had lost.' He was further asked: '... are you not the principal person to whom the prisoners apply if they have any request to make or any grievance to complain of, or anything to tell?' 'Certainly, if a prisoner thought himself under punishment he would speak to me or if he thought himself aggrieved by any officer.'[92]

In the light of this description of the chaplain's duties and the extent of his authority it might be asked what scope remained for the governor to exercise his command. He was responsible for controlling the prisoners, for staff management and the general maintenance of the organisation.[93] In contrast to this the chaplain was the director and principal instrument of penal therapy. From their very nature the tasks that lay within the governor's sphere caused considerable problems. Those that fell to the chaplain, because they were intangible and largely beyond evaluation, evidenced fewer failures and gave the committee greater cause for optimism. For political reasons the work of the governor earned scant praise and was given little public mention. Like the committee when it acted in staffing matters, the governor could not succeed — all he could do was to stave off failure. Should he root out corrupt staff or curb inmate indiscipline, his efforts could not be fully acknowledged for fear of occasioning scandal. There was, on the other hand, scarcely any way in which the chaplain could fail. Religion was tightly woven into the organisational fabric of the prison; the committee spoke of 'The great Christian objectives of the institution'.[94] The committee were quite explicit about the weight they attached to religion as a means of bringing about reformation. They were convinced, they said, 'that no discipline which is not combined with a zealous and fruitful inculcation of religious instruction, can effectively promote the

---

92 1823 *SC*, *op. cit.*, 302.
93 He rarely even came into prolonged personal contact with prisoners, but operated rather by means of written reports and orders. The turnkeys (in charge of wards) passed their reports up to the taskmasters (who had charge of pentagons), who summarised them for the governor the following morning. Orders were passed down from the governor via the taskmasters. Holford commented that 'The regular examination of the taskmasters' reports and a promptness in giving orders thereupon are the most important parts, or I should rather say, form the most important part of the governor's duty'. If the governor did not receive and act upon these reports, 'The offences of prisoners reported for misconduct shall be left unnoticed for a day or two [and] it cannot be expected that the prison should be in good order' (1823 *SC*, *op. cit.*, Appendix E, No. 8, 378-9).
94 *RCGP*, PP, 1839, XXXVIII, 403.

reformation of the criminal'.[95] The disciplinary interests of the governor were thus always likely to be sacrificed to the reformist ambitions of the chaplain.

In these circumstances reformatory efforts easily displaced purely organizational priorities. This was most significantly shown by the issue of remission, which had been recognised by the 1823 select committee as a useful disciplinary tool. Even so, the management committee, by the late 1830s, were prepared to countenance its abolition on religious grounds. The abolition, they said,

> is most important in principle as, by depriving the prisoner of all hope of obtaining his liberty before the expiration of the appointed period of his confinement, it removes temptation to hypocrisy, and tends to reduce his mind to a quiet and submissive state, and to render him more accessible to good impressions. If the moral character of a prisoner is really reformed, he ought not, by mere conformity to the rules of discipline, which in truth is no real test of reformation, to obtain any indulgence.[96]

This viewpoint minimised the elements of Southwell's behaviourism which had been incorporated in the policy and administration of the prison, and gave greater weight to the reformism of Gloucester. The clash between the two ideologies had been resolved by effectively dismissing the aims and methods of one of them.

In truth there was no room in the penitentiary for two officers, 'each supreme in his own department'. From the outset the Millbank governor's authority was eclipsed by that of the chaplain, and this adverse relationship developed during the 1830s to its logical conclusion, the abolition of the post of governor.

The Select Committee on Secondary Punishments set up in 1831 in response to public alarm at a supposed increase in crime reached two main conclusions: that crime was related both to the uncertain enforcement of the law and to inadequate secondary punishments. Even though the select committee had been favourably impressed with the disciplinary system of the penitentiary,[97] the management committee decided on a major review of their own. Their sub-committee reported that 'The prosperity and well-being of the establishment must depend

---

95 *RCGP*, PP, 1835, XLV, 221.
96 *RCGP*, PP, 1837-8, XLII, 311. Remission of sentence was abolished by 7 Will. IV, c.13.
97 'As a place of punishment it [Millbank] possesses one great advantage over any other in the country – in being generally dreaded for the strictness of the discipline and the irksomeness of the confinement.' 'Nothing can exceed the order and cleanliness which characterises every department' (*Select Committee on the Best Mode of Giving Efficacy to Secondary Punishments*, PP, 1831-2, VII, 10).

upon effecting a more strict seclusion of the prisoners, one from another'.[98] This led them to a number of recommendations, including the abolition of the second class and the replacement of the partner system by silent, single-file exercise. To make the more rigorous separation acceptable they called for shorter sentences and for more educational classes.[99] Within a few years, and under the influence of the newly appointed inspectors, William Crawford and Whitworth Russell (the latter being promoted directly from the Millbank chaplaincy), the committee in 1836 went on to seek an even more complete form of separation: the cells were altered, 'with a view to the introduction of a system of complete separation of prisoners from each other', which was to 'render the punishment of prisoners more certain and severe'.[100] The following year remission was abolished, as were the prisoners' shares in the profit of their labour, and the discharge gratuity besides. Inmates were no longer allowed to hold positions of trust within the prison.[101] The removal of these disciplinary incentives resulted in an increase in charges of misconduct against prisoners, but the committee showed how far it had moved in the direction of reformist priorities by the bland observation that the increase was due to the 'removal of those indulgences which had a natural tendency to produce insincere and temporizing conformity'.[102] They were no longer interested in mere compliance.

In April 1837, in the midst of these far-reaching changes, Captain Chapman tendered his resignation. 'The changes that have taken place,' he wrote,

> those about to be introduced by the new Bill, his advanced age
> and indifferent health, induced him to consider it due to the
> public service to retire, for the purpose of enabling the
> Committee to supply his place by the appointment of an officer
> who might begin the new system at its commencement.[103]

The meeting which received Chapman's resignation proposed that the chaplain, the Rev. Daniel Nihill, who had suggested many of the changes in discipline, should succeed Chapman and hold the combined

---

98 *Cit.* Griffiths, *op. cit.* (1875), p. 180.
99 *RCGP*, PP, 1833, XXVIII, 659. By 1835 each prisoner was given six hours' instruction per week in classes.
100 *RCGP*, PP, 1837, XLVI, 305.
101 All these changes were introduced by 7 Will. IV, c.13, which was enacted largely as a result of the recommendations of William Crawford and Whitworth Russell.
102 *RCGP*, PP, 1837-8, XLII, 311.
103 The committee thanked Chapman for the 'unwearied assiduity, zeal and ability' with which he had carried out his duties, and recommended him 'for the most liberal and favourable consideration of the Secretary of State on account of his long and faithful services' (Griffiths, *op. cit.* (1875), I, p. 201).

office of chaplain and governor.

Even in an institution as novel as Millbank amalgamation of the offices of governor and chaplain was thought to be sufficiently radical to require the endorsement of the home secretary, then Lord John Russell.[104] He initially approved the move, but then had second thoughts and called for further justification from the committee. Their reply brought into the open many of the organisational difficulties that had dogged the penitentiary over the years. They argued that they had found it unsuitable to have

> two officers, each supreme in his own department; the governor as the head of the penal, the chaplain of the religious part of the system. In a penitentiary these two parts are so intimately blended that jars and jealousies between the governor and the chaplain are inevitable when the authority is thus divided. The governor, being responsible for the maintenance of the discipline of the establishment and having the sole direction and control of the inferior officers, is naturally satisfied with their conduct provided they maintain the discipline; whereas the chaplain, if a conscientious man, is anxious that together with the maintenance of discipline, the great reformative purposes of the institution should be promoted, or at the least, not counteracted by the inferior officers. The Rev. W. Russell, late chaplain, in his evidence before Parliament, complained that his ministerial labours were often thwarted by the indifference to religion which was too generally manifested on the part of the inferior officers, and the present chaplain concurs in the same complaint. . . . The supreme authority over every part of the Penitentiary system being now exercised by the same individual he [i.e. the chaplain] will be enabled to select and superintend the inferior officers, both with a view to the maintenance of discipline and also to the promotion of the moral and religious objects of the institution. This will put an end to the collision which has so frequently occurred between the rival departments.[105]

The home secretary, not without misgivings, then confirmed Nihill's appointment, making it clear to the committee that

> this arrangement may be considered only as an experiment, it appearing to him that the strict enforcement of discipline in a

104 The only other example which I have noted of joint office-holding is given by Eric Stockdale in his interesting history of Bedford prisons: in February 1849 when the governor absconded from the prison, the chaplain, George Maclear, acted as governor for about three months until a new governor was appointed (*A Study of Bedford Prison, 1660-1877*, pp. 187-8).
105 *Cit.* Griffiths, *op. cit.* (1875), I, p. 203. The committee added that Nihill had been suggested for appointment because he was personally fitted for the combined post.

165

prison is a duty hardly to be reconciled with the consoling and charitable offices of a minister of religion, and that the governor and chaplain must lose by a combination of the two characters.[106]

Immediately on taking up his enlarged appointment Nihill issued a circular to all staff outlining the manner in which he intended to run the prison:

> The reformation of persons who have engaged in criminal acts and habits is the most difficult work in the world. God alone, who rules the heart can accomplish it, but God requires means to be used by man, and amongst the means used here, none are more important than the treatment of prisoners by the officers in charge of them.[107]

Thereafter those subordinate members of staff who offended against certain religious standards were dismissed. Nihill's approach, whilst supposedly removing the temptation to hypocrisy on the part of inmates, virtually forced it upon the officers. They either behaved in an appropriately religious manner, or ran the risk of being charged by colleagues and the prisoners with impropriety, and possibly losing their positions entirely. Griffiths claims that the new policy totally undermined the discipline of the establishment. Inevitably and understandably some of the staff took to scriptural language and went about ostentatiously carrying large Bibles. They became known to the inmates as 'Pantilers'.[108] And, of course, prisoners reacted similarly:

> As the most successful simulator of holiness became the most favoured prisoner, sanctified looks were, as a matter of course, the order of the day, and the most desperate convicts in the prison found it advantageous to complete their criminal character by the addition of hypocrisy.[109]

Theoretical distinctions were far more easily detected than were the practical differences between a truly reformatory demeanour and mere compliance.[110]

---

106 *Ibid*., p. 205.
107 *Ibid*., p. 211.
108 *Ibid*., p. 208 *et seq*.
109 Mayhew and Binny, *op. cit*., p. 236.
110 A rather obvious point which had been made a decade before by John Orridge, the experienced and widely known gaoler at Bury St Edmunds. He was asked: 'Have you known prisoners ever pretend to be reformed who in fact were not?' 'Oh! yes; hypocrisy goes to a great extent in prisons. I am sorry to say there are many whom I have never known properly till I had no power over them.' 'Do you find that the worst are generally the best behaved?' 'Yes, a complete scoundrel conceals himself; I had thought that after 30 years I had a knowledge of criminal character, but I believe I shall die a novice at last.' (*Select Committee on Criminal Commitments and Convictions*, PP, 1826-7, V, 50.)

In the first years of the new administration the committee seemed confident and well satisfied. Nihill was in many respects a competent and innovative administrator.[111] In 1840 the committee commended his work and reported that there had been 'A diminution in those temptations, which not only give rise to frequent breaches of discipline, but indispose the mind to the reception of serious and salutary impressions'.[112] But then, very rapidly, things began to go wrong, and the tone of the committee's report changed dramatically.

> Great alterations have been made in the discipline of the Institution. In consequence of a distressing increase in the number of insane prisoners, the Committee . . . came to the resolution that it would be unsafe to continue a strict system of separation for the long periods to which the ordinary sentences of prisoners in the Penitentiary extend.[113]

Accordingly, prisoners were permitted a form of association after their first three months' confinement. This privilege could be suspended for misbehaviour and was, in any case, subject to a classification system to 'render the indulgence as little injurious as possible, on a moral point of view'. Voicing their great disappointment at the change that had been forced upon them, the committee said that they were

> inclined to believe that no scheme of discipline in which intercourse between prisoners, however modified, forms an essential part is ever likely to be made instrumental, either to the prevention of crime, or to the personal reformation of convicts, in the same degree as a system of separation.[114]

The changed discipline appeared to them to have accomplished its object, namely a reduction in cases of insanity,[115] but Nihill made very

---

111 He introduced the system of morning reports and adjudications in place of the previous on-the-spot justice, and established the rule that tools should be left outside the cells at night, as a measure to counter escape attempts. It was also Nihill who set up the system of fining officers for lapses in punctuality, or failure to adhere to the rules (Griffiths, *op. cit.* (1875), I, pp. 221-2).

112 *RCGP*, PP, 1840, XXXVIII, 679.

113 *RCGP*, PP, 1842, XXXII, 623, 1.

114 *Ibid*.

115 *RCGP*, PP, 1842, XXXII, 623. Nine prisoners had to be removed from the prison during the year covered by the report because of insanity. It is probable that the actual incidence of insanity was greater, but that the symptoms had to be very pronounced before medical action was taken by the authorities. Playfair's comment seems plausible: 'Daniel Nihill was inclined to equate manifestations of mental derangement with deliberate "sauciness" or, rather, to regard all such manifestations as *prima facie* feigned and therefore curable by disciplinary action' (Playfair, *op. cit.*, p. 39).

obvious his sense of frustration: 'What I object to is a nominal separation accompanied with secret fraudulent communication. Health is certainly a consideration, but are morals less?' This outlook showed astonishing single-mindedness and political naïvety and it is hardly surprising that he was unable to persuade the committee to maintain the new régime.[116]

Evidence suggests that growing dissatisfaction with the disciplinary system of the penitentiary, as well as public criticism of the rate of recidivism and insanity, combined with certain other matters at this time to demoralise the committee.[117] Committee membership and attendance significantly declined[118] and it is clear that the penitentiary's ambitious reformatory objectives (what Nihill had called 'the most difficult work in the world') were overhung with ominous and growing clouds of failure. Under the influence of his Home District prison inspectors, Whitworth Russell and William Crawford, Sir James Graham, the home secretary, had decided to transfer the reformatory endeavour elsewhere. A juvenile penitentiary had been established at Parkhurst and, in the last few days of 1842, Pentonville Model Prison was opened as the keystone of a reformed system of transportation. On 5 May 1843 the home secretary introduced a bill to terminate the use of Millbank as a penitentiary;[119] henceforth the prison was to be used as a convict assembly depot. During a confinement of up to nine months the Millbank inmates would be assessed; the juveniles would be sent to Parkhurst, the more promising adults to Pentonville, and the rest to the hulks. Of the prisoners remaining at Millbank most would be transported, but some would gain conditional pardons and others would serve out their sentences there. Nihill refused to hold office in the convict depot (in effect a government gaol), and informed the committee that 'he should deem it wholly incompatible with his character as a clergyman to consent to hold the office of governor under the new system'.[120] On 16 June 1843 the penitentiary committee met for the last time. They thanked Nihill

---

116 Griffiths, *op. cit.* (1875), I, p. 302. See also *Returns of the Number of Prisoners Sent to the Penitentiary in Each of the Last Five Years – of Prisoners Removed on the ground of Insanity, etc.*, PP, 1841, XVII, 655.
117 See, for example, p. 139, n. 17.
118 *Penitentiary (Milbank) Return to an address of the Honourable The House of Commons etc.*, PP, 1840, XXXVIII, 689.
119 This became 6 & 7 Vict., c.26: 'An Act for Regulating the Prison at Millbank'.
120 *Cit.* Griffiths, *op. cit.* (1875), I, pp. 308-9. Nihill eventually repented of his decision, however, and within a few years was trying to obtain another appointment at Millbank. On 6 February 1847, he wrote to Jebb, the surveyor-general of prisons, pointing out that he had been unable to obtain a suitable living:

Seeing that Lords Chichester and Seymour have recommended Govt. to put Millbank Prison under *paid* Superintending Commissioners, instead of

governor and chaplain, for the zeal, ability and humanity with which he had discharged his onerous duties, and especially for the earnestness with which he had uniformly endeavoured to render the administration of the discipline subservient to the great moral and religious ends of the Penitentiary.[121]

With thanks to the other senior and subordinate officers, the business of the committee ended, as did the short-lived penitentiary establishment at Millbank.[122]

---

the Inspectors, I wrote to Sir George [Grey, the home secretary] to request he would appoint me to one of the new offices, referring to my qualifications from my experience and the familiarity I have acquired with both the principles and details of Prison discipline. . . .

Now, my dear Sir, you may very possibly have it in your power to put a spoke in my wheel in some way that I cannot suggest, but which will easily occur to you in your conferences with the Home Office. Our friendly intercourse when we were together in the Military Prisons Commission, and indeed at all times inspires me with a very strong hope you will kindly do so.

You will oblige me by considering this communication as most confidential and not mentioning it to any one connected with Millbank Prison. . . . (Jebb Papers, box 3).

Nihill was unsuccessful in his request and was not again appointed to government service.

---

121 *Cit.* Griffiths, *op. cit.* (1875), I, p. 310.
122 *The Times* (4 July 1843, 7c) made little of the event. It simply noted the new name and that the prison was henceforth to be headed by inspectors, and drew special attention to the restriction on visitors and to the revival of a discharge allowance. It also referred to a provision of the Act that no prisoner was to work more than twelve hours a day, unless the prisoner himself requested an extension of work to accumulate funds for discharge.

7 Central government prisons, 1835-50

The inspectorate

By the mid-1830s the Whig reforms had significantly redefined the relationship between central and local government, and enforcement of more uniform standards of prison administration had become a political and practical possibility. In these favourable circumstances the recommendations of the 1835 Select Committee on Gaols speedily produced new legislation, namely 5 and 6 Will. IV, c.38, 'An Act for effecting great Uniformity of Practice in the Government of the Several Prisons in *England* and *Wales*; and for appointing Inspectors of Prisons in *Great Britain*'. The Whig government thus applied to prisons its two leading assumptions – 'the value of uniformity of administration throughout the country and the impossibility of attaining this uniformity without a large increase in the activity of the central government'.[1]

The novelty and effectiveness of this legislation lay chiefly in the appointment of inspectors. They were given no executive powers, nor were any other executive powers increased;[2] yet by the act of inspection and by public and private exhortation the inspectorate became a potent instrument for changing the local administration of prisons. The appointment of inspectors also added another section to central government's prison establishment.

From an early stage it was recognised that the inspectors would need to be men possessed of uncommon qualities:

> They must be a high Class of Persons; the Selection of an efficient Person to perform a most important Duty, in which Discretion, Judgement and Knowledge of Law are required, would be a difficult thing and, no Doubt, great Consideration would be necessary in

1 S. and B. Webb, *English Prisons Under Local Government*, p. 110.
2 See n. 114, p. 254, below.

selecting a proper Man; I should say that they should be men of the same Class as the Factory Commissioners.[3]

The initial appointment was of five inspectors, each autonomous in his district and of nominally equal standing.[4] This latter aspect of the establishment was criticised at the time for perpetuating the very diversity that the inspectorate had been designed to counteract. A recent writer adopts the same argument:

> The indolent Lord Melbourne had set the pattern in 1835 by rejecting the idea of an Inspector General of Prisons because he could not abide the prison philosophy of the man most qualified for the job, William Crawford. Crawford was the protagonist of separate confinement and an inspector of prisons. Melbourne neither had the courage to dismiss Crawford nor the desire to allow him to extend separate confinement to all the prisons of England; so he appointed four equal and autonomous inspectors each with his own favorite policies.[5]

Melbourne's historical reputation may well include a name for indolence, but the criticism on this occasion is not entirely justified. Some fifteen years after the foundation of the inspectorate the Duke of Richmond recounted the circumstances of this decision to a select committee. He said that the home secretary thought that it would be injudicious to appoint a chief inspector and thus commit the inspectorate to the enforcement of one system of discipline throughout the country.[6] If weight is given to the fact that the separate system was, in the rigorous form envisaged by Crawford, untried in England and that, in any case, a very careful approach to magistrates was essential for the new inspectorate, Melbourne's decision seems to spring from common sense rather than from indolence. Moreover, he may have been comforted by the knowledge that, although no formal hierarchy was established among the inspectors, there was from the outset, on the part of government and their own colleagues, a *de facto* recognition of the primacy of the two Home District inspectors,[7] namely until 1847

---

3 *Select Committee of the House of Lords on Gaols and Houses of Correction*, PP, 1835, XI, 252.
4 The Act stipulated a maximum of five appointments for Great Britain.
5 David Roberts, *Victorian Origins of the Welfare State*, pp. 123-4. Roberts is inaccurate on two matters of fact: there were four districts, but five inspectors (two being appointed to the Home District), and Crawford was not an inspector prior to the appointment of his four colleagues. He had previously reported (in 1834) on US penitentiaries for the British Government, but all five inspectors were appointed and took up their posts at about the same time.
6 *Select Committee on Prison Discipline*, PP, 1850, XVII, question 958, 68.
7 They were paid higher salaries, carried out special inquiries, and prepared and presented the national prison statistics. There even arose the practice of

171

William Crawford and the Rev. Whitworth Russell.

William Crawford had wide experience of the problems of penal policy and administration. Before he had been commissioned by the government to report on the United States penitentiaries,[8] he had been joint secretary (with Peter Bedford) of the Committee for Investigating the Causes of the Alarming Increase of Juvenile Delinquency in the Metropolis and later was a foundation member and a secretary of the Society for the Improvement of Prison Discipline.[9] The Rev. Whitworth Russell was chaplain of Millbank Penitentiary when his uncle, Lord John Russell, in April 1835 became home secretary and leader of the House of Commons in Lord Melbourne's government. Lord John Russell promptly appointed his relative to the Home District inspectorate.[10] Both men were separate system zealots — Crawford from long investigation and consideration, confirmed by his assessment

---

promoting inspectors from other (supposedly equal) districts to the Home District. On the presentation of statistics see, for example, the *Tenth Report of the Inspectors of Prisons (Home District)*, PP, 1845, XXIII, 1; *Eleventh Report of the Inspectors of Prisons (Home District)*, PP, 1846, XXI, 1, and the *Fourteenth Report of the Inspectors of Prisons (Home District)*, PP, 1850, XXVIII, i.

For details of the salaries of the inspectors see the various estimates: *Estimates to Defray Salaries and Expenses of Inspectors of Prisons*, PP, 1836, XXXVIII, 387; PP, 1837, XL, 336; PP, 1843, XXXI, 424; PP, 1850, XXXIV, 356. The salary differential between the Home and other districts remained the same during these fifteen years: Home District £800, other districts £600. The inspectors received travelling expenses, at an average of £300 each.

The inquiry conducted in 1843 by Whitworth Russell into a complaint about the governor of Carnarvon gaol illustrates the national duty of the Home District inspectors. It was undertaken on the instructions of Sir James Graham, then home secretary, over the head of the inspector appointed for that district. See *Report and Evidence on the Inquiry into the Conduct of the Governor of the County Gaol of Carnarvon*, PP, 1843, XLIII, 261.

William John Williams, previously inspector for the Northern and Eastern Districts, was appointed to the Home District on the death of Crawford and Whitworth Russell. His first report in his new capacity makes it clear that he considered the appointment as a promotion. (See *Twelfth Report of the Inspectors of Prisons (Home District)*, PP, 1847-8, XXXIV, 373.)

---

8 His report was published as *Report on the Penitentiaries of the United States*, PP, 1834, XLVI, 349.

9 Gordon Rose, *The Struggle for Penal Reform*, pp. 21-2. Crawford (1788-1847) was the son of a well-to-do wine merchant.

10 Lord John Russell, it was said, 'was reproached with showing undue favour to members of his own party and family, yet he was never convicted of exercising his patronage to the detriment of the public welfare, and, while remembering his relatives, he did not neglect his friends' (*Dictionary of National Biography*, XVII, p. 463).

Whitworth Russell was the son of Sir Henry Russell, Chief Justice of Bengal, and his mother was the daughter of Sir Charles Whitworth.

of the North American penitentiaries,[11] Russell because of his experience as Millbank chaplain. The impressions that they created when carrying out their duties differed considerably. Clay recalled Crawford as 'one of the earliest founders of the Prison Discipline Society ... for many years he and Mr. Samuel Hoare, the Chairman of the Committee, had been about the least vocal and most practical among its members'.[12] George Chesterton, who differed from Crawford over prison discipline, could yet describe him as 'an honest advocate', but found Russell, on the other hand, although possessed of 'very considerable abilities',

> dogmatical and arbitrary to the last degree. He was singularly indifferent to the feelings of others, and some of his discourteous exhibitions in the metropolis — and at least one provincial gaol, in particular — would shock the minds of all those who deem it the duty of a clergyman to be mild and courteous, at least.[13]

Chesterton was governor of Cold Bath Fields house of correction which, by the 1830s, had the largest prison population in the kingdom. Crawford and Russell were anxious to win his support for the separate system, and paid him several visits:

> Nothing could exceed their courtesy up to a certain point; but so soon as they discovered that I was inexorable, and was not to be moved by their reasoning and eloquence, a total change marked their demeanor towards me and the personal rudeness of Mr. Whitworth Russell became unworthily insulting and was enough to evoke keen resentment.[14]

Chesterton's impression of Russell — somewhat arrogant and overbearing scion of a powerful family — is supported to a considerable extent by the tone of the numerous and lengthy contributions that Russell made to various committees of inquiry. There is some evidence, moreover, that Russell was the dominant partner in the working relationship between the two inspectors.[15]

---

11 Crawford's favourable report on the Philadelphia penitentiary was to be expected, as there were close links between the Philadelphia prison reformers and the Society for the Improvement of Prison Discipline.

12 Rev. Walter Lowe Clay, *The Prison Chaplain: A Memoir of the Rev. John Clay, B.D.*, p. 169.

13 George Laval Chesterton, *Revelations of Prison Life; with an Enquiry into Prison Discipline and Secondary Punishments*, I, pp. 316-17.

14 *Ibid.*, I, pp. 316-18, *passim.*

15 This is partly a personal impression from the tone of the two men's various writings, contributions to committees, etc. It is perhaps significant that (according to Chesterton) Russell was the author of the crucial *Third Report of the Inspectors of Prisons (Home District)*, even though the document was supposedly of joint authorship.

The main task of the inspectors[16] was to influence the development of local prison administration and management, and to ensure that the various requirements of prison legislation were being met. To do this effectively they had to establish candour in their working relations with the magistrates and keepers. Much time was also spent drafting their reports for publication. This essential task was in itself enormous, entailing detailed inspection of many prisons for the first time since James Neild and Thomas Buxton. The inspectorate was conscientious, as the several thousands of pages of reports and commentaries in the Parliamentary Papers indicate. From the very first report of Crawford and Russell it is also clear that their inspections were far from perfunctory: both showed that they were well acquainted with their milieu; they were persistent, sceptical and meticulous in their methods and displayed self-confidence and shrewdness in their dealings with the sometimes devious explanations, protestations and rationalisations of magistrates, staff and prisoners alike. This high quality of reporting compared favourably with that of the most effective and perceptive of parliamentary inquiries.[17]

The physical conditions of work of the early inspectors were arduous and demanding. They commenced their duties before the rail network had been established, and travelled on horseback, by coach and by ship. Frederic Hill, when inspector for Scotland, took almost seven months to cover his district, which extended from the Borders to Shetland and the Orkney Islands. Even so, at a later point the home secretary thought that he could cope with more work and added Northumberland and Durham to his district!

Had their duties been restricted to the inspection of prisons, the task of the inspectorate would have been sufficiently daunting. But as central government expanded its convict establishment the inspectors, particularly those for the Home District, were required to undertake quite intricate preliminary planning and then administrative duties for the prisons at Parkhurst (from 1838), Pentonville (from 1842) and

---

16 See for greater detail Chapter 8, below.
17 Bisset Hawkins, inspector for the Southern and Western District, was not so efficient. His first report gave promise of extraordinary complacency:

> In all the County Gaols which I entered a remarkable degree of cleanliness and neatness has reigned throughout, equalling that which is usually maintained among the middle-classes in England, and largely surpassing the standard which generally prevails in the most splendid residences of Continental Europe (*First Report of the Inspectors of Prisons (Southern and Western District)*, PP, 1836, XXXV, 269).

> To be fair, he did make a few mild comments about the poor state of diet in some prisons. His career as an inspector was, however, relatively short and he submitted his last report in 1842. The other inspectors seemed to work as effectively as those for the Home District.

Millbank (from 1843). At the last-named, for example, it was ordered that the responsible inspectors should

> personally inspect every prisoner, examine the documents transmitted with him, and inquire into all the particulars of his previous life and character. The great number of convicts who in the course of the year pass through this prison, amounting in the last year to 3,928, renders this investigation a task of onerous performance, as well as of heavy responsibility.[18]

In 1843 Crawford and Russell listed their extensive tasks:

> Our official duties, arising from the establishment of Pentonville Prison — The preparation of the Official Code of Rules — the reorganization of the Queen's Prison, and the Prison at Millbank — and the frequent occasions on which we have had to report on various documents connected with the Prison Discipline of this Country and our Colonies.[19]

Frederic Hill was similarly burdened with business in the administration of the newly centralised Scottish prisons.[20]

Despite the original intention that the inspectorate should be permitted a fairly liberal rein in decisions on penal ideology and administration, by the early 1840s central government had given substantial support to the separate system and encouraged its adoption by the local authorities. Enabling legislation was brought in and much favourable emphasis was placed on the effectiveness of the new Model Prison at Pentonville.[21] Crawford and Russell's colleagues were not so enthusiastic or clear about the desirability of the separate system. Williams scarcely concealed his opposition to it; he claimed with approval that in his district the silent system had been widely adopted: 'I have found this treatment of prisoners, when rigidly maintained, to

---

18 *Royal Commission on the Management of Millbank Prison*, PP, 1847, XXX, 13.

19 *Eighth Report of the Inspectors of Prisons (Home District)*, PP, 1843, XXV, and XXVI, 31, III.

20 Over the years the establishment of inspectors was reduced and it is likely that many of the duties and the pace of work of the early period became unnecessary as the regulative effects of inspection made themselves felt. A similar process occurred in the Poor Law Commission. But in the prisons' inspectorate the burden of work remained formidable for some years, and government finely related the easing of demands to the process of reducing the number of inspectors. As late as 1850 the inspectors still referred to the heavy volume of work as a reason for failing completely to execute all their duties. (See, for instance, the *Fourteenth Report of the Inspectors of Prisons (Home District)*, PP, 1850, XXVIII, 1.)

21 The legislation was 2 and 3 Vict., c.56, 'An Act for the Better ordering of Prisons'. This set out certain minimum standards and conditions for the enforcement of separate confinement.

be so irksome as to induce a deterring influence, and so sufficiently exclusive to prevent mutual corruption.'[22] In the same year (1842) Frederic Hill, whilst giving his general support to the separate system, called none the less for its excesses to be avoided.[23]

But from the sixth report (1841) there was a noticeable muting of criticisms of the separate system. With the establishment of Pentonville the government's prestige was firmly committed, and whereas Crawford and Russell were quite cock-a-hoop,[24] Williams was apologetic in his disagreement:

> I deferentially abstain from adverting to or reurging former opinions, however strengthened by maturer experience, which may provoke discussion upon the subject of the separate or seclusive system of prison discipline; but I feel it incumbent on me to recommend most strongly that its danger and inapplicability as a penal infliction for juvenile offenders should be impressed generally on the justices.[25]

That tone of forced and uneasy acquiescence probably reflected the attitude of the majority of the inspectors, which persisted until developments at Pentonville and the death one after the other, in 1847, of Crawford and Russell removed the strongest and most uncompromising influences in favour of the separate system acting upon the Home Office.

22 *Seventh Report of the Inspectors of Prisons (Northern and Eastern District)*, PP, 1842, XXI, 1, iv. He complained that the magistrates in his district were reluctant to effect any alterations because they believed that the home secretary would approve only those which served to introduce the separate system. In an attempt to persuade them that this was not the case he referred them to the relevant section (s.56) of 2 and 3 Vict., c.56 – 'which enacts that it shall not be lawful to disapprove of plans for the re-building, enlarging, or altering of prisons on the sole ground that such plan does not allow the separate confinement of prisoners' (*ibid*., p. iii).

23 'I am of the opinion that there are some cases in which it cannot be judiciously applied; and that there are others in which it is desirable to modify it.' He would not have applied it to prisoners serving life-sentences, or to young offenders, and wished in all cases (presumably by a progressive-stage system) to combine it with a period of association. (*Seventh Report of the Inspectors of Prisons (Scotland, Northumberland and Durham)*, PP, 1842, XXI, 369.) Bisset Hawkins was also cautious about the possible harm of overdoing the separate system.

24 They referred to their direct interest in the success of Pentonville, stating that they were 'Deeply interested in, and responsible for its results; and as this prison is situated in our district, it is our duty, and our intention to give from time to time . . . a full account of its discipline and management' (*Seventh Report of the Inspectors of Prisons (Home District)*, PP. 1842, XX, 1, iv).

25 *Eighth Report of the Inspectors of Prisons (Northern and Eastern District)*, PP, 1843, XXV and XXVI, 249, vi.

The surveyor-general

Once government had embarked, at the end of the 1830s, on the modification of Millbank cells, the conversion of Parkhurst and the construction of a model separate system prison, it was decided to provide the Home Office with the services of a scientific and technically skilled adviser on a regular and permanent basis. Captain Joshua Jebb, RE, at that time an engineer officer stationed at Birmingham, was selected to fill this post, and took up his duties on 20 September 1839.[26]

Jebb, a graduate of the Royal Military Academy at Woolwich, was particularly well qualified for this task. He had previously given assistance to Crawford and Russell in matters affecting prison construction.[27] Although he had not come to prison administration until his middle years, his background in the Royal Engineers had made him familiar with the business of large-scale public works and the recruitment, management and discipline of men. Indeed these qualities had made the sappers a prop of civil administration throughout the nineteenth century.[28]

Even before taking up his appointment Jebb had been given a glimpse of prison administration, becoming, in May 1839, a visitor at Parkhurst Juvenile Prison, the conversion of which from a military hospital he had at one time supervised. Within a few years he was promoted to act (December 1842) as a commissioner of Pentonville prison and in 1844 became the first holder of the newly created post of Inspector-General of Military Prisons.[29] In this capacity Jebb had responsibility for the construction of military prisons and for the drafting and administration of their system of discipline. In 1844 the importance of Jebb's services to the Home Office was recognised by his

---

26 Whitworth Porter, *History of the Corps of Royal Engineers*, II, p. 352.
27 Julius Carlebach, 'Major-General Sir Joshua Jebb, K.C.B., 1793-1863', *Prison Service Journal* (April 1965), IV, no. 15, p. 26. Jebb was first mentioned in their *Third Report* (1837-8).
28 This specialised and somewhat elite military body has an 'unbroken record of permanent service to the Crown going back to the military engineers of Norman times, hand-picked by the Monarch for their professional knowledge and holding their appointments by Royal Patent' (Derek Boyd, *The Royal Engineers*, p. xxii).
29 This post had been created on the recommendation of a Royal Commission headed by Earl Cathcart and comprising Colonel Grant, Colonel Goodwin, Jebb and Nihill.

Evidence was brought before the Commission showing that the local authorities objected greatly to the reception of military offenders in their civil gaols. They found them a very turbulent and unmanageable class, occupying space which was much wanted for their own criminals (Porter, *op. cit.*, II, p. 353).

appointment to the specially created office of Surveyor-General.[30]

Jebb's extremely varied civilian duties put him in the way of exercising some authority in the administration of the government prisons, as well as responsibility for the supervision of conversions and the construction of new buildings.[31] He was frequently consulted by the local authorities on matters of prison design and construction, keeping up a brisk correspondence with them and travelling to all parts of the country in the course of such undertakings.[32] He was regularly called upon to advise the Home Office on various matters of policy and had frequent meetings with the home secretary.[33] In common with Russell and Crawford, Jebb was credited by many of the county magistrates with having wider Home Office responsibilities than he had and, consequently, was sent correspondence about administrative matters and criminal justice in general, such as alleged wrongful conviction and commutations of sentence.[34]

30 This new post was authorised by 7 and 8 Vict., c.50.
31 Carlebach lists his works between 1842 and 1857 as the conversions at Dartmoor, Millbank, Brixton and Newgate, and new prisons at Portland, Portsmouth, Chatham, Holloway, Wandsworth, Clerkenwell and Woking. In addition he was responsible for various public works, such as the breakwater and fortifications at Portland and the extension of Chatham dockyard.
32 See box 3 of the Jebb Papers. His correspondents on local prison matters included the Earl of Yarborough, Lord Wharncliffe, Viscount Melville, the Duke of Northumberland, the Earl of Shaftesbury, the Earl of Spencer, the Marquess of Devonshire, the Earl of Devon, and, on wider interests, the Duke of Richmond and the Earl of Chichester. In 1854 Jebb became the brother-in-law of Lord Chichester, by taking as his second wife Lady Amelia Rose Pelham, Chichester's sister. Chichester (1804-86) was Lord Lieutenant of Sussex from 1860 until his death, and chairman of East Sussex quarter sessions continuously from the age of thirty-one. He exerted a significant influence on national penal policy through his membership of the 1835 Select Committee on Gaols. He also gave evidence to the 1850 Select Committee on Prison Discipline. The relationship between the two men seems to have been close and cordial, whereby Jebb's position was greatly strengthened.
33 See the numerous letters referring to these meetings in box 3 of his papers. Even before his appointment as surveyor-general he was consulted about parliamentary problems affecting the prisons: on 28 February and 1 March 1842, for example, Lord Shaftesbury twice wrote to him about a motion which was about to be discussed in the House of Commons.
34 See, for instance, a letter from Lord Morpeth (14 May 1844) stating that he had reason to believe that two men recently convicted at York assizes and sentenced to fifteen years' transportation were innocent of the crime with which they had been charged. Morpeth appealed to Jebb, 'if it is not too late as I greatly fear, to take whatever steps may be in your power to stop [their] sailing . . .'. He went on to say that he thought Jebb 'would be better able than any other person to make out whatever there is known respecting the acknowledgement made by the Prisoner Johnson, as it would materially confirm the rest of the evidence we have collected on this case' (Jebb Papers, box 3). Another example is the letter from Lord Chichester (11 October

In contrast to Crawford and Russell, Jebb was no ideologue. Carlebach (doubtless with intentional paradox) describes him as being a believer in 'absolute pragmatism'; 'whatever is found to be practically right is not theoretically wrong. That was his dogma and his creed'.[35] His approach to penal policy was broader than that of the two Home District inspectors; he 'always maintained that the problem of juvenile delinquency could not be divorced from the larger issues of child education and welfare in an industrial society'[36] and therefore emphasised prevention of crime and differential treatment according to age:

> an older criminal knows the consequences of crime, and may deserve it; but, looking to the lamentable ignorance of criminal children, their neglected state, the circumstances in which they are generally placed and even the instruction they may have had in vice from abandoned parents, it is not just to hold them so severely and personally responsible for the acts they commit.[37]

This outlook, of course, enabled him to advocate a more uniformly deterrent policy as appropriate to the older offender whilst favouring what today would be called the 'short, sharp shock' as punishment for the first and second offences of juveniles. More hardened young offenders should spend some years at Parkhurst, followed by industrial school and arranged employment. Generally he agreed that reformation and deterrence were the objectives of imprisonment, but insisted that

> the only difficulty that occurs in the consideration of the subject is the due proportion in which these two elements should be administered. I think that for short periods of imprisonment you should look more to the deterring influence of the punishment, and that the object of reforming prisoners arises when they are in

---

1849) regarding a convict at Portland, 'who if Sir George Grey [then home secretary] ever commutes sentence of this class, I think might be most fairly considered as a proper subject for this kind of mercy. I merely mean that he should not be transported'. Chichester detailed the various extenuating factors and concluded: 'If you can properly recommend the case to Sir Geo. I shall be much obliged – or if Sir Geo. requires an official letter from me – please let me know' (Jebb Papers, box 2). The inspectors acted in a similar manner, when occasion demanded. (See evidence of Whitworth Russell to the *Select Committee of the House of Lords on the Execution of the Criminal Law*, PP, 1847, VII, 78.)

35 Carlebach, *op. cit.*, p. 20. But a citation from Jebb in a contrary vein could be given. Writing of the classification system of discipline he observed: 'There can be no question as to its being wrong in theory, and if so, it will be difficult to prove it right in practice' (Jebb, *Modern Prisons: Their Construction and Ventilation*, p. 9).

36 Carlebach, *op. cit.*, p. 22.

37 *Cit.* Carlebach, *op. cit.*, p. 24.

custody for a sufficient time to give the opportunity of reforming them.[38]

Jebb's military training probably contributed to his disagreement with Crawford and Whitworth Russell. The army and the prison population were recruited from much the same group of people. In the early part of the nineteenth century 'the respectable working classes continued to regard enlistment in the army as a sign of failure in life, if not of positive disgrace'.[39] A large proportion of those who enlisted were unskilled or ill-fitted for routine work, were one step outside the law, or joined up to placate a threatening magistrate. It was a matter of pride to the army that it could refashion such recalcitrant and unpromising material.[40]

In itself, therefore, the army offered a régime that had much in common with penal discipline. But unlike the reformism of Crawford and Whitworth Russell, the army's philosophy and methods were markedly utilitarian: it did not need to produce a fundamental change in attitudes or personality; indeed, many qualities thought undesirable or antisocial in civilian life were well suited to a nomadic fighting life. Even in the treatment of military delinquents the army sought merely to produce a change of behaviour. This point was strongly emphasised by one nineteenth-century commentator: 'It is essential to bear in mind that the object of military law is not to punish moral delin-quencies, in other words, to make men virtuous and good, but to produce prompt and entire obedience.'[41] A battery of rewards and punishments had been evolved for this purpose, reinforced by effective supervision and control and some inculcation of certain social habits and beliefs. Military penal theory was strongly mixed with elements of the doctrine of maximum general deterrence[42] and this, together with

38 1850 *SC, op. cit.*, question 340, 27.

39 G.M. Trevelyan, *English Social History*, p. 502.

40 The Duke of Wellington said that the privates in his army had been drawn from the lowest ranks in society, 'the very scum of the earth', and added:

People talk of their enlisting from their fine military feeling – all stuff – no such thing. Some of our men enlist from having got bastard children – some for minor offences – many more for drink; but you can hardly conceive such a set brought together, and it is really wonderful that we should have made them the fine fellows they are (Philip Henry, 5th Earl Stanhope, *Notes of Conversations with the Duke of Wellington*, p. 18).

41 Du Cane Papers, sheet 184. See sheets 178-93 generally, for a useful and concise account of the philosophy and administration of military punishment up to about 1880.

42 This had been carried, in the previous century, to inordinate lengths:

a drummer boasted that he had received twenty-six thousand lashes in fourteen years, and his officers could testify that he had received four thousand more between February 1727 and February 1728. 'And yet',

the nature of army tasks and organisation, led to more direct punishment in place of imprisonment.[43] Coming from such a background there is some irony in the fact that Jebb the 'absolute pragmatist' should have been responsible, with the two inspectors, for the construction of reformatory Pentonville, and through that and his book *Modern Prisons: Their Construction and Ventilation* that he should so profoundly have affected the design of 'subsequently erected places of imprisonment all over the world'.[44]

The inspectorate and the surveyor-general

The great difference in their backgrounds made some clashes between Jebb and the two Home District inspectors inevitable:[45] while Jebb put practical matters first, Crawford and Russell, with their eyes on the reformist promise, bent practice to the requirements of theory. Yet

---

comments the chronicler, 'the man is healthy and well, and no ways concerned' (Hon. Sir John Fortescue, 'The Army', in A.S. Turberville (ed.), *Johnson's England*, pp. 72-3).

See also S.P. Adye, *A Treatise on Courts Martial*, pp. 231-92, *passim*, for an extensive discussion of the exemplary and deterrent elements in military punishment.

---

43 Viscount Hardinge, then secretary of war, pressed this case in a letter to Sir James Graham, home secretary, on the subject of the 1844 Report of the Commission on Military Prisons. He approved of the proposal to construct three large district prisons, largely on grounds of economy, but called for a simplification of the proposals for barracks' cells (for regimental punishments) 'by constructing some on the old principle of the Black Hole for short punishments – other more expansial [*sic*] for longer periods and different treatment'. Though he thought that the new scheme would be more successful than the existing use of civil gaols, yet he hoped

the Government will never be induced to make any concession of the power of inflicting Corporal Punishment which with an Army scattered as ours is over the globe, in small fragments, is, in the critical circumstances in which it is frequently placed, the only effective mode of maintaining discipline and constitutes the secret (combined with good faith in the Soldiers) of never having any mutinies.

Imprisonment as a substitute for corporal punishment would in various situations in our Colonies totally fail. It can only be used as an auxiliary in large Garrisons in quiet times and even then in cases of insubordination flogging is the proper remedy (Jebb Papers, box 3, letter of 15 May 1844).

44 S. and B. Webb, *op. cit.*, pp. 177-8, n. Although Jebb in *Modern Prisons* condemned the classified (ward) system of discipline, dismissed the silent system with faint praise, and recommended the separate system, his emphasis was more on prevention than reform: he was primarily concerned to prevent contamination (see pp. 7-10).

45 For a short account of the relationship between Jebb and the inspectors see Eric Stockdale, 'The Rise of Joshua Jebb, 1837-1850', *British Journal of Criminology* (1976), XVI, p. 164.

such differing outlooks and talents could be powerfully complementary, and seeming opposition be actually of mutual benefit. But when ambitions and differences of personality aggravated the underlying friction due to unlike beliefs less productive intercourse resulted.

The nature and course of the relationship was clearly presaged by the inspectors' letters of congratulation on Jebb's becoming surveyor-general. There had been an acrimonious dispute about the powers to be vested in the new office, and this was referred to by Crawford:

> My dear Jebb,
>
> Accept my cordial congratulations.
> The objection I entertained to the Claim proposed last Septem. was that it withdrew from the Inspectors the power of certifying cells. I am sure that the retention of this power is not only just in itself, but will, I trust, enable us all to work together harmoniously.[46]

Russell's congratulations were characteristically far more grudging:

> My dear Major Jebb,
>
> I trust I have too good a heart not to rejoice at your promotion, and I therefore cordially congratulate you on the appointment you have received. I should, however, be wanting in candour if I did not say I am as much opposed to the office which has been created, and to the assignment of duties, as I understood them. Whilst you feel the office essential to you as placing you in a better position to do your duties, I complain that it places us and the public in a worse. The Office, however, is now created by Law, and the Secretary of State has conferred it upon you. I therefore cheerfully fall in with your wish that we should cordially co-operate, and I sincerely hope that there will be an end to all squabbles of which I am heartily weary.[47]

These objections and reservations were not due entirely to the establishment of another senior post as such.[48] Long before the new post

---

46 Jebb Papers, box 3. Letter of 12 August 1844. The certification of cells refers to the requirement in 2 and 3 Vict., c.56, that cells to be used for separate confinement in local prisons had first to be certified as suitable by the inspectors. Retention of this power was a crucial factor in relations between the two parties. Crawford concluded his letter with a friendly enough reference to other prison business: 'Dr. Crichton who was to have gone to Western Aust. with the [Parkhurst] boys, died yesterday morning. I hope that matters went off well at Parkhurst yest.?'

47 Jebb Papers, box 3, letter of 10 August 1844.

48 From the outset Jebb was on a par with Crawford and Russell. In a letter of 30 November 1839 to S.M. Phillips, under-secretary at the Home Office, on the question of his salary Jebb wrote, 'Having hitherto been on the same

and title had been created Jebb had been able to act independently of the inspectors and, indeed, on occasion the latter had to apply to him for his recommendation for schemes which they wished to place before the home secretary.[49] The objection was based on the new division of duties, which the inspectors felt detracted from and diluted their powers, mainly in relation to the magistrates but also in respect of national penal policy. On his part, Jebb insisted that it was his prerogative, not the inspectors', to give advice to the magistrates on prison construction.[50]

That the conflicts were not directly due to, but only exacerbated by, innate incompatibility of temperament is shown by Jebb's quarrels with inspectors other than Crawford and Russell. A letter from John Perry, inspector for the Southern and Western District, well illustrates the intensity of the clash of overlapping authorities, and is worth citing in full:

My dear Major Jebb,

I now proceed to reply to your Letter of the 8th inst., which has remained so long unanswered in consequence of my absence from London.

I am glad to find that you consider my request to see and observe upon the plans of Prisons in my District to be both natural and reasonable, and that the same arrangement for that purpose will be adopted with me as with the Home Inspectors.

Let me assure you that I have no wish to interfere improperly between you and the Magistrates — I only desire the opportunity

---

footing as the Inspectors of the Home District with whom I am associated, I trust also that my claim of being continued on that footing will be admitted' (*cit.* Stockdale, *op. cit.*, p. 164).

49 As shown in the letters from Crawford and Russell to Jebb on 19 September 1839. The latter urged him to give his support to the scheme (not made clear in the letter), as

your silence . . . may be interpreted into a disinclination on your part and our interference. . . . If you concur with the principle of the application I think it very important that you should without any delay (I mean *today*) make it known by letter to Lord Normanby.

Crawford wrote in similar terms:

I cannot help feeling very nervous respecting the fate of the second letter which was sent in today, relating to the Plans, and think that unless it is backed by a corresponding one from yourself the Inspectors generally will be the parties appointed to confer with you. If you do not *strongly* object to write, I think that it would be highly desirable that you should do so; and that as soon as possible (Jebb Papers, box 3).

50 See Jebb's letter of 25 and 26 November 1844 concerning Russell's advice to the Buckinghamshire magistrates on the building of the Aylesbury county gaol.

of offering my objections and suggestions at the commencement of the works rather than after they shall have been completed, by which much expense and disappointment *might* be avoided.

I feel sure that when you call to mind the course I pursued in the case of Portsmouth Gaol, you will admit that there was little necessity for 'strongly impressing upon my mind' the importance of avoiding such interference. When I accidently [*sic*] discovered in the progress of the building that all provision for ventilation had been neglected, I did not 'interfere between you and the Magistrates', but I privately drew your attention to the omission in time to enable you to rectify it. I acted then, as I hope I always shall act, in the spirit of friendly assistance and support of a Colleague in the execution of his duty — and let me add that I should feel much disappointed if under similar circumstances, my Colleagues should not manifest the same good feelings towards me.

I must now reply to another passage in your letter in which you infer from some words in mine that I mean to impute to you ignorance or neglect of your duty, and in which you challenge me to state more explicitly the particulars of the cases in which I found the opinion that a timely inspection of the Plans would have had the effect I anticipated.

I feel much concerned that you should have received so unfavourable an impression of my meaning from my words which do not seem to me to admit of such a construction, and which are certainly not written with such an object. I have no hesitation in saying that I did not mean to impute blame to you, or any body else: — my sole object was to request that the same arrangement might be made with me as had been already made with the Home Inspectors, as I thought it likely to prevent inconveniences I had several times felt.

After this disavowal of my intention of imputing blame to you, it seems hardly necessary to go into the details of the cases I alluded to; but as you desire it, I will just state that the Prisons of Peterborough, Shepton Mallet and Hereford (City) are those I chiefly referred to — in the first two of which I was obliged to decline to certify the Cells from the want of ventilation and in the last from want of light.

I repeat that I have no desire to step out of my Province and would, on the contrary, maintain a broad line of demarcation between the duties of a Surveyor and Inspector; but as some questions of Construction involve points of discipline, I desire only the opportunity of making my objections and suggestions concerning them, which I may think necessary and useful, at the Commencement rather than at the end of the works, in order that they may be obviated without much increase of expense or trouble.[51]

Russell's dispute with Jebb over the demarcation of duties began about six months before the trouble with Perry. Russell had protested about Jebb's plans for Aylesbury gaol, claiming that the surveyor-general had overestimated the amount of accommodation required and that, had he consulted the two inspectors, the lavish space for debtors and male criminals and an unnecessary wing for females might have been avoided. Russell also objected to the unreasonable thickness of the walls between the cells, to the extent of land enclosed by the boundary wall, and to the rash expenditure of iron to line cell doors. Altogether it was claimed that several thousand pounds had been wasted. The news had been opportunely communicated to the magistrates direct by Russell who actually stopped the work of construction to do so. This serious slight to Jebb's authority left Russell quite unrepentant:

> I cannot admit for a moment your definition of our respective duties. An Inspector of Prisons is not to be precluded from giving the Magistrates of his own District any benefit which may arise from any knowledge or experience he may have, as to nature and amount of the accommodation to be provided in any Prison, because the Surveyor-General of Prison Buildings prepares and recommends his plans without any communication with such Inspector. I beg distinctly to state that I shall always feel it my duty to make known my sentiments with reference to Prison Arrangements whenever the opportunity is first legitimately offered by yourself — my opinion shall be cordially and readily expressed to you, and you shall be the channel of communication with the Justices; if it arises otherwise I shall endeavour to avail myself of it in the manner least likely to occasion collision, which is consistent with the public interests and my own duties.[52]

51 Jebb Papers, box 3, letter of 23 May 1845. There had been a letter from Crawford dealing with similar issues, about the new county gaol at Springfield, Essex, in the previous month (26 April 1845).
52 Jebb Papers, box 3, letter dated 26 November 1844. There had also been a strident protest from Russell over Jebb's failure, in the *First Report of the Surveyor-General*, properly to acknowledge the part played in the design of Pentonville by the two inspectors. He argued that the Pentonville plans should have appeared separately with joint authorship:

> The erection of a Model Prison is . . . as much ours and ours alone, as Paradise Lost is Milton's. This is sad egotism — and will disgust you perhaps to read [as] it does me to write. That 'Justice to Ireland' must not absorb all justice — Justice to Crawford and Russell also; now Russell needs some — for he has had scant measure amongst you all. I leave the whole matter confidently in your hands.

185

All the evidence points to increasingly bitter quarrels in the two years following Jebb's appointment as surveyor-general; as such conflicts inevitably promoted scandal, in July 1846 Jebb received a strong rebuke from the home secretary, Sir James Graham.[53] The letter, marked 'Private', was short and to the point:

> I have no doubt that your conduct has proceeded from the purest and best Intentions . . . but I would not fail to express my regret that angry differences should have arisen between Public Servants, when cordial co-operation is necessary for the public Good, and when quarrels, unless speedily terminated, must lead to consequences which I should regret.
>
> I had have occasion to be highly satisfied with your demeanour and with the trustworthy execution of any duty confided to you, since I have held the Seals of the Home Department.[54]

Following this warning from the home secretary the parties seem to have held their fire. In any event, the deaths of Crawford and Russell

---

Russell noted the various points in Jebb's report at which acknowledgment should be paid and reminded Jebb that in the inspector's second report — several months before Jebb's appointment — he and Crawford had published a full and careful article on improved prison construction (Jebb Papers, box 3, letter of 26 August 1844).

It is difficult to say, in this case, whether Russell's complaint was justified. Some years later the Rev. W.L. Clay was convinced that it was to Jebb that credit for Pentonville was due:

> when Messrs. Crawford and Whitworth Russell were bungling, for want of professional knowledge, over their plans for the model prison, Lord John Russell had appointed Captain Jebb, R.E., who was already well known as a very clever engineer, to help them through their difficulties. He took up their crude designs and built the Pentonville Prison, a work of which he may well be proud, considering the difficulty and the entire novelty of the task. His success in this undertaking earned for him the Surveyor-Generalship of Prisons, a new office then just created, in virtue of which he became Prison Architect-in-Chief to the whole Kingdom (*Our Convict Systems*, p. 24).

Clay was far from being a sycophantic follower of Jebb, but it is probably only fair to note that by 1862, when Clay's work was published, Jebb had held the highest position in the government prison service for some fifteen years — quite long enough persuasively to disseminate his own account of events. Robin Evans, an architectural historian, states:

> The architect, Sir Charles Barry, restricted himself to applying the stonework decoration of machicolations and pilasters to the parts visible from outside the entrance. The planning, design and details of the interior was the work of the Surveyor-General of Prisons, Joshua Jebb (thesis: 'Prison Design 1750-1842', p. 19).

---

53 It is likely that the inspectors received letters of admonition, but if such were sent they have not survived.

54 Jebb Papers, box 3, letter of 5 July 1846.

just over a year later removed two of the protagonists from the scene.

The decline of transportation

The volleys of accusation and recrimination between the inspectorate and Jebb were exchanged against a background of changing policy towards transportation which was to have far-reaching consequences for the whole system of imprisonment in England. Discontent with transportation mounted through the 1830s, and arose from doubts about its efficacy as a deterrent and from condemnation of its fiscal, political and moral effects on the colonies.

That transportation failed to meet the test of less-eligibility had been pointed out by Sydney Smith in his sardonic letter to Peel in March 1826:

Because you have committed this offence, the sentence of the court is that you shall no longer be burdened with the support of your wife and family. You shall immediately be removed from a very bad climate and a country over-burdened with people to one of the finest regions of the earth, where the demand for human labour is every hour increasing, and where it is highly probable you may ultimately regain your character and improve your future. The Court have been induced to pass this sentence upon you in consequence of the many aggravating circumstances of your case, and they hope your fate will be a warning to others.[55]

A couple of years later a witness expressed a similar opinion to a parliamentary committee in the context of a story so variously repeated thereafter that it must have been apocryphal:

I believe that, latterly, offenders have not been afraid of a sentence that leads really to transportation . . . I saw a letter from a convict in New South Wales addressed to a friend in the village where he had lived in Bedfordshire, stating that he was now the owner of a considerable estate; that he had a great stock of cattle; that he served upon grand juries, and was in every respect comfortable; that a mutual friend of theirs, who had been transported with him, was also extremely comfortably situated; but that he was only the tenant of a large farm; that neither of them had any intention of

---

55 Charles Stuart Parker (ed.), *Sir Robert Peel*, I, pp. 401, 402-3. Smith recommended the deterrent effects of the treadwheel in sentences of imprisonment ranging from one day to life. Peel replied that the number of offenders was too great for proper and effectual punishment: 'I despair of any remedy but that which I wish I could hope for — a great reduction in the amount of crime' (*ibid*., p. 402).

returning to England, but were quite happy and comfortable; and the impression produced by that letter on the minds of their former village acquaintances was, that transportation was rather a benefit and an improvement of situation than a punishment.[56]

This theme was taken up by several witnesses who gave evidence to the 1831 Select Committee on Secondary Punishments, and the committee suggested that convicts under sentence of transportation should first be punished by a spell of imprisonment in the home country.[57] The point was powerfully pressed by Archbishop Whately, who condemned transportation both on grounds of the corrupting effect that it had on the colonies and his belief in its encouragement of crime rather than its deterrence.[58] Doubts of this kind and Treasury desires to reduce the expenses led in 1837 to the setting up of a select committee under the chairmanship of Sir William Molesworth to consider the whole question.

It has been objected that the Molesworth Committee, strongly attracted by Wakefield's schemes for colonisation,[59] made recommendations which bore little relation to the evidence which it received.[60] Be that as it may, the committee's members included Lord John Russell, the home secretary, Sir George Grey, under-secretary of the Colonial

56 *Select Committee on Criminal Commitments and Convictions*, PP, 1826-7, VI, 41. The witness was the Rev. Dr Hunt. So strong indeed were the fears in legal circles that transportation had little deterring effect that some judges experimented with two-part sentences – a period of imprisonment with hard labour (which usually meant stone-breaking or the treadwheel) followed by transportation. This arrangement was brought to an end when doubts were raised about its legality (Chesterton, *op. cit.*, I, p. 215).

57 *Select Committee on Secondary Punishments*, Second Report, PP, 1831-2, VII, 559, 12.

58 Richard Whately, *Thoughts on Secondary Punishment*, p. 3, and *Substance of a Speech on Transportation Delivered in the House of Lords, May 19th 1840*.

59 Wakefield (1796-1862) argued that the development of the Australian colonies was hindered because of the ease with which labourers could obtain their own land, leading to a shortage of labour and preventing the exploitation of the colonies' abundant natural resources. He proposed that the free land grants should be discontinued, that a local tax should be raised in order to bring more free labourers into the colonies, and that immigration should be regulated carefully. In pursuit of these aims Wakefield helped to found the South Australian Association in 1834, of which Sir William Molesworth was an early member. The association almost immediately obtained an Act establishing the colony and implementing the Wakefield proposals by providing for land to be sold rather than granted and for the resultant funds to be used to aid immigration. It also forbade the introduction of convicts into the colony. Wakefield's interest in imprisonment and kindred judicial sentences was a personal one, having served a term for bigamy in 1826, an experience which he described in the pamphlet, *Facts Relating to the Punishment of Death in the Metropolis*.

60 A.G.L. Shaw, *Convicts and the Colonies*, p. 273.

Office, Lord Howick, secretary at war, Fowell Buxton and Sir Robert Peel, and its views could not be regarded but as authoritative. Indeed, even as the committee was appointed the government was deciding that the system of assigning convict labour to colonists at the place of transportation should be stopped.[61] Responding to criticisms of a lack of certainty in punishment the plan was now to assign convicts to labour in the public works for a fixed period.

The Molesworth Committee's recommendations went much further than these changes in the assignment system. In Du Cane's words, the committee 'entirely condemned the system of transportation as it had been carried on, as being unequal, without terrors to the criminal class, both corrupting to convicts and very expensive'.[62] The committee proposed that transportation to New South Wales and to the settled districts of Van Diemen's Land should cease as soon as possible and be replaced by confinement with hard labour at home or abroad for a term between two and fifteen years, and that penitentiaries should only be set up in the colonies in places where there were no free settlers. Finally, the committee, reflecting its Wakefieldian persuasions, suggested that because of their difficulties in securing employment at home, the very best behaved of the home-punished convicts might be encouraged to emigrate on their release.[63]

As one of the reasons for setting up the Molesworth Committee was to seek means of avoiding or reducing the heavy expense of transportation there was some reluctance on the part of the government to endorse too readily the resultant recommendations even though Lord John Russell, the home secretary, had been a party to them. Howick urged Russell to set trial measures in hand without delay, in particular to provide home penitentiaries for those sentenced to less than fourteen years' transportation. He suggested that 'In the meantime, as large a number as possible of such convicts should be sent to the hulks and to Bermuda'.[64] As secretary of war and a very energetic member of the government, with ministerial experience at both the Colonial and Home Offices, Howick's was a voice which could not easily be disregarded; moreover, the stream of convicts sentenced to transportation continued to run at about 4,000 a year, and decisions could not indefinitely be postponed.

Howick's memorandum was sent on 23 November 1838. On 2 January 1839 Russell made his own proposals. While endorsing the Molesworth Committee's condemnation of transportation he pointed

61 *Ibid.*, p. 268.
62 Sir Edmund F. Du Cane, *The Punishment and Prevention of Crime*, p. 139.
63 *Report from the Select Committee on Transportation*, PP, 1837-8, XXII, 1, xlvi-xlvii.
64 *Papers Relative to the Transportation and Assignment of Convicts*, PP, 1839, XXXVIII, 749.

to the variety of conflicting considerations which hitherto had gone some way towards impeding a clear evaluation of the system:

> Crime is not punished as crime. . . . The question of colonial profit and loss mixes with the award of justice. A man is estimated by his capacity as a colonist, not by his crime as a felon . . . inequality of punishment, and the good fortune of many of the convicts, destroy the dread of transportation among the worst part of our population – the habitual and hardened criminals.[65]

Russell calculated that the cost of keeping the convicts at home in silent system prisons would be some £220,000 a year and in separate system establishments probably more than £360,000, as compared with the expense of only £7 14s. 2d. per head per year for the New South Wales establishment and a profit of £13 3s. 6d. per head in Bermuda.[66] He referred to Bourke[67] and Maconochie, both of whom had stated that

> a certain period of no less certain punishment should be endured by the convict. It is in this respect that, as a penal system, transportation chiefly fails. . . . There can be no doubt that the establishment of a fixed period of punishment, under the eye of persons employed by Government, would tend more effectually than the present system to deter from crime.[68]

Russell's survey of the issues did not lead him to a complete acceptance of Howick's proposals. Instead of keeping at home those sentenced to less than fourteen years Russell proposed that, as far as practicable, convicts sentenced to seven years should be employed in dockyards at home and in Bermuda while lodged in hulks. They would spend at least two years in confinement engaged in irksome penal labour, the daily record of conduct being by the award of marks; confinement completed, the convict would enter on a period of probation in associated labour. Finally, Russell proposed the construction of a separate system penitentiary with a capacity of at least 500.[69]

---

65 *Ibid.*, 749, 2.
66 *Ibid.*, p. 5; *Papers Relative to the Transportation and Assignment of Convicts*, PP, 1839, XXXVIII, 741, II, Appendix A.
67 Sir Richard Bourke (1777-1855) was Governor of New South Wales from 1831 to 1837.
68 *Papers Relative to the Transportation and Assignment of Convicts*, PP, 1839, XXXVIII, 749, 8.
69 *Ibid.*, 9-10. Jebb was instructed to look into the practicabilities of the proposed home-based convict system, as he later recalled:

> With a view to the consideration of the means by which such a system of penitentiary discipline could be established for the great body of convicts, I received the directions of Lord John Russell . . . to report on the localities that would be best adapted for the purpose of erecting suitable prisons.

Apart from the building of the Model Penitentiary at Pentonville which was put in hand, these proposals were only partly implemented. At the end of 1839 it was decided to abandon Maconochie's experiment on Norfolk Island; and in 1840 what had been a reduced flow to New South Wales was finally stopped, leaving Van Diemen's Land as the main depository for transported convicts. Unfortunately the number sent there doubled as a consequence of a Commons decision in 1841 to transport the seven-year convicts whom Russell had proposed to keep at home, and a 'disastrous influx' was steered into a colony which, between 1838 and 1841 had received only 2,000 free migrants,[70] resulting in a near breakdown in the penal administration through overcrowding, a lack of separation and classification and inadequate supervision.[71] These difficulties were exacerbated by and at the same time contributed to the economic depression and stagnation of the colony. With revenue actually falling, the requirement that the colonists should pay for convict labour on the public works and for a large prison and a police service could not but produce much resentment and tension in relations with the home government.[72]

With Peel's accession to power in 1841 Stanley replaced Russell at the Colonial Office and in November 1842, after extensive consideration, set in hand his 'probation system' for the reorganisation of transportation. This divided sentences of transportation into five main stages of progressively easing discipline, the most severe of which was detention at Norfolk Island. This was reserved for all those transported for life and to the more aggravated cases in which sentences in excess of fifteen years had been imposed. The second stage was to be served in one of the probationary gangs, which were composed of convicts who had completed a period at Norfolk Island and those who had been transported for terms of less than life and who had bypassed Norfolk Island but were thought to merit a period of punishment of this type. The probationary gangs were to be graded, with some performing less arduous toil and having extra indulgences, so that by transferring the convicts from one gang to another 'an effective system of rewards and penalties might be established, of which the enjoyment or the terror

---

Public works were not yet in Jebb's mind for this purpose:

> I recommended generally, that if Penitentiaries were established they should be situated in manufacturing districts or the neighbourhood of London in order that there might be no difficulty in obtaining employment for the prisoners, which was an essential element in the contemplated discipline (Jebb Papers, box 12: confidential report by Major Jebb to Sir George Grey on convict discipline, 5 November 1846).

---

70 Shaw, *op. cit.*, pp. 278-9.
71 Crawford and Whitworth Russell to Sir George Grey, 12 December 1846 (PRO HO 45/OS. 1393).
72 Shaw, *op. cit.*, pp. 299-307, *passim*.

would be immediate'.[73] Having completed his period of assignment in a probation gang, and provided he obtained a certificate of general good conduct, the convict next became the holder of a probationary pass; this authorised him to engage in private paid service. This stage was also sub-divided into three classes, during the first of which the convict needed government approval before entering into employment, and was paid only half his wages directly, the balance being placed in a savings bank. In the second class no prior authority was required to enter into employment, and two-thirds of wages were paid immediately; members of the third class could keep all of their earnings. Transition from holding the probationary pass was partly determined by length of sentence and partly by conduct: the rule was that time in the first three stages — Norfolk Island, a probationary gang and a probationary pass — should amount to at least half the sentence. The last two stages were a ticket-of-leave and a pardon, conditional or absolute.

The objective of this elaborate scheme was to control more closely the transported convict, and to propel him into good courses by keeping alive 'an invigorating hope and a salutary dread at every stage of the progress . . . from the commencement to the close of his punishment'.[74] As an extra refinement the most promising of the short-term convicts were to undergo, prior to their transportation, a period of separate discipline at Pentonville (or the modified discipline of Parkhurst, in the case of juveniles), their performance during which period determining the stage to which they would be allocated upon arrival overseas.[75] The probation system was intended only as a means of regulating the operation of transportation, not of diminishing it, and it did not, therefore, affect the rate of flow of convicts to the colony.

By the mid-1840s the difficulties in Van Diemen's Land had reached critical proportions. With the penitentiaries at Parkhurst and Pentonville (which, in any case, dealt with only a tiny proportion of those transported) failing to achieve their hoped-for success, attempts were made to suspend transportation altogether from March 1846 until April 1847.[76] Another and more urgent review of convict policy was becoming peremptory when in July 1846 Lord John Russell came into power and appointed Sir George Grey as home secretary. There could hardly

---

73 *Copies or Extracts of any Correspondence between the Secretary of State and the Governor of Van Diemen's Land, on the Subject of Convict Discipline*, PP, 1843, XLII, 451, 6.
74 *Ibid.*, 4.
75 *Ibid.* See pp. 205-7, below.
76 Gladstone, who became colonial secretary in March 1846, decided to suspend transportation to Van Diemen's Land in order to give a breathing space, a decision endorsed by his successor, Earl Grey. However, the suspension was not complete and convicts still arrived there, though much reduced in numbers (*Correspondence on Convict Discipline and Transportation, op. cit.*, 322).

have been a more favourable political combination to ensure an extensive change in convict policy. Lord John Russell had failed to achieve fruition of his earlier plans, but they had been firmly anti-transportation so as to prepare him to back radical amendments to what he saw as a basically unsatisfactory system; and he had a strong partner in Sir George Grey who had both the inclination and the ability to oversee such a reform,[77] while of his political career it was said: 'Entering parliament just after the passing of the Reform Bill, he took the work of the Whig party to be the adjustment of the rest of the institutions and organization of the country to the level of the ideas which the Reform Bill expressed.'[78] On both moral and administrative grounds the system of transportation and the state of the penal colony in Van Diemen's Land appalled him. At the end of April 1846 the governor of the colony had been recalled because of his neglect of the moral condition of the convicts and also because of very serious allegations as to his behaviour in private life.[79] This must have strengthened government desire for a change in the convict system which would free it from the economic and political obligations of colonial administration and place it in the hands of the home penal administrators.

On 5 September 1846 a note to Jebb informed him that consideration was again to be given to the home employment of convicts on public works. The letter shows that the home secretary had very specific proposals in mind and a good idea of the pitfalls he wished to avoid:

I am directed by Secretary Sir George Grey to inform you that it has been proposed that a certain number of Convicts should be employed in the construction of some works about to be undertaken by the Board of Admiralty at the Isle of Portland. Sir George Grey is of opinion that there are peculiar facilities for the employment of Convicts at Portland but he thinks it of importance that care should be taken to combine with the profitable labour of the convicts to be so employed effective means of improved Prison Discipline and Moral Superintendance. He would therefore entertain great objection to their being placed in Hulks and he thinks it essential that provision should be made for their being lodged on shore in buildings erected for the purpose and so arranged as to secure as far as possible the separation of the convicts from one another when

77 His mother was a friend of William Wilberforce, and had exerted a strong religious influence over Grey which never left him.
78 *Dictionary of National Biography*, VIII, p. 627.
79 *Correspondence Relating to the Recall of Sir Eardley Wilmot from Van Diemen's Land*, PP, 1847, XXXVIII, 513, 2-5. See also the letter to Earl Grey from the Bishop of Tasmania entitled 'Notes on Transportation and Prison Discipline as Applied to Van Diemen's Land' (*ibid.*, p. 559).

not at work or receiving instruction and especially that they should have separate sleeping places. . . .[80]

In supporting the public works scheme Grey was hopeful that the full flow of transportation to a penal colony would never be resumed, although he accepted that, at the end of their separate and public works terms of imprisonment, convicts would 'in ordinary cases' be exiled or banished for the remainder of their sentence,[81] but under a very different arrangement from the erstwhile contaminating association of transportation. In this scheme, at least, there seemed to be common ground between Grey and some of those who still maintained that a reformed system of transportation could be an effective deterrent: Whitworth Russell, in his evidence to the 1847 select committee, strongly expressed his view that transportation was indispensable, but emphasised that convicts ought not to be sent to penal colonies or held under any penal restraints once transported, unless they committed further offences.[82]

Although Crawford's and Whitworth Russell's opposition to the public works prisons probably rested on their detestation of any system of discipline which brought convicts into close association, they defended transportation as an alternative on the grounds that the prospect of retaining and releasing large numbers of convicts in the home country was unacceptable.[83] They urged that for 'a considerable number of comparatively minor offences' imprisonment might be more appropriate than transportation. This class of offenders would present few accommodation problems in view of the improvement in the local prisons, whilst 'the Government having already recognised the principle of providing for the maintenance of convicted Prisoners it might be so far extended as to prevent any additional burthen being thrown upon the County or Borough . . .'. Those who had committed the most serious crimes they singled out as a distinct class and proposed sending them to a special penal colony. For the intermediate sort they suggested an extension of the policy already being followed at Pentonville and Parkhurst – a period of separate discipline, to be followed, for those who had been of good behaviour, by removal to the colonies, or 'by liberation in this country in the case of those who may be able to provide Bail for their good conduct during the remaining period of their original sentence'. In the colonies a strengthened penal administration

---

80 PRO HO 43/71/201. See also the *Select Committee on the Execution of the Criminal Laws*, Minutes of Evidence, PP, 1847, VII, qs 2014-19.
81 *Correspondence on Transportation: Letter from Sir George Grey to Earl Grey*, 20 January 1847, PP, 1847, XLVIII, 93, 196-7.
82 1847 *SC*, *op. cit.*, q. 558.
83 Crawford and Whitworth Russell to Sir George Grey, 12 December 1846, *op. cit.*; *SC on Execution of the Criminal Laws*, *op. cit.*, qs 543-5; Shaw, *op. cit.*, p. 312.

should be provided, together with sufficient accommodation to ensure that each convict had a separate sleeping cell. Besides combating the indulgence in homosexuality which was thought to be widespread, this last would have the advantage of giving 'full employment for a considerable time to the Convicts first sent out ...'. The inspectors suggested that whilst these measures were being put into effect temporary accommodation could be found in Bermuda and Gibraltar by enlargement of the convict stations and that cells might be rented in some of the newly constructed county prisons.[84] These proposals of the inspectors, largely reproductions or extensions of schemes already tried, were insufficiently persuasive to head off the public works project backed by Grey and then being investigated by Jebb.

In evidence to the Select Committee on the Execution of the Criminal Law Jebb pointed out that he had seen something of the employment of convicts at public works whilst he had been an officer of the Royal Engineers at Woolwich, where he had also discussed it with fellow sappers who had served in Bermuda and on Gibraltar. These references served not so much to establish Jebb's credentials before the select committee as to underline the fact that the use of convict labour on public works was already a well-tried practice. He was careful, none the less, to draw a distinction between the 'far superior' system as it was then being conducted by the Engineers on Bermuda and Gibraltar and the old convict system.[85]

The scheme which Jebb had put before the government was not complicated:

assuming that the sentences which had heretofore been Seven and Ten years transportation were commuted to periods of three, four, or five years imprisonment in this Country, and that we had by our experience at Pentonville ascertained pretty nearly the period which would be safe for enforcing separate confinement ... I assumed that four years might be the average period which possibly would be passed by the great mass of the adult Convicts in this country; one year of which would be passed in separate confinement and the remainder on public works.

On this basis Jebb estimated that about 6,000 convicts would be employed on public works. Some would be engaged in the construction of a harbour of refuge at Portland, and about 1,000 at each of the dockyards. Looking ahead he spoke of 'fortifications and other great national works under the Admiralty, which in consequence of the vast expense would not be undertaken by the Government unless they had

84 Crawford and Whitworth Russell to Sir George Grey, 12 December 1846, *op. cit.*
85 *SC on Execution of the Criminal Laws, op. cit.*, q. 2014.

some available labour'.[86]

Jebb also made a point of answering the criticisms of Crawford and Whitworth Russell of the public works scheme, as expressed in their memorandum to Sir George Grey of 23 April 1846.[87] He argued that convicts working in the public eye in gangs and clad in uniform would not necessarily be degraded: whilst the old convict system had always been 'very properly reprobated', a preliminary period of penitentiary imprisonment, to which all but about 10 per cent of convicts might be subjected, would diminish the dangers of association; and

> if they were brought from the Pentonville System into a modified system of association, with a view to their industrial training on public works, and if a small proportion of wages were given them, and they had the same stimulus to labour which has been applied at Gibraltar and Bermuda by the Engineer Department . . . I think it would confirm in a great measure the industrial training which they had received.[88]

By taking so seriously the claims which Crawford and Whitworth Russell had made for the reformatory effects of Pentonville, Jebb was outflanking the inspectors in a manner which must have been particularly galling to them, especially as Jebb's obeisance to the penological accomplishments of the separate system provided government with a useful means of distracting attention from the fact that the venture into public works had been stimulated by the collapse of transportation arrangements.

The public works scheme went ahead rapidly and Portland Prison was opened in November 1848. But, whatever the inclinations of Sir George Grey, public works could not be an immediate substitute for transportation as the press of numbers was too great.[89] In August

---

86 *Ibid.*, q. 2019.
87 They objected on a number of grounds – the undesirability of exposing convicts engaged on the works to public scrutiny, contamination and the problems of eventually releasing the convicts in the home country. They were also doubtful about the security implications posed by congregating large bodies of working convicts, suggesting that chaining 'would be almost inevitable'. They queried the cost and wisdom of erecting the necessary temporary accommodation (PRO HO 45/OS 1847).
88 *SC on Execution of the Criminal Laws*, *op. cit.*, qs 2020-4, 2040, *passim*.
89 On 31 December 1846 it was necessary for Grey to send a circular to the chairmen of quarter sessions seeking temporary accommodation in the local prisons for those convicts who were not to be transported. He pointed out that the last session of Parliament had voted to defray the costs of maintaining convicted prisoners in gaols, so no additional expense would be imposed on the localities (*Circular Letter Addressed to Her Majesty's Secretary of State to the Justices in Quarter Sessions, Relative to the Confinement of Convicts after Sentence, and of the Replies Received Thereto*, PP, 1847, XLVII, 5).

1848 Earl Grey (colonial secretary) sent a circular letter to some of the colonies to inquire which would be willing to take the 'exiles' produced by the new arrangement combining terms of separate confinement and of public works labour. Only Western Australia replied favourably. Despite the opposition of the Pentonville commissioners, who hoped that their reformed prisoners might be sent to a larger and more developed colony, Western Australia was, on 1 May 1849, designated as a place fit to receive convicts, and, together with Van Diemen's Land (which continued to receive convicts until 1853), provided a sufficient outlet for the mother country's convicts during the period that penal servitude was in the making. But the new system, much as Jebb outlined it to the 1847 select committee, bade fair to become what Jebb in a letter to Earl Grey in 1856 called 'a more certain and deterring punishment ... which, as regards the great majority of the Convicts shall render the country entirely independent of the Will of a Colony, and at the same time be more efficacious and economical'.[90]

The hulks

The history of the hulks during this period closely followed developments in transportation policy and administration, and, in the case of the bases in Bermuda and on Gibraltar, was also influenced by issues in colonial and naval policy. The importance of the hulks to the convict establishment can be seen from Table 7.1, providing as they did until 1844 the main form of convict custody at home. As late as 1842 and 1843 they held over 70 per cent of home-based convicts; but by the beginning of 1844 Pentonville was available, Millbank had been converted into a depot, and its holding had almost doubled, whilst the number of convicts in rented cells in the local prisons had trebled. In addition to those held in the hulks in home waters there were also, by 1847, some 1,800 convicts stationed in Bermuda and on Gibraltar,[91] all of whom (in England and abroad) came under one administration, headed by a superintendent.

John Henry Capper became superintendent of the hulks in July 1815 and, during the thirty-two years of his management, ran the hulks according to the entrepreneurial methods of prison-keeping prevalent at the time of his appointment.[92] In conjunction with the office of superintendent, Capper held a clerkship in the Home Office. He made biannual reports (published annually) to Parliament, but no other system of scrutiny was provided. Even with a superintendent many

90 Jebb to Earl Grey, 11 July 1856, Grey Papers, 112-14.
91 The average daily population in Bermuda in 1847 was 1,191 and on Gibraltar 627 (see *Report of J.H. Capper*, PP, 1847, XLVIII, 1, 3).
92 He had been appointed under the 1815 Transportation Act (55 Geo. III, c.156), s.11 of which specifically defined his powers as equivalent to gaolers'.

times more energetic and attentive than Capper, it would have been difficult to maintain an efficient and honest system of administration and staffing in the hulks: the establishment consisted of several vessels which shifted their moorings between Woolwich, Chatham, Devonport and Portsmouth from time to time; supervision was difficult, and the nature of the dockyard work made trafficking between prisoners, staff and civilians impossible to prevent. By the 1840s Capper had become virtually an absentee office-holder, when old age, infirmity and possibly idleness had led him, while still drawing a salary of £400 and office allowance (for a non-existent office) of £131 per annum, to depute most of his duties to his clerk and nephew, Robert Capper, earning an honest £257.

TABLE 7.1   *The accommodation of convicts in custody in England and Wales, 1839-47*

Establishment	1839	1840	1841	1842	1843	1844	1845	1846	1847
Millbank	417	359	810	662	586	1,034	1,094-	629	1,270
Parkhurst	49	123	232	284	236	284	540	648	620
Pentonville	–	–	–	–	28	501	333	484	341
Hulks:									
Justitia	316	513	451	514	327	326	435	414	324
Leviathan	536	653	607	689	615	356	–	–	–
Stirling Castle	–	21	460	548	424	315	422	294	289
Warrior	357	416	663	671	567	485	392	343	311
York	279	556	566	692	597	322	445	217	262
Total in hulks	1,488	2,159	2,747	3,114	2,530	1,804	1,694	1,268	1,186
Total in local prisons	269	345	189	253	174	511	272	138	218
Overall total	2,223	2,986	3,978	4,313	3,554	4,134	3,933	3,167	3,635
% in the hulks	66.9	72.3	69.1	72.2	71.2	43.6	43.1	40.0	32.6

Source: Derived from the *Return of the Number of Convicts under Sentence of Transportation Confined on 1st January in Each Year*, PP, 1847-8, LII, 1.

In accordance with his statutory powers and duties, Capper appointed and promoted staff, disciplined his charges (by corporal punishment if necessary), recommended for pardons and transportation, purchased supplies and disbursed payments and was responsible for the regular inspection and superintendence of the vessels and for making quarterly returns.[93] Experience in the local prisons had for many years taught that benefits were to be gained by separating many of these responsibilities and powers. Nor was there any compensating level of administration between the officers in charge of each hulk and Capper; each of

93 5 Geo. IV, c.84, ss. 11-16.

the hulks was run more or less independently, both with respect to staff management and the discipline of the convicts.[94] Medical officers — from whom a responsible attitude might have been expected — were too wrapped up in their own more absorbing affairs, according to contemporary evidence, to act upon a sense of duty.[95]

The convicts slept in wards on board and were employed in the dockyards on Admiralty and Ordnance work, which varied greatly in the demands it made on their strength and endurance. Heavy tasks such as landing and loading coal, excavating, hauling timber and cleaning shot were performed in gangs of ten to twenty, each gang under a superintending officer and convict wardsman, and working the same hours as free labourers.[96] Other employments entailing less hardship were reserved for the trusty, either in superintending their fellows or in bookkeeping.[97]

Although a small number of refractory convicts had occasionally been transferred to the hulks from Millbank, until 1843 most convicts were taken to the hulks directly from the local gaols.[98] From the middle of that year Millbank became a marshalling depot and convicts were taken there by gaolers rather than to the hulks. These changes quickly affected the size and quality of the hulk population, as Capper made clear in his report for 1845:

> the only Convicts received on board the Hulks at home during
> the past year have been Prisoners received from the Pentonville
> and Millbank prisons, who were at the time, either from disease,
> old age or infirmity, wholly unfit for Transportation, Confinement
> in a Gaol, or for Hard Labour.[99]

The *Euryalus*, a hulk which succeeded the *Bellerophon* in being reserved for juvenile offenders, was withdrawn in the autumn of 1843,[100] so in the decade after 1845 the home hulks increasingly became depositories for the sick as the sentences of the remaining healthy convicts progressed into transportation or release[101] and the opening of the public works prison at Portland reduced the means of their full replenishment.

The gradual disuse of the hulks must have been a source of satisfaction to Sir George Grey who, in his instructions to Jebb in September 1846, made it clear that he had 'great objection' to their being used for

94 *Report of an Inquiry into the General Treatment and Condition of the Convicts in the Hulks at Woolwich*, PP, 1847, XVIII, 1, xxix.
95 *Ibid.*, xxx. Peter Bossy, the Woolwich surgeon, also ran a large private practice, as had his predecessor.
96 *Ibid.*, xix.
97 *Ibid.*, xxi.
98 See p. 168 above and pp. 275-6 below.
99 *Report of J.H. Capper*, PP, 1845, XXXVII, 315, 1.
100 *Report of J.H. Capper*, PP, 1844, XXXIX, 397, 1.
101 *Report of J.H. Capper, Esq.*, PP, 1847, XLVIII, 1.

public works convicts.[102] Neither can the home secretary have been greatly displeased when in January 1847 T.S. Dunscombe, member for Finsbury, made allegations in the House about the ill-treatment of convicts at Woolwich and moved for a select committee of inquiry.[103] On Grey's instructions William J. Williams, the newly appointed inspector for the Home District, started to investigate and, in his report, touched on one of Grey's chief concerns, the imparting of religious and moral instruction, which was 'a very minor consideration ... regarded more as a matter of routine than the most important element of penal treatment'.[104] Williams reported the state of cleanliness of the hospital ships *Justitia* and *Unité* to be 'most disgraceful and discreditable', a large proportion of the convicts showing symptoms of scurvy, and he implied that men were not always allotted work which was within their strength.[105] He condemned the trafficking that went on, the use of convicts for officers' private work and he also drew attention to the plight of the lunatics. Many of these had been received from other prisons, especially Millbank, and kept for 'very considerable periods' without efforts being made by the surgeon to secure their removal to lunatic asylums.[106] More generally he saw clear signs of laxness in authority:

> The distance at which the Superintendent resided, combined with his feeble and imperfect exercise of the controlling power, and the want of system in the management, have been the obvious causes of the neglects and irregularities which have so generally prevailed.

He thought that the instructions and regulations were generally adequate had they been accompanied by the appointment of a deputy superintendent resident in a place convenient to the moorings.[107] As for the senior officers, several were

> manifestly incapable of performing their duties satisfactorily in consequence of age and infirmity, others are so tainted by long habit with the vicious system of employing the convicts in work for themselves, and other irregularities, that ... I feel I can do no less than advise a thorough reorganization of the whole body.[108]

102 See p. 193, above.
103 *Hansard* (Third series), LXXXIX, cols 511-28.
104 *Report of an Inquiry into the General Treatment and Condition of the Convicts in the Hulks at Woolwich*, *op. cit.*, xiv.
105 *Ibid.*, xv-xix, *passim*. The hospital ship, *Unité*, in service by 1847, was not included in the returns made of the numbers of convicts confined to the hulks (see Table 7.1, p. 198 above).
106 *Ibid.*, xx-xxvi.
107 *Ibid.*, xxix.
108 *Ibid.*, xxxiv.

A thorough reorganisation followed; but such was the demand for convict labour from the Admiralty and the Arsenal that the hulks could not have been abolished overnight, even had sufficient shore accommodation existed. Capper was allowed to retire immediately after the inquiry, with a pension of £240, and the superintendence of the hulks was taken over on 1 October 1847[109] by Herbert Voules, a clerk in the Home Office, who shortly after this was given equal responsibility with Jebb and O'Brien. The practice of working the convicts with free labourers in charge was discontinued; more guards were appointed and a closer record of convicts' misbehaviour kept. Unfortunately there were drawbacks to the new régime:

> Formerly the well-conducted men remained to work out half the period of their sentence, at the expiration of which time they were recommended for free pardon in this country; but now they are sent abroad with tickets of leave, and the worst characters alone remain, and are accumulating on board as each party of well-conducted men are embarked for the colonies. The power formerly possessed by the overseers of recommending three or four times in each year those persons for immediate transportation to a penal colony, who persisted in their misconduct was a powerful check, and did much to strengthen the discipline.[110]

In 1850 a report signed by Jebb, O'Brien and Voules expressed what was to become the often repeated view of the Directorate of Convict Prisons:

> In closing our Report for the past year, we would state our decided opinion that the Hulks are unsuited for the confinement of convicts, and so long as they continue to be occupied for such a purpose, it will be impracticable fully to develop the advantages of the system which Her Majesty's Government have determined to adopt . . . we cannot too strongly recommend that immediate measures be taken for abolishing them and building convicts' prisons on shore, both at Portsmouth and Woolwich.[111]

The hulks in Bermuda and on Gibraltar

The home hulks continued to operate despite strong government and administrative misgivings, partly because of a lack of alternative accommodation, but also because of the value to the Admiralty and Ordnance Department of convict labour. This latter reason was even

109 PRO HO 9/16, p. 9.
110 *Report of the Manager of the Convict Hulk Establishment, for the Years 1848 and 1849*, PP, 1850, XXIX, 1, 2.
111 *Ibid.*, 15.

stronger as regards the hulk establishments in Bermuda and on Gibraltar. In both places a sufficient supply of suitable local labour was not available, whilst the projects being undertaken were considered to be of high military, naval and political importance. Such was the weight attached to these considerations that the overseas hulks outlasted the home establishment by many years.[112]

The Bermuda establishment owed its origin to the Admiralty's fears of a French or American seizure of the islands during the Napoleonic War. Work on fortifications was started in 1810, but progressed only slowly, and after the 1812 war with America border disputes continuing between the United States and Canada led to a confirmation of the earlier decision to fortify. Since little had so far been accomplished, it was decided to make the place a convict station, preference being given to the islands over Sierra Leone or Canada.[113] The first 300 convicts were dispatched from England on 6 January 1824 by the authority of an Order in Council under 4 Geo. IV, c.47.[114] Within five years the number of convicts in Bermuda had grown to more than 1,300.[115] Such was the demand for convict labour that despite recurrent outbreaks of yellow fever and attendant fatalities the number remained around that level until the late 1840s and early 1850s.[116]

The convict establishment set up in 1842 on Gibraltar was also intended to supply labour for the repair of the fortifications.[117] The numbers transferred there grew steadily and by 1850 there was accommodation for over 900.[118] Although regarded as part of the hulk establishment, most of Gibraltar's convicts were held in on-shore buildings, only the hospital being a hulk.[119] If Capper's fulsome 1846 report is to be credited, the convicts, at least in the early years, proved to be highly satisfactory labourers:

A considerable addition has been made during the past year to
the number of Prisoners employed at Gibraltar, where works of

112 The *Defence*, the last home-based hulk, was destroyed by fire on 14 July 1857. The Bermuda establishment did not close until 31 March 1863 and the Gibraltar establishment until 30 May 1875.
113 J.C. Arnell, 'Bermuda as a Naval Base', *Bermuda Historical Quarterly* (Winter 1978), XXXV, no. 4, pp. 60-2, *passim*.
114 *Account of the Number of Convicts Transported to the British Colonies*, PP, 1824, XIX, 181; PRO CO 38/21, 61.
115 *A Return of the Expense for the Convicts in the Hulks at Bermuda*, 1824-9, PP, 1830, XXIII, 17, 2.
116 *Estimates, etc. Miscellaneous Services*, PP, 1847-8, XL, 349; PP, 1849, XXXI, 347, 10; 1849, XXXI, 347; PP, 1850, XXXIV, 364.
117 *Reports by J.H. Capper*, PP, 1842, XXXII, 523, 10; PP, 1843, XLII, 337, 5.
118 *Estimates, etc. Miscellaneous Services*, PP, 1850, XXXIV, 356.
119 According to Du Cane, the Gibraltar convict prison 'was constructed after the model of a hulk prison, its hospital was a hulk, and many of the greatest evils of the hulks remained in full activity in it until the last' (*The Punishment and Prevention of Crime*, p. 118).

great magnitude are in progress. . . . The principal Offices of the
Ordnance and Naval Departments at Gibraltar appear to be in
every way satisfied with the labour performed, and the general
demeanour of the Convicts . . . and that the work of three
civilians, being generally Spaniards, is not equal to the work
of two of the Convicts. . . .[120]

By the mid-1840s there was a decline in the demand for convict
labour in the home dockyards, the events in Van Dieman's Land were
reaching their crisis and Millbank and then Pentonville were being used
as marshalling places for convicts. As the unsuitability of the home
hulks became recognised, healthy convicts appear to have been transferred immediately to Bermuda and Gibraltar,[121] the overseas hulk
establishments thus came to preponderate both in numbers held and
funds expended: in 1846 there were more than 1,800 convicts in
Bermuda and on Gibraltar and only 1,300 in the English hulks,[122] and
the annual cost overseas likewise exceeded that at home.

The difficulties experienced in supervising and controlling the hulks
at home were present on an even greater scale at the overseas depots;
even before Capper's fall steps were being taken to tighten the hand of
government. In January 1846 the governor of Bermuda was appointed
assistant superintendent of convicts,[123] the intention being to place
under his

immediate control and authority . . . every branch of the Convict
Establishment and all the Officers engaged in the superintendence
of it . . . the Govr. should exercise every requisite power of control,
inspection and discipline over the Convicts while on Board the Hulks
and not actually engaged in their appropriate labours.[124]

This action was followed eighteen months later by an order to the
Gibraltar overseer informing him that the Home Office was relin-
quishing responsibility for the establishment under his charge: similar
arrangements were made at both bases to divide authority between the
local colonial authorities (who reported to the Colonial Office) and the
Engineers, who directed the actual labour of the prisoners. Henceforward for some years there was silence on the overseas hulk depots in
Home Office reports.

120 *Report of J.H. Capper, Superintendent of Hulks*, PP, 1846, XXXIV, 491,
   1.
121 *Report of J.H. Capper, Superintendent of Hulks*, PP, 1847, XLVIII, 1.
122 *Ibid.*, 3.
123 By s. 7 of 11 Geo. IV and 1 Will. IV, c.39.
124 PRO CO 38/22/429.

The penitentiaries

There had been developments in the provision and administration of government penitentiaries long before the crisis had been reached in the system of transportation. The 1835 Select Committee on Gaols had recommended the establishment of a juvenile prison,[125] intended to serve two purposes: on the one hand adding the deterrent element which transportation was said to lack, and on the other providing such occupational training as would enable fit young convicts, with little or no criminal record, to make a new and better life for themselves in the colonies. A juvenile penitentiary was a good starting-point for expanding central government's prison system. It had long been felt that youthful offenders were more open to beneficial influences than the mature; moreover, they constituted a very large proportion of those sentenced to transportation (some 47 per cent in 1840 being below the age of twenty-one).[126]

In August 1838 the Act establishing Parkhurst was passed.[127] The nucleus of the prison was formed by the buildings of a former military hospital, so there was comparatively little delay before the first prisoner was received, on 26 December 1838. The supervising committee of visitors consisted of Lord Yarborough, J.P. Kay, William Crawford and, as his first involvement in penal administration, Captain Joshua Jebb. The régime was intended to be at once deterrent and reformatory and the visitors recognised, at least in theory, the difficulty of simultaneously seeking these two goals:

> In carrying the first of these objects into effect, the utmost care must be taken to avoid any species of discipline which is inconsistent with the habits and character of youth, or calculated in any degree to harden and degrade. The second object can only be effected by a judicious course of moral, religious and industrial training, but the means adopted for this purpose should not be of such a nature as to counteract the wholesome restraints of the corrective discipline.... There should be nothing, throughout the arrangements at Parkhurst, of a tendency to weaken the terrors of the law, or to lessen in the minds of the juvenile population at large (or of their parents) the dread of being committed to prison.[128]

Accordingly, the régime the visitors designed was split up to suit the governor's argument that 'the treatment of criminal boys, for the

125 *Select Committee of the House of Lords on Gaols and Houses of Correction*, PP, 1835, XII, 1, iv-v.
126 Sixty-four per cent were under twenty-five years of age and only 20 per cent were over the age of thirty (*Tables Showing the Number of Criminal Offenders in the Year 1840*, PP, 1841, XVIII, 255).
127 1 and 2 Vict., c.82, 'An Act for Establishing a Prison for Young Offenders'.
128 *Reports Relating to Parkhurst Prison*, PP, 1839, XXII, 643, 1.

double purpose of punishment and reformation, is a question wholly distinct from that of the convicted adult . . .'.[129] There was an extensive system of trade-training and education, and the inducement of a progressive-stage easing of discipline. At the same time discipline was all-pervading under such conditions as

> deprivation of liberty, wearing an iron on the leg, a strongly marked prison dress, a diet reduced to its minimum, with regard to the mental and bodily demands made on the prisoners, the enforcement of silence on all occasions of instruction and duty, and uninterrupted surveillance by officers.[130]

All Parkhurst prisoners (with the exception of a few whose sentences were restricted to imprisonment) were destined to be transported; but the visitors and governor assessed each prisoner's performance and decided whether he was to be transported as a free emigrant, or under a conditional pardon, or, having been deemed incorrigible, he was to be kept in confinement on arrival. Appropriate recommendations were then made to the home secretary. Boys in the first two categories were provided with clothing, money and other necessities for the voyage and the immediate period thereafter.

With the introduction of Lord Stanley's scheme for changes in the system of transportation in 1842, the home secretary, Sir James Graham, wrote to the Committee of Visitors at Parkhurst emphasising the intimate connection between their régime and Lord Stanley's reformed system: good behaviour would continue to earn a boy his freedom or conditional pardon; the penal gang, located at Puer Point, 'where the most rigid discipline, combined with forced labour and instruction, is severely maintained, to an extent which amounts to hardship and to unremitted punishment', awaited the incorrigible.[131] Graham pronounced grimly upon the fate of the juvenile convicts:

> Every boy who enters Parkhurst, is doomed to be transported; and this part of the sentence passed on him is immutable. He must bid a long farewell to the hopes of revisiting his native home, of seeing his parents, or of rejoining his companions. These are the hopes and pleasures which his crimes have forfeited: but he should be made to understand, that his future prospects in life entirely depend on his conduct at Parkhurst.[132]

Whilst he did not comment in any detail upon the prison's system of discipline the home secretary observed that, though experience might

---

129 *Reports Relating to Parkhurst Prison*, PP, 1841, XVIII, 701, 10.

130 *Ibid.*, PP, 1840, XXXVIII, 637, 4.

131 *Copies or Extracts of any Correspondence between the Secretary of State and the Governor of Van Dieman's Land on the Subject of Convict Discipline . . .*, PP, 1843, XLII, Appendix to Part 1, 1.

132 *Ibid.*

suggest further improvements, he himself desired to effect no change.[133]

Pentonville was to provide for adults what Parkhurst had provided for juveniles. It was intended to increase the reformatory and deterrent elements in transportation, and also to act as a national model, by its success in persuading the magistrates to adopt the separate system. At first the inspectors had thought that Millbank could be adapted for these purposes:

> we have proposed the construction of large airy separate cells at Millbank, with every needful accommodation for the prisoner. The value of the plan suggested will be further felt, when it is considered that by carrying it into effect in a place so central and important as the Metropolis, at a time when the magistrates in several parts of the Kingdom are contemplating the erection of separate cells a model will be presented for general imitation.[134]

As was seen in the last chapter, these experiments produced no satisfactory results and in their lengthy third report, in which they strongly advocated national adoption of the separate system, Crawford and Whitworth Russell called for the building of a completely new model prison:

> Such a building would serve as a model for every other prison on the same principle; and it would serve as a normal school for the instruction and training of officers for other prisons. It might be appropriated to the confinement of prisoners sentenced to long terms of imprisonment, in order to put the system to its severest test.[135]

In response to this plea the government in 1842 legislated for the building of Pentonville at a cost of £84,000 to accommodate 520 prisoners.[136] Although many elements of the Pentonville system were drawn from Parkhurst,[137] nevertheless its régime and objectives, and

133 *Ibid.*, p. 2.
134 *First Report of the Inspectors of Prisons (Home District)*, PP, 1836, XXXV, 1, 81.
135 *Third Report of the Inspectors of Prisons (Home District)*, PP, 1837-8, XXX, 1, 100. They ended their argument for the model prison with an appeal to patriotic sentiment: 'Let England resume her own; let her reclaim that system to which herself gave birth . . . national honour requires that after a long suspension it should be effectively resumed . . .' (*ibid.*, 101).
136 5 and 6 Vict., s.2, c.29.
137 Sir James Graham's letter to the first commissioners of Pentonville explicitly referred to Parkhurst:

> Pentonville shall be for adults what Parkhurst now is for juvenile offenders — a prison of instruction and probation, rather than a gaol punishment; excepting the more severe discipline of the Separate System is in Pentonville applied to those of riper years, while the tender youth of

the fact that it dealt with adult prisoners, made Pentonville a new and unique venture.[138] Almost from the outset, however, the commissioners were in a state of turmoil about the effects of the system of discipline — particularly about the undefined role of the chaplain and the tendency of vigorous evangelical preaching to upset the strictly separated prisoners. In September 1843 — just over nine months after the opening of the prison — there were complaints that the chaplain's preaching and visitations had produced 'morbid symptoms' in the prisoners. Lord Wharncliffe sent Jebb two letters, one from Sir Benjamin Brodie (a commissioner and very distinguished physician) and the other from Dr Rees (the surgeon); the covering note was marked 'Private and Confidential'. Wharncliffe wrote that he had confidence in Jebb's discretion and knew that he was not

disposed to view Mr. Ralph's [the chaplain] proceedings, in what he thinks his duty, with that degree of [favourable] prejudice which some other members of the Board labour under. You will see from the contents of these letters that they must not be produced at the board, but I should recommend that the following course should be taken with reference to the matter to which they refer.

You should have Dr. Rees before the Board, and ask him whether he has perceived, of late, any of the indications of morbid religious feeling, among the Prisoners which he formerly, and some time since, complained of, as likely to lead to very serious consequences, and if so, ask him to state the particular instances, and whether the physical state of those prisoners has been or is likely to be affected by these indications. This will bring the whole matter before the board, and when Dr. Rees has made his statement to you, you must have Mr. Ralph before you and he must be told that the Governors had hoped from what passed upon a previous occasion, and the communication I had personally with him upon this subject, in which he appeared to be fully sensible of the results which might follow from want of due consideration of the peculiar circumstances

---

Parkhurst is not exposed to the full rigour of the salutary discipline (cit. Pentonville Prison, Report of the Surveyor General, PP, 1844, XXVIII, 127, 26).

---

138   In 1842 Lord Stanley framed the improved system which was intended thenceforth to be followed. . . . It was termed the Probation System, and was based on the idea of passing convicts through the various stages of control and discipline. Pentonville Prison was . . . to afford means (with Millbank) of applying that part of the system which was to be carried out in England (Du Cane, op. cit., pp. 140-1).

However, Du Cane probably underestimated the extent to which Parkhurst had provided the prototype and experience.

under which the inmates of Pentonville are placed, that he would have exercised greater caution than he appears to have done lately in respect of his ministrations, and intercourse with the Prisoners. That we must insist upon their having other books besides religious books, placed always in their cells, that they may enjoy some relaxation from the constant confinement of their minds, to that one subject, and that when the medical officers state to him that they apprehend ill effects from the state of spirits of any prisoners, he must attend to their suggestions and alter his mode of communicating with some prisoners on religious subjects. You will further say that this matter is of vital importance that we the Governors are responsible for the conduct of the Prison in that as well as all other respects and that altho' we are quite aware that Mr. Ralph is led only by an exaggerated estimate of his duty as Chaplain, into the errors of which we complain, it is quite impossible that we should not do, what is absolutely necessary to maintain not only the bodily but the mental health of the prisoners, and that we must have a person in that situation, in whom we can place our confidence, for tempering his zeal with discretion.

All this which relates to Mr. Ralph, you may, if you think fit, read to him before the Board, and I hope it will produce the proper effect upon him. If not, however sorry I may be, I will not allow the mental health of the Prisoners to be risked, as it appears to be now.[139]

This dispute continued over the succeeding years, although no allusion to it was made in the various published reports. By the mid-1840s it was becoming apparent that Pentonville had not fulfilled the original and rather extravagant expectations and promises of Crawford and Russell and their supporters, and a deepening sense of anxiety and hostility was expressed in public opinion, chiefly because of the high rates of insanity.[140] In 1847 Crawford and Russell died. The most

139 Jebb Papers, box 3, letter of 22 September 1843. The matter seems, then, to have been resolved by a temporising response from the chaplain and agreement to introduce a secular library (letter of 26 September). Not all of the commissioners were convinced of the ill effects of the chaplain's ministrations. Chichester wrote to Jebb: 'The whole subject is a most delicate and painful one — It will take a great deal to convince me that Mr. Ralph is to blame or that his *mode* of preaching or teaching has anything to do with the unfavourable results produced on the Prisoners' minds. I am afraid however that if our own physician and the Medical Commissioners stoutly maintain the contrary opinion *we* must give way' (Jebb Papers, box 2, letter of 13 December 1843).

140 From the beginning *The Times* had been wholeheartedly against the separate system, which it thought ineffective, cruel and dangerous to health. Less than a year after the opening of the prison, a leader drew attention to section 23 of the Pentonville Prison Act which allowed for the removal to

powerfully placed proponents of the separate system gone, Pentonville sank under the weight of public disapproval, its own unfulfilled promises, and the requirements of the new public works prisons. In 1849 the special selection for Pentonville of the most fit and promising convicts ceased and, with various other changes in the régime, the reformatory experiment was effectively abandoned. Henceforth Pentonville differed little in objectives, methods or population from Millbank convict depot; in both, convicts were disciplined before being sent, as a preliminary to transportation, to labour in association at the new public works prison at Portland, thus irrevocably wrecking the scheme of careful penitential preparation followed by ejection into completely new circumstances.

Long before Pentonville's failure as a reformatory was recognised, however, there had been evidence that Parkhurst had also disappointed the high hopes of its sponsors. As on the former occasion the clear signs of failure were ignored in the public reports, which continued to be drafted in terms of measured optimism. Privately there was much heart-searching. Crawford wrote to Jebb on 5 February 1845:

> I send you the Report on the Conduct of the Parkhurst Boys in VD Land.
>
> This is a very heart-breaking Document; but the distressed condition of the Colony when the Boys arrived out, and the shameful manner in which they have been treated by the

---

and return from lunatic asylums of certified prisoners, and commented that this showed that the government 'cooly contemplated suicide . . . as a necessary result from its regimen and discipline' (25 November 1843). A few days later (29 November 1843) *The Times* again expressed strong criticism of the Pentonville discipline. It returned to the attack on 27 January 1844, with a scathing comment upon the visiting justices at the separate system county gaol at Springfield, Essex.

The period of separate confinement at Pentonville had been reduced in the first few years by successive stages from eighteen to nine months, yet even as late as 1852 there occurred an 'unusually large' number of cases of insanity. The amount of exercise in the open air was increased, and ceased to be taken in solitary airing pens: 'brisk walking' was introduced, following the practice at Wakefield. In 1853 the plan seemed to have worked, as there were no removals on grounds of insanity, but in the following years the figures increased again.

Removals from Pentonville on grounds of insanity (per 10,000)

1842-9	27
1850	32
1851	16
1852	16
1853	0
1854	10
1855	20

The proportion for all other prisons was 5.8 per 10,000 (Mayhew and Binny, *The Criminal Prisons of London*, p. 115, n.).

Government there, will account for much of the Evil described.
After making, however, due allowances for these circumstances
I fear the boys would never have turned out so badly had there not
been something radically wrong in our System at Parkhurst, or a
total want of Judgement exhibited in the selection of Objects
[boys for favourable transportation].

You may recollect, from the reading of Mr. Innes' Journal that
many of these boys began to steal soon after the Mandarin left
Cowes. Woollcombe and England would have had no real
acquaintance with the character of the Boys when they reported
so favourably as to induce us to recommend them as Emigrants. . . .

I begin to be very dolorous about Parkhurst. The failure of
Colonial Outlets is here, as at Pentonville, a serious blow to us. The
disposal of the junior boys is a most anxious question, and we
should meet immediately on your return to Town, to consider
whether we should not recommend Sir James to stop at all events
this part of the System. Magistrates sentence these children to
imprism. under the impression that by being sent to Parkhurst
they are providing for them.[141]

Millbank, of course, had long been abandoned by the reformists as a
bad job, and Russell went so far at one stage as to urge Jebb (perhaps
half jokingly) to pull it down.[142]

Administration and staffing

By the end of the 1840s the government penitentiaries rather resembled
the patient whose operation was a success, but who nevertheless died:
the régimes had failed to achieve their objectives, but the methods of
administration were comparatively successful. The decorative, high-
ranking committees of management had been stiffened by the addition
of inspectors and surveyor-general (as at Pentonville) or replaced by
them entirely (as at Parkhurst and Millbank).[143] Many of the earlier
inconveniences of Millbank were avoided: officers' families were not
introduced into the prisons at Parkhurst and Pentonville, and the new

---

141 Jebb Papers, box 3.
142 *Ibid.*, undated letter (but probably some time in the early 1840s). Jebb had
    sent Russell some plans in relation to Millbank. Russell thanked him but said
    that the best service he could do the cause of prison improvement would be
    to pull down the buildings which, he said, had already swallowed up millions
    of pounds: the soil being peat would not be drained and moisture from the
    river seeped in.
143 Du Cane looked back with some contempt, forty years later, at the old-
    fashioned management committees, which he described as 'a number of
    persons with high-sounding names' and 'the least effective and most
    irresponsible mode of administration that could be devised' (*op. cit.*, p. 185).

buildings were very much more manageable and functional. There were no more unwise experiments with the dietary scales,[144] and the governor's authority was not displaced by superior committee intervention.

One problem — the handling of subordinate staffing — prominent at Millbank continued to fester, and it was becoming obvious that it would long remain a foremost concern of prison administration and management.

Pentonville's reformatory régime had imposed considerable demands upon the subordinate staff, who, in line with Millbank Penitentiary, were expected to be exemplars of proper conduct as well as custodial officers.[145] In the early years along with their charges they were obliged to attend services in the chapel twice a day, and the names of all absentees who were not sick or engaged in essential duties were noted in the governor's journal.[146] As a means of closer supervision, a system

144 Mannheim makes too much of his distinction between 'less-eligibility' and 'non-superiority', claiming that 'the acceptance of the principle of non-superiority, on the surface of it, seems to eliminate the function of deterrence from the penal system at least for the lowest strata of society'. Pentonville could not avoid offering physically superior conditions to those enjoyed 'by the lowest strata of society'. What slum-dweller had an air-heated, well-ventilated room equipped with a w.c.? And what unskilled labourer had an adequate diet and clothing? As indicated in the discussion of Millbank, in the last chapter, what was achieved *in practice* on this issue was a recognition that less-eligible conditions had to be sought by psychological methods. Mannheim is vague: 'It was probably regarded as the utmost level of indulgence when this principle of less-eligibility was sometimes exchanged for what I should call the principle of *non-superiority*. . . .' Millbank and Pentonville, the two most significant reformatory prisons in the nineteenth century, do not provide support for the distinction which he wished to draw. (See Mannheim, *The Dilemma of Penal Reform*, pp. 56-8, *passim*.)

145 The Pentonville staffing structure was quite complex, consisting of the secretary-cum-accountant and his clerk (both under the direct authority of the commissioners), governor, deputy governor, clerk to the governor. Subordinate discipline staff consisted of the four principal warders, fourteen warders and eight extra warders. The chaplain's department consisted of the chaplain, assistant chaplain, schoolmaster and two assistant schoolmasters. On the medical side were a medical officer, resident surgeon and an infirmary warder. The various building and manufacturing services were provided by a steward and his clerk, and an assistant clerk and eight assorted porters, cooks, bakers, etc. There was a clerk for manufactures, five trade instructors, and nine assistant trade instructors. Additionally there were a clerk of works, engineer and smith, and eight assorted labourers, porters and the like. Out of a total of seventy-five superior and subordinate staff only twenty-eight (including a governor and deputy governor) had direct disciplinary duties. This was a feature of the separate system. (See *Second Report of the Commissioners of Pentonville Prison*, PP, 1844, XXVIII, 71, Appendix D, 46-8; *Third Report of the Commissioners of Pentonville Prison*, PP, 1845, XXV, 53, Appendix E, 22-4, and *Routines Carried out at Pentonville Prison*, HMSO, 1848.)

146 Hoskins, R. (ed.), 'Pentonville Prison, Governor's Journal 1842-44'.

of 'tell-tale' clocks was installed, leading automatically to staff fining so extensive that a tariff had to be drawn up.[147] If offences were repeated the matter could be reported to the commissioners and end in severe reprimand or dismissal.[148] Since many plans hatched by staff-inmate collusion involved the officers in shady business at off-duty times, regulations were framed to curtail their leisure hour liberty, and within the first few months of the opening of the prison the warders were informed of

> two resolutions of the Board, expressive of a want of confidence on the part of the Commissioners in any of the warders who could so far forget the respect due to their situations, as to frequent Public Houses or Beer Shops etc.[149]

After all the posts on the disciplinary staff had been filled in 1842, any new recruits were first appointed to the probationary grade of extra warders, and if they then proved satisfactory they were promoted to the rank of warder and sworn in as constables by the commissioners of the peace of the metropolis — 'to keep the peace within the Prison and within 500 yards thereof' (the oath presumably being seen, at least in part, as an additional means of staff control).[150]

---

147 Robin Evans describes the tell-tales, which were located in various parts of the prison:

> Projecting pegs on a revolving dial denoting quarter-hour intervals could be pressed down only by use of a lever fixed to the body of the *tell-tale*. If an officer did not proceed on his rounds in the right order and at precisely the right time of day, he would be unable to press down the correct peg. His omission was thus recorded and disciplinary action followed, usually in the form of a deduction from his wage (*op. cit.*, p. 16).

> Fines were imposed mainly for leaving the place of duty, or for forgetting to lock cells, withdraw hammocks, etc. Among the incidents recorded in the governor's journal, there is a fine imposed on a principal warder for waving to his wife (who lived in a staff cottage on the boundary wall). Many instances of quarrelling among officers were also punished with fining (*ibid.*, pp. 24-5).

148 On the third offence the governor was obliged to make a report to the commissioners. Not all of the officers in the government prisons passively accepted the system of fining. An officer of Millbank (who had served under the penitentiary system, and remained when the prison was converted into a convict depot) alleged in 1847 that the fining system was an abuse of authority by the governor in that it was being administered in an illegal manner. A Royal Commission investigated his allegations and, while finding the specific charges unsubstantiated, concluded that 'the offences for which officers are liable to a pecuniary penalty have never been properly defined, nor the amount of fines imposed regularly recorded' (*Royal Commission on the Management of Millbank Prison*, PP, 1847, XXX, 1).

149 'Pentonville Prison, Governor's Journal', p. 13.

150 *Ibid.*

212

It seemed to the public, in the first few years, that Pentonville staff were responding well to the exacting standards required of them. But some staff had found the discipline so unbearable that they had simply taken themselves off without warning,[151] and the commissioners agreed among themselves to omit delicate staffing topics from their reports.[152] The first public hint of difficulties with staff was not given until the fourth report, and was then expressed in the oblique manner previously adopted at Millbank Penitentiary for such matters. 'The conduct of the officers, with few exceptions, has been satisfactory.'[153] Such damningly faint praise was repeated in the fifth report and, except in the sixth, in all subsequent reports up to 1850 when the administration of the prison was brought under the Directorate of Convict Prisons.[154]

The unsatisfactory conduct of the subordinate staff was keenly felt by the Pentonville commissioners, and towards the end of 1845 Wharncliffe wrote to Jebb:

> The Warders must not be allowed to be going drinking and behaving like Blackguards, from alehouse to alehouse, any more than Serjeants of a Reg; not only upon their own accounts, but because their misconduct brings disgrace upon all that are employed in the Prison.[155]

Some commissioners thought that the whole standing of the institution was hopelessly undermined; the Duke of Richmond, who blamed the governor for this, resigned from the board.[156]

151 One such officer, noted in the governor's journal, was 'Warder W.'. His family lived in a prison cottage, to which the police traced him and returned him for formal dismissal. The governor noted that it had been discovered that the man was of indifferent character and had absconded from his family before ('Pentonville Prison, Governor's Journal', entry of 12 April 1843).
152 Jebb Papers, box 3. See, for instance, Lord Chichester's letters of 7 March 1844 and 26 September 1846. In 1846 (day and month omitted) Viscount Eversley wrote to Jebb regarding the commissioners' report: 'we have agreed to omit that part of our Report which relates to the Conduct of the Officers'.
153 *Fourth Report of the Commissioners of Pentonville Prison*, PP, 1846, XX, 97, Appendix A (Governor's Report), 12.
154 See the *Fifth Report of the Commissioners of Pentonville Prison*, PP, 1847, XXX, 481, Appendix A (Governor's Report), 17: 'With few exceptions brought under your notice at the times of their occurrence, the conduct of the subordinate officers, warders, trade-instructors and other servants, has been very satisfactory.' See also *Pentonville Prison – First Report of the Directors of Convict Prisons*, PP, 1851, XXVIII, 1, 8: 'The conduct of the officers generally has been satisfactory.'
155 Jebb Papers, box 3, letter of 12 November 1845. See also the letters of 13 and 18 November.
156 He wrote to Jebb that he could not consent to hold office as he could not perform all the duties of inspection:

> I have no confidence in the Governor. I think the Prison therefore should be most frequently visited. The Monthly Inspection is only a

213

However, the standards of behaviour expected from subordinate staff do not appear to have fallen, and in some respects were raised so as to make greater demands on a man's self-respect over the years. In the 1850s the chaplain, Joseph Kingsmill, noted that officers were dismissed for drunkenness on or off duty, and that 'swearing and improper language; knowingly incurring debts which they are unable to pay; the habit of frequenting public houses, all will severally be considered a sufficient reason for the dismissal of an officer', as would disclosure of information.[157]

Parkhurst, although it had a smaller staff and dealt with juvenile offenders whose command of ready cash must have been unequal to any vicious amount of trafficking, and which was geographically remote, none the less suffered as much as Millbank and Pentonville from dereliction of duty on the part of warders. The annual reports were equally non-committal: the first report merely noted that no officer had been discharged or had resigned. The first significant though still elliptical references were made in 1845 to staff performance: 'On this point,' wrote the governor, 'I have reason, generally to feel satisfied.'[158] Then in 1846 there were no less than seven staff changes, all seemingly for disciplinary reasons; and, while in 1847 misconduct resulted in an officer's dismissal, in 1849 there were more signs of incipient unreliability:

The conduct of the Subordinate Officers has been generally in accordance with the regulations and orders issued for their guidance, and though I have had occasion, in some instances, to inflict fines for slight breaches of punctuality etc., I have not found it requisite to recommend to the visitors that any officer should be discharged for misconduct.

In the following year a graver series of offences involved the governor in consultations with the home secretary, and it seemed that staff management was to be an early challenge to the new directors of convict prisons, who noted in 1851: 'Four officers have been discharged from the prison for misconduct and some minor irregularities have been reported; but otherwise the general conduct of the officers must be regarded as satisfactory.'[159]

---

form. I have no time to go there often enough and therefore by resigning the Secretary of State has the opportunity of appointing a Gentleman who will better perform a most necessary duty (Jebb Papers, box 3, letter of 9 July 1845).

157 Rev. Joseph Kingsmill, *Chapters on Prisons and Prisoners and the Prevention of Crime*, p. 307.
158 *Reports Relating to Parkhurst Prison*, PP, 1839, XXII, 643, and PP, 1845, XXV, 29, respectively.
159 *Reports Relating to Parkhurst Prison*, PP, 1846, XX, 69, 3; PP, 1847, XXX, 457; PP, 1849, XXVI, 327; PP, 1850, XXIX, 95; and *Parkhurst Prison – First Report of the Directors of Convict Prisons*, PP, 1851, XXVIII, 69, 3.

The Directorate of Convict Prisons

The 1840s had been a decade of rapid expansion and consolidation in central government's prison interests: the inspectorate had been consolidated, a new surveyor-general appointed, and the on-shore prison accommodation enlarged; transportation had been curbed and the basis of an alternative system laid down; administration of the hulks had been reorganised and responsibility for the overseas depots shifted to the Colonial Office, the department of government whose interests they most directly served. Additional space for the confinement of convicts had been found at Portland, Shornecliff (a former barracks, acting as a reservoir for the overflow from Millbank), and government-rented cells in local prisons at Bath, Leeds, Leicester, Northampton, Preston, Reading and Wakefield.[160] Administration of new government prisons had been provided on an *ad hoc* basis, step by step with expansion, and a miscellaneous range of bodies, titles and powers was the result. Millbank prison was run by inspectors and then visitors, Pentonville by commissioners (including some of honorary status), and Parkhurst by visitors; Portland with its extensive public works, was Jebb's special responsibility. The inspectors, the surveyor and the criminal clerk at the Home Office[161] all operated under different Acts and codes of rules. There were strong criticisms from a select committee of the variety in payments and costs in government prisons;[162] and government, which had long impressed on local authorities the benefits of uniformity in prison administration, at last saw that a greater degree of consistency would be appropriate for its own establishments. While regularising administrative duties connected with the prisons, it was also felt necessary to give statutory recognition to the largely informal advisory and mediating roles which had been taken up by the inspectors and Jebb, and in 1850 the Directorate of Convict

---

160 The government prisons at this time were described in some detail in evidence given by Captain D. O'Brien to the Select Committee of 1850 (*op. cit.*, 103, questions 1466-9, and 133, question 1880).

161 For a full discussion of the work of the criminal clerk see A.P. Donajgrodski, 'New Roles for Old: The Northcote-Trevelyan Report and the Clerks of the Home Office 1822-48', in Gillian Sutherland (ed.), *Studies in the Growth of Nineteenth-Century Government*.

Until his retirement in 1847 John Capper was the criminal clerk, in which capacity he corresponded with the sheriffs and with the Colonial Office and Admiralty on transportation matters. He was responsible for the preparation of a quarterly report on the convict establishment and for accounts, estimates and any returns called for by Parliament; recommendations for convict pardons passed through his hands before going to the home secretary.

162 *Select Committee on Expenditure for Miscellaneous Services*, PP, 1847-8, XVIII, Pt 1, 619.

Prisons was established.[163] The first three directors were Jebb (by then a lieutenant-colonel), Captain D. O'Brien (the senior inspector) and Mr H.P. Voules.[164]

A central board for government prisons, indeed for all prisons, had long been mooted, though there had been various disagreements about the form which it should take.[165] Its eventual establishment had more than administrative significance: it made a coherent group of the highest prison officials, and enabled them further to exercise considerable influence over the policy; in particular, it greatly enhanced Jebb's public and political standing, and placed extensive powers of patronage in his hands.

The directorate was established at a time of significant disillusionment at the end of the decade that had seen the fantastic flowering of reformist imprisonment, followed straightaway by the destruction and discrediting[166] of the hopes that had been raised. The chaplain's

163 The Act was 13 and 14 Vict., c.39 – 'An Act for the better Government of Convict Prisons'. This Act provided for the appointment of not fewer than three fit persons to be directors of Parkhurst, Pentonville and Millbank and other places for the confinement of male offenders under sentence of transportation in England. The directors were to assume the powers of the previous administrators, thus finally excluding honorary appointments from the administration of the convict prisons; one of them was to be chosen as chairman.

164 Although Voules had been appointed in Capper's place he had not been given the title of superintendent (being referred to in official papers as 'a person') because the directorate was then in the process of preparation. He subsequently took special responsibility within the directorate for the hulks. He had been deputy governor of Millbank, but after a quarrel with the governor, on Jebb's recommendation had been appointed to the hulks; 'he failed in this office – the hulks which were put in his charge were not well looked after and some trouble occurred with the accounts' (Du Cane Papers, sheet 311). Captain O'Brien supervised Pentonville, Millbank, Parkhurst and Shornecliff. He was a manager of Portland and the hulks, though he left the bulk of duties there to his colleagues. He was also responsible for the government prisoners in hired local cells.

   The directorate formalised the duties which the three men had effectively been carrying out for the previous two years.

165 See Chichester's letter to Jebb, 21 December 1846, in which he queried the scheme that Jebb then had in mind, on the grounds that it was provided with insufficient Parliamentary control (Jebb Papers, box 2).

166 In view of Whitworth Russell's public standing, the notoriety that attended such a desperate act and its condemnation in the eyes of contemporary society, his suicide cannot but have affected his penological cause. He took his own life in Millbank, as the prison secretary reported to Sir George Grey on 2 August 1847: 'It is with deep concern that I communicate to you the death of the Revd. Whitworth Russell, which Melancholy event took place at this Prison between the hours of four and five o'clock this day, by an Act of self destruction' (PRO, HO 45/OS 1790). Joseph Kingsmill, then chaplain of Pentonville, sent a distraught letter to Jebb:

reformatory role and administrative importance, supreme under the separate system, had given way to the authority of the governor, who sought the behavioural ends of inmate discipline, organisational efficiency and staff control. William Crawford and Whitworth Russell, ambitious, theoretically brilliant, and brooking no opposition at the beginning of the 1840s, had left the stage to the politically sensitive and pragmatic Jebb with far more effective power than they had ever held. The events, personalities and decisions of the 1840s shaped English penal thought and administration until almost the end of the century.

Oh what a lesson, my dear Sir, not to have the mind absorbed with worldly cares so as to have no room for him who should be all and in all – the First and the Last – our rest – our stay – our hope – Poor Mr. Russell's ruin was his ambition and attempts which could brook no check.

It is a relief to hope that the mind had lost its balance and that other Causes besides prison affairs contributed to the dreadful act.

M . . . says he had speculated in Railways for advancing his daughter [who] was going into gay life so into expence. Oh what a lesson to parents . . . (Jebb Papers, box 3; see also Russell's obituary in *Gentleman's Magazine*, NS, XXVIII (1847), no. 2, p. 550).

By a strange coincidence William Crawford also died in a prison. The *Fifth Report of the Commissioners of Pentonville Prison* stated: 'Previous to the final adoption of this Report, the deliberations of the Board were arrested by the death of Mr. Crawford, who was suddenly seized in the Boardroom, and expired within a few seconds' (PP, 1847, XXX, 481, 16).

---

8 Local prisons 1800-50: policies and conditions

Social conditions and social thought

At the time of Waterloo England was in the midst of a profound economic and social upheaval. Law and order were of particular political importance because of the disorder and crime that followed in the wake of the demobilised army.[1] Moreover, no observer could fail to be impressed by the deep-seated rifts in the fabric and stability of the nation. Enclosure had been completed and agricultural production revolutionised, supplying both food and labour for the rapidly expanding manufactories. The population was growing at an unprecedented rate: in 1811 the census was 11,000,000; in 1851 over 21,000,000. The increase was mainly concentrated in the towns, some of which more than doubled their populations in a few decades.[2] At the time of Waterloo agriculture was the main employment of the nation; by 1831 'probably half the population already lived under urban conditions'.[3] One reason for the increase in population was a fall in the infant mortality rate which was in turn a reflection of general material improvements in the living conditions of the people, both town-dwellers and country-dwellers.[4]

Internal migration and immigration from abroad swamped the towns, physically and administratively. Methods of urban finance, policing and administration, established in medieval times to meet different demographic conditions, simply could not cope. Crime, social disorder and urban distress increased at a rate far beyond that of the population. The swollen towns had a predominance of young people, who faced difficult economic and social problems, which they had to

1 Ted Robert Gurr et al., The Politics of Crime and Conflict, pp. 62-3.
2 Sir Ernest Llewellyn Woodward, The Age of Reform 1815-1870, pp. 1-2.
3 David Thomson, England in the Nineteenth Century, p. 11.
4 Woodward, op. cit., p. 2.

meet with few personal resources. Very frequently the solutions they found were based on:

the techniques, the habits and the attitudes of the criminals. There was thus, in London and the other large towns in the latter part of the eighteenth century and the earlier part of the nineteenth century, an upsurge of crime which was the fruit of a society in rapid transition.[5]

Social change and upheaval on this scale generated perplexity and confusion. Many of the old ways still thrived and doubtless provided consolation and security. Well into the century,

survivals . . . are to be found round every Victorian corner. Habits, patterns of behaviour, attitudes of mind, conditions of living which had come down from the eighteenth century persisted not only in the life and practices of the aristocracy but also in the ways of life and thought, and where there was not much conscious thought, in the instincts and customs of people much lower down the social scale, particularly of people at the very base of society.[6]

But this inertia was matched by a will to change of considerable proportions:

in the first quarter of the nineteenth century it was becoming increasingly clear that what was politically, socially, intellectually and spiritually a new society was growing up in England for which neither the institutions, nor the ideas that had been inherited from the eighteenth century would suffice.[7]

The greater part of that urge for institutional change was given form and purpose by the Evangelicals and Utilitarians, now politically established with achievements that began increasingly to be consolidated. In 1797 William Wilberforce's *Practical View of the Prevailing Religious System of Professed Christians in the Higher and Middle Classes in this Country Contrasted with Real Christianity* was published and became 'the handbook of the Evangelicals'.[8] The evangelical theology, certainly stark and dramatic, made its appeal directly to the emotions. It taught that

all mankind were utterly sinful, and therefore in danger of Hell; that God had provided deliverance in the atoning death of Christ; and that, if only we would accept the offer of salvation so made,

---

5 J.J. Tobias, *Crime and Industrial Society in the Nineteenth Century*, p. 42.
6 G. Kitson Clark, *The Making of Victorian England*, pp. 58-9.
7 *Ibid.*, p. 39.
8 Ian Bradley, *The Call to Seriousness*, p. 19.

we were forgiven, reconciled and safe. That acceptance was conversion.[9]

Wilberforce's hard-fought victory against the slave trade, Peel's reforms in the administration of criminal justice and Lord Shaftesbury's achievements on behalf of lunatics and the factory workers were all testimonies to the power of the evangelical drive. It went straight to the heart, and had something to say about all aspects of life, possessing ' "the eternal microscope" with which it pursued its arguments into the recesses of the heart, and the details of daily life, giving to every action its individual value in this life, and its infinite consequences in the next'.[10] The evangelical world view had relevance both for the remoulding of educational, welfare and penal institutions, and for the individual fates and outlook of those who passed through or administered them.

This was also the time of the triumph of utilitarian principles in law, social policy and public administration. In the last quarter of the eighteenth century utilitarian thought had been closely associated with liberal principles in politics and economics — the notions of a non-interventionist state and *laissez faire*. Now its emphasis changed;

> The 'utilitarian' philosophy was not solely, nor even perhaps fundamentally, a liberal system; it was at the same time a doctrine of authority which looked to the deliberate and in a sense the scientific interference of Government to produce a harmony of interests. . . . In Bentham's view, when the authority of the state had been reconciled by a universal or at least a very wide suffrage with the interests of the majority there was no further reason to hold it suspect, it became an unmixed blessing.[11]

John Stuart Mill's revision of Benthamism rescued it from the ethical charge of epicureanism and permitted considerable reconciliation with Christian doctrines, and at the same time supported a constructive and interventionist view of the state.[12] Utilitarianism in the first part of

9 *Cit. ibid.*, p. 20.
10 G.M. Young, *Victorian England*, pp. 1-2. G.F.A. Best has written of Shaftesbury:

> His religion kept him in a state of constant involvement with the world, and his religious meditation, profound and elaborate though it often was, directed him all the time to look outwards into the world where God's grace and providence were at war with man's sin and folly, and to participate in that momentous conflict (*Shaftesbury*, p. 54).

11 Elie Halévy, *A History of the English People in the Nineteenth Century*, 111, p. 100.
12 Geraint L. Williams (ed.), *John Stuart Mill on Politics and Society*, pp. 121, 129. See, for example, the passage:

> As between his own happiness and that of others, utilitarianism requires him to be strictly impartial as a disinterested and benevolent spectator. In

the nineteenth century was thus enabled to combine both competitive individual endeavour and a measure of state regulation. Particularly, as applied by Chadwick, it reduced progress 'from an aspiration to a schedule', which was to be implemented by toil:

> And always and everywhere competition is reducing the profits of the employer, and the wages of the workman, to the level of bare subsistence. . . . But Nature has not left her children without all hope of escaping the fate to which her mathematics seem to have consigned them. By industry, and abstinence, the employer may enlarge his market for his goods; by industry and continence, the workman may increase the purchasing power, and limit the numbers of his class: progress, like salvation, is the reward of virtue; of diligence and self-education; of providence and self control. . . .[13]

This, too, was a philosophy immensely relevant to social and penal policy and the 'improvement' of the individual.

By noting the broader intellectual drives and concerns of the time, the criminological and penological theories that were current in the various localities are placed in this chapter in a suitable context, so as to adumbrate their subsequent development. A wide variety of political and economic interests had to be accommodated in the construction of policy, as the constraints of unequal access to limited material resources had to be allowed for. These preliminary observations pave the way to a brief consideration of the state of the local prisons.

---

the golden rule of Jesus of Nazareth, we read the complete spirit of the ethics of utility. To do as you would be done by, and to love your neighbour as yourself, constitute the ideal of perfection of utilitarian morality. As the means of making the nearest approach to this ideal, utility would enjoin, first, that laws and social arrangements should place the happiness or . . . the interest of every individual as nearly as possible in harmony with the interest of the whole; and secondly, that education and opinion, which have so vast a power over human character, should so use that power as to establish in the mind of every individual an indissoluble association between his own happiness and the good of the whole. . . .

See also Thomson (*op. cit.*, pp. 30, 32) who observes that Bentham's utilitarianism

soon became glaringly inadequate in the conditions of early Victorian England. His principle was capable of much wider and more positive interpretation, permitting of every extensive State action. It was Bentham's disciples, Mill and Chadwick, who saw this and built on it the liberal philosophy of social reform.

---

13 Young, *op. cit.*, pp. 9-10.

Prison conditions

It is very difficult to be precise in statements about early nineteenth-century imprisonment. Attempts of central authority to gather and record facts and figures upon which the machinery of government depended were spasmodic and the local response was always uneven. Before 1800 it was not even known how many subjects the kingdom possessed. Regular annual returns of the basic statistics on indictable offences did not begin until 1805. Because of the comparative strengths and political relationships between central and local government, systematic and reliable information on local prisons was nearly impossible to obtain.

The collection of criminal statistics was stimulated by the efforts of Romilly, Mackintosh and Buxton to mitigate the penal code.[14] Two attempts were made to secure prison statistics, the first by an Act of 1815 which required annual returns, giving committal details, in respect of every prison in the country,[15] and the second by Peel nine years later, when, having been baulked in his attempts to reform the gaols, partly because of lack of information, he carried through an order for quarterly returns.[16] Even so, the inefficiency and indifference of central and local government largely nullified the effect of this measure.[17] In the years that followed, under the influence of Benthamite utilitarianism the adolescent science of statistics played an important part in the 'intellectual revolution' of the 1830s. The 1835 Select Committee on Gaols, hampered by the lack of information on prisons, laid upon the newly appointed inspectors of prisons the task of remedying this deficiency. So ineffective had Peel's measure been in securing regular and accurate returns that the inspectors discovered many prisons that had been omitted altogether;[18] and it took five years of determined effort, aided by far-reaching changes in local government, before the

14 K.K. Macnab, thesis: 'Aspects of the History of Crime', p. 36.
15 55 Geo. III, c.49.
16 By 5 Geo. IV, c.85, which supplemented the Gaol Act of the previous year.
17 A letter in *The Times* reported in June 1832 that accurate returns had been submitted the previous year only by Tynemouth, Hexham, Guildford and Petworth.

> Thus it appears that the gaoler makes a wrong return, the clerk of the peace neglects to examine it, the sessions and Secretary of State omit to look at it, and so one of the most important Acts of Parliament, which relates to thousands of criminals in this country, is permitted, in this respect, to become worse than a dead letter (*The Times*, 6 June 1832, 5c).

18 *Select Committee of the House of Lords on Gaols and Houses of Correction*, First Report, PP, 1835, XI, 1, 3, and Minutes of Evidence, PP, 1835, XI, 1, 275-6; *First Report of the Inspectors of Prisons (Scotland, Northumberland and Durham)*, PP, 1835, XXXV, 357, 18.

inspectors could claim a reasonable degree of accuracy for their prison statistics.[19]

Before 1840, therefore, national figures relating to imprisonment must be treated with great caution. Even the number of prisons is uncertain: whereas in 1812 James Neild reported that there were 317 prisons in England and Wales, and in 1818 the Society for the Improvement of Prison Discipline counted a total of 518 for the whole of the United Kingdom,[20] parliamentary returns for England and Wales gave 335 and 291 in 1819 and 1833 respectively.[21] It is highly probable that the smaller prisons were often overlooked in all these calculations, since many were used infrequently and had no full-time, or even regular part-time, staff to attend to correspondence.

But if the precise number were hard to obtain, their general condition was widely advertised. In the last decade of the eighteenth century Parliament had been persuaded to consolidate existing prison legislation and to intervene more systematically in the discipline and administration of the local prisons in accordance with the underlying intention of 31 Geo. III, c.46, 'An Act for the better regulating of gaols and other places of confinement'. The Webbs described it as 'a high-water mark in the conception of prison discipline'. Sir George Paul, however, pointed to the utter indifference with which the magistrates received it. Had 31 Geo. III, c.46, contained

> an ordinance for committing to the flames the modern statutes for the construction and regulation of prisons, the purposes of these laws could not have made a less general progress, or have been more disregarded. I have reason to think that in no one county of

19 See the *Sixth Report of the Inspectors of Prisons (Home District)*, PP, 1841, IV, 1, vi.

20 James Neild, *The State of the Prisons in England, Scotland and Wales*, pp. lx-lxiv, and H. Mayhew and J. Binny, *The Criminal Prisons of London*, p. 97, n.

21 *An Account of All the Gaols, Houses of Correction or Penitentiaries in the United Kingdom*, PP, 1819, XVII, 371, and *Return of All the Gaols and Houses of Correction in England and Wales, Including those under Corporate Jurisdiction*, PP, 1833, XXVIII, 549. These latter figures include county, municipal and franchise prisons, which ranged in size from mere lockups to multiple-winged establishments with hundreds of prisoners. Prisons in some of the smaller towns seemed to be little more than cages, or extensions of the parish stocks. For example, at Dinas Mwddy in Merioneth in the mid-1830s it was reported that

> Besides the Pinfold and the Stocks there is a Crib, a little Prison, in which a drunken Man was lately confined for a few Hours until he was sober, or at least fit to be set at liberty. The Crib was built not long since, and the Country [*sic*] it was said is unwilling to pay for it ('Extracts Relative to Gaols' from Appendix to *Report on Municipal Corporations*, Appendix No: 1, Minutes of Evidence, 1835 *SC, op. cit.*, 589).

England have the powers of the three Acts of the 22nd, the 24th and the 31st George III, been fully carried into effect.[22]

Indeed, the eighteenth-century practices in general continued unabated, and entrepreneurial keepers were left, in most places, to preside over neglected fee- and garnish-ridden establishments, into which prisoners were still promiscuously herded and left, very often, literally to rot: 'although some 46 new gaols had been built on the cellular plan by 1800 . . . by and large the state of the prisons was hardly less deplorable than it had been in Howard's day'.[23]

Howard's work, however, had ensured that some sanitary precautions were taken, and there seems to have been a reduction in the incidence of gaol fever. And in some localities the magistrates had provided new, regulated prisons, which the Webbs list as the West Riding, Lancashire, Norfolk, Suffolk, Cornwall, Devon, Hampshire, Hereford and Derby;[24] to these must be added the prisons at Gloucester, Southwell, Horsham and Petworth. William Waddington, writing in 1798, referred to Gloucester and Dorchester as model regulated prisons;[25] and Bridewell, of which he was a governor, provided itself with a new prison in 1797.[26]

Because of the decentralised system of prison administration, however, change was slow in coming. Traditional prisons and their practices predominated for many years, and there was even some

---

22 *Cit.* S. and B. Webb, *English Prisons Under Local Government*, p. 53.
23 Giles Playfair, *The Punitive Obsession*, p. 76. Neild argued that the reformation produced by Howard had been, in several places, merely temporary: 'some prisons that had been ameliorated under the persuasive influence of his kind advice were relapsing into their former state of privation, filthiness, severity or neglect' (*cit.* Babington, *The English Bastille*, p. 167).
24 S. and B. Webb, *op. cit.*, p. 56 and p. 56, n. 2. Robert Alan Cooper mentions several other local authorities which attempted to bring their prisons within the provisions of the new laws. These included Hertfordshire, Wiltshire, Bedfordshire, Northamptonshire, Warwickshire, Berkshire, Surrey and the towns of Liverpool, Manchester and Nottingham (thesis: 'English Prison Reform 1773-1835', pp. 94-7, *passim*).
25 William Waddington, *Considerations on the Proper and Original Objects of the Royal Hospital of Bridewell*, p. 37, n. Dorchester Penitentiary, completed in 1791, followed closely the design and administration adopted at Gloucester.
26 E.G. O'Donoghue, *Bridewell Hospital*, II, p. 215. Before the opening of the new prison, a delegation of Bridewell governors went to visit Cold Bath Fields house of correction to learn what they could about its classification, employment and separation systems. This prison was opened in 1794 and adopted rules much influenced by those put into force by Paul at Gloucester. Indeed, the Cold Bath Fields Regulations explicitly drew the keeper's attention to Paul's ideas on separate confinement (Richard Herrick Condon, thesis: 'The Reform of English Prisons, 1773-1816', p. 135).

backsliding in the pioneering establishments at Gloucester and Southwell.[27] In 1818 the Society for the Improvement of Prison Discipline discovered that, of the 518 prisons in the United Kingdom,

> in 23 . . . only the inmates were separated or divided according to law; in 59 of the number, there was no division whatever − not even separation of males from females; in 136 there was only one division of the inmates into separate classes, though the 24th Geo. III, c.54 had enjoined that eleven such divisions should be made; in 68 there were but two divisions, and so on. . . . Again, in 445 of the 518 prisons no work of any description had been introduced. And in the remaining 73, the employment carried on was of the slighest possible description. Farther in 100 jails, which had been built to contain only 8545 prisoners, there were at one time as many as 13,057 confined.[28]

The corporate and franchise prisons were particularly noted for their resistance to change. Clay described the 140 municipal prisons of the late 1820s as 'the filthiest and most abominable in the Kingdom . . . containing about eight thousand inmates', and referred to the several

27 The Gloucester régime had in fact been modified several years *before* the setting up of the Holford Committee because the numbers committed were too great to be separately confined. (See the *Second Report of the Inspectors of Prisons (Home District)*, *op. cit.*; see also J.R.S. Whiting, *Prison Reform in Gloucestershire 1776-1820*, pp. 87-8.) A memorandum from the Nottinghamshire magistrates to those of Essex dated 14 January 1822 makes it clear that the reward-based system at Southwell house of correction was by then abolished (Essex County Record Office, QS bundles, ref. Q/SBb-489/81). In October 1821 the Nottinghamshire quarter sessions initiated an inquiry into means for the more effectual employment of the Southwell prisoners, resulting in a recommendation in January 1822 that the diet should be changed and a treadmill set up for those sentenced to hard labour; by February 1823 the new machinery was installed and in use (Nottinghamshire Record Office, refs QAG/5/50, 5/51, 5/54, 5/72, 5/73). This reflected a change in Becher's views on the function of labour in an institutional régime. His pessimism in this regard was shown by his comment in *The Antipauper System* (published in 1828):

> to realize actual profit by servile and involuntary Labour, I can affirm, after long and fruitless experience, to be an impracticable attempt. The Expense of additional Buildings and Machinery, the Superintendence, the Interest of Capital, and the Losses occasioned by defective Workmanship, and irrecoverable Debts, counterbalance any apparent Emoluments, if the Accounts be correctly stated. Forced labour can never compete successfully with free Industry. Indeed one of the fundamental Errors in the Management of Workhouses has been a false notion, that they might be converted into profitable Manufactories; which project, considering the constitution of such Establishments, and the mental degradation, as well as the physical inability of the Inmates, never can be substantially realized (pp. 15-16).

28 *Cit*. Mayhew and Binny, *op. cit.*, p. 97, n.

semi-private franchise prisons, which by then were used only for debtors, as 'miserable, filthy dens for the most part, where the wretched debtor, without any allowance from the county, without the means of wringing his alimentary sixpence a week from his creditor, was left to starve'.[29]

The 1835 Royal Commission on Municipal Corporations provided a wealth of detail on the condition of municipal prisons.[30] The commission was particularly struck by their proliferation, which was due to the fact that, whatever their size and resources, nearly all the boroughs which possessed criminal jurisdiction exercised their right to have a gaol, the administration and financial arrangements of which were consequently much more irregular than the larger and more aptly funded county establishments. In some towns the corporation was responsible for them, in others the borough magistrates. Financial support was in some cases provided by the corporation, but equally it might be raised by a borough rate, or even a poor rate. Inefficiency in the control of the corporation's finances and administration made prison management difficult. Many corporations were heavily in debt: 'In some the payment of the interest absorbs a very large proportion of the revenue; others are absolutely insolvent.'[31] The low ability of municipal officials was also a factor increasing maladministration: 'The corporate magistrates are often selected from a class incompetent to the discharge of judicial functions, and the consequence has been a great defect in the administration of justice.'[32]

29 W.L. Clay, *The Prison Chaplain*, pp. 98, 99. These views were supported by Samuel Hoare, chairman of the Prison Discipline Society, in his evidence to the select committee of 1835. The franchise prisons were, he stated,

> great nurseries of crime. Where there is a very small number of Prisoners confined in one Place Prison Discipline cannot be enforced; they have not the Requisites. Many Gaols are without any Religious Instruction, many without any Place of separate Confinement, almost all without Employment – a Gaoler who is occupied about other things perhaps a great Part of the Day – the Establishment is not sufficiently large to employ proper Officers; in short they are so exceedingly bad that the sooner they are abolished the better; They cannot be carried on as at present without great Evil (1835 *SC*, *op. cit*., First Report, Minutes of Evidence, 25).

30 *Royal Commission on Municipal Corporations*, First Report, PP, 1835, XXIII, 5.
31 *Ibid*., 32.
32 *Ibid*., 39. The commission gave illustrations to back their point:

> At East Retford . . . one of the magistrates was in the habit of conversing familiarly with the culprits brought before him, and endeavoured to impress them with the idea that he was performing an unwilling office. On one occasion he (the witness) saw the magistrate fighting with a prisoner, and struggling with him on the floor. At Malmesbury the magistrates are often unable to read or write . . . (*ibid*.).

In an effort to economise many municipalities followed an old-established convention by siting their prison in the town hall; at Berwick the gaol was on the third floor of the town hall, and at Bishops Castle in a dungeon beneath it. Tamworth gaol, also a town hall dungeon, was described by the Royal Commission as 'a single Room with Excavations in the Wall, in which the Prisoners sleep. There is no sufficient Admission of Light or Air, nor any Yard or Place in which the Prisoners may take Exercise'.[33]

Lack of resources and training were not the only factors inhibiting change. The City of London, which once, with its Bridewell and other royal hospitals, was a pioneer in social and penal philosophy and management, was now in the grip of politicians favouring non-intervention, being of the 'whig frame of mind'. With righteous parsimoniousness it obdurately resisted criticisms and rejected suggestions for any change in the running of its prisons. In 1814 the Middlesex grand jury presented Newgate as a public nuisance,[34] whereupon a parliamentary select committee was set up to investigate the condition of the City prisons. Its report condemned the grossly overcrowded and unsatisfactory state of Newgate,[35] in terms which repeated those of Sir Richard Phillips who had visited in 1808, and were replicated in turn by Henry Bennet in 1817, and by Sir Thomas Buxton in 1818[36]

33 *Ibid.*, 193.
34 Woodward, *op. cit.*, p. 467.
35 *Select Committee on City of London Prisons*, PP, 1813-14, IV, 1, 249.
36 Sir Richard Phillips complained of the corruption, overcrowding and unhealthy conditions at Newgate, and the overcrowding and ruinous conditions at the various Compters (*A Letter to the Livery of London*, pp. 80-98, 118-21 and 131-5, *passim*).

Henry Bennet inspected Newgate just a few years after the passing of gaol legislation which forbade the taking of fees. The sole effect seemed to be a shift in the practice of corrupt enterprise and extortion from the newly salaried keeper to the turnkeys. Bennet's survey catalogued all the usual grievances – the lack of classification, overcrowding, drunkenness, bribery, prostitution and so forth – but commended the keeper who, though handicapped by the bad design of the building, had none the less introduced certain reforms. He reported that the keeper

is endeavouring to check the abuses which have prevailed in the management of the prison: among these abuses the sale of offices has been the most serious; and I have been informed that the place of wardman to the different wards has often been purchased, not of Mr. Newman (the former keeper), who was ignorant of the transaction, but of the turnkeys. I know an individual . . . who offered fifty guineas for one of these situations, and was refused, no doubt because a better price was got (Hon. H.G. Bennet, 'A Letter to the Common Council and Livery of the City of London, on the Abuses Existing in Newgate; Showing the Necessity of an Immediate Reform in the Management of that Prison', *Pamphleteer* (1818), XI, no. 277, p. 15).

Buxton compared Newgate to the Maison de Force at Ghent in a memorable paragraph:

227

whose report on the Borough Comptor was found truly shocking by a wide circle of informed opinion. Elizabeth Fry's missionary work, which commenced in earnest about this time, also brought Newgate conditions to public notice. But City members of Parliament ignored the criticisms and the aldermen declared that 'their prisoners had all they ought to have unless gentlemen thought they ought to be indulged with Turkish carpets'.[37]

City rejection of outsiders' complaints over the next twenty or so years meant that most of the grievances remained in place to incur the condemnation of the inspectors in their first report in 1836.[38] In their second report the inspectors turned to the other City prisons, and found even worse conditions to write about:

> In the description of these prisons, which it has been our painful duty to lay before your Lordship, we have been consoled by the reflection that the very enormity of the evils which we have exposed releases us from the necessity of expatiating upon them.[39]

But the inspectors failed to appreciate how thick-skinned the City authorities could be: the least defensible practices and most flagrant abuses were grudgingly corrected or modified, but even several years

---

The most boisterous tempest is not more distinct from the serenity of a summer's evening: the wildest beast of prey is not more different from our domesticated animals, than is the noise, contention, licentiousness, and tumult of Newgate, from the quietness, industry, and regularity of the Maison de Force (*An Enquiry Whether Crime and Misery are Produced or Prevented* . . . , p. 87).

Newgate was also subjected to a critical survey by a select committee in 1819 (*Select Committee on the State of Gaols*, PP, 1819, VII, 1, 266), in 1835 (*Select Committee of the House of Lords on Gaols and Houses of Correction*, PP, 1835, XI), and in 1836 (*Select Committee on the Laws Relating to Prisons*, PP, 1836, XXI, 301). It was described in condemnatory detail by the inspectors of prisons (*First Report of the Inspectors of Prisons (Home District)*, PP, 1836, XXXV).

---

37 *Cit.* Babington, *op. cit*., p. 161.
38 This document gave rise to the famous libel case of *Stockdale v. Hansard*. John Stockdale sued the firm of Hansard because they had, in keeping with the instructions of the Commons, published the report in which, *inter alia*, Crawford and Russell referred to one of Stockdale's books, uncovered in the course of an inspection of Newgate, as being 'of a most disgusting nature . . . the plates are indecent and obscene in the extreme'. The case turned on the privileges of parliament and the powers of the courts. Stockdale won his case, and in 1840 the Parliamentary Papers Act (2 and 3 Vict., c.9) was introduced to protect from such suits persons employed in the publication of parliamentary papers, thus ensuring the unhindered reporting of the proceedings of parliament (*First Report of the Inspectors of Prisons (Home District)*, PP, 1836, XXXV, 1, 7; (1839) 112 ER 1112).
39 *Second Report of the Inspectors of Prisons (Home District)*, PP, 1837, XXXII, 1, 68.

on, in their tenth report, the inspectors were repeating substantially the same objections.[40]

The other prisons of the metropolis were not very different. Although, strictly speaking, they were not local prisons, there is some advantage in briefly considering the Fleet, Marshalsea and King's Bench prisons. Theoretically these institutions, for debtors and civil prisoners only, came under the authority of the courts they served; both judiciary and Parliament (which had, indeed, exempted them from certain legislation) by an acquiescent attitude gave countenance to the methods of their entrepreneurial management. Until their amalgamation in 1842 they continued to display most of the administrative and disciplinary features of eighteenth-century prisons; indeed, the legislation by which they were amalgamated sealed the legality and propriety of the preceding state of things by providing compensation to the officials for their loss of profits.[41]

40 *Tenth Report of the Inspectors of Prisons (Home District)*, PP, 1845, XXIII, 1.

Staff corruption in the City prisons was apparently rife late into the century. A pickpocket, sent to the City bridewell at Blackfriars, was thus able considerably to ease the pains of his incarceration:

During my imprisonment I did not live on the prison diet, but was kept on good rations supplied to me through the kindness of my comrades out of doors bribing the turnkeys. I had tea of a morning, bread and butter, and often cold meat. Meat of all kinds and pastry was sent to me from a cook-shop outside, and I was allowed to sit up later than other prisoners. During the time I was in prison for these three months I learned to smoke, as cigars were introduced to me (J.J. Tobias, *Prince of Fences*, 1974, p. 24).

Another notable instance of corruption at Newgate occurred as late as 1877 when certain prisoners established regular communications with the outside world and obtained 'an apparently unlimited amount of money, with which, it would seem, they were able to seduce from his duty and allegiance every person with whom they came in contact' (Montague Williams, *Leaves of a Life*, p. 232).

41 They were amalgamated in 1842 by Act of Parliament, 5 and 6 Vict., Sess. 2, c.22, 'An Act for consolidating the Queen's Bench, Fleet and Marshalsea Prisons, and for regulating the Queen's Prison'.

In 1816 Henry Bennet expressed doubts whether any reforms had been achieved in the King's Bench:

It would hardly be believed that the marshal had derived 800 l. a year from a per-centage on the beer drank in the prison, in defiance of Act of Parliament: and 2,500 l. a year from the rules: that is to say, this sum of money was taken from the pockets of debtors, to the injury of their creditors, for the benefit of the marshal. He could not imagine that these abuses could continue, unless the marshal was supported by some person of high authority (*Hansard* (First Series), XXXIV, col. 1262).

The prisons were subjected to an inquiry in 1819 by a sanguine, and at times openly sympathetic, Royal Commission. The Fleet, then a prison of about

At Cold Bath Fields, the Middlesex house of correction, initial provisions for regulation and inspection had proved ineffective or had lapsed, and enormous profits were made. When he became governor, in 1829, George Chesterton found that

> There was scarcely one redeeming feature in the prison administration, but the whole machinery tended to promote shameless gains by the furtherance of all that was lawless and execrable . . . widespread defilement . . . polluted every hole and corner of that Augean stable.[42]

By this time, as at Newgate, payment of an adequate salary to the keeper had shifted profitable extortion down the hierarchy to the yardsmen (prisoners) and the turnkeys. One turnkey had boasted in a neighbouring public house that 'his perquisites averaged at least twenty-five shillings a day . . . in my own judgement, some of them [the turnkeys] by the multiplicity of their illicit transactions, must have realized an average even exceeding the above ample estimate'.[43] Such an income was very substantial for the time.[44] Chesterton himself

---

240-50 inmates, had a further sixty or seventy in the rules (i.e. free to be at large in a certain district). At the time of the commission there were, in addition to the prisoners, thirty-nine of their wives and fifty-four of their children living in the prison. Remuneration of the staff was entirely by means of fees; offices were farmed out and there were absentee officials. Unrestricted admission of women and liquor, a tap-room, cellar-head, and coffee house, 'occasionally' gave rise to rioting and disorder, the commission noted. (It recommended the closing of these amenities during Sunday chapel.) 'Chummage' or garnish was practised, as was extensive trading in food, bedding and utensils of all kinds. As the prison had a great turnover of inmates, the annual net income of the deputy warden (after he had paid all expenses, including £500 to the absentee warden) amounted to about £2,238. The other two prisons were in most respects in a similar state. (See the *Royal Commission on State, Conduct and Management of the Fleet, Westminster Palace and Marshalsea*, PP, 1819, XI, 325.) Besides providing considerable detail about the offices and administration of these prisons, the commission in its recommendations substantially endorsed all the rationalisations for the continuation of the practices.

By 43 Eliz., c.2, and 11 Geo. II, c.20, and 12 Geo. II, c.29, amended by 53 Geo. III, c.113, every county was required to contribute to the upkeep of poor prisoners in these three prisons. As has been seen (Chapter 1) charges were extremely high, with an inflationary effect upon the levy laid on the counties, many of which bitterly criticised this provision (see S. and B. Webb, *op. cit.*, p. 69, n. 2). The practice of allowing prisoners to purchase the privilege of 'going abroad' continued in the Queen's Prison until it was prohibited by s.12 of 5 & 6 Vict., Sess. 2, c.22.

---

42 George Laval Chesterton, *Revelations of Prison Life; with an Enquiry into Prison Discipline and Secondary Punishments*, I, p. 44.
43 *Ibid.*, I, p. 124.
44 All forms of prison trading were pursued at Cold Bath Fields, with the usual preponderance of foodstuffs, alcohol and tobacco. Money to finance the

at first received all kinds of offerings from tradesmen and prisoners' friends:

> ... house-lamb, game, poultry and fish, all neatly packed, and accompanied by propitiatory notes, poured in rather thickly, and, one day, a twelfth cake, of costly size, denoted a trader's opportune provision for a seasonable festivity.[45]

The multitude of prisoners, the indifference or hostility towards regulation shown by some magistrates and aldermen, the organisation and traditions of local criminals, all probably made the metropolis an exceptionally rich province for enterprising gaolers and turnkeys. But there is little doubt that in the 1840s, and later, opportunities to make money were found with little trouble and grasped in prisons throughout the country. Whilst vigorously exposing its corruptions, Chesterton argued that condemnation should by no means be reserved only for his prison:

> let it be remembered that the disclosures which then set the seal of infamy upon the prison at Coldbath Fields, would equally have been elicited by an inquiry into the details of almost every other prison in the kingdom. Such establishments reeked with corruption.[46]

---

trade was brought in from the outside, and the turnkey and yardsman deducted about 50 per cent for their services in transmitting it. The remaining amount was then spent on highly priced illicit goods. Parcels were also smuggled in, and a levy exacted on their contents. There were some fairly ingenious devices employed to exact money from the prisoners, besides the widespread system of intimidation; the hospital turnkey, for example, sold 'nights' in the infirmary beds at the rate of $2s.$ $6d.$ a time; prisoners, anxious to sleep comfortably and between sheets, were easily found to meet this tariff. Other turnkeys connived at meetings between the male prisoners and prostitutes from the female side.

Chesterton wrote that his unexpected night-time visit to the infirmary which uncovered the beds racket also uncovered a trade in tobacco, writing-paper and the like. The infirmary turnkey accepted goods as well as money in payment, and even granted credit, to control which he kept ledgers.

---

45 Chesterton, *op. cit.*, I, p. 110. Sir Richard Phillips (*op. cit.*, p. 221) reported the debauchment of a female prisoner by the son of the governor of Cold Bath Fields in 1807.

46 Chesterton, *op. cit.*, I, p. 55. Between the surveys of Neild and Buxton and the inspectorate, accounts of the state of prisons were only local and fragmentary; but whatever evidence that emerged supports Chesterton's assertion, although it is likely that the magistrates and municipal officials grew more mindful of their duty in the late 1820s and early 1830s. Some of the many incidents that can be mentioned may give an insight into prevailing conventions in prison administration and management. At Preston gaol convicted felons were *usually* hired out to neighbouring factories in the 1820s. Clay records that a convict serving a sentence of a year's imprisonment 'was employed, during the whole of that term in the capacity of gardener at the residence of a gentleman within two miles of the town:

None the less, although trafficking, collusion and corruption were rife in most prisons, such activities generally amounted to mere peccadilloes when compared to the extortion and torture of Huggins and Bambridge in the Fleet a hundred years previously, or the fatal neglect and heartless cupidity catalogued by Howard and Neild. Moreover, an increasing number of municipal authorities waived their prison-keeping rights and used the county gaol and bridewell, paying on a *pro rata* basis, while some of the large borough gaols, newly built, were reasonably well administered and managed. Elsewhere, despite a certain amount of idiosyncrasy, fairly efficient and economical arrangements were made: at Newcastle-under-Lyme, for example, the gaol was attached to the parish workhouse, enabling the common use of certain facilities and of staff.

By the end of the 1830s reformatory pressures on the corporate prisons had intensified; not only had their deficiencies been authoritatively given publicity by the Royal Commission, but they had been thrown into sharp relief by the efficient regulations of a growing number of county establishments. Harried by the conscientious Inspectorate of Prisons and increasing insistence of legislation, many of the smaller municipal authorities closed their prisons (a course which raised certain legal difficulties)[47] or contracted for accommodation with

---

this "prisoner at large" merely coming *home* in the evenings to sleep' (Clay's report for 1843, cited in W.L. Clay, *op. cit.*, pp. 146-7).

Very many instances of the overcharging and exploitation of debtors are recorded; it continued to be legal to levy fees for the hire of the keeper's own utensils, rooms and bedding after 1815. Debtors at Chelmsford, for example, complained to quarter sessions in 1820 that the gaoler had increased the rental for a bed from 3*s.* to 6*s.* per week, and that by crowding them together he was able to let out parts of the prisons for sums of £4 and £5 per week (Essex County Record Office, QS bundles, ref. QSBb/459/5/1). Even the segregation of the sexes was not effected in many places until the late 1820s or mid-1830s: at Berwick town gaol it was not ordered until 1828 (1835 *SC, op. cit.*, First Report, Minutes of Evidence, 276), and at Horsemonger Lane Gaol (the Surrey debtors' and remand prison) prostitutes freely visited the male prisoners as late as 1835 (*ibid.*, 227-8).

Male staff seem frequently to have taken sexual advantage of female prisoners. A newly appointed chaplain at Preston incurred the enmity of the governor when he obtained the appointment of a matron which (Clay laconically recorded) 'considerably embarrassed his [the governor's] household arrangements' (Clay, *op. cit.*, p. 113). At Chelmsford gaol a woman prisoner became pregnant as a result of a liaison with a male member of staff. The magistrates were obliged to appoint a matron and, pending her arrival, withdrew the relevant keys from the staff and gave them to their wives (Essex Record Office, QS, Gaol Visitors' Report, Easter 1822, ref. QSBb/24/2).

---

47 As late as 1848 Frederic Hill, then inspector for the Northern District, criticised the state of the law on prison closures. He cited an Act of Parliament which had to be passed 'for the sole purpose of discontinuing a

the county. At the end of the decade one inspector, whilst still denouncing the condition of the smaller borough prisons in his district, noted that they were by then rarely used for more than remand purposes.[48]

Conditions in the franchise prisons, which existed solely to provide rents for owners and livings (usually miserable) for keepers, changed more slowly. Due to alterations in the laws respecting debtors, these prisons could no longer take fees, and survived financially in a hazardous way only because of the profits that could be made from trading with the prisoners.[49] The inspectorate repeatedly urged their abolition and gave accounts of their condition that conjured up the reports of Howard:

> Independently of the precarious supply of food, the condition of
> the debtor in many of these local gaols is very pitiable – there being
> no provision either of light, fuel, bedding, medical assistance, nor
> the means of cleanliness; and in one prison the water is so bad as to
> compel the prisoners, even with their scanty means, to purchase it
> from without.[50]

Garnish[51] was levied by the destitute inmates; often there was no separate accommodation for female prisoners, nor were female staff employed. Despite the continual urging of the inspectors[52] it was not until 1850 that legislation permitted abolition,[53] the first application of which was to the gaol of the liberty of St Albans.

Thus it can be seen that for several decades conditions in the local prisons – particularly those under corporate or franchise administration – remained in many significant respects unaltered from the eighteenth-century pattern. The financial interests of the administrations, keepers and turnkeys continued strongly to militate against change. How

small prison at Rothwell, a little village in Yorkshire' (*Thirteenth Report of the Inspectors of Prisons (Northern and Eastern District)*, PP, 1847-8, XXVI, 361, XX fn.).

48 *Fourth Report of the Inspectors of Prisons (Northern and Eastern District)*, PP, 1839, XXII, 1.
49 *Fifth Report of the Inspectors of Prisons (Northern and Eastern District)*, PP, 1840, XXV, 565, iii-iv. William Williams, the inspector for this district, was particularly concerned because he had no fewer than nine franchise gaols in his area.
50 *Seventh Report of the Inspectors of Prisons (Northern and Eastern District)*, PP, 1842, XXI, 1, iv.
51 See p. 52, n. 10, above.
52 See, for example, the *Eighth Report of the Inspectors of Prisons (Northern and Eastern District)*, PP, 1843, XXV and XXVI, 249, and the *Ninth Report of the Inspectors of Prisons (Northern and Eastern District)*, PP, 1844, XXIX, 227.
53 This was 13 & 14 Vict., c.105, 'An Act for facilitating the Union of Liberties with the Counties in which they are situate'.

was this reluctance to improve affected by developments in social and penal philosophy?

Explanations of crime

It can be argued that the risks of exploitation run by inmates of state prisons were not inappropriate for a penal policy of maximum deterrence.[54] That policy in turn involved Hobbesian assumptions about the causes of crime; and there is a commonly held belief that nineteenth-century criminological thought was little more than an extension of this, namely, that it was confined to moralistic explanations which resulted in a purely repressive penal policy. But such a belief ignores the fact that most of the elements in modern criminological thought were then anticipated. It is true that some of the theories were intensely idiosyncratic; some were religious, harping upon man's fallen state (but as all men were sinful that did not have to lead particularly to repression); others brought in environmental influences, physical, social and economic; others again were a combination of types. Our terminology differs from that of the nineteenth century, but the theories ranged over the same ground as now.[55]

However, most of the criminological theories of the early nineteenth century lacked an empirical base, and were highly speculative. They could thus more easily become vehicles for the fashionable prejudices of the time. Then (as now) policy was shaped only in part by aetiological tenets, ideas and theories being otherwise determined by a variety of factors, namely, ideology, personal interest and national economy. Thus we find the religious creed of the Roman Catholic Irish the central component of one theory — admittedly put forward by the fanatically anti-popery chaplain of Pentonville:

> They are wholly given to lying, and are as clever as they are deceitful. . . . I would warn their own priests not to trust them too

54 See above, Chapter 3.
55 See, for example, *Select Committee of the House of Lords on Gaols and Houses of Correction*, First Report, Minutes of Evidence, PP, 1835, XI, 393; Anon., *Old Bailey Experience, Criminal Jurisprudence and the Actual Working of our Penal Code of Laws. Also, An Essay on Prison Discipline, to which is added a History of the Crimes Committed by Offenders in the Present Day*, p. 4; Chesterton, *op. cit.*, I, 161; Rev. Henry Phibbs Fry, *A System of Penal Discipline*, pp. 72-3; *Eleventh Report of the Inspectors of Prisons (Scotland, Northumberland and Durham)*, PP, 1846, XX, 461, xlv; *Eleventh Report of the Inspectors of Prisons (Home District)*, PP, 1846, XXI, 1, 3; Cobbett's *Rural Rides*, ed. Cole, I, p. 330; Sir Walter Scott, *Journal*, ed. Tait, 1827-8, p. 192.
     In modern terminology these various theories were concerned with factors such as sub-cultural deficiencies in child-rearing and family life, peer-group pressures, lack of education, urbanisation, poor housing, criminal areas, poverty and the effects of the trade cycle.

far, but even in their most solemn intercourse with their catechumens, to take care of their pockets, and to consider nothing, *however sacred*, safe which is within their reach, and which can be turned into money or tobacco.[56]

And the astute John Perry, one of the inspectors of prisons, without a shred of firm evidence, sweepingly stated: 'It is generally believed that about nine-tenths of our criminal population are not strictly sound in intellect, and my own observation does not permit me to doubt it. . . .'[57] Some writers, such as the chaplain of Preston gaol, John Clay, because of their extensive experience and long research, were not content with one-factor explanations, but rather listed several.[58] Others attempted to explain the unequal propensity to crime of different groups in the population, and were aware of the criminogenic effects of the law itself. A witness told the 1827 Select Committee on Criminal Commitments and Convictions that in the rural areas crime had to be associated with 'the degradation of the moral character of the labouring classes' and placed the blame for this on bad laws which led to excessive gaoling and the purveying of moral infection by released offenders, who went into the community like 'scabbed sheep going into a flock'.[59] The lack of education among the lower classes was long debated as a cause of crime, and attention was drawn to the breakdown in social control which attended urbanisation: Sir Walter Scott, who in the 1820s was influenced by the penal philosophy of Sydney Smith, found the great concentrations of population which had taken place repulsive and corrupting.

> The state of society now leads so much to great accumulations of humanity, that we cannot wonder if it ferment and reek like a compost dunghill. Nature intended that population should be diffused over the soil in proportion to its extent. We have accumulated in huge cities and smothering manufactories the numbers which should be spread over the face of a country — and what wonder that they should be corrupted? We have turned healthful and pleasant brooks into morasses and pestiferous lakes — what wonder if the soil should be unhealthy?[60]

56 Rev. Joseph Kingsmill, *Chapters on Prisons and Prisoners and the Prevention of Crime*, p. 306.
57 *Sixteenth Report of the Inspectors of Prisons (Southern and Western District)*, PP, 1851, XXVII, p. 669, VII.
58 Clay categorised the causes of just over three hundred crimes under seven headings, Drinking; Various and Uncertain; Idleness and Bad Company; Want and Distress; Weak Intellects; Temptation; and Bad Habits (*cit.* Macnab, *op. cit.*, pp. 299-300).
59 *Cit.* Macnab, *op. cit.*, p. 298.
60 Scott, *op. cit.*, p. 192.

A similar opinion was less colourfully expressed: 'The collection of large masses of population in crowded cities conduces more than anything else to the creation of those causes, whatever they be, which stimulate the commission of crime.'[61] Joseph Fletcher was far more specific and argued that 'the masses employed in mining and manufacturing pursuits' were 'brought into close neighbourhood, and estranged from the influence of superior example' and

> subject to temptations, hazards and incitements far beyond those which approach the rural cottage; ignorant and largely depraved, they are likewise capable of combination; and combined, they form bodies little prepared to stoop to the exigencies of a reeling alternation of prosperity and adversity; to say nothing of all the evils which improvidence and heathenism pour out upon themselves.[62]

It is little wonder that the notion of a 'criminal class' had wide credence,[63] or that many theories, dealing with both individuals and groups, were strongly Hobbesian.[64] Indeed, as various prophylactics were unavailingly tried, the attraction of such explanations increased. The chaplain of Cold Bath Fields house of correction, for example, collected statistics which showed that out of 967 prisoners questioned in one week only 104 were illiterate, and concluded from this that 'it is not the want of education, but the Absence of Principle, which leads to the Commission of Crime'.[65]

The path from criminological theory to penal policy was no more simple in the nineteenth century than it is today, separate theories being welded together in contributory and main causal relations: adverse trade cycles and poor urban conditions could combine to harden into crime the low moral behaviour of the poorer classes. By such an argument the perennial misgiving of the advocate of prison

61 R.W. Rawson, 'An Inquiry into the Statistics of Crime etc.' (1839), cit. Macnab, op. cit., p. 317.

62 Cit. Macnab, op. cit., pp. 27, 25.

63 'The first point that has to be made in relation to crime in the nineteenth century is that contemporaries were convinced that the crux of the question was the existence of a separate criminal class' (Tobias, op. cit., p. 59).

64 Thus a Royal Commission (dominated by Edwin Chadwick) suggested that crimes against property arose from the

> temptations of the profit of a career of depredation, as compared with the profits of honest and even well-paid industry; and these temptations appear to us to arise from the absence of appropriate and practicable arrangements by means of a constabulary such as forms the main subject of our inquiry. The notion that any considerable proportion of the crimes against property are caused by blameless poverty or destitution we find disproved at every step (Royal Commission on Constabulary Force, PP, 1839, XIX, 1, 67).

65 Select Committee on Gaols, First Report, Minutes of Evidence, PP, 1835, XI, 76.

discipline that he is dealing with an individual, even while recognising the environmental elements in the causation of crime, is set at rest. The ingredients of a penal régime can then be selected and justified, according to the emphasis placed on individual and environmental factors in the chosen theory of crime, which may in turn be constrained by other factors.

The construction of criminological theories did not necessarily lead to a practical *penal* policy. Robert Owen's social determinism spurred him to no less a task than completely to recast society. It was to demonstrate the strength of environmental factors that he ensured that his New Lanark factory was 'staffed largely by thieves and drunkards'.[66] Other determinists were less ambitious and concerned themselves with programmes of slum-clearance, education, temperance campaigns, and rescue missions and the provision of special facilities for women and children. Some reformers attempted to improve the standing (and therefore the efficiency) of the law. Capital penalties, relics of a more ruthless age, too unjust to be imposed, were revoked and the Game Laws modified. The New Police was not a simple repressive instrument, but was, as Chadwick insisted, preventative.

But none of these measures could succeed in diverting more than a fraction of the criminally minded from being caught up in the machinery of justice. Curtailment in the use of the death penalty and the desuetude or abolition of other punishments such as whipping, the stocks and the pillory gave a greater role to imprisonment as punishment of most common recourse. The world remained harsh and strewn with temptations; at the very least, as all theorists agreed, the exigencies and discomforts of prison had so to be ordered along the lines of direct discouragement to crime. And in that simple requirement alone there was room for almost endless speculation, experiment and contention. It must be stressed, however, that in none of the influential theories of crime current in the early nineteenth century (apart, possibly, from the more extreme City views) was it possible to continue the teleological rationalisations which for most of the seventeenth and eighteenth centuries had so happily justified an attitude of *laissez faire* towards prison administration and encouraged a blind eye as regards the dangers and exploitation encountered by the prisoner. The scene was set for an upsurge in interest and agitation over the policy and administration of imprisonment, which was to reach a peak in the 1840s.

---

66 At New Lanark, 'Every aspect of modern welfare-work was undertaken, ranging from public health, temperance and education to provision of social security' (Thomson, *op. cit.*, p. 45).

Prison policies

The extreme decentralisation of prison administration, variation in prison conditions and resources, different interpretations of current social and religious philosophies and criminological theories produced such diversity in local prison policy and management that an observer commented in the 1840s:

> It is a mortal impossibility to find any two prisons where the discipline is the same, excepting the House of Correction, Cold Bath Fields, and Westminster Bridewell, where the management, government and discipline are more closely allied to each other than any two other prisons throughout the country....[67]

In the various localities objectives were often unclear, contradictory and unrealistically combined. It was argued that, at one and the same time, prisons should provide safe, healthy conditions of custody, reconcile the aim of deterrence with that of reform, and approximate as closely as possible to self-sufficiency of management. Methods of achieving such exorbitant ideals were heatedly debated, even abusively and nearly always dogmatically. Each locality's crotchet consisted in its unique regulation, combination and use of buildings, diet, clothing, lighting, heating, hours of sleep, beds and bedding, labour, religion, letters, visiting, reading material, staff management, payment and uniforms — and many other matters touching on the most paltry aspects of prison life. The improvement in communications during the 1830s enabled interested magistrates and burghers to keep abreast of every latest infallible method.[68] To the student, quite embarrassed by the mound of contemporary penological documents, it seems almost as though the pent-up polemical energies of centuries had suddenly burst forth. However, certain common themes are recurrent in the various debates and require special comment at this point.

Less-eligibility

The concept of less-eligibility, which was derived partly from utilitarian psychology, partly from the requirements of practical politics,

---

67 Augustus Such, *Remarks on Prison Discipline, and the Model Prison*, p. 4. See also pp. 8-18, *passim*, for his discussion of some of the main differences.

68 There was much correspondence between the prison authorities. Prison rules were very often produced in printed form and circulated to other areas, or supplied on request. Certain prisons developed reputations for particular systems and were much studied and visited. For example, Becher corresponded with, and even sent his keeper to, Wakefield house of correction in 1834, when the Nottinghamshire magistrates were considering introducing the silent system to Southwell house of correction (Nottinghamshire Record Office, refs QAG 5/79, 80 and 82).

was an important consideration in the policy and management of all local prisons.[69] During most of its early history the régime at Reading gaol, for example, came under severe criticism for what was seen as its violation of the requirements of less-eligibility.

> An inspector is compelled to believe not only that thousands would gladly resign liberty for the remainder even of their lives to be received into such an asylum, but that many would purchase admission were it permitted them to do so.[70]

John Field, the Reading chaplain, whilst denying that 'civilians' had committed offences in order to be imprisoned, agreed that workhouse inmates had so acted: 'We have had many boys committed from the workhouses who for the sake of the diet, and because they have exceedingly disliked their treatment in the workhouses, have committed offences with a view of getting into prison.'[71] In the 1830s, Hill reported that five prisoners had asked, and had been allowed, to remain in the rigorously separate and reputedly deterrent Glasgow bridewell after the completion of their sentences (there being no poor-law relief for the able bodied in Scotland at that time). By the winter of 1842-3 (a time of very severe economic recession) the voluntary prisoners numbered forty. This practice was discontinued, because it had no legal sanction (much to Hill's regret).[72]

In the harsh social and economic conditions of the poor, the relationship between the prisons and the no less deterrent system of workhouses was uneasy, and remained so until well into the twentieth century. The poor-law guardians and overseers repeatedly complained that prison held no terrors for workhouse inmates: prison diets, in particular, remained comparatively generous; and experienced governors were convinced that offences were committed on the approach of winter by those who preferred the prison discipline to that of the

69 Sir Walter Scott's opinion would be shared by many: 'I do not see the propriety of making them Dandy places of detention. They should be a place of punishment, and that can hardly be if men are lodged better, and fed better, than when they are at large' (*Journal*, p. 191).

70 Fry, *op. cit.*, p. 26. Robin Evans notes that at Pentonville, the model which Reading followed, the £158 which each cell cost was 'the same amount of money as would house an entire family in a commodious new artisan's cottage . . .' (thesis: 'Prison Design 1750-1842', p. 7).

71 *Select Committee on Prison Discipline*, Minutes of Evidence, PP, 1850, XVII, question 3790, 249.

72 Glasgow having no workhouse, Hill felt that to discharge destitute and desperate men, such as the voluntary prisoners obviously were, was an incitement to crime: they would simply offend again in order to be recommitted. See *Third Report of the Inspectors of Prisons (Scotland, Northumberland and Durham)*, PP, 1843, XXVI, 441, and *Tenth Report of the Inspectors of Prisons (Scotland, Northumberland and Durham)*, PP, 1845, XXIV, 399.

workhouse. In one case a woman wrote to her sister from Westminster bridewell highly approving of the clothing and food, and advised her to get committed — 'which advice was duly followed'. Chesterton claimed that 'the regularity and sobriety enforced within the prison is the means of considerably benefiting the health of habitual drunkards'.[73]

The problem of less-eligibility was raised in complaint by many of the magistrates in the 1840s, when an officially recommended prison dietary was issued. The inspectors sought to reassure them by the traditional argument, which distinguished the life of the prisoner from that of the free labourer:

> Other enjoyments, viewed in the light of comforts (as for example, well ventilated cells with good light, and sufficiently warmed in cold weather) are so necessarily connected with the prisoner's health that no denial or diminution of them could be safely recommended. But coarse diet for a convict is a prison infliction at once safe and efficacious.[74]

Constrained as they were by health considerations, by the complaints of workhouse keepers, and by public opinion, many prison authorities

---

73 1850 *SC*, *op. cit.*, question 7319, 508, and 1835 *SC*, *op. cit.*, First Report, Minutes of Evidence, 399. The perplexing relationship between the prisons and the New Poor Law workhouses was highlighted by the comment of one assistant commissioner: 'Our intention is to make the workhouses as like prisons as possible.' Another noted: 'our object . . . is to establish therein a discipline so severe and repulsive as to make them a terror to the poor and prevent them from entering' (*cit.* E.P. Thompson, *The Making of the English Working Class*, p. 295). If this was the intention of the commissioners, then very substantial problems arose if their system of discipline was seen to be more deterrent than that of their chosen model, the prisons. Becher, who had designed both prison *and* workhouse régimes, attempted to resolve the problem of less-eligibility by emphasising the perverse (but, for the administrator, fortunate) reactions of the inmates to order and cleanliness:

> Many Persons, on surveying the regularity and neatness which characterise our Workhouses, have been erroneously induced to imagine that the Poor will be tempted to prefer such a Residence to their customary abodes. But we know from experience, that the cleanliness, temperance, decency, subordination, and seclusion, which administer essentially to the health and comfort of the friendless, impotent and orderly Poor, are regarded with abhorrence by those who have depraved their feelings by habits of vagrancy, filthiness and immorality. With this abandoned Class, Discipline and Punishment are convertible terms (*The Antipauper System*, p. 16).

74 *Third Report of the Inspectors of Prisons (Home District)*, *op. cit.*, p. 11. See also *Eighth Report of the Inspectors of Prisons (Home District)*, PP, 1843, XXV and XXVI, 31, and *Ninth Report of the Inspectors of Prisons (Home District)*, PP, 1844, XXIX, 1. For a useful description of the problems arising from the requirements of less-eligibility in the design of prison dietaries see M. Heather Tomlinson, ' "Not an Instrument of Punishment": Prison Diet in the Mid-Nineteenth Century'.

placed great faith in the treadwheel as a means of enforcing the required degree of less-eligibility. While condemning its unproductive, depressing and degrading effects, the Webbs concluded, none the less, that it was an effective deterrent, preventing persons 'from using the gaol as a convenient place of refuge in seasons of adversity'.[75]

Often less-eligibility is caricatured as some type of neurotic obsession of nineteenth-century social and penal administrators. Yet in the context of the social and political order, of the economic conditions and welfare provision of the times, and of the development of psychological thought, it can be seen as a genuine dilemma in penal policy.

Deterrence

Some prison administrators and penal theorists closely analysed the experience of imprisonment in the hope of uncovering elements that were particularly vexatious for the prisoners. One witness told the 1835 select committee that the only proper means of deterring the criminal youth of the metropolis was to make gaols 'So irksome that self-convenience and self-interest, in the absence of virtue or repentance, may induce a person to abstain from the Commission of Evil'. To this end he recommended a régime based on constant inspection, sparse diet, little sleep, separation and silence. He also held, on the basis of a kind of homeopathic principle, that the reduction to a state of boredom could efficaciously be applied to the young criminal as a deterrent measure:

> As it is evident that Labour becomes a Relaxation, where Silence especially is enforced, I should suggest that it should be used not so much as a constant Punishment as for the Purposes of preserving Health. It would be a severe and irksome Punishment if Prisoners were compelled to sit for a Number of Hours in the Yards, on Forms with Partitions on each Side in Rows one above another, facing a blank Wall.[76]

75 S. and B. Webb, *op. cit.*, p. 99. C.C. Western was extremely enthusiastic about its deterrent qualities (writing a few years after the invention of the famous treadwheel at Bury St Edmunds by W. Cubitt):

> nothing was ever contrived so admirably adapted to the application of corrective labour, as the treadwheel. The work is severe, tedious and irksome, but not injurious to the human frame: the most artful cannot escape his share of the work. . . . They retire from it in the evening in that state of fatigue of body, and exhaustion of the animal spirits, which renders them far less inclined to mischief than when in the full possession of vigor and a restless spirit (C.C. Western, *Remarks Upon Prison Discipline*, 1821, p. 27).

76 1835 *SC, op. cit.*, Second Report, Minutes of Evidence, PP, 1835, XI, 395, 397-8, *passim*. The witness was W.A. Miles.

Charles Dickens strongly disputed Frederic Hill's view that an orderly and abstinent régime was possessed of sufficient deterrent qualities:

> What kind of work does the determined thief, or the determined swindler, or the determined vagrant, most abhor? Find me that work; and to it, in preference to any other, I set that man relentlessly. . . . I have not the least hesitation in avowing to Mr. Hill that it is a satisfaction to me to see that determined thief, swindler, or vagrant, sweating profusely at the treadmill or the crank, and extremely galled to know that he is doing nothing all the time but undergoing *punishment*.[77]

Some were even less subtle in their choice of a deterrent element in a system of prison discipline. John Orridge, governor of Bury St Edmunds gaol, another witness to the 1835 select committee, thought that nothing was as effective as a good flogging: 'I never had a Complaint against a Man when that Punishment was awarded to him at the End of his Imprisonment.'[78]

Whether the means of deterrence were of a sophisticated psychological nature, or of a cruder physical kind, no disciplinary system could afford to step out of line by overlooking this ingredient in the nineteenth century. The new-fangled goals of reformation, or even prevention of moral deterioration were acceptable to many, because their practical application required disciplinary systems that were not incompatible with the old instincts of expiation and retribution:

> If we cannot apply motives of the pleasurable sort, to induce the party to abstain from committing the act, we must apply such motives, of the painful sort, as will outweigh the motives which prompt to the performance. To prevent, by such means, a theft of £5, it is absolutely necessary to affix to that act a degree of punishment which shall outweigh the advantage of possessing £5.[79]

At the time, 'All the penologists were influenced by the narrow Hartleian psychology of impressions and association. They hoped to enforce associations of crime with punishment and pain, honest industry with advantage and pleasure'.[80] Whereas, in present-day discussions of

---

77 *Cit*. P.A.W. Collins, 'Dickens and the Prison Governor, George Laval Chesterton', p. 24.
78 1835 *SC, op. cit*., First Report, Minutes of Evidence, p. 236.
79 James Mill, *Essays on Government, Jurisprudence, Liberty of the Press, Prisons and Prison Discipline, Colonies, Law of Nations and Education, Reprinted from the Supplement to the Encyclopaedia Britannica*, p. 19.
80 U.R.Q. Henriques, 'The Rise and Decline of the Separate System of Prison Discipline', p. 91.

penal discipline, punishment is counterposed to reformatory and rehabilitative measures, no such dichotomy was recognised by the vast majority of theorists and administrators in the nineteenth century; consequently they saw no disabling contradiction in a system that aimed to be retributive, deterrent and reformatory.

Separation or silence?

Although the separate system sought reformation, its proponents claimed that it also promoted the minor objectives of less-eligibility and deterrence; after all, on such or similar grounds it was introduced into the government prisons.[81] Its cardinal advantage was that no experience could more certainly reduce the obdurate, or so terribly impress, as separation. Given acceptance of that premise other regulatory elements could easily be introduced specific to reformation.[82]

Those who, like George Chesterton, adhered to the silent system,

---

81 See Chapter 7, pp. 187-8.
82 This would be carried to what was often viewed by contemporaries as extreme lengths, and yet, because of the punitive nature of separation, such régimes could survive official and public opposition. In Reading gaol, one of the Pentonville type, opened in 1844 (see above, p. 206), separation was linked to religion and 'corrective education' as the basis of the régime. Prisoners committed large portions of Scripture to memory from morning until night. Enthusiastically presided over by the Rev. J. Field, the prison allegedly became known to criminals as 'Read-Read-Reading Gaol'. A clergyman rather acidly described the memorisation industry: 'Two or three gospels, nay, almost the whole New Testament, were sometimes learnt by rote by eminently studious felons' (Clay, op. cit., p. 195). To Lord Brougham Reading gaol was 'a public nuisance'; it was 'more like a place for students and professors than for prisoners convicted as felons', and it 'might rather be called Reading university' (House of Lords debate, 6 July 1849, Hansard (Third Series), VI, cols 1368-70, passim). Crawford and Russell, on the other hand, cited it as a 'gratifying example' of the separate system:

> Religion appears to act upon the prisoner, whilst in separation, with a power and adaptation to his circumstances of which no other prison system can exhibit an example . . . The earnestness with which the prisoners devote themselves to the perusal of the Scriptures – the readiness with which they make themselves acquainted with the facts and doctrines contained in them – and the care they bestow in acquiring by heart large portions of the sacred volume – are indications, as convincing as they are satisfactory, of the hold which the great truths of religion are calculated to take upon the mind of the prisoner placed in circumstances favourable to their reception, and of the permanence of those impressions when so received (Tenth Report of the Inspectors of Prisons (Home District), PP, 1845, XXII, 1, iv).

Peter Southerton (The Story of a Prison, Chs 4, 5 and 6, passim) gives an interesting, if somewhat limited, account of the new prison in the early 1840s and some aspects of its régime and administration.

entertained few hopes of reformatory success.[83] They certainly wished to avoid contamination and deterioration and to make their disciplinary conditions less-eligible and deterrent, and to those ends relied greatly on devices like shot-drill, the crank and the treadwheel. Although they frequently accused the separate system of promoting hypocrisy and encouraging religious morbidity, hysteria and insanity, as well as ill preparing prisoners for their return to society, the main objections entertained by many magistrates against it were financial and practical rather than philosophical; unlike the silent system it required expensive new buildings or modifications of old ones. The silent system could be commenced with minimal preparation, literally overnight; thus, on 29 December 1834, George Chesterton, appropriately deploying his staff, simply issued the necessary order and

> a population of 914 prisoners were suddenly apprized that all intercommunication by word, gesture or sign was prohibited; and, without a murmur, or the least symptom of overt opposition, the silent system became the established rule of the prison.[84]

At first, by employing prisoner-monitors, he was even able to operate the system without a great increase in staff. But subsequent legislation prohibiting the employment of prisoners in positions of trust made it

---

83 Although there were some claims that the silent system offered a more probable road to individual reform. Dickens supported the silent system not only because he thought separation cruel, but because the silent system tested prisoners. He also thought highly of Maconochie's mark system of discipline which was based on 'the principle of obliging the convict to some exercise of self-denial and resolution in every act of his prison life' (Philip Collins, *Dickens and Crime*, p. 164). Collins further remarks that in his attack on Pentonville in *Household Words* Dickens emphasised that removal from all temptation was not an adequate preparation for re-entry into a world of temptations; and 'it seems to me that the objection that nothing wholesome or good has ever had its growth in such unnatural solitude, and that even a dog, or any of the more intelligent among beasts, would pine, and mope, and rust away beneath its influence, would be in itself a sufficient argument against this system' (Dickens, *American Notes*, p. 127). An inspector asserted the advantage of the silent system in this one testing respect:

> It must, however, be admitted to possess one superior quality among others – the placing men under trying circumstances where they are compelled to exercise, and may acquire, the valuable habits of self-control. At the same time social duties are kept in view; for it exacts respect to authority, order, cleanliness, decency at meals, and industry at labour.

He added that 'The harshness of all this is little more than what the rustic undergoes during the period of his transformation into a soldier' (*Third Report of the Inspectors of Prisons (Northern and Eastern District)*, PP, 1837-8, XXXI, I, 6).

84 Chesterton, *op. cit.*, I, p. 303.

necessary to increase considerably the establishment of officers.[85] Even so, especially in the small prisons, the silent system remained a very much less expensive option. It had the further advantage, in the eyes of many magistrates, of allowing productive labour — favoured for a variety of reasons — to continue.

Whereas the separate system played into the hands of the chaplain,[86] the silent system conversely enhanced the importance of the governor. It necessitated, in the larger prisons, the development of skills in staff control and the management of prisoner groups. Such qualities were pre-eminently fostered by military discipline and experience, as Captain William Williams, inspector for the Northern and Eastern District, reported, with evident complacency.

> To such as are unacquainted with the precision, regularity and minuteness, attained without difficulty under military discipline, the details of the system of silence must naturally seem cumbrous and prolix; while to myself, after some experience in the army, this does not at all appear to be the case.

Indeed, he went on,

> The management of prisons should be as near as possible upon the same principles as a military organisation. The prisoners should be formed into divisions; and officers appointed to their charge; all orders and reports should be made in writing; the responsibility, duties and precedence of the officers should be defined; the daily routine of services laid precisely down and never departed from; the interior of a well-regulated prison should present the same aspect as a garrisoned fortress.[87]

85 This was 2 & 3 Vict., c.54, s.6, clause 4. Introduced at the behest of Crawford and Russell, this provision was specifically intended to make the silent system less easy to apply in the local prisons. See p. 254 below.
86 See above, Chapter 6.
87 *Third Report of the Inspectors of Prisons (Northern and Eastern District)*, PP, 1837-8, XXXI, I, 5, 6 respectively. Nowhere in his district did Williams encounter such a desirable state of affairs, except at Derby gaol, whose governor, Sims, a former subordinate of Chesterton's, had been appointed for his military qualities. But in London, the Middlesex house of correction and Westminster house of correction, at Cold Bath Fields and Tothill Fields respectively, followed his prescription. The governors of both prisons, Chesterton and Tracey, were personal friends and, as an interesting parallel, former military men. Similar views on management were held by Elam Lynds, the superintendent of Sing Sing, which was then run on silent system lines. He thought that the quality more desirable in the director of a prison was

> The practical art of conducting men. Above all, he must be thoroughly convinced, as I have always been, that a dishonest man is ever a coward. This conviction which the prisoners will soon perceive, gives him an irresistible ascendency, and will make a number of things very easy,

In their campaign against the silent system, William Crawford and Whitworth Russell concentrated upon its staffing structure. They were not greatly concerned with the extra running costs which it involved, but with the discretion that it necessarily allowed governors and other officers. Consistently with their rationalistic perspective (paradoxically shared by many of their opponents among the Utilitarians and adherents of the silent system),[88] they thought that prison management approached perfection in the same measure as it succeeded in eliminating the human element, and they condemned discipline

> influenced, as to strictness or lenity, by the character of the moral agents by whom it is administered. . . . The severity which arises, not from the system itself, but from the character and temper of the governor and his assistants, implies in its very nature the exercise of a discretionary power which cannot safely or legally be lodged in any hands. The same may be said of laxity of discipline.[89]

By contrast a good system possessed the

> capacity of being administered with *exact uniformity* in every prison, unaffected by the diversity of character and disposition which must be expected in the keepers and subordinate officers of the various establishments. The law obviously makes no difference in the sentence; none should be made therefore in the mode or degree of its infliction; nor should the same crime be punished with severity in the metropolis, which is leniently dealt with in other districts.[90]

> which, at first glance, may appear hazardous (Gustave de Beaumont and Alexis de Tocqueville, *On the Penitentiary System in the United States and its Application in France*, p. 185).

These views were echoed almost word for word by Chesterton in his account of his governorship of Cold Bath Fields.

---

88 Philip Collins uses the phrase 'rationalistic error' to characterise some of the debates of the 1840s. This, he argues, involves

> expecting far too much from a mere change of system, organisation, or architecture. Enthusiastic system-mongers tended to forget that prison governors and officers and prisoners, were all individuals, and that talking about '*the* system' and '*the* prisoner' concealed the actualities of the situation (Collins, *op. cit.*, pp. 18-19).

Perhaps 'local prison conditions' should be added to the factors neglected by the system-mongers in their speculative debates.

89 *Third Report of the Inspectors of Prisons (Home District)*, *op. cit.*, 8.
90 *Ibid.*, 27. The nearly obsessional lengths to which they were prepared to go in order to ensure that the very minimum of discretion was allowed to staff is shown in the publication *Routines Carried Out at Pentonville Prison*. This was a book of 159 pages which, if not written by Crawford and Russell themselves, was certainly produced under their immediate and close supervision. It contains a *literally* minute-by-minute account of the routines

Thus although contenders on both sides raised questions such as expense, incidence of insanity, contamination, excessive punishment and the use of prisoners in positions of authority, even more fundamental disagreements were involved. Besides the basic belief in the possibility of reform — the ability to procure a 'change of heart' — there were two quite distinct strategies of management. Supporters of the separate system generally believed in maximum restriction in the use of official discretion (their chaplains being priests transmitting the Divine Word, whilst governors merely facilitated this sacred work within a close network of rule and regulation). Always on the defensive about staffing, many advocates of the silent system nevertheless claimed that *any* system of prison management was only as reliable and efficient as the capabilities of staff permitted, and that the issue of the staff's discretionary powers could not be side-stepped.

Legal changes and government intervention

Considering the decisive role of finance in prison administration it is surprising that the Act of 1815, which totally prohibited the taking of gaol fees, has not received greater attention in penal histories. Even the Webbs, although giving it a passing mention, fail fully to appreciate its significance and far-reaching effects.

This legislation was mainly the work of Henry Bennet,[91] who argued that fee-taking was at the root of most defects in prison administration and management. He was fortunately able to secure the support of the powerful City interest, which was worried that reforms already in hand, if confined to City prisons alone, would result in severe overcrowding and consequent financial burdens.[92] Although making a drastic alteration

---

and states that in every large prison 'the nicest adjustment of time, and of labour is required; and without routines embracing all essential points, however minute, the duties could not be satisfactorily performed' (p. 5).

---

91 Henry Grey Bennet (1777-1836), the second son of Lord Tankerville, was a Whig and member of Parliament for Shrewsbury in 1806-7 and 1811-26. Statute 55 Geo. III, c.50, was also sponsored by Romilly, Holford and Whitbread. At this time 55 Geo. III, c.48, was also enacted, which amended the Gaol Chaplain's Act of 1773 (13 Geo. III, c.58); it permitted the justices to pay twice the original salary provided, obliged the chaplain to keep a journal and allowed for the additional appointment of a bridewell chaplain.

92 See *Hansard* (1st Series), XXVII, 1814, cols 90-1. Later on central government sought to exempt the Fleet, King's Bench and Marshalsea from Bennet's legislation on the ground that as they came under direct judicial administration an abolition of fee-taking in their case would mean a charge on national revenues. Not unreasonably the City argued that it would suffer financially if this exemption were allowed: debtors would avoid arrest in Westminster in order to make sure of confinement in City prisons where no prison fees could legally be taken (*Hansard* (1st Series), XXIX, 1814-15, cols 1048-50). The City was defeated on this issue.

247

in prison finance and administration the bill met with little opposition and, eventually enacted in 1815 as 55 Geo. III, c.50,[93] its provisions became the prototype of all subsequent local prison legislation.

By the peremptory prohibition of its first clause, it became a criminal offence for a gaoler to exact a fee:[94] 'from and after the First Day of October next, all Fees and Gratuities paid or payable by any prisoner, on the Entrance, Committment, or discharge, to or from Prison, shall absolutely cease, and the same are hereby abolished and determined'.

Thus the position of the magistrates in prison administration, within a very short space of time, was given far more immediacy. Dilettante attitudes towards their duties of regulation and inspection were no longer permissible when the magistrates were made accountable for the disbursement of public funds to meet the salaries of gaol staff,

> And whereas in some Places such Fees and Gratuities as aforesaid are payable to the Gaoler or his Servants and are to him or them as a Salary; be it enacted, that it may be lawful for the Justices of the Peace for any County, City or Town, assembled in General or Quarter Sessions, to make such Allowances to the aforesaid Gaoler or Servants, as may to them seem fit, in the way of Salary or Compensation, for the Fees or Gratuities payable by Prisoners, now abolished by this Act.[95]

The next major piece of prison legislation, concerned in this case more with discipline than administration, was Peel's Gaol Act of 1823 (4 Geo. IV, c.64), the gist of which would class it as preventative and deterrent.

> It is no less the interest than the duty of every government, to take care that the individuals who by the laws are subjected to imprisonment, do not, by the effect of that sentence, become worse members of society, or more hardened offenders. It is also of much importance, that Prisons be so managed, that confinement within them may be an object of terror, and may operate as real punishment upon those for whom it is so intended; at the same time that the exercise of all unnecessary severity is restrained by wholesome regulations. With a view to these objects, the means of a judicious classification of Prisoners and of constant employment and labour are essentially necessary. . . .[96]

---

93 It was subsequently subject to some minor amendments by 56 Geo. III, c.116.
94 55 Geo. III, c.50, s.13 provided that any gaoler who exacted a fee 'on account of the Entrance, Committment or Discharge of such Prisoner, or who shall detain any Prisoner in Custody for non-Payment of any Fee or Gratuity, shall be rendered incapable of holding his Office, be guilty of a Misdemeanour, and be punished by Fine and Imprisonment'.
95 55 Geo. III, c.50, s.3.
96 *Select Committee on the Laws Relating to Prisons*, PP, 1822, IV, 67, 3.

These objectives were to be sought by means of a disciplinary system which on the one hand emphasised non-contamination, and on the other drew on the experience of the administrations at Gloucester and Southwell with a combination of their utilitarian and religious methods. Separate confinement was rejected in favour of association regulated by a five-fold method of classification; and due weight was given to the value of religious and educational instruction. However, the effectiveness of the classification used was widely criticised for being based on offence rather than character and antecedents. Clay went so far as to describe it as 'universally impotent to prevent ruinous corruption'.[97]

Among its clauses was one consolidating twenty-three previous prison statutes, a measure which was a step towards the amalgamation of gaols and houses of correction.[98] Moreover, supplementary legislation required the justices to make quarterly prison returns to the home secretary, this being an important prerequisite for the development of national penal policy — even if very imperfectly executed.[99]

Peel's Act was restricted in its application, and included only 130 of the country's prisons, namely all the county prisons, those of the City of London and of Westminster, and seventeen provincial towns: 'it did nothing to reform either the three great debtors' prisons in London or the one hundred and fifty or so gaols and bridewells in the franchises and minor municipalities'.[100] As it seemed rather perversely to ignore prisons most in need of regulation, the legislation attracted much criticism from reformers, as well as from penal historians.[101] Some of the objections to the Act are unjustified as they fail to pay adequate attention to its contemporary circumstances.[102] From available evidence

97 Clay, *op. cit.*, p. 164.
98 Lionel W. Fox, *The English Prison and Borstal Systems*, p. 34.
99 The important pensioning provision will be discussed in Chapter 10.
100 S. and B. Webb, *op. cit.*, p. 110.
101 See Leon Radzinowicz, *A History of English Criminal Law and its Administration from 1750*, I, pp. 570-1.
102 Some of the criticisms imply that Peel and his colleagues were oblivious of the condition of the excluded borough and franchise prisons. This was not the case. The select committee which prepared the ground for the Act noted the unsatisfactory state of the smaller prisons, but were aware that the smaller local authorities did not have sufficient resources to provide proper accommodation and management; and chose to bring in enabling measures rather than mandatory legislation. (They probably had in mind the provision of powers to contract and amalgamate.) The committee concluded that general measures could not equally be applied to large and small authorities and establishments, and 'before any specific measure with respect to these [small prisons] can be safely adopted, further information appears to be necessary' (1822 *SC*, *op. cit.*, p. 14). This was the not unreasonable basis of the restriction of the 1823 Act. It was also the explanation for the seemingly arbitrary inclusion of the larger municipalities with the counties which the Webbs found themselves unable to explain: action on the municipal prisons was restricted to those upon which the authorities had information. The

it appears that most counties sought to bring their prisons into conformity with the new Act and considerable funds were expended on new buildings and on alterations. The Act was often disregarded, sometimes ostentatiously so, in the municipal jurisdictions.[103]

In their efforts to influence local prison policy and administration the inspectors, appointed under 5 and 6 Will. IV, c.38, faced a difficult and delicate task.[104] Until this point permissive legislation and a great deal of mandatory legislation had been implemented according to the beliefs and interests and resources of the magistrates and municipal officials. Actions of enforcement in the higher courts were extremely rare, owing partly, perhaps, to the very small size of the Home Office staff, a stronger reason being the undiminished sense of the inviolability of local authority. As has been noted, the constitutional and legal reforms of the 1830s wrought a fundamental alteration in the relationship between central and local government, not amounting, however, to anything like central government dictation.

Fifteen years before the appointment of the inspectorate, such a move had been denounced by Sydney Smith, largely because he thought that they would be parasitical 'placemen':

We object to the office of prison inspector, for reasons so very obvious that it is scarcely necessary to enumerate them. The prison inspector would have a good salary; that, in England, is never omitted. It is equally matter of course that he would be taken from among Treasury retainers, and that he would never look at a prison.[105]

large London debtors' prisons were excluded because the very considerable charge for their upkeep would otherwise have fallen on central government (see n. 92, p. 247, above), as would direct responsibility for their regulation. Public administration was not politically, organisationally or financially prepared for such a move.

Peel had promised that the situation would be reviewed in 'a year or two', and if at that time local administrations had not rebuilt and improved their establishments or had not contracted with the county authorities, he said, 'I shall not hesitate to ask Parliament for powers to compel them to make the necessary alterations' (cit. S. and B. Webb, op. cit., p. 104, n.). This promise to review he did not keep. Peel's sense of the futility of imprisonment as a solution to the wave of crime is sh⁄wn in his letter to Sydney Smith (see p. 187, n. 55, above). Radzinowicz (op. cit., p. 572) points out that during the period of Peel's secretaryship there was an 86 per cent increase in committals in England and Wales (excluding London and Middlesex).

103 Cooper, op. cit., pp. 248-52, passim.
104 See Chapter 7 for the effect of their appointment upon the central government prison establishment. Discussion here will, therefore, be confined to some aspects of their relationships with the local prison authorities.
105 Cit. S. and B. Webb, op. cit., p. 75, n.

But if Sydney Smith objected to the prospect of an ineffective inspectorate, others equally or more strongly objected to the possibility of a
body of dedicated and efficient interlopers. Thus Sir Peter Laurie, a
City spokesman (and president of Bridewell), while acknowledging to
the 1835 select committee that there were defects in prison administration, very probably expressed a substantial magisterial consensus when
he none the less urged that the justices themselves should be left to
correct them. Asked for guarantees that corrective action would be
taken without an inspectorate he replied:

> That comes to the sore Part again; I call it the sore Part, because
> I am convinced that in the working of it you will find it a very
> sore Part. Leave it to the Honour of the Magistrates, send round
> these Queries, and get bona fide and good Answers to them, and
> I will pledge myself that it will have a good effect; but if you
> send a Spy upon us, then it will create Dissatisfaction with every
> body. . . . The very Notion of a Person coming to see whether you
> have done your duty or not to a high-minded Man is an extremely
> degrading Thing.[106]

The local administrations still, and very firmly, held the purse-
strings. In such financial and political circumstances there was little
question but that the functions of the inspectorate should be restricted
to advice in their dealings with the magistrates and municipalities, and
that their strongest sanction should be the publication of their
reports.[107]

---

106 1835 SC, op. cit., Fourth and Fifth Report, Minutes of Evidence, XII,
      464-5. Sir Peter agreed that officers in the army were men of honour, and
      yet were inspected without that honour being insulted, but he claimed that
      this was not applicable to the situation of the magistrates, since unlike army
      officers they were employed in a voluntary service; hence 'this new
      Regulation gives the Idea that one is suspected, because one naturally says,
      it should have been otherwise, or no Inspector would have been appointed:
      the very Appointment of an Inspector says it has not been properly done'
      (ibid.).
107 Samuel Hoare, secretary of the Society for the Improvement of Prison
      Discipline, thought that it was best 'if the Inspectors were not armed with
      any Authority, but were limited to suggesting to the Magistrates and
      reporting to the Home Office, [so] that their Co-operation would not be
      offensive to the Magistrates, but highly beneficial'. He distinguished between
      advice and superior authority: 'they [the magistrates] would not like any
      Authority to be exercised over them and have the Inspectors say such and
      such a Thing must be done, but they would be very glad to receive their
      Suggestions' (1835 SC, op. cit., First Report, Minutes of Evidence, XI, 19-20).
      T.C. Higgins, a visiting justice at Bedford, and William Seymour, a
      Brighton magistrate, argued similar cases, the latter opposing an inspectorate
      with executive power:

> I think if more was given they would not assist but supersede the
> Magistrates, that the Magistrates would not act with them; and I think

Even in cases where malpractices in prison administration and management were uncovered the powers of the inspectorate remained severely circumscribed. Although the law might have been broken, the home secretary himself had no executive authority or powers of direction, and could intervene only through the courts. Some local authorities resisted both inspection and advice. In their prolonged war of attrition with Crawford and Russell the City authorities went so far, at one time, as to prohibit a prison official from communication with the inspectors.[108] Other hostile or indifferent authorities allowed inspection, but ignored the resultant findings and advice. In 1843 an inspector, after investigating the conduct of the governor of Carnarvon gaol, recommended to the home secretary that the governor should be dismissed from his post; the home secretary wrote to the magistrates pointing out that the charges against the governor had been upheld, and requested that 'you will inform me of the course which you decide on taking for preventing the repetition of such violations of the law', the clear implication being that the governor should be dismissed — although it is interesting that no direct request was made. In their reply the magistrates informed him that 'it is not expedient to dismiss Mr. George [the governor] from his situation', adding that steps were being taken to prevent a repetition of the irregularities. The home secretary could only note their decision with the comment, 'I very much regret that [you] have decided that it is not expedient to dismiss Mr. George from the office of Governor . . .'.[109]

---

the effect of Inspectors should be leaving the Magistrates with the same power they now have under Rules and Regulations, and that the Magistrates should see them well performed; and after a short time Inspectors would have nothing more to do than to report that they are performed; whereas there being no Inspectors now, I believe there is not a prison in the Kingdom where the Rules and Regulations have not been broken (*ibid.*, 177).

A few reformers advocated an executive inspectorate. Sir Frederick Adair, who was involved in a more general campaign for local government reform, wished to give the inspectors 'Power of acting in addition to the Duty of Reporting' (*ibid.*, p. 252).

---

108 The Gaol Committee of Aldermen of the Corporation of the City of London resolved: 'That the Ordinary of Newgate be restricted from making any communication to the Home Office or Inspectors of Prisons, and that he is required wholly to confine himself to the performance of his duty as prescribed by the Act of Parliament' (resolution of 18 March 1842, *cit.* Joseph Adshead, *Prisons and Prisoners*, p. 159).

109 *Report and Evidence on the Inquiry into the Conduct of the Governor of the County Gaol of Carnarvon*, PP, 1843, XLIII, 12, 49, *passim*. The incident is interesting in itself, as a measure of the changed standards of prison management which existed even by the early 1840s: the governor had been guilty of what would probably at most have been seen as minor improprieties a few decades previously. The inspector reported:

But such stubborn resistance to advice and to public condemnation was comparatively uncommon, and most local authorities corrected the defects and abuses which were brought to their attention; even the City was induced to make *some* changes.[110]

Few governors would wish to resist the suggestions of an inspector if the alternative was the risk of a scathing public report. Such an attitude could be struck only with the support of the magistrates; and unless an issue of principle was involved why should the magistrates take a stand? But the boundary between the pressing of advice and the issue of a direct command can be narrow, and on at least a few occasions in their dealings with governors the inspectors crossed it. On a visit to Cambridge gaol in June 1846, for example, an inspector ordered that a prisoner be punished for writing on walls and doors, and on another visit stopped a special tobacco allowance which had been made to a cook-prisoner (thereby precipitating a running dispute between the governor and the prisoner which lasted long after the inspector had gone).[111] As a safeguard against any direct interference the inspectors were, strictly speaking, obliged to give their reports and observations not to the governors, but (through the home secretary) to the justices. As evidence, however, that this procedure was not always followed, Whitworth Russell, on his first visit to Hertford county gaol, demanded an immediate explanation from the governor as to why prisoners were not being kept in proper classes.[112]

Even though instances of direct intervention by inspectors can be found it must be remembered that their extensive duties and arduous working conditions were severe constraints against any widespread interference.[113] Not even the prodigious energy and enthusiasm of

I am of opinion that [he] is not of strictly sober habits; that he has treated with cruelty some of the prisoners committed to his charge; that he has exercised his authority in a vexatious and unlawful manner; that he has permitted, if not promoted, great irregularities in the prison; that he is in the habit of cursing and swearing . . . (*ibid.*, 12).

110   We are glad to find that the full and faithful exposure which we . . . felt it our duty to make of that prison has been productive of at least some advantage inasmuch as it has aroused the attention of those upon whom Parliamentary Reports and Grand Jury Presentments had hitherto failed to make the slightest impression (*Second Report of the Inspectors of Prisons (Home District)*, PP, 1837, XXXIII, 1, 68).

111 'Extracts from the Journal of John Edis' (MS in Radzinowicz Library), entries of 25 June 1846 and 15 April 1850. The governor had been acting illegally in allowing a tobacco allowance. This was prohibited by s.6, clause 5, 2 & 3 Vict., c.54.

112 Hertfordshire County Record Office; Hertford County Gaol and House of Correction — Governor's Journal, 1834-8, ref. Shelf 44. Entry for 22 April 1836.

113 See pp. 174-5, above.

Crawford and Russell would suffice to do more than occasionally to tinker with the management of the local prisons in their district.[114]

The influence of central government over the policy administration and management of local prisons was greatly increased by 2 and 3 Vict., c.54. This was enacted in 1839 and its main provisions reflected the opinions and interests of Crawford and Russell. It aided rather than compelled adoption of the separate system of discipline, but did much to discourage the silent system. Prisons which had not been covered by Peel's Gaol Act were obliged to enforce minimum classification; and a set of general rules 'in addition to and in amendment of the other Rules and Regulations which shall be in force' were provided for every prison in England and Wales. Boroughs were directed to appoint chaplains to their prisons, and powers were given to appoint deputy governors in all prisons where it was thought necessary. It was also required that cells used for separate confinement should be certified by the inspectors, and that all plans for new prison buildings, alterations or extensions, should be approved by the secretary of state.[115]

In the early 1840s central government attempted in various other ways to influence the course of local prison policy. Pentonville was presented as a national model to the magistrates and, with the active encouragement of Crawford and Russell and various other devotees, the separate system was adopted in several localities along with imitation of building design and the system of management.[116] The increased

114 Cooper (*op. cit.*, p. 292) argues that the power given by s.5 of the 1835 Act to the home secretary to alter or add to the regulations was the significant feature of the Act, rather than the appointment of inspectors. He says that by this provision 'For the first time the central government was made the final authority for the administration of all English gaols'. It is hard to follow the logic of this argument. What had previously been lacking was not sets of rules, but means of enforcing them. Moreover, as long as prison administration rested upon locally raised finance and supervision, central government could *not* be the final administrative authority in any but a theoretical, constitutional sense. (See 1850 *SC*, *op. cit.*, p. iii.)

115 The secretary of state (in practice Jebb) could refuse to approve plans, but was obliged to give in writing his reasons for so doing. He could not disapprove on the sole grounds that the separate system had not been adopted (s.12).

116 Although the extent of Pentonville's influence has been grossly exaggerated by many penal historians, Sir Edmund Du Cane bears the main responsibility for propagating this misunderstanding. Fox (*op. cit.*, p. 38), for example, cites Du Cane's claim 'in six years after Pentonville was built 54 new prisons were built after its model, affording 11,000 separate cells'. This has often been used as an illustration of the massive Victorian commitment to prison building, and if Du Cane's were an accurate statement it would indeed reflect an enormous national effort. But the true picture is not nearly so dramatic. The error arises from a misreading of the evidence of Jebb, the surveyor general of prisons, to the 1850 select committee. Handing over to the committee a list of fifty-five prisons Jebb said: 'I have a list of 50 or 60

confidence felt by the inspectorate and the home secretary was shown by the circulation of a new code of rules and a dietary scale in January 1843. In his covering letter to the magistrates the home secretary made several recommendations about construction, education and staffing and made clear his intention of ensuring a greater measure of uniformity. He had forborne to exercise the power which he held as secretary of state

> of introducing into the Prison Rules now in force the Alterations and Amendments which seem to me desirable. I have thought it better, in the first instance, to call the Attention of the Magistrates in Gaol Sessions and of the Municipal Authorities to those Alterations which I consider most necessary; I confidently anticipate the Adoption of the Recommendations which I have offered to them. . . .[117]

By the end of the following year the Home District inspectors reported that both the dietary and the code of rules had been widely adopted 'with advantage to the discipline and health of the Prisoners'.[118] But while many benches doubtless welcomed official guidance, some continued to feel that they were themselves the best draftsmen of rules suitable to local conditions.

Despite the formidable accumulation of prison legislation and central governments powers and influence, policy and administration in local prisons retained, in many respects, a heterogeneous character. But constitutional and political positions had shifted very considerably

---

(prisons), which have been built, containing, I should think, altogether, those completed and those that are in progress, about 11,000 cells' (1850 *SC, op. cit.*, question 31, 3). But the list that Jebb handed in as evidence was headed: 'Statement showing the prisons which have been Erected or Improved on the Pentonville Plan during the last Few Years, or that are now in the course of Erection or determined'. Under a heading 'Prisons in Progress' there was an additional list of six prisons (making sixty-one mentioned in all). Jebb was asked: 'You do not mean that those 50 or 60 have all been built since the passing of the Act of Victoria, but that the prisons have been increased, and that additions have been made with a view to adapt them to the requirements of that Act?' He replied:

> In some instances they are additions, as in Stafford, to the old gaol, leaving the old gaol perfectly intact; in others, as at Leicester, and Chelmsford, the wings which existed have been pulled down, and large blocks of separate cells have been erected in their places. In others, as at Shrewsbury and Hertford, the cells have been altered (*ibid.*, question 32, 4).

It is quite clear, therefore, that nothing like fifty-four or fifty-five *new* prisons had been built in the period between 1842 and 1850.

---

117 PRO, HO 158/1.
118 *Ninth Report of the Inspectors of Prisons (Home District)*, PP, 1844, XXIX, 1, 3.

since the 1830s as the recommendations of another select committee made clear in 1850, when they criticised the existing arrangements for the supervision of local prisons, which rested largely on the home secretary's moral influence and right to veto:

> But although the Secretary of State has the power to lay down rules, he has no direct means of enforcing them. If the plans for the construction or alteration of a Prison do not obtain his approbation he may express his dissent but he has no power to order his own views or alterations to be adopted. . . .[119]

The committee thought that prison conditions had improved, but considered that there was too great a variety in prison discipline and construction. Carried away by the logic of their own argument and possibly influenced by Jebb's lobbying, they contended that greater powers should be entrusted to a central authority which would be given the responsibility of 'enforcing uniform adherence to rules laid down from time to time by Parliament in these respects ... such increased powers would be best exercised by a Board, subject to the authority of the Secretary of State'.[120]

This formula 'enforcing uniform adherence' would have commanded little support a generation before, and was to be a recurrent and eventually dominant theme in considerations of penal policy and administration in the decade and a half that followed.

The development of grants-in-aid

The payment by central government of a substantial subsidy towards local prison expenses, which began simply as a part of more general fiscal reform in the 1830s, became an increasingly important means of ensuring local compliance with statutory obligations and ministerial directions. Before 1835 only a few such expenses were paid by the Treasury, namely the maintenance of convicts, soldiers imprisoned by courts martial, and smugglers and revenue prisoners. Localities paid in full for the conveyance of prisoners to gaol, whether under sentence or to take their trial, and for the building, maintenance, repair and staffing of gaols, houses of correction and lockups.[121] In 1833 the Select Committee on Agricultural Labourers held that the expense to ratepayers of improvements in the gaols and administration of justice which had been brought about by changes in the law were

---

119 1850 *SC, op. cit.*, iii.
120 *Ibid.*
121 *Report of the Commissioners Appointed to Inquire Respecting County Rates*, PP, 1836, XXVII, 1, 47-8.

anomalous from the circumstance that purposes of general utility are thus defrayed by local taxation, subject to abuse because placed under the control of authorities not personally responsible and requiring, therefore, the early and deliberate attention of the Legislature.[122]

This attempt to reclassify the punishment of crime as a national rather than a local responsibility was in violation of what another committee called the 'sound principle of municipal law . . . that crime should in its pecuniary consequences be a local burthen. . .'.[123] It was decided, nevertheless, to offer some relief, and the estimates for 1835 provided for payment of half the expenses of assize and quarter session prosecutions, and the whole expense of conveying convicts from gaols to the convict prisons.[124] The Commission on the County Rates opposed a complete shift in prison expenses, but stated that

> should it be found practicable to charge on the public revenues the expenses connected with gaols and bridewells throughout the country, we see many advantages in a plan of that description, if the management of those institutions were also placed in the hands of Your Majesty's Government, and conducted upon general and uniform principles.[125]

This view was to reappear many times in subsequent policy discussions.

In 1840 it was decided that local rates should be levied only on immovable property. This decision set in hand the struggle between the ratepayer and the taxpayer which became a major force in the shaping of fiscal policy in the latter part of the nineteenth century, and which set the interests of the local ratepayer against the national taxpayer.[126] Some five years later the government were pressed to extend the financial assistance being given to local government. Mr W. Miles, member of Parliament for Bristol, moved that due regard should be had to the agricultural interest in the reduction or remission of taxation, and urged that, in addition to the grants made since 1835, government should also contribute half the running and maintenance costs of county prisons and of coroners' inquests. His argument was another version of that put by the county rate commission in 1835: that those responsible for the direction of the prisons should meet

122 *Select Committee on the Present State of Agriculture, and of Persons Employed in Agriculture*, PP, 1833, V, 1, vi.

123 *RC on County Rates, op. cit.*, 24.

124 *Estimates etc., Miscellaneous Services*, PP, 1835, VI, 539. £80,000 was provided for assize and quarter sessions' prosecutions, and £30,000 for the conveyance of convicts.

125 *Report of the Commissioners Appointed to Inquire Respecting County Rates, op. cit.*, 24.

126 Edwin Cannan, *The History of Local Rates in England*, p. 132.

their cost. In his view, because of the proliferation of legislation and increasing regulation, central government was already playing a substantial part in local prison administration: 'The magistrates acted, in many respects ... in a mere ministerial capacity to the Home Office – for instance, in respect of the prison rules and regulations, and in respect to prison dietries ...'. County prisons had become a *divisium imperium* and therefore 'there should be no difficulty, and should be no shame, in asking the Government to bear half the expense of the salaries of the officers employed in them, as well as half the incidental expenses'.[127]

Peel's government resisted this appeal. The home secretary, Sir James Graham, contended that landed proprietors had no right to claim exemption from liability for these expenses, while at the same time they retained the financial protection arising from the Corn Laws and that, moreover, the proposed transfer to the Treasury of responsibility for more prison charges would not really benefit the agricultural interest, since the cost of the services would certainly increase and have to be met by the ratepayers in their role as taxpayers.[128] But when in June 1846 the Corn Laws were repealed part of the case put forward by the government against this transfer of financial responsibility ceased to be valid. Peel had, in fact, recognised that changes in the Corn Laws would have to be accompanied by measures to reduce the burden on local rates. With regard to prisons he told the House,

> You have already taken off one-half the expense of maintaining prisoners in Great Britain and Ireland, who are under sentence for felony or misdemeanour; and I propose to relieve the counties of this charge altogether, and take from the Consolidated Fund, the expense of the maintenance of such prisoners.[129]

The Finance Act introduced in the summer of 1846 allowed up to £40,000 to be applied to the maintenance of prisoners under sentence for felony or misdemeanour and other similar charges, for the half-year beginning on 1 October 1846.[130] A Treasury circular of 15 December 1846 stated that the £40,000 was thought to be sufficient

> to relieve the several Counties throughout the United Kingdom (and also such Boroughs as have Quarter Sessions and in which the cost of maintenance of convicted Prisoners is paid by a Rate raised by the Borough in the nature of a County Rate).[131]

127 *Hansard* (Third Series), LXXVIII, 17 March 1845, col. 979.
128 *Cit. Royal Commission on Local Taxation*, Memorandum by Sir E.W. Hamilton, KCB, PP, 1899, XXXVI, 1, 685.
129 *Hansard* (Third Series), LXXXIII, 27 January 1846, cols 272-3.
130 9 & 10 Vict., c.116, s. 18.
131 PRO, L.C08/2.

A form was issued and half-yearly returns were requested from the local prison authorities;[132] the funds disbursed amounted to between a quarter and a third of the total cost of the maintenance of prisoners.[133] The same year 9 & 10 Vict., c.95 (Small Debts Act, 1846), ss. 49 and 99, provided for a similar Treasury subsidy for the maintenance of debtors. The restriction of the grant-in-aid to prisons supported from a local rate intentionally excluded the franchise prisons, and those prisons located in boroughs which had escaped the municipal reforms of 1835; this became a further pressure in the campaign to effect closures and amalgamations of the smaller prisons.[134]

The local prisons in 1850

By mid-century the local prisons, in common with many other English institutions, had undergone an administrative transformation. Most of the very small prisons had been closed. Although many variations in policy and régime persisted, prisons were more thoroughly regulated than ever before.

After the heated ideological contention of the 1830s and early 1840s a certain calm descended. This was true of fields other than penal policy. The messianic appeal of evangelical and utilitarian thought had abated:

> in both cases the doctrine was the reflection of an exceptional experience, the religious experience of a nation undergoing a moral revival, its social experience during a revolution in the methods of production; and in both cases a larger view was certain to show that neither was a more than provisional synthesis.[135]

But there were more specific reasons why penological experiment and controversy had so noticeably diminished. The system of record-keeping and statistics, although still unreliable, had developed to the point where some empirical and comparative assessment of penal régimes was possible. The instinctively pragmatic stance of English government and administration had probably never provided a fully congenial milieu for the growth of the systems, and now the attention of criminologists and penologists became increasingly concentrated on 'better bets' — reformatory and industrial schools and other kinds of preventative measures.

This trend was strengthened when, often supported by statistics, the

---

132 West Sussex Record Office, QAP/15/W13/14.
133 See the returns in PRO TI/5337/2950.
134 Berwick borough gaol, which was supported out of a corporate fund, rather than a borough rate, was refused a grant in February 1847 (PRO T.13/2, TI/5338).
135 Young, *op. cit.*, p. 12.

effects of 'advanced' and 'backward' régimes were compared. Of course these comparisons were extremely crude, with little or no realisation of the need to control for significant differences in conditions. Nevertheless, the results were destructive of many confident and hitherto unchallenged claims: none of the systems, including the most deterrent, seemed to have any discernible effect on recommittal rates.

Frederic Hill, probably the most accomplished and reflective of the inspectors,[136] reviewed his several years' work in the Scottish prisons in terms which showed that he measured success by standards considerably less ambitious, but much more realistic, than those of the various disciplinary zealots.

> Although, therefore, the moral improvement in the prisoners may not always be great, there is at least the consolation of feeling that the prisons are no longer schools of crime, and that there is now little danger of a person, sent to prison for a small offence, or committed on a charge of which he is ultimately found to be innocent, leaving the place skilled in those arts of crime, of which, on his admission, he was ignorant; accustomed to scoff at all which he had hitherto held sacred, and with his character blasted for ever.[137]

Elsewhere Hill pointed out that the recommittal figures were in any case difficult to ascertain, and that some of the worst country prisons had fewest recommittals owing to their being in districts 'where the whole population is small, where from the extent to which every one's actions become known it is difficult for an offender to continue to reside ...'.[138] A few years later he was much more definite in his

136 By 1850 in terms of service and experience Frederic Hill was *primus inter pares* in the inspectorate. Originally in charge of the Scottish District, he was moved in 1847 (at his own request) to the Northern District. In view of his seniority, it is difficult to know (especially as he had expressed a wish to be near London) why he was not offered the Home District, which was *de facto* the superior inspectorate position. It may well have been that, though he was not opposed to the separate system then favoured by the government, his frequent public warnings about its extreme forms, and his developing scepticism about the effectiveness of any system of prison discipline, rendered his presence in such a senior post unacceptable.

137 *Tenth Annual Report of the Inspectors of Prisons (Scotland, Northumberland and Durham)*, PP, 1845, XXIV, 399, vii.

138 *Thirteenth Report of the Inspectors of Prisons (Northern and Eastern District)*, PP, 1847-8, XXXVI, 361, xvii. To overcome some of the statistical problems Hill advocated the foundation of a central record office. Hill's scepticism extended to criminal statistics in general:

> Nothing can be more fallacious than taking the returns, from time to time, of the number of persons apprehended and of the offences of which they are convicted, as indications of the comparative amount of crime. . . . These returns take no notice of the increase of population,

judgment that almost all reformatory and deterrent claims to success should be viewed with extreme caution:

How greatly the number of prisoners in any case is affected by other causes than prison discipline is shown by the report on the city prison at Norwich . . . where it will be seen that, at a prison conducted neither on the separate system nor silent system, where there is but little work, little instruction, and little supervision, where many of the prisoners congregate, to their general corruption, in idleness and unrestrained conversation, the number of prisoners during the last ten years has steadily decreased, and is now but little more than half what it was. Had such a result been obtained in a prison under some peculiar system conclusions would probably have been drawn highly favourable to its effects.[139]

Hill was possibly the most articulate and influential of those who doubted the relevance of prison discipline to the prevention of crime, in any but a negative sense; but similar observations appeared in other official documents; the *First Report of the Directors of Convict Prisons*, for example, provided some substantiation for Hill's views. This described the results obtained from the hulks which had no credible reformatory facilities whatsoever:

Notwithstanding the many disadvantages inseparable from the use of hulks, we are enabled to speak favourably of the conduct of those prisoners who were embarked with tickets of leave in 1849, and the early part of the year 1850, even though the greater proportion of them had never been subjected to any probationary discipline or separate confinement.[140]

---

the greater efficiency of the police, the increased willingness to give evidence . . . a less reluctance to prosecute . . . and they take no account also of the increases of wealth, and the changes in what the law declares to be crime (*Crime: Its Amount, Causes and Remedies*, p. 19).

---

139 *Sixteenth Report of the Inspectors of Prisons (Northern and Eastern District)*, PP, 1851, XXVII, 461, xii-xiii. Pressing the point home Hill added:

in giving full value to good prison discipline as a means of diminishing crime, it is necessary to keep in mind other operating powers, such as education, the general condition of the country, the poor-laws, police, and the state and administration of the criminal law (*ibid.*, xiv).

140 *Report of the Directors of Convict Prisons: The Hulk Establishment*, PP, 1851, XXIV, 197, 7. The 1850 select committee also received evidence of this kind; William Musson, governor of Leicester gaol, who claimed that because of changes in the system of discipline in his prison, committals had dropped, also stated that 'the recommittals have decreased very little indeed' (*op. cit.*, 269). George Pinson, governor of the county gaol at Norwich, argued on the basis of comparative recommittal rates that his (silent) system was 'succeeding as well as they were doing elsewhere'; at Wakefield, which

Reports from Van Diemen's Land showed that the convicts in question had been well behaved and had committed very few offences, and usually those of a trivial character, such as drunkenness and neglect of work.[141] Such views and findings helped to emphasise the uncertainty of the links between crime and penal policy, and made appropriate and acceptable goals of a more modest type aiming at safe custody and the prevention of the further moral deterioration of the prisoner. For political reasons these objectives had still often to be set in the framework of individual and general deterrence, and due or full obeisance had still to be paid to the requirement of less-eligibility.

The exhaustion of penal ideology did not result in new lurches in policy, however. It is not necessary to be a total pragmatist to recognise that ideological persuasions never totally or directly determined the policy in the several score of still mainly small local prisons of the 1840s. Local resources, the state of buildings, the quality and interests of staff and the persistence of inspectors, were far more likely to be the drums to which local administrators marched than was the very distant rumble of abstract ideological dispute. But, as has been shown, the prolonged debate on objectives and régimes, the interest, energy and involvement of the various participants, had a significant general effect on the state of the prisons. No matter which régime was adopted, which system of administration or style of management followed, few establishments could avoid the new legislative requirements and the application of new standards of probity by the informed public, justices and inspectorate alike.

---

was something of a model prison, the number of recommittals was indeed greater (*ibid*., 300). Frederic Hill also submitted an interesting paper to this committee, comparing the results of different régimes (Appendix No. 5, 708-9). In most cases he considered that the change in committal rates (which included both increases and decreases) could be explained by circumstances other than the alteration in the system of discipline or 'a general increase or decrease of crime in the country'.

---

141 Even John Burt, the assistant chaplain at Pentonville, and a fervent believer in the separate system was obliged to accept the failure of its claims to dominate penal policy:

I do not advocate an indiscriminate application of the Pentonville modification of separate confinement to all classes of criminals. A classification of criminals for different kinds of punishment, no less than for different degrees, appears to me to be the only basis for a rational penal system. . . . But to define the exact criminal classes to whom it ought to be applied, and the modifications which it ought to undergo with other classes of criminals, would require nothing less than a solution of the whole problem of secondary punishments (*Results of the System of Separate Confinement*, p. 248).

9 Governors' duties and working conditions, 1800-50

Governors' tasks

Custodial duties

Peel's Gaol Act of 1823 did not set out a governor's duties in detail, but merely stipulated that he was to visit each cell at least once every twenty-four hours, and that he was to keep a journal.[1] His primary task, at common law, was to maintain the safe custody of the prison. It was largely as a guarantee of diligence in this respect (although indemnification of loss by embezzlement may also have had something to do with it) that a governor provided sureties to the sheriff (and often to the magistrates as well). The history of imprisonment is liberally studded with corruptly assisted 'escapes', and very naturally the first to be suspected in the circumstances were the staff. By the 1830s a successful bid for freedom seems almost invariably to have been carefully scrutinised by the visiting justices, with a view to taking disciplinary or even court action against the governor and his staff.[2] George Chesterton

---

1 4 Geo. IV, c.64, s.10.
2 At Bedford in the 1820s, for example, the justices were not entirely satisfied with the governor's explanation of how two prisoners had made a daylight escape. Whilst they carried on their investigations the governor was directed to distribute hue-and-cry handbills offering a reward of £20. As the prisoners were recaptured within a short time the incident was closed without the governor being censured. There were further escape attempts, however, and the justices, in an expression of dissatisfaction, issued new directions: the governor was, on such future occasions, to have handbills printed, inform the nearest visiting justice and to offer a reward

> proportionate to the nature of the case — all such expenses to be borne by the gaoler, in addition to such fine or other punishment as may be awarded, if it shall appear that he has been negligent or inattentive in any respect, as to have given or allowed any facility to temptation to such escape — but . . . all such expense shall be borne by the County, when it

remarked in his memoirs that the possibility of an escape had been a source of 'ceaseless discomfort' to him — a feeling probably shared by most governors.[3]

Besides the prevention of escapes, the custodial task also required that adequate control be exercised within the prison, and that fighting, thieving, intimidation and rioting be suppressed. In most cases this meant regular direct contact with prisoners, as few prisons were large enough to warrant a sufficient complement of staff to insulate the governor from the petty routines of institutional life.[4]

A large proportion of inmates in local prisons were young males; minor offenders, incarcerated for short periods.[5] This made for a fairly

---

shall appear to the Visiting Justices, after due examination, that no fault or negligence is imputable to the gaoler (Bedfordshire County Record Office, Bedford County Gaol and House of Correction, Minute Book of Visiting Justices, 1825-33, entry for 19 April 1825).

Nevertheless the justices were sometimes willing to accept a plea in mitigation even when, as at Huntingdon in 1835, a breach of quite elementary security precautions enabled two prisoners to escape (Huntingdon Record Office, Huntingdon County Gaol and House of Correction, Keeper's Journal, 1833-8, entries for 22 and 27 April).

---

3 George Chesterton, *Revelations of Prison Life*, II, pp. 56-7. John Treganza, gaoler at Bedford, was faced with a catastrophic bill for nearly £260 in 1840, following the escape of a debtor. The £260 was made up of the debt owed and the creditor's costs, together with the expenses of the attempt to recapture the prisoner. Only a collection among the magistrates of more than £200 prevented Treganza's ruin (Eric Stockdale, *A Study of Bedford Prison, 1660-1877*, pp. 170-1).

4 The division of labour between governors and turnkeys was not clear in this respect, even in medium-sized prisons. An incident reported at Cambridge town gaol (one of several) perhaps makes this point:

C.G. a convict under sentence of transportation for life was this afternoon detected by the under turnkey secreting a quantity of oakum about his person [presumably to make into a rope for purposes of escape] and on the officer's attempting to take it from him, he most violently assaulted and resisted him. On my going to his assistance the prisoner assaulted and strongly resisted me and it was with the greatest possible difficulty that we were able to remove him from the yard. I placed him in the refractory cell for the night, but from his continual violence was obliged to put him in irons ('Extracts from the Journal of John Edis', MS, Radzinowicz Library, Cambridge, entry for 3 April 1844).

5 Macnab notes that in the period 1823-38 'just over 2/5ths of the persons committed for trial were aged twenty-one years or less' (thesis: 'Aspects of the History of Crime', p. 343). Whitworth Russell calculated that 'In 1843 89.2% of those imprisoned on summary convictions received three months or less, while 83% imprisoned after trial received six months or less'. The sex ratio of committals for trial averaged out for the years 1842-4 was: females 63.3 per 100,000; males 297.8 per 100,000 ('Abstract of the Statistics of Crime', *Journal of the Statistical Society of London* (1847), X, pp. 51-3, 40). See also Tables 11.1 and 11.2.

unstable and troublesome population. In many rural prisons staff often had personal knowledge of the prisoners' backgrounds and some contact with their families and friends, which would have assisted control; and in these establishments disciplinary offences rarely appear to have offered very serious threats to the maintenance of security and mainly involved brawling, trading and gambling, and tardiness or refusal to obey orders to rise and to work.[6] Some notion of the strict standard against which transgressions were measured in county prisons in the late 1830s can be gained from an incident at Hertford gaol, in which an inmate used blasphemous language and was reproached by the governor as 'one of the most depraved boys I ever had under my care; this is the second time of his being in prison',[7] and sentenced to three days in the solitary cell. Assaults on prison staff and damage to prison property were not common, as far as can be seen, and were punished condignly by the authorities.[8]

As might be expected, more serious incidents of indiscipline and licentiousness arose in the towns and cities, and were often aggravated by administrative ineptitude. As late as 1850 Hepworth Dixon was shocked by disciplinary conditions in the City of London prisons:

> no work, no instruction, no superintendence . . . idleness, illicit gaming, filthiness, moral and material disorder, unnatural crowding together, unlimited licence − broken at times by severities at which the sense of justice revolts. . . .[9]

Penalties included whipping (which could be imposed only by order of the magistrates) and solitary confinement; the restraint harness seems to have been used more as a means of controlling a violent burst of temper than as a punishment. Rewards and privileges had their place in the régime for encouraging orderly behaviour: in many prisons it was customary for the governor to draw to the attention of the justices

6 See Huntingdonshire County Gaol and House of Correction, Keeper's Journal, 1833-8, and Hertford County Gaol and House of Correction, Governor's Journal, 1834-8. June 1836, in which there were ten minor offences, was a bad month for discipline by the standards of Hertford gaol. In two separate months at Huntingdon, in 1847 and 1848, the total number of offences (all trivial) were five and eighteen respectively (Huntingdonshire County Gaol and House of Correction, Keeper's Journal, 1844-52; see entries for 8 July and 11 August 1847 and July and August 1848 generally).

7 Hertfordshire County Record Office, Hertford County Gaol, Governor's Journal, 1834-8, entry for 6 October 1837.

8 In one incident a prisoner who caused damage and insulted the chaplain was sentenced to fifty lashes and seven days' solitary confinement (*ibid*., entry for 29 October 1835). Increased severity was shown to minor offenders who did not respond to repeated punishments: a boy who committed the same trivial offence on ten successive occasions was brought before the visiting justices and received forty-eight lashes (*ibid*., 1847-51, entry for 1 April 1850).

9 *Cit*. Anthony Babington, *The English Bastille*, p. 206.

instances of particularly good conduct; any that were thus thought suitable for clemency were recommended to the secretary of state, and might earn a pardon.[10] Some governors actively concerned themselves with prisoners' home circumstances, probably finding that this assisted in the maintenance of discipline, since outside developments were often a source of disruptive behaviour in the prison.[11] It was fairly common practice, in any event, for governors to correspond with the family or friends of young or sick prisoners.[12] These gratuitous services were not always traceable to purely disciplinary reasons and on at least some occasions were motivated by altruistic concern for the general welfare of a prisoner.[13] But as the smaller prisons were closed and more and more of the lesser boroughs contracted with the county authorities, the governors' local knowledge declined and ties loosened and the requirements of other duties made this type of charitable intervention less practicable.

Requirements of the disciplinary régime

Besides the paramount requirements of custody and control, governors' duties were determined to a significant extent by the type of discipline

10 See, for example, Hertford County Gaol and House of Correction, Governor's Journal, 1838-44, entry for 20 May 1838, and 1834-8, entry (as a letter in rear portion of journal) for July/August 1841.

11 John Edis, the Cambridge governor, described one such incident in his journal:

J.N. is labouring under considerable excitement in consequence of his wife not visiting. I have endeavoured to soothe him, but without much success. He is a man of very ardent passions — jealous in the extreme, but I cannot call him insane. Fearing, however, that he may be tempted in his present mood to do something wrong, I have placed him with two other prisoners to sleep, and directed that he be most carefully watched.

The wife did not visit for some time, and eventually the governor intervened 'In consequence of N's continual excitement I deemed it prudent to see his wife and advise her to come and see him, which she did' ('Extracts from the Journal of John Edis', entries for 15 and 24 September 1844). The wife's visit was of little avail, however, and 'J.N.' eventually suffered what seems to have been a total mental breakdown.

12 The governor of Ilford gaol wrote to the friends of those of his prisoners who were under the age of twenty-one, 'apprizing them of the time they will be Discharged from the Gaol, and if any Prisoner should be taken ill the Friends are written to' (Essex Record Office, 'General Duties performed by the Governor of Ilford Gaol', ref. QACP/3).

13 John Edis watched the behaviour of various ex-prisoners around Cambridge, occasionally advising and helping them by finding employment or securing a place in a welfare refuge:

I have today placed H.H., a little girl 13 years of age, in one of the female houses at Wandsworth. This child has been three times convicted of felony under the Juvenile Offenders Act. She is shrewd and clever for her age, but has evidently been much neglected by her father and mother in town (*op. cit.*, entry for 17 October 1855).

which they were charged to enforce.[14] Both silent and separate systems governed inmate and staff routine more rigidly than that of classified association provided by Peel's Act. It is ironical that, despite their disapproval of military personnel and military methods in prisons, Crawford and Russell intended the daily routine of separate system governors to be an endless military-type inspection of records, staff and inmates. They argued that only in this way could a governor, within a few hours, visit some five hundred cells:

> his visits are not like those of the Chaplain and Schoolmaster, who must devote a longer period of time to the instruction of the convicts. But in the case of the Governor or Surgeon, no such delay with each individual is called for. An officer precedes them in their rounds, and has already opened two or three cells in advance, and the Governor or Surgeon passes on from one cell to another, almost as an officer passes down a line of troops, stopping whenever a case requires further inquiry or communication. . . . Considering the importance of attending to the daily inspection of the cells, of making regular visits to each prisoner, and of constantly observing the manner in which the subordinate officers perform their duty, we cannot help expressing our decided opinion, that the Governor's time ought not to be unnecessarily occupied with matters of detail, for instance with bookkeeping and such other business as may safely be confided to a clerk. The appointment of a clerk, with proper qualifications, is indispensable in every prison of ordinary size, and when his duty is properly performed the Governor's other engagements can be more effectually attended to: half an hour every evening will be sufficient to enable him to enter [in] his journal for the guidance and information of the visiting justices, references to those places, in the proper books, in which a detailed account of all the important incidents of the day may be found.[15]

In contrast to this energetic but intentionally remote surveillance of the separate system governor, his 'classified' or silent system counterpart was obliged to participate much more directly in the daily business. Inmates were congregated in day-rooms and work-rooms, where his duties centred on the supervision of staff and industrial activity, and the control of the assembled prisoners.[16] In an 'associated' system,

14 See above, pp. 245-7.
15 *Third Report of the Inspectors of Prisons (Home District)*, PP, 1837-8, XXX, 1, 89. Such a picture of the governors' duties was particularly attractive to Crawford and Russell because of their desire to limit the effects of staff discretion as far as possible, and thus to promote uniformity of practice throughout the prisons (see p. 246, above).
16 See, for example, the 1834 rules and regulations of the Wakefield house of correction, a silent system prison which placed a strong emphasis on

moreover, the governor was fully engaged in his duties until locking-up had taken place which, in summer months, could be late evening.[17] In 1844 the governor of Ilford gaol (run on 'associated' lines) thus described to the visiting justices his working day:

> In the Morning I see that the Prisoners are unlocked at the Proper time, and set to Work. Afterwards, I see that the Breakfast is served at Eight O'Clock, with any Extra Allowances that are Ordered by the Surgeon. At 9 O'Clock the Schoolmaster brings his Books into the Office to me, with the General Report Sheet, for the Previous Day. Before Unlocking after Breakfast I see that the Turnkeys have on the Uniform as Ordered, and I then Examine the Daily Report, and the Turnkeys' Report Books.
>
> About 10 O'Clock, I attend Chapel, and after Service is Over, make a General Inspection of all the Yards, Cells and Infirmaries, and Enquire into Reports of Misconduct, or Complaints, for or against, any of the Prisoners, and Investigate, or award such Punishment as I may think the Justice of the Case Demands. I also see that my Orders of the Previous Day are executed, and write such Others in the Order Books as may be requisite. I Examine all the Commitments and also the Prisoners recently Committed, and Discharge such Prisoners, whose term of Imprisonment has Expired. I also see that the Dinner is Delivered agreeably to the Regulations.
>
> The Afternoon is Devoted to the General Duties of the Office, in which the Books are kept . . . I also make out Parliamentary Returns, and Copies of all Warrants under the Game Laws, for the Secretary of State.
>
> In the Afternoon I again go round the Prison, to see that the Prisoners are properly Enlarged, and frequently Visit the Prisoners at Night after Locking up. . . .
>
> In conclusion, I beg to State, my time is Occupied in the General Supervision of the Prison, and in Seeing the Officers Discharge their Duties Properly, and that the Establishment is conducted in as Economical a manner, as the proper Enforcement of the Regulations will allow. . . .[18]

But, as variants of the separate system became more widely adopted, there were consequent changes in governors' duties. Less intimate

---

productive labour (a copy of this document is held in the Nottinghamshire Record Office, ref. QAG5/83).

---

17 Locking and unlocking had no comparable significance in the routine of the separate system; the only equivalent was the release from their cells of batches of closely supervised prisoners for exercise.

18 Essex Record Office, 'General Duties performed by the Governor of Ilford Gaol', ref. QACP/3.

contact with inmates and staff was required, and the model suggested by Crawford and Russell was more closely followed.

Staff management

Staffing levels were determined by the size of the prison, the volume of receptions and the system of discipline.[19] As will be seen from Table 9.1 a large establishment of staff was unusual, even by the mid-1830s.

TABLE 9.1   *Staff establishment of 143 prisons in 1835*

Number of staff	Number of prisons
1–4	45
5–9	60
10–14	23
15–19	8
20–4	4
Over 24	3

Source: *Select Committee of the House of Lords on Gaols and Houses of Correction*, PP, 1835, XI, Appendix 2, 612 *et seq*. These figures were compiled from responses to a House of Lords questionnaire. No guidance was given to the local authorities to assist them in making their returns, so some errors were made. Some small prisons failed to make returns and so these establishments are under-represented as a proportion of the total distribution of staff.

The great majority of prisons had fewer than ten on the staff, and a staff of more than twenty was rare. The most common staffing complement in the 1830s and 1840s probably was limited to the governor, his wife (acting as matron), a few assistants or turnkeys, and a visiting chaplain and part-time surgeon. In such circumstances it would be futile to discuss the relationships between the governor and his subordinates in terms of formal management; but, as the trend of prison policy

19 As noted above (pp. 244-6), the silent system required a much larger staff than the separate system and most systems of punitive or reformatory discipline required many more officers than a merely custodial prison, like the Fleet, which held 240-50 inmates, and employed a staff of only ten, including superiors. In practice the number was even less than ten: the warden was superannuated and the clerk had little direct contact with prisoners (*Royal Commission on the Fleet, Westminster Palace and Marshalsea*, PP, 1819, XI, 325). By contrast, Cold Bath Fields, which applied the silent system, required about 135 officers to supervise around 1,000 prisoners (Chesterton, *op. cit.*, II, p. 3, n., and *Abstract of Answers to Queries Sent by Order of the House of Lords to the Governors of Gaols*, PP, 1835, XI, 612).

favoured the establishment of larger prisons, formal methods of enforcing staff discipline and a stricter division of labour between superior and inferior officers became more common.

The control, in large prisons, of a poorly paid, hard-worked subordinate staff of low status and ill-educated, in social conditions which favoured a climate of corruption, posed almost intractable management problems.[20] Some commentators had emphasised the need to isolate

20 See above, pp. 211-14. Frederic Hill recorded that subordinate officers were paid only 14s. a week in Scotland in the early 1840s (*Sixth Report of the Inspectors of Prisons (Scotland, Northumberland and Durham)*, PP, 1841, V, 413). He considered £1 a week to be a living wage. But in some English prisons wages were at least as low: an assistant turnkey at Cambridge town gaol in 1850 was paid only 6s. a week, with rations and lodgings, and in addition to the duties of turnkey was obliged to act as schoolmaster and trade instructor. Another turnkey in the same gaol had his wage increased to 18s. only when he took on the work of the cook. After thirty-two years' service the senior turnkey at Cambridge was paid 22s. a week; this was as late as 1864 ('Extracts from the Journal of John Edis', entries for 21 October 1850, 7 April 1846 and 5 February 1864). Indeed annual increments in wages for subordinate officers were unknown before the 1840s, when they were introduced at Pentonville, 'with a view to secure and retain the services of an efficient body of subordinate officers'. This practice spread and in 1847 was introduced at Hertford; it was recorded at Cambridge in 1864 (*Second Report of the Commissioners of Pentonville Prison*, PP, 1844, XXVIII, 71, 8; Hertford County Gaol and House of Correction, Governor's Journal, 1844-52, ref. Shelf 44, entry for 4 December 1847; and 'Extracts from the Journal of John Edis', entry for 5 February 1864). Holidays for subordinate staff, at the rate of one week per year, were first introduced at Pentonville in 1844 ('Pentonville Prison, Governor's Journal', p. 28). One can be certain about the unusual nature of subordinate staff holidays from examinations of governors' journals which, by this time, were regularly kept in almost all prisons. Minor incidents of staff illness and lateness for duty were reported, but very rarely any absence that could at all be defined as a holiday. Hours of work were little short of what would today be described as slavery. An Edinburgh warder stated that 'he seldom saw his children except on Sunday; that he was obliged to leave house before they were awake in the morning, between five and six o'clock, and that he did not get back till between nine and ten at night when they were gone to bed'. The governor of Glasgow prison claimed that the work of a warder was as hard as that of ordinary mechanics, over fourteen hours a day with additional Sunday duties on rota (*Seventh Report of the Inspectors of Prisons (Scotland, Northumberland and Durham)*, PP, 1842, XXI, 369, 5). These remarks seem to have had some effect, for Hill noted in his next report that the problem of warders working long hours had been eased a little and that 'in some of the chief prisons, the warders are not now required to be on duty more than 72 hours per week (which is still a long time), and . . . they have each a week's holiday in summer' (*Eighth Report of the Inspectors of Prisons (Scotland, Northumberland and Durham)*, PP, 1843, XXV and XXVI, 441, 5). Hours of work for staff in English prisons were not very different. A Newgate officer reported that his duties occupied seventeen or eighteen hours a day, a claim which was confirmed by a fellow officer who had worked these hours for some twenty years (*First Report of the Inspectors of Prisons (Home District)*, PP, 1836, XXV, 1, 43). Nor were such hours worked only in the

subordinate officers from the 'civilian' working-class neighbourhood — the social environment from which most prisoners sprang. For this reason many local authorities insisted that subordinate officers, as well as the governor, should reside in or under the shadow of the prison, in special accommodation.[21] The desirability of a general adoption of this policy was explained in the evidence of a witness to the select committee of 1835: 'The Economy is not in my Opinion, the chief Recommendation. I think the Discipline of the Prison could be much improved, and there would be much less Communication from without than there is at present.'[22]

The quality of subordinate staff was obviously a matter of considerable consequence to the justices and governors alike. But the part that governors should be permitted to play in staff selection was debated for many years, being a matter upon which the inspectors themselves disagreed fundamentally. Williams (inspector for the Northern and Eastern District) was opposed to governors having any significant role in staff selection.

> The appointment and discharge of the under officers is in many cases left entirely with the keeper, and they are not infrequently preferred for possessing qualifications as gardeners, or grooms, etc., and the relation between the parties is more that of master and servant, than of officers entrusted, in common, with the performance of public duties. The prisoners under such circumstances have no respect for the turnkeys, beyond that which physical force inspires.[23]

This view he reaffirmed some years later when, as *de facto* senior inspector, he gave evidence to the select committee of 1850:

> I should say the whole of the discipline of a prison depends upon the character of the governor. A great mistake arises at times, which I have very great difficulty in putting to rights; the magistrates

---

metropolitan prisons. The governor of Stafford gaol told the 1835 select committee that his subordinates worked a sixteen-hour day, from 6.00 a.m. until 10.00 p.m. (*Select Committee of the House of Lords on Gaols and Houses of Correction*, First Report, PP, 1835, XI, 1, Minutes of Evidence, 245). Even at the Model Prison of Pentonville warders assembled for duty at 5.30 a.m. and remained in the prison until 10.00 p.m. (*Second Report of the Commissioners of Pentonville Prison, op. cit.*, 18-20, *passim*).

---

21 As, for example, at Hertford gaol and house of correction: see rule eighteen of the 'Rules and Regulations', 1824 (Hertfordshire County Record Office, ref. County Gaol, 5).

22 1835 *SC, op. cit.*, Fourth and Fifth Reports, Minutes of Evidence, PP, 1835, XII, 157, 500.

23 *Third Report of the Inspectors of Prisons (Northern and Eastern District)*, PP, 1837-8, XXI, 1, 2.

necessarily suppose that the governor of the county gaol . . . has the appointment of the sub-officers, and a very great mischief arises therefrom.[24]

On the other hand, his colleague, Frederic Hill, held a diametrically opposite view:

> The principle of leaving the unfettered choice of the subordinate officers to the keeper appears to me to be of the highest importance in the management of a prison, and to its full adoption at the Glasgow Bridewell I have always attributed much of the success and excellence of that prison – the high degree of discipline among the prisoners, the productiveness of their labour, and the economy of the prison funds.[25]

Hill maintained that it would be in the governor's own interest to select the best staff; moreover, that a governor who had been entrusted with such authority would be precluded from resorting to the excuse of incompetent subordinates:

> He it is who has the best opportunity of judging their qualifications, and who has the strongest interest in seeking the best men; for without good subordinates it will be in vain for him to expect that the state of his prison will redound to his credit, or give him any prospect of promotion. Indeed, unless the governor have this power, it is difficult to say, in case of success or failure, to whom the credit or disgrace is due; without it, the important principle of responsibility cannot exist; and endless trouble may be created in determining, in every case of mismanagement, with whom the fault really rests.[26]

Against the objections that staff appointed by governors might be under greater pressure than staff appointed by the justices to collude in any wrongdoing, Hill riposted that it was for the justices, in the first instance, to appoint reliable governors. However, this prescription ignored the advantage – by then well recognised – of dividing the loyalties of prison staff as a guard against tyranny and corruption. Perhaps it was because the arguments on both sides were so plausible that by the 1850s there was still no uniformity of practice in this matter.[27]

---

24 *Select Committee on Prison Discipline*, PP, 1850, XVII, Minutes of Evidence, 751.
25 *Sixth Report of the Inspectors of Prisons (Scotland, Northumberland and Durham)*, PP, 1841, V, 413, 5.
26 Frederic Hill, *Crime: Its Amount, Causes and Remedies*, p. 312.
27 In 1850 Hill suggested that a compromise be effected by following the course adopted at Preston: every subordinate officer was there taken on trial and if he proved unsatisfactory he was dismissed by the governor; if he was

Serving the courts

Corporal and capital sentences Imprisonment was not the only penalty under a court sentence which brought a man to prison. In the nineteenth century both floggings and hangings took place on or near prison premises. Flogging was ordered as a punishment for prison offences, but it was also a frequently used court sentence. As the number of strokes, or the weight, design and construction, of the instrument with which the punishment was to be inflicted were not usually specified in the sentence, these matters were decided by the governor.[28]

---

satisfactory he was then recommended to the magistrates for the ratification of his appointment; the governor selected but the magistrates had a right of veto (see *Fifteenth Report of the Inspectors of Prisons (Northern and Eastern District)*, PP, 1850, XXVIII, 291, xxvi-xxvii). At Hertford county gaol and Cambridge town gaol the Preston system was followed, i.e. the governors were authorised to select subordinate staff, but appointment had to be confirmed by the magistrates.

Many local magistrates were well aware of possible abuses by governors of their rights to select and appoint subordinate staff. When extra turnkeys were required at Bedford in 1832 to enforce the newly adopted silent system, selection was left to the governor, on the condition that 'neither Turnkey nor Assistant Turnkey be employed in stable-work or other domestic services for the gaoler' (Bedfordshire County Record Office, Bedford County Gaol and House of Correction, Minute Book of Visiting Justices, 1825-33, entry for 25 June 1832). In government prisons the supervising committee was responsible for staff appointments, but in the reformed and consolidated Queen's Prison the governor was empowered to appoint his own subordinate staff, subject to the approval of the home secretary (5 & 6 Vict., Sess. 2, c.22, s.22).

---

28 Which moved Samuel Hoare to complain:

I believe that few Judges, or Magistrates are aware what the Punishment is; it is not known what the Instrument is with which it is to be inflicted, and the Instrument is seldom the same in Two Prisons; it is not known what Number of Lashes are to be inflicted — all is left to the Discretion of the Gaoler. This surely ought not to be; the Sentence of Whipping ought to be defined; a certain Number of Lashes with a certain Instrument should be a part of the Sentence, always to be executed in the Presence of the Surgeon. I have heard of Several Cases in which it has been very improperly exercised.

John Orridge, governor of Bury St Edmunds gaol, and a strong believer in the efficacy of corporal punishment, agreed with Hoare: 'I think the Number of Lashes should be defined, and the Instrument' (1835 *SC*, *op. cit.*, First Report, Minutes of Evidence, XI, 29 and 236 respectively). The select committee was impressed by these objections and recommended that 'in Cases where the Punishment of Whipping is resorted to it is expedient that it should be defined, as regards both the Extent to which it may be carried and the Instruments with which it may be inflicted' (*ibid.*, First Report, iv-v). But this recommendation applied to prison punishment, not to court sentences. In any event the governor's considerable discretion was little undermined, for although a maximum number of strokes was ordered, this was usually so large

273

In most county prisons flogging was carried out by a turnkey, but in some of the smaller establishments it fell to the governor. Floggings took place in public until well into the century, and were regarded by some governors as a particularly degrading task; George Chesterton angrily remembered the first public flogging that he had attended as governor: 'I and the police had been degraded, and the public outraged by so savage a spectacle, and I heartily rejoiced when the custom fell into desuetude or became prohibited.'[29] Frederic Hill's views were much the same; he was opposed to the use of flogging for offences against prison discipline and thought that the duty of inflicting a flogging affected adversely the relationship between officers (superior and inferior) and prisoners. Presumably he would have liked an outsider to perform this duty.[30]

By the 1830s and 1840s hangings had ceased to be very frequent, even at county and large borough gaols,[31] and, although they aroused

---

that the attending governor had to remit a substantial portion to avoid killing or severely maiming the prisoner. It was not until the Royal Commission investigating Millbank prison in 1847 condemned this practice, that a maximum of thirty-six strokes for prison punishment was established (*Royal Commission on the Management of Millbank Prison*, PP, 1847, XXX, 1, 13). Before this, the order had frequently been for a hundred lashes, and occasionally for as many as several hundred. As late as 1861, however, a Home Office circular to visiting justices expressed concern at the considerable diversity in both the mode of administering corporal punishment and the number of cases to which the punishment was applied (PRO, HO 158/2/60).

Floggings, if ordered by quarter sessions, were usually carried out on the day following the close of court proceedings, as the earliest opportunity when the governor, along with any of his subordinates, would be free from his obligatory attendance at the court.

---

29 Chesterton, *op. cit.*, II, pp. 135-6.
30 *Thirteenth Report of the Inspectors of Prisons (Northern and Eastern District)*, PP, 1847-8, XXXVI, 361, xvi; see also Hill, *op. cit.*, pp. 282-3.
31 From the middle of the eighteenth century there had been a steady decline in the number of hangings. In the years 1749-55, 66 per cent of capital convictions resulted in execution; by 1812-18 this had declined to 11.5 per cent (Macnab, *op. cit.*, p. 94). In the period 1828-34, of the 8,483 convicts sentenced to death in England and Wales 'only 355, or less than five per cent, were executed' (J.J. Tobias, *Crime and Industrial Society in the Nineteenth Century*, p. 233). Not only was the law liberally interpreted in the courts, but from 1808 the statute-book was steadily being rid of capital penalties, so that by 1837 it 'was in practice almost entirely reserved for murder' (J.J. Tobias, *Nineteenth Century Crime: Prevention and Punishment*, p. 135). In 1835 there were thirty-four hangings in England, and in 1845 only eleven (*Tables Showing the Number of Criminal Offenders Committed for Trial or Bailed for Appearance at the Assizes and Sessions . . . and the Result of the Proceedings*, PP, 1836, XLI, 11 *et seq.*; PP, 1846, XXXIV, 1 *et seq.*). Eric Stockdale reports that, from the time of its opening in 1801 until it was nationalized in 1877, there were only seventeen hangings in Bedford county's new gaol; of the seventeen, however, only four took place after 1837 (*op. cit.*, p. 194).

considerable public interest, these events do not seem to have affected the routine duties of the officers of the prison; they receive only a cursory mention in governors' journals, having mainly involved the chaplains.[32] In the conduct of capital executions division of labour was strictly enforced and the governor's duty was discharged when he delivered the condemned prisoner to the sheriff or his agent.

Transportation Transportation was the responsibility of central government and therefore during or immediately after the assizes or sessions the sheriff applied to the secretary of state for authorisation to remove the convicts. This request was usually granted forthwith (speed being very important, as shall be seen) and the convicts were escorted to the hulks.[33]

Sentences of transportation were imposed at nearly every assize and sessions and entailed a journey to London by the governor to escort those condemned. If the number of convicts was small and the governor thought the risk of their escape slight, he might act alone; if, however, he were anxious about security he would arrange for one or two constables to accompany him. Turnkeys occasionally carried out the transfer instead of the governor, but custody could not, in law, be delegated, and the governor would have had very firm trust in his subordinates in these cases. By the mid-1840s when it became fairly common for deputy governors to be appointed in the larger county prisons, the governor and his deputy usually shared escort duty equally.[34] At a small prison, with a correspondingly small staff available, escort duties could pose great problems, so that often special staff were

32 Occasionally, however, the crowds which collected to watch a hanging caused problems, as appears in a letter from the governor of Bedford county gaol and house of correction to the magistrates, complaining about the events which surrounded a recent execution: 'As considerable damage has been done to the *Fence* belonging to my Field opposite the Gaol, by the *Spectators* at the late *Execution of Reach and Fletcher*, I should esteem it a favour if you would be kind enough to allow me a carpenter to put it into repair.' His request was refused. (Bedfordshire County Record Office, Bedford County Gaol, Governor's Journal, 1834-8, letter-book portion.)

33 Evidence of John Capper, superintendent of the hulks, to the 1819 select committee (*Select Committee on Gaols*, PP, 1819, VII, 1, 299). By a subsequent Act (5 Geo. IV, c.84, ss.4 & 10) governors were obliged to supply certificates with each convict stating:

the Description of his Crime, his Age, whether married or unmarried, his Trade or Profession, and an Account of his Behaviour in Prison, before and after his Trial, and the Gaoler's Observations on his Temper and Disposition, and such Information concerning his connexions and former course of life as may have come to the Gaoler's Knowledge. . . .

. 34 Gloucestershire Records Office, County Gaol Deputy Governor's Minute Book, November 1844-April 1845, ref. Q/GC. 14. See entry for 12 December 1844.

employed to take charge of the prison during the absence of the regular officers.[35]

Court duties Besides the escort to the hulks, there was escort for prisoners – criminal and civil – to be provided whenever they made court appearances. Governors and other staff also frequently travelled to give evidence of identity which was often in dispute since, by adopting an alias, prisoners could avoid the heavier penalties to which they would otherwise become liable. In the absence of a central criminal register, photographic aids and fingerprinting, affirmation that a person had previous criminal convictions had to be made in person and upon oath. In addition prison staff frequently recognised the description of a suspect in the *Police Gazette*, and would inform the relevant authorities, who might in due course call upon them for testimony.[36] The use of photography to identify suspects (which was initiated in Bristol in the 1850s) gradually reduced the volume of these particular demands upon governors during the latter half of the century. The removal of insane prisoners was a less common type of escort: the asylum in some cases was in a neighbouring county.[37] Above all, the requirement that governors should attend their local sessions and assizes was criticised as 'productive of much loss of time ... [it] must interfere greatly with the proper discharge of the governor's duties'.[38]

Accordingly prison governors, especially in districts remote from London, could be away from their duties for a large proportion of their time, as the governor of Wakefield prison explained to Frederic Hill in 1848:

I am seldom at home for more than three weeks together. Eight times a year I am obliged to leave Wakefield to attend Quarter Sessions, and three times to attend the Assizes. With the time occupied in going and returning, I am seldom detained less than a

---

35 'Extracts from the Journal of John Edis', entry for November 1852.

36 At Hertford in August 1847, for example, the governor identified as a begging-letter imposter a man then in his custody on a vagrancy charge (Hertfordshire County Gaol, Governor's Journal, 1844-52, entry for 10 August 1847).

37 Huntingdon governors had occasionally to convey insane prisoners to the asylum at Bedford (see Huntingdon County Gaol and House of Correction, Keeper's Journal, 1847-51). It was not until 1845 that boroughs and counties were obliged by 8 & 9 Vict., c.126, to provide asylums. See pp. 339-40 below.

38 *Thirteenth Report of the Inspectors of Prisons (Northern and Eastern District)*, PP, *op. cit.*, p. xix (1850 *SC, op. cit.*, Minutes of Evidence, question 4584, 299). At Newgate, where movement of prisoners to and from court was very frequent, the governor complained that he was often left with a full gaol staffed by only three officers out of the twenty or so who were normally available.

week, and sometimes the period extends to a fortnight, or even longer. This causes a great interruption to my prison duties.[39]

The establishment of the railways during the 1840s eased some of the administrative pressures arising from repeated and prolonged absences,[40] which were now cut, in many cases, from several weeks to a matter of days or even hours.[41]

By way of contrast to the burdens they imposed, these travelling duties had a significant effect in promoting understanding and comradeship among a far-flung body of fellow administrators. On their various journeys governors got to know colleagues from neighbouring, and even distant prisons, meeting one another in courts or in the London receiving-prisons or hulks, provincial governors encountering metropolitan counterparts and vice versa.[42] News of associates and vacant posts could be exchanged, different disciplinary systems, legal and penological views, technical matters and even notorious prisoners discussed; both knowledge and values could be shared. Entries in the journals and letter-books of county prison governors show that details of disciplinary methods were passed from one locality to another by this means, as was information about penal devices. Using the information obtained on a few of such trips, for example, a Hertfordshire

39 *Thirteenth Report of the Inspectors of Prisons (Northern and Eastern District)*, *op. cit.*, xxiii. The governor of Ilford gaol, besides all his local court attendances, had to attend the Central Criminal Court twelve times a year (Essex Record Office, QS bundles, ref. Q/ACP3).

40 And expense, one might add. In the decades immediately preceding the establishment of the railways the costs of the conveyance of prisoners to and from courts and to the hulks had risen enormously, at least in some counties. The preliminary report of the Commission of Inquiry into the County Rates particularly mentioned Somerset and Sussex in this regard. In the latter costs had risen by 525 per cent between 1792 and 1832, from £4,865 to £25,201 (PP, 1835, XXXVI, 17, 25).

41 The effect of the railways on escort duties can be illustrated by the Gloucestershire records. Thomas Cunningham (who was governor during Sir George Paul's time) was frequently absent for periods of several weeks on London escorts. At one point he escorted to King's Bench in London and was absent for fourteen days (11 to 25 November 1802). On 26 November Cunningham set off once again for London, returning on 10 December. On 26 December he again went to London (this time on private business), and came back on 5 January 1803. From 12 to 16 January he was again away from the prison, and was in London for several weeks at various times during the rest of 1803. Altogether, between 1802 and 1803 he was absent from the prison for about eighteen weeks (Gloucestershire Records Office, County Gaol, Governor's Journal, 1802-5, ref. Q/GC 3/3). Just one transportation escort to Millbank prison in the 1840s shows the contrast. The deputy governor left Gloucester by train at 6.00 a.m. and returned, escort completed, at 3.30 a.m. the following morning (Deputy Governor's Minute Book, entries for 21 and 22 December 1844).

42 George Chesterton, for instance, had visited many provincial prisons, and had been as far afield as Glasgow (Chesterton, *op. cit.*, I, p. 297).

governor recommended to his justices the punishment diet in use at Westminster bridewell and the work of a particular treadwheel repairer.[43]

Even a cursory examination of prison records of the first part of the nineteenth century produces a strong sense of the compactness and intimacy of the world of prison staff and administrators. In correspondence between benches, in competitions for posts, in evidence to committees and in the reports of the inspectors, the same names occur again and again. And where a sense of colleagueship and association was established, a political tendency, an impulse to influence policy, was bound to emerge. Whilst in the first several decades of the century the establishment of anything like a common approach to policy among governors was barely discernible, its development was clearly presaged in the networks of contacts of which so much evidence remains.

Bookkeeping

Books and journals played an important part in the regulation of prisons.[44] Besides their being a means of controlling staff, however, administrative records served various legal purposes. From an early point in the century new prisons, such as Petworth house of correction, were equipped with an extensive and elaborate system of entry-books, account-books and journals;[45] by the 1840s this recording system had become a general requirement in prisons, and in 1845 the governor of Ilford gaol listed twenty-five books kept mainly by himself together with three others which came under his supervision.[46]

43 Hertford County Gaol, Governor's Journal, 1834-8, entries for May and August 1839.
44 See above, p. 128.
45 In 1826 the Petworth books numbered thirty-three in all, of which twenty-six were kept by the governor (West Sussex County Record Office, ref. QAP/15/W5(74)).
46 The books were: Governor's, Chaplain's, Matron's, and Surgeon's journals, General Prison Register, Provision Delivery Book, Bread and Flour Book, Bedding and Clothing Book, Quarterly Account Book, Ledger, Cash Book and Day Book, Prisoners Received After Trial Book, Prisoners Removed for Trial Book, Book of Fines and Penalties, Chaplain's School Register, Copies of Letters Received from Secretary of State, Copies of Orders of Courts, Magistrates' Minute Book, Magistrates' Order and Contract Book, Prisoners' Discharge Book, Governor's Order Book, Monthly Account of Prisoners Committed, Prisoners' Misconduct Book, Inventory of Books Furnished by the Chaplain, and the Liberty Prisoners' Account Book. Three additional books, the Receiving, Labour and Locking-up books, were kept in the turnkeys' lodge and regularly inspected by the governor (Essex Record Office, 'General Duties performed by the Governor of Ilford Gaol', ref. QACP/3).
   The governor of Bedford gaol kept thirteen books and journals, and four more were in the charge of other senior officers (Bedfordshire County Record

But bookkeeping did not end with the prison registers and journals. The growth in inspection and other central government intervention brought a considerable increase in Home Office circulars, questionnaires and returns. Some of the older governors, who had been appointed to carry out less complicated duties, were quite overwhelmed. It is apparent, even to present-day inspection, that prison journals and registers, instead of being completed on a daily basis, were occasionally completed in arrears.[47] George Smith, governor of Huntingdon gaol rather bitterly (if a trifle histrionically) blamed increased clerical duties for his retirement in 1856:

> In the midst of the pressure incident to making up my late Returns and Quarterly Accounts I have received directions from the Home Office for a Return on a *'simplified'* form for the Inspectors of Prisons in lieu of the former — Now this 'simplified' Return contains *8* principal Tables, including *126 sub divisions* All of which I trust a degree of returning health will enable me to accomplish thereby affording another opportunity of *dying in harness*.[48]

This change in the nature of duties demonstrates how some types of governors were eased out, and how changing circumstances made it necessary to appoint men of different backgrounds and abilities.

Conditions of work

Hours of work

Following the principle laid down by John Howard, the 1823 Gaol Act obliged governors to reside in the prison. But even without such a specific provision the rigid common-law insistence that the gaoler had sole custody of the gaol on behalf of the sheriff would have ensured

---

Office, Minute Book of Visiting Justices, 1838-44, ref. QGR5, entry for 15 November 1841).

---

47 For example, at Huntingdon county gaol in 1850 there was a note in the Keeper's Journal on 2 August that both he and the matron had been away, on ten days' leave of absence. Yet the journal was fully kept up as though he had been in the prison during that period. Obviously, therefore, entries were made in arrears, probably based on roughwork records of the chief turnkey (Keeper's Journal, 1847-51).

48 Huntingdon Record Office, Quarter Sessions Miscellaneous, 1856. However, it is possible that clerical duties were a perennially favoured excuse, since even in the 1820s the governor of Petworth house of correction claimed that it was not so much the number of prisoners that had increased his work as the number of books which he was obliged to keep (West Sussex County Record Office, ref. QAP/15/W5 (75)).

long hours of attendance.[49] Moreover, a small staff (as in the majority of prisons) made it obligatory that the governor be on the premises and actively undertaking the supervision of the prisoners. His responsibility being continuous, it was possible for him to be roused by the night-watchman to decide, for example, whether to summon the surgeon for a sick inmate or to take action about an escape.[50] Even if the prison was large enough for the governor to depute to responsible subordinates the handling of all but the gravest night emergencies, he still had to check the staff on duty. Certainly by the end of the 1840s night visiting (a common army procedure) was generally recognised as an essential part of an efficient governor's work.[51] Governorship thus involved an almost complete tie to the prison: any absence had to be noted in the journal and approved in advance by a visiting magistrate.[52] So strong was the presumption that the governor would be in the prison – ill or well – that a Bedford governor who, for reasons of health, requested a short break from duty during the day had his request recorded in an obviously sarcastic manner by the visiting justices.[53]

In 1845, anxious to reduce prison expenses, the justices at Springfield gaol, in Essex, mooted a proposal to charge the governor for his use of the prison garden. His indignant petition, in reply to quarter sessions,

49 As mentioned in Chapter 4, the new prisons at Horsham, Petworth and Gloucester had, from their opening, a residence requirement for governors. So strictly was it interpreted that in 1809 Sir George Paul expressed concern that Thomas Cunningham (the governor of the Gloucester Penitentiary) should be 'eating out in the city and not returning until midnight' (J.R.S. Whiting, *Prison Reform in Gloucestershire 1776-1820*, p. 25).

50 By the 1830s there seems to have been a night-watchman in most medium-sized and large prisons. John Edis, governor of Cambridge town gaol, recorded one such night-call in his journal: 'I was called up this morning about two o'clock to B.J. who was suffering from severe pains in the body. I . . . sent for the surgeon early in the morning' ('Extracts from the Journal of John Edis', entry for 26 October 1843).

51 Governors of George Chesterton's calibre and military background had adopted this practice even in the late 1820s. The governor at Huntingdon began to record regular night checks from the middle of 1849 (Huntingdon Record Office, Huntingdon County Gaol and House of Correction, Keeper's Journal, 1847-51, ref. Accessions 320). At Hertford the new governor started night checks immediately he assumed office in 1844, and continued them throughout his period of office; the previous governor had not followed this practice (Hertfordshire County Record Office, County Gaol and House of Correction, Governor's Journal, 1844-52, ref. Shelf 44).

52 The 1834 rules of the Wakefield house of correction were probably typical, and provided that the governor 'shall not be absent from the Prison at night, except on unavoidable business relative to the duties of the Prison, without permission from two Visiting Justices' ('Rules and Regulations for the Government of the House of Correction at Wakefield', Nottinghamshire Record Office, ref. QAG5/83).

53 Bedfordshire County Record Office, Minute Book of Visiting Justices, County Gaol and Old House of Correction, 1825-33, ref. QGR4, entry for 23 April 1832.

graphically describes the pressures which some governors thought arose from continuous attendance. Headed: 'The Gaoler is bound to be in the Prison on his Duties', the petition read, in part:

> Is it intended to charge him for the liberty of walking about the Prison — if not upon what principle is he to be charged with a Garden? — surely it is not too much for him to expect to have as much convenience and comfort as is consistent with the discipline — does he expect too much — when he asks to take as much exercise in the open air as the prisoners do — and if that is to be allowed — instead of an airing yard he might without too much damage to the County be allowed a Garden without being made to pay for it — it is very much like a deserter being made to pay for his handcuffs.[54]

Certainly the constraints of duty were eased to some extent by escorts and visits to courts, but on these occasions the governor was still on official duty. This arrangement of work must have had a strong tendency to isolate governors from wider social contacts and to heighten the physical and nervous strains of their work.

Leave

Until a system of annual leave was introduced at Pentonville no regular leave provision was made in English prisons.[55] The health of many governors broke down as a result of the unremitting demands of duty. Absences for medical purposes (at least ostensibly) account for most of the 'holidays' discoverable in the archives of local prisons. In August 1832, for example, the visiting justices at Bedford gaol allowed the governor several weeks' leave (during which time he hoped to visit his wife, already on sick leave); similar periods of leave were granted in 1842, 1844 and 1848.[56] At Huntingdon the first extended allowance of

---

54 Essex Record Office, QS bundles, ref. Q/AC, p3. He went on to argue (in the third person) that the paths and garden should be kept up, but not at his expense, and concluded: 'This certainly was not the opinion of the Magistrates when Mr. Neale was first appointed — he was then led to believe that his comfort and convenience would be studied where they did not interfere with his duties and he has always found it so.'

55 Nor were vacations allowed, as such, in many other areas of official employment. In the customs, 'Vacations for officers were not a general provision. Leave of absence though was granted ad hoc for various reasons. Bad health, "need of the waters", visits to ill or dying relatives seem to have been the common excuses' (Marios Raphael, thesis: 'The Origins of Public Superannuation Schemes in England, 1684-1859', p. 19).

56 In 1842 the matron was allowed four to six weeks' leave by quarter sessions. Health was not given as a reason in this case, but the fact that the request had to be put to quarter sessions shows it to have been unusual. The 1844 leave was also granted only to the matron — on health grounds — and the 1848 leave was granted for a fortnight to the governor on health grounds (Bedfordshire

leave which appears to have been granted was in 1850: 'Leave of absence owing to ill health having been granted by a Visiting Justice to the Keeper and the matron during ten days they this day returned to their usual duties.'[57]

In the early 1840s Hertford justices were relatively generous in granting leave, but they seem to have grown more parsimonious over the years. It would thus be hard to claim, at least in some localities, that the granting of leave was a practice which won increasing favour up to mid-century.[58]

An obvious solution to some of the problems which arose from the demanding custodial requirements of governorship was the provision of deputies. A legally authorised and responsible deputy could ease the pressure of work for his superior and allow for much greater scope for planning and pacing in the distribution of duties. With the active support of the inspectorate this approach was endorsed by government in the 1839 Prisons Act, though the governor still remained civilly responsible for the acts and omissions of his deputy.[59] This last stipulation meant that the measure was hardly a generous easing of the governors' bonds, although it was probably as great an alteration as the legal circumstances and administrative conventions of the day would allow.

The pace of work

Pressure of work was determined mainly by the size and location of the prison, staffing arrangements, system of discipline, sittings of the courts and the seasonal variations in the number and type of offences.

Epidemics continued to be a dangerous feature of prison life, and

County Record Office, Minute Book of Visiting Justices, County Gaol and Old House of Correction, 1825-33, ref. QGR4, entry for 27 August 1832; *ibid.*, 1833-44, ref. QGR5, entries for 13 April 1842, 13 April 1844; *ibid.*, 1844-8, entry for 14 February 1848).

57 The Huntingdon governor was granted no leave of any sort in 1834, 1835 and 1837 (Huntingdon Record Office, Huntingdonshire County Gaol and House of Correction, Keeper's Journal, 1833-8, ref. Accessions 320, entries for 1834, 1835 and 1837; *ibid.*, 1847-51, entry for 2 August 1850).

58 In 1841 the governor had a month's holiday, and, without the usual 'reasons of health' formula, another month the following year. In 1844 another vacation was granted ('his health requiring a change'). The new governor at Hertford in the mid-1840s received no leave in 1846, 1847 and 1848; in 1849 he was granted a one-week health leave. Finally in July and August 1850 he had a one-month unqualified holiday (Hertfordshire County Record Office, Hertford County Gaol and House of Correction, Governor's Journal, 1838-44, entries for 23 August 1841, 5 August 1842 and 16 April 1844; *ibid.*, 1844-52, entries for 1846, 1847, 1848, 1 August 1849 and 16 July-14 August 1850).

59 2 & 3 Vict., c.56, s. 8.

were more likely to occur during the spring. At Bedford, for example, this season consistently was marked, in years as far apart as 1827 and 1842, with outbreaks of typhus; other local prisons followed a similar pattern.[60] Such epidemics doubtless caused governors anxiety for their own health and that of their families, besides involving periods of arduous extra work attending the sick. Preventative medicine and forms of treatment were still rudimentary, so the outbreaks had to be allowed to run their course and to be contained in whatever way possible.

The changing seasons also brought changes in the types of offenders committed to prison. In winter, the peak period of hardship and destitution, workhouse inmates destroyed their clothes and bedding in order to be removed to the more ample prison diet.[61] In rural areas summer brought a high level of employment and flow of money, and the number of committals for assaults and drunkenness increased. In autumn, the prevalent offences were apple-stealing and other acts of illicit harvesting.

Security requirements also differed from season to seaon. Until gas was laid on at many prisons in the 1840s the prison day had been determined largely by the hours of daylight; outside exercise or employment was not possible without adequate light. Artificial lighting permitted the establishment of a more regular, equitable and healthy routine for the year as a whole.

As would be expected, the legal calendar had a marked effect on prison routine. But besides the pattern of court duties which it set, remands in custody caused fluctuations in the size of prison populations. At Bedford, for instance, the number of inmates varied between about twenty-five and eighty in a matter of months;[62] at Huntingdon such was the pressure of numbers on accommodation as sessions approached that on at least one occasion the governor recorded in his journal his anxiety for the security of the prison. Generally there was a build-up of remands for trial, many of whom had little to lose by an escape attempt, and to whom an opportunity might be presented, when staff were most stretched. For this reason it was common practice at

---

60 Influenza was also a regularly recurring and virulent illness. At Bedford in January 1831, for example, there was one of a series of such outbreaks. Cholera, too, was familiar, and Hertfordshire gaol had *two* bouts in 1849 (Bedfordshire County Record Office, Minute Book of Visiting Justices, 1825-33, ref. QGR4, entry for 23 April 1827; *ibid.*, 1833-44, entry for April 1842; Huntingdon Record Office, Huntingdonshire County Gaol and House of Correction, Keeper's Journal, 1833-8, ref. Accessions 320, entry for January 1837).

61 See the discussion of the relationship between the workhouses and prisons above (Chapter 8, pp. 239-40).

62 Bedford County Gaol and House of Correction, Minute Book of Visiting Justices, 1833-44, entries for 26 December 1833 and 1 September 1834.

these times to employ extra temporary turnkeys or watchmen.[63] With the imposition of a large number of non-custodial sentences (fines and floggings) and with the usually quick removal of convicts for transportation, there was a sharp reduction in the population, until the slow build-up began again.

Such were the main short-term factors which determined the pace of prison work.[64] It would be inaccurate, however, to see the work entirely as subject to continuous anxiety, punctuated by risky and prolonged escort journeys, and excursions to courts; periods of smooth prison routine, when not even a minor breach of discipline disturbed the calm, are also regularly to be interpreted from entries in governors' journals.

Working relationships with the justices

Since the level of authority and responsibility granted to governors had a direct bearing on the organisational efficiency of the prison,[65] a balance for each prison had to be found, which avoided undermining the governor's authority by too much magisterial intervention, and at the same time allowed proper regulation. That such a balance was rarely achieved to perfection goes without saying, but despite the example of Millbank the significance of the issue was poorly grasped

63 An extra warder was employed at Huntingdon for a time following an escape attempt by convicts awaiting transportation in November 1847 (Huntingdon County Gaol and House of Correction, Keeper's Journal, 1847-51, entry for 1 November 1847). During one of the many tense pre-sessions periods at Bedford the visiting justice authorised the ironing of prisoners and the employment of an extra night-watchman (Bedford County Gaol and Old House of Correction, Minute Book of Visiting Justices, 1825-33, entry 12 March 1832).

64 Other factors had a *long-term* effect on the prison population, and thus on the work of governors. As Macnab points out, there were a number of years during the first part of the century when crime (and thus committals) notably increased: 'The "reeling alternation" between depression and prosperity produced in certain years – 1812-13, 1817-19, 1831-32, 1839-42 and 1842 – high points of spontaneous violence and crime' (*op. cit.*, p. 28). He describes 1842 as 'The Everest of committals in this whole period [1805-60]' (*ibid.*, p. 62).

Changes in the law exerted an even more general and gradual influence on the prison population, both in terms of numbers and the type of persons imprisoned. These included such measures as the removal of the general provision of the death penalty for felony in 1827 (by 7 & 8 Geo. IV, c.28) and the Vagrancy Act of 1824 (5 Geo. IV, c.83), which deprived the justices of their power to impose whippings on minor offenders. The pattern of sentencing also affected the prison population, as did the efficiency of the police, and the extension of summary jurisdiction. That these factors had an influence on the level and nature of the prison population is clear, but the lack of accurate national statistics before 1856 makes it difficult to provide even a general national analysis.

65 See above, Chapter 6.

by many magistrates and commentators. Thus in the 1820s Thomas Le Breton was in favour of justices' keeping their governors on a short rein: 'It behoves the magistracy not to leave discretionary power in the hands of their officers; a Gaoler should act to the letter of his instructions, a good servant will not require more, a bad one ought not to be trusted.'[66]

Le Breton's advice was based on the observation that governors were not gentlemen, and the assumption that the justices wished, and were able to give, a high priority to prison management. It is doubtful whether, when they were appointed, gentlemen governors would have tolerated a close regulation by the justices, but in any event one of the main reasons for their appointment was the recognition that no amateur committee could successfully and continuously carry on the detailed management of a prison or a very close control of its governor. Eventually, therefore, Le Breton's first premise became untenable as the standing of governors in the community rose. Chesterton's authority at Cold Bath Fields, for example, was consistently respected by the great majority of Surrey magistrates, even though they were frequent visitors to the prison.[67]

As for Le Breton's second premise, magisterial neglect of prisons was far more common than excessive interest. Quarter sessions seem to have left the visiting justices very much to their own devices, and even within the committee of visiting justices the burden of the work of establishing policy and regulating the prison was frequently undertaken by one or two active members. The committees of the county prisons were often drawn from a wide geographical area and it was usual for duties to fall particularly heavily on members who lived in the county town.[68] Moreover, the effectiveness of their management being related closely to their level of experience could not but suffer when, as sometimes

---

66 Thomas Le Breton, *Thoughts on the Defective State of Prisons and Suggestions for their Improvement*, p. 18.

67 One particular magistrate spent long periods in the prison, consulting with the engineer and seeking improvements in the buildings. Even so Chesterton was able to comment that he 'studiously avoided any interference with my authority as governor, but on the contrary, extended towards me such ceaseless kindness as to kindle in my mind a very grateful sense of his consideration and attention' (Chesterton, *op. cit.*, I, pp. 114-15). Chesterton found that Benjamin Rotch was the exception to the generally satisfactory relationship which he had with the magistrates. Rotch was a noted opponent of the silent system that was followed at Cold Bath Fields, and had crossed swords with Dickens over the separate system. At one time Rotch visited Cold Bath Fields regularly, mainly to preach abstinence sermons, and Chesterton alleged that he showed favour to those staff and prisoners who were converted (see P.A.W. Collins, 'Dickens and the Prison Governor, George Laval Chesterton', pp. 22-5).

68 See the evidence of Higgins, a visiting justice at Bedford, to the 1835 select committee (1835 *SC, op. cit.*, First Report, Minutes of Evidence, XI, 68).

happened, membership changed as often as four times in a year.[69]

Sometimes the work of the justices became ritualised, as at Bedford where the committee, scrupulous in the regularity of its meetings and thorough in its inspections, arranged that for several years in the 1820s visits should take place every Tuesday and invariably found prison staff alert and diligent. The arrangement was only slightly altered in the 1830s when visiting day was changed to Mondays. Unexpected visits were eventually found to work better.[70] During the Bedford visits prisoners were asked (out of the governor's hearing) if they had complaints to make, and books and registers were examined in some detail. Occasionally an omission or breach of duty was discovered and the governor or other officer was reprimanded.[71] Sometimes wrongdoing was so blatant that it was uncovered without reference to the journals and registers, but even so the books would probably be used to present the case to sessions. Yet whilst prison records might be used to demonstrate a breach of duty, they could also give staff a measure of protection against unsound charges brought about, perhaps by magisterial ineptitude, a clash of personalities or by malice.[72]

69 *Thirteenth Report of the Inspectors of Prisons (Northern and Eastern District)*, PP, 1847-8, XXXVI, 361, xix.

70 In 1832, following the introduction of a new (silent) system of discipline, inspections became more thorough and on at least one occasion the justices returned unexpectedly, immediately after a routine visit (Bedfordshire County Record Office, Minute Book of Visiting Justices, County Gaol and Old House of Correction, 1825-33, ref. QGR4. See also the Minute Book for 1833-44, ref. QGR5).

It seems to have been an accepted practice in many counties to fix the dates of the visitation of the magistrates publicly, and in advance. Item nine on the agenda for the Michaelmas Quarter Sessions at Chichester in 1842 was to 'appoint three days for the Visiting Justices of Petworth House of Correction to visit and inspect the same between each Quarter Sessions during the current Year, the same to be printed on a card and sent by the Clerk of the Peace to each such Visiting Justice'. Item ten was 'The like as to Horsham Gaol' (West Sussex Record Office, ref. QAP/5/W15(5)).

71 At the end of April 1844 a Bedford prisoner told one of the visiting magistrates that he and three fellow inmates had been employed in the governor's garden. The allegation was investigated and upheld. As a result, the governor was strongly reminded that private use of prison labour was a breach of the regulations. On another occasion a convict was returned from Millbank because he had the itch. The surgeon was called before the visiting committee to explain how this had happened, and subsequently regulations were strengthened (Minute Book of Visiting Justices, County Gaol and Old House of Correction, 1833-44, ref. QGR5, entries for April and May 1844). On another visit a justice inspected the books in the governor's absence. The justice complained that the committee should have been informed in advance of the governor's (official) absence, and also that the journal was three days out of date. The matron's book was found to be eight days behind (*ibid*., entry for 30 January 1843).

72 In 1822 a visiting justice complained to sessions about the keeper of Chelmsford gaol. He wrote that, though he had long thought him unsuitable,

One duty of the governor — the ordering of supplies — seems often to have been subject to particularly close supervision. The requisitions which the Hertford and Bedford justices considered at their monthly meetings and solemnly recorded in their minute books were usually handfuls of brooms and mops, a few pairs of shoes and small amounts of linen. Even commodities in regular use, such as coal and candles, with a known depletion rate, were ordered in this way.[73] But more often than not the visiting justices probably did little more than countersign the governor's requests and, after the habit of committees, spent much time debating insignificant detail, whilst taking more important matters for granted.

Prison work by mid-century

Although, as was shown in the previous chapter, the reformist promises of the separate system were widely seen by mid-century not to have been redeemed, the debate in which they had played such a prominent part none the less had its effect on the duties and working conditions of governors. The zeal of Crawford and Russell and the other inspectors, the legislation which they were instrumental in obtaining and the more critical temper which had been stimulated among justices had closed many of the very small prisons, and had improved and more closely regulated the remainder. When compared with their condition at the turn of the century, the general state of the prisons, both physically and administratively, could be described only as a transformation.

'general conduct though sufficient to disqualify a Man for his situation is often incapable of that proof which may be thought necessary to justify his dismissal [sic]'. Only this requirement had prevented charges being brought at an earlier time. He made a number of specific charges, ranging from rudeness to the trade instructors, to improper behaviour, abuse and even threats of violence against them. He also charged the keeper with insolence to himself, a visiting justice, and with using 'disrespectful, degrading, contemptuous and scurrilous expressions of and concerning the visiting and other Magistrates'. Other charges included taking illegal fees, embezzlement, and trading with the prisoners. New charges were being made daily which the complainant himself had not been able to investigate, but which he wished to have examined.

This incident illustrates the degree of security of employment which governors enjoyed. If the visiting justice is to be believed at all he had obviously been subjected to some insolence, yet was unable to take action against the governor until specific violations of the regulations had been shown (Essex Record Office, QS bundles, 1822, ref. Q/SBb 469/17).

---

73 Hertfordshire County Record Office, County Gaol and House of Correction, Governor's Journal, 1834-8, ref. Shelf 44, entries for 15 January and 12 March 1838; Bedfordshire County Record Office, Minute Book of Visiting Justices, County Gaol and Old House of Correction, 1825-33, ref. QGR4, entries for 24 and 30 April 1827.

287

These changes in the tasks and the working conditions of the governors might be summarised not too misleadingly by the phrase 'fewer but better'. Although by modern standards, or even the standards which were to prevail a quarter of a century or so later, many of the prisons of the 1850s were small and difficult to manage efficiently, their governorship generally required greater skills of literacy and administration and a higher degree of probity than had been the case a couple of generations previously.

There was widespread adoption of the separate system, which even in its reformatory heyday tended to make governors remote from prisoners and staff alike. With their lives being spent in cells, prisoners were suffering a drastic reduction in their opportunities for association with both fellow inmates and prison staff. Such education and exhortation as the prisoners received was at the will of the chaplain and (where provided) the schoolmaster who worked under his supervision. And even the silent system, in prisons of large or medium size, removed governors from direct contact with the minor and demeaning routines of the prison; and, with its larger staffing requirement, it made necessary the exercise of control and custody through efficient staff deployment and supervision. Alongside these new requirements of the disciplinary systems a general attitude of distance-keeping between governor and turnkey was established. After reading mid-century memoirs, advertisements for posts, prison records and penological books and tracts one cannot escape the conclusion that no place remained for the old, easy relationships of keeper and turnkey, each collusively drawing income from the needs of prisoners, and the one subordinate to the other often only in the fashion of master and familiar household servant.

Prisons continued to be highly undesirable places — social lazars populated in the main by the uneducated, undernourished and lower class, prone to and carriers of disease both by their physical state and their frequently brutish way of life. Although not the charnel-houses of earlier years, prisons still were swept by epidemics which struck down members of the staff, their families or the surrounding community.

Prison staff remained in isolation, though in the case of most governors not suffering from social opprobrium as in the past. The literally incessant custodial responsibility, the long hours of duty, only relieved by sometimes protracted absences escorting prisoners, continued to confine governors for the greater part of their lives to a world which they shared with others in the service of the criminal justice system.

10 The recruitment of governors, 1800-50

Remuneration of governors

Salaries

When fee-taking was prohibited by Bennet's Act in 1815 magistrates were empowered to compensate gaolers and turnkeys with a remuneration charged upon the rates; by the early 1820s the changes seem generally to have been made. Regulation of trading (as distinct from fees and gratuities) had been left to the local authorities, but in nearly all the large prisons trading with criminal prisoners was already forbidden. In 1823 Peel's Gaol Act gave this prohibition the force of law.

Because prisons differed greatly in their annual turnover, the principle of compensation so worked as to continue the previous inequalities in the substituted remuneration. But local authorities' resources[1] were also a factor in determining salary levels, not only negatively but positively, as in Middlesex, where the magistrates wished to abandon the notion of compensation and to attract candidates of superior calibre by paying appropriately large salaries.[2]

Peel's Act laid no restrictions upon the purchase of certain goods and services from prison staff by civil prisoners; and for many years vestiges of the entrepreneurial system lingered on in the form of charges

---

1 In England governors in the small county and borough prisons received salaries which appeared beggarly compared with those sums paid in the metropolis, but the contrast in Scotland was even greater, with rural annual salaries of £3 and £4 not uncommon. This led Frederic Hill, when inspector for Scotland, to comment that 'The only wonder is that, under the present circumstances, men comparatively so respectable and well disposed as the Gaolers, even of the small Prisons, generally appear to be, can be obtained' (*Second Report of the Inspectors of Prisons (Scotland, Northumberland and Durham)*, PP, 1837, XXXII, 759, 10).
2 See pp. 303-7, below.

for special facilities – mainly the hire of the governor's own rooms, furniture and utensils. Traces of the old system of payment could also be discerned in the non-monetary emoluments, and in the necessity for prison rules and regulations to contain explicit prohibitions of fee-taking.[3]

The balancing of these different values in the computation of governors' salary levels – previous fee-income, a generosity in the current salary to attract suitable recruits and the resources of the locality – led to many anomalies. As late as 1850 Fry was moved to complain that 'the salaries of the governors of prisons are very unequal, disproportionate to their duties, and founded upon no fixed principle'.[4] Yet in comparison with the early years of the century many of the extremes in income had been curbed.[5] The application of Bennet's Act, the decline in the proportion of debtors and closer regulation by inspectors and justices had greatly reduced legitimate profits, whilst other legislative requirements and the critical reports of the inspectorate had closed many of the small prisons which had paid very small wages. In 1850 Perry (one of the inspectors) reported that the salary for governors of county gaols varied between £100 and £350, 'with a residence and generally some allowance of coal and candles'.[6] By then no fees at all were paid by debtors and other allowances were rarely made. Table 10.1 shows salary distribution of governors and keepers in 1840.

A fairly typical range of salaries was paid at the medium-sized

3 At Hertford county gaol, for example, the governor's salary was fixed at £417. 10s. 6d. net, and he was forbidden to levy fees except upon self-supporting debtors for the use of his own furniture (Hertfordshire County Record Office, County Gaol and House of Correction Rules and Regulations, 1824, ref. County Gaol 5). In 1836 the governor of Newgate thus charged between half a guinea and one guinea a day for prisoners committed by Parliamentary process. Such large fees were exceptional, but the practice was not (see *First Report of the Inspectors of Prisons (Home District)*, PP, 1836, XXXV, 1).

The usual non-monetary emoluments were apartments, lighting and heating for governors, and board and lodging for subordinates.

4 Rev. Henry P. Fry, *A System of Penal Discipline*, p. 130.

5 The Fleet provides a good example of this process. In 1819 the warden had a net income of £2,238, which a Royal Commission thought entirely appropriate: 'under present circumstances, we do not think that . . . he is overpaid, considering the duties he has to perform and the responsibility to which he is subject' (*Royal Commission on the Fleet, Westminster Palace and Marshalsea*, PP, 1819, XI, 325). But when the Fleet, the Queen's Bench and Marshalsea prisons were merged to form the Queen's prison the governor of the new establishment was given a salary of only £800. This figure had been arrived at by reference to other government prisons rather than previous fee-income.

6 *Select Committee on Prison Discipline*, Minutes of Evidence, PP, 1850, XVII, 1, question 1131, 83.

county gaol and house of correction at Northampton: governor £400 (plus house, washing, coal and candles); chaplain £210; visiting surgeon £60; first turnkey £60 (plus coal); second turnkey £52 (plus coal); third, fourth, fifth and sixth turnkeys, all £52. The matron was paid £35 and the night-watchman £52. It can be seen that governors were paid substantially more than other prison officials, including chaplains. In the central government prisons the position was much the same, although the differential between governors and chaplains was not quite so pronounced (see Table 10.2).

TABLE 10.1   *Salaries of governors and keepers of 178 gaols and houses of correction, 1840*

Salary	Number of prisons
Less than £100	73
£100-99	38
£200-99	26
£300-99	21
£400-99	7
£500-99	8
£600-99	2
£700+	3
Total	178

Source: *Abstract Return of the Establishment of, and Persons Confined in, and Expenditure of Each Gaol and House of Correction in England and Wales*, PP, 1840, XXXVIII, 241.

Note: In compiling this table non-monetary emoluments have been ignored, as it is difficult to calculate their value. Only a few governors did not receive these emoluments, which ranged from house, coal and candles, in most cases, to the provision of bread, soap, potatoes and other vegetables, washing, clothes, taxes and a garden or field. In a few instances fees or allowances for escorting those under sentence of transportation were listed as extra emoluments, though strictly speaking these were prison expenses (see also *Return of Salaries Paid to Governors or Keepers*, PP, 1843, XLIII, 257).

As has been noted, these emoluments in kind were a survival of the old entrepreneurial system. When the system of public finance was introduced some authorities retained these goods and services as emoluments in order to prevent peculation. The governor of Springfield gaol in Essex reminded his local magistrates of this historical motive when they queried the expense of providing these 'extras':

> Charges of Peculation are easily made, and rebutted with difficulty – and therefore it was thought better to allow the Governors all they required and thus there would be no ground for charging them with stealing the County

property. The principle is in some prisons extended to soap, and even to provisions. After a lapse of years the motive is forgotten by the older Magistrates and the New Magistrates may look only at the Expense either not knowing the Reasons — or not deeming them sufficient. But however viewed the Governor does not deserve censure (Essex Record Office, QS bundles, ref. Q/ACP 3).

In eleven of the 178 prisons no salary at all was paid. Of the eleven all but three (Harwich, Leominster and Faversham gaols) were franchise prisons. At one of the franchise prisons (Eccleshall Debtors' Gaol) the gaoler reported a fee-income of £250 per annum. This was probably higher than in the other franchise establishments.

Generally the returns show that outside the metropolis the keepers of borough prisons were paid less than those of the county establishments, and keepers of county houses of correction less than governors of county gaols.

The highest salaries (£800) were paid at York Castle and Giltspur Street Compter (the City house of correction); Newgate came next at £700. A previous return had shown that the keeper of Lancaster Castle was paid £1,000, but he contributed £200 to the payment of staff. No details were given of other emoluments (*Return of the Establishment of Officers and Servants Employed in Each County Gaol and House of Correction in England and Wales*, PP, 1833, XXVIII, 391).

At that time the keeper of Springfield gaol was paid £500, with free accommodation, heating and lighting. Similar amounts were paid at Salford and Kirkdale gaols. Chesterton, at Cold Bath Fields, was then paid £600.

TABLE 10.2   *Salaries of senior officials in central government prisons, 1850*

Prison	Governor	Deputy governor	Chaplain	Assistant chaplain
Millbank	£600	£200	£400	£200
Parkhurst	£500	£110	£300	£200
Pentonville	£600	None	£400	£200
Portland	£500	£200	£300	£200

Source: *Estimate of the Sum to defray the charge of Inspection and General Superintendence over All the Prisons in the U.K.*, year ending March 1851, PP, 1850, XXXIV, 356.

It is interesting to note that after 1823 chaplains' salaries were also calculated by a method analogous to fee-compensation, even though they had never enjoyed fee-income. This was due to Peel's Gaol Act which provided that chaplain's salaries should accord with prison capacity. In a fifty-inmates prison £150 was to be paid, the rate rising to £250 in one of 200 inmates. Magistrates had discretion to fix a still higher rate in larger establishments. But, as Table 10.3 suggests, even allowing for extra-mural income[7] many gaol chaplains in medium to large establishments seem to have had lower total incomes than the governors. In most small local prisons chaplains worked only part-time, or even on an occasional and voluntary basis; therefore comparisons between their rate of payment and that of governors could be misleading.

TABLE 10.3   *Salaries paid to chaplains in 114 gaols, 1835*

Salary	Number	Other income	Number
£0-49	19	£0-49	56
£50-99	25	£50-99	26
£100-49	23	£100-49	14
£150-99	18	£150-99	8
£200-49	16	£200-49	4
£250-99	3	£250-99	0
£300+	10	£300+	6
Totals	114		114

Number with no salary:	4	Highest non-gaol income:	£700
Number with no other income:	48	Highest combined income:	£725
Highest gaol salary:	£400	No gaol or other income shown:	3

Source: *Return of Salaries Paid to Chaplains in Gaols*, PP, 1835, XLV, 187. In this table all amounts have been rounded up to the next pound. Chaplains were generally not given non-monetary emoluments, and in only a few instances was the provision of a house shown in the returns at this time. Several chaplains refused to disclose their non-prison income (one or two minced no words in pronouncing the inquiry an impertinence), which is therefore under-represented in the table. Even allowing for this omission, it would appear that a number of respondents had low prison salaries and no supplementation from other sources. As with governors, the borough chaplains were usually poorly paid, but this was often balanced by some enjoying a substantial urban parochial stipend. A great number of borough and franchise gaols made no returns, and it seems reasonable to assume that most of these had no paid chaplain at all. The returns showed that the chaplains' performance of their duties ranged from perfunctory occasional visits to the prison, to regular attendance for morning prayers, education, censoring and other tasks. See also the *Return of the Salary Paid to the Chaplain of Every Prison in England and Wales*, PP, 1831-2, XXXIII, 533.

7 At the beginning of the 1830s there were about 10,000 beneficed clergymen in England and Wales. Approximately a quarter (2,268) of them held two or more livings.

By mid-century chaplains were regarded by some observers as unfairly disadvantaged in comparison with the governors. Perry thought that an improvement in salaries was the only means of raising the standard of chaplains' qualifications, whilst Kingsmill (the Pentonville chaplain) warned the justices:

> Some of my brethren, it is to be feared, domiciled in the spacious and costly edifices which ornament the grand entrances of new prisons . . . are in danger of getting into the debtors' side of their own prison, from the disproportionate style of their stipends.[8]

Yet the chaplaincy was not well placed to improve its financial standing. Whilst by mid-century governors had benefited from closures and amalgamations which made for larger and financially more satisfactory units, the chaplains were increasingly being called upon to provide full-time services in return for payments that had been first calculated in the days when it was common for such prison earnings to be a marginal or supplementary income. The eclipse of the reformist separate system robbed the chaplains of their strongest argument for parity (let alone superiority) based on the relative importance of their contribution to prison discipline.[9]

Pensions

Salaries were the most obvious item for attention in the regularisation of prison finance and it was some years before the less pressing matter of pensioning was raised. In common with occupants of most other public positions gaolers had been expected to provide for old age out of income. Ability to do this varied greatly from one prison to another; most gaolers in the large metropolitan and county establishments would have found it a matter of little difficulty. Indeed, as has been mentioned, under the entrepreneurial system of finance such was the

---

In those days, when a curate or dissenting minister could be expected to live on £80 a year or sometimes less, £200 a year could be considered a reasonable income. Of these 2,268 pluralists, 643 held livings each of which was over £200 per annum and 711 held two, one of which was over £200 (G. Kitson Clark, *The Making of Victorian England*, pp. 152-3).

---

8 Rev. Joseph Kingsmill, *Chapters on Prisons and Prisoners and the Prevention of Crime*, p. 340.

9 For a fuller discussion of chaplains' salaries see W.L. Clay, *The Prison Chaplain*, Ch. 4. By way of comparison it is interesting to note Mishra's report that in 1850 the salary of a poor-law relieving officer averaged £82, which was similar to that of a schoolmaster. There was great variation in salaries between the counties: 'In the County of Bedford the average salary was £142 10s. and in the County of Radnor in Wales, £37' (thesis: 'A History of the Relieving Officer', pp. 35-6).

proprietary nature of office that agreements were often made between incumbents and their successors for the provision of annuities.[10] This kind of arrangement was made by John Eyles, warden of the Fleet prison in 1804; he appointed a deputy to perform all duties, who contracted to pay him an annuity of £500, and in return received all the substantial emoluments of the wardenship.[11] Whereas the Fleet yielded large revenue, income in provincial prisons was generally insufficient for these purposes. In any event when public finance was introduced governors lost the control of office necessary to bind their successors.[12]

In the early years of the nineteenth century there were various moves to provide pensions for civil servants. Schemes dependent upon contributions and means tests already existed for some officials, but in 1810 an Act was passed which created 'a comprehensive and generous public superannuation system for all civil servants'.[13] Behind this provision,

> were the powerful motives which had as their objective the
> elimination of patronage and corruption. The abolition of
> contributions on the one hand, and of tests of means on the other,
> were part of the price that was paid to further this objective.[14]

The staff of local prisons were not, of course, covered by this legislation, but it is highly probable that the example of the earlier measure

---

10 See Chapter 3, p. 67.
11 *Royal Commission on the Fleet, Westminster Palace and Marshalsea*, PP, 1819, XI, 325 *et seq*. Eyles had not visited the prison at all in the fifteen years the agreement had been in force.
12 Gerald Rhodes points out that it was impossible to operate pension schemes *before* salaries began to be paid to active full-time holders of public office:

> To begin with, no precise line [could] be drawn in the modern sense
> between salaries paid to those who were at work and pensions paid to
> those who had retired from work. Some civil servants were remunerated
> by fees as well as or instead of salaries; some held sinecures providing an
> income with no duties; others again held office for life but paid a deputy
> part of the remuneration to perform the actual duties of the office.

He goes on:

> Those who held sinecures . . . were not necessarily retiring in the modern
> sense, although the acquisition of a sinecure might well serve as a means
> of providing an income in retirement. But apart from sinecures and offices
> performed by deputies, there were other means of making the necessary
> provision, as in the Post Office where public servants 'were generally
> allowed to make private bargains for annuities with their successors'
> (*Public Sector Pensions*, p. 16).

13 Marios Raphael, thesis: 'The Origins of Public Superannuation Schemes in England, 1684-1859', p. 129. The Act was 50 Geo. III, c.117.
14 *Ibid*.

and the same reasoning lay behind the inclusion of a pension provision in Peel's Gaol Act of 1823. This gave justices powers to superannuate gaolers and keepers on grounds of sickness, old age or infirmity.[15] They were also permitted to pension chaplains, but not the subordinate officers of the prison. Several administrative disadvantages arose from this latter neglect and until appropriate legislation was finally provided in the early 1840s this was another significant differential in the remuneration of governors and their staff.[16]

15 They were allowed to

> grant such Gaoler or Keeper such an Annuity as they in their Discretion shall think proportioned to the Merits and Time of his Service, and may order the Payment thereof out of the Rates lawfully applicable to the building or repairing of such Gaols and Prisons: Provided always that the annual amount paid by way of Superannuation or Allowance to any retired Keeper of any Prison shall not exceed the Amount of Two Thirds of the salary fixed for the succeeding Keeper of such Prison (4 Geo. IV, c.64, s.26).

16 The legislation which eventually empowered magistrates to superannuate subordinate staff was 5 and 6 Vict., c.98. This had been obtained after an extended campaign of pressure upon government by the inspectorate. For some it was largely a moral issue. Augustus Such wrote that 'a turnkey at the close of an active life, whose salary has been such as would only find him in the common necessaries of life, finds himself no longer able to get his living, and may end his days in a workhouse' (*Remarks on Prison Discipline, and the Model Prison*, pp. 17-18). The workhouse was obviously no fitting place for a faithful public servant. The inspectors, who pressed their argument over several successive reports, stressed administrative considerations. William Williams (inspector for the Northern District) outlined his case:

> I have in several cases observed great inconvenience to result from the retention of turnkeys in their situations beyond the periods when they were capable of duty. The magistrates, from motives of humanity, are always unwilling to discharge officers under such circumstances, and the absence of any provision for old age or infirmity must prevent a more respectable class of persons from seeking these offices (*Third Report of the Inspectors of Prisons (Northern and Eastern District)*, PP, 1837-8, XXXI, 1, 2).

William Crawford and Whitworth Russell put forward a similar case and held that powers to superannuate would enable the magistrates to remove, without harshness, officers appointed in earlier years whom they had come to view as unsuitable for new conditions (*Fourth Report of the Inspectors of Prisons (Home District)*, PP, 1839, XXI, 1).

When legislation was not provided as quickly as they had hoped, the inspectors outlined other administrative advantages, headed by staff recruitment and control and a removal of a possible motive for corruption:

> Such a measure is called for not less with reference to the interests of prison discipline than the welfare of a large and deserving body of public officers who have important trusts confided to them − whose credit and respectability as a class are daily increasing − but whose salaries are generally too small to enable them to lay by an adequate provision as a

The granting of pension requests was no simple process. At that time retirement was not associated with any age limit:

> Old age was an undefined condition which could not lead as such to any sort of special treatment. Illness, infirmity, even 'great melancholy', however, occurring to elderly people more frequently and with far more severe results, were concrete conditions, accepted causes, leading to practical inability to perform certain duties. . . . The essential fact, therefore, which led to a pension was incapacity to work. Biological age was not, by itself, a material condition.[17]

The pension application in 1827 at the Halstead house of correction in Essex provides an appropriate illustration of the system just described. The keeper's submission, based on old age and infirmity, was made to Michaelmas Sessions. He had no baptismal certificate, and to prove his age was obliged to make deposition that (according to an entry in the family Bible) he was sixty-five years of age; he also produced a surgeon's certification of his infirmity. His application was addressed to the sessions as a petition, supported by the visiting justices of his prison:

> Your petitioner would have continued his services for a longer period had he not been rendered incapable by loss of health and increase of Years. Your petitioner has obtained a Certificate from his medical attendant which is hereto annexed, and he humbly prays the Court to grant him such an allowance as his services may be considered to merit.[18]

---

resource against the evils of old age and infirmity (*Fifth Report of the Inspectors of Prisons (Home District)*, PP, 1840, XXV, 1, 111).

The arguments were repeated in the sixth report (1841), when Crawford and Russell were supported by most of their colleagues from the other districts. The legislation was provided the following year.

---

17 Raphael, *op. cit.*, p. 44.
18 Essex Record Office, Quarter Sessions bundles, ref. Q/SBb489/12/4, 12/5. A similar letter was submitted by the keeper of the Lewes house of correction in 1838. It was addressed to Lord Chichester, the chairman of the quarter sessions:

> My Lord, I beg leave most respectfully to represent to your Lordship that in Consequence of my Advanced Age (being now in My 70 year) and the declining State of my health, I find myself under the powerful necessity of tendering my resignation of Keeper of the House of Correction at Lewes, to the Court of Quarter Sessions.
> Having discharged the duties of an Office of considerable responsibility and requiring the most unremitting attention for . . . 13 and 14 years and having at all times endeavoured to discharge these duties to the best of my abilities I humbly hope the Court will be pleased to take a favourable view of my past Services, and grant me the means of support during the period

After consideration the sessions voted an appropriate sum.

This system of petitioning and certification continued to operate until the nationalisation of prisons in 1877. In 1850, for instance, James Banfield, the governor of Bedford County Gaol and Old House of Correction petitioned and produced a certificate from the surgeon stating:

> the Governor had been suffering for the last year or two from aggravated Dyspepsia accompanied with nervous depressions and irregular action of the Heart in a great measure induced by the exertions and anxieties of his office.[19]

When the governor of Huntingdonshire county gaol resigned on health grounds in 1856, he too produced a certificate of ill-health, even though he had been advised to resign by a visiting justice, who had discovered him to be unwell.[20]

As might be expected, the rate of payment of superannuation varied considerably from one authority to another. The level was influenced by a number of factors, chief of which (apart from the size of the prison and resources of the prison authority) seems to have been the governor's standing with the magistrates. The Bedford petition of James Banfield cited above resulted in a pension of £80. Banfield had served (first as turnkey) for eighteen years; yet as against a pension of £75 given in 1845 on request to the governor of Hertford county gaol and house of correction who had held office for only seven years,[21] Banfield was not treated with particular generosity. As Banfield had been a turnkey, one reason for this decision may have been the differential in pension rates between governors and subordinates (when eventually legislation permitted their superannuation). The difference this could make is shown in the pension allowed to a turnkey of Cambridge town gaol in 1864; having held his position satisfactorily for thirty-two years he was granted £45 per annum (half his salary); his wife, who had been matron for twenty-three years, was granted £6. 17s. 4d., 'which is the

---

that it may yet please God to spare me (East Sussex County Record Office, ref. QAP/L/E7, 58).

It would seem that the justices did not feel that they had had full value for money from this keeper, because he was already in his late fifties when he took up his post. It was stipulated that the next keeper should not be older than forty-five on appointment.

---

19 Bedfordshire County Record Office, Quarter Sessions Minute Book, 1850, QSM36, p. 464.
20 Huntingdon Record Office, Huntingdonshire Quarter Sessions, Miscellanea, 1856. The surgeon stated that the governor's poor state of health 'has been accelerated and increased by too long and too close personal application to the duties of his office, these particularly the last three or four years'.
21 Hertfordshire County Record Office, ref. QS Misc. B 108(B)7.

full sum fixed under the Act of Parliament in such cases'.[22]

This method of pensioning gave the justices a considerable hold over their governors. Even modern entitlement pensions can act as significant constraints on the behaviour and attitudes of employees. Control must therefore have been very much greater when a pension was granted on what was virtually a grace and favour basis — especially when no feasible alternative means of provision for old age and incapacitation was available.

TABLE 10.4   *Length of service of 178 governors in England and Wales, 1840*

Years of service	Number
Up to 4	55
5–9	34
10–14	24
15–19	28
20–4	19
25+	9
Not stated	9
Total	178

Source: Abstract Return of the Establishment of, and Persons Confined in, and Expenditure of Each Gaol and House of Correction in England and Wales, PP, 1840, XXXVIII, 241.

The governor of Norwich county gaol and house of correction, who had been appointed in 1797, had been longest in a post — forty-three years. His length of service was almost equalled by the redoubtable John Orridge, governor of Bury St Edmunds gaol (forty-two years) and by the governor of the Beccles house of correction (forty-one years).

Decentralised pensioning militated to a significant extent against the movement of governors from one prison to another and thus perhaps prevented many capable men from extending their experience and improving their skills. Before deciding on a change of prison a governor would need to calculate how many years he could serve in his new post, and would need to offset whatever increase in salary he might obtain against a possible loss in superannuation. On the other hand, so large was the differential in both payment and pensions between governors

22 'Extracts from the Journal of John Edis', MS, Radzinowicz Library, Cambridge. Entry for 5 February 1864.

and subordinates that an aspiring turnkey had great inducement to move in search of a governorship. In 1840, as can be seen from Table 10.4, almost two-thirds of governors had held office for five or more years and just under half had been in the post for ten years or above. No solution to this problem of immobility of governors came until centralisation, although the difficulties and disadvantages were well understood by writers such as Fry, who saw a central administrative board as the remedy.[23]

Despite its cumbersomeness the localised pension system had a certain personal and ritualistic character which provided the magistrates with an opportunity of expressing public gratitude to valued servants. In his memoirs George Chesterton proudly recalled as a form of public honour the pension voted to him on his retirement in 1854, which had been accompanied by a testimonial acknowledging his services to the county.[24] This *rite de passage* was a unique advantage that grace and favour had over an entitlement to superannuation.[25]

The social status of governors

Occupational status is notoriously difficult to determine with any precision. It is obviously impossible here to follow or to utilise the results of the ambitious methodology of some modern studies, which attempt to order different occupations according to the prestige accorded to them by sample respondents.[26] But two criteria of social worth current in early nineteenth-century England may loosely and descriptively be used as measures of social standing – respectability and gentility.

Respectability was shown by hard work and self-reliance and reflected a strong sense of duty and knowledge of correct behaviour. In the 1830s and 1840s the powerful political appeal of the concept of respectability was shown by the many movements for moral and social improvement.

23 Fry, *op. cit.*, p. 139.
24 George Laval Chesterton, *Revelations of Prison Life* (1856), II, pp. 301-2.
25 It is of interest to note the way in which some kindred occupational groups acquired pensions schemes. Poor-law officers had to wait until the 1860s before the guardians were given discretion to grant them pensions. Many of the reasons for introducing this benefit were the same as those given in respect of prison officials. Mishra notes that many old and infirm officials were, prior to the measure, kept in service on compassionate grounds until, in some instances, they were in their eighties and nineties (*op. cit.*, pp. 181, 184, 189, *passim*). As for the police, 'as early as 1829 in the Metropolis and 1840 elsewhere, pensions could be granted to policemen who were disabled or "worn out by length of service", but not until 1890 was a police pension scheme established' (Rhodes, *op. cit.*, p. 28).
26 As, for example, in John Goldthorpe and Keith Hope, *The Social Grading of Occupations*.

The overall aim was the strengthening of a common culture, based on middle class social norms, into which the working classes could be integrated. Respectability was the goal to be striven for, and self-improvement the way to attain it.[27]

When the prisons were run on entrepreneurial lines the staff were severely stigmatised.[28] But with the introduction of public finance, 'trust-management' and regulation, it became increasingly possible for them to lay claim to respectability. It was, at the same time, expedient for the justices as prison administrators to encourage such claims and expectations. The process of acquiring the new reputation was, however, slow and uneven, and it is impossible to date the change as uniformly applicable to all the existing prisons. The small borough and franchise establishments undoubtedly exercised an influence on the public image of imprisonment that was only slowly dispelled by the advances made in the large regulated prisons. Yet it seems reasonable to assume that at least some sections of the public were capable of distinguishing between the new, morally rigorous Pentonville, for example, and the antiquated, sordidly commercial franchise prisons. Certainly the importance of redefining the position of prison staff was grasped by many commentators. In 1840 Crawford and Russell described the subordinate members as 'a large and deserving body of public officers who have important trusts confided to them — whose credit and respectability as a class are daily increasing'.[29] Gentility was an indicator of social standing equally as strong as respectability but maybe more difficult to define:

When anyone in early Victorian times was asked to define exactly what he meant by gentleman he had as much difficulty as we do today. Anthony Trollope . . . confessed . . . that although a man might be defied to define the term gentleman, everyone knew what he meant. Essentially the term was held to include gentle birth, ownership of a landed estate, and an income sufficient to permit the enjoyment of leisure. But the concept of gentility also implied certain moral qualities — honour, courage, consideration for others — which were embodied in a fairly strict code of what was 'done' and 'not done'. What was most clearly expected of a gentleman was public service, given voluntarily and if necessary at his own expense. In return he was accorded immense respect and his authority and privileges were accepted. The concept of gentility functioned as an agency of social discipline.

27 J.F.C. Harrison, *The Early Victorians 1832-51*, p. 163.
28 See above, Chapter 3.
29 *Fifth Report of the Inspectors of Prisons (Home District)*, PP, 1840, XXV, 1, 111.

This was the 'ideal type' of gentleman; but the less 'perfect', among whom might be numbered the early governors, belonged to a class a little further down in the social order:

> Moreover, in a deferential society some of the attributes of gentility rubbed off on those lower down the social scale. Every foreign visitor knew that Englishmen loved to ape their betters . . . and the Victorian middle classes were no exception in their anxiety to rise socially.[30]

Indeed, the concept of gentility has its place in a discussion of governors precisely because of its ambiguities. Governors made steady and substantial progress away from disreputability, but contemporary literature gives a clear impression that very often the term 'gentleman' was allowed in referring to them out of kindly condescension as much as out of respect. And doubtless these upwardly aspiring officials ignored any ambiguity of intent and were mightily consoled by the form.

Whatever the uncertainties of such terms they were very much a part of the discourse and preoccupation with social status which prison officials shared, broadly speaking, with the rest of their society.[31] This emerges clearly in the writing of Thomas Le Breton, governor of the county gaol and keeper of St Augustine's House of Correction, near Canterbury, in the early 1820s. Le Breton was one of the earliest 'gentleman governors'. He was keenly aware of his anomalous position and much concerned to explain his background and to justify his choice of occupation. He felt a strong interest in penal policy, but found that

> Theory was but slender ground to work upon. . . . The track of Prison Reform could only be formed in practice. . . . The way to acquire which would divert me for a time from that society with which I had been accustomed to move, but the reflection that a gentleman is recognised in every situation induced me to waive private consideration, and the instant I was placed upon half pay . . . I acquired some information through the much respected and venerable Governor of Gloucester Prisons [Cunningham, appointed

---

30 Harrison, *op. cit.*, pp. 125-6.
31 A point which Kitson Clark makes well in relation to the professions:

> The later eighteenth and the early nineteenth centuries saw the beginning of the development of other organised professions in their modern form. In many walks of life − in medicine, in the army and the navy, in architecture and in engineering − it came to be realized that an increasingly higher standard of technical capacity would be required by anyone who wished to do their work successfully, and at the same time in many of these professions the reward became greater, and it seemed at least for many of those who practised them that they had a claim to a more assured and distinguished social position that their predecessors might have had in the past (*op. cit.*, p. 260).

by Sir George Paul to Gloucester Penitentiary] who subsequently introduced me to the Magistrates of Glamorganshire where I became the Keeper of the County Gaol.[32]

But the social stigma – loss of caste, almost – was oppressive:

> many respectable individuals are alone prevented from devoting their time and talents to such useful employment, because public opinion, founded on the assertion of a great man in many respects [Sir William Blackstone] . . . has branded Gaolers with being a merciless race of men, and steeled against every tender sensation; this stigma has done more to deteriorate gaol discipline than all the indifference of the age; there is not a lawyer's clerk but at every Assize or Session points at the Gaoler as an inferior being, one beneath the human species; the abandoned culprit commands the sympathy of thousands, whilst the unoffending officer of justice is considered (and that from public prejudice) a much worse man than his prisoner; how different this would be, if the Directors of Prisons were countenanced by respectable persons as useful members of society, and (when merited) treated with common courtesy; The advantage of such treatment is well known where the Magistrates have condescendingly made the experiment.[33]

Le Breton realised that social labelling was self-reinforcing. Until the magistrates adopted more generally a policy of social upgrading in the recruitment of governors, the only break in the circle of stigmatisation would come from oddities like himself.

Le Breton's view of the public standing of governors was confirmed by Clay, in his recollection of the governor at Preston in the 1820s when he himself was first appointed chaplain:

> He had been appointed to the office many years before, when a rough and ready bully, with a flavour of good nature, and wit enough to manage the prison cheaply, was the kind of gaoler commonly approved by justices. He had been successively a sergeant in the army, butler to a county magistrate, and a publican. His military experience, his old master's influence and (it was said) the excellence of his tap, procured him the post.[34]

After a scandal about the bridling of a female prisoner, other offences of peculation, neglect and gambling were discovered and the governor was dismissed. His successor was a gentleman, a captain in the Royal Navy. The justices had decided that their supervision was an insufficient

32 Thomas Le Breton, *Thoughts on the Defective State of Prisons and Suggestions for their Improvement*, p. x.
33 *Ibid*., pp. 15-17, *passim*.
34 Clay, *op. cit*., p. 113.

guard in itself against possible abuses of office, and that the 'social discipline' of gentility was a necessary addition for control.

In 1829, shortly after the appointment of the new Preston governor, and under very similar circumstances, George Chesterton was appointed to Cold Bath Fields. Their poor experience with his predecessor had made the Surrey magistrates (who included Samuel Hoare, William Crawford's colleague in the Society for the Improvement of Prison Discipline, and brother-in-law of Elizabeth Fry) determined to elect a socially superior candidate to the post. To that end they increased the salary and it was this that enabled Chesterton — at that time studying for the priesthood — to overcome his initial rejection of the notion of employment as a governor.[35]

Within a generation of the adoption by some localities of the new recruitment policy the beneficial effects on the public attitude towards governors had become apparent. The 1835 Select Committee on Gaols heard clear evidence of this new standing; even Whitworth Russell, who was generally no great admirer of governors, conceded that they had become a better class of men.[36] But the attention which the committee paid to the opinions of governors was an even more convincing testimony to their improved status: in the course of its extensive deliberations seventy-five witnesses were called, of which governors constituted by far the largest single group — some twenty in all.[37] Yet despite this recognition of professional expertise, fine but firm gradations in gentility were maintained. Governors who had formerly held naval or army rank were unfailingly accorded their service rank in the minutes, but a distinction was made between the 'civilian' governors and other gentlemen who gave evidence — the former titled plain 'Mr'

---

35 Chesterton, *op. cit.*, I, pp. 38-40, *passim*; P.A.W. Collins, 'Dickens and the Prison Governor, George Laval Chesterton', pp. 12-13.

36 *Select Committee of the House of Lords on Gaols and Houses of Correction*, PP, 1835, First Report, Minutes of Evidence, XI, 138, *passim*.

37 Two turnkeys, four prisoners, six visiting justices and six chaplains also appeared. Other witnesses included penal reformers, surgeons and magistrates. Governors stand out remarkably clearly in the proceedings as a group of 'expert' witnesses. Kitson Clark draws attention to the marked increase in the numbers and influence of administrative experts at this time:

At least from 1833 when the factory inspectors were appointed, or with the appointment of the Poor Law Commissioners . . . expert administrative opinion was being developed. It was accumulated through the activities of a number of newly appointed public servants, commissioners and assistant commissioners, inspectors, servants of enlightened local authorities and men in a variety of public offices. They learnt the science of what was to be done and applied their knowledge by influencing legislation or by administrative methods. What was done by such men in the middle of the century with, at best, uncertain support from Parliaments and Ministers, and confronted by a wayward, or recalcitrant, public opinion, is in retrospect very remarkable (*op. cit.*, pp. 280-1).

and the latter properly recognised with 'Esquire'. This practice was also followed by the select committees of 1850 and 1863. Such a distinction draws attention to the social position of the military in Victorian society: together with the Church it was (from the establishment of the standing army after Waterloo) a favourite choice of career for the younger sons of gentry, who, although lacking in landed estates, were none the less gentlemen. The other factor may have been the social transformation worked by the sovereign's commission – it was all but inconceivable that an officer was not a gentleman.

By 1850 a prison governorship could be taken up by a gentleman without loss of self-respect. Some contemporary observers were inclined to credit this change almost entirely to the scale of remuneration: Fry noted that 'Gentlemen are willing to take charge of prisoners, but they would think it degradation to be governors of poor-houses', and concluded that this attitude to the two establishments derived from the different scales of salaries offered.[38] This idea was examined by the 1850 select committee who were anxious to establish the minimum salary necessary to attract gentlemen to governorships. One witness tried to give them an estimate:

> The appointment must be somewhat influenced by the size of the gaol and the amount of the salary. If you were to appoint none but gentlemen to offices of £100 a year I am afraid you would often have to take a man who had fallen from better circumstances, and perhaps by his own fault, into a situation to make £100 a year an object to him; but in all prisons where you can offer a sufficient temptation you may ensure the services of an educated man.[39]

This argument probably hypothesised too crude a connection between salary and status. Whilst an adequate salary was necessary for a governor to meet the social obligations of an acceptable life-style, it was not in itself sufficient to establish a claim to gentility. Entrepreneurial prison staff had sometimes achieved incomes many times greater than

38 Mishra reports that

> The qualifications for the relieving officer's position as laid down by the Poor Law Commissioners were no more than the ability to 'read and write and keep accounts'. He was to live 'within the area of his district . . . and devote . . . his whole time to the employment, not following any other trade or profession whatsoever' (*op. cit.*, p. 32).

He also notes that 'Although some ex-N.C.O.s were recruited, the majority of the relieving officers were local men, drawn from amongst the existing parish officers' (*ibid.*, pp. 33-4).

39 1850 *SC*, *op. cit.*, 83-4, *passim*. The poor-law commissioners were also much taken with the idea that salary and quality of official were closely connected. 'The Commissioners believed that a good salary would not only help to attract better candidates, but a well-paid officer would be less likely to misappropriate funds' (Mishra, *op. cit.*, p. 35).

gentleman officials later received in the publicly financed prisons. Yet, as has been shown, no gentleman could have maintained his social position had he become an entrepreneurial gaoler.[40] Moreover, by the 1850s there had been a couple of decades during which men as literate, able and socially worthy as George Chesterton had done much in key governorships to change the public image of their occupation. Such men could regard their careers with a pride and self-confidence that would have been impossible a generation earlier:

> I have a word to say upon my own claims as a prison reformer, a character which I feel it a pride to assume. I cannot expunge from my memory the foul abominations which I had to suppress, nor the danger that menaced me in the fulfillment of that task. My pecuniary recompense has not been proportionate with my labours, nor should I have any difficulty in showing that the majority of the magistrates, at the period of my retirement, were of that opinion. . . .
>
> But although I consented to forgo pecuniary advantages, I cling the more tenaciously to the credit of my past exertions, when, beset with fraud, ferocity and moral pollution, I achieved a triumph fraught with civilizing influences. . . . In that retrospect I find a consolation for many subsequent trials, and for later disappointments.[41]

Chesterton and his colleague Tracey (governor of Tothill Fields house of correction) were capable publicists. Both were friends of Charles Dickens, and through his writings many of their penological views were communicated to a broad public, together with an image of public service, integrity and dignity which corresponded closely to that of the recognised culture of the gentleman. Had these occupational qualities not been projected it is extremely doubtful whether higher salaries would of themselves have had sufficient attraction for able men from the respectable middle section of society. This very point was made by de Beaumont and de Tocqueville in their report to the French government on the American penitentiaries:

> As soon as the penitentiary system was adopted in the United States, the personnel changed in nature. For jailer of a prison, vulgar people only could be found. The most distinguished persons offered themselves to administer a *penitentiary* where a moral direction exists.[42]

40 See above, Chapter 3.
41 Chesterton, *op. cit.*, I, p. v.
42 Gustave de Beaumont and Alexis de Tocqueville, *On the Penitentiary System in the United States and its Application in France*, p. 63.

While there was no unanimity even by mid-century about the advisability of appointing gentleman governors, it seems clear that those who dissented from this policy were in a minority.[43] In any case, it was not necessary that all governors should actually be gentlemen. With a few significantly placed appointments new standards could be set.

The term 'governor'

One other point about the social status of governors remains to be mentioned. Although the term 'governor' has been used here to refer to salaried officers as distinct from entrepreneurial gaolers, there was no such neat consensus on usage in practice. Even so, although somewhat erratically employed, the title 'governor' was associated with the rise in social standing of the occupation; many authorities introduced the term in an attempt to improve the dignity of the office: it would have been unthinkable, for example, to sully the sense of moral mission and social prestige of Millbank or Gloucester Penitentiaries by giving their chief officials the title of 'gaoler' or even 'keeper'. 'Governor' was evocative of deputising duties on behalf of higher authority; an image reminiscent of colonial administration. It is significant that when Le Breton called for a change in social attitudes he specifically asserted the need for Parliament to abolish 'the offensive term gaoler' and for the office to be renamed. In some cases, the magistrates, although formally incorporating the new title into their prison rules, lapsed in their various minutes and communications and referred instead to 'gaoler' or 'keeper'. In one set of correspondence relating to Petworth house of correction in 1824 the terms 'keeper' and 'governor' were used interchangeably.[44] At Bedford, the magistrates began to use 'governor' irregularly towards the end of 1840 and for some time employed both titles indiscriminately in their minutes.[45] Eventually use of the old term must have been felt as anachronistic, just as use of the old-fashioned and inaccurate 'warder' is today.

Then, in 1839, to avoid possible technical difficulties with the law, sanction was given for use of the new title. An enactment provided that

43 Thus Clay's biographer, writing in 1861, observed in a footnote that

> Sheriffs and magistrates are not even yet unanimous about the necessity of gentlemen keepers. . . . A few years ago the vacant governorship of another county prison was filled up on the avowed principle that 'it was better not to have a gentleman, he wouldn't be submissive enough' (Clay, *op. cit.*, p. 114).

44 West Sussex County Record Office, ref. QAP/15/W5 (5) and (6).
45 Bedfordshire County Record Office, Minute Book of Visiting Justices, County Gaol and Old House of Correction, 1833-44, ref. QGR5, entries for July 1840, September 1840 and March 1841.

if the Persons authorized by Law to appoint the Gaoler or Keeper of any Prison shall appoint such Keeper by the Style of Governor such Governor shall have all the Powers and Duties of the Gaoler or Keeper of that Prison; and all Enactments made with regard to the Gaoler or Keeper shall apply to the Governor so appointed.[46]

The recruitment of governors

Attributes of candidates and procedures of appointment

Whilst a search for gentility and respectability in applicants played an essential part in raising the social standing of the office, it would be misleading to suggest that the prisons suddenly came under the management of a new breed. In determining their appointments policy the justices were faced with a conflict between status and experience; for many benches the issue presented itself as that of raising the experienced to respectability. But social standing was only one of several factors to be weighed in making an appointment.

For the benefit of those who, as he hoped, would follow his lead Thomas Le Breton listed various desirable characteristics of the governor: 'firmness, humanity, cool deliberation, some education and considerable knowledge of human nature . . . the cast off livery servant is no longer competent to the task . . .'. But generally the aspiring governors of the 1820s were of 'cast-off-livery-servant' quality:

> no sooner is a vacancy known than a host of Police or Sheriff's Officers are clamorous candidates, and in some instances they succeed. If Prisons are to be considered as merely places of security, either they or any strong man may be competent to the task, but I doubt whether in such a case they would be more serviceable than a keeper of wild beasts.[47]

Yet the low social standing of the candidates in the field had not been without its compensations for some appointing justices. Only a few

46 2 & 3 Vict., c.56, 'An Act for the better ordering of Prisons', s.24.
47 Le Breton, *op. cit.*, pp. 15, 38-9, *passim*. Although, as will be shown, the quality of applicants improved in the 1830s, the 'cast off livery servant' still entered the lists. In 1838 the Rev. E. Thompson of Portman Square, London, wrote to the clerk of the peace at Lewes about the vacant keepership of the house of correction:

> I have in my service a man six feet high and as stout in proportion, and who can have the strongest recommendations from the different families he has lived in. He is at present my footman.
> Will you be kind enough to inform me, if he would have a chance for the vacant Governorship of the jail at Lewes? If there be any person who has prior claims, please tell me, as it would save much trouble and expense (East Sussex County Record Office, ref. QAP/2/7, 14).

years before, Sir George Paul, when seeking no mere gaolers for the Gloucestershire prisons, had none the less expressed a clear preference for ingenuous and obedient officials, and spoke especially warmly of William Stokes, keeper of the Horsley house of correction, whom he regarded as:

> an extraordinary instance of the effect of application of a simple mind to a duty which is mere attention to rule. I think him the best keeper of a house of correction I ever met with. He was taken from the Regiment of Horse Guards Blue, as have been all the present keepers of our house of correction; this man, far advanced in years, with his wife (as matron) keeps forty prisoners in a state of perfect obedience to the rules with no other assistance than a porter at the gate.[48]

Within a relatively short time the type of applicant had changed and was no longer quite as Le Breton feared or as Paul desired. Though it was partly due to the size and importance of the prison, Chesterton, when applying for the governorship of Cold Bath Fields, found himself competing with a miscellaneous but by no means educationally deficient or socially insignificant group of men: 'military, naval, men of law, a high constable, and the police officer Plank'.[49]

These changes were marked when, in 1836, the governorship at Gloucester Penitentiary fell vacant. In response to the advertisement the candidates ranged from military and naval men to workhouse and prison officials (including the governors of Dorchester and Bedford gaols) and one who described himself simply as a gentleman.[50] Even at a much less important prison competition was keen by the end of the 1830s and in 1838 the post of keeper of the Lewes house of correction was sought after by a Millbank schoolmaster, several army and naval officers, workhouse keepers, turnkeys and prison and military clerks.[51]

Many applicants were quite unsuitable, which could be an expensive and time-wasting nuisance to the authorities.[52] For this reason when in

48 *Select Committee on the State of Gaols*, PP, 1819, VII, 1, 405.
49 Chesterton, *op. cit.*, I, p. 244.
50 Gloucestershire Records Office, ref. Administrative: Gaols, Applications for post of governor of the county gaol, 1836.
51 East Sussex County Record Office, 1838 election to keepership of Lewes House of Correction, ref. QAP/L/E1, 55. There is a definite contrast in the quality of this bunch of candidates and those who competed for the keepership at Petworth house of correction some fourteen years previously. Then the thirty-nine applicants included a police constable, officers from the hulks (who produced testimonials from Wm Capper) and two sheriff's officers. As a whole they appeared to be on an NCO level (West Sussex County Record Office, refs QAP/15/W5 (5), (6) and (69)).
52 As was shown by a particularly persistent local candidate for the Lewes keepership in 1838. He addressed the following letter to the clerk of the peace (spellings and grammar as in the original):

1856 the governor of Huntingdon gaol resigned he apprised them confidentially 'so that the Magistrates may be saved from the annoyance of ineligible applicants before the proper time'.[53] Even if unsuitable applicants were excluded, rivalry to win the appointments was fierce, especially, as Perry testified to the select committee of 1850, for the higher and more lucrative ones.[54]

Advertisements were usually placed in local newspapers and, if the

---

Sir, On my Lewes paper arriving I found an Advertisement in it stating – a Keeper to the House of Correction at Lewes – would be appointed by the Court at the next Epiphany Sessions – and as I have a large family of Children to bring up with a decrease of Income – by the depreciation of Property at Brighton – I shall like to get appointed to this Vacant place – I have 1600L in hands – a Freehold at Nottinghamshire let for 25L per a. 12 houses at Brighton – also this villa with 130 acres of Ground Worth 150L per acre – and at Druid's Lodge – 70 acres let for 70.15.0 – in this parish – and I hope after living 20 years here I shall not be deemed uneligible or unfit to undertake such a trust – The Cuckfield Bench of Magistrates and the Board of Guardians have accepted my sole indemnity – to the amount of 50L as security, for the Collector of the Poor Rates for three parishes of this Union. I merely mention this to show that my request is not an improper one and having now stated my Station in Society here I shall beg it as a great favour and eternal obligation conferd on me – if you will support me with your powerful aid and interest – and also inform me what steps I am to take to procure the vacant place – I shall not hesitate to say I will give a Cheque on my Bankers for 50L or over 100L to any person or persons who could place me in this situation to be laid out by them for the benefit of the poor of the said House of Correction – or in any other way they might deem fit – As it would enable me to bring up 9 Children all Girls (but One) and lay by a little yearly – for them out [of] my Income for their Support at my Death – And as to honesty – Sobriety or any other qualaty required – I leave all the World to speak to that – for I am confident – if One Chosen – no one will have occasion to repent their choice. I am, your Obt. Servt., J. Barrowcliffe.

When it was discovered that Barrowcliffe was over the age limit (forty-five) stipulated in the advertisement the hapless clerk of the peace was treated to two further letters in the same vein, one making the offer of '50 or over 100L' more explicit, and the other implying that Barrowcliffe would take legal action. Despite such exertions, however ('a post like the one I am contending for is not to be obtained every day – and a faint heart never won anything'), Mr Barrowcliffe was unsuccessful, and indeed appears to have given some offence ('I appeal to you in the name of Charity – to lend me your Aid – I am sure you are too much a Gentleman and Man of business – to be offended with me in anything I have written – if you consider I am the Father of a large Family who I wish to provide for – and this by my own exertions') (East Sussex County Record Office, ref. QAP/L/E7, 16).

---

53 Huntingdon Record Office, Quarter Sessions bundles, 1856, letter of 8 October.
54 1850 SC, op. cit., 83-4, passim.

post were sufficiently important, in the national press as well.[55] Applications were directed to the clerk of the peace and supported with testimonials. Canvassing was customary and many either personally approached every magistrate in the county or, to avoid expense, canvassed by means of advertisement in the local newspapers.[56] But the majority simply circulated their printed testimonials to the names on the magistrates' list.[57]

55 The Gloucestershire vacancy of 1836 was advertised in *The Times, Morning Herald* and *Sun*, thrice weekly for three weeks. Widespread advertising had obviously been the custom for some time: the keepership of Lewes gaol and house of correction was advertised in *The Times, Hampshire Telegraph* and *Lewes Journal* in 1825 (East Sussex County Record Office, ref. QAP/15/W5 (69)).

56 This procedure was followed at Gloucester during the 1836 selection, when the following notice, addressed to the High Sheriff and County Magistrates, was placed in the *Cheltenham Journal*:

> I have the honour to solicit your Vote and Interest for the situation of Governor of the Penitentiary and Gaol of the City of Gloucester. [The candidate here made a mistake: the vacant post was at the county, not the city, gaol.] Encouraged by the uniform support Officers of His Majesty's Navy and Army, have received on all occasions from the Authorities, Magistrates of Counties, etc. etc. has induced [*sic*] me at this late period, to offer myself as a Candidate. From experience and continual active service of ten years in the East and West Indies, Africa and Ireland, during which time I have filled important trusts in His Majesty's Service, and consequently have seen a great deal of the human character, I have no hesitation in declaring that I shall be able, should you think fit to elect me, to uphold the high and important name for which the Institution of Gloucester, under its last Governor, has stood pre-eminent.
>
> Gentlemen, for testimonials as to character, I beg leave, humbly but with confidence, to submit to you − 1st my Commissions which I have the honour to hold, not by purchase, but by gift from our most gracious Sovereign, out of consideration, and friendship for my Grandfather, Byam Edwards, Historian of the West Indies, feeling assured that you will at once be convinced that an unworthy individual would not be allowed to hold so honourable a distinction. 2nd, from my former and present commanding officers; and 3rdly, from a few Resident Gentry of the County of Wilts, and also from Magistrates in Ireland under whom I have served.
>
> On these, then, Gentlemen, do I rely, confident that he who has faithfully served his King and his Country, will not be forgotten by you on the day of election. I can only add further that should I be deemed by you worthy of the appointment, that application and firmness, blended with humanity, will be exercised by me to merit your unqualified approbation, and the trust reposed in me.
>
> I have the honour to be,
My Lords and Gentlemen,
Your obedient humble Servant.

57 Similar procedures were followed by both applicants and authorities in the case of prison chaplaincies. The Hertfordshire authorities, for example, when seeking a chaplain in 1836 and again in 1838, advertised extensively in the

These recruitment and selection procedures were expensive and inefficient. Even at the time the inappropriateness was recognised of involving the whole body of magistrates, frequently resulting in factionalism and political bickering; and some critics claimed that it would have been better to restrict the duty of selection to the visiting justices, others that changed selection procedures were the key to an improvement in the quality of governors.[58] But a governorship was one of the most important appointing powers of the local authorities, and the understandable desire of the magistrates for maximum participation in the selection procedure was probably why such methods were employed for so long and against such strong objections.

Promotions to governorships

Despite different disciplinary and administrative systems and the problem of non-transferable pensions, there was a certain amount of staff interchange between local prisons, the main inducement being promotion, either in rank or to a post of the same rank but at a larger, grander and better paid prison.[59] For instance, Lieutenant Tracey's deputy at Tothill house of correction, Lieutenant William Austin, left metropolitan Tothill Fields to serve as deputy to Maconochie at Birmingham — a larger provincial prison,[60] a quite common type of movement; many justices thought that metropolitan experience was a valuable qualification for a higher provincial post.[61] Likewise George

---

London and County newspapers, morning and evening (Hertfordshire County Record Office, ref. County Gaol 12). In 1844 the Gloucestershire authorities also advertised for a chaplain, but seemingly confined their advertisement to the *Ecclesiastical Gazette*. One respondent apologised that he had no local influence, whilst another wished to know if any of the interviewing magistrates were noblemen, so that he might address them by their correct titles (Gloucestershire Records Office, ref. Q/AG 30/2).

58 Perry told the 1850 select committee that while an increase in salaries would attract better quality applicants to the chaplaincy, the quality of governors could be improved only by a better method of selection (1850 *SC, op. cit.*, Minutes of Evidence, 83-4, *passim*).

59 Mishra describes similar movements among poor-law officials (*op. cit.*, p. 34).

60 Austin eventually achieved a terrible notoriety at Birmingham where his 'over-lavish use of the punishment cells and of illegal punishments led to a boy's suicide, a Royal Commission and Austin's serving a six months' sentence for these abuses' (Philip Collins, *Dickens and Crime*, p. 66). His callous and tyrannical behaviour was portrayed in Reade's *It is Never Too Late to Mend*. See also the Report of the *Royal Commission Appointed to Inquire into the Condition and Treatment of the Prisoners Confined to Birmingham Borough Prison*, PP, 1854, XXXI, and the *Annual Register*, vol. 93 (1855), pp. 120-4.

61 Joseph Becket, for example, after a time as storekeeper at Cold Bath Fields, moved to Southampton to be keeper of the house of correction (*Select Committee on Gaols*, PP, 1819, VII, 1, 334).

Chesterton's chief turnkey Sims (who had assisted in the purge of staff corruption at Cold Bath Fields) obtained the governorship of Derby county gaol. Chesterton thought that his subordinate had over-reached himself by applying for this post, but circumstances combined favourably to procure Sims's unanimous election.[62] Another governor, John Treganza, of the county gaol at Bedford from 1834 to 1849, had previously been chief turnkey at Ilchester gaol; although his pension would have raised some difficulties for a transfer after only a couple of years as governor at Bedford he applied in 1836 (unsuccessfully) for the more important governorship at Gloucester.[63] Movements to local prisons from government ones were also common, as might have been expected since many local authorities looked to government prisons for guidance on a number of points of prison management, including staffing. Parkhurst, Pentonville and Millbank all sent officers to higher positions in local prisons.[64] A successful application by William Linton for the governorship of Petworth gaol and house of correction in 1856 gives a good account of the progressive movements of an officer who worked his way up from the ranks. He stated, *inter alia*:

I have been engaged in the performance of Prison duties for the last fourteen years, having during that period held various Offices in the following Establishments, namely: in the Pentonville Prison (separate system); in the New County Prison for Bucks (separate system); Horsley House of Correction (silent congregated system); and in the above Gaol [he was governor of Nottinghamshire County Gaol] where the separate system prevails as far as the construction of the Building will allow. I have thus had abundant facilities for

62 Chesterton, *op. cit.*, I, 251.
63 Gloucestershire Records Office, ref. Administrative: Gaols, Application for the post of governor of the county gaol, 1836.
64 In 1846 the governor of Parkhurst lost three subordinate officers who had moved to other prisons (*Reports Relating to Parkhurst Prison*, PP, 1846, XX, 69, 3). The commissioners of Pentonville prison noted in 1847 the similar loss of two of their officers, one of whom − a principal warder − had become deputy chief officer at Stafford county gaol (*Fifth Report of the Commissioners of Pentonville Prison*, PP, 1847, XXX, 481). Charles Foster, chief clerk at Millbank, was appointed governor of Bedford county gaol in 1850. The appointment was ill-fated, however, Foster eventually fleeing the prison, leaving a deficit in his accounts (Eric Stockdale, *A Study of Bedford Prison, 1660-1877*, pp. 183-4). In earlier years hulk officers also moved by way of promotion to local prisons. Giving evidence to the 1819 select committee, Sir John Acland, chairman of Somerset quarter sessions, stated that the governor of Ilchester gaol who had been selected had formerly been mate of the hulk *Retribution*. Sir John explained: 'we had a very excellent character with him; and Mr. Graham who had the superintendence of that vessel, offered if he would remain with him to obtain a separate command, but he preferred coming to us' (*Select Committee on Gaols*, PP, 1819, VII, 1, 377).

acquiring a complete practical knowledge of the main features and general working of the most approved systems of Prison Discipline – whether of Separate Confinement or of Classification and silence.

I am a member of the Church of England, 32 years of age, unmarried, and in the enjoyment of perfect health. . . .[65]

By the 1850s varied prison experience had become a recognised qualification and highly desirable advantage in candidates for governorships in many localities, of which Huntingdon is a good example. In 1856 the first preference of the justices was George Hulme, governor of Appleby gaol in Westmorland, who had worked, first as warder, and then as superintendent of manufacturing, in two gaols, prior to his Westmorland appointment; the second choice, William Ingram, was governor of the borough gaol at Devonport, and had previously been a warder at Bath borough gaol; the third also had experience of more than one prison, while the fourth and fifth had served in only one. The short-listing sub-committees thought it just to include the upper turnkey at Huntingdon as their fifth choice, 'though with the exception of Benjamin Rust, he is the only one included who has not had the benefit of experience in more than one gaol'.[66]

The changing social status of governors upset this pattern of migration and promotion. While it was impossible for a gentleman to be a subordinate prison officer – by definition – the candidacy of subordinate staff for governorships could pit occupational expertise against the social advantages of gentility, an issue probably raised most acutely in the medium-sized prisons with funds enough to pay a gentleman's salary, yet compact enough for the more able subordinates to compete with fair hope of success for higher positions. If Gloucester and Huntingdon were at all typical, experience outweighed social status in very many cases, recognition was given to the desirability of an appropriate opening for the ambitious subordinate officer, and of a

much more just, advantageous and natural arrangement to raise the character and degree of the subordinate officers, so that persons of

---

65 West Sussex Record Office, ref. QAP/15/W5 (81).
66 Huntingdon Record Office, Quarter Sessions Miscellanea, 1856. A similar decision was made by Bedfordshire justices in 1849 when James Banfield, a prison officer of long-standing, keeper of the house of correction and acting governor, was told that his appointment as governor was to be for one year only. The justices minuted that Banfield

be distinctly informed that the magistrates, though they have the highest opinion of his past services, are very doubtful whether it will not be necessary that the governor should be a person who has already had some experience in the new system (*cit.* Stockdale, *op. cit.*, p. 182).

proved ability and experience might be selected from among them and promoted to the vacant situations of governor.[67]

The contradiction between these two objectives — promotion and the employment of gentlemen — was still pronounced by mid-century. But one solution, with far-reaching implications, had been offered by a permissive clause in the 1839 Prisons Act:

> It shall be lawful for the Keeper of every Prison, with the Approval of the Visiting Justices, to appoint an Officer of the Prison to Act as Deputy Keeper whenever the Keeper shall be necessarily absent from the Prison; and during such necessary Absence of the Keeper the Deputy Keeper shall have all the Powers and Duties of the Keeper of the Prison, and the Keeper shall be civilly responsible for all Acts and Omissions of his Deputy Keeper.[68]

This legal and public recognition of what hitherto had been only an internal arrangement of duties extended the promotion ladder in a way which made more likely an increase in outside — particularly military — recruitment, since army and navy officers, until now handicapped in competition for governorships, could henceforth gain the requisite experience in an acceptable manner, and deputy governorships thus opened up a second career for them.

Governorship as a post-military career

Indeed, apart from prison officials, military men were by far the most numerous among the applicants for governorships. But in spite of the qualities of reliability and the number of relevant skills that military experience was supposed to inculcate and the social standing it conferred, appointment of such candidates was not without controversy. Whitworth Russell strongly opposed the appointment of military men both as subordinate officers[69] and as governors. In 1838 he wrote to

67 Fry, *op. cit.*, p. 132.
68 2 & 3 Vict., c.56, s.7.
69 In evidence to the 1835 select committee Russell, then chaplain of Millbank Penitentiary, disclosed that he disagreed with its committee on this point. (The governor of Millbank at the time was Captain Chapman upon whom Russell's criticisms were a thinly veiled attack.) He insisted that

> Twenty or Thirty years of a Barrack-yard life and Habits are not very likely to form such a Moral and Religious Character as we ought to require in an Officer of this Establishment. . . . Indulgence in Drink is another Habit too often acquired by that Class of Men, amongst whom Intoxication, except upon Duty, is not considered an offence. . . . A general Feeling of Disrespect exists on the Part of the Prisoners towards their Officers; they think them tyrannical and unprincipled . . . they assert that there are few who are not, sooner or later in some way or another, seduced from their Duty.

315

Lord Chichester (who was chairman of the quarter sessions) recommending the schoolmaster at Millbank for the post of keeper at the Lewes house of correction:

> I feel it to be most desirable, that, not only judicious, educated and experienced men, but those of a decidedly religious character should be appointed to govern the Prisons of this Country. Such men, whilst they manifest in their own conduct, temper and habits, what it is the aim of all penal restraints to produce; by a similarity of objects, means, and principles with a good Chaplain, produce that unity of purpose and action in the Prison which is so essential to success in any undertaking. It too often happens that there exists a kind of rivalry rather than co-operation between discipline and Religion. . . .
>
> I have always been of opinion that Military and Naval men, however gentlemanly, intelligent and moral, make bad Governors of Prisons; and my experience of those who have been appointed confirms my impression; their system is [? constraint] without looking to moral effects; much less to renovation of heart, as the only basis for permanent improvement of conduct, and generally they gather around them subordinates of similar opinions and course of proceeding.[70]

Fry also questioned the suitability of military experience as a preparation for governorship, but was more moderate than Russell in his argument:

Russell maintained that subordinate officers should be men of higher quality – men of judgment, sobriety, decency, benevolence, and religion – and he suggested that such men might be found among Sunday School teachers (1835 *SC*, *op. cit.*, First Report, Minutes of Evidence, 43-4, *passim*). Crawford concurred in this view.

The Millbank Committee of Management responded by saying that they had been careful to select only highly recommended candidates, but that their choice was restricted by the limited remuneration which they could offer:

> which seems hardly adequate to the expectations of such a Class as Mr. Crawford appears to point out. This has led in a Majority of Instances to the Appointment of Retired Non-commissioned Officers of the Army, who, in addition to their Salaries, are in the Enjoyment of small Pensions for their Services.

Significantly, the committee thought that, while the disciplinary qualities of such men were an advantage, it was none the less necessary, in order to ensure sobriety and regularity of behaviour, to impose great strictness of discipline on the men and 'to visit with Severity even very slight Deviations from Correctness of Conduct' (*ibid*., 257-9, *passim*).

---

70 Letter of Whitworth Russell to the Earl of Chichester, 1 December 1838 (East Sussex County Record Office, ref. QAP/L/E1, 55).

Their honourable conduct and habits of regularity and strict
discipline are certainly highly advantageous; but their sympathies
are with another service; their habits are those of command; orders
and submission comprise their entire discipline; they cannot usually
employ gentle exhortation or moral influence to win respect; they
in general know not how to obtain obedience by inducements of
attachment, and appeals to reason or feeling.

He also felt that the former social rank of military officers was 'an
obstacle to their performing the subordinate duties of their office'.[71]

That many benches preferred not to appoint former military men to
governorships is clear. Some would have shared the objections of
Russell and Fry, whilst others were possibly struck by the social incon-
gruity of a prison post. Many would have shared Sir George Paul's
preference for governors who were accommodating and malleable. In
some cases it is possible that the appointment of a military man may
have cut across local patterns of obligations and jobbery,[72] prison
appointments remaining, until late in the century, one of the most
lucrative and important areas of local government patronage.

Yet, despite this contention, naval and military men applied for
posts in droves and found many benches content to accept them,[73]

---

71 Fry, *op. cit.*, p. 131.
72 In respect of poor-law appointments, 'Patronage was all important and in the
rural Unions a failed farmer and in urban Unions a failed tradesman was
occasionally jobbed in' (Mishra, *op. cit.*, p. 34).
73 The relevance of military training to the tasks of the Millbank governor has
already been discussed in Chapter 6; a few more general observations may,
however, be appropriate at this point. George Chesterton, perhaps the most
significant example of military man turned governor in the first part of the
century, indicated in his memoirs the various ways in which his army
experience helped him to solve the problems of his new occupation. For
example, he initiated a weekly kit inspection, which brought order to the
previously unregulated issue of bedding, utensils and uniform. Since any
deficiencies uncovered in the inspection were held to be the personal
responsibility of the inmate concerned, Chesterton estimated that by this
measure alone he saved over £10,000 of county money during his first seven
years of office (*op. cit.*, I, p. 172). He also organised more efficiently along
military lines the distribution of discharge clothing, and carried out systematic
thrice-daily searches of prisoners to prevent the circulation of contraband and
the preparation of escapes.

Army and navy officers had experience of victualling, and all governors
were responsible for checking the quantity and quality of food that entered
their establishments. Constant vigilance was necessary to combat the
underselling, dilution, adulteration and other tricks of contractors. Two
governors in succession had trouble of this kind with the local merchants at
Hertford gaol; one, embroiled in longstanding disputes with the butcher and
the baker, reached the end of his tether when, in addition, the gas company
began to default on its contract (Hertfordshire County Record Office,
Governor's Journal, 1838-44, and 1844-52, ref. Shelf 44).

and by mid-century they held sway in central government prisons. With Jebb's accession to the chairmanship of the Directorate of Convict Prisons, a post which carried with it very considerable powers of patronage, this predominance was consolidated, heightening the contrast with local government prisons in this respect.[74]

The control of patronage

As noted in Chapter 4, the justices, who had always had undivided power over the houses of correction, became increasingly involved in the appointment of staff to the local gaols during the last quarter of the eighteenth century. The sheriff's legal custody of the gaol and choice of gaoler was undermined by the practice of uniting the gaolership with the keepership of the house of correction as well as by legislation which increased the financial and regulatory powers of the justices over the gaols. In 1815 the justices acquired total control over the salaries of gaolers and their staff. Peel's Act, however, whilst reaffirming this power, also expressly saved the formal rights of the sheriffs to appoint the gaoler. Quarter sessions was empowered to

nominate and appoint such Keepers, Matrons, Taskmasters, Schoolmasters and Officers as to them may seem expedient for every prison within their jurisdiction to which this Act shall extend,

---

The military were also familiar with problems of peculation, embezzlement and corrupt liaison between contractors and subordinate staff. Chesterton who had served in the Field Train Department was particularly well equipped to cope with such difficulties; but most officers would have had some knowledge of the various ruses and the appropriate countermeasures (see George Laval Chesterton's *Peace, War and Adventure*, 1853, I, p. 10).

Finally, military aptitude and governorship completely overlapped when, in the economic, social and political upheavals of the 1830s, law and order was secured at times only precariously by the militia, and governors were sometimes required to undertake the physical defence of their establishments with carbines, grenades and even light field guns (see Chesterton, *op. cit.* (1856), I, pp. 202, 204, 251, *passim*, and Clay, *op. cit.*, p. 161).

---

74 A more extensive survey would be needed to establish the exact degree of military dominance in the staffing of government prisons in the 1830s and 1840s; some examples can be given, however. The first governor of Parkhurst was a Captain Robert Wollcombe; his steward was an ex-naval purser. The first governor of Millbank Prison (i.e. after the closure of the penitentiary) was a Captain Groves, and the administration of the time had a policy of recruiting as subordinates suitable men of non-commissioned rank. The military were well represented at Pentonville (particularly after the deaths of Crawford and Russell) and at Portland. Jebb, himself, continued to hold military rank and to carry out military duties for several years whilst serving as a director, and one of his two fellow directors (Captain O'Brien) also had an army background (see *Reports Relating to Parkhurst Prison*, PP, 1839, XXII, 643, and PP, 1843, XLIII, 447, and *Royal Commission on the Management of Millbank Prison*, PP, 1847, XXX, 1).

except the Keeper of the Common Gaol, and to remove as occasion
may require, all Officers so by them nominated and appointed.

But the extent of the justices' staffing powers highlighted the very
nominal nature of the sheriff's right of appointment. The justices were
authorised to

> fix Salaries and Allowances, to such Amount and subject to such
> Conditions as to them shall seem meet for the Keeper of the
> Common Gaol, and for every Keeper, Matron, Taskmaster,
> Schoolmaster and Officer of each Gaol and House of Correction
> within their jurisdiction, and to order such Salaries, and the Expence
> [sic] of such Allowances, to be paid out of the Rate lawfully
> applicable thereto. . . .[75]

Out of courtesy in most localities the formality of consultation with
the sheriff continued, but the provisions of the law were such that
when conflicts arose the outcome depended almost entirely on the
resoluteness of the justices.[76]

75 4 Geo. IV, c.64, ss.25 and 26. The retention of a measure of divided authority
between the justices and the sheriffs may have been in part due to a belief that
total control by one or the other would be unconstitutional. This certainly
was the view of Sir Richard Phillips, who had argued in 1808 that the liberty
of the subject could be protected only by ensuring that remands were not held
in houses of correction:

> for as it is the duty of the Sheriff or his deputy to prepare the calendar at
> the Sessions of Oyer and Terminer, or of general Gaol Delivery, it is
> obvious that no man can be secretly imprisoned or be imprisoned contrary
> to the provisions of the Constitution while he is in the custody of the
> Sheriff. But if these bulwarks are destroyed, and if it be permitted that
> persons accused of crimes may be committed to any secret prison, *not
> under the controul, or within the jurisdiction of the Sheriff or officer who
> prepares the calendar for the Judges of assize*, then we may indeed possess
> the forms of liberty, but the substance will be lost! Persons obnoxious to a
> minister or a magistrate, may be committed to such a prison and never be
> heard of more (*A Letter to the Livery of London*, pp. 27-8).

76 Not all magistrates were satisfied with this situation. Mr H.C. Higgins, a visiting
justice at Bedford, told the 1835 select committee that the appointments
system was inefficient. Sometimes political considerations prevented the
justices from appointing the most suitable candidate. Higgins claimed that:

> the real and legal responsibility attaches to the Sheriff, and he legally is the
> Appointer, and he is the party to whom the surety is given, therefore
> perhaps it is unreasonable to expect the Sheriff always to defer to the
> Choice of the Justices; but . . . it would be very unjust that the Sheriff
> should have the Power of appointing a man over whom the Justices ought
> to have a continual control.

Higgins argued that either the lord lieutenant or the visiting justices (not the
quarter sessions, because of political wrangles) should have the power of
appointment. He was certain that this responsibility should be removed from

319

Even so, sheriffs from time to time sought to exercise their titular patronage. Perry told the 1850 select committee that, while such disputes were unusual, they were not unknown and caused great inconvenience: 'In one instance which I would rather not more particularly name, the sheriff appointed an old servant of his to a very important prison, and the magistrates reduced his salary, as the only means of getting rid of him.'[77] The unwanted governor in this case resigned, but only after a year of financial pressure.

A few years later an almost identical set of circumstances arose at Huntingdon, when the sheriff proposed to make his own appointment to the vacant governorship without consulting the justices. When rumour of the sheriff's intention reached James Rust, one of the visiting justices of the county gaol, he wrote to a colleague:

> I hope the Sheriff will leave it to us to choose *subject, of course to his approval*. But I have reason to know that he is aware that the appointment is formally with him, and has had applications – *we* appoint as far as it is a House of Correction, he, as far as it is a gaol – and *we* fix the salary in both cases, so *we* must be satisfied, or else might be driven to use our power as to the salary. I hope we shall get it done without any such misunderstanding. . . . It is rather absurd that an *annual* officer like the Sheriff should have such an appointment – and particularly so when he has, as in this instance, no connection with the County beyond his annual office now nearly at an end.

Rust then ensured that the sheriff's candidate was informed of the difficulties he would encounter should he be appointed against the wishes of the magistrates:

> I have written to Mr. Gale Lownby, who had sent me a letter in favour of Mr. Burrows the sheriff's nominee – and asked him to let Burrows know the probable consequences of his accepting an appointment from the sheriff without any . . . communication with the magistrates of the County. Our power over his salary is absolute – and his situation obtained by such an unusual course would be extremely unpleasant in every respect and not likely to be of much pecuniary value or of long continuance. It seems to me that it would

---

the sheriff who, he said, was often a man of very small income who found the obligations of office difficult. Higgins wanted the justices to take total legal responsibility for the gaols. These views were not adopted by the select committee and both sheriffs and justices continued in their respective obligations and rights (1835 *SC, op. cit.*, 138).

77 1850 *SC, op. cit.*, Minutes of Evidence, question 1148, 84.

be an act of the greatest indiscretion on his part to attempt to force himself in such a way on the County.[78]

The justices won this test of will and the appointment was delegated to a sub-committee of quarter sessions. Burrows, the sheriff's nominee, did not even appear on the short-list.[79]

This incident shows how unassailable by mid-century were the staffing powers of the justices. The relationship between them and the sheriff doubtless varied greatly from one county to another and miscellaneous factors determined the manner of consultation and the reconciliation of sometimes conflicting interests. Since many localities would have continued, for reasons of etiquette, to allow the sheriffs a display of authority, Table 10.5 can be interpreted as showing that by 1840 the majority of appointments of governors were made by the justices.[80]

Governors and policy at mid-century

From this and the previous chapter it should be clear that though it is possible to speak of certain general changes in prison staffing by mid-century, the transformation was by no means uniform: considerable disparities existed in income, conditions of service and status. It is equally clear, however, that the old stigma which had so vexed Le Breton and others even in the 1820s no longer held universal sway. Apart from in the very small prisons a governor had great latitude to make for himself a social position and a working relationship with his magistrates.

Governors were, by 1850, more on an equal footing with the justices and at the same time subject to more regulation and control. Regulation flowed from legislation and central government inspection and from the greater awareness of their obligations which these had stimulated in governors and justices alike. If anything, however, justices were less likely to intervene in the day-to-day running of the prisons, as had Paul at Gloucester and Holford at Millbank. Control of the governors

78 Huntingdon Record Office, ref. QS 1856. The two letters are dated 21 October 1856 and 30 October 1856. A résumé of these letters is given in a transcript of Huntingdonshire quarter sessions (Historical Manuscripts Commission, 1958), though the description given is inaccurate on a point of detail.

79 Huntingdon Record Office, ref. QS 1856, 'The Report of the Committee Appointed at the Michaelmas Sessions . . .'. A similar difficulty had arisen in 1830.

80 The exclusion of the sheriff from staff appointments was formalised by the Prison Act 1865 (28 and 29 Vict., c.126), which defined 'prison authorities' as the relevant justices or municipal officers (s.6) and abolished the distinction between the gaols and houses of correction (s.56). The only prison powers and responsibilities left to the sheriff by the 1865 Act were in respect of the execution of the death sentence and the custody of debtors (ss.58-60).

321

TABLE 10.5   *Appointing authorities for 178 prisons, 1840*

Appointing authority	Number
Sheriff	20
Justices	72
Sheriff and justices	28
Town council	30
Hereditary rights and franchise	14
Crown	2
Others	11
Not shown	1
Total	178

Source: Abstract Return of the Establishment of, and Persons Confined in, and Expenditure of Each Gaol and House of Correction in England and Wales, PP, 1840, XXXVIII, 241.

Boroughs differed from the counties in their procedures for prison appointments. The basic conflict of authority was between the corporations and town councils on the one hand, and the magistrates on the other. As the corporations and councils eventually accepted financial responsibility for the town prisons they also sought to control the appointment of governors. The magistrates resisted and the matter was taken to the High Court. According to Frederic Hill, the inspector, it was decided 'that this power [of appointment] lies with the magistrates, and not with the town council' (*Thirteenth Report of the Inspectors of Prisons (Northern and Eastern District)*, PP, 1847-8, XXVI, 361, xix).

Crown appointments were made at Chester and Durham. 'Others' in the table includes the lord warden of the Cinque Ports; the mayor acting with the justices; the mayor alone; the sheriff and court of aldermen; the mayor, justices and town council; and the sheriff and the town council.

The appointment of governors in the government prisons (not covered by this table) did not involve the same conflicts in authority. Nevertheless there was no uniform procedure until the establishment of the directorate. Some of the governors (at Millbank Penitentiary and Pentonville, for example) were appointed by the Board of Management or commissioners. Others (Parkhurst and Queen's Prison) were appointed directly by the secretary of state (see 1 & 2 Vict., c.82 (Parkhurst Act); 5 & 6 Vict., Sess. 2, c.22 (Queen's Prison Act); 5 & 6 Vict., Sess. 2, c.29 (Pentonville Act); and 6 & 7 Vict., c.26 (the Act which terminated Millbank Penitentiary). Millbank Prison appointments were made directly by the secretary of state.

was exerted by more subtle and effective means – their 'respectable' background or aspirations and their increased financial dependence on the justices. In the old prisons men who were pariahs had no reputation or standing to lose by ill-doing; in the new prisons not only would a desirable place in society be forfeited by unmasked illegalities, but so also would a pension; indeed, even short of illegal activity, service which displeased the justices would almost certainly depress the rate of pensioning. The independence of the gaoler or keeper based on the purchase of office and enjoyment of fee and trading income had long since been displaced by the accountable and limited autonomy of a salaried position.

Within the prison the governor's position became more secure *vis-à-vis* the chaplain, and more distant, at least in the medium-sized and large prisons, with regard to the subordinate staff. This left the way open for the very ablest and determined of the subordinate staff to seek promotion, and at the same time rendered possible applications for governorships from outside the prisons.

The recruitment policies of magistrates varied a lot and were to some extent inconsistent. The basis of these inconsistencies was the desire to employ as governors those who had a reasonably wide experience of different prison régimes. This experience obviously could best be obtained by working at more than one establishment. This was made difficult because of the pensioning arrangements and by the awkwardness of the social transition from a subordinate and socially inferior office to the superior position of governor. The establishment of deputy governorships helped to ease entry into the work of those who had held naval or military rank and created a social as well as an occupational bridge for others.

Despite the growth of central government influence over the local prisons, the justices remained firmly in control of administration. Not only had they been left a good deal of leeway in which to implement nationally determined policy, but the scope for local policy still remained considerable. Together with their control over locally gathered finance, the justices' prerogative to staff their prisons secured substantial administrative autonomy for them.

But the justices did not make or apply policy in a vacuum and the governors more and more became one of the influences that shaped their decisions. There were several reasons why the voice of the governor attracted more attention. In the first place he tended increasingly to be a person of some social weight and credence, drawn very often from a background similar to that of many of the justices. Moreover, some governors had experience of several different disciplinary systems, or could, from their contacts with other prison officials, tender informed advice upon such matters. The more established position of governors was reflected in the extent to which they were called before parliamentary committees of inquiry, where they had come to replace, at least in numbers, the justices themselves.

As has been shown, there was not much movement between major governorships; governors gathered their practical knowledge of other

323

systems either in the smaller prisons (which taught only the basics of the custodial trade) or in subordinate positions in the larger prisons. This would have given them a clear sense of the primacy of the justices in matters of policy. Such a progression between different systems would be likely to militate against governors having an undue attachment to their own penological crotchets and to make them willing to carry out the decisions of the justices.

Despite the contacts which they established in their progression from one establishment to another and in the course of their court and escort duties, the governors did not establish a joint sense of occupational identity and interests; the diversity of local conditions and problems, and the backgrounds of governors themselves, substantially impeded such a development. This is not to retract what has been noted about the exchanges of experience and values that undoubtedly took place, but simply to contend that these had their effect on policy in a general rather than specific fashion, and worked through individuals rather than groups.

11   The local prisons, 1850-77

The changing setting of penal policy

The disillusioned and sceptical mood which had so markedly overtaken penological discussions by the early 1850s was matched in social policy and public administration generally by a more agnostic, sober and pragmatic temper. In Burn's opinion

> there is some evidence, scattered and imperfect as it is, that England in the 'fifties and 'sixties had lost or was losing certain characteristics which had distinguished it in the preceding forty or fifty years: the capacity for single-minded belief . . . the impetuosity of thought and action, the rapid alternation between radiant optimism and abasing pessimism.

And in the 1860s

> One is conscious of a note of impatience; the impatience, not of the fanatic or the revolutionary but of the rational, tidy-minded man resolved to clear his premises of an accumulation of junk. Some of the junk was institutional . . . some was human. . . .[1]

Attitudes towards the poor hardened, at this time, and the administration of relief took on a noticeably deterrent emphasis.[2] Alongside the harshness, however, came greater discrimination between categories of paupers, culminating in the Goschen Minute of 1869 which decreed that only the totally destitute should be relieved by the guardians, and that those merely on the verge of pauperism should be directed to the charitable agencies, where more individualised forms of assistance might be given. The effect of this policy was to restore, to some extent,

---

1 W.L. Burn, *The Age of Equipoise*, pp. 87 and 194.
2 R.C. Mishra, thesis: 'A History of the Relieving Officer', p. 87.

the distinction between the 'deserving' and 'undeserving' poor which lay at the heart of the 1834 Poor Law.[3]

Public administration still offered many opportunities for tidying and junk-clearing. The administrative failures highlighted by the Crimean War led to a new campaign for civil service reform,[4] and the Northcote-Trevelyan Report, and the resultant Civil Service Commission, began a transformation in the administration of central government. Even the army, pillar not only of the state but of 'society', was subjected to far-reaching reforms. The protracted campaign against flogging and the deplorable living conditions of enlisted men secured in 1868 an amendment to the annual Mutiny Bill which abolished the lash for the home army. The purchase of office and of promotion was condemned by a Royal Commission in 1858[5] but was not forbidden until Gladstone's First Ministry in 1870. In 1875, open examinations for officers were introduced. Army officers became more professional and among the enlisted men the outcast and misfit became ever less prominent.

New powers continued to accrue to Whitehall. Although Chadwick's constitutionally suspect and unpopular Board of Health had fallen in 1854, its extensive authority had passed to the Home Office and the Privy Council. Following the cholera outbreak of 1865-6, local authorities were compelled to provide water, sewers and refuse disposal, and to appoint sanitary inspectors. The Local Government Board was set up in 1870 to supervise the performance of these duties, together with the workings of the new locally elected school boards and the schools' inspectorate. Such had been the growth of social legislation since the 1834 Poor Law that there was by this time 'an amazing multiplicity of special local authorities, often with overlapping and confused duties and areas'.[6] This confusion, and the anomaly by which since 1835 municipal councils elected by the ratepayers had been provided for the more important towns, whilst the counties continued to be governed by the non-elected justices, made further reform of local government inevitable. It was slow in coming, however, and the elected borough councils and county councils, which took over the non-judicial duties of the justices and many of the other local bodies, did not make their appearance until 1888.

The extension of central government responsibilities necessitated a larger and ever more complex administrative apparatus, which was

3 *Twenty-second Annual Report of the Poor Law Board*, PP, 1870, XXXV, 1, Appendix A, 9-11, *passim*.

4 Emmeline W. Cohen, *The Growth of the British Civil Service 1780-1939*, pp. 110-12.

5 *Report of the Commissioners Appointed to Inquire into the System of Purchase and Sale of Commissions in the Army*, PP, 1857, Sess. 2, XVIII, 1; PP, 1857-8, XIX, 233.

6 David Thomson, *England in the Nineteenth Century*, p. 179.

largely centred on the Home Office and Privy Council. The civil service, more confident and effective in the wake of the reforms, increased from 21,300 in 1832 to more than 50,000 in 1880.[7] At the same time administration was made easier through the expansion and improvement of transport and communications.[8]

The population increased by about five million to nearly twenty-three million between 1851 and 1871 and, despite a slight halt in the 1860s, numbers in rural areas continued to decline. By 1881 there were, besides London, some twenty-six towns with populations of more than 100,000.[9] The improved machinery of local and central government ensured that this increase and transference of population caused less disruption to public health and order than had occurred in the early part of the century. Indeed, apart from the destitute, virtually all sections of society enjoyed a period of unprecedented well-being.[10]

Theories of crime

Habitual criminals were a growing subject of concern in the formulation of penal policy. They were one of the groups most liable to transportation, and the gradual closing of this outlet meant that more and more of them had to be dealt with at home. The fear that the community thereby became prey to depredations of a new type was a major factor in the garrotting scare which resulted in the Carnarvon Committee and the Royal Commission of 1863 and, apart from political agitation, improvements in methods of identification, communication and statistical recording brought the repeated offender to the forefront of discussions.

Habitual offenders found a central place in theories of a criminal class. Sir Walter Crofton wrote of

A dominant criminal class in our midst, able to throw us periodically into a state of panic, and to afford, through their immunity, an evil example to those upon whom we expend both time and money to instil better things.

---

7 *Ibid.*, p. 178. This figure excludes those employed in the telephone and telegraph services.
8 Railways being the pivot upon which this transformation turned; by 1852 more than 7,500 miles of track were in use. Postal and (from 1868) telegraph facilities expanded and improved apace, providing cheap, flexible and reliable means of communication (Phyllis Deane and W.A. Cole, *British Economic Growth, 1688-1959*, pp. 238-9; H.J. Dyos and D.H. Aldcroft, *British Transport – An Economic Survey from the Seventeenth Century to the Twentieth*, p. 129).
9 Geoffrey Best, *Mid-Victorian Britain 1851-75*, p. 29.
10 Asa Briggs, *The Age of Improvement*, p. 403.

He distinguished this criminal class from the 'unemployed poor' and 'roughs' and towards the end of the 1860s saw it becoming ever more 'aggressive and dominant'.[11] C.P. Measor, one-time deputy governor of Chatham Convict Prison, claimed that the criminal class was 'luxuriating ... in the treble immunity of freedom from identification as old offenders, and of the mildest administration of the lightest possible sentences'.[12]

The criminal class was thought to be distinct not only from the non-criminal population, but also from other offenders. The chaplain of Petworth prison in Sussex, writing in 1867, spoke of the influx into his prison of vagrants and men from what he termed 'the dangerous classes of society'. These were criminals drawn in large numbers from London and other places to 'the Towns on our sea coast and who attend the attractions on or near it during the summer months in order to pursue their nefarious practices', and consisted of persons

> who live either wholly or in part by crime. They are intelligent
> and shrewd but with minds much hardened against good impressions
> and they are consequently not by any means so hopeful as the
> residents of our own county who may be convicted of a solitary
> act of crime.[13]

John Campbell, a surgeon in the convict service, developed his views as to the peculiar characteristics of criminals into a crude theory of physical determinism. He argued that

> The physiognomy of prisoners as well as the conformation of the
> skull, is often remarkable; and the result of many *post-mortem*
> examinations has proved that the brains of prisoners weigh less
> than the average, and that a large brain is an exception.[14]

And in a powerful but brutal passage Thomas Carlyle described prisoners as

> Miserable distorted blockheads, the generality: ape-faces, imp-faces,
> angry dog-faces, heavy sullen ox-faces; degraded underfoot perverse

---

11 Sir Walter Crofton, *The Criminal Classes and Their Control*, pp. 5, 8 and 9.
12 C.P. Measor, *Criminal Correction*, pp. 8-9. He wished there to be especially severe means for dealing with habitual offenders:

> Although in ordinary cases and first offences, the scale of punishment
> can only be apportioned to the actual offences committed, a further
> scale and classification is essential in respect of those habitual offenders
> upon whom all the appliances of corrective discipline have been in vain
> tried over and over again, but who as constantly return to crime like a
> dog to his vomit (*ibid.*, p. 6).

13 West Sussex County Record Office, QAP/5/W18 606.
14 John Campbell, *Thirty Years' Experience of a Medical Officer*, p. 74.

creatures, sons of *in*docility, greedy mutinous darkness, and in one word, of stupidity, which is the general mother of such.[15]

Notions about juvenile crime and habitual criminals dovetailed in the theory that the criminal class was constantly regenerated by the transmission through upbringing of criminal dispositions.[16] If juveniles could be reached before they became firm in the mould the vicious process might be stayed and the criminal class would diminish. This hope led to calls for the inclusion of elements both of education and repression in penal and social policies.[17] The Newcastle Commission of

15 Thomas Carlyle, *Latter Day Pamphlets*, p. 70. He went on to condemn reformatory attempts with such materials:

> Hopeless for evermore such a project. The abject, ape, wolf, ox, imp and other diabolic-animal specimens of humanity, who of the very gods could ever have commanded them by love? A collar round the neck, and a cartwhip flourished over the back; these in a just and steady human hand, were what the gods would have appointed them. . . .

16 W. Bayne Ranken, honorary secretary of the Discharged Prisoners' Aid Society, described habitual criminals as the 'lowest class' – children of criminals trained in crime from an early age (*English Convicts Before and After their Discharge*, p. 8).

17 The Brougham Committee reported that

> Upon one Subject the whole of the Evidence and all the Opinions are quite unanimous – the good that may be hoped from Education, meaning thereby a sound moral and religious training, commencing in Infant Schools and followed up in Schools for Older Pupils; to these, where it is practicable *industrial* training should be *added*. There seems in the general Opinion to be no other Means that afford even a Chance of lessening the Number of Offenders, and diminishing the Atrocity of their Crimes (*Select Committee of the House of Lords Appointed to Inquire into the Execution of the Criminal Laws, Especially Respecting Juvenile Offenders and Transportation* (Brougham Committee), PP, 1847, VII, 1, 12).

> In the early 1860s W. Bayne Ranken argued that habitual offenders – incorrigibles – should be subject to special measures: 'All very bad cases should be treated separately, and perpetual imprisonment would seem in some instances to be the only termination of a career spent in the perpetration of repeated and desperate crimes' (*op. cit*., 7). Frederic Hill and his brother, Matthew Davenport Hill, had put forward similar views in the 1850s. In a charge delivered in December 1856, in his capacity as recorder of Birmingham, Matthew Hill held that

> Surely all who give themselves the trouble of mastering the subject, must feel that what we ought to aim at is, to prevent criminals once apprehended and convicted from being so placed as to have the power of offending again, until we have some proof that their dispositions and habits are changed for the better. And if the discipline of the gaol should fail to produce its intended effect, then is it not unquestionably right that the seclusion of the prisoners, should continue even if it last for their lives? (*Frederic Hill: An Autobiography of Fifty Years in Times of Reform*, ed. Mary Constance Hill, p. 278).

1861, for example, was told by one witness that whilst he opposed compulsory education for all, it might be introduced for 'certain classes' including paupers and prisoners.[18]

Drunkenness was another important theme in discussions of crime. Herbert Voules, when inspector for the Northern District, observed that during the nine months of the Preston strike of 1854 there had been a fall in the number of adult offenders committed to prison and that, because of the strike, spending on alcohol in Preston had dropped in the same period by over £1,000 per month. From this he deduced that 'drunkenness is the source of almost all crime, and that destitution arising from want of employment acts far less prejudicially on the working classes than this monster vice of our large towns'.[19] Although drunkenness was frequently linked to other malign conditions, discussions of crime or prisoners rarely omitted some reference to the dangers of alcohol. The comments of a chaplain, made in the late 1850s, are representative:

> On the Causes of crime, as they are discoverable in a prison, I will only say that, next to parental neglect and defective education, Intemperance still immeasurably exceeds all others. From Cell to Cell and from day to day, the lamentation is heard — ''Twas Beer that did it', and if it were not for drink I shouldn't be here. O how much has yet to be done in checking the facilities and the progress of this overwhelming vice, as well as in promoting the religious training, and the proper comforts of the poor.[20]

The availability of reasonably reliable crime statistics from the mid-1850s onward gave a new firmness to criminological debates, but the range of views remained as great as in the earlier part of the century, and the connection between these theories and penal policy continued to be complicated and uncertain. The popularity of a criminological theory and the weight which it brought to bear on penal policy were largely determined by the level of political anxiety about crime, and particular types of offender and offence. Juvenile crime, habitual criminals, the criminal class and drunkenness were the strongest threads

---

18 The witness, J. Snell, added that in the case of prisoners, compulsory education 'Should be confined to moral, religious and industrial education, as anything tending to sharpen their wits would probably be productive of greater mischief than ignorance itself' (*Report of the Commissioners on the State of Popular Education in England*, PP, 1861, XXI, Pt 1, 198).

19 *Twenty-second Report of the Inspectors (Northern and Eastern District)*, PP, 1857-8, XXIX, 1, 7-8.

20 West Sussex County Record Office, Report of Chaplain of Lewes Gaol and House of Correction (1858), p. 13. The chaplain did, however, qualify these observations: 'Still, the abolition of drunkenness would not secure the abolition of crime; and experience among criminals by no means confirms the extravagant statements sometimes made upon the subject.'

in discussions of crime, and this led to attempts to isolate the wilful and persistent criminal. One way of doing this was to provide alternative means for dealing with those whose imprisonment could more easily be attributed to misfortune or incapacity. The way was then cleared for a policy of uniform repression, deterrence and retribution in the prisons.

Changes in the use of imprisonment

Sentence and committal lengths

The length of sentences of imprisonment and the frequency of custodial remands determined the rate of turnover of the local prison population. A great fluctuation in numbers increased administrative problems and led to an uneconomic use of resources, since levels of staffing and accommodation had to be fixed in accordance with maximum populations, which meant that there were prolonged periods of under-employment and under-use. A high turnover, with the consequent greater frequency in receptions and releases, was also expensive in that it incurred higher medical, laundry and clothing costs.

Sentences of imprisonment on summary conviction rose steadily between 1857 and 1877, from 62,293 to 100,525 per annum,[21] whilst the number of fines imposed by magistrates increased from 143,463 to 358,053. Imprisonment as a percentage of total summary convictions declined from 26.7 per cent in 1857 to 19.3 per cent in 1877 and fines rose from 61.4 per cent to 68.9 per cent. The use of short sentences by magistrates' courts noticeably grew between 1857 and 1867. As can be seen from Table 11.1 sentences of fourteen days and under made up 30.7 per cent of custodial sentences imposed in magistrates' courts in 1857, but 44.9 per cent in 1877. This increase in the proportion of short sentences was clearly associated with the greater recourse to fining and the consequent necessity to imprison more defaulters for short periods.[22] The higher courts' use of imprisonment did not change very much, the most marked development being a 50 per cent increase in the proportion of sentences of from one and two years in the period 1857 and 1877, even though the *numbers* receiving this sentence continued to be very small. Overall recourse to imprisonment increased slightly. In 1857 they sentenced 12,198 persons to imprisonment (79.7 per cent of convictions), in 1867 11,801 (83.1 per cent) and in 1877 9,793 (82.0 per cent). Rather less use was made of penal servitude

21 All figures and calculations, unless otherwise stated, are taken from the *Judicial Statistics*: see Tables 11.1 to 11.6 for a summary. Between 1857 and 1877 the population of England and Wales increased from 19,256,000 to 24,700,000.
22 See Table 11.3, n. 2.

in the same period; in 1857 this sentence was imposed on 16.2 per cent of those convicted; in 1877 upon 13.7 per cent.[23] The proportion of sentences of between six months and one year passed at sessions and assizes also increased. In 1856 legislation on the powers of courts diminished by about 40 per cent the number of sentences of under six months imposed by the higher courts;[24] but this failed to affect the overall proportion of short sentences, which in the magistrates' courts rose immediately by several thousand. This Act made savings in court expenses and, by removing the need for so many custodial remands which fell from 20,212 in 1857 to 14,005 in 1877, eased that demand on prison services. The drop was proportionately the greater since total committals had risen in the period. Remands for trial made up 14.3 per cent of total committals in 1857, but only 7.5 per cent in 1877. Another, but less marked, decline in the use of imprisonment was in respect of persons unable to find sureties, who accounted for 2.2 per cent of committals in 1857, but only 1.8 per cent in 1877. On the other hand, the use of civil prisons for naval and military offenders committed under the Mutiny Act by courts martial increased from 2.0 per cent of total committals in 1857 to 3.2 per cent in 1877.

These various changes in the use of prison both for convicted and unconvicted prisoners resulted in a slight stabilisation of the population, with the average length of stay between 1857 and 1877 increasing from nine to ten days. The greater proportion of short sentences passed in magistrates' courts was offset to some extent by the reduction in the proportion of persons remanded in custody for trial. Moreover, the greater numbers sent to prison by the magistrates steadied the prison population in another respect: because they met much more frequently than the higher courts the sentences of the magistrates' courts made a less fluctuating contribution to the prison population. Accommodation became more efficiently used; whereas the average daily population accounted for only 73 per cent of available accommodation in 1857, it took up 86 per cent in 1877.[25] But the closure of many of the small prisons and the greater recourse to contracts between jurisdictions also played a major part in this increased level of efficiency, in addition to the various changes in the practice of the courts.

23 See Table 11.2.
24 The statute was 18 & 19 Vict., c.126 which authorised the magistrates at petty sessions (with the defendant's consent) to deal with charges of petty larceny involving property of less than five shillings. The drop in the proportion sentenced to terms of under six months by higher courts is reported in the *Judicial Statistics* for 1856, x.
25 See Table 11.5.

TABLE 11.1   *Sentences passed by the magistrates' courts, 1857-77*

| Year | 1857 | | 1867 | | 1877 | |
Punishment	Number	%	Number	%	Number	%
Imprisonment for:						
above 6 months	101	0.2	38	0.1	188	0.2
3-6 months	2,479	4.0	2,677	3.6	3,708	3.7
2-3 months	8,604	13.8	6,957	9.3	8,248	8.2
1-2 months	10,586	17.0	10,600	14.2	13,291	13.2
14 days-1 month	21,386	34.3	22,764	30.4	29,913	29.8
14 days and under	19,137	30.7	31,778	42.4	45,177	44.9
Total sentences of imprisonment[1]	62,293	100.0	74,814	100.0	100,525	100.0
		26.7		22.3		19.3
Total fined	143,463	61.4	213,671	63.7	358,053	68.9
Total whipped	525	0.2	705	0.2	1,333	0.3
Sent to reformatory and industrial schools	768	0.3	2,554	0.8	3,622	0.7
Other punishments: to find sureties; delivered up to army or navy, etc.	26,710	11.4	43,615	13.0	56,306	10.8
Total convicted by justices	233,759	100.0	335,359	100.0	519,839	100.0

Source: These figures are abstracted from the *Judicial Statistics* for 1857, PP, 1857-8, LVIII, 383, ix; for 1867, PP, 1867-8, LXVII, 519, xvi; and, for 1877, PP, 1878, LXXIX, 1, xviii. Detailed figures for the results of summary procedure were collected for the first time in 1857. See PP, 1857-8, *op. cit.*, viii.

1: Total sentences of imprisonment given as a percentage of total convictions, and the figures for the different terms of imprisonment are given as a percentage of the total of sentences of imprisonment.

Providing alternatives to imprisonment

Juveniles   For many years there had been attempts to separate youthful offenders from other prisoners, to provide special régimes for them and, if possible, to keep them out of prison altogether. The Brougham Committee of 1847 contended that

333

TABLE 11.2   *Sentences passed by the higher courts, 1857-77*

Year Punishment	1857 Number	%	1867 Number	%	1877 Number	%
Imprisonment for:						
above 2 years	17	0.1	–	0.0	2	0.0
1-2 years	1,014	8.3	1,379	11.7	1,198	12.3
6 months-1 year	3,291	27.0	3,485	29.5	3,046	31.1
3-6 months	4,128	33.9	3,531	29.9	2,929	29.9
1-3 months	2,648	21.7	2,433	20.6	1,774	18.1
1 month and under	1,100	9.0	973	8.3	844	8.6
Total sentences of	12,198	100.0	11,801	100.0	9,793	100.0
imprisonment		79.7		83.1		82.0
Sentenced to:						
death	54	0.3	27	0.2	34	0.3
transportation	110	0.7	–	0.0	–	0.0
penal servitude	2,473	16.2	1,846	13.0	1,639	13.7
reformatories	309	2.0	270	1.9	184	1.5
whipping, fine, etc.	163	1.1	263	1.8	292	2.5
Total convicted by the higher courts	15,307	100.0	14,207	100.0	11,942	100.0

Source: These figures are abstracted from the *Judicial Statistics* for 1857, PP, 1857-8, LVIII, 383, xiv-xv; for 1867, PP, 1867-8, LXVII, 519, xxii-xxiii; and, for 1877, PP, 1878, LXXIX, 1, xxvii-xxviii.

> the contamination of a gaol or gaols as usually managed may often prove fatal, and must always be hurtful to boys committed for a first offence, and thus for a very trifling act they may become trained in the worst of crimes.[26]

This view had induced certain sentencers to use existing legal arrangements to keep less hardened young offenders out of prison. As early as the 1820s some Warwickshire magistrates in suitable cases committed young offenders to the care of their employers.[27] Matthew Davenport Hill expanded upon this idea when he was appointed recorder of

26 Brougham Committee, *op. cit.*, 9-10.
27 Dorothy Bochel, *Probation and Aftercare: Its Development in England and Wales*, p. 4.

TABLE 11.3   *Total commitments to local prisons, 1857-77*

Year Type of commitment	1857		1867		1877	
	Number	%	Number	%	Number	%
Remanded and discharged	14,653	10.3	10,788	7.4	11,999	6.4
For trial at assizes and sessions	20,212	14.3	17,251	11.9	14,005	7.5
Convicted at assizes and sessions[1] (not previously in custody)			1,883	1.3	1,711	0.9
Convicted summarily[2]	86,795	61.1	98,636	67.9	144,562	77.1
Want of sureties	3,163	2.2	2,840	2.0	3,379	1.8
Debtors and on civil process	14,339	10.1	11,647	8.0	5,754	3.1
Military and naval offences	2,808	2.0	2,139	1.5	6,002	3.2
Total commitments	141,970	100.0	145,184	100.0	187,412	100.0

Source: These figures are abstracted from the *Judicial Statistics, op. cit.*, xxi, xxvii and xxxii.

1: Not counted separately in the figures for 1857.

2: This figure is greater than that noted in Table 11.1 for the total sentences of imprisonment on summary conviction because Table 11.3 includes those imprisoned in default of payment of a fine. See the *Judicial Statistics* for 1866: 'of the large number sentenced to be fined . . . many are sent to prison in default of payment of the fine, and these are included in the prison returns, along with those sentenced to imprisonment under the heading "convicted summarily" ' (PP, 1867, LXVI, 523, xxviii). Thus the number of defaulters is in each case in 1857, 24,502; in 1867, 23,822; and, in 1877, 44,037. These figures make up 17.3%, 16.4% and 23.5% of the total commitments in those years.

Birmingham in 1839; offenders were handed over to suitable guardians and Hill kept a register and received reports on their subsequent behaviour. This scheme became quite widely known and was adopted by other courts.[28] The legal basis of these experiments was uncertain. Often a nominal penalty such as a day's imprisonment was imposed, in addition to placing the offender in the care of a supervisor. The

28 *Dictionary of National Biography*, IX, p. 855.

TABLE 11.4   *Turnover of prisoners in local prisons, 1857-77*

Year	1857	1867	1877
Number in prisons at the beginning of the year	17,073	17,532	20,499
Number committed during the year	141,970	145,184	187,412
Removals between local prisons	4,099	4,536	3,211
Total	163,142	167,252	211,122
Removed from the local prisons:			
to government and other prisons	9,041	6,850	5,170
to reformatories, etc.	1,121	1,513	1,598
to lunatic asylums	114	122	182
Total	10,276	8,485	6,950
Discharged:			
On pardon or commutation	405	153	144
On ticket-of-leave	7	6	1
On termination of sentence or commitment	132,548	139,231	182,206
Escaped	14	13	9
Committed suicide	15	17	22
Died	172	148	186
Executed	19	7	20
Bailed		996	1,184
Overall total removed and discharged	143,456	149,056	190,722
Number remaining in prisons at the end of the year	19,686	18,196	20,400
Average length of stay/prisoner (approx.)[1]	9 days	9 days	10 days

Source: These figures are abstracted from the *Judicial Statistics, op. cit.*, xxv, xxxii, xxxviii.

1: Calculated by dividing daily average number into total prisoners received during the year, rounded to the nearest whole day. This calculation does *not* take account of repeat committals.

TABLE 11.5   *Use of accommodation, 1857-77*

Year	1857	1867[1]	1877
Maximum available accommodation	26,022	20,131 (17,609)	27,151 (24,614)
Greatest number during the year	23,639	22,282	24,466
Daily average number	19,009	17,995	23,220
Daily average number as a percentage of maximum available accommodation	73%	89% (102%)	86% (94%)

Source: Taken from *Judicial Statistics*, *op. cit.*, respectively, xxvi, xxxii and xxxviii.

1: The definition of 'maximum available accommodation' had changed by this time to the 'number of separate sleeping cells', with certified sleeping and punishment cells counted separately. (See 28 & 29 Vict., c.126, s.18, which required the inspector to certify cells and the purpose for which they were intended.) The number of certified sleeping cells is shown in brackets.

TABLE 11.6   *Juveniles as a percentage of total committals to prison, 1857-77*

Year	1857		1867		1877	
Age	Number	%	Number	%	Number	%
Under 12 years	1,877	1.5	1,690	1.3	1,065	0.6
12 years and under 16 years	10,624	8.5	8.041	6.1	6,517	3.7
Number of juveniles removed to reformatories	1,121		1,513		1,698	

Source: Taken from *Judicial Statistics*, *op. cit.*, p. xxiii, p. xxix and p. xxxv.

drawback with this was that the court had no remedy should the offender or his supervisor fail to comply with its directions. To meet this difficulty Edward Cox, recorder of Portsmouth, released suitable offenders on recognizance, with or without sureties. This device became the basis of the Summary Jurisdiction Act of 1879,[29] which permitted

29 42 & 43 Vict., c.49.

a conditional discharge on the giving of sureties for good behaviour or reappearance for sentence. Following the enactment of this measure the courts began to use missionaries of the Church of England Temperance Society as supervisors.

In 1851 a movement began to provide alternative custodial means of dealing with juveniles, when Matthew Davenport Hill and Mary Carpenter convened a national conference on criminal and destitute children. This led to the setting up of a select committee[30] and to the passing of the Youthful Offenders Act[31] which empowered courts to send to a reformatory school on the completion of a prison sentence certain offenders below the age of sixteen. These schools were administered by voluntary bodies and aided by a state grant. Other Acts followed, and in 1866 two statutes consolidated the legislation on both reformatory and industrial schools.[32] By that year there were sixty-five reformatory schools accommodating rather fewer than 5,000 offenders, and fifty industrial schools providing for some 2,500 needy children.[33]

Reformatory and industrial schools reduced, but did not stop, the flow of young offenders to prison, and in 1863 John Perry complained of the very great number of boys in the prisons of his district.[34] The initial legislation had stipulated that a reformatory school sentence was to follow a period of imprisonment of not less than fourteen days, and this meant that the reformatory could not be a direct substitute for imprisonment, even though by taking youthful criminals out of circulation the reformatories helped to keep a proportion of them out of prison. Moreover, young offenders frequently spent long periods in prison before reformatory places could be found for them.[35]

Attempts were made to keep youthful offenders who were sent to prison apart from adults, but the establishment of a juvenile department or a special juvenile prison depended on there being sufficient numbers of young prisoners available to make the project reasonably economical. This was possible in a few large urban areas; Tothill Fields house of correction in Westminster had separate boys' and girls' wards, as did Holloway, then the City house of correction.[36] But only on a

30 *The Select Committee on Criminal and Destitute Children*, PP, 1852-3, XXIII, 1. The committee reported in June 1853.
31 17 & 18 Vict., c.86.
32 29 & 30 Vict., c.117, dealt with reformatories and 29 & 30 Vict., c.118, with industrial schools.
33 *Report of the Commissioners on Reformatories and Industrial Schools*, PP, 1884, XLV, 1, Appendix A6, lxxix.
34 *Select Committee of the House of Lords on Gaol Discipline* (Carnarvon Committee), PP, 1863, IX, para. 1428, 138-9.
35 *Twenty-third Report of the Inspectors of Prisons (Southern District)*, PP, 1857-8, XXIX, 69.
36 M. Mayhew and J. Binny, *The Criminal Prisons of London*, pp. 376-97, 578-80.

national footing was it feasible to establish a special juvenile prison — Parkhurst juvenile penitentiary. This was part of the convict service and therefore dealt only with those sentenced to penal servitude or transportation, but from 1854 boys under the age of sixteen who had been sentenced to one or two years' imprisonment were also accepted at Parkhurst. However, the juvenile penitentiary closed in 1864 and this outlet ceased to be available to the courts.[37]

The development of non-custodial supervision and reformatories took some time to gain momentum, but by the end of the 1870s there had been a large drop in the proportion of prisoners who were under the age of sixteen. In 1857 1.5 per cent of the total committals to prison were of children under the age of twelve and 8.5 per cent were aged between twelve and sixteen; during that year 1,121 juveniles were removed to reformatory schools. In 1877 0.6 per cent of persons committed were aged under twelve and 3.7 per cent between twelve and sixteen.[38]

Lunatics Before 1845 a variety of institutions, both public and private, dealt with lunatics. The publicly financed establishments included gaols, houses of correction, workhouses and county asylums. Of the last there were only sixteen. There were also 139 private institutions for the insane, run on business lines. Although most of the private madhouses catered for those from well-to-do families there was money to be made even from paupers, and some large establishments catered for this group,[39] drawing their income from the inmates' responsible local authority (after 1834 usually the poor-law guardians). In addition to the public and private institutions there was a small number of charitable foundations. In London these included the old established Bethlehem (or Bethlem or Bedlam, as it was variously called), and wards at Guy's Hospital and at St Luke's. Similar foundations existed in the provinces, but never dealt with more than a small proportion of the insane.

Many of the leading figures in penal reform also campaigned for reform of the lunacy laws, including Sir Samuel Romilly, Samuel Whitbread and Sir George Onesiphorus Paul. Although they may have had philosophical or religious reasons for extending their interest in reform to the treatment of lunatics, many would have found it difficult to draw a distinction between penal institutions and methods for dealing with the insane: the prisons, particularly the houses of correction, were the means of last resort of responding both to feckless pauperism and bothersome lunacy.

37 See pp. 428-9, below.
38 See Table 11.6. As noted below (pp. 428-9), the drop in the number of young persons sentenced to penal servitude was even more marked.
39 Andrew T. Scull, *Museums of Madness*, pp. 52-3.

In the early 1840s pressures for the reform and regulation of provision for lunatics resulted in a major national inquiry by the Metropolitan Commissioners in Lunacy. Many parts of their report are reminiscent of the prison surveys of Howard and Neild. The issue was taken up with great vigour by Ashley (later Earl of Shaftesbury), who introduced two measures in the summer of 1845. One of these, the Lunatics Act,[40] set up a Lunacy Commission, which was vested with extensive powers of inspection. The other Act[41] obliged borough and county authorities to provide asylums for lunatic paupers, and by the 1850s almost all authorities had complied with this statute. Criminal lunatics, who had almost invariably been consigned to gaols, gradually became the responsibility of central government, and therefore of the convict service. Those criminal lunatics detained at Her Majesty's pleasure had at first been sent to a special wing at Bethlehem or (the less dangerous) to Fisherton House. After much consideration and indecision a national criminal lunatic asylum, designed by Jebb, was opened at Broadmoor in 1862. As can be seen from Table 11.7, by 1876 more than two-thirds of the country's criminal lunatics were confined there.

TABLE 11.7   *The detention of criminal lunatics, 1856, 1866, 1876**

Place of confinement	1856	1866	1876
County and borough asylums	260	361	144
Hospitals	108	8	1
Metropolitan licensed homes	33	11	2
Provincial licensed houses	180	193	73
State Criminal Asylum	–	440	494
Total	581	1,013	714

*Years ending on 1 January 1857, 1867 and 1877.

Source: Abstracted from the *Reports of the Commissioners of Lunacy*, PP, 1857 (Sess. II), XVI, 1; PP, 1867, XVIII, 201; PP, 1877, XLI, 1. See also Kathleen Jones, *A History of the Mental Health Services*, pp. 145, 158; *Mental Health and Social Policy 1845-1959*, p. 7; and Nigel Walker and Sarah McCabe, *Crime and Insanity in England*, pp. 3-9.

Reliable figures of any kind on the numbers of mentally disturbed persons in prisons, apart from criminal lunatics, are impossible to

40 8 & 9 Vict., c.100.
41 8 & 8 Vict., c.126.

obtain. The incomplete returns of information which undermined all prison statistics until the inspectorate got well into its stride is one reason for the paucity of information; the other is the perennial problem of defining and diagnosing mental disorder. Even with modern techniques and relatively systematic examination, the exact number of the mentally disordered in English prisons remains a matter of some speculation.[42] Returns of the number of persons sent from local prisons to lunatic asylums show a total of 182 in 1877,[43] but a fairly large number of weakminded or imbecile prisoners continued to be received and kept in the prisons – some 541 in 1879.[44] In the absence of other useful figures relating to the mentally disordered it seems reasonable to suppose that, as the number of places in the county and borough asylums increased, the courts made less use of prisons for this category of person. This policy would certainly have been urged by prison staff, since this type of prisoner was frequently the source of great difficulties for prison discipline and management.[45]

Debtors   For several hundred years debtors were one of the largest groups of prisoners – their increase in the eighteenth century probably being a major factor in the overcrowding which then arose.[46] In 1709 Daniel Defoe estimated there were 5,000 of them[47] and John Howard found in 1776 that of a total of 4,084 inmates 2,437 (60 per cent) were imprisoned for debt. Any change in this use of imprisonment was therefore a matter of major significance for the administration of prisons.

Until 1869 imprisoned debtors could not be subject to the same régime as those charged with or convicted of criminal offences.[48] They were allowed extensive visiting privileges, their own food and clothing, could continue to work at their trade or profession to the extent that their confinement allowed, and were exempt from many of the prison rules. At Bedford gaol in the 1830s one well-known local figure had over thirty applications to visit him on one day alone, prompting the

42 See, for example, the *Fifteenth Report from the Expenditure Committee* (1978), xxxviii-xxxix.
43 See Table 11.4.
44 *Report of the Commission on Criminal Lunacy*, PP, 1882, XXXII, 1, Appendix A, 150.
45 See the reports of governors of the invalid prisons for convicts, pp. 416-17 below.
46 Duffy recognises that the lack of statistical material makes precise judgments on this matter difficult, but he thinks it likely that insolvency and committals increased because of the growth in population and the economy (thesis: 'Bankruptcy and Insolvency in London in the late Eighteenth and Early Nineteenth Century', p. 7).
47 Daniel Defoe's 'Review', 1 March 1708-9, *cit*. R. Paulson, *Hogarth: His Life, Art, and Times*, p. 32.
48 Prison Act 1865 (28 & 29 Vict., c.126, sch. 1, rules 16-18, 31 and 46).

governor to complain to the justices that extra staff would be needed if the visits continued at the same rate.[49] In 1846 the Reverend J. Field, chaplain of Reading gaol, and an enthusiastic advocate of the separate system, had argued, ostensibly on liberal and humanitarian grounds, against exempting debtors from the separate system during their imprisonment:

> What a violation of equity, to subject the unfortunate, the friendless, the comparatively innocent, and the most fraudulent, to the same penalty, the same temptations, and the same distress! I sincerely hope that the day is not distant when this [debtors'] prison shall be identified with the rest: when the insolvent who is the subject of suspicion, shall be committed for trial; and the man convicted of fraud, shall be treated as a felon.[50]

But this policy was not adopted and in 1846 the County Courts Act obliged the justices to continue to provide special conditions for debtors.[51] There were some attempts to circumvent this requirement by magistrates who thought it improper to give preferential treatment to this class of prisoner; but the Home Office insisted on special treatment for debtors, and complained to the local authorities about departures from this requirement. Moreover, the home secretary refused to approve any local prison rules which failed to provide proper treatment for debtors.[52]

Throughout the 1850s and 1860s, therefore, debtors continued to be subject to special rules, although at some of the smaller gaols, which held only one or two debtors at a time, *de facto* separation or, alternatively, association with misdemeanants, may have been imposed. Most magistrates probably did not need to be compelled to treat debtors as a distinct class, and willingly continued to extend to them the privileges which they had always enjoyed. In 1860 one of the inspectors noted that

49 Eric Stockdale, *A Study of Bedford Prison*, p. 144.
50 Rev. J. Field, *The Advantages of the Separate System of Imprisonment*, p. 66.
51 See p. 344, below.
52 The Home Office Out-Letters to County Courts (PRO HO 86, vols 2 & 3) contain many items of correspondence on this matter, following the County Courts Act of 1846. In December 1847 the clerk to the justices at Preston was informed that the home secretary could not sanction any departure from the recommended rules to be applied to imprisoned debtors which increased their penal character. The rules proposed by the Preston magistrates were unacceptable because the dietary was insufficient and because debtors would be obliged to work and to comply with the silent system (PRO HO 86/1/361). A similar matter arose respecting Coldbath Fields house of correction in January 1849 (PRO HO 86/1/500).

The visiting justices of many prisons feel a delicacy in subjecting debtors to any discipline beyond that of safe custody; but there are generally troublesome characters among that class, who take advantage of that laxity of discipline. . . .

He continued, 'I should be glad to see debtors while in prison kept under the discipline of good order, to be enforced by punishment when necessary, for I think it would be beneficial to themselves.'[53] That debtors were also seen by many governors in a very different light from criminal prisoners is evidenced by their occasional employment in positions of trust, and the consequent need for the justices sometimes explicitly to forbid their use as turnkeys.[54]

Debtors, perhaps because there were probably among them more educated men than there were among the criminals, were apt to complain about the conditions of their confinement. In 1860, Herbert Voules, inspector for the Northern District, reported that in the debtors' section of York Castle

I found the inmates of one or two of the wards very full of complaints, and very much disposed to be disorderly. The debtors, as a class, are generally the most unsatisfactory that I meet with in any prison.[55]

In 1862, Kincaid, then inspector for the Northern District, was directed by the Home Secretary to investigate allegations made by debtors in Manchester city gaol[56] and was occupied with this work during the early part of that year. Debtors' wards also posed disciplinary difficulties because of the trafficking which went on between them and the criminal prisoners. Certain prisons, moreover, suffered from the reputation of providing superior living conditions or easier access to transport for visitors, and this made them particularly attractive to debtors. In 1861 the serious overcrowding at Lewes gaol was in part attributed to there being so many debtors from other counties who had chosen to be arrested locally.[57]

For many years there had been much perplexity about the operation

---

53 *Twenty-fifth Report of the Inspectors of Prisons (Northern District)*, PP, 1860, XXXV, 381, 426.
54 See Stockdale, *op. cit.*, p. 89.
55 *Twenty-fifth Report (Northern District)*, *op. cit.*, p. 426. Certainly there are many instances of complaints by debtors of their treatment, both in central and local government papers.
56 *Twenty-seventh Report of the Inspectors of Prisons (Northern District)*, PP, 1862, XXV, 237.
57 A large number had also speeded up their committal, so as to be dealt with before the coming into effect of the new Bankruptcy Act (24 & 25 Vict., c.134) (East Sussex Record Office, QAP/2/24: governor's reports to Epiphany and Michaelmas Sessions: visiting justices' report to the Midsummer Sessions).

of the bankruptcy and debt laws. It was clear that dishonest debtors frequently used them to their own advantage; on the other hand, it was recognised that many persons had come to be in prison as the result of misfortune or the action of a pitiless creditor, and often suffered lengthy imprisonment, leaving their dependants without support, because of some trifling sum. Partly because of such considerations and also because of the overcrowding of the gaols, Insolvent Debtors Acts were passed at frequent intervals from the late seventeenth century onwards, releasing considerable numbers of debtors. This was an arbitrary and unfair method of dealing with overcrowding, since the Acts applied only to those in prison at the time of the enactment. Some debtors contrived to be arrested in order to take advantage of an imminent Act, occasionally returning from abroad for this purpose.[58]

The overhaul of the debt laws began in earnest only in 1813, when the Act for the Relief of Insolvent Debtors in England[59] set up a court to deal with insolvent debtors, thus making the frequent provision of insolvency Acts unnecessary. More than forty different measures on debt and bankruptcy followed before the 1844 Insolvency Act[60] abolished imprisonment for debts under £20, and extended to private persons the right (hitherto restricted to traders) to go into bankruptcy. Further changes were made in 1845[61] with the intention of making it easier to recover small debts; and the following year it was permitted under the County Courts Act[62] to imprison debtors in a convenient gaol or house of correction, should the gaol of the jurisdiction be located at an inconvenient distance from the court.[63] Other statutes

58 Duffy, *op. cit.*, p. 79; Stockdale, *op. cit.*, p. 47.
59 53 Geo. III, c.102.
60 7 & 8 Vict., c.96.
61 8 & 9 Vict., c.127.
62 9 & 10 Vict., c.95.
63 This Act legalised what seems to have been a not uncommon practice. The Act was amended by 12 & 13 Vict., c.101, s.3, which made it necessary for the home secretary to designate a house of correction as suitable for debt committals and allowed him to alter the regulations of the designated house of correction 'in order that such Persons may be treated as nearly as may be in like Manner as if they had been committed to a Gaol in which such Debtors . . . may be confined . . .'. Authorisation of the use of the most convenient gaol or house of correction by the county courts was a source of embarrassment to those localities whose prisons were in a poor state. In 1848 the visiting justices at Tothill Fields house of correction at Westminster were told that their request that the county court should be directed not to commit to their prison could not be met since 'the County Courts Act appears to give in express terms the powers of committing to the House of Correction for the County' (PRO HO 86/1/433). A similar appeal was directed in 1849 to the judge at the Lancashire county court with respect to Salford house of correction, because the visiting justices claimed to have been unable to make provision there for debtors, within the spirit and letter of the law (PRO HO 86/2/11). New Romney gaol, long under attack by the

followed in 1849, 1850 and 1856.[64] As a consequence of the 1858 Act which, *inter alia*, dealt with the collection of small debts, the number of imprisoned debtors noticeably increased. The governor of Bedford prison reported this to the Easter Sessions, and representations were made to the home secretary, which eventually resulted in the passing of an amending Act.[65] This measure sought to restrict the power of county court judges to commit small debtors to prison to cases where credit had been obtained by fraud. A further clarifying measure was enacted in 1860[66] and a major consolidating and amending Act on bankruptcy was passed in 1861.[67] This last Act authorised registrars of the court of bankruptcy to visit the gaols and adjudge bankrupt those imprisoned for debt who satisfied them as to the genuineness of their insolvency;[68] once declared bankrupt the person could then be released from prison. This proved to be a highly effective means of clearing the prisons of numerous debtors without, as the lord chancellor observed a few years later, leading to complaints 'that the remedy of the *bona fide* creditor had, in consequence of the operation of the measure, been abridged'.[69]

Although the 1861 Act reduced the number of debtors in prison, it did not altogether eliminate them. In 1865 it was claimed that those then in prison had made their way there with the intention of seeking their discharge under the 1861 Bankruptcy Act[70] and this was one of the matters considered by a select committee which was then sitting on the bankruptcy laws.[71] The committee made its final report in March 1865, and in 1869 three measures affecting bankruptcy and debt

---

inspectors, was also obliged, because of this statute, to make improvements. The Home Office wrote to the county court stating that should the judge report to the home secretary that

the prison is unsuitable or unfit for the confinement of prisoners of this class [debtors], he will make a communication on the subject to the Corporate Authorities, with a view to confirm their liability – and require a Government Inspector of prisons to visit and report to him upon the state of the prison (PRO HO 86/1/266).

---

64 12 & 13 Vict., c.101; 13 & 14 Vict., c.61; 19 & 20 Vict., c.108.
65 22 & 23 Vict., c.57. Stockdale (*op. cit.*, p. 203) notes that the part played by the governor of Bedford prison in obtaining this legislation has gone unacknowledged.
66 23 & 24 Vict., c.147.
67 24 & 25 Vict., c.134.
68 24 & 25 Vict., c.134, s.101. The registrar had regularly to be informed by the gaols of the names of those in custody for debt.
69 *The Times*, 10 March 1865, 5e.
70 *Ibid.*
71 *Report from the Select Committee Appointed to Inquire into the Working of the Bankruptcy Act 1861*, PP, 1864, V, 1, and PP, 1865, XII, 589.

were enacted.[72]

Following the passage of the first of these three Acts the home secretary issued a circular instruction to the magistrates, requiring them to change their rules on the treatment of debtors. Those imprisoned in default of the payment of an instalment, or under the Bankruptcy Act of 1869, were to be subject to the same rules and to be treated as were prisoners awaiting trial on criminal charges; persons committed because of a misdemeanour under s.2 of the Bankruptcy Act were to be treated in the same way as sentenced criminal prisoners. Only those committed under warrant by the sheriff for contempt or under mesne process under s.6 of the Act were to be treated according to the existing rules for debtors.[73]

The Acts of 1869 did not therefore entirely stop imprisonment for debt. It was possible for the bankruptcy courts to commit debtors for such contempts as failing to co-operate to the satisfaction of the court or to make a full disclosure; failure to pay an instalment of a settlement ordered by the court could also result in imprisonment for contempt.[74] Imprisonment for debt was, moreover, sanctioned by the Bankruptcy Act for debts of £50 or less; any court was allowed to commit such a debtor to prison for a term of up to six weeks if it was convinced that he had means to settle the debt but had refused or neglected to do so.[75] Imprisonment under such circumstances did not extinguish the debt, for which the debtor could at a future time again be committed. This provision was strongly attacked in 1877 by Robert Lowe[76] on the grounds that it perversely discriminated against those in debt for small sums, and that it contrasted unfavourably with earlier laws under which any imprisonment − even for a day − automatically cancelled the debt. According to Lowe the cost of imprisoning a debtor (apart from his maintenance there) was fifteen shillings, and that of the 4,438 persons imprisoned by the county courts in 1874, just under a half were committed for amounts of £2 and above; the remainder were imprisoned for sums of less than £2 − twenty-three persons being

72 32 & 33 Vict., c.62, which abolished imprisonment for debt and provided for the more effective punishment of fraudulent debtors; 32 & 33 Vict., c.71, which was a major overhaul of bankruptcy law and administration, and 32 & 33 Vict., c.83, a consolidating measure.

73 West Sussex Record Office, QAP/5/W13: letter from secretary of state, 7 February 1870. The Webbs are therefore inaccurate when they state that after the 1869 Act debtors were treated in the same way as ordinary criminal offenders (see *English Prisons Under Local Government*, p. 195).

74 See s.4, sub-sections 1-6 of the 1869 Debtors Act.

75 S.5.

76 Robert Lowe (1811-92), later Viscount Sherbrooke, settled in Australia in 1842, becoming a member of the legislative council for New South Wales the following year. In this office he was instrumental in securing the abolition of imprisonment for debt. On his return to England he became a leader-writer for *The Times* and (in 1852) MP for Kidderminster.

committed for debts of between one and five shillings.[77]

Despite such criticisms, and the many reasons why further reform may have been desirable, the committal figures clearly indicate the effectiveness of legal changes in reducing imprisonment for debt. As can be seen from Table 11.3, the numbers of persons imprisoned for debt or on civil process declined sharply from 8 per cent of committals in 1867 to 3.1 per cent of committals in 1877. The trend is all the more marked when these figures are considered against the background of an increase in the population of the country and in the volume of trade.

The general consequences for prison administration of the reduction in the prison population of the proportion of debtors were such that in 1862 the debtors' gaol, the Queen's Prison, closed,[78] subsequently becoming a military prison and then a discharge depot for the convict service; it was demolished in 1868.[79] Despite the contribution which the 'Bench' and the other debtors' prisons made to literature, and the place which they established in the popular consciousness, few can have regretted their passing.

Prison discipline

Reformatory or punitive?

After 1850 the reformatory objective in penal policy underwent an almost total eclipse. Some commentators, such as Frederic Hill, doubted whether prisons *could* be reformatory;[80] but others, particularly during the 1860s, wondered whether they should aim to be reformatory. Jebb, pragmatic as ever, answered that imprisonment was both reformatory and punitive:

> There is very little difference of opinion concerning these two objects of prison discipline; as far as my experience goes, the only difficulty that occurs in the consideration of the subject is the due proportion in which these two elements should be administered.

And even the difficulty of proportion could be resolved by giving different objectives to different lengths of sentence:

> for short periods of imprisonment you should look more to the deterring influence of the punishment, and ... the object of reforming prisoners arises when they are in custody for a sufficient time to give an opportunity of reforming them.[81]

77 'Have we Abolished Imprisonment for Debt?', *Fortnightly Review* (March 1877), XXVII, pp. 311, 314.
78 By 25 & 26 Vict., c.104.
79 See the *Illustrated London News* (14 March 1868), LII, p. 262.
80 See pp. 260-1, above.
81 *Select Committee on Prison Discipline* (Grey Committee), Minutes of Evidence, PP, 1850, XVII, 1, 24, q. 298.

He maintained this opinion throughout his career, and told the Carnarvon Committee that 'no one can hope to reform during very short periods, and if you fail to deter, you miss both the objects of a sentence'.[82] But this was his view only of sentences of imprisonment: with penal servitude it was right and possible to attempt reformation.[83]

Whether punishment or reformation should have precedence was a matter which sorely vexed the Carnarvon Committee. John Perry, whose response to their questions patently riled the committee, insisted that reformation should have first place; and as for deterrence he contended that

> if it were possible to reform a man without inflicting pain, I should conceive it to be our duty to do so; but that as pain is necessary to produce reformation in the present constitution of the human character, pain must be inflicted; but we do not do it for the purpose of inflicting punishment, but to make punishment a means of improving the prisoner.[84]

According to Sir Walter Crofton, chairman of the Board of Directors of Irish Convict Prisons between 1854 and 1862, the penal element in imprisonment had become all the more essential since the establishment of juvenile reformatories. Having done what was possible to train the young offender and to prevent crime it was necessary to be all the more severe with those who still offended. Indeed, he was quite satisfied that 'the managers of reformatory schools would consider their hands strengthened by its being known that pursuing a course of crime would lead to really stringent punishment . . .'.[85]

The weakness of the reformatory cause was shown by the quality of evidence given to the Carnarvon Committee, the calibre of its advocates and the temper with which the committee received their views.[86] The committee's recommendations were entirely in keeping with their proceedings, and the thoroughness with which they rejected the primacy of reformatory objectives, and emphasised the need for deterrence and behaviourist inducements in penal régimes, set firm the direction of penal policy and administration for the thirty years which followed. Reformatory influence, they fully admitted to be

> a necessary part of a sound penal system, but they are satisfied that, in the interests of society and the criminal himself, it is essential

82 Carnarvon Committee, *op. cit.*, Minutes of Evidence, PP, 1863, IX, 5, 140.
83 *Ibid.*, 146; see pp. 396-429, *passim*, below.
84 *Ibid.*, 100.
85 *Ibid.*, 327.
86 Their explicit and almost total rejection of the penological views of the inspectors dealt a heavy blow to the inspectors' standing with government and their authority with the magistracy.

that the other means employed for the reformation of offenders should always be accompanied by due and effective punishment. . . .

They also believe that the inefficiency of the present system of administering the law in ordinary prisons is shown by the large proportion of prisoners who, after undergoing a period of confinement, are again committed to prison under fresh sentences. . . .

The Committee, whilst they are compelled to admit that the reformation of individual character by any known process of prison discipline is frequently doubtful, believe that the majority of prisoners are, within certain limits open to the influences of encouragement and reward.[87]

These views were embodied in the 1865 Prison Act[88] and had consequences for all aspects of life in prison, which was systematically put on a footing as austere and vexatious as possible. Hard labour and separate confinement were the two devices most central to these ends.

Penal versus productive labour

By and large the inspectorate favoured productive labour, which they considered had beneficial moral effects. Frederic Hill described penal labour as 'utterly worthless, and must tend strongly to confirm rather than to remove that dislike of labour which is one of the chief causes of crimes against property'.[89] John Perry was also a staunch opponent of punitive labour, and diplomatically but determinedly persisted in his opinion long after the Carnarvon Committee had pronounced on the issue.[90] Herbert Voules was of a similar mind, being particularly opposed to the crank, and scornfully drew attention to such bizarre versions of

87 Carnarvon Committee, *op. cit.*, 12.
88 28 & 29 Vict., c.126.
89 *Fifteenth Report of the Inspectors of Prisons (Northern and Eastern District)*, PP, 1850, XXVIII, 291.
90 As a central government official Perry could not properly argue against established policy, so he resorted to the ploy of citing sections of the annual reports of governors favourable to his own views. He thus drew attention to the 1868 report of the governor of Bedford prison, which noted the steady increase in profits from £350 in 1864 to £600 in 1868 and which lamented, 'But the operation of the new Prisons Act, rendering the labour of the prisoners more penal and consequently less remunerative, will hereafter affect materially the pecuniary advantage hitherto derived from this source of employment . . .' (*Thirty-third Report of the Inspectors of Prisons (Southern District)*, PP, 1868-9, XXIX, 1, 13). The report of the governor of Shrewsbury prison reinforced this point. Referring to those prisoners serving over three months, who were allowed under the 1865 Act to engage in productive labour, the governor said that because of their employment in this fashion punishments were almost unknown and that scarcely any re-convictions had as yet occurred among them (*ibid.*, 170).

penal employment as the separation of black and white oats.[91] Even
W.J. Williams, who was not opposed to the use of the treadwheel, crank
and other forms of unproductive hard labour during short sentences,
thought that from those serving longer sentences only a limited amount
of hard labour should be required, 'the residue of their time being
devoted to moral and religious training'.[92] Alone of the inspectors Sir
John Kincaid had an uncritical belief in the value of penal labour[93] and
one witness told the Carnarvon Committee that because the prison
inspectors had 'set their faces against it entirely as an irritating and
useless labour ... crank labour had been discountenanced so entirely,
that it is scarcely practised in any prison in England'.[94]

All this was changed by the Carnarvon Committee, whose recommendations aimed to revive the crank and the treadwheel and added
only shot-drill as suitable penal labour, in the belief that industrial
labour 'is so much less penal, irksome, and fatiguing that it can only be
classed under the head of light labour'.[95] It is quite clear that they had
thoroughly taken to heart Jebb's aphorism that 'The labour that is most
productive, as far as the county rates are concerned, is that which will
keep a man out of prison ...'.[96] The home secretary, Sir George Grey,
refused to limit hard labour to the severe forms recommended by the
Carnarvon Committee, but was unable himself to propose a satisfactory
alternative definition[97] and so listed acceptable forms of hard labour in
the Act and gave the magistrates power, in consultation with the home
secretary, to introduce others.[98]

The cause of productive labour in prisons lay dormant for a generation, but such were the financial benefits that it was never totally
abandoned. Encouraged by the observations of a new set of inspectors[99]

91 This was at Wisbech county house of correction. Three pints of separated
    oats were considered a day's work (*Seventeenth Report of the Inspectors of
    Prisons (Northern and Eastern District)*, PP, 1852-3, PP, LII, 1, 14).
92 *Fifteenth Report of the Inspectors of Prisons (Home District)*, PP, 1850,
    XXVIII, 1, v-vi.
93 See his *Twenty-second Report of the Inspectors of Prisons (Scotland)*, PP,
    1857, Sess. 1, VII, 505, 8.
94 Carnarvon Committee, *op. cit.*, Minutes of Evidence, 147. The witness was
    William Musson of Leicester gaol.
95 *Ibid.*, 7. The committee classified oakum-picking as intermediate labour.
96 *Ibid.*, 146.
97 *Hansard* (Third Series), CLXXVII, col. 215.
98 See s.19 of the 1865 Prison Act (28 & 29 Vict., c.126). To the crank, wheel
    and shot-drill were added the capstan and stone-breaking. Oakum-picking
    was not acceptable to the home secretary as a form of first-class labour
    (PRO HO 158/2/39: circular to quarter sessions, 9 December 1865).
99 See Henry Briscoe's *Thirty-eighth Report of the Inspectors of Prisons
    (Southern District)*, PP, 1874, XXIX, 1, vii-viii. His attack on the hard labour
    provisions of the 1865 Act was quite direct:

some magistrates in the 1870s used their remaining discretion and leeway[100] to maintain and reintroduce various forms of money-making labour.[101] On the eve of nationalisation so extensive was industrial production in some prisons that travelling salesmen and even agents in foreign countries were employed to market their goods.[102] But it was not until after nationalisation that the introduction of a four-stage system of discipline, promotion through which was earned partly by work, again gave productive labour a central place in prison life.[103]

Separation

The separate system won the strong approval of the Grey Committee of 1850, who thought it 'more efficient than any other system which has yet been tried, both in deterring from crime and in promoting reformation'.[104] In the years that followed the system was more and more widely adopted. As has been noted, magistrates were urged to extend its benefits even to untried prisoners, and the system was made more acceptable by the abandonment of some of its more ridiculous and

---

By this rule the hands of the gaol authorities are tied, and instances are of daily occurrence where the services of various tradesmen, tailors, shoemakers, carpenters, etc. are much required for prison use and would be of great value in saving expense, if not in making money, but the authorities are precluded from availing themselves of such labour. . . . Prison labour of a remunerative kind might be made sufficiently penal by enforcing daily task-work in the performance of the several trades.

Briscoe went on to recommend the practice of giving prisoners a pecuniary interest in their work. He returned to this theme in his *Fortieth Report* (PP, 1876, XXXV, 1, vii).

---

100 By rule 34 of the Regulations for the Government of Prisons, annexed to the 1865 Act, the justices could put a prisoner to hard labour of the second class after he had served three months of his sentence or if his sentence did not exceed fourteen days. Second-class hard labour was defined as any form of bodily labour apart from first-class labour 'as may be appointed by the Justices in Sessions assembled with the Approval of the Secretary of State' (28 & 29 Vict., c.126, s.19).

101 At Lewes prison the justices decided to introduce industrial labour in place of the crank in April 1873. The home secretary gave his approval to this change the following month (East Sussex Record Office, QAP/2/37/E16).

102 S. and B. Webb, *English Prisons Under Local Government*, p. 197. See also R.B. Orr's thesis, 'In Durance Vile', p. 231, for comments on the profit-making at pre-nationalisation Holloway, and J.H. Turner, *The Annals of Wakefield House of Correction*, pp. 242-4, for a discussion of the Wakefield magistrates' attitude to penal labour.

103 *First Report of the Commissioners of Prisons*, PP, 1878, XLII, 1, 8. The payment to prisoners of a part of the profits of their labour had been forbidden by 2 & 3 Vict., c.56, s.8; only prisoners committed in custody for trial who were subsequently acquitted might be allowed such payments for work performed whilst on remand.

104 Grey Committee, *op. cit.*, 1, v.

inhumane features, such as stalled chapels and masks, and by a recognition that it should not be applied to the sick.[105] But régimes which permitted the association of prisoners were not easily or swiftly eliminated. Even as late as 1863, Cold Bath Fields, with upwards of 1,600 prisoners, still adhered to the silent rather than the separate system. Indeed, the classified association of Peel's Act of 1823 continued to be followed at the important county gaol at Maidstone.[106] Besides these large establishments, associated régimes were maintained at many small prisons throughout the country. Voules did report in 1858 that with only two exceptions all the English counties had either wholly or partly adopted the separate system. This statement was slightly misleading, however, since one of the most important counties – Middlesex – still remained outside the fold and, moreover, the formula 'wholly or partly' covered a multitude of adaptations and evasions. Further, only one prison in eight Welsh counties was equipped for separate confinement. This was the county gaol of Merionethshire, but although separate cells were available 'the prisoners there, as in the other prisons in Wales, are exposed to all the evil influences inseparable from unrestricted association in a gaol'.[107] Failure to adopt the separate system was not, as the inspectors seemed to imply, always a matter of sloth or indifference on the part of the magistrates. Many quarter sessions continued to resent the expense of the building alterations required to effect separation; whilst others worried about its possible ill-effects and were sceptical about its efficacy. Although *The Times*, a staunch opponent of separation, gradually switched its interest from the local prisons to the convict service, pamphleteers such as Charles Measor kept up the attack:

> Except as affording the initiatory means of prison training and forming the first step in the ladder of ascension, by self-control and exertion, I entertain the settled conviction that separate confinement is useless, if not worse; that the reformatory effects attributed to it are a delusion, and that, instead of softening the heart, its permanent though frequently unappreciated result is softening of the brain.[108]

105 *Eighteenth Report of the Inspectors of Prisons (Southern and Western District)*, PP, 1852-3, LII, 113, 235; *Nineteenth Report of the Inspectors of Prisons (Northern and Eastern District)*, PP, 1856, XXXIII, 358, 407; *Carnarvon Committee*, *op. cit.*, Minutes of Evidence, p. 219; *Royal Commission on the Condition and Treatment of the Prisoners Confined in Leicester County Gaol and House of Correction*, PP, 1854, XXXIV, 1.
106 *Carnarvon Committee*, *op. cit.*, Minutes of Evidence, pp. 470-1, 430.
107 *Twenty-third Report of the Inspectors of Prisons (Midland District)*, PP, 1859, Sess. I, XI, 1, 5.
108 Measor, *op. cit.*, p. 54.

The separate system had been promoted by Crawford and Russell as a means of reformation, but even its most fervent reformist advocates did not hesitate to point out that it was also happily possessed of marked punitive properties. Burt, the assistant chaplain of Pentonville, recommended prolonged separation as a means of breaking or bending the will of the habitual offender, believing that 'One end to be aimed at in dealing out punishment, is to impress the prisoner with the conviction that there is over him an irresistible power', and that separation was the best means to that end:

> The passions of the criminal by which he is chiefly actuated, are
> usually excessive and malignant. Penal discipline finds the will
> vigorous, but vicious, propelled powerfully, but lawlessly. It is
> this vicious activity that is subjugated by protracted seclusion and
> wholesome discipline . . . the will is . . . subdued . . . bent or broken,
> and the moral character is . . . made plastic by the discipline. . . .
> The will is bent in its direction; it is broken in its resistance to
> virtue, its vicious activity is suppressed only to leave it open to the
> control of better motives.[109]

The Carnarvon Committee heard from several witnesses of the powerful coercive and punitive effects of separation. Voules told of some men who so disliked separate confinement that they would beg to be put on the treadwheel rather than remain in their cells.[110] Musson, the governor of Leicester, where the separate system was rigorously enforced through separate cells and exercise and a stalled chapel and black maria, emphasised that 'the separate system cojoined with the hard labour is a very powerful element'.[111] Jebb advocated separation as the indispensable partner of penal labour in short deterrent sentences.[112] Even William Merry, chairman of the visiting justices at Reading, and whose disciplinary opinions in general were viewed with obvious disfavour by the committee, affirmed how hard it was for prisoners to endure solitude: 'What we call our punishment is a man's being shut up doing nothing; that is the real sting; every hour that they are taken out of their cells is a relaxation or relief.'[113]

Such punitive properties were to the liking of the Carnarvon

---

109 John T. Burt, *Results of the System of Separate Confinement*, p. 81.

110 *Carnarvon Committee, op. cit.*, Minutes of Evidence, 217.

111 *Ibid.*, 197.

112 *Ibid.*, 142.

113 *Ibid.*, 268. Indeed, so beneficially irksome was separation that it was held to be instrumental in the conversion of a Jew, who had asked for a New Testament after he had been locked up, and having read it became a Christian. In Merry's opinion: 'All the argument and all the persuasion upon earth would have had no weight with that man; but the irksomeness of his cell compelled him to do something. If we had put him upon the treadwheel, he would have been a Jew now' (*ibid.*, 273).

Committee and they recommended the universal adoption of the separate system, which they contended 'must now be accepted as the foundation of prison discipline, and that its rigid maintenance is a vital principle to the efficiency of county and borough gaols'.[114] They paid lip-service to the reformatory qualities of separation, but it is clear that its main attraction was its ability to increase the pains of imprisonment. In this they were probably at one with the majority of prison administrators, since it was only at Pentonville under Crawford and Russell, and at a few other prisons such as Gloucester, Petworth and Reading, that separation had been employed mainly for its reformatory rather than its punitive possibilities.

Less-eligibility

Catering as they did for overlapping groups, it was inevitable that the conditions in the workhouses built under the Act of 1834 would frequently be compared with those in prisons. Problems arising from the relationship between the two were raised with both the Grey Committee[115] and the Carnarvon Committee. Major Fulford, the governor of Stafford gaol, told the latter that his prison was superior to the workhouse not only in diet, but also in bedding and general comfort, and that workhouse inmates frequently committed offences in order to be imprisoned.[116] Similar occurrences were described by Edward Shepherd, governor of Wakefield house of correction,[117] and by William Oakley of Taunton gaol. Oakley had compiled a list of the dietaries of forty-six poor-law unions and fifty county gaols, and the comparison between the two was greatly in favour of the gaols.[118] Both Shepherd and Oakley were of the opinion that paupers preferred prison to the harsh treatment which was meted out to them by the poor-law guardians. But not all governors were of one mind on this issue, and not to be outshone by workhouse keepers, Musson, the governor involved in the Leicester gaol scandal of 1853, proudly

114 *Ibid.*, report, 5.
115 Grey Committee, *op. cit.*, Minutes of Evidence, 249-50, 309-10, 508.
116 Carnarvon Committee, *op. cit.*, Minutes of Evidence, 183. Similar evidence had been given by John Field, the chaplain of Reading gaol, to the Grey Committee. See p. 239, above.
117 Carnarvon Committee, *op. cit.*, Minutes of Evidence, 292.
118
　　... on the average of the 50 county gaols, 267 ounces of solid food, and 17 pints of liquid food, is given per week to the prisoners; and in the 46 union workhouses in Somerset, Devon, Dorset, Wilts. and two in Middlesex, the solid food given to adult paupers is 202 ounces, and 16 pints of liquid food (*ibid.*, 341).

　　The convict prisons compared even more favourably with the workhouses: see pp. 417-18, below.

proclaimed that he had succeeded in deterring workhouse offenders and vagrants alike: 'Leicester gaol used to be a red letter gaol, it is a black one now.'[119] A poor-law inspector claimed that offences such as refusing to work and the destruction of workhouse property arose from 'the lenient discipline, liberal dietary and general comforts of the county gaol [which] render [it] a desirable object with these persons'.[120] A prison matron, on the other hand, was sure that the fault lay firmly with the workhouse régimes which meant that female prisoners

> are better off than those women consigned to the tender mercies of the poor-law guardians. They are more cared for, their health is more scrupulously regarded, their food is better, their task-masters are — if we may believe the cruel reports which shame us as Christians and fellow-men and women — more considerate and kind.
>
> Some day, when the Government takes the case in hand, and workhouses as well as prisons are under its surveillance, so 'odious' a comparison may not be drawn: but sad and certain it is that there are, in prison, advantages which are denied to the honest working-classes, who have come at last to the 'House'.[121]

John Campbell, a prison surgeon, gave an instance from his own experience to show with what dread the workhouse was viewed:

> An infirm old man had just completed his last sentence. He was without friends, and had no means of support. When about to be discharged he was very abusive. On my inquiring into the cause, he apologised to me for his intemperate language, adding 'But you must allow it is enough to make a man angry when he finds he is to be sent to a union after spending thirty years of his life in prison.[122]

So strongly deterrent was some of the indoor relief offered by the Poor Law that prisons were sometimes used as substitute welfare institutions. In a charitable gesture of doubtful legality insane old men were kept in Lewes prison in 1856 for some months after their discharge date because they were unable to provide for themselves.[123] At the same prison in 1858 a prisoner who was disabled by an abscess was kept in the infirmary for six months after his release date, leaving only when his health was thought to be sufficiently strong for him to journey

119 *Ibid*., 201.
120 *Cit*. William E. Passey, thesis: 'Houses of Correction in England and Wales', p. 95.
121 'A Prison Matron', *Female Life in Prison*, p. 11; see also pp. 100-1.
122 Campbell, *op. cit*., p. 52.
123 East Sussex Record Office, QAP/2/E14: surgeon's report to 1856 Michaelmas Sessions.

to his friends in Somerset.[124]

Despite rising prosperity critical comparisons continued to be drawn between the condition of the free labourer and that of the prisoner. In the mid-1850s, for example, Voules pointed out that in many districts affected by diarrhoea and cholera the prison had escaped the epidemic: 'This immunity can only be ascribed to the attention which is paid to the ventilation and drainage, and to the diet of the prisoners.'[125] But while some commentators had condemned the Poor Law and employers, others condemned the penal reformers. In his scornful 'Model Prisons' article of 1858 Thomas Carlyle asked,

> What sort of reformers and workers are you, that work only on the rotten material? That never think of meddling with the material while it continues sound; that stress it and strain it with new rates and assessments, till once it has given way and declared itself rotten; whereupon you snatch greedily at it, and say, now let us try to do some good upon it![126]

This approach attracted much support in the 1860s and 1870s, in line with the greater moral discrimination shown by the Poor Law administration itself. It is no wonder that Frederic Hill's proposal that prisons should be places of cheerfulness should be condemned as ludicrous by the *Civil Service Gazette*, which asserted that prisoners should be rewarded only by 'the moral satisfaction of working harder than the generality of mankind for their daily bread, and of living upon coarser fare'.[127]

Other components of penal discipline

Religion   Religion, one of the most favoured topics in the 1830s and 1840s, was conspicuously absent from discussions of penal discipline after 1850. Such mention as it was given in inspectors' reports, or in the proceedings of committees of inquiry, was confined almost entirely to technical matters such as the advisability of having stalls in chapels and allowing prisoners to join in responses during services. William Linton, governor of Petworth gaol, suggested to the Carnarvon Committee that for disciplinary reasons the number of visits made to the chapel should be reduced, and this was probably typical of the prevailing attitude towards prison religion.[128] The Carnarvon Committee made no major reference to religion in their report, but two of their

124 *Ibid.*, governor's report to 1858 Midsummer Sessions.
125 *Eighteenth Report of the Inspectors of Prisons (Home District)*, PP, 1856, XXXII, 1, 6.
126 Carlyle, *op. cit.*, p. 75.
127 *Civil Service Gazette*, 19 December 1857, p. 816.
128 Carnarvon Committee, *op. cit.*, Minutes of Evidence, 431-2.

minor recommendations, that instruction should take place only in the evening and that the chaplain's discretion over the issue of books should henceforth be shared with the visiting justices,[129] lowered the standing of the chaplain in the hierarchy of the prison. This demotion was confirmed when the duty previously entrusted to the chaplain to be a check against possible abuses by all prison staff was substantially modified by the requirement in the Prison Act that he should 'communicate with the Gaoler any Abuse or Impropriety in the Prison which may come to his Knowledge, and shall enter the same in his Journal'.[130] So far had religion and the office of chaplain been relegated to a largely ornamental position that by 1870 it was necessary for Henry Briscoe, inspector for the Southern District, to question the restrictions placed upon the chaplain by certain visiting justices;[131] a far cry indeed from the halcyon years of clerical pre-eminence during the 1840s.

Dietaries   Jebb had told the Carnarvon Committee that his recipe for deterrent imprisonment was 'hard labour, hard fare and a hard bed',[132] and the committee devoted much time and effort to the discovery of how best to implement this infelicitous formula. The punitive possibilities of the diet and of the hours and conditions of sleep had long been obvious to some justices, and allegations about inadequate dietaries had occasioned several clashes with the inspectorate.[133] The requirements of less-eligibility constantly preoccupied the justices, and, in any event, a quarter sessions sensitive to ratepayers' grumbles would almost invariably light upon prison food as an item upon which economies might be made. But the Carnarvon Committee had only punishment in mind when they drew attention to 'The low animal natures of too many of the criminal class, and the admitted efficiency of reductions in food in cases of prison offences, which render plain the value of diet as one form of penal correction.'[134] Dr William Guy, the medical superintendent at Millbank, gave the committee clear warning about the dangers of tampering with the dietary, and reminded them that the

129 *Ibid.*, Report, 11 and 12.
130 28 & 29 Vict., c.126, Sch. 1, rule 49; see also Rule 93: 'All Officers of the Prison shall obey the Directions of the Gaoler, subject to the Regulations of this Act. . . .'
131 *Thirty-fourth Report of the Inspectors of Prisons (Southern District)*, PP, 1870, XXXVII, 1, 54.
132 Carnarvon Committee, *op. cit.*, Minutes of Evidence, 135.
133 See, for example, the reference to Carlisle gaol in the *Seventeenth Report of the Inspectors of Prisons (Northern District)*, PP, 1852-3, LII, 265; the reference to Gloucester gaol in the *Twenty-sixth Report of the Inspectors of Prisons (Southern District)*, PP, 1861, XXIX, 1, 22, and the reference to Exeter county gaol in the *Thirty-fourth Report of the Inspectors of Prisons (Southern District)*, PP, 1870, XXXVII, 1, 34.
134 Carnarvon Committee, *op. cit.*, Report, 9.

357

recommended dietary for local prisons was based on that adopted at Millbank after the epidemic, and which was subsequently confirmed to be suitable and safe by experiments carried out at Pentonville.[135] His reference to the epidemic was too pointed prudently to be ignored,[136] so even though they desired to employ food as an instrument of punishment the Carnarvon Committee were vague in their recommendation on dietary scales, observing that they should not be 'in more favourable contrast to the ordinary food of free labourers or the inmates of the workhouse, unless sanitary conditions render it necessary'.[137] For his part Sir George Grey did not think that it was possible to fix an acceptable dietary for all areas of the country and the Prison Act, therefore, largely left control over diet to the justices.

Sleeping arrangements   In the early 1850s, much to the satisfaction of their respective governors, guard-beds[138] were introduced at Carlisle and at Durham county gaols. The Carlisle governor stated that

> As the prisoners thoroughly detest them . . . it is to be hoped they
> will be the means of rendering the prison exceedingly
> uncomfortable; and I should be glad to see all convicted prisoners
> placed upon them for a more lengthened period than one month.[139]

135 *Ibid.*, Minutes of Evidence, 390. A similar observation was made about the convict diet (see p. 418, below).

136 After 1823 the diet was raised: they raised it immediately; medical men were called in, in consequence of the outbreak of those diseases; they took the requisite steps for the treatment of those diseases, and then recommended an improved dietary; which improved dietary, with alterations . . . has continued in existence up to the present time (*ibid.*, 391).

137 *Ibid.*, Report, 9. There had, moreover, been a strong statement on dietaries by a committee the previous year:

> The duty which the authorities have to discharge in respect of the diet of prisoners, seems to us to be strictly analogous to that which they already perform in regard to other matters which involve their health and strength: and just as it would not be thought right to subject the inmates of our prisons to the dirt, overcrowding and defective ventilation to which the majority of them had been subject when they are free, so ought it to be with their food. The quality and amount of it ought to be determined not by the standard of any class of labourers, but by the actual necessities arising out of the prisoners' altered circumstances (*Report of the Committee on the Dietaries of County and Borough Gaols*, PP, 1864, XLIX, 22).

138 Beds of wooden planks used by soldiers on guard duty and in military prisons.

139 *Eighteenth Report of the Inspectors of Prisons (Northern District)*, PP, 1842-3, LII, 361, 432.

The governor of Durham thought this plan 'likely to prove useful as well as deterring',[140] a view endorsed by Sir John Kincaid, inspector for the Northern District, for whom the particular advantage of the beds was that they were possessed of punitive qualities 'without being in the slightest degree detrimental to health'.[141] Herbert Voules, however, claimed that use of the guard-bed was prima facie a breach of Peel's Gaol Act.[142] Despite this doubt about their legality guard-beds were widely used in the 1850s and early 1860s on what was sometimes termed 'the summary side' of the prison (the house of correction) for those committed for offences such as poaching and vagrancy for periods of up to three months.[143]

The Carnarvon Committee heard much evidence favourable to the use of guard-beds. The governor of the Admiralty prison at Lewes reported that the prisoners greatly missed their usual beds: 'they dislike it very much; but I have not the power to order it for more than three days at a time'.[144] Dr Guy was not opposed to use of the beds, and even William Merry, of the supposedly 'soft' Reading gaol, approved of the substitution of the guard-bed for the hammock.[145] Encouraged by this evidence the committee proposed that during short sentences, or the earlier stages of a longer sentence, prisoners should sleep upon planks. This recommendation was embodied in the Prison Act, but its implementation was left entirely to the discretion of the justices.[146]

---

140 *Ibid.*, 434.

141 *Twenty-second Report of the Inspectors of Prisons (Northern District)*, PP, 1857, Sess. 1, VII, 505, 512. Charles Measor thought otherwise:

> I know, from having visited . . . at all hours of the night, how fearful are the cramps and sufferings which result from a continuance of this miscalled 'rest'. . . . I do their Lordships' better feelings . . . no injustice when I say that they cannot have fully considered this fearful suggestion; or when I suggest that they would revolt from its practical effect, could they for one moment realize what a continued punishment of this nature would be to men taken from eight hours' treadwheel, or other hard labour (*op. cit.*, p. 52).

142

> Although I see no hardship in requiring a certain class of prisoners to sleep on the same description of bed as our soldiers use when on guard, the gaol act requires that 'Every prisoner shall be provided with suitable bedding' and the term 'suitable bedding' is clearly defined in the general regulations for prisons which direct that 'The following articles of bedding shall *at least* be always supplied, viz. hammock or bedstead, mattress and pillow, a sufficient number of blankets and coverlet' (*Twenty-third Report of the Inspectors of Prisons (Midland District)*, PP, 1859, Sess. 1, XI, 1, 13).

143 See, for example, evidence of Major A. Fulford, governor of Stafford gaol, to the Carnarvon Committee (*op. cit.*, Minutes of Evidence, 179).

144 *Ibid.*, 263.

145 *Ibid.*, 284.

146 28 & 29 Vict., c.126, Sched. 1, rule 26.

There was no uniform practice regarding the hours of sleep of prisoners, and from time to time there were complaints from the inspectors in this regard. Voules was particularly concerned:

> Some of the prisoners continue to pass far too much time in bed, — a practice in every way most injurious. The prisons in which this system is permitted are generally those in which a large majority of the prisoners are associated throughout the day, without supervision or employment.[147]

In the opinion of the Carnarvon Committee the usual nine and a half to ten hours' sleep exceeded 'the fair allowance due to health, and is injurious both to the prisoners and the prison discipline', and they therefore strongly insisted that a limit of eight hours should be set.[148] This recommendation also was not given the force of law, and policy continued to be determined by the magistrates, but the deliberations of the committee probably influenced many justices, especially since the provision in most prisons of gas lighting by the end of the 1850s made evening work or instruction possible throughout the year.[149]

Rewards and punishments   The balance struck between reformation and repression was directly reflected in the system of rewards and punishments. The Grey Committee of 1850 held the view that as

> a great majority of convicted prisoners are open to the same good motives and good impulses which influence other human beings . . . a system of encouragement to good conduct and endeavours to inspire feelings of self-respect, self-reliance, and hopefulness for the future, which have been tried in some of our largest establishments, ought to be adopted as far as is practicable without impairing the penal and deterring character essential to any system of imprisonment.[150]

No remission of sentence was allowed in local prisons[151] and payment of a portion of the profits of their labour was forbidden, so this 'system of encouragement' usually took the form of a relaxation of discipline in progressive stages. At Wakefield promotion through the stages was determined by the number of marks earned, and the top class with its

---

147 *Eighteenth Report of the Inspectors of Prisons (Northern and Eastern District)*, PP, 1856, XXXIII, 1, 5.
148 Carnarvon Committee, *op. cit.*, Report, 11.
149 See the *Twenty-third Report of the Inspectors of Prisons (Midland District)*, PP, 1859, Sess. 1, XI, 1.
150 Grey Committee, *op. cit.*, v.
151 Though it remained open to magistrates to recommend a prisoner to the home secretary for pardon, this practice appears to have grown much less frequent than in the early part of the century.

more generous diet, extra exercise, letters and other privileges could be reached after nine months' very good conduct.[152] A variation of this scheme at Petworth ensured that time spent in the various stages was affected by the number of previous convictions: for those serving a sentence for a second conviction the time in each stage was doubled, and for those with three convictions it was trebled.[153] The stage system was at this time considered to be of great importance in the organiza- tion of the convict service, and the value of a progressive easement of discipline was represented by Jebb to the Carnarvon Committee.[154] Crofton, whose high reputation in penological matters had been estab- lished through his application of marks and progressive stages to the Irish convict service, took a similar line.[155] Musson of Leicester was, predictably, unhappy at the prospect of any stage system which included rewards, as distinct from an easement of punishment.[156]

As a result of the urgings of Jebb and others the 1865 Act provided for a two-stage system; the first part, based on heavy labour, lasted for three months; the justices were given some discretion over the hours to be worked, and also over promotion to and demotion from the second class.[157] As can be seen from Tables 11.1 and 11.2, however, such a small proportion of sentences exceeded three months that this discretion was of only limited value.

A great diversity remained in prison punishments, both in respect of the amount and the nature of the punishment. Strait-jackets, handcuffs, irons, dark cells, baths, showers and even the brank supplemented the whip and reduction in diet.[158] As late as 1870, the visiting justices at Leeds sought permission from the home secretary to use stocks for refractory women.[159] Flogging was highly favoured for the stubborn:

152 Carnarvon Committee, *op. cit.*, Minutes of Evidence, 292.
153 *Ibid.*, 423-4.
154 *Ibid.*, 143.
155 *Ibid.*, 331.
156 His objection was the old one that it was difficult to be sure that good behaviour meant that a prisoner was reformed: 'A man may be a very good prisoner, as many of the old ones are, and yet not be reformed' (*ibid.*, 200).
157 28 & 29 Vict., c.126, sched. 1, rule 34.
158 The brank (a kind of metal gag) was inflicted on an unruly female at Shrewsbury county gaol in 1860, although its use was subsequently held to be illegal (*Twenty-sixth Report of the Inspectors of Prisons (Midland District)*, PP, 1861, XXIX, 45, 49-50). Dr Guy, of Millbank, recommended the use of a device he called the hobbles on obdurate female prisoners (Carnarvon Committee, *op. cit.*, Minutes of Evidence, 399-400).
159 The inspector objected to their use of the stocks and the magistrates had argued that 'some mechanical means of this nature are indispensable to secure proper discipline and good government in the Gaol . . . but the stocks are not used as a means of punishment'. Correspondence on this matter continued for over two years, but the home secretary refused to yield on the issue (PRO HO 45/9685/A48397/1 and 2). Even after nationalisation the

The most experienced witnesses are unanimous as to the wholesome influence of corporal punishment; some, indeed, have stated, that they have never known it ineffective; and the Committee wish to record their opinion of its great value as one form of disciplinary correction.[160]

The 1865 Act restricted prison punishments to a reduction in the dietary, cellular confinement and corporal chastisement; irons were to be employed only in cases of 'urgent necessity' and their use for periods exceeding twenty-four hours required a magistrates' order.[161] Some breaches of these regulations by justices and governors were reported after 1865, but they were few and far between and, when compared with earlier incidents, of a comparatively minor character.

Assistance for discharged prisoners   Private assistance to discharged prisoners had been given since the earliest days, both through bequests and acts of individual charity, and magistrates had been empowered by Peel's Act of 1823 to make 'moderate' payments to enable destitute prisoners to return to their families or to take up employment.[162] In the 1850s such assistance began to be put on a wider and more systematic footing, with the formation of discharged prisoners' aid societies. These societies, supported by voluntary subscriptions, soon won wide support, being seen as an economical and flexible means of helping to prevent released prisoners from returning to a life of crime. Herbert Voules commended them in his annual reports, noting in 1859 that in Birmingham more than two hundred persons had been assisted in two years for an expenditure of just over £172. In their methods of work the societies were careful to avoid any impression of molly-coddling. They did not, reported Voules,

> bring together under one roof a number of persons of criminal
> habits to be fed and clothed without any effort on their part
> beyond the performance of a certain daily task; the object is
> to place discharged prisoners in a position to maintain themselves
> by honest labour; with this view, if destitute, they are provided
> with food, and placed in lodgings in the cottages of persons of good

---

justices (then a visiting committee) continued to urge use of the stocks (letter of 10 February 1888, *ibid*., A48397/5).

---

160 Carnarvon Committee, *op. cit*., Report, 13. But even with regard to corporal punishment there were considerable variations between prisons, both in the method of its administration and in the number and type of cases in which it was imposed. In May 1861, in a letter to visiting justices, the home secretary expressed disquiet at such a lack of uniformity (PRO HO 158/2/60).

161 28 & 29 Vict., c.126, sched. 1, rules 56-60.

162 4 Geo. IV, c.64, s.39.

character, until work is obtained for them. Clothing and tools are also occasionally given.[163]

In response to the urgings of Voules and others the societies were given official recognition and support in 1862, when legislation was brought in to permit quarter sessions to grant a certificate of recognition to a prisoners' aid society, and to make payments to such a society of up to £2 per head for the assistance of suitable prisoners.[164] This Act further stimulated the development of the societies which, although locally based, also began to assist discharged convicts.[165]

The disciplinary system which grew up in the 1850s and was embodied in the Prison Act of 1865 was almost exclusively deterrent and retributive. This policy was all the easier to apply because many of those offenders whose lapses might be attributed to misfortune had, at least in theory, been removed from the prisons. Even the establishment of philanthropic organisations to aid discharged prisoners was justification for treating all the more harshly those who spurned or abused assistance, and again committed offences. For their own good those whose first time it was in prison should be impressed with its unremitting and painful discipline; those who returned again fully deserved rigorous chastisement.

The Carnarvon Committee were told that as the law stood and was administered in some localities imprisonment was already a very severe punishment. Major Fulford, of Stafford gaol, claimed that

> if I had the means of giving every man who is sentenced to hard labour in Stafford prison the full amount of discipline I am empowered to do by Act of Parliament, for two years, no man alive could bear it: it would kill the strongest man in England.[166]

Yet the committee found even this standard of severity to be inadequate to their purposes. An offender who served time in the 1870s left an account of the degree of harshness which by then had been attained:

> This sentence of four years' imprisonment[167] is said to be the severest punishment, with the exception of death, known in the

---

163 *Twenty-third Report of the Inspectors of Prisons (Midland District)*, PP, 1859, Sess. 1, XI, 1, 6. See also the Midland District reports for 1860, 1861 and 1863.
164 25 & 26 Vict., c.44, ss. 1 and 2. The extent to which the societies had won approval may be gauged from the fact that this Act went through all its readings without debate.
165 See pp. 423-5, below.
166 Carnarvon Committee, *op. cit.*, Minutes of Evidence, 186.
167 Two years' imprisonment was then the maximum to which a person might be sentenced, but it was possible that for a simultaneous second conviction up to another two years could be imposed. This general maximum had been

English law. I have heard on very good authority that a learned judge . . . after passing this sentence upon a man turned to the high sheriff and remarked I have only passed that sentence twice before; in the one case the man died, in the other he went raving mad; and I believe it a sentence that no man can survive and retain his senses.[168]

Citing no less an authority than the lord chief justice in his support, Charles Measor insisted that

In the mode of confinement, and by reason of the differences in diet, labour, and gratuities, punishments of eighteen months or two years, in county gaols have come to be infinitely heavier inflictions than the three or four years' sentences to convict prisons.[169]

By the 1870s the deterrent policy of local prisons was becoming self-defeating, much as overuse of the capital sentence in the eighteenth century had made it impossible properly to discriminate between greater and lesser offences. Severity had reached such a pitch that it could not, without endangering mental or physical health, be increased. Jebb's defence of the less rigorous discipline of penal servitude, which held that its punitive quality arose from its greater length, was open to objection because, allowing for remission, a minimum sentence of penal servitude was three years and nine months. Some commentators saw this difference between a minimum term of penal servitude and maximum sentence of imprisonment as a weakness in the structure of sentencing; others held that the balance of severity between the local and central government prisons was unsatisfactory. One way or the other the contention grew that the different parts played in the criminal justice system by the convict service and the local prisons were in need of reconsideration and adjustment.[170]

---

laid down by the various criminal law consolidation Acts of 1861 (Advisory Council on the Penal System, *Sentences of Imprisonment*, p. 23).

---

168 'One Who Has Tried Them', *Her Majesty's Prisons*, pp. 164-5.

169 Measor, *op. cit.*, p. 10.

170 It is impossible . . . that we can continue so inconsistent a national system of punishment: and its conspicuous discrepancies and anomalies must in some manner be primed and adjusted. If the extremely mild views as to labour and diet advocated for convicts by the Royal Commissioners are to be adopted, the resolutions of the Lord's Committee must be modified when carried out into practice; or if on the other hand punishment is to be made as formidably deterrent as their Lordships suggest upon small offenders, it will be necessary that the larger culprits should in due proportion be compelled to taste the same bitter waters (Measor, *op. cit.*, pp. 10-11).

The condition of the local prisons

Although W.J. Williams told the Grey Committee of 1850 that during his time as a prison inspector some prisons had improved almost beyond recognition,[171] it is quite clear that many of the conditions and practices current in the 1830s persisted right up until the nationalisation of 1877. Among the prison buildings in use in 1850 there were some erected before Peel's 1823 Gaol Act, others built in accordance with that Act, and yet others which followed the separate system provisions of the Prisons Act of 1839.[172] In the pre-1823 buildings even limited classification was frequently difficult,[173] whilst the Peel's Act prisons were equipped with small night cells originally intended for one person, but which in 1850 were frequently used for two or three prisoners.[174]

Overcrowding was particularly a problem in the borough prisons. Newcastle borough gaol is a good example of the type, being described by the inspector as a 'nursery of crime'.[175] Difficulties in maintaining order led the Newcastle authorities to resort to 'unbending severity' in their punishments, including an illegal use of the shower-bath. Even when the authorities enlarged their prisons, committals often overtook the new capacity and, as at Liverpool, instead of being separated as was intended, prisoners were, within a couple of years, once more sleeping three to a cell.[176]

---

171 Grey Committee, *op. cit.*, 31, q. 393.

172 *Ibid.*, p. 3, q. 23.

173 Newgate being the most notorious example of this type (*ibid.*, p. 297, q. 4546).

174 *Ibid.*, p. 86, q. 1173.

175 It was also so poorly constructed that prisoners could communicate quite easily with each other and with their friends outside (see the *Twenty-third Report of the Inspectors of Prisons (Northern District)*, PP, 1857-8, XXIX, 209). In his *Twenty-fourth Report* Sir John Kincaid described one aspect of Newcastle's defective construction:

> Accompanied by the head warder, I was examining a piece of ground between the boundary wall and the end of the prison wings, when all at once, on some understood signal, a regular heavy shower of missiles commenced flying over my head, some from the prison yard, but the greater part from beyond the boundary wall. . . . I picked up one parcel containing a pound of tobacco, and it was written on the cover that a similar quantity would be thrown over on the Saturday following. The missiles thrown from the prison were chiefly pieces of bread, which probably conveyed some communication; 'the shower' lasted about five minutes (PP, 1859, Sess. 1, XI, 213, 264).

176 *Twenty-third Report of the Inspectors of Prisons (Northern District)*, PP, 1857-8, XXIX, 209, 255; *Twenty-first Report of the Inspectors of Prisons (Northern and Eastern District)*, PP, 1857, Sess. 2, XXIII, 1, p. 25. Despite some easing of pressure at the end of the 1860s, Liverpool was again in 1873 reported to be grossly overcrowded (*Thirty-seventh Report of the Inspectors of Prisons (Northern District)*, PP, 1873, XXXII, 337, 387).

The metropolitan prisons were particularly afflicted by the pressure of numbers. In the early 1860s Cold Bath Fields had to squeeze some 1,500 prisoners into 900 cells. The magistrates had not helped matters by deferring improvements, in the hope that a falling trend in the level of commitments at the end of the 1850s would continue. When this optimism proved to be unfounded, the chronic overcrowding which resulted led to a high incidence of punishments.[177] The pressure of numbers at the Middlesex house of detention at Clerkenwell also precipitated a crisis in discipline and control:

> Both officers and prisoners feel the ill-effects of it, and those who at other times are quiet and well-conducted prisoners become talkative both in the chapel and at exercise; the good effects of the system are banished, while the officers, with energies over-taxed, have not the power of checking misconduct, or even seeing that the cells are kept clean and in order and thus things continue for even days after the pressure has passed.[178]

At the opposite extreme the spirit of the law was evaded by the *small* populations of some municipal prisons. In 1865 Perry noted that a woman had been kept for five months in solitary confinement whilst awaiting trial in Helstone borough gaol where for much of this time she was the only inmate.[179] Perry reported many similar cases over a period of at least ten years: Bradninch borough gaol was even worse than Helstone in that it did not even possess a resident officer. These cases demonstrated

> how fruitless is the law which prohibits separate confinement in cells uncertified by an Inspector of Prisons, since it can be and is continually defeated in prisons of the description of that under consideration. In truth this prison and several others attached to small borough jurisdictions should only be kept as lock-up houses for prisoners before they are committed for trial or summarily convicted.[180]

---

177 See the *Twenty-seventh Report of the Inspectors of Prisons (Southern District)*, PP, 1862, XXV, 5, pp. 49-50, and the *Thirtieth Report of the Inspectors of Prisons (Southern District)*, PP, 1865, XXIII, 1, 140.
178 *Ibid.*, 146.
179 *Ibid.*, 55, 74.
180 *Ibid.*, 55. Even where cells were adequate a lack of other facilities often rendered the prison unsuitable. Perry noted that at Buckingham borough gaol

> There are 12 cells for males and one for females, which might easily be brought into conformity with the Prison Act, 1865, but the want of every other appliance for separation and hard labour opposes insurmountable obstacles to conformity, and as the very small number of prisoners would render it unwise to build another prison, and the present

The inspectors were unremitting in their attempts to secure the closure of many of these small prisons throughout the 1850s and 1860s. They raised the issue with the Carnarvon Committee, before which the examination of George Whitehall, the governor of Poole borough gaol, so clearly illustrated the condition of the minor establishments. Whitehall told the committee that his average of prisoners was two, his largest number eleven, and that twice he had had an empty prison for eight days. He received prisoners from the sessions but not the assizes, and no prisoner came to him with a sentence of more than nine months. The full-time staff consisted only of himself and his sister, who acted as matron. Because of this it had been arranged that in emergencies he could call upon the nearby police station to which an alarm bell had been fitted. When Whitehall left the locality the police and matron took charge of the gaol, but when he left the premises for only short periods the prisoners were locked in the yard, which had a twenty-two foot wall, over which he said the prisoners' friends 'did not often' throw tobacco. The dietary was the same as at Dorchester county gaol, but was contracted out to a local innkeeper. Borough magistrates visited once a month; a surgeon visited twice a week and was 'on call'. In violation of the law no chaplain had been appointed, but a local clergyman called voluntarily every Friday. Disciplinary arrangements were as primitive as the staffing. The only means of effecting classification was a debtors' ward, and if it was occupied by debtors then, in violation of Peel's Act, all the other prisoners, tried and untried, felon and misdemeanant, were allowed to mingle.

The justification for keeping this unsatisfactory prison was the cost of sending prisoners the twenty-six miles to Dorchester:

> the cost for the conveyance of two prisoners down there keeps one man in Poole gaol for a month; it costs the borough in six years for the conveyance of 72 men, and their keep down there, £450;

---

one on account of its position does not admit of enlargement, I would strongly advise that the building should cease to be regarded as a gaol and house of correction, and be used only as a lock-up house (*Thirty-first Report of the Inspectors of Prisons (Southern District)*, PP, 1866, XXXVII, I, 25).

In some localities Perry's advice was reversed and lockups were used to hold convicted prisoners. At Walsall convicted prisoners were kept for up to seven days, and at Newcastle-under-Lyme sentences of one and even two months had been served in the lockup. In these borough police cells, convicted prisoners and those being detained on a charge overnight mixed freely and no provision was made for their health or discipline (*Twenty-sixth Report of the Inspectors of Prisons (Midland District)*, PP, 1861, XXIX, 45, 49-50).

whereas for the same term it would have cost them in the borough gaol £172 for 182 men.[181]

Similar descriptions were given to the Carnarvon Committee of Worcester city gaol and Falmouth. In the latter establishment the governor also acted as superintendent of police; the magistrates had appointed a warder (the governor's son) but the town council refused to confirm the appointment and so had never paid him.[182] These glimpses of administration and discipline would not have seemed out of place in the pages of Howard or Neild, and such had been the general improvements in prison administration that the Carnarvon Committee were as firmly struck by that impression as one would be today.[183]

Despite the Act of 1858 some liberty prisons continued to receive debtors as late as 1865.[184] Voules had three in his district — Peterborough, Halifax and Ripon (although Ripon had not actually been used for several years). The persistence of these private gaols and some very small borough and county establishments is quite remarkable. The Carnarvon Committee noted that according to the *Judicial Statistics* for 1862, out of the 193 prisons in England and Wales

there were 63 which, during the entire year, gave admittance to less than 25 prisoners; and that of these there were 22 prisons which received between 11, and more than six; and 27 prisons which received less than six prisoners; or in some cases were absolutely tenantless.[185]

It was only in 1872 that Folliott Powell reported the closure of Hexham borough prison, noting at the same time that two Westmorland county prisons — Appleby and Kendal — were unfit for the reception of prisoners;[186] yet despite his repeated remonstrances these two prisons

181 Carnarvon Committee, *op. cit.*, Minutes of Evidence, 461-7, *passim*.
182 *Ibid.*, 450-87, 488-93, *passim*.
183 They were, for example, very obviously incensed when they heard that the authorities at St Albans gaol had defended their withdrawal of beds from the prison by saying that 'they were afraid of the prisoners breaking them up, and making use of them as weapons against their officers, and for the purposes of effecting their escape' (*ibid.*, 42).
184 The Franchise Prisons Abolition Act of 1858 (21 & 22 Vict., c.22) had closed eight of these establishments: the liberty of Gower prison, Newark liberty prison, Halifax home gaol for the manor of Wakefield, the gaol for the Forest and Forest liberty of Knaresborough, the gaol for the borough and township of Knaresborough (both belonging to the duchy of Lancaster), Sheffield debtors' gaol for the liberty of Hallamshire and Hexham debtors' prison. By schedule 2 of the Prisons Act 1865 the prison for the liberty of Romney Marsh was closed.
185 Carnarvon Committee, *op. cit.*, Report, xv. The number of prisons reported to be *in use* in 1850, 1867 and 1877 are given in Table 11.8.
186 *Thirty-sixth Report of the Inspectors of Prisons (Northern District)*, PP, 1872, XXXI, 169, 175-6. The *Thirty-seventh Report* notes the closure of

continued in use until 1875.[187] In the Southern District there were equally unsuitable prisons at Yarmouth and Sandwich. The latter was an old thorn in the inspector's flesh:

> there are but 14 uncertified male cells in the prison, and the average greatest number of prisoners taken from the greatest number at any one time during each of the preceding five years is 36, showing a deficiency of 22 cells.[188]

And though its closure seemed always to be imminent, Poole borough prison also survived as a family-run concern long enough to be censured in the 1875 report of the inspector.[189]

Since the appointment of the inspectors many of the smaller jurisdictions had contracted with larger authorities, but there were a number of reasons why some authorities were reluctant to follow this course. These might have included the administrative convenience of the local prison or, as at Poole borough prison, the fact that it met the requirements of the jurisdiction more cheaply than would the higher standard of service provided by a contract.[190] Moreover, whilst the various parties were sometimes agreeable in principle to a contract, they were unable to fix terms.[191]

---

poorly constructed prisons at Louth and Kirton in Lincolnshire, and the transfer of prisoners to Lincoln. There were similar developments in other counties (PP, XXXII, 337 *et seq.*).

---

187 Work was then begun on two new prisons. Powell thought this a wasteful plan as the average daily population of the two prisons together was less than fifty and one establishment could have served the whole county (*Thirty-ninth Report of the Inspectors of Prisons (Northern District)*, PP, 1875, XXXVII, 417, 422).

188 *Thirty-ninth Report of the Inspectors of Prisons (Southern District)*, PP, 1875, XXXVII, 1, 7. By the next year Yarmouth had been closed, but Sandwich borough prison continued to operate in an 'inefficient' state (*Fortieth Report of the Inspectors of Prisons (Southern District)*, PP, 1876, XXXV, 1, vii).

189 There was still no male warder to assist the governor, whose wife, as matron, was often left in charge of the establishment. The inspector described this as 'most objectionable' (*Thirty-ninth Report of the Inspectors of Prisons (Southern District)*, op. cit., 8).

190 In the early 1860s the borough magistrates at Falmouth, who wished to contract with the county gaol, sent a great many prisoners there at a cost of £300. The town council was in favour of a contract, but the borough gaol, as long as it was under-staffed, was cheaper than the terms offered by the county. The Home Office eventually took a part in the affair, and refused to pay the fees for those convicted at the sessions and assizes for whom the borough was otherwise liable to the county (Carnarvon Committee, *op. cit.*, Minutes of Evidence, pp. 494-6).

191 In other cases boroughs claimed that they could not afford to contract. This problem seems to have arisen particularly when they had already incurred heavy expenditure in one of the various town improvement schemes which

Local political sentiment also played a significant part in the unwillingness of some of the smaller authorities to contract. Even in the 1860s public administration was still largely decentralised, many of the medium and small towns had little movement of population and a strong sense of local community appears to have sustained mild forms of xenophobia.[192] Sometimes a prison was kept as little more than a legal fiction in order to dignify and ornament the municipality. John Constance, who was governor of a prison that had no inmates, or staff other than himself, told the Carnarvon Committee that New Radnor (which also employed him as serjeant of police and serjeant-at-mace) had contracted with the county two years previously because this appeared to be cheaper than maintaining a local prison. Constance stated that it was 'merely to keep the right in the borough that I am appointed at all'.[193]

The stubbornness that local authorities could display over their prisons probably reached its peak at Abingdon, which had a contract of many years' standing with the county, one of whose gaols was located in the town. An attempt was made as early as 1818 to close this prison, and this course had since then repeatedly been urged by the inspectors, who suggested that much expense might be avoided by sending the prisoners to the county gaol at Reading.[194] The borough did not wish to lose the prestige (and trade) consequent on its being an assize town, but without a prison the court would be moved elsewhere. In 1860 the inspector stepped into an already heated controversy by again pressing the case for closure.[195] A resolution to this effect was promised for the next quarter sessions, and he thought that the prison's days were

---

were common at the time. W. Griffiths, governor of Worcester city gaol, told the Carnarvon Committee that the city had just paid out some £80,000 on water and sewerage and so could afford neither the improvements suggested by the inspectors, nor a contract with the county (*ibid*., 484-5).

---

192 The annual reports of the chaplain to the prisons of East and West Sussex (Lewes and Petworth) from time to time showed hostility towards 'strangers' – prisoners who came from outside the district. (See the reports of the chaplain and the governor of Lewes county gaol and house of correction to the 1856 Michaelmas Quarter Sessions (QAP/2/E4) and to the 1858 Michaelmas Quarter Sessions; also the reports of the chaplain of Petworth prison to the 1867 Michaelmas Sessions (QAP/5/W18) (606) and the 1869 Midsummer Sessions (QAP/5/W18/638) (East and West Sussex County Record Offices).)

193 Carnarvon Committee, *op. cit*., Minutes of Evidence, 468.

194 *Twenty-ninth Report of the Inspectors of Prisons (Southern District)*, PP, 1864, XXVI, 1, 9. Perry (the inspector for the Southern District) made clear that by closing Abingdon the county could save £629 per annum, and that it cost three and a half times more to keep a prisoner at Abingdon than at Reading.

195 *Twenty-fifth Report of the Inspectors of Prisons (Southern District)*, PP, 1860, XXXV, 153, 162.

numbered. However, the borough successfully used the legal rights arising from its contract with the county to keep the gaol open, despite three quarter sessions' resolutions to the contrary.[196] The row over Abingdon's proposed closure even pushed its way into the debates on the 1865 prison bill,[197] and after intensive parliamentary activity the borough succeeded in having the prison omitted from the list of scheduled closures. The inspector returned to the attack in the hope that the more stringent standards of the 1865 Act would of themselves force the borough to relent;[198] but the townspeople proved obstinate and in 1867 with some ingenuity threatened to turn the Act to their own advantage by a writ of mandamus to compel the county justices to make the improvements necessary to bring the prison into conformity with the new Act! Nevertheless, Abingdon was subdued the following year and ceased to be an assize town in 1869.[199]

196 *Twenty-ninth Report, op. cit.*, 9.
197 The member for Devizes had sharp exchanges with both the home secretary and the member for Abingdon (*The Times*, 9 March 1865, 6e, and 10 February 1865, 6c). The matter was raised again in committee (*Select Committee on the Prisons Bill*, Minutes, PP, 1865, XII, 425, 435). Sir George Grey, the home secretary, prevaricated and said that as the justices were themselves divided, and that as the matter was one of expense

> and therefore to be decided by the inhabitants and the magistrates, and as the desire to discontinue it came from another part of the county, I think that the case stands on an entirely different footing from that of the other prisons inserted in the schedule, and which, by the reports of the Prisons Inspectors, are unfit for the reception of prisoners (*The Times*, 14 February 1865, 6c).

198
> It is to be hoped that this prison, which is so universally admitted to be unnecessary and unfit for carrying out any system deserving of the name of discipline, will ere long be abandoned, and that all prisoners of the county will thus be subjected to the salutary influence of the other county prison (*Thirtieth Report of the Inspectors of Prisons (Southern District)*, PP, 1865, XXIII, 1, 21).

199 *Victoria County History*, Berkshire, IV, p. 440. It was found elsewhere that contracts could limit the freedom with which policy decisions were made. In 1866, for instance, the county justices and Lewes town council fell into disagreement over the contract fee. The justices wished to improve the prison, but could not do so unless Lewes paid more for its prisoners. Lewes refused to increase its payment so the proposed alterations had to be abandoned (East Sussex County Record Office, Report of Visiting Justices, Michaelmas Quarter Sessions, 1866, QAP/2/E4).
    At Leicester in the mid-1850s the county declined to accept any prisoners from the badly overcrowded borough gaol because of the prior contract into which they had entered with the Directorate of Convict Prisons (*Twenty-first Report of the Inspectors of Prisons (Southern and Western District)*, PP, 1856, XXXIII, 485, 524). This may, however, simply have been a convenient excuse for the county justices to settle an old score since, in the late 1840s, claiming that they could accommodate them more cheaply

Some county establishments with accommodation to spare welcomed contracts with central government for convicts undergoing the discipline of the first, separate stage of their sentences. Such prisoners were kept apart, and were subject to convict regulations. Overhead costs, and thus the burden on local ratepayers, were reduced by such arrangements.[200] The justices were obliged to accommodate certain central government prisoners without the option of refusal and, not unnaturally, this frequently caused problems and resentment. This unwelcome obligation arose from the Mutiny Act, which authorised the committal of military offenders to civil prisons, where the expense of their upkeep was paid by the War Office.[201] Frequently these prisoners arrived at extremely short notice, or with no warning at all,[202] and in numbers which could be considerable. By the mid-1870s military prisoners had become a major administrative embarrassment in some establishments.[203]

Another type of contracting began in the 1860s, when efficient railway transport made practicable the transfer of inmates from overcrowded metropolitan prisons to the counties. It was only economical to remove those prisoners serving the longer sentences, which meant that many of the more hardened and troublesome prisoners were likely to be sent to the provinces; a possibility which was increased by the quite understandable desire of the metropolitan prisons to be rid of their more difficult charges. Certainly the Cold Bath Fields prisoners, who were removed to Bedfordshire, Northamptonshire and Somerset in the early 1860s, were an especially irksome lot. Taunton gaol received

---

themselves, the borough had caused offence when it had terminated its contract with the county (Grey Committee, *op. cit.*, 68, qs 958-96).

200 After its enlargement in 1847 the West Riding's prison expenses were reduced by a contract with the convict service. Almost a third of the enlarged prison of 1,374 cells were rented.

201 Under s.42 of the 1848 Mutiny Act (11 & 12 Vict., c.11) the military authorities paid 6d. per day for the confinement of their prisoners. In March 1860 this was increased to 1s. per day (Mutiny Act, 23 & 24 Vict., c.9, s.32).

202 The visiting justices at Lewes reported to Midsummer Quarter Sessions in 1858 that there were ten soldiers in the prison, under sentence of courts martial, the longest sentence being 168 days: 'These soldiers have been sent without any previous communication with the Visiting Justices as to the accommodation which could be afforded' (East Sussex County Record Office, QAP/2/E4). In 1859 the chaplain at Petworth gaol had complained of the influx of soldiers (Midsummer and Michaelmas Reports, 1859, West Sussex County Record Office, QAP/5/W18/446 and 451). In April 1859, to help overcome this difficulty, the army requested a weekly return of accommodation from prisons in certain districts (PRO HO 158/2/49).

203 See Table 11.3. On the eve of nationalisation there were 138 military prisoners at Lewes and about 200 civilian prisoners (Chaplain's Report to Michaelmas Quarter Sessions 1876, East Sussex Record Office, QAP/2/E4; *First Report of the Commissioners of Prisons*, PP, 1878, XLII, 24).

its first hundred in 1863,[204] and almost immediately the governor complained that there were too many sickly prisoners among them. In 1864 the Taunton surgeon 'prudently took the precaution of causing 15 prisoners, whose health seemed to be failing to be removed to Cold Bath Fields prison, from whence they with others had been received on contract'.[205] Because of similar difficulties the Bedfordshire justices would not renew their contract with Middlesex, the Bedford governor reporting to the inspector that several Middlesex prisoners

> had committed unprovoked and repeated assaults upon the officers, besides other acts of insubordination, and he congratulates himself that they passed through his prison without inflicting permanent injury upon some or other of the officers.[206]

It can be seen that although amalgamations and contracts offered some solutions to the problems of prison administration after 1850, many difficulties remained. Nevertheless the press of legislation and inspection, and a willingness by the justices to accept higher standards of prison-keeping, ensured that in the decade or so after 1865 improvements, closures and contracts continued to change the condition of the local prisons.[207] One of the most striking features of these developments (as can be seen from Table 11.8) was the reduction by almost one-third of the number of prisons between 1850 and 1877.

---

204 Carnarvon Committee, *op. cit.*, Minutes of Evidence, 344.
205 *Twenty-ninth Report of the Inspectors of Prisons (Southern District)*, PP, 1864, XXVI, 1, 65.
206 *Thirtieth Report of the Inspectors of Prisons (Southern District)*, PP, 1865, XXIII, 1, 14. Provincial dislike of the London prisoners was readily reciprocated: some Londoners complained that the treadwheel labour at Taunton was more severe than at Cold Bath Fields (*Thirty-second Report of the Inspectors of Prisons (Southern District)*, PP, 1867-8, XXXIV, 203, 444). This may not simply have been indolence on their part, since it was clear that many of them were in poor health, to the extent that at Wakefield it was thought that the treadwheel labour might endanger their lives (Turner, *op. cit.*, p. 244).
207 But in the two years immediately prior to nationalisation there was a general halt in building and renovation. Folliott Powell reported that 'Consequent upon the uncertainty that has prevailed during the past year as to whether the County or Borough Prisons would be taken over by Government, very few additions or alterations have been made in the prison accommodation for the Northern District' (*Forty-first Report of the Inspectors of Prisons (Northern District)*, PP, 1877, XLIII, 421, 427). He made similar comments in his next report (*Forty-second Report of the Inspectors of Prisons (Northern District)*, PP, 1878, XLI, 417). Although there were some improvements undertaken in the Southern District, the picture there was similar (*Forty-first Report of the Inspectors of Prisons (Southern District)*, PP, 1877, XLIII, 1).

TABLE 11.8   *The closure of local prisons, 1850-77*

	1850	1867	1877
Number of prisons reported to be in use in the year[1]	187	126	112
Number of prisons closed in the intervening period[2]		68	16
Number of county prisons closed[3]		18	9
Number of borough/town prisons closed[4]		41	6
Number of debtors' prisons closed		7	1
Number of liberty prisons closed		2	0

Source: Abstracted from the *Annual Reports of the Inspectors of Prisons.*

1 The totals for 1850 and 1867 include Lichfield city gaol, which was disused but not discontinued by 1867, and Buckingham which Perry described thus: 'The number of prisoners of both sexes who have been committed to this prison has been only 9. . . . There are twelve cells which are said to have been certified but by whom or at what time, I have never been able to ascertain' (*Report of the Inspector of Prisons (Southern District)*, PP, 1867-8, XXXIV, 236).

2 Some new prisons were opened during these years so the number of prisons reported in use cannot be computed simply by subtracting closures from the previous 'in use' figure.

3 County prisons which were closed were generally situated in those counties which also possessed a large central prison to which, as communications improved, committals could easily be made. In Gloucestershire four county houses of correction were closed between 1850 and 1867, leaving only the main gaol and penitentiary in operation.

4 Twenty-three of the local prisons inspected in 1850 had an annual turnover of fewer than ten prisoners and, as these figures show, it was mainly these small borough gaols which were closed. For example, between 1850 and 1867 seven town prisons were closed in Kent.

Enforcing uniformity in discipline and administration

Convinced of its moral and technical superiority, Crawford and Russell had campaigned with great vigour and with considerable success to ensure nationwide adoption of the separate system. Even when its tendency to cause insanity and its indifferent reformatory results had become obvious, it was argued that should it be adopted throughout the country the system would prove itself since

> no great result can be expected from the separate system until it is universally practised, because I consider one of the chief advantages of the separate system to be, that it will relieve the public from apprehension of employing criminals after they are discharged from prison. At the present time, with the best

intention, a master is afraid to receive into his employment again a prisoner after his discharge from prison, because he has been associated during his imprisonment with persons who could not fail to corrupt him; but if the public were relieved from the apprehension that the man was made worse from being sent to gaol, I think, generally the humane disposition of the public would lead to the man's being employed again by his master.[208]

When separation became a mainly deterrent and punitive rather than a reformatory instrument the demand for uniformity was pressed even more strongly in the belief that justice required that sentences imposed upon offenders, whether reformatory or deterrent in intent, should equally be carried out. Why, it was asked, should a criminal be subjected to a lesser penalty simply because of the policies of local administrators? This was clearly the view of the Grey Committee, who held that Parliament had long been anxious

> to see established such a uniform system of Prison Discipline as would ensure the sentences of Courts of Justice being strictly carried into effect, and which would at the same time tend to improve the morals of convicted persons.[209]

The Carnarvon Committee was of a similar mind. Lack of uniformity in construction, labour, diet and general discipline led, in their opinion, to 'an inequality, uncertainty and inefficiency of punishment, productive of the most prejudicial results'.[210] Failure to achieve uniformity the committee ascribed to 'the different construction placed by the local authorities upon the sentence of hard labour ordered by the court', with regard to which their evidence had shown 'the widest possible differences in the opinions held as to what constitutes hard labour'.[211] Charles Measor held that lack of uniformity in all matters affecting prison construction, administration and discipline meant that 'In no two places does six months or a year's imprisonment mean the same thing; each term of punishment, to know its true signification, requiring to be translated locally . . .'.[212] The inspectors noted the great variation between counties in the matter of prison punishments,[213] a point taken up by the *Civil Service Gazette*, which drew attention in 1853 to the fact that the average imposition of a flogging in England and Wales was

---

208 Perry in evidence to the Grey Committee, *op. cit.*, q. 1735, 120. Sir George Paul of Gloucester had employed similar arguments half a century earlier.
209 *Ibid.*, Report, iii.
210 Carnarvon Committee, *op. cit.*, 3.
211 *Ibid.*, pp. 3, 7.
212 Measor, *op. cit.*, 10.
213 *Twenty-third Report of the Inspectors of Prisons (Southern District)*, PP, 1857-8, XXIX, 1, 73-4.

one per 1,200 inmates, whereas at Leicester gaol the rate was one in 22.[214]

These arguments, which appealed to notions of justice and equity, were backed by more pragmatic fears that criminals would exploit any unevenness in penal administration, by migrating from 'hard' to 'soft' areas in order to commit their offences. In 1839 Rowan and Chadwick had argued that the uneven introduction of a constabulary throughout the country had increased the likelihood of such movements of criminals.

> In respect to the general course of delinquency, for example, it appears that a large proportion of the more pernicious crimes against property in the rural districts is committed by bands of depredators who migrate from the larger towns as from centres; the metropolis being the great centre from which they spread over the country; the chief provincial cities and towns being the subject of complaints as minor centres from whence depredators regularly steal out or make inroads into the adjacent rural districts.[215]

Rowan and Chadwick subscribed to the widely held belief that after the establishment of London's New Police in 1829 there had been an exodus of criminals to the provinces. This was a factor in the reform of borough policing in 1835, commentators argued, which led to a further criminal migration to rural areas, and made necessary the police reforms of 1839. William Merry, chairman of the visiting justices of Reading gaol, told the Carnarvon Committee that so deterrent was his prison that Buckinghamshire magistrates had claimed that all the Berkshire tramps and vagrants were migrating into Buckinghamshire.[216] Whether or not these views were supported by evidence is immaterial: that they were held by policy-makers shows how fears of roving criminals led to calls for greater uniformity. After the country-wide establishment of constabulary forces after 1859 such views developed and became even more influential. Arthur Griffiths, a convict governor, and an inspector under Du Cane, wrote that during the 1860s and 1870s

> It began to be understood . . . that the prisons under local jurisdictions were not always conveniently and economically situated. Crime, with the many facilities offered for rapid locomotion to those who committed it, had ceased to be merely local, and the whole state rather than individual communities ought to be taxed. . . .[217]

---

214 *Civil Service Gazette*, 22 January 1853.
215 *First Report of the Constabulary Force Inspectors*, PP, 1839, XIX, 1, 1-2.
216 Carnarvon Committee, *op. cit.*, Minutes of Evidence, 271.
217 'Prison', in *Encyclopaedia Britannica* (1911), p. 365.

The extreme variation in costs between the local prisons was also a source of great concern, which was particularly taken up by Herbert Voules in his annual reports at the end of the 1850s. The comparisons which he made reflected poorly on the smaller prisons; for instance, the annual cost of maintaining a prisoner at Grantham, which had a daily average of only nine inmates, was £39. 7s. 4d., whereas at Birmingham the cost was £23. 9s. 8d.[218] Ten years later Charles Measor noted even more extreme differences in annual maintenance expenses: £16.17s. 0d. to keep a prisoner in Hull gaol for a year, but £83. 13s. 3d. at Oakham and £114. 3s. 2d. at Alnwick. From these figures he concluded,

> Of the 130 gaols in England and Wales a large number might be advantageously abolished, for the necessity of keeping up a staff at each of them leads to most unnecessary expense, and even then the superior officers cannot be of that class by whom the most perfect discipline can be maintained, or the best prison routine carried out.[219]

On grounds of equity, efficiency and economy the case for further closures and a greater measure of uniformity seemed to be overwhelming, yet witnesses told the Carnarvon Committee that the home secretary had failed fully to take advantage of his existing powers. John Perry disclosed that the power to alter the rules and regulations of the local prisons was rarely exercised 'because the magistrates generally prefer making the rules themselves, and they very often object to the alterations that are made, which leads to very long correspondence'.[220]

---

218 *Twenty-fifth Report of the Inspectors of Prisons (Midland District)*, PP, 1860, XXXV, 229, 278, 356-9.

219 Charles Measor, *The Utilization of the Criminal*, p. 13. The average annual cost of keeping a prisoner in 1869 (as computed from the *Judicial Statistics*) was £24. 14s. 10d. All figures on prison expenditure before nationalisation must, however, be treated with some caution. In their fourth report the prison commissioners explained that under local administration

> The prison expenditure was defrayed by 84 different bodies, who formed the prison authorities, and their treasurers no doubt furnished periodically accounts of the disposal of funds that came into their hands, and among these, in some shape or another, the prison expenditure must have appeared; but these bodies were not bound to any particular and uniform mode of keeping and rendering their accounts. Thus, some showed gross expenditure and some only net, they did not follow a uniform principle as to what should be classed as prison expenditure; such expenditure as was received from funds which did not pass through their hands was often ignored altogether, and the accounts of the different bodies did not run between the same dates. It is not possible to obtain from this source, even if available, any complete information as to the former cost of prisons (*Fourth Report of the Commissioners*, PP, 1881, LI, 501, Appendix 19).

220 Carnarvon Committee, *op. cit.*, Minutes of Evidence, 36.

This account was confirmed by Everest, the principal criminal clerk at the Home Office, who stated that the home secretary did not exercise his power to provide rules where none had been drawn up by the magistrates, largely because of his disinclination 'to do anything which may be, or may be considered to be, distasteful or offensive to the magistrates'.[221] Even where the law was flagrantly being broken by the magistrates little could be done;[222] and in other instances the law was so badly drawn up that its intention could easily be evaded.[223] Evidence of these defects and loopholes led the Carnarvon Committee to conclude that obligatory rules and regulations for prisons should be embodied in a statute; that the Treasury grant should be withheld from all gaols where the rules were not enforced; and that the statutes on the county and borough prisons should be consolidated.[224] What they did not recommend, but what was implicit in their entire report, was that the Home Office itself should be more determined in seeking and securing a greater measure of uniformity.[225]

The recommendations of the Carnarvon Committee were both numerous and far-reaching, and it was a full ten months later that the resultant gaols bill was introduced by Sir George Grey. Grey stated that he was in general agreement with the Carnarvon Committee's recommendations, but believed it to be impossible to obtain absolute uniformity

> unless you subvert the existing system of local administration, which I for one, should be sorry to see superseded in regard to borough and county prisons. . . . You must submit to some

---

221 *Ibid.*, 246.

222 Perry gave the instance of one prison where, over a period of fourteen years, the law was broken by prisoners being put two in a bed. This was continually reported and published but no action was taken by the magistrates. As the law prescribed no penalties for violations the power of the home secretary in these matters was, in effect, null (*ibid.*, 38-9).

223 Perry here referred to the section of the Prisons Act of 1839 which made it necessary for a cell to be certified by the inspector before being used for separate confinement – ostensibly a most valuable and important safeguard. Perry explained that as the Act did not define what length of confinement in the cell constituted separate confinement 'in some prisons, where the cells are not certified the prisoners are really kept as long in them as they are in certified cells' (*ibid.*, 55).

224 The Treasury grant, which covered the entire cost of the food, fuel, clothing and bedding for convicted prisoners, amounted to between one quarter and one third of the total expenses of local prisons. That it might be withheld in whole or in part in order to procure the obedience of the magistrates to the home secretary's directions was suggested to the committee by the principal criminal clerk at the Home Office (*ibid.*, 248).

225 Their comment on the inspection of prisons indicates that they were dissatisfied with the amount of supervision being exercised by the Home Office over the local prisons (Carnarvon Committee, *op. cit.*, Report, xiii).

inequalities and anomalies, and some variety both in the
punishments awarded and the mode in which they are carried
into effect.[226]

There were a number of objections to the bill, centring mainly on its
vagueness and upon the discretionary power which it vested in the
home secretary to make prison rules; it was argued that the measure
should go further to ensure uniformity and that the prison rules should
be a part of the Act.[227] C.B. Adderley, member for North Staffordshire,
urged the House not to listen to local objections against the separate
system:

Any gaol of any size which refused to carry out the [separate]
system was injuring the prison discipline and the beneficial effects
of confinement throughout the country, because such a refusal
would only tend to foster in the minds of criminals that speculation
on uncertainty and that gambling on crime which tended to paralyze
the power of all law.[228]

Other points which emerged in the debate included disapproval of the
appointment of Roman Catholic clergy to prisons and of the omission
of a definition of hard labour, and objections to power being taken
from magistrates to make rules. But on Sir George Grey's promise that
he would be willing during the committee stage to listen to all suggestions for amendment, the bill was given its second reading.[229]

In the event it proved impossible to complete the committee stage
on the bill before the end of the session, and it had, therefore, to be
withdrawn and a new measure submitted the following year. On that
occasion the home secretary showed that he had taken to heart many
of the criticisms of the earlier bill: the prison rules were annexed to the
measure and, although a definition of hard labour had not been provided, examples were given, and the home secretary's approval was
required for any departure therefrom.[230] In addition, the new measure
followed the Carnarvon Committee's proposal and consolidated existing
prison legislation, a task which had not been performed since Peel's
Gaol Act of 1823. Grey also made clear his determination to use the
sanction of withdrawal of the grant-in-aid in order to enforce uniform
adherence to the separate system and the enforcement of hard labour.[231]
Aside from a prolonged (and rather irrelevant) skirmish on the suggested
closure of Abingdon gaol,[232] there was little debate on the bill, detailed

226 *Hansard* (Third Series), CLXXV, 1864, col. 2046.
227 *Ibid.*, cols 2063-4.
228 *Ibid.*, col. 2057.
229 *Ibid.*, cols 2073-88.
230 28 & 29 Vict., c.126, s.19.
231 *Hansard* (Third Series), CLXXVII, cols 214-5.
232 See pp. 370-1, above.

examination being left to a select committee. There, too, it encountered no major difficulties, and so passed into law in July 1865. Grey had been correct, however, when he had told the Commons the previous year that it was impossible to obtain absolute uniformity under a system of local administration. The new Act went further than any previous legislation in placing the visiting justices under the supervision of the Home Office,[233] but it still left substantial powers and initiative in their hands, sufficient indeed to ensure that prison discipline, construction and staffing in the decade that followed fell well short of 'absolute uniformity'.

233 Two provisions, of little practical import, though of some historical significance, should not be passed over. Section 56 of the Act, by formally terminating the distinction between gaols and houses of correction, ended what by this time had become a legal fiction. Since for gaols and houses of correction there was thereby substituted a hybrid institution, known by the generic term 'prison', it has not been strictly correct since 1865 to refer to 'gaols' in England; although both the noun and verb continue to flourish in popular usage. Sheriffs, the failure of whose tussle with the justices for a controlling place in prison administration is described above (pp. 318-21), were finally and indubitably displaced, retaining only certain rights conferred by their responsibilities for debtors, and for executing the capital penalty (ss. 5, 10, 58 and 59).

12 The convict service, 1850-77: policy and régime

Transportation and penal servitude

Removal overseas

The gradual abandonment of transportation from the late 1840s onward was accompanied by doubts, confusion and public controversy. One lesson which had been well learned, and about which there was a wide measure of agreement, was the need to avoid swamping the colony of consignment with convicts: if a colony were to prosper, enough free settlers had to be available to help to establish those institutions, activities and standards of behaviour upon which stability and development depended. It was on the basis of these assumptions that in June 1849 Western Australia was designated as a suitable area for a penal establishment. This was at the colonists' request, since their settlement had not proved successful, being, indeed, 'on the verge of extinction', and they hoped that a convict station might stimulate economic growth.[1] By sending out free emigrants equal in number to the transported convicts it was expected that the colony would be enabled to expand at a pace sufficient to allow it to absorb annually a reasonably large number of convicts. But the discovery of gold in New South Wales and Victoria in 1850 proved a strong counter-attraction to most of those contemplating emigration and the government was faced with the fact that their plans were shaping badly and that the public works prison system would have to be enlarged and adapted to house all but a small proportion of convicts, with the prospect besides of their

---

1 Major-General Sir E.F. Du Cane, 'Lieutenant-Colonel Sir Edmund Yeomans Walcot Henderson', *Royal Engineers Journal* (1 February 1897), p. 4; see also *Correspondence on the Subject of Convict Discipline and Transportation; Despatches from Governor Fitzgerald*, PP, 1849, XLIII, 606 and PP, 1852, XLI, 345.

release in the home country. In the meantime the first party of convicts arrived at Fremantle in June 1850, under the charge of Captain Edmund Henderson, who commanded a small group of Engineers. Those convicts who could not find employment with private individuals or firms were made use of by the government as labourers in road-making and the building industry for the benefit of the settlement. Henderson (who later became chairman of the Directorate of Convict Prisons) was a very capable administrator: as comptroller he had charge of convict discipline as well as public works, in a unified control that precluded the friction and deadlocks occasioned by the separation of these responsibilities in Van Diemen's Land.[2] The home government did not make immoderate demands upon the new depot which was regarded as markedly more successful than other ventures in transportation. Du Cane, who arrived in Western Australia as a subaltern in December 1851, and served there for four years, became strongly convinced of the benefits of well regulated transportation as a result of his experience:

> Considered as a penal system, transportation, as carried on to Western Australia, was undoubtedly very successful, for a very large proportion of men, who would most likely have drifted back into crime in England, became peaceful and law-abiding citizens.[3]

Yielding to pressure from the colonists the government finally terminated transportation to Van Diemen's Land in 1853,[4] but the introduction of penal servitude during the same year meant that the only convicts thenceforward transported were those whose sentence exceeded fourteen years.[5] Besides reducing the numbers sent to Western Australia from an anticipated 2,000-3,000 a year to about 500 a year,[6] the new legislation thus removed the power of selecting only the best elements for transportation. The 1856 Select Committee on Penal Servitude pointed out that this meant that 'the worst and most flagitious class of offenders (some of them, indeed, utterly unfitted for trans-portation under any system) is now sent out instead of the less depraved one as before'. The committee therefore decided: 'it is essential to

2 Du Cane, 'Lieutenant-Colonel Henderson', p. 5.
3 Major-General Sir Edmund Du Cane, 'Early Days in Westralia', *Cornhill Magazine* (May 1897), LXXV old series (no. 2, third series), p. 625.
4 In 1853 a total of 1,480 convicts were shipped to the colony, the last consignment of 207 arriving on 26 May 1853 (*Correspondence on the Subject of Convict Discipline and Transportation*, PP, 1854, LIV, 1, 51). The change in policy was communicated to the governor, Sir William Denison, by the colonial secretary, Sir John Pakington, in December 1852 (*Correspondence on the Subject of Convict Discipline and Transportation*, PP, 1852-3, LXXXII, 1, 105). The Order in Council making Van Diemen's Land a penal colony was revoked on 29 December 1853.
5 16 & 17 Vict., c.99, s.1.
6 Du Cane (1897), *op. cit.*, p. 627.

revert without delay to the previous practice of selection in this respect'.[7] But, according to evidence laid before them, 'a considerable difficulty' had arisen over the wording of the 1853 Act: though persons subject to penal servitude might be kept in any lawful prison in the United Kingdom 'or in any Part of Her Majesty's Dominions beyond the Seas, or in any Port or Harbour thereof',[8] this power in the opinion of the Crown Law Officers was probably rendered nugatory by the uncertainty of any 'power in the colony of dealing with them exactly as persons under sentence of transportation were dealt with'.[9]

As a result of these difficulties the 1857 bill was drafted so as to remove the distinction between transportation and penal servitude. It did so by apparently abolishing the sentence of transportation altogether[10] and at the same time empowering the authorities to treat any person sentenced to penal servitude as though he had been sentenced to transportation. This meant, said the bill, that such persons could be

> conveyed to any Place or Places beyond the Seas to which Offenders under Sentence or Order of Transportation may be conveyed, or to any Place or Places beyond the Seas which may be hereafter appointed . . . and all Acts and Provisions now applicable to and for the Removal and Transportation of Offenders under Sentence or Order of Transportation to and from any Places beyond the Seas, and concerning their Custody, Management and Control . . . and all other Provisions now applicable to and in the Case of Persons under Sentence or Order of Transportation, shall apply to and in the Case of Persons under Sentence or Order of Penal Servitude as if they were Persons under Sentence or Order of Transportation.[11]

In a circular letter to all judges, recorders and the like, on 27 June 1857 (the day after the Act received the Royal Assent) Sir George Grey indicated how it was intended to exercise the discretion given to the home secretary under the new measure either to remove or to confine

---

7 *Report of the Select Committee of the House of Lords Appointed to Inquire into the Provisions and Operation of the Act 16 & 17 Vict., c.99*, PP, 1856, XVII, 561, iv, paras 8-9.

8 16 & 17 Vict., c.99, s.6.

9 1856 *SC, op. cit.*, evidence of Waddington, under-secretary at Home Office, q167. The doubts arose, presumably, from a possible conflict between s.6 of the Act and s.3, which allowed the courts discretion to sentence those liable to transportation for fourteen years or more to transportation *or* penal servitude. It might have been argued, therefore, that if the court's sentence were properly to be executed a person sentenced to penal servitude would have to be treated differently from one sentenced to transportation, whether penal servitude were served at home or abroad.

10 20 & 21 Vict., c.3, s.2: 'After the Commencement of this Act, no Person shall be sentenced to Transportation . . .'.

11 *Ibid.*, s.3.

at home those sentenced to penal servitude. Grey described this as the most important change made by the new Act because it would 'enable the Government to avail itself, to the fullest extent, of facilities which may from time to time exist for removing to a penal settlement abroad convicts sentenced to penal servitude'.[12] All convicts sentenced to penal servitude would, in the separate and public works stages of their sentences, generally be treated alike. From the public works a certain number would be selected for removal to a penal colony; as far as possible this selection would be from those serving more than seven years, and would take place after they had served about half their sentence.[13] Shortly after their arrival in the penal colony the convicts would, by good conduct, become eligible for a ticket-of-leave and, after a further interval of good conduct, to a conditional pardon; persons retained in the home country would undergo a longer term of imprisonment before earning their ticket-of-leave than would those removed abroad. As there was no colony available at the time to receive female convicts, these provisions applied to males only.[14]

From 1857 until 1861 some 1,600 convicts were shipped to Western Australia, 1,200 to Bermuda and 540 to Gibraltar.[15] Following the garrotting scare and fears raised about the release at home of ticket-of-leave men in the winter of 1862-3, the 1863 Royal Commission urged that *all* persons sentenced to penal servitude, except those physically or otherwise unfit, should ultimately be sent to Western Australia. This course, they insisted, had advantages both for society and for the criminals.[16] The commissioners' proposal was not acted upon, however, as settlers in the east were agitating against the relegation of convicts to the Western colony, being convinced that they would sooner or later be drawn to the richer side of the continent, attracted thither by the gold finds. Du Cane, in commenting on this campaign some years later, referred to the impossibility of their getting across the then trackless interior and the right of the eastern colonies in any event to make laws forbidding persons who had been prisoners in Western Australia from making their way to any of the other colonies by sea.[17] Although the

---

12 Circular from Sir George Grey, 27 June 1857, addressed to all Judges, Recorders, etc., Appendix I.E. to *Royal Commission on Transportation and Penal Servitude*, PP, 1863 (3190), XXI, 1, 129.

13 Convicts likely to become lunatics or idiots were excluded from selection for Western Australia, as were those too old or infirm to earn a livelihood, the incorrigible or those convicted of bestiality or unnatural crimes (Standing Orders no. 38 (31 March 1857), no. 56 (28 May 1858) and no. 98 (4 August 1863)).

14 *Ibid.*

15 *Reports of the Directors of Convict Prisons* (henceforth *RDCP*), PP, 1861, XXX, 237, v. For a further discussion of Bermuda and Gibraltar, see pp. 393-6, below.

16 1863 *RC, op. cit.*, p. 72, para. 86.4.

17 Du Cane (1897), *op. cit.*, pp. 627-8.

Western Australian colonists *wanted* to continue to receive convicts, the home government decided to discontinue the shipments, giving as its reason the scarcity of long-term prisoners and the dangers arising from their concentration in penal settlements.[18] The last consignment of 451 men was sent out in 1867.[19] In its regulated form, from 1850 onward, transportation or 'removal' as an administrative measure seems to have had much to commend it, and hardly deserves the condemnation almost uniformly meted out to it in general.

The home convict service

When, in 1850, it became clear that transportation to Van Diemen's Land would shortly have to be discontinued, and that only a minority of the convicts could be transported to Western Australia, the Home Office recognised that it must seek a change in the law.[20] The 'change' however, was of a very limited character, since the main measures which were eventually to be combined in the Penal Servitude Act were

18 See the 'Letter from the Colonial Office to Signatories of a Petition from Western Australia Asking that Transportation be Carried On, 6th February 1865', in *Correspondence Relating to the Discontinuance of Transportation*, PP, 1865, XXXVII, 1, 53-4. The political considerations apart, it also seems likely that the home government was influenced by the unfavourable comparison of costs between home imprisonment and removal to Western Australia, a comparison made much of by Jebb in his initial proposals for penal servitude. Information published in 1867 emphasised this point:

> The results of a comparison of the cost of convicts in these distant establishments with the cost of convicts in prisons in this country are important. The net cost of each convict per annum in the convict prisons in England was in 1865 £31.12.4d. . . . in Western Australia the 'actual expenditure' for 1865 cannot be calculated at less than £50 for each convict in confinement, exclusive of the cost of transportation (*Digest and Summary of Information Respecting Prisons in the Colonies in Answer to Circular Despatches of the Secretary of State for the Colonies*, PP, 1867-8, LVII, 557, 48).

19 Between 1861 and 1867 convicts were sent out as follows: 1861, 306; 1862, 782 (of whom 192 were from the closure of the depot at Bermuda and 590 from England); 1863, 727; 1864, 261; 1865, 845; 1866, 410; 1867, 451 (*Report of the Commissioners Appointed to Inquire into the Working of the Penal Servitude Acts*, PP, 1878-9, XXXVII, 1, Appendix no. A.16, 1152).

20 Waddington (1799-1867), permanent under-secretary at the Home Office, in evidence to the 1856 Select Committee on Transportation explained:

> It was considered that when the number who could be transported bore so small a proportion to the number who would probably be sentenced to transportation if the law were not altered, it would be improper to continue passing a sentence which could be carried out in so few instances . . . (PP, 1856, XVII, 1, 3).

A similar point was made very strongly by Earl Grey in a Lords' debate in May 1853 (*Hansard* (Third Series), LXXVII, col. 1).

already in operation. Convicts had been released directly from the hulks, on pardons or (in the case of men on short sentences) on the expiry of their sentences, ever since the hulks had first been established in 1776. This practice had continued over the years, and between 1843 and 1847 3,400 prisoners were thus discharged.[21] By then the system of release in the home country had lost some of the haphazardness of earlier years. The convicts involved were those who because of their poor state of health could not be transported, and the practice had become established of recommending them for pardons when they had served half their sentences.[22] In September 1852 the home secretary issued a directive clarifying arrangements. Only in exceptional circumstances would a mitigation of sentence to allow their release at home be granted to those serving sentences of ten years and over, but

> When the Convict is under Sentence of Transportation for Seven Years only for a crime of no particular atrocity, and he has not been previously convicted, he may be permitted to remain in the Country if his services are likely to be useful on the Public Works, and if his conduct is specially reported on both by the Governor and Chaplain.[23]

Other ingredients which were to be included in penal servitude and which had already been tested were associated labour and the progressive stage system. Convicts on the hulks had been put to labour from the beginning and since 1848 Jebb's reformed system of public works labour, which was preceded by a period of separate confinement, had been in operation at Portland. The progressive stage system, as has already been pointed out,[24] became an integral part of transportation as a result of the directives of Lord Stanley and Sir James Graham in 1842. The practice of remitting a portion of sentence, and of easing the conditions under which a person was transported, was also very well established. Although legal difficulties prevented its operation, the fact that the 1853 Act even allowed removal to the colonies of those sentenced to penal servitude, at the discretion of the convict authorities, narrowed further the distinction between the existing and new arrangements.[25] All the essentials of penal servitude were in full operation considerably before 1853: all that the 1853 Act added to these was the *certainty* of release on licence in this country for all those whose sentences would not, before the passing of the Act, have exceeded fourteen years' transportation. This was no leap in the dark, but rather

21 Lieutenant-Colonel Jebb, 'The Convict Question', p. 19.
22 1856 *SC*, *op. cit*., q18.
23 PRO, HO 22/6, p. 76.
24 See pp. 191-2, above.
25 16 & 17 Vict., c.99, s.6. See pp. 383-4, above, for an account of the legal problems which arose with this provision between 1853 and 1857.

a regularisation and combination of existing measures, renamed and presented in a manner calculated to allay and soothe public anxieties.

Jebb was asked by the home secretary to draw up detailed proposals for the 'new' scheme. These were submitted on 1 November 1852, and printed on 17 November for discussion in cabinet. That the changes were being brought about because of colonial difficulties, rather than through a desire for penal innovation, was made clear by Jebb at the outset:

> I believe the system as it stands, though not yet fully developed, has hitherto fulfilled, both at home and abroad, the different objects which require to be provided for; and it will be much to be regretted if through a change of circumstances in the Colonies, the final disposal of the men, which is one of the main elements on which its success depends, should so far fail as to render necessary any great alteration.[26]

The 'final disposal of the men' at home was in fact the great difficulty, and raised problems of finance for accommodation and maintenance, as well as the politically sensitive matter of public security.[27] Jebb put forward two sets of proposals to meet these difficulties, one based on a calculation of the partial substitution of imprisonment for transportation, and one on complete substitution. The first drew on the recommendation of the 1850 Select Committee on Prison Discipline (the Grey Committee) that district prisons should be established, to which long-term prisoners, having first spent a preliminary period in separate confinement, might be sent. In these prisons the silent rather than the separate system was to be followed and prisoners were to engage in productive labour.[28] Jebb thought that district prisons,

---

26 Jebb, *op. cit.,* p. 3. Jebb also argued that, by 1851, Van Diemen's Land was not as demoralised by the presence of convicts as had been claimed (*ibid.*, pp. 6, 7). Elsewhere, he held that Van Diemen's Land was flourishing (p. 17). He somewhat contradicted this contention that the system, at home and abroad, was meeting its various objects when later he stated that because of the greater frequency of emigration transportation had ceased to have a deterrent character and, indeed, had become a 'boon' to convicts (p. 18).

27 This had been forcibly pointed out to Jebb five years before by Sir James Graham, the home secretary, in a note of 6 February 1847. Jebb had sent him proposals for dealing with the transportation crisis. These included the release of convicts at home on the expiration of sentence. Graham described this as 'the weak part of your plan' and went on

> I fear that the British Public, which has the expense, will lose all the benefit of annual relief to Society from the Transportation or Exile of Criminals, if yearly . . . the Ranks of the Thieves and Cutthroats are to be recruited by public servants from our Hulks and Gaols. The new System may be less expensive; but I doubt whether the Community will gain, if the value of Life and Property is to be considered (Jebb Papers, box 3).

28 *Select Committee on Prison Discipline*, PP, 1850, XVII, iv-v.

maintained by central government, could provide a useful intermediate disposal, bridging the gap between the maximum sentence of imprisonment (three years) and the minimum sentence (seven years) of transportation.[29] He suggested that seven-year transportees and those sentenced to more than one year's imprisonment could be dealt with in this way.[30] Only an extra 700 cells would be needed,[31] and the annual cost of the convict service would actually fall by a substantial amount, chiefly because of the savings achieved in the reduced amount that would be paid to the Australian colonies for maintenance and for transport costs.[32]

Jebb's second set of estimates assumed a total substitution of home imprisonment for transportation and was set out on both minimum and maximum predictions of the numbers of convicts involved. The minimum, which supposed that convicts would serve an average of three and a half years each,[33] required no extra accommodation at all, if Bermuda and Gibraltar continued to be used, and if Western Australia was also run as a public works convict station.[34] The maximum assumed an average term of imprisonment of four years and, in addition to the three overseas convict stations, required an extra 3,220 cells, mainly on the public works. Jebb summarised the estimates as shown in Table 12.1.[35]

29 Few persons beyond those whose duties bring them into immediate connexion with prisons, are aware of the great inequality of sentences passed in the different courts for similar offences; nor is it generally known that so few are sentenced to long terms of imprisonment, and so large a proportionate number to short terms of transportation, thus omitting altogether such an intermediate and lengthened term of imprisonment as would give a more just and proper gradation of punishment for different offences . . . it would appear proper that imprisonment should be carried to its fullest extent before recourse were had to transportation; but, practically, neither the deterring nor the reformatory effects of imprisonment have ever had a trial on a sufficient scale to test their efficiency, excepting in the case of convicts under sentence of transportation. The experience, however, of the last few years carries with it the most conclusive evidence in favour of such a system; and if it were only to avoid the inconvenience and expense of transportation, it is well deserving of attention, especially in an economical point of view . . . (*Fifth Report of the Surveyor-General of Prisons*, PP, 1852-3, LI, 1, 63-4).

30 Jebb, *op. cit.*, p. 8.
31 *Ibid.*, p. 65.
32 *Ibid.*; cf. pp. 5, 10.
33 Jebb thought that it would be reasonable to substitute on average between three and four years' imprisonment for existing sentences of transportation. The average served would be further reduced by deaths and by pardons on medical and other grounds (*ibid.*, p. 12).
34 Jebb emphasised that he was not recommending the establishment of a new penal colony but a public works convict station of the Portland type, located overseas (*ibid.*, p. 16).
35 *Ibid.*, p. 16.

TABLE 12.1   *Comparative cost of transportation, 1852*

	Existing system	Modified system	Discontinuance of transportation	
	15,720 prisoners	Imprisonment for a proportion 16,070 prisoners	Assumed minimum no. of 15,050 male prisoners and 1,200 females including Ireland	Assumed maximum no. of 19,250 male prisoners and 1,200 females including Ireland
Gross estimate	£587,294	£507,284	£324,050	£431,800
Real cost to the country after deducting value of labour[1]	£419,476	£337,366	£175,400	£232,750

1 Although most of the savings which imprisonment showed over transportation were made on transport and colonial costs, much was made of the value to the country of convict labour. From 1849 to 1851 at Portland this had risen from £7,214 to £20,541, and during 1852, Jebb wrote, 'the earnings have exceeded the entire cost of the establishment and there is no reason to doubt that wherever there exists the same facilities of employment, a similar result will be obtained' ('The Convict Question', p. 11).

In the event of imprisonment being substituted completely for transportation, Jebb suggested that the facilities at Woolwich, Portland and Western Australia should be expanded, new prisons provided at Chatham and Plymouth, and a penal station established on Lundy Island or another isolated spot. The last proposal arose from his belief that with free emigration to prosperous colonies becoming more common, transportation had lost much of its terror for criminals and that an overseas establishment such as Norfolk Island, which had been reserved as a place of condign punishment for the most incorrigible convicts, had become ineffective as a deterrent, 'a remote place ... where a criminal and his fate are alike soon forgotten'. Jebb was aware of the likely difficulties involved in supplying and superintending any island penal station but had little doubt that a suitable location could be found and 'an establishment ... formed with discipline of so severe a character as to render it a constant terror to evil-doers'.[36]

There remained the problem of the release of convicts in the home country on the expiry of their sentences. To Jebb 'the disposal of prisoners on their discharge is the only real difficulty of the Convict Question. A sentence expires, and the man must be discharged somewhere'.[37] He was obviously much more uneasy about this than any other part of his proposals. He explained how important it was to assess the character and circumstances of convicts in order to provide for their most appropriate disposal: the very best behaved might be encouraged by a remission of sentence to emigrate to Western Australia or elsewhere on tickets-of-leave;[38] the worst characters might be imprisoned for the whole of their lives, or at least for the full period of their sentences. Between these two extremes he advocated conditional pardoning, encouragement to emigrate and, for some, service in companies of labourers, under military discipline.[39] Although Jebb described the last proposal in some detail, it remained implausible: at the very best it would have been suitable for only a limited number of convicts. Conditional pardoning appeared to be more soundly based, and had indeed already been employed in Barbados, where local convicts were released on tickets-of-leave. According to Sir William Colebrooke, the governor of Barbados:

> The success during the last two years of the Act for granting tickets-of-leave has proved that under a reformatory system of prison discipline, by which incentives to good conduct are held out to prisoners, it is practicable, with the assistance of the magistrates, aided by a rural constabulary, to guard against the renewal of bad habits, to which discharged prisoners are exposed in populous places; and adverting to the difficulties attending the deportation of convicts, arising from the reluctance of other communities to receive them as such, it is *important to have ascertained that they can be corrected and controlled at home, although in many cases their*

36 *Ibid.*, p. 18.
37 *Ibid.*, p. 20.
38 *Ibid.*, p. 16. So convinced was Jebb that transportation had become a benefit rather than a deterrent that he suggested that those choosing to emigrate on tickets-of-leave should be obliged to contribute to the cost of their passage from their earnings.
39 *Ibid.*, p. 20. Jebb held that it would be of great assistance in the operation of the range of disposals if sentencers could classify prisoners according to character and offence. This would affect allocation to the proposed penal station and ultimately, therefore, mode of release. In this regard Jebb emphasised 'the importance of the Secretary of State's receiving more accurate information than at present concerning the characters of convicts and the crimes of which they may have been convicted' (*ibid.*, p. 23).

voluntary emigration may be afterwards encouraged with advantage to themselves and the public.[40]

Jebb saw a partial remission of sentence as being an important inducement to convicts to consent to reasonable conditions being attached to their release, and as a device to ensure their good behaviour during imprisonment. With this provision, and under good management, he considered that only rarely would it be necessary to enforce the whole of a sentence,[41] and he therefore proposed the scale of sentences illustrated in Table 12.2.

TABLE 12.2   *Proposed scale of sentences, 1852*

Sentence of transportation	Ordinary term of imprisonment	Minimum term of imprisonment
7 years	3	2
10 "	4½	2¾
15 "	7	4
20 "	9½	5
Life	11½	6

When the Penal Servitude Bill eventually appeared it fixed the minimum sentence of transportation at fourteen years; although it extended penal servitude to those who would otherwise have received a sentence of less than fourteen years' transportation, it made no reference to the intention to substitute the new sentences for terms of ordinary imprisonment. For sentences of fourteen years and over courts were empowered to impose either transportation or penal servitude according to the scale of equivalents shown in Table 12.3.

Not only were Jebb's original equivalents thought to be excessively lenient, but his suggestions regarding remission were substantially disregarded. The Act did allow the release on licence of those under sentence of transportation or 'any Punishment substituted for Transportation by this Act'.[42] But from the outset it was the intention of the Home Office, whilst granting remission generally to those under sentence of transportation who merited it, only in exceptional cases to

---

40 *Cit. ibid.*, p. 23. The emphasis is probably Jebb's.
41 In only about 2½ to 4 per cent of cases: this was the proportion of those who under the existing system of transportation were sent to the penal colony at Norfolk Island (*ibid.*).
42 16 & 17 Vict., c.99, s.9.

extend it to those sentenced to penal servitude.[43] This policy was adopted because of the likelihood of a hostile public and judicial reaction to sentences, already reduced in length in comparison with transportation, further being diminished through remission,[44] even though with regard to transportation it was recognised that conditional release would probably prove to be a useful disciplinary aid.[45]

TABLE 12.3   *Equivalents for transportation and penal servitude, 1853*

Transportation	Penal servitude
Up to 7 years	4 years
7-10 years	4-6 years
10-15 years	6-8 years
15 years +	8-10 years
Life	Life

43 Waddington's evidence to the 1856 Select Committee (*op. cit.*, PP, 1856, XVII, 1, q20).

44 In a note to Jebb of 26 September 1853, Waddington pressed strongly the case against allowing remission of sentences of penal servitude:

> It appears to me that a general promise of a remission of a portion of these new punishments would be highly injudicious and to speak plainly, an abuse of the Prerogative of the Crown. A general commutation of those sentences of Transportation *which could not be carried out*, was just and necessary. But these new sentences were substituted to obviate that difficulty and were intended to be certain and definite and to be enforced, generally speaking, to their full extent. Why should they not, as well as sentences of Imprisonment with hard labour in a Gaol or House of correction? Why is the Secretary of State to enter into an engagement to interfere with the due course of Law in the one case rather than the other? As to the necessity of such a step for maintaining order and discipline, I cannot admit such a reason for a moment (Jebb Papers, box 3).

Waddington described to the 1856 select committee the very limited number of occasions upon which remission was granted,

> it might happen that there might be cases in which it would be desirable also to let them out before the expiration of their sentence; some upon medical grounds, others for remarkably good conduct, assisting in preserving order and other matters of that sort. . . . It was thought that it might be better in sentences of penal servitude to give that mitigation in the shape of a free pardon (1856 *SC, op. cit.*, 4).

45 Waddington put it thus:

> It was thought that the power of revoking the licence, without assigning any cause whatever, at the pure pleasure of the Crown, would hang *in terrorem* over these unfortunate persons, and would hold out the very

The hulks

Jebb and his colleagues were steadfast in their opinion that the hulks were possessed of 'radical and irremediable disadvantages', and did not waver in a campaign for their discontinuance.[46] In this they were aided by the natural processes of decay and disintegration. By 1855 the Woolwich hulk *Warrior* had become so rotten that it was feared that it might not last until a new prison at Chatham had been completed.[47] It was broken up the following year as soon as the new accommodation was available.[48] The *Defence*, the last hulk to be used in home waters, was destroyed by fire on 14 July 1857.[49]

In 1848 the colonial governors of Bermuda and Gibraltar were given responsibility for their respective convict establishments;[50] their officials took charge of the discipline and accommodation, whilst sappers were responsible for all matters appertaining to works. As in England, staffing was a perennial problem and large numbers of warders had to be disciplined or dismissed because of drunkenness.[51] Whether because of the high rate of turnover, or because the establishment level had been set too low, an insufficient number of staff was available to

---

strongest possible inducement to conduct themselves properly, and to abstain from any violation of the law (*ibid.*).

---

46 *RDCP*, PP, 1854-5, XXV, 33, 311. See also the *Reports* for 1852 (PP, 1852-3, LI, 385, 621 and 655) and 1853 (PP, 1854, XXXIII, 181, 256-7).
47 *RDCP*, PP, 1856, XXXV, 1, 230.
48 *RDCP*, PP, 1857, Sess. 2, XXIII, 65, 349.
49 The convicts were at first transferred to Millbank and then, on 1 September, to temporary accommodation in the Admiralty prison at Lewes. This prison had been a house of correction, and subsequently as a naval institution had been the abode of Russians captured in the Crimean War; it then became a barracks for marines (*Sussex Advertiser*, 8 September 1857). The convicts were moved from Lewes to the new prison at Woking in April 1859.
50 See Chapter 7, above.
51 Local living conditions appear to have aggravated these difficulties. In 1859 it was reported from Bermuda that

The conduct of the officers generally has been satisfactory, although I regret to add six assistant warders have been dismissed for drunkenness and one assistant warder for disgraceful conduct. . . . Three warders and 19 assistant warders have resigned, their places being filled mostly by discharged soldiers of the 26th Regiment. I consider it preferable to fill vacancies in this manner than by persons sent from England, who, being unused to discipline and a warm climate, soon get dissatisfied, many of them are discharged for drunkenness.

The Gibraltar chief of establishment reported similarly: 'I cannot but regret to add that the habit of drinking the cheap and abominable preparations of the place has obtained with some to such an extent as to render it necessary . . . to remove them from the service' (*Annual Reports on the Convict Establishments at Bermuda and Gibraltar*, PP, 1859, Sess. 2, XXII, 233, 9 and 31).

meet the requirements of the two depots.[52] Quarters were scarce and, for a time at least, of poor quality.[53] On Gibraltar there were quarrels between the civil and military authorities over the control of the prisoners,[54] and bitter disputes between the colonial and prison officials over the purpose, state and usefulness of the Bermuda establishment.[55] The convicts seem to have been an especially troublesome lot, there frequently being among them men who had proved to be intractable or mutinous in England,[56] and despite a generous recourse to flogging they fought among themselves and assaulted both the discipline and works staff.[57] As if routine brawling were not enough the English and Irish convicts fought each other in groups, resulting, on one occasion, in a fatality and twenty-four injuries.[58] As in England at the same time,

52 See, for example, the comments made by Griffiths in his first report as comptroller from Gibraltar (*Report on the Convict Establishment at Gibraltar* for 1868, PP, 1870, XXXVIII, 424, 425).

53 *Annual Reports on the Convict Establishments at Bermuda and Gibraltar* for 1859, PP, 1860, XLV, 279, 5; *Papers Relative to the Convict Establishment at Bermuda*, PP, 1860, XLV, 269, 4.

54 *Annual Report on the Convict Establishment at Gibraltar* for 1863, PP, 1864, XL, 475, 3.

55 In 1859 the chaplain and comptroller in Bermuda criticised what they described as the moral contamination and deterioration of the hulks. On his return from leave the colonial governor, who obviously thought that the colony derived substantial benefit from the continued operation of the convict establishment, attacked both men's reports. A small extract indicates the flavour of the dispute:

> As to the enormities and foul sins said to prevail amongst the convicts, it is remarkable that ever since my arrival in the colony in 1854 I do not call to mind a single instance of a charge of that nature being brought. . . . The convicts are remarkably healthy, and the hulks kept in a most remarkable state of cleanliness, which is sufficient proof that the Chaplain's estimate of the sufferings of these unfortunate men is founded on erroneous information (*Papers Relative to the Convict Establishment at Bermuda, op. cit.*, 269, 5).

The following year the quarrel became even more bitter:

> I fear that the Chaplain, being so completely under the influence of some of the most artful of the prisoners, greatly deteriorates his usefulness, and that the nature of his representations is tending to undermine the discipline of the establishment by encouraging prisoners to make groundless complaints (*Report on the Convict Establishment in Bermuda and Gibraltar* for 1860, PP, 1861, XL, 425, 7. See also the *Annual Reports on the Convict Establishments at Bermuda and Gibraltar* for 1859, op. cit., 14).

56 Many of the Chatham mutineers (see pp. 439-40, below) were sent to Gibraltar, including seven described as ringleaders (*Report on the Convict Establishments at Bermuda and Gibraltar* for 1862, PP, 1863, XXXIX, 373, 32).

57 *Annual Reports*, PP, 1859, Sess. 2, XXII, 233, 10.

58 *Annual Reports*, PP, 1860, XLV, 279, 5.

there was dissatisfaction with the legislative changes affecting penal servitude, and the convicts staged a go-slow and strike.[59]

Bermuda was the first of the two stations to be wound up. The criticisms of the hulk officers, and particularly the chaplain, had probably had some effect in Whitehall despite the protestations of the colonial governor. During the latter's absence, moreover, the acting governor had drawn the attention of the Colonial Office to the 'numerous grave irregularities [which] have occurred in this establishment of late years'.[60] It is likely that the familiar prison vices of misusing convict labour and prison stores and equipment were in full bloom, to the profit of both colonial and prison officials. In 1860 the supply of prisoners markedly dwindled and, despite the favour with which a new governor viewed the establishment, the decision was taken to wind it up.[61] In August 1862, the Duke of Newcastle, then colonial secretary, informed the governor of Western Australia that those Bermuda convicts liable to transportation (not all were so liable since some had been sentenced to penal servitude only) were to be sent to Western Australia. This done, the establishment was closed down in the spring of 1863.[62]

For more than a decade Gibraltar continued to go on in the same old way, even though the convict prison, situated in the dockyard which its inmates had helped to build, was pulled down and replaced by what Griffiths, who became comptroller in November 1868, described as 'a long, low two-storied wooden shed of fragile, flimsy appearance'.[63] Apart from fifteen punishment cells this prison, which could accommodate as many as 800 prisoners, had no facilities for separate confinement:

> The wards, when full give only 176 cubic feet per head, the hammocks then almost touching. . . . The water is very impure. . . . The management appears to be as excellent as the building and system will allow. The visitors have visited only eight times in five years.[64]

---

59 *Report on the Convict Establishment in Bermuda and Gibraltar* for 1860, *op. cit.*, 30-2.

60 *Papers Relative to the Convict Establishment at Bermuda*, *op. cit.*, 3.

61 *Report on the Convict Establishments at Bermuda and Gibraltar* for 1861, PP, 1862, XXXVI, 423, 3; PP, 1863, XXXIX, 373, 3. There had been mention of an insufficient supply of convicts in May 1860 (PRO CO 37/176, letter 5401).

62 *Correspondence on Convict Discipline and Transportation*, PP, 1863, XXXIX, 263, 56.

63 Major Arthur Griffiths, *Fifty Years of Public Service*, pp. 143-4.

64 *Digest and Summary of Information Respecting Prisons in the Colonies*, *op. cit.*, p. 63.

The decision not to rebuild in stone underlines the fact that the future of the convict station was already in doubt in the mid-1860s. Numbers remained at around 500, however, and a 'large amount' of convict labour was said still to be required on the military and naval works.[65] Griffiths left in 1870 to take up the deputy governorship of Chatham. Since he was an able, energetic and articulate official, who later became a close colleague of Du Cane, his adverse view of the Gibraltar establishment probably helped to confirm the directors of convict prisons in their opinion that its closure should be speeded up. In the early 1870s numbers began to be run down and no prisoners at all were sent out from England in 1873. In their report for that year the directors of convict prisons were unstinting in their condemnation:

> Gibraltar prison continues to be our only weak point. It seems to exist in order to remind us of the condition of our prisons under the hulk system, and to prove the wisdom of the changes of system and management effected in this country within the last 30 or 40 years. . . .
> The prison itself is hardly better than a hulk. Depravity and demoralization were the result of the associated system in the hulks, and the reports of the superintendents and chaplains in this and former years . . . show that for the same reasons Gibraltar Convict Prison is very far indeed from the standard at which an English prison should be maintained.[66]

The directors deplored the seemingly unavoidable demoralisation produced among the warders by local conditions and concluded that as the accommodation was no longer needed by the convict service 'there can be little doubt that following the similar precedent of Bermuda it should cease to be a station for carrying out sentences of penal servitude'.[67] On 15 May 1875 the remaining 127 English convicts embarked for England, the prison was handed over to the colonial authorities for local use,[68] and the English convict system shed the last vestiges of the hulks.

The convict disciplinary system

Labour

As the very name of the punishment implies, labour was at the heart of penal servitude.[69] Jebb wrote of 'a confiscation of labour in which the

65 *RDCP*, PP, 1871, XXX, 1, 514.
66 *RDCP*, PP, 1874, XXX, 55, x-xi.
67 *Ibid*.
68 *RDCP*, PP, 1876, XXXVII, 1, 587.
69 Jebb said that the term was chosen 'in order to describe the condition under which a convict would work out the main part of his sentence – a condition

Crown has a vested interest', and of convicts being put 'at the mercy and disposal of the Crown'.[70] Labour was thought simultaneously to accomplish a number of desirable objectives: the drudgery and toil of the dockyard or construction site was painful and therefore both retributive and deterrent. Through such work convicts were forced to contribute to their own upkeep by producing tangible benefits for the community; they were at the same time undergoing a form of industrial training. There was, of course, some recognition that in practice not all the objectives of punishment could equally be accomplished, and the directors were apt to chop and change their minds as to the relative importance and benefits of the various results. Both Jebb and Du Cane, in their public pronouncements, gave greater priority to production than to industrial training. Du Cane contrasted public works labour, which he claimed to be of an interesting nature, in the course of which convicts supposedly acquired useful trades, to the 'hard, dull, useless, uninteresting, monotonous labour' of the local prisons, but the greater part of the article in which he made these comments concentrated on the financial advantages which accrued thereby to the public.[71] In later years he did a complete about-turn and poured scorn on the notion that trade-training was an effective penal measure.[72]

The various tasks which Du Cane described as interesting also happened to be of a particularly heavy and demanding nature. These included quarrying, stone-dressing and placing, brick-making, timber-sawing and iron-casting and forging. In fact, not only were quarrying and the dockyard work, in which they were used as little more than beasts of burden, intensely disliked by the convicts but they were,

---

intermediate between imprisonment and a revokable pardon popularly known as a Ticket-of-Leave' ('Memorandum for the Right Honourable Sir George Cornwall Lewis, Bart., etc. etc., on different Questions relative to the Management and Disposal of Convicts, together with Abstracts of Returns, etc. 1860-61, by Sir Joshua Jebb, Chairman of Directors, etc.', *RDCP*, PP, 1861, XXX, 237, xvii).

---

70 *Third Report of the Surveyor-General of Prisons*, PP, 1850, XXIX, 151, 32.
71 Major E.F. Du Cane, *An Account of the Manner in which Sentences of Penal Servitude are Carried Out* (1872), pp. 24-9, *passim*.
72 It is assumed as a general rule that by teaching a prisoner a trade he will be less likely to fall again into crime, and this is apparently founded on the idea that people fall into crime from want of employment or ignorance of any mode of earning their own livelihood. I believe that it is an entire delusion to suppose that this is true of any considerable number of criminals, and, moreover, I believe that it would be rather a misfortune than otherwise if any large number of men who are in the habit of earning their bread by outdoor or unsedentary labour should be tempted to adopt indoor work instead, especially any such as they could be taught in prison (Du Cane, 'The Unavoidable Uselessness of Prison Labour', p. 641).

for the most part, unused to these tasks and prone to accidents.[73] Some, indeed, were unaccustomed to any form of physical labour and could be driven to it only by continual punishments.[74] Some labour was so arduous that even the health of warders at Parkhurst and Dartmoor was damaged simply through their having to be out of doors supervising it.[75] In these circumstances malingering became a major problem, provoking a sweeping and sometimes harsh response from the authorities. At Parkhurst, for instance, even on occasions when boys were recognised to be unfit and in a poor state of health, they were not spared outdoor labour.[76] And when the marks system was introduced it was decreed that only six marks per day could be earned by those in the infirmary: this was sufficient to allow the convict to maintain but not to improve his position with regard to progress through the stages.[77] Medical officers claimed that this had the desired effect on the rate of malingering,[78] as apparently had the use of separate confinement in infirmary cells.[79] John Campbell, a convict prison surgeon for many years, used both galvanism and the cold douche as treatments. He noted in his memoirs that 'Patients suffering from the real disease gladly submit to this or any other remedy likely to benefit them, but malingerers show a great repugnance'.[80] So strong was the determination to reduce to the minimum absences from labour that medicines were administered during meal-breaks.[81] Faced with what was, very probably, a uniformly disbelieving attitude to the claims of all but the most obviously and gravely ill, some prisoners inflicted injuries on themselves in order to escape work. At Chatham alone in 1871 forty-one injuries were said by the medical officer to have been of this kind.[82] Prisoners even sought punishment in order to avoid

---

73 It was reported in 1860 by the medical officer at Portland that many accidents in the quarries occurred because the convicts were unused to the implements (*RDCP*, 1861, XXX, 237, 149).

74 *RDCP*, PP, 1868-9, XXX, 1, 165.

75 *RDCP*, PP, 1854-5, XXV, 33, 88; *RDCP*, PP, 1854, XXXIII, 181, 338.

76 *RDCP*, PP, 1852-3, LI, 384, 86-8.

77 Although this could be increased by a special recommendation of the governor of the prison to the responsible director (Du Cane, *op. cit.* (1872), p. 46). The 1878 Royal Commission on Penal Servitude objected to a convict being denied his full marks simply because illness or physical incapacity prevented his employment at heavy labour, but Du Cane defended the practice on the grounds that 'convicts are so prone to malingering and to indolence' (1878 *RC, op. cit.*, p. xlv).

78 *RDCP*, PP, 1865, XXV, 1, 117-18.

79 *RDCP*, PP, 1868-9, XXX, 1, 184-5.

80 John Campbell, *Thirty Years' Experience of a Medical Officer*, p. 67.

81 This practice was condemned by the Royal Commission in 1878, *op. cit.*, p. xlvii.

82 *RDCP*, PP, 1872, XXXI, 385, 269. In the report for 1878 this number was down to only three – but was referred to as 'self-mutilation'. It is not clear if 'self-mutilation' differed from 'self-injury', but it might be reasonable to

labour. Twelve assaults on officers, during 1877, were committed by men described as 'irreclaimable offenders, probably for the sole purpose of obtaining a skulk in the punishment cells; some prisoners of the class unfit for corporal punishment being so thoroughly depraved that neither reduction of diet nor loss of remission has the slightest deterrent effect'.[83] Disquiet with the degree of severity and the uniformity with which convicts were put to labour was expressed in a muted, but still clear manner, by the 1871 Royal Commission on the Treatment of Treason-Felony Convicts, which recommended periodic weighting as a means of ascertaining which prisoners were too weak to carry out certain tasks. The commission also suggested a degree of individualisation whereby

> after a preliminary stage of probation, a discriminating adjustment of prison labour to the previous habits and individual capacity of prisoners, might not afford a valuable means of rewarding good conduct, and likewise a wholesome reformatory influence on character.[84]

This recommendation failed to gain the acceptance of the directors and labour continued to be exacted uniformly from all convicts except those able to convince the medical authorities of their being too unwell, and a small number of craftsmen whose skills were of particular use to the directorate.[85]

'Invigorating hopes and salutary dreads': the progressive stage system

The difference between the penal philosophy of Crawford and Russell on the one hand and Jebb and his successors on the other is most marked in the system of stages, classes, marks and remission which was an integral part of penal servitude. Crawford and Russell had spurned threats and inducements as being likely to promote hypocrisy and

---

assume that it refers to a more permanent form of self-injury, in which case a direct comparison between the two figures would be misleading (see *Reports of the Officers of Convict Prisons*, PP, 1878-9, XXXV, 1, 66).

83 *Reports of the Officers of Convict Prisons*, PP, 1878, XLIII, 1, 266.
84 *Commission of Inquiry into the Treatment of Treason-Felony Convicts*, PP, 1871, XXXII, 1, para. 30.
85 These included printers and the 1878 Royal Commission strongly objected to the policy of exempting them from penal labour:

> The first object ought to be the infliction, as nearly as may be, of equal punishment; and the mere saving of expense, or the convenience of employing skilled men in their own trade, are not sufficient to justify the entire exemption of a particular class of artisans from the severe penal labour which is undergone by other less fortunate prisoners (1878 *RC, op. cit.*, p. xlvi; *RDCP*, 1871, XXXI, 1, 381).

dissimulation.[86] Yet even while their views were apparently predominant in the convict prisons, their political superiors took a different line with regard to the administration of transportation. The very behaviouristic balancing of rewards and threats which Crawford and Russell so scornfully rejected clearly lay at the heart of Lord Stanley's policy instruction of 25 November 1842:

> We do not . . . contemplate a state of things in which the convict, suffering under the sentence of the law, should ever be excluded from the hope of amending his condition by blameless or meritorious behaviour, or from the fear of enhancing the hardships of it by misconduct. On the contrary, to keep alive an invigorating hope and a salutary dread at every stage of the progress of the prisoner . . . appears to us to be an indispensable part of the discipline to which he should be subjected. Further, we contemplate the necessity of subjecting every convict to successive stages of punishment, decreasing in rigour at each successive step, until he reaches that ultimate stage . . . of a pardon, either absolute or conditional, though not ever entitled to demand the indulgence of right.[87]

This was the formula according to which transportation was organised throughout the 1840s. After the transportation crisis of 1846-8, and with the opening of the public works prisons, the number of stages was reduced to four: separate confinement; associated labour on the public works; a ticket-of-leave in Van Diemen's Land or Western Australia and a conditional or absolute pardon. Under penal servitude there were only three stages — separate confinement, associated labour on public works and (after 1857) release on licence.

The stage system had the theoretical advantage of allowing the various different (and partly contradictory) aims of punishment each to be given different priorities, as Du Cane noted:

> The most practical way of carrying out the . . . three aims of prison punishment, viz: deterrent, reformatory, pecuniary, is to divide the period of punishment into different stages, during one of which the penal or deterrent object should be considered almost exclusively and during the other the reformatory and pecuniary may prevail in various degrees.[88]

The Home Office decision not to allow remission of sentences of penal servitude led Jebb to conclude that successful operation of the

86 See p. 164, above.
87 *Correspondence on Convict Discipline and Transportation*, PP, 1843 (502), XLII, 451. See pp. 191-2, above, for a description of the stage system as applied by Stanley to transportation.
88 Du Cane, *op. cit.* (1872), p. 24.

stage system would have to rest on keeping alive Stanley's 'invigorating hope and salutary dread' *within* each stage. Convicts who could not by good behaviour diminish by a day the period of their confinement had to have offered to them other tangible inducements. Progress through the various stages and the granting of privileges, Jebb decided, should rest on detailed assessment of character and institutional behaviour – 'a combination of the various reasons which bear upon the question in each several instance'.[89] This very imprecise formula greatly enlarged the discretionary power of the prison officials, and to provide a measure of regulation governors were issued with character-books. In these books they recorded their impressions of the convicts' conduct and character, and they referred to them when making decisions about classification, the granting of good behaviour badges and recommendations respecting release. Jebb directed that prisoners should be reminded 'at every opportunity' of the existence of the character-book and of the effect of their behaviour, good or bad, upon the length of their imprisonment.[90]

The award of conduct badges was one of the ways of impressing upon the convicts the fact that they were continually under assessment. Badges, worn upon the uniform, publicly denoted the progress towards the attainment of the ticket-of-leave of every man in the establishment. The satisfactory nature of this system was confirmed to Jebb by the anxiety 'of even the ill-conducted prisoners to regain a lost good-conduct mark and the efforts to keep subsequently clear of the misconduct-book'.[91] Convicts on the public works were divided into three classes, allocation to which, in the first instance, was based on the report sent with the prisoner from Pentonville or Millbank; after that, however, classification was determined by 'conduct, industry and observed character under the discipline of the establishment' and demotion as well as promotion was possible, the higher classes being awarded greater gratuities and privileges.[92]

Despite the advantages of the progressive stage system as applied during these years Jebb remained convinced of the disciplinary benefits of rewarding good behaviour with remission. He told the 1856 select committee: 'if the penal servitude is to be carried out during the whole period of the sentence, I cannot hope ever again to see the high standard of moral discipline maintained which has been established at Portland'.[93] This time his advice was heeded. The 1857 Act therefore provided that sentences of penal servitude should be of the same

---

89 *Fourth Report of the Surveyor-General of Prisons*, PP, 1851 (1419), XXVIII, 213, 62.
90 *Third Report of the Surveyor-General of Prisons, op. cit.*, 26-7.
91 *Ibid.*, 28.
92 *Ibid.*
93 1856 *SC, op. cit.*, 103-4.

length as the former sentence of transportation, with the exception that where a seven-year sentence of transportation might have been passed this could now be as short as three years' penal servitude.[94] This lengthening of sentences made acceptable the systematic granting of remission to those who were of good behaviour. In June 1857, Sir George Grey sent a table (reproduced here as Table 12.4) to judges, recorders and magistrates to indicate the amount of remission which would henceforth normally be granted.

TABLE 12.4   *Remission under the 1857 Penal Servitude Act*

Sentence, penal servitude	Proportion to be undergone		Proportion which may be remitted in case of good conduct
3 years	Five-sixths	= 2 years 6 months	One-sixth
4 years	Four-fifths	= 3 years 3 months	One-fifth
5 years	Ditto	= 4 years	Ditto
6 years	Three-quarters	= 4 years 6 months	One-quarter
7 years	Ditto	= 5 years 3 months	Ditto
8 years	Ditto	= 6 years	Ditto
10 years	Ditto	= 7 years 6 months	Ditto
12 years	Ditto	= 9 years	Ditto
15 years and upwards	Two-thirds		One-third

Source: Taken from Appendix I.E., *Royal Commission on Transportation and Penal Servitude*, PP, 1863 (3190), XXI, 1.

There was a further change in the granting of remissions in 1864. One of the central concerns of the Royal Commission on Penal Servitude of the previous year had, of course, been the supposed ill-effects of the ticket-of-leave system.[95] The commissioners had been impressed by the marks system in operation in Western Australia, and recommended its introduction in a modified form in England. The essence of the system was that

> The amount of remission which a convict would be enabled to earn by industry, would be determined by the number of marks required

94 20 & 21 Vict., c.3, s.2.
95 The 1864 Act, which followed the Royal Commission, increased the minimum sentence of penal servitude from three to five years (seven years in the case of a person previously convicted of an offence punishable by penal servitude).

to gain a day. If three marks were the maximum given for the best day's work, and also the number required to earn one day's remission, a convict who gained the maximum credit every day, from the beginning to the end of his sentence and never incurred a single fine for misconduct, would abridge his punishment by one half. . . .[96]

Since remission of sentence was a matter already within the discretion of the authorities no new legislation was necessary. The directorate followed the recommendations of the Royal Commission in general terms, although not permitting such a great remission of sentence as had been suggested and, less importantly, recording behaviour by means of a greater number of marks, thus enabling a more precise correspondence to be reached between behaviour and the mark granted.[97] The chairman of the directorate, then Lieutenant-Colonel Henderson, outlined the narrowed criterion which would govern a convict's progress:

The broad principle on which we propose to act is that the period of a convict's imprisonment shall be measured by the actual quantity of work which he performs, no remission being granted for 'good conduct', which must be indispensable to entitle him to any reward for his industry, a reward which he will forfeit by misconduct.[98]

That the marks system was concerned with ensuring obedience and productivity, and that reformation was viewed as an incidental benefit, were shown by the directors' observations three years later:

It is difficult, and indeed almost impossible, to express any decided opinion upon the real amount of good conduct effected upon the

96 1863 *RC, op. cit.*, PP, 1863, XXI, 1, 29-30; see also Appendix 18, 260-4.
97 Until the introduction of the marks system the convict's prospects on release in many cases affected the amount of remission granted. His likelihood of obtaining employment and the willingness of his friends to receive him were ascertained by the chaplain and communicated to the directors (see Standing Orders nos 25 (3 February 1855) and 31 (13 December 1855). Shortly after Jebb's death Henderson condemned these inquiries as 'almost useless' and stated

It would not be just to make the liberation of convicts dependent on their being able to give satisfactory references; indeed after the lapse of many years, this would be probably impossible. Neither is it at all desirable that they should be forced or induced to return to their former haunts, to which this system tends (Standing Order no 101, October 1863).

98 *RDCP*, PP, 1864, XXVI, 209, 218. A number of skilled tradesmen were employed as instructing warders 'for the purpose of assisting in the direction, supervision and measurement of the works executed by convict labour'. It was their special duty to record the work actually performed by the convicts for the purpose of allocating marks (Standing Order no. 136, 22 June 1864).

minds of the convicts by the efforts made for their reformation; secluded as they are from the world, they are more parts of a machine than free agents. . . .[99]

Soon after his reception into prison the convict's sentence was represented to him in terms of a number of marks which he had to earn. The maximum number of marks which could be earned each day was eight — 'for steady hard labour, and the full performance of their allotted task'; 'a fair but moderate day's work' earned only six marks. A convict who earned the maximum number of marks throughout his sentence would gain a one-quarter remission of his sentence. No marks could be earned during the separate stage, in the penal class or on second probation, and marks could be forfeited for misconduct; those who lost all their remission marks were liable to be kept in separate confinement during the last six months of their sentences.[100]

The marks system quickly established itself as a powerful disciplinary device. Two years after its introduction the directors described it as 'the true principle of dealing with convicts'.[101] Many governors and other officials were equally fulsome. The chaplain at Chatham reported, for instance, that

increased life and activity are visible in the convicts themselves, attributable to the interest which the men take in perceiving beneficial results from their work under the mark system, which puts into their own hands the means by the full stretch of manly labour to shorten the period of their imprisonment.[102]

The 1878 Royal Commission stated:

That the allotment of marks is no mere form, is shown by the fact that a large number of convicts do not attain the maximum remission of their sentences, that many obtain but a small proportion of that amount, and that in some cases no remission whatever is earned. . . . We need scarcely point out the value of this system, both as an aid to the maintenance of order and discipline, and as a means of inducing the prisoners to acquire habits of steady industry and obedience.[103]

Separation

The separate confinement of prisoners was regarded as the most important part of convict discipline only as long as the Pentonville experiment

---

99 *RDCP*, PP, 1867, XXXVI, 1, 10.
100 Standing Order no. 146: 'Regulations — Mark System', 22 July 1864.
101 *RDCP*, PP, 1866, XXXVIII, 1, 11.
102 *RDCP*, PP, 1867-8, XXXIV, 519, 7.
103 *Report of the Commissioners Appointed to Inquire into the Working of the Penal Servitude Acts*, PP, 1878-9, XXXVII, 1, xxvi-xxvii.

continued under Crawford and Russell; Jebb regarded a period of separation merely as a salutary prelude to association on public works. His view of the matter was well represented in an 1852 statement of William Clay, the governor of Portland:

> I must here state, what has always been my opinion ever since I became a prison officer, that without undergoing the probation of separate confinement where they are subject to discipline and receive instruction convicts could not be brought with good effect into a state of association on public works as established here, and I conceive that the high moral tone and discipline among the prisoners here as it now stands could not have proved so gratifying to myself and all interested in Portland prison without the first stage of probation, — 'separate confinement'.[104]

The directors were, however, convinced that a direct relationship existed between prolonged separation and insanity,[105] and several alterations were therefore put in hand. The separate exercise yards at Pentonville were demolished to allow the convicts to take more vigorous associated but non-communicating exercise; this was followed by reports of an improvement in the health of the prisoners. Even Kingsmill, the Pentonville chaplain, who had not stinted his praise of the old arrangements, welcomed the changes, although he did point out that under the earlier allocation policy debilitated (and therefore by implication unsuitable) prisoners were excluded from Pentonville.[106] In 1859, after much discussion and consultation, the directors decided to remove the stalled chapel.[107] At the same time as the stalls were

104 *RDCP*, PP, 1852-3, LI, 385, 545.
105 In two months of 1852 five cases of mental illness occurred at Pentonville. As a result of this the directors compared the insanity rates of some strictly separate prisons with those at some more moderate prisons. From this comparison they concluded that 'there was an absolute relation between the amount of mental disease and the rigour with which the separate system was carried out' (*RDCP*, PP, 1852-3, LI, 385, 397).
106 *RDCP*, PP, 1852-3, LI, 385, 397.
107 A comparison had been made between Pentonville and some other prisons where stalls had been taken out which had shown that removal of the stalls resulted in a saving of space and an increase in the efficiency with which prisoners could be supervised. Once more there was retrospective criticism of the old system and praise for the new from the prison officials. The directors reported that

> The chaplains and the Governors reported the 'separate stall' system, introduced about seventeen years ago, to have failed altogether in preventing prisoners from communicating with each other, or in affording an effective supervision by the discipline officers. Nevertheless, as the necessity for the change had been combatted by some whose opinions we respected, we have watched for an indication of the result with considerable interest though without doubt or apprehension . . . (*RDCP*, PP, 1860, XXXV, 429, 437).

removed the long-peaked caps or masks which were intended to prevent recognition and communication whilst the prisoners were out of their cells were taken out of use.[108]

Throughout Jebb's chairmanship of the directorate the rigours of the separate system continued to ease. In part this arose simply from the pressure of numbers, which meant that some prisoners spent as little as five months on the separate stage,[109] but there was also a deliberate shift towards less severity. The character of this movement in policy was well exemplified by the observations of Ambrose Sherwin, the new chaplain of Pentonville, just before Jebb's death. Sherwin asked, 'will any amount of severity in treatment secure the desired end? Is punishment, per se, reformative?' He answered his own question with the claim that 'It remains problematical whether severity of regimen is so potential in deterring the convict from a repetition of crime as is supposed'.[110] In the same document (the annual report of the directors) the medical officer of Pentonville reviewed the various easements in the régime which had occurred since 1850, pointing to the consequent improvements in mental health.[111]

Jebb's death in 1863 deprived the convict service of a powerful moderating influence. The Royal Commission on Penal Servitude reported in the midst of an apparent panic of public opinion, and recommended an increase in the punitive and deterrent elements in the discipline of convict prisons. They urged that the period of separate confinement, which had fallen to an average of seven months, should be restored to the full nine months, and that the cellular visitations of trade instructors should cease, as they necessarily mitigated the irksome nature of the discipline.[112] Succeeding reports of the directors showed the impact of these recommendations. The 1863 report (written whilst the commission was still in progress) showed that the full nine-month period of separation had been reinstituted and various changes effected at Millbank (always more lax in its separation than Pentonville) to make separation more complete and deterrent.[113] Even at Dartmoor invalid prison (where association had hitherto been permitted) separation was enforced and special punishment cells were installed.[114] By 1866 William Morrish, governor of Millbank, reported that

> there can be very little doubt but that separate confinement as at present administered is much more deterring than formerly, and

108 *RDCP*, PP, 1860, XXXV, 429, 437.
109 *Select Committee of the House of Lords on Gaol Discipline* (Carnarvon Committee), Evidence, PP, 1863, IX, 31, 378.
110 *RDCP*, PP, 1862, XXIV, 1, 17.
111 *Ibid.*, 29 *et seq*.
112 1863 *RC, op. cit.*, 39-40.
113 *RDCP*, PP, 1864, XXVI, 209, 216.
114 *RDCP*, PP, 1865, XXXVIII, 1, 8.

if it is not associated generally with a higher degree of reformation, it is certainly regarded by all, and especially by the most hardened and habitual offenders, as the most obnoxious element of their imprisonment, and it is especially noticeable in their eagerness to secure the earliest removal to public works.[115]

The Royal Commission of 1878 decided that the directors had achieved the right balance in their use of separation and rejected calls for a prolongation of the period during which it was enforced, with the observation that the existing practice was the result of much experience and that nothing could really be gained by its alteration.[116]

Religion

Religious instruction and exhortation had been another important feature in the disciplinary scheme of Crawford and Russell. After 1850 there was in the convict system an almost total subordination of religious objectives and interests to the concerns of discipline and administration. Kingsmill did attempt to lay claim to some of the chaplain's old moral authority and independence, but he was careful to give full recognition to the over-riding authority of the directors:

> It appears to me especially important that we, who fill the office of chaplains, should place before you our views without reserve; feeling at the same time that whatever opinions we may entertain as regards the discipline and management of the institutions to which we are attached, we are bound to leave the responsibility of judging in your hands, and to give effect in every way to your decisions.[117]

Kingsmill proved himself to be a flexible and temporising subordinate. At one point he held to the penal value of separation, but a few years later agreed to its amelioration.[118] In the year of Kingsmill's

115 *RDCP*, PP, 1867, XXXVI, 1, 46.
116 1878 *RC*, *op. cit.*, xxvii. They also rejected the proposal that convicts should be subject to a period of separate confinement immediately before their release.
117 Even though, somewhat unctuously he continued,

> There can be only one exception to this as a rule, namely, when the direction is such as to violate conscience, or prevent us from the exercise of our ministry in its great and essential features. This has happily never yet been the case, to my knowledge, in the whole service in a single instance (*RDCP*, PP, 1854-5, XXV, 33, 57).

118 He wrote in the 1854 report,

> If the value of separate confinement, in its effect upon the moral condition of prisoners, has been over-rated, I think its use as a penal agency has been as unduly undervalued. No species of imprisonment so

retirement (1860) the chaplain at Portland prison went almost as far in the deprecation of the penal value of religion as it was possible for a chaplain to go. He noted that

> the influences of religion in the minds of the majority of the men are not wholly wanting, but the improvement in the outward character of the prison is rather owing to the wise and encouraging measures taken by the discipline authorities for the comfort and advantage of the men in the system of stages and classes for good conduct, than the influence of religious truth.[119]

This opinion about prison religion provided little challenge or irritation for Jebb and his colleagues: it was religion relegated to an ornamental role and under the ministry of chaplains whose acceptance of the structure of authority avoided conflict and embarrassment. The extent of their retreat into the purely liturgical side of their duties was shown by the recommendation from the 1863 Royal Commission (not a body taken with reformist notions) that chaplains should return to the practice of making frequent private cellular visits to prisoners.[120]

Nevertheless, as part of the tightening up of discipline and security which followed the same Royal Commission, religious observances were further restricted. From July 1864 morning services were shortened to the reading of a few prayers and a piece of scripture, and evening prayers were discontinued.[121] Instead of being conducted in the chapel, these services were held in the prison wings by chaplains or schoolmasters, and apparently lasted no more than twelve minutes. The report of the Portland chaplain in 1865 creates a clear impression that even this shortened time was threatened with further erosion by the secular demands of the institution.[122] The chaplains complied quietly enough with these changes, and only an occasional flicker of dissatisfaction found its way into their written reports in the years that followed. One such complaint in 1878 shows how restricted within the penal system religion had by then become: the chaplain of Chatham lamented the downgrading of what, under Crawford and Russell, had been seen as the essential and central duty of cellular visiting:

> thoroughly punishes the bad, and at the same time so effectually protects the less criminal from contamination and instruction in villainy. My objections, on the ground of severe pressure on the bodily and mental functions . . . apply only in its excess of extension and indiscriminate application, especially in the case of men under such a heavy sentence of transportation (*RDCP*, PP, 1854-5, XXV, 33, 62).

---

119 *RDCP*, PP, 1861, XXX, 237, 440-1.
120 1863 *RC*, *op. cit.*, 49.
121 Standing Order no. 143, 21 July 1864.
122 *RDCP*, PP, 1865, XXV, 1, 115-16.

As has been noticed on former occasions the shortness of the time
during which prisoners can be visited in their cells seems very short
[*sic*] in comparison with the importance of the duty. During the
eight summer months scarcely half an hour each night can be thus
employed. If it were possible to revert to the old system of prisoners
being seen by Chaplains for religious purposes as they are seen by
the Medical Officers for the health of their bodies, it would
considerably increase the opportunities for doing good to the
prisoner at the cost only of the time of the warder in charge.[123]

But this was an unheeded plea and restrained, and, laconic though he
was, Du Cane barely concealed his contempt in his assessment of the
contribution of religion to the life of the prison:

The advantage of inculcating religious feelings will not be contested
by any one; and, notwithstanding the doubts which have arisen from
injudicious exaggerations of the results of these influences, and by
misconception of the true position of and functions fulfilled by the
chaplains of prisons, it is certain that these advantages are much
appreciated by prisoners, and that the exertions of the ministers of
religion bear perhaps as much fruit as in the world outside.[124]

Education

Secular education, which at Millbank Penitentiary and Pentonville had
come under the charge of the chaplain, was also curtailed by the
directors; but among the chaplains themselves there had long been
scepticism about its benefits. In 1852 Kingswell expressed these doubts.
He agreed that basic learning in reading and writing was necessary but
confessed that

To confer the advantages of a superior education on criminals I hold
to be wrong in principle. A superficial one is worse than useless.
What such men need is principle, and not mere intellectual
development. That mere education does not produce moral elevation
is too apparent, from the fact that our convicts on the whole have
had as large a share of its advantages as the non-criminal classes in
society to which they belonged.[125]

In 1856 it was noted that convicts had far higher educational attainments than prisoners in local establishments — 'probably because many
of the convicts learned to read and write during their previous imprisonment'. This, the directors concluded, was unfortunately 'one of many

123 *Reports of the Officers of Convict Prisons*, PP, 1878, XLIII, 1, 106-7.
124 Du Cane, *The Punishment and Prevention of Crime* (1885), p. 160.
125 *RDCP*, 1852-3, LI, 385, 408.

convincing proofs that "the greater the crime the higher will be found the degree of education" '. They quoted Kingsmill:

> Mere education cannot be received either as a panacea or preventative of serious crime; it is plainly a power which acts both ways, for evil and for good, according to the religious principles and moral habits of those who possess it.[126]

Education was also reorganised in 1863. The allowance to each convict in the public works prisons of half a day's education a week ceased, and in the separate prisons cellular instruction took the place of classes.[127] Education in the public works prisons was organised to give priority to labour and even at Broadmoor classes were pushed into the evening (between 6 and 8 p.m.) rather than being held during the day.[128] It was claimed that the greater separation of prisoners during educational activities, as part of the general discontinuance of association, had improved the discipline of the establishments.[129] Great importance was still attached, nevertheless, to basic educational attainments. Although it was admitted that education was not as potent a reformatory influence as once had been hoped, there was a belief that 'a knowledge of reading and writing afford ... much opportunity for mental and moral improvement'.[130] In May 1868 systematic educational testing of convicts began, and prisoners were assessed on reception and at six-monthly intervals thereafter.[131] In order to provide the maximum inducement to prisoners to equip themselves with a basic education, instructions were issued that no convict should be promoted to the first class unless he could read and write. Any exceptions to this rule, based on considerations such as old age or obvious gross incapacity, had to be reported to the directors.[132] Education remained a privilege as well as a duty, however, and it was not until they had served an initial month of separate confinement and 'by their industry and good

---

126 *RDCP*, PP, 1857, Sess. 2, XXIII, 65, 73-4.
127 *RDCP*, PP, 1865, XXV, 1, 6-9, *passim*.
128 *Ibid.*, 9.
129 *RDCP*, PP, 1866, XXXVIII, 1, 6-8.
130 Du Cane, *op. cit.* (1872), p. 12.
131 *RDCP*, PP, 1868-9, XXX, 1, viii (Millbank, Portland, Fulham). The chaplain of Portland reported that no one in the prison was above the standard of grade four, and that it was not until he had reached grade five in all subjects that a prisoner's name was removed from the books.
132 'System of Classification for All Convicts' (22 July 1864), *cit.* Du Cane, *op. cit.* (1872), p. 45. Convicts who were thought not to have given sufficient attention to the instruction which they were given and who remained illiterate on their emergence from the third class (the class above the probation class) were to forfeit their gratuity, which would be restored only when they could read and write (*ibid.*, p. 46).

conduct, gained promotion to the second stage' that convicts were allowed to receive visits from the schoolmasters.[133]

Punishments

Effective as the stage system was in reducing disciplinary problems, some prisoners failed to respond to its threats and inducements. For such persons other sanctions were needed. These included bread and water diet, confinement in a dark cell, allocation to a penal class, flogging and the use of restraints such as cross-irons and handcuffs (for women a canvas dress and ankle-straps). Governors' powers to inflict these punishments were limited: only the directors or (after 1864)[134] magistrates could order corporal punishment, whilst the period for which governors could impose bread and water diet could not exceed three days at a time, as compared with the twenty days which the directors could order.[135] Sometimes punishments would be combined: the anonymous author of *Five Years Penal Servitude* reported that a fellow convict at Dartmoor in the early 1870s who had struck an officer had been flogged and, in addition, put in chains which he wore day and night.[136]

There were a number of changes in the use of punishments over the years. The dark cells, upon which great reliance had been placed at Millbank, fell into disuse, and by 1878 were used only for women.[137] The cat-o'-nine-tails was replaced by the birch, and the Royal Commission of 1878 drew attention to the instruction that restraints should not be used as punishments.[138] The main changes, however, arose from successive attempts to deal with persistently troublesome offenders. Prior to 1853 those convicts whose behaviour was especially bad in the home prisons could be consigned to the penal colony on Norfolk Island, and until its closure in 1863 it was still possible to send such persons to Bermuda. The closure of these stations denied to the

133 Du Cane, *op. cit.* (1885), p. 81.
134 William Guy, medical superintendent at Millbank, had complained to the Carnarvon Committee of delays between the commission of an offence and its punishment by the visiting director – thus the recourse to magistrates (Carnarvon Committee, *op. cit.*, Evidence, 402). Corporal punishment could be ordered not only for the more serious offences, such as striking an officer or mutiny, but also for threats of violence, grossly offensive or abusive language to any officer, the destruction of prison property and making a disturbance in the punishment cell (Standing Order no. 86, 10 May 1862).
135 Though it was noted by the 1878 Royal Commission that governors sometimes ordered repeated periods of three days: 'the only limit to the punishment appears to be the convict's power of endurance' (1878 *RC*, *op. cit.*, xlviii-xlix).
136 'One Who Has Endured It', *Five Years Penal Servitude*, p. 81.
137 1878 *RC*, *op. cit.*, xlviii.
138 *Ibid.*, xlix-l.

home prison administrator an effective safety valve and deterrent. Henceforth no matter how difficult they might prove, even the most refractory of convicts had to be dealt with at home.

The progressive stage system allowed the authorities to send back to the probationary (separate) stage those who seriously misbehaved on public works. There was some objection to this, however. Kingsmill, the Pentonville chaplain, considered that the idea was 'no doubt sound in principle', but in view of the disciplinary difficulties which then arose in the separate prisons he urged that special punishment units should be established in the public works prisons.[139] Although this suggestion was not to be adopted for over twenty years, from 1855 special penal classes were established at Millbank both for men and for women.[140] In 1861 another penal class for males was set up at Pentonville; two years later penal class cells were provided at all the public works prisons and at Dartmoor invalid prison.[141] The penal class ranked below the probationary stage; its deprivations were more stringent than even those of the basic level and its discipline was described as 'severe'. In 1873 a special party for convicts who had committed violent offences on the public works was set up at Portland. Convicts in this party were subject to 'rigid discipline' under experienced officers and were denied the benefit of associated exercise on Sundays. Those who were of good behaviour for three months could return to normal routine.[142] In February 1876 the principle of imposing deprivations in order that convicts might win their release therefrom by good behaviour was extended to other prisons when single-file, silent exercise was instituted for those in the probation and third classes in the public works prisons.[143] Considerable success was claimed for this new departure, the governor of Dartmoor reporting that 'the whole spirit of the men when confined to single exercise appears to undergo a great change, the restlessness of disposition encouraged by exercising in company giving place to a quiet demeanour and bearing'.[144] But when, in violation of what had become the axiom that relaxations and inducements should reward good behaviour, the silence rule was extended beyond the lowest classes, discontent and insubordination markedly

139 *RDCP*, PP, 1854-5, XXV, 33, 55.
140 *RDCP*, PP, 1856, XXXV, 1, pp. 74, 78. Prisoners spent between nine and twelve months in the penal class. They underwent a second period of separation and, from July 1855, were put to work on a specially installed treadwheel – the only one ever used in the convict service (*ibid*., 74, 82).
141 *RDCP*, PP, 1864, XXVI, 209, 220. The directors observed that the absence of suitable facilities on the spot had 'proved of serious detriment to the service, which will be hereafter removed by the measures we have sanctioned'.
142 *RDCP*, PP, 1875, XXXIX, 1, 318.
143 *Reports of the Officers of Convict Prisons*, PP, 1878, XLIII, 1, 3.
144 *Ibid*., 123.

increased.[145] The governor of Portsmouth convict prison described the extension of the silence rule as 'the most stringent rule that has as yet been laid down in our penal disciplinary system', and urged that 'its effect upon the mental fibre ... of prisoners under long sentences of penal servitude may not improbably be such as to render its modification advisable ...'.[146]

In 1878 a system of 'second probation' was introduced in an attempt to deal with what was sometimes described as the 'contaminating class' of convicts. This was simply the separate confinement, normally operated at Millbank and Pentonville, applied to certain offenders in the public works prisons. These were men who had lost hope of recovering any part of their remission. Their isolation was necessary because among them

> every kind of misconduct is indulged in by turns for the admiration
> or amusement of their fellows, who encourage them in the
> commission of serious offences with the assurance that 'they have
> nothing to lose'. Men of this stamp also appear to derive a certain
> gratification from committing themselves in the presence of others,
> creating scenes of which they become the heroes.[147]

The governor of Portland, a prison much plagued by ill-behaved convicts, welcomed the second probationary class. He did not think that it reformed the refractory, but saw it as a boon to the well-conducted class, leaving them free from corrupting influence.[148] The second probation scheme was supported by the 1878 Royal Commission, who saw in it a suitable means for dealing with those prisoners who did *not* prefer the solitary cells to labour.[149]

Refractory women presented special difficulties. The small number of female convict establishments and the fact that there was no public works stage meant that trouble-makers could not easily be moved elsewhere. Moreover, even the most violent of them could not be subjected to corporal punishment. In their report for 1855 the directors asked the question, 'How are the reckless ones to be treated?'

> If only advised and reasoned with, they ascribe leniency to
> weakness, and presume upon the kindness shown to them. If
> punished, they must be punished according to the ordinary methods
> laid down by the Statute.... And yet, the oftener a female convict
> is punished, the less she is physically able to endure punishment.

---

145 The daily average of punishments at Brixton increased by 40 per cent, largely, the governor thought, because of this measure (*Reports of the Officers of Convict Prisons*, PP, 1878-9, XXXV, 1, 37).
146 *Ibid.*, p. 420.
147 *Ibid.*, 119.
148 *Ibid.*, 345.
149 1878 *RC, op. cit.*, xlviii.

The female constitution will neither bear long nor repeated deprivation of food. Though no immediately perceptible effect may be produced the medical officer is of opinion, from the experience of the last two years, that the seeds of permanent disease may nevertheless be sown, and the utmost caution must be exercised lest lasting injury be inflicted consequent upon breaches of discipline or the wanton destruction of prison property, which last is the prevailing offence. Hence it follows, that after a certain point of physical endurance is passed, the worse a woman behaves the less she suffers. If with failing powers came amended lives, some counterbalancing good at any rate would be the result. But this is not so, as the health deteriorates irritability increases; violence and passion remain so strongly in the character as when she was in full health, and in compassion for her bodily condition she is borne with and coaxed by those who are over her, to her own detriment and the subversion of wholesome discipline throughout the prison.[150]

That female convicts were a source of well-nigh intractable disciplinary problems is confirmed in their not unsympathetic portrayal by 'A Prison Matron', who frequently refers to the 'break-outs' and 'smash-ups' and other hysterical outbursts which occurred at Brixton; female convicts as a class are described by this author as 'desperately wicked — deceitful, crafty, malicious, lewd, and void of common feeling. . . . In the penal classes of the male prisons there is not one man to match the worst inmates of our female prisons'.[151] When it was further decided, in 1855, to provide a penal class for women at Millbank, the accommodation rapidly proved to be insufficient for the demand. In 1859 the lady superintendent of Brixton reported that only eight women had been transferred to Millbank with the comment that the number was small 'not because many more did not deserve it, but because there was not room for them . . .'.[152] The following year she lamented the fact that overcrowding compelled her to accept for association at Brixton

150 *RDCP*, PP, 1856, XXXV, 1, 273. The picture of persistent defiance of punishment leading to breakdowns in health was confirmed some twelve years later by the medical officer at Brixton:

> They [women in the refractory ward] are a constant source of trouble and anxiety in the prison, and equally so as regards their health. Punishment fails to deter or reform them, and the ultimate result on health of life spent under such circumstances is, I believe, unknown. Many of them certainly die prematurely, either in or out of prison (*RDCP*, PP, 1868-9, XXX, 1, 366).

151 'A Prison Matron', *Female Life in Prison*, p. 26. See also Chapter 11, *passim*. Solitary confinement seems to have been the most frequently resorted to punishment for women; sometimes the cells were darkened or semi-darkened which, noted the 1878 Royal Commission, was said to exert a calming effect on the women (1878 *RC*, *op. cit.*, xlviii).

152 *RDCP*, PP, 1860, XXXV, 429, 684.

incorrigible females, who were proving an evil influence.[153] In the long run there could, of course, only be imperfect solutions to these problems. The difficulties encountered on the male side following the closure of the outlets offered by transportation were magnified in the very much smaller female system, with its necessarily restricted range of punishments and possibly more disorderly inmates.

Health

The epidemics of typhus, cholera and influenza, which had decimated prison populations well into the nineteenth century, were now well under control. There was an outbreak of cholera at Millbank in 1854, but the removal of 700 convicts to Dorchester barracks and other measures taken by the medical superintendent, Dr Baly, kept fatalities to a low level.[154] During the outbreak of smallpox which occurred in London in 1871, the convict prisons did not remain immune, but fatalities were relatively few. The health of prisoners (and presumably staff) at Millbank was improved dramatically through the relatively simple expedient of sinking artesian wells instead of using the heavily polluted waters of the Thames.[155] It is difficult, however, to assess with any great exactitude the standard of medical care provided for the convicts since, as has been mentioned, some convicts went to any lengths to avoid labour. The medical authorities responded to this with a profound scepticism and a certain callousness in respect of any claim to sickness. Although these two circumstances must throw into doubt the official figures for mental and physical illness,[156] it does seem fairly clear that despite developments in the provision of county asylums from the 1840s onward, and an increasing availability of infirmary services through the Poor Law, fairly large numbers of feeble-minded, insane and diseased persons continued to find their way into the convict prisons.

From the outset the directors acknowledged that there was an inappropriately high death rate among convicts. In 1855 it was 15.4 per 1,000, in 1865 18.6 and in 1870 12.6;[157] which compared with rates of 22.6, 23.2 and 22.9 respectively for the whole civilian population.[158] The high death rate was attributed to the poor health in which

---

153 *RDCP*, PP, 1862, XXV, 331, 616.
154 *RDCP*, PP, 1854-5, XXV, 33, 123-4.
155 *RDCP*, PP, 1855, XXXV, 1, 76-7.
156 See pp. 339-41, above.
157 Du Cane, *op. cit*. (1872), p. 34.
158 B.R. Mitchell, *Abstract of British Historical Statistics*, p. 36. The 'civilian' death rate includes the very young and the very old. Most convicts, by contrast, were 'in the prime of life'.

many of the convicts were received,[159] an opinion which was reiterated by Du Cane:

> when it is considered that convicts are, as a class, men of low physical type, born and brought up under conditions unfavourable to health, early given up to vicious courses, and with constitutions in many cases ruined or impaired by excess, it may fairly be said that the statistics of mortality show that prisoners are duly cared for in all that pertains to health, and that in that respect the conditions of their life, their habitation, clothing and diet, are more favourable than they probably are in a state of freedom.[160]

A hope expressed by the Pentonville medical officer in 1861 that the health of convicts was improving proved to be unfounded. In 1866 the directors reported that

> The general deterioration in the physical condition of the class of men now received into the convict prisons is a remarkable fact. A few years back the large majority of convicts were men of robust health and appearance; these are now the exception rather than the rule, and a large proportion of the men being of weakly, enfeebled constitutions and unfit for hard labour are necessarily drafted either to an invalid prison or placed in light labour gangs.[161]

The following year it was noted that 'Of 6,552 male convicts in confinement on the 7th of April 1868, no less than 1,981 were either confirmed invalids or fit only for light labour'.[162] Indeed, of the 1,237 convicts who were allocated to other establishments from Millbank during the year only 55 per cent were sent to the public works prisons certified as fit for hard labour, and a further 11 per cent certified fit only for light labour; the remaining third of the convicts had to be sent to invalid prisons.[163] A light labour class was formed at each of the public works prisons, but the need for extra accommodation for this group led, in December 1869, to Brixton being taken over as a light labour prison for males.[164]

The insanity rate continued to be an acknowledged problem.[165] Indeed, mental illness appears to have been a cause of some disputation among the medical staff, and whereas the medical officer at Brixton

---

159 *RDCP*, PP, 1854-5, XXV, 33, 121. This claim is all the more credible in the light of the uniformly sceptical attitude shown by the prison authorities towards claims of illness (see pp. 398-9, above).
160 Du Cane, *op. cit.* (1872), p. 34.
161 *RDCP*, PP, 1867, XXXVI, 1, 6.
162 *RDCP*, PP, 1867-8, XXXIV, 519, 5.
163 *Ibid*.
164 Standing Order no. 162, 15 October 1864; PRO, PCOM 7/224.
165 *RDCP*, PP, 1862, XXV, 331, 346.

reported that he had difficulty in diagnosing mental illness among women convicts, his colleague at Millbank asserted that such conditions were comparatively rare among women.[166] It is clear, in any event, that both the mentally and physically unwell were difficult to manage. The directors attempted to segregate them, at first in the hulks, then in a special pentagon at Millbank, and eventually in Dartmoor. This allowed for some easing of discipline without provoking the resentment that would have been inevitable had they been held alongside healthy convicts. Even so, many problems were reported. The governor of Millbank described the invalids in his charge as 'a class of prisoners exceedingly difficult to deal with, by reason of the many impediments imposed by their state of health to the ordinary enforcement of discipline'.[167] At Dartmoor, by the mid-1850s, there were scarcely any non-invalids, but it was still necessary to separate the weak-minded from the physically unwell.[168] Despite what seems to have been a reasonably sympathetic consideration of their plight, the imbeciles in particular were a great inconvenience: 'they not only obstruct the course of discipline, but are in reality a very dangerous class of men . . .'.[169]

In April 1859 Woking invalid prison was opened and soon began to take the most helpless imbeciles;[170] Broadmoor Criminal Lunatic Asylum received its first inmates in March 1862. Prisoners could be committed to Broadmoor directly from the courts, and also could be transferred from the convict prisons. From October 1864 Millbank was used as an assessment centre to which convicts thought to be insane were sent; if the diagnosis was confirmed they were sent to Woking. From 1877 this procedure was changed and all insane male convicts were held at Woking.[171]

The place of the diet in a penal régime continued to be a contentious issue. Convicts on the public works received thirty-nine ounces of meat a week, at a time when only four ounces were served to workhouse inmates, and this disparity inevitably and understandably was a cause of public concern. Some witnesses who gave evidence to the 1863 Royal Commission claimed that dietary scales in the public works prisons were too generous, and that convicts were better fed not only than paupers but also than free labourers. On the other side it was argued that food of superior quality was consumed by free labourers who did the same type of heavy work as the public works convicts, and that therefore the diet of the latter was not better than was necessary

---

166 *RDCP*, PP, 1861, XXX, 237, 284; *RDCP*, PP, 1862, XXV, 331, 385.
167 *RDCP*, PP, 1854, XXXIII, 181, 264.
168 *RDCP*, PP, 1856, Sess. 2, XXIII, 65, 284; *RDCP*, PP, 1862, XXV, 331, 525.
169 *RDCP*, PP, 1860, XXXV, 429, 599.
170 *RDCP*, PP, 1864, XXVI, 209, 219-20.
171 Standing Order no. 161, 6 October 1864; 1878 *RC*, *op. cit*., xli; *Reports of the Officers of Convict Prisons*, PP, 1878, XLIII, 1, 517.

'considering the labour that is extracted from them'.[172] The commission recognised that the existing scales had evolved as a result of lengthy experience and on the basis of good medical advice. Whilst not being prepared to make a positive recommendation that there should be a reduction they thought that experiments might be conducted in order to ascertain what might safely be done in this regard.[173]

The following year a departmental committee under the chairmanship of Dr William Guy, then medical superintendent of Millbank, again considered convict dietaries. Cautious approval was given for a limited reduction in the separate prisons' dietaries, with the rider from the committee that 'they wish it to be understood that they cannot take upon themselves the serious responsibility of advocating any such reduction or alteration of diet as was made at Millbank in 1822, and at Wakefield in 1849 and 1862'.[174] As a result the public works dietaries were left unchanged, and indeed the committee criticised existing scales for carrying monotony to an extreme and for being 'less calculated to maintain health than a more varied dietary'.[175] Monotony in the penal-class diet they found acceptable, and suggested that there might be some reduction in quantity to make it even less attractive.[176] Guy and his colleagues thought that dietary policy should have the objective of preserving the convicts in an efficient and productive state of health. This meant, for example, that at the end of the period of their separate confinement those convicts selected for public works should

> be able at once to perform such labour at our dockyards and arsenals as could be required of men who, whether in prison or out of prison, had led a comparatively inactive life, or had been engaged in comparatively light labour indoors.[177]

The directors endorsed the committee's recommendations and forwarded the report to the home secretary for his approval. A growing knowledge of the relationship between health and diet, and of the earlier epidemics, thus ensured that even at a time when convict discipline generally was being toughened, dietary decisions continued to be made on the basis of medical rather than penal considerations. Although dietaries were scrutinised by the Royal Commission on the Treatment of Treason-Felony Convicts in 1870, and the Royal Commission on Penal Servitude in 1878,[178] there was no change in this approach to

172 1863 SC, op. cit., p. 42; see Appendix 21 for the workhouse comparison.
173 Ibid.
174 Report of the Committee Appointed to Inquire into the Dietaries of Convict Prisons, PP, 1864, XLIX, 1, 323.
175 Ibid.
176 Ibid.
177 Ibid., 322.
178 1871 RC, op. cit., paras 22-5; 1878-9 RC, op. cit., xxxvi-xxxix.

convict dietaries. The 1878 Royal Commission reported that they were satisfied that the convicts' food was 'fairly proportioned to the amount of labour required of the prisoners, whether in separate confinement or at public works'. As for the ingredients, 'though they are coarse in quality, they are good of their kind and nutritious, and . . . sufficient in quantity to maintain ordinary convicts in good health and vigour'.[179]

Arrangements for release

The release of convicts was affected by two separate developments — the introduction of a licensing or ticket-of-leave system and the growth of voluntary societies to aid discharged prisoners.

Decisions about licensing were taken largely on the basis of institutional behaviour, on the advice of the governor and chaplain, transmitted through the directors to the secretary of state.[180] High standards of behaviour were required for favourable consideration. The 1863 Royal Commission were told that no convict was put forward for a ticket-of-leave unless he had been clear of all prison reports for misconduct for at least six months before being considered and that it was also required that he had been industrious at his work.[181] In 1870 it was decided that greater weight should be given to prisoners' criminal records and a restriction was imposed upon the granting of licences to men who had previously served a sentence of penal servitude. This, asserted the directors, would 'add to the motives a discharged prisoner has for not getting into trouble'.[182]

---

179 1878 RC, op. cit., xxxvii. It is interesting to note that even as long after the event as this, cautionary reference was still made to the Millbank epidemic of 1822, which arose from an attempt to subordinate health to penal requirements (ibid.).

180 PRO, PCOM 7 68HN08404, p. 13. Though Jebb was at some pains to explain that the chaplains' comments played only a limited part in release procedures. He told the 1856 select committee that

> There exists an erroneous impression that the chaplains have been required in all cases to satisfy themselves that a convict is a reformed man before he is recommended to the Secretary of State for a license — such a condition would be both impracticable and unjust; impracticable, because no sufficient means exist of forming an accurate opinion of the religious state of any one, much less of a prisoner; and unjust, because a prisoner should not be deprived of any privilege he might gain on an opinion unsupported by evidence . . . there is little doubt that the ministerial usefulness of a chaplain would be greatly impaired if much weight were assigned to it in the distribution of rewards. It would besides be open to the objection of holding out a bonus to hypocrisy, which under present circumstances is not one of the sins of prisoners (1856 SC, op. cit., q1076).

181 1863 RC, op. cit., 16.
182 RDCP, PP, 1871, XXXI, 1, vi.

As has been noted, the release of convicts at home was probably the matter which caused greatest concern about the ending of transportation and Jebb had recommended adoption of the licensing system which had been introduced in Barbados.[183] This scheme provided for the superintendence of discharged convicts by both the magistracy and the constabulary. The 1853 Act, intentionally vague about licensing procedures, vested in the secretary of state complete powers over the issuance and revocation of licences.[184] The licence was intended to be a deterrent against further law-breaking and, indeed, since no system of supervision was provided, revocation was ordered only in the event of a further conviction or, occasionally, after repeated complaints of association with known thieves.[185] When it was decided to withdraw a licence a metropolitan magistrate was directed by the Home Office to issue a warrant; this was executed by the relevant local constabulary who brought the prisoner before the issuing magistrate who then recommitted him for the unexpired portion of his original sentence to the prison from which he had been released.[186] The 1857 Act only slightly altered this procedure by allowing recommittal to be ordered to any convict prison.

The 1863 Royal Commission heard a good deal of evidence on the granting of release on licence, since the supposed misdeeds of ticket-of-leave men had been one of the main reasons for its establishment.[187] The commissioners agreed that there were difficulties in the establishment of an effective supervision of convicts, but argued that this was a matter of 'such extreme importance' that an attempt to provide surveillance should be made. Their suggestion was that an official of the directorate, supported by the necessary assistants, should, following the practice of the Irish convict system, closely supervise the licence-holders. Police support should be given when required but 'in other

---

183 See pp. 390-1, above.
184 S.9 of the Act provided that a licence could be granted

> during such Portion of his or her Term of Transportation or Imprisonment, and upon such Conditions in all respects as to Her Majesty shall seem fit; and it shall be lawful for Her Majesty to revoke or alter such Licence by a like Order at Her Majesty's Pleasure.

185 1856 *SC, op. cit.*, qs. 52-5, p. 7.
186 16 & 17 Vict., c.99, s.11.
187 It was Jebb's opinion that the public outcry against ticket-of-leave men had the effect of driving them into crime:

> In 1854, when we released 1,895 men, the number re-convicted was 9.6 per cent. The outcry against the granting of tickets-of-leave was made at that time, and the reconvictions rose in 1856 to 17.2 per cent, showing clearly the effect of branding these out of doors and making them a class to be avoided, had the effect of driving them into crime by the loss of any means of employment (1863 *SC, op. cit.*, q535).

cases the police should abstain from any interference with the licence-holders, in order not to increase the difficulty of their obtaining employment'.[188] They also desired that power should be given to arrest licence-holders thought to be guilty of misbehaviour, *before* the actual revocation of their licences, and recommended that convicts should be obliged to preserve their licences, and that it should be an offence not to produce a licence when duly required so to do.[189]

In the subsequent Act the recommendation that the directorate should assume responsibility for licence supervision was set aside in favour of police supervision. It was required that within three days of his arrival in a district, and once each month as thereafter directed, a male licence-holder should report to the local police station; he could not then change his address without reporting it to the police.[190] Failure to comply with these conditions was a misdemeanour, summary conviction of which led to forfeiture of the licence. Failure to produce a licence without reasonable excuse, or breach of any of the other conditions of the licence, such as association with notoriously bad characters, or living an idle or dissolute life, were in themselves criminal offences punishable on summary conviction by imprisonment for up to three months,[191] in addition to the forfeiture of the licence. Should a licence-holder be sentenced to imprisonment for a new offence, he would on completion of that term of imprisonment be returned to a convict prison to serve the portion of his sentence of penal servitude which was outstanding at the time when he was granted a licence.[192] The police were empowered to arrest without warrant any licence-holder suspected of having committed any offence or having broken any of the conditions of his licence.[193] The provisions affecting arrest on suspicion and reporting to the police were continued and made rather more stringent in general by Acts passed in 1869 and 1871.[194] The 1871 Act obliged a licence-holder who changed his district of abode to notify the police of both districts. Failure to report within forty-eight hours of arriving in a new district, or to notify a change of residence, or to report once a month, made a licence-holder liable to forfeiture of licence, and, should his sentence of penal servitude be

188 1863 *RC, op. cit.*, 32.
189 *Ibid.*
190 27 & 28 Vict., c.47, s.4. In February 1863 it was decided that convicts' gratuities would in future be paid through the police, in order to increase the pressure on the convict to report as required (Standing Order no. 93, 13 February 1863). This did not apply to convicts who were under the charge of a prisoners' aid society (Standing Order no. 95, 1 April 1863), see n. 207, p. 424, below.
191 27 & 28 Vict., c.47, s.5.
192 *Ibid.*, s.9.
193 *Ibid.*, s.7.
194 The Habitual Criminals Act and the Prevention of Crimes Act, respectively.

expired at the time of conviction for breaching these conditions, or be thought to be insufficiently long, up to one year's imprisonment.[195] The Act also provided for the keeping of registers and the photographing of criminals and made those convicted of any indictable offence liable for a period of seven years thereafter to imprisonment if it appeared to a summary court that they were living by dishonest means, that they were apprehended in suspicious circumstances, or for giving a false name and address.[196] Indeed, the whole licensing system was extended, by granting to the courts the power to subject reconvicted criminals to police supervision for up to seven years after the completion of the last sentence passed upon them.[197]

These changes were intended to make possible the close supervision of discharged convicts, and to subject them to continual pressure to desist from crime. From the outset, however, there were objections that the notoriety arising from being under close police supervision might make it more difficult for an offender to secure and keep honest employment. Jebb favoured the granting of free rather than conditional pardons for the remitted portion of the sentence. He argued that

> One great disadvantage under which ticket-of-leave men have laboured has been that they have been regarded as a distinct proscribed class. 30 or 40 per cent of the prisoners who circulate through other prisons are habitual criminals, but excite no notice whatever, because when they have endured their sentence they are free. Not so with the man who continues under a legal restriction after his release; he becomes a *marked* man.[198]

There was some support for the view that police supervision handicapped the man who wished to make a fresh start. In 1868 the chaplain

---

195 34 & 35 Vict., c.112, s.5.
196 *Ibid.*, s.7.
197 *Ibid.*, s.8.
198 1863 *RC, op. cit.*, Appendix 2, 144. In July 1856 Jebb wrote to Earl Grey about his doubts concerning the creation of the class of ticket-of-leave men:

> I think it has operated seriously against them, and the balance of my opinion is in favour of a shorter remission of the original sentence, and the release of the men perfectly free, just as they are from the County Prisons at the expiration of their sentences (Grey Papers).

After Jebb's death his brother-in-law, the Earl of Chichester, explicitly dissociated Jebb from the ticket-of-leave system:

> he was neither the author of it nor the adviser of its introduction into this country . . . he was only responsible for some of the regulations under which it was carried out . . . neither of us wholly approved of the particular form in which it has been hitherto applied in this country (Earl of Chichester (ed.), *Reports and Observations on the Discipline and Management of Convict Prisons . . . by Jebb*, p. vi).

of Dartmoor disclosed the fact that some former prisoners had in their letters to him complained of the police betraying their secret to their employers, and of their resultant dismissal.[199] The 1878 Royal Commission rejected this criticism, but recommended that special plain-clothes police officers should be used to supervise licence-holders;[200] they also rejected the policy of the Gloucestershire magistrates, who allowed the police to inform employers of a discharged prisoner's record.[201] They contended that the system of supervision had an unavoidable defect in that whilst

> convicts who are really desirous to earn a living by honest means report regularly to the police, those who on their release return at once to a life of crime are quite prepared to run the risk of not reporting themselves, and thus those criminals who most require to be constantly watched often evade supervision altogether. . . .

They concluded, nevertheless, that 'police supervision is a valuable means of controlling the criminal classes'.[202]

One important effect of these measures upon prison management was to make more reliable the statistics relating to reconvictions. From the early 1860s onward there were attempts in both the local and convict prisons to improve the means of identifying habitual criminals. Photographic equipment was installed in some of the convict prisons in 1863,[203] but it was not until a central registry was set up under the 1869 Habitual Criminals Act that such devices could be used with reasonable effectiveness.[204] In 1871 the directors claimed that the higher number of reconvictions appearing in the statistics was due to the increased facility provided by the Acts of 1869 and 1871 for the detection and conviction of habitual criminals. This was one of the first statements upon a theme which, over the years, became of increasing importance in assessing the work of the administrators of prisons.[205]

Because it dovetailed so well with official objectives and endeavours, the decision of the local societies aiding discharged prisoners to extend

199 *RDCP*, PP, 1868-9, XXX, 1, 265-6.
200 1878 *RC*, *op. cit.*, xxxv.
201 *Ibid.*, xxxix.
202 *Ibid.*, xxxiv.
203 Standing Order no. 103 (13 October 1863); see also *RDCP*, PP, 1866, XXXVIII, 1, 116.
204 The registry was set up in September 1869, and initially consisted of a registrar, sub-registrar and two clerks. The governors of both local and convict prisons had to submit weekly returns of discharged prisoners who had been sentenced to one year and over. At first under the charge of the metropolitan police, the registry in January 1875 came under the direct charge of the Home Office, where it was kept in the Convict Department (PRO HO 45/9509/16260/1; HO 45/9518/22208/32, 34A).
205 *RDCP*, PP, 1872, XXXI, 385, vi.

their activities to convicts was warmly welcomed by the authorities. Jebb was of the opinion that these societies should be aided by the government and pointed out to the 1856 select committee that there would be a saving to the public purse should crime thereby be prevented.[206] The following year the directors indicated their support for the societies by making arrangements whereby, in certain circumstances, a convict's release gratuity might be paid over to the society.[207] The chaplain of Portsmouth urged increased public support to enable the societies to extend their operations.[208] By 1860 the expansion of activities was such that Folliott Powell, the governor of Chatham, drew attention to the large number of convicts who were helped by the societies and praised the 'amount of practical good' being carried out.[209] There was no provision for female convicts for a time, however, an omission described by Jebb as a great drawback which 'hangs like a cloud over the exertions of both officers and prisoners'.[210] Du Cane shared Jebb's estimation of the importance of the work of the societies:

> It is a work of charity which for every reason it is desirable to encourage and develop, for nothing can be imagined more hopeless than the condition of a man cast out on the world with a ruined character and without friends to help him, surrounded by temptations from which he has been long removed, or open to the influence of former evil associates.[211]

Growth of the societies was greatly stimulated when, in 1862, the justices were empowered to assist them with grants from public funds,[212] and by 1871 nearly half the male and more than two-thirds of the female discharged convicts were assisted by the societies.[213]

Not only was there agreement between the convict service and the societies over objectives, but the method by which the societies kept an eye on their charges fitted well with the official requirements for

---

206 1856 *SC, op. cit.*, 110-11. A convict released in England was given official assistance in the form of a discharge gratuity, an outfit of clothing and free travel to the place at which he had been convicted 'or to any intermediate point at which he may desire to stop' (Standing Order no. 19, 7 November 1853).

207 *RDCP*, PP, 1857-8, XXIX, 483, pp. 634-5. Gratuities over £5 were paid to the convicts in instalments (Standing Order no. 40, 6 July 1857). Where a prisoner applied to a prisoners' aid society or a refuge, for assistance, the whole of the gratuity could be handed over to the society or refuge and disbursed as was thought appropriate (Standing Order no. 47, 20 November 1857).

208 *RDCP*, PP, 1857-8, XXIX, 483, 152-3.

209 *RDCP*, PP, 1861, XXX, 237, 538.

210 *RDCP*, PP, 1862, XXV, 331, 632.

211 Du Cane, *op. cit.* (1872), p. 18.

212 Authorisation was given by 25 & 26 Vict., c.44. See pp. 362-3, above.

213 Du Cane, *op. cit.* (1872), p. 17.

licensing and supervision.[214] On release the convicts were interviewed by the society in order to determine their intentions. They were given suitable clothing, lodgings and pocket-money (the last from their prison gratuities) and efforts were made to obtain employment for them. A system of regular visitation was established. This was described by W.B. Ranken, secretary of the London-based Discharged Prisoners' Aid Society:

> The men employed in the Metropolitan District are visited, periodically, by Agents of the Society, and a daily report is made by these Agents of the cases they have visited. . . . A correspondence is also kept up with the Chief Constable of any place to which a man is sent beyond the Metropolitan District, and communications respecting him opened with any Magistrate or Clergyman likely to interest himself on his behalf.[215]

There still remained, in the 1870s, a certain nostalgic regard for transportation, and in particular for the opportunity which it had offered for 'making a fresh start'. Du Cane shared this view,[216] as did some of his governors, and in 1872 we find the governor of Parkhurst lamenting the fact that the prisoners' aid societies did not operate an emigration scheme 'as certain classes of prisoners who have once fallen, and are without friends to assist them, would in all probability, be thus reclaimed to an honest and industrial life'.[217]

Special categories of convicts

Women　From the outset women had been accommodated in their own Millbank pentagons, and subjected to a semi-independent administration. With the introduction of penal servitude Jebb estimated that an extra one thousand places would have to be found for convicts in England,[218] and in the decade or more that followed there was much chopping and changing in the use of the various prisons. In October 1853 the directorate purchased Brixton prison from the Surrey magistrates,[219] and almost immediately transferred to it all the female convicts from Millbank.[220] There were considerable organisational, staffing and disciplinary problems in the new establishment, which rapidly

214 The 1878 Royal Commission recommended that the plain-clothes police whom they proposed for supervision duties should work alongside the Royal Society for the Assistance of Discharged Convicts (*op. cit.*, xxxv).
215 *Cit*. Du Cane, *op. cit*. (1872), p. 20.
216 *Ibid*., pp. 18-19.
217 *RDCP*, PP, 1872, XXXI, 385.
218 Jebb, *op. cit*., p. 15.
219 *The Times*, 10 October 1853, 6f.
220 *RDCP*, PP, 1854-5, XXV, 33, 365.

became overcrowded after the introduction of penal servitude, and in February 1855 a pentagon at Millbank was reallocated for female use.[221] Further accommodation was made available with the opening of Fulham Refuge in April of the following year,[222] and in March 1863 part of Parkhurst juvenile prison was temporarily adapted for women,[223] the whole prison being given over to them in April 1864. Parkhurst and Brixton were both used for women until January 1869, when the latter was taken into use as a light labour prison for men. Work was begun at Woking in 1865 on a new convict prison for women and this was completed and the buildings occupied in April 1869, at which time the use of Parkhurst for women ceased.[224] By 1872 the three female convict prisons – Millbank, Fulham and Woking – had between them just under 1,400 places, all but 186 consisting of separate cells.[225]

Disciplinary arrangements for women were distinct in several respects. They served six rather than nine months in the probationary class, before moving to the associated stages. As on the male side, different levels of gratuity were paid to each class – fourpence per week in the third class, sixpence in the second, eightpence in the first and one shilling per week at the top of the first class – the labour-women. In addition women in the second class were allowed 'the woman's luxury of tea three times a week'; in the first class there was tea every day and more 'talking time'. Women who behaved especially well were awarded one of the twelve special service dresses which entitled them to extra privileges and allowed them to be sent unescorted around the prison. Women under the age of forty who had reached the first class became eligible to spend the last twelve or more months of their sentence at Fulham Refuge.[226]

Fulham, to which Jebb gave special attention, was intended to be for the women what public works prisons were for men. Tuition was given in skills such as baking, cooking and washing, which it was hoped would fit the women for service or housekeeping.[227] Refuge women could apply for a place in the home run by the Discharged Prisoners' Aid

---

221 *RDCP*, PP, 1856, XXXV, 1, 78.
222 *RDCP*, PP, 1857, XXIII, 65, 415.
223 *RDCP*, PP, 1864, XXVI, 209. The directors noted of this change: 'It does not appear to us to be a proper place for the permanent accommodation of female convicts, and we hope arrangements will be made for otherwise disposing of them.' It was later questioned whether the change in use of Parkhurst in 1863, and again in 1869 (when it became a prison for male adults) was strictly legal, as the original Parkhurst Act (1 & 2 Vict., c.82) had not been repealed. (See 'The Powers and Duties of the Directors of Convict Prisons', in PRO PCOM 7 68HN08404, p. 8).
224 *RDCP*, PP, 1870, XXXVIII, 1, 367.
225 Du Cane, *op. cit.* (1872), p. 39.
226 All details from 'A Prison Matron', *op. cit.*, pp. 121-2.
227 *RDCP*, PP, 1857, XXIII, 65, 415.

Society. Selection for the refuge was made not so much on the basis of a slight criminal record or favourable antecedents but 'from showing by their conduct, whilst in the previous stages at Millbank and Brixton that they are inclined to profit by the instruction imparted'.[228] Accommodation was limited, and at the end of 1860 when the population of all the female institutions was 1,283 the daily average at Fulham was 174, or 13.5 per cent of the total.[229]

From about the mid-1860s onward the function and character of Fulham began to change. The directors, under Henderson, had hoped to maintain it in a distinctive role – 'a place of Refuge for female convicts on discharge, and not the last stage of imprisonment';[230] but the opposite happened, and it became ever more like a prison. In 1864 there was a serious disturbance following which it was decided that the women should eat in their cells rather than in association.[231] The following year two new refuges were opened, the Eagle House Refuge in Hammersmith for Roman Catholics, and the Carlisle Memorial Refuge in Winchester. To these was added, in 1871, the Westminster Memorial Refuge at Streatham. All three new refuges were administered and staffed by voluntary bodies, assisted by government grant. Du Cane claimed that they were not prisons 'either in appearance or in discipline – they are *homes*'.[232] Concurrent with the opening of the Streatham refuge a new wing was added to Fulham for second- and third-class women, and thereafter the institution was referred to as Fulham Prison.[233]

Women received more favourable treatment than men in the remission of their sentences. In October 1853, when release on licence was provided for those sentenced to transportation, it was decided that women should be allowed remission on a sliding scale of between one-sixth for sentences of three years and one-third for fifteen years and more.[234] And under the marks system women (unlike the men) could earn marks even whilst in the probationary class, and could earn up to one-third remission of sentence, as compared with the maximum of a quarter granted to men.[235] Women released on licence were obliged to report to the police only upon their release and not, as were the men, at monthly intervals thereafter.[236]

The contrast between male and female convict management in these decades is pronounced: on the one hand uniformity and harsh

---

228 *RDCP*, PP, 1859, Sess. II, XIII, Pt 1, 191, 523.
229 'A Prison Matron', *op. cit.*, p. 275.
230 *RDCP*, PP, 1864, XXVI, 209, 220.
231 *RDCP*, PP, 1865, XXV, 1, 299-300.
232 Du Cane, *op. cit.* (1872), pp. 16-17.
233 *RDCP*, PP, 1872, XXXI, 385, 471.
234 'A Prison Matron', *op. cit.*, p. 289.
235 Standing Order no. 150, 5 August 1864.
236 *RDCP*, PP, 1865, XXV, 1, 13.

regimentation, on the other a strict régime, but with considerable toleration of refractory episodes and even a degree of individualisation. Odd little foibles were allowed which certainly would have met with severe punishment had they been attempted on the male side. There were many 'improvements' in the prison uniform and in the women's appearance, and one reads of mouse-training and sparrow-taming, of attempts to mix punishments and threats with persuasion, of the humouring of the obdurate offender and of ties of affection between staff and inmates. All of these were to remain strictly forbidden irregularities on the male side for many years to come.

Juveniles   The establishment of many new reformatory schools from 1854 onward increasingly limited the role of the convict system with respect to juvenile offenders. In 1854 the home secretary decided that in addition to those boys under sentence of transportation or penal servitude, boys aged sixteen and under who had been sentenced to one or two years' ordinary imprisonment should also be sent to the juvenile penitentiary. Despite this decision the number of juvenile convicts declined from 536 on 31 December 1854 to 68 on 31 December 1864.[237] In the spring of 1863 the directors decided to send Parkhurst boys to Dartmoor. This transfer was completed on 1 April 1864[238] and a couple of years later the directors reported that

> All the juvenile convicts removed from Parkhurst having been
> either discharged or having grown into men, have been removed
> to the public works. No boys being now sent to the Government
> prisons, the remnant of the juvenile prison has been abolished.[239]

Nevertheless a small number of young offenders continued to be sent to the convict prisons. Ninety-five convicts under the age of eighteen (of whom eighteen were under sixteen) were received at Portland during 1866; these included the party from Dartmoor. The chaplain reported that they were kept apart from the adults in their own work party, and at school, but that a few were scattered among the adult parties.[240] It was not too difficult to accommodate these young convicts at Portland, since the régime to which they were subjected differed

237 *Royal Commission on Reformatories and Industrial Schools*, PP, 1884, XLV, 736.
238 *RDCP*, PP, 1864, XXVI, 209, 11; PP, 1865, XXV, 1, 77.
239 *RDCP*, PP, 1866, XXXVIII, 1, 8. The number of juveniles at Dartmoor fell during 1865 from sixty-eight to twenty-six boys, who were reported by the governor to have been moderately good in behaviour — 'but they are more troublesome than adults, and require as strict a system of discipline' (*ibid.*). The following year all the juveniles were removed from Dartmoor, twenty-seven going to Portland and one each to Millbank and Woking (*RDCP*, PP, 1867, XXXVI, 1, 182).
240 *Ibid.*, 108.

only slightly from that of the adults. They had a short separate stage of four months, and more schooling, but otherwise were employed on the public works.[241]

The number of those aged under fifteen sentenced to penal servitude continued to decline, and in 1875 the directors reported that there were only two boy convicts, one at Portland and one at Pentonville;[242] by 1877 only one remained, at Dartmoor.[243] The Royal Commission of 1878 noted that it remained lawful to pass sentences of penal servitude upon juveniles, and that occasionally this was done. They recommended that, with certain exceptions, such as when a juvenile was sentenced for murder, criminals under the age of sixteen should no longer be subject to penal servitude.[244]

Accommodation

The stage system and the segregation of various special categories of convict led in the period up to 1878 to a considerable expansion and renewal of convict accommodation, as well as many changes in the use of individual establishments. A summary of these changes is given in Table 12.5.

No mention has so far been made of the practice of renting cells in certain local prisons, in which convicts were subject to separation under the directorate's rules. This was an inescapable expedient in the first decade of the directorate, but in the early 1860s the convict service became self-sufficient in this regard. The main disadvantage of rented accommodation was that the justices, quite naturally, put local needs first. As a result, the convict service was 'exposed to the great inconvenience of having its agreements with county prisons terminated at the most inconvenient periods'.[245] In each of the three years up to 1865 there was a 20 per cent drop in convictions and reconvictions. This, together with an increase in the separate accommodation available at Millbank, enabled the directors to discontinue their agreements at Aylesbury, Bedford, Leicester, Northampton and Nottingham, and still leave themselves with two hundred or more spare cells.[246] The following year renting stopped altogether with the release to the West Riding of the 412 contract cells at Wakefield.[247]

241 1863 *RC*, para. 17, pp. 17-18; *RDCP*, 1868-9, XXX, 1, 87.
242 *RDCP*, PP, 1876, XXXVII, xxxii.
243 *RDCP*, PP, 1878, XLIII, 1, Appendix 18, xxx. Normally by this time convicts aged under fifteen were sent to reformatories (1878 *RC*, *op. cit.*, evidence of Capt. Lewis, governor of Pentonville, qs. 1540-1).
244 1878-9 *RC*, *op. cit.*, xxx.
245 *RDCP*, PP, 1864, XXVI, 209, 216.
246 *RDCP*, PP, 1866, XXXVIII, 1, 5.
247 *RDCP*, PP, 1867, XXXVI, 1, 67.

TABLE 12.5   *Convict service accommodation, 1850-77*[1]

| Establishment | | | Population on 31 December | | |
			1850	1865	1877
		Millbank	910	925	499
		Pentonville	527	475	1,009
		Portland	782	1,358	1,595
		Dartmoor	173	599	991
		Parkhurst	516	319	561
Hulks	*Warrior* } *Justitia* }	Woolwich	444	–	–
			422	–	–
	Stirling Castle } *York* }	Portsmouth	447	–	–
			421	–	–
Invalid depots	*Defence*	Woolwich	395	–	–
	Shorncliff		259	–	–
	Rented cells in eight local prisons		832	–	–
		Chatham	–	1,054	1,339
		Portsmouth	–	998	1,312
		Woking	–	482	1,416
		Broadmoor	–	73	–
		Brixton	–	523	302
		Fulham Refuge	–	112	278
		Borstal	–	–	396
		Wormwood Scrubs	–	–	459
Total			6,128	6,918	10,157

Source: Abstracted from *Report on the Discipline and Management of Convict Prisons*, PP, 1851, XXVII, 213; 2; *RDCP*, PP, 1866, XXXVIII, 1, 41-272, *passim*; *RDCP*, PP, 1878, XLIII, 1, Appendix II, xxi.

1 Excluding overseas establishments.

13   The convict service, 1850-77: administration and staffing

Senior staff

The directors

Powers and duties   The first three chairman of the Directorate of Convict Prisons were officers of the Royal Engineers. Lieutenant-Colonel Jebb was appointed chairman upon the formation of the directorate in August 1850, remaining in the post until his death in June 1863. He was succeeded by Colonel Edmund Henderson (1821-96) who resigned in 1869 to become Commissioner of the Metropolitan police. Henderson's friend and protégé, Captain Edmund Du Cane (1830-1903) was then promoted to the chairmanship, which was held jointly with the posts of Surveyor-General of Prisons and Inspector-General of Military Prisons. Of Jebb enough has probably been recounted, except to note that a mark of the acceptance of prison administration as a respectable part of public service was given when he was awarded the KCB in 1859.[1] Henderson had served for thirteen years as a captain in the Royal Engineers in Western Australia, as Comptroller of Convicts in charge of the penal settlement, where his success was such that a public presentation was made to him by the colonists on the completion of his tour of duty.[2] Although in his six years as chairman he showed little of the interest evinced by Jebb and Du Cane in the broader issues in penal policy, he was responsible for carrying out the extensive changes which followed the Royal

---

1 On the recommendation of Home Secretary Walpole. (See letter of Chichester to Jebb, 17 November 1857, Jebb Papers, box 2.)
2 Major-General Sir Edmund Du Cane, 'Lieut-Colonel Sir Edmund Yeomans Walcot Henderson', *Royal Engineers Journal* (1 February 1897), p. 6.

Commission of 1863.[3]

Du Cane's first appointment was as an engineer assistant on the staff of the Great Exhibition of 1851. He was then posted to Western Australia, where he had charge of public works at Guildford, York and Toodyay,[4] and became acquainted with Henderson. On his return to England in 1856 he served in the War Department under the inspector general of fortifications. In 1863, as a result of the recommendations of the Royal Commission, it was decided to appoint an additional director and two assistant directors. Henderson, whom Jebb intended to appoint to the extra directorship, recommended Du Cane for an assistant directorship. This proposal was unsuccessful because Jebb was displeased with an article critical of the English convict system which Du Cane had published in *Bentley's Miscellany*. But Henderson took over the directorate in July 1863 and was then free to appoint Du Cane.[5]

Jebb, Henderson and Du Cane each for a time, whilst holding their civil offices, continued formally in military service. This pluralism was allowed under a ruling of the Office of Ordnance of 30 December 1836, permitting officers of the Ordnance to be appointed to civil duties, at their existing rate of pay and retaining their claim to promotion; a limit of ten years was fixed, within which they were entitled to return to their corps.[6] Because of the time limit Jebb was obliged to resign his army appointment on full pay retirement in January 1850; in November 1854 he received the honorary rank of colonel, and in July 1860 that of major-general. Henderson, who had been appointed chairman of the directorate in July 1863, resigned from the army in October 1864, but Du Cane was able to resist the attempt to retire him on his completion of ten years of civil duties in 1873 by claiming that of his two appointments of 1863, Director of Convict Prisons and Inspector of Military Prisons, the latter which was a military office was the principal one.[7] His formal service with the Royal Engineers continued until 1887.[8]

3 Something of the energy with which he applied himself to this task may be gauged from the fact that whereas between 1850 and June 1863 ninety-five Standing Orders were issued by the directors, in the eighteen months which followed (until the end of 1864) Henderson issued as many again.

4 R.B. Orr, thesis: 'In Durance Vile', p. 42.

5 Du Cane was at the same time appointed to the newly created post of Inspector of Military Prisons. This post had been created in order to relieve the chairman of the directorate of the actual work of inspecting military prisons (Du Cane to Lord Ripon, 23 October 1873, Du Cane Papers, ref. c. 647, 205; Du Cane, *op. cit.* (1897), p. 6).

6 PRO HO 45/9297/9408. See also the 'Royal Warrant for the Pay and Promotion, Non-effective Pay and Allowances of Her Majesty's British Forces Serving Elsewhere than in India, 3rd February 1866, Part 1', p. 17.

7 Du Cane to Lord Ripon, 23 October 1873, *loc. cit.*

8 Orr, *op. cit.*, pp. 48-9. Besides their possession of relevant skills and experience, the comparative ease with which secondment could be arranged,

Directors' duties were not specified in the Act which established the directorate, but were implicit in the various powers and responsibilities then taken over from existing bodies and offices.[9] These were the visitors of Parkhurst prison, the commissioners of Pentonville prison, the visitors of Millbank prison and the superintendent of convicts, all of whom were directed by their respective Acts of establishment to visit, to inquire into the behaviour of the officers and into the treatment, behaviour and condition of the prisoners. Parkhurst visitors were required to make biannual reports to the home secretary as well as a rather more general annual report.[10] The powers of the Pentonville commissioners were more extensive than those of the Parkhurst visitors and allowed them to appoint or dismiss senior staff, subject only to the approval of the home secretary, whilst over subordinate staff they had unfettered control. The commissioners were vested with the powers of visiting magistrates, could make and alter rules for staff and convicts (also subject to the approval of the home secretary) and were empowered to enter into contracts for the domestic and industrial supplies required by the prison. They could order the prosecution of a convict for an assault on a member of staff and could inquire upon oath into trafficking.[11] The Millbank visitors (formerly inspectors) had almost identical powers and duties.[12] From the superintendent of hulks, directors inherited (in addition to supervisory responsibilities) the powers and duties of both sheriff and magistrate; they were answerable for any escapes and could inflict moderate punishment for prison offences.[13]

The operation of these statutory provisions was regulated by rules approved by the home secretary in March 1851 and December 1858. *Inter alia*, these rules required the directors to be familiar with the

---

and the extent to which pension and rank entitlement continued to accumulate, undoubtedly made the convict service a particularly attractive second career to army and navy men. Secondment with entitlement to rank and other rights did not, however, extend to the prisons under the control of local government.

---

9 By 13 & 14 Vict., c.39 – 'An Act for the Better Government of Convict Prisons', which created the directors as a body corporate.

10 1 & 2 Vict., c.82, ss.9, 10, 17.

11 5 Vict., c.92, ss.6-29, *passim*.

12 These were derived from three Acts: 5 & 6 Will. IV, c.38, s.7; 6 & 7 Vict., c.26, ss.8, 9, 11, 15, 24 and 27; 11 & 12 Vict., c.104.

13 5 Geo. IV, c.84, ss.11 and 16. It was made clear to the directors in Standing Orders that their powers and duties as sheriffs and justices were limited to their prison responsibilities. They were allowed to arrest escaping convicts and could call in the military to assist in the putting down of a dangerous riot, for which purpose they could, if they thought such a course absolutely necessary, and without reading the 'Riot Act', order the military or the warders to fire upon or bayonet charge rioters.

legislation affecting prisons and the management of convicts, and with the rules for convict prisons. With regard to their charge of staff, they were authorised to fine subordinate grades up to three months' pay, or to suspend them. The rules specified that they should visit in his cell every convict in separate or solitary confinement and hear complaints or applications, and that they should take appropriate action in cases where convicts were likely to be mentally or physically injured by the discipline. They could investigate upon oath disciplinary offences alleged against convicts, were given extensive powers to remove from association or otherwise punish, and to select convicts for release on licence. As well as inspecting the prison buildings, journals and accounts they were required to ensure that convict labour was profitably being applied.

In the 'Rules and Regulations for the Government of Convict Prisons' a number of other matters were specially reserved for the attention of the directors. These included religious questions such as the employment of substitutes by chaplains, the approval of books and prayers, and convicts' applications to change religion. Certain privileges such as smoking and extra visits and letters could be granted only by their authority. They had to approve the provision of assistance for medical officers and the use of painful tests for malingering.[14]

Standing Orders also dealt with directors' duties,[15] including their inspection of the convicts' extra diet book on each visit, and their decisions as to the restoration of marks lost by prisoners whilst on light labour or in hospital. They had oversight of the selection of female convicts for refuges, and their consent was necessary to inflict the punishment of cutting a convict's hair within three months of his release, for a letter to be written on behalf of a convict, and for any person other than a governor to contact a prisoner's friends. The directors had particular concern with possible staff malpractices, and therefore kept a specially close watch over the sale of produce to officers, the scrapping of fixtures and other articles, the leave of superior officers and the restoration to officers of leave lost through sickness.

From this description of duties and responsibilities it is clear that the directors were as closely involved in administration as in policy. The railways, the relatively small number of prisons (and the fact that once the renting of cells at Wakefield had ceased all were located in the south of England) allowed them to make frequent visits, and to get to know staff and, in many cases, individual prisoners. Prior to their appointments Henderson and Du Cane had acquired substantial experience of convict discipline, whilst Jebb had a wide knowledge of

14 See, for example, rules 56, 69, 75 and 84 of the 1886 edition of the Rules.
15 These are usefully summarised in PRO PCOM 768 HNO8404, p. 25.

all matters connected with prison construction and management. This expertise was augmented from time to time by the promotion of serving governors to directorships.[16] All these circumstances helped to make the directorate a compact administrative unit in which responsibilities were clearly demarcated and decisions could be reached fairly quickly, much as Du Cane claimed:

> When in 1863 I took up an appointment in the Prison Department under the Home Office, I was at once struck by the immensely greater facility with which the business of my particular department was done. The reason was that the Prison Department was like a satellite with an organic life of its own; whereas in the War Office each department could run only as part of the whole machine.[17]

Nevertheless, the directorate was not without its flaws. From the outset the prisons were divided up between the directors for purposes of visiting and general oversight.[18] The 1863 Royal Commission criticised this method of work, which made it hard for the directors to exercise the collective responsibility with which they were charged. It was therefore suggested that regular consultative and decision-taking meetings should be held.[19] Although this recommendation was followed, directors continued to take special responsibility for particular prisons, leading to the 1878 Royal Commission to recommend that work should periodically be redistributed, in order that the prisons might, from time to time, be viewed with a fresh eye, and directors could acquire a thorough knowledge of all establishments.[20]

Prisons were inspected once a month (in London every week), and between times for special purposes, a procedure which Du Cane thought most advantageous and effective:

> The Director not coming in daily contact with the officers and prisoners, but only visiting the prison magisterially at uncertain intervals, it is, of course, felt that he can give a fresh and an impartial consideration to any question or complaint.[21]

Some staff regarded the visits in a different light, as an 1861 article in the *Civil Service Gazette* revealed. The author claimed that Jebb quite unjustly flattered himself in his supposed knowledge of prisons:

16 See n. 64, p. 445.
17 Major-General E.F. Du Cane, 'The Civil Service and Reform', *Monthly Review* (April 1900), pp. 35-6.
18 See n. 164, p. 216, above.
19 *Report of the Commissioners Appointed to Inquire into the Operation of the Acts Relating to Transportation and Penal Servitude*, PP, 1863, XXI, 1, 49.
20 *Report of the Commissioners Appointed to Inquire into the Working of the Penal Servitude Acts*, PP, 1878-9, XXXVII, 1, lx.
21 E.F. Du Cane, *The Punishment and Prevention of Crime*, p. 167.

... when he makes his appearance, of course all is *en regale* and *couleur de rose*. His business is not with the convicts, but with the buildings and grounds, to see that they are in proper repair and order. The Governor is all smiles and attention; the Deputy-Governor touches his cap à la militaire, and shakes hands ... the warders present arms; Sir Joshua walks round the prison and grounds, and a gracious 'good morning' finishes the inspection.

As for the regular visiting director:

In theory an appeal lies from the Governor to the Visiting Director, but in practice such appeal is a delusion and a snare. Woe to the poor wretch of a convict or 'subordinate' who would dare attempt such an act of rebellion against superior authority! If an official he would be marked, entrapped and dismissed, as 'too much of a lawyer'; if a convict, the prospect of his moral reformation is not thought of seriously, or, if thought of at all, it is only decided as an impracticable theory, as a visionary idea never to be realised.[22]

Perhaps not surprisingly a former convict agreed with the contention that directorial inspections were largely show:

Much in the same way that an audience at a theatre witnesses a drama; he sees and knows nothing about the wires, and the ropes, and the traps, and the wings; he sees only what is made visible by the footlights. ... The director is merely ornamental. He makes a formal visit of two or three hours' duration eleven times a year, in order to flatter everything that the governor has done. ... He nods, he eats eleven luncheons ... praises the claret, nods again, and has then earned his thousand pounds.[23]

A less partisan report describes how before the weekly visit of the director to Brixton, applications were vetted by the lady superintendent. There does not appear to have been any sinister reason for these preliminaries. Indeed the author estimates that about two-thirds of those seeking an interview had only one question to ask: the date of their release and what good behaviour was likely to speed it.[24]

The powers of the directors over the inmates, staff and activities of the convict prisons were greater by far than the powers exercised by local prison officials. But whilst there were strong criticisms of policy, particularly in the decade 1853 to 1863, and not infrequent complaints of inefficient inspection or unfair dismissal, there were few allegations about systematic maltreatment such as had led to the

22 *Civil Service Gazette* (18 May 1861), IX, no. 438, p. 313.
23 'A Ticket-of-Leave-Man', *Convict Life; or Revelations Concerning Convicts and Convict Prisons*, pp. 158-9.
24 'A Prison Matron', *Female Life in Prison*, pp. 45, 49.

Birmingham and Leicester scandals. Despite this record the Royal Commission of 1878 thought that the system of inspection might be strengthened since

> it would conduce to public confidence in the system, and would be a valuable safeguard against any abuses creeping into it, if means were taken to secure the inspection of the prisons from time to time by persons appointed by the Government, but unpaid and unconnected with the prisons department.

The commission noted the objections of Du Cane and others, who were fearful that the authority of the directors might be undermined, but suggested that it would not be difficult to find competent persons, such as chairmen of quarter sessions, to act as unpaid inspectors:

> It seems to us inconsistent that such jealous precautions should have been taken as regards the local prisons, in which prisoners are only confined for comparatively short terms, and that no similar safeguard should be provided in the case of convict prisons, in which prisoners are confined for long periods, and even for life.[25]

The home secretary agreed with the commissioners and a system of visitors was established and began to operate as from 1 January 1880.[26] That Du Cane was rather grudging in his acceptance of this change, was indicated in his 1882 *Punishment and Prevention of Crime*. Although noting that visitors could visit a prison at any time and make various inquiries, he was careful to add that 'they have no power to give any order, or to interfere in any way with the administration of the prison'.[27]

Du Cane's unease about outside inspection is difficult to understand since the justices had, from the earliest days, played a part in convict disciplinary proceedings in those local prisons where cells had been rented.[28] Here they carried out with respect to the convicts the same duties of inspection, the hearing of applications and adjudication as for their own local prisoners. Moreover, following a recommendation of the 1863 Royal Commission, certain county magistrates were given authority by the secretary of state to order the infliction of

---

25 1878 *RC, op. cit.*, pp. xi-xii. Du Cane's former colleague Dr W.A. Guy, formerly medical officer at Millbank, and a member of the Royal Commission, issued a dissenting memorandum on this issue: see lxv-lxvi.

26 *Return . . . of Persons . . . Appointed to be Unpaid Inspectors of Convict Prisons in England*, PP, 1880, LIX, 527.

27 Du Cane, *op. cit.*, p. 167.

28 Earl of Chichester (ed.), *Reports and Observations on the Discipline and Management of Convict Prisons by . . . Jebb*, p. 53.

corporal punishment in convict prisons.[29]

These incursions into the powers of the directorate were minor. By the end of the 1870s there was no threat of any major change in the system, and no want of public confidence. Jebb had faced such problems, but the system which was taken over by his successors was politically secure. The virtual absence of internal disturbances, a decline in the number of convict receptions[30] and the endorsement of two Royal Commissions[31] contributed to an obvious feeling of confidence which, as manifested in published reports and discussions of policy, sometimes verged on self-congratulation. But it was not without passing through severe difficulties that the directorate had won this secure and respected position in public esteem.

Under pressure, 1853-63   The directorate faced a series of difficult issues and strong criticisms in the decade which followed the introduction of penal servitude. The politically sensitive circumstances in which the convict service operated were reflected in the fact that within seven years it was the subject of two major inquiries: a select committee in 1856 and a Royal Commission in 1863. The service was also the subject of continual comment in newspapers, pamphlets and books; from policy to the practical details of administration, scarcely any aspect of its work escaped close appraisal. At times Jebb found the criticism and attacks almost too much to bear, and his morale and that of some of his staff clearly suffered.

---

29 1863 *RC, op. cit.*, PP, XXI, 1, 43. This recommendation was implemented by s.3 of the 1864 Penal Servitude Act (27 & 28 Vict., c.47), which empowered the home secretary to appoint two county magistrates to adjudicate and order corporal punishment in a convict prison situated in their county. Their authority was to be 'exercised under the same Conditions as One of the Directors of Convict Prisons would have, and no greater'.

30 As Du Cane pointed out in his *Punishment and Prevention of Crime*, whereas on 31 December 1869 there were 11,660 persons undergoing penal servitude, by the end of 1885 this had fallen to 8,790 (*op. cit.*, p. 191).

31 The 1871 Royal Commission on the Treatment of Treason-Felony Convicts had said of the convict prisons,

> we feel justified in reporting favourably of their general administration in respect of treatment, diet and discipline. The governors and other officers appear to us, as a body, well qualified for the discharge of their arduous duties, while careful frequent and responsible supervision by the central department is calculated to provide a wholesome safeguard against possible abuses of power (PP, 1871, XXXII, 1, 7).

The 1878 Royal Commission on Penal Servitude concluded that

> the present system of penal servitude is on the whole satisfactory, that it is effective as a punishment, and free from serious abuses. . . . We believe that a sentence of penal servitude is now generally an object of dread to the criminal population (PP, 1878-9, XXXVII, 1, xxvi).

The first major problem arose from the convicts' reaction to the substitution of penal servitude for transportation. It has been noted[32] that, as a general rule, those sentenced to penal servitude under the 1853 Act were not allowed remission of sentence. If Jebb was correct in his judgment transportation had, by the middle of the century, come to be viewed by most offenders as preferable to continued confinement in a home prison, and the prospect of remission of sentence added to its attraction. When convicts subject to transportation and penal servitude were consigned to the same prisons and given numerous opportunities to compare their respective sentences the mixture became explosive. This first eruption of serious trouble began in the hulks and public works prisons in 1856, as a result of dissatisfaction on the part of prisoners under sentence of penal servitude at the regular release on licence of those who had received sentences of transportation, but who had, nevertheless, been kept in the home prisons.[33] Jebb had forecast that discipline would suffer should remission not be applied to penal servitude, but this did not prevent him from claiming after the first troubles had subsided that 'a much better state of feeling now exists', and holding out hopes that the existing disciplinary system of privileges and rewards would prove to be adequate in maintaining order and control.[34]

The Penal Servitude Act of 1857 ended the distinction between penal servitude and transportation, and thus made necessary the granting of remission to all. In the long term this dissipated the feelings of unfairness and inequity, but more immediately additional strife was created, since there were soon in the same prisons persons sentenced after July 1857, who benefited from the new measure's dispensations, and those whose sentences, being imposed before that date, continued to be subject to the old Act. At Portland there was an outbreak of insubordinate behaviour, which resulted in ten floggings for assaults or threats against officers, offences which previously were almost unknown. These condign punishments were to little avail, and in September 1857 open displays of concerted disobedience occurred. Some who had benefited from the new Act apparently added to the unrest by baiting their less fortunate fellows. The directors reported that 'the 1857 Act men taunted them ... and jeered at them for working so hard for nothing. This feeling at last showed itself by large bodies of men striking work and refusing to labour any more'.[35] Large numbers of troops were brought in to enforce order. Two hundred and thirty men were removed to Millbank; one hundred were put in chains

---

32 See pp. 391-2, above.
33 *Reports of the Directors of Convict Prisons* (henceforth *RDCP*), PP, 1857, Sess. 2, XXIII, 65, 201-2.
34 *Ibid*.
35 *RDCP*, PP, 1859, Sess. 2, XIII, Pt 1, 191, 338.

and on a bread and water diet, and those identified as the ringleaders were flogged.[36]

The convicts' sense of grievance was eventually dissipated and, as those subject to the 1853 Act completed their sentences and were released, one dangerous source of tension was removed from the system. By the early 1860s governors were reporting that the remission offered under the 1857 Act was indeed proving helpful in the maintenance of discipline.[37] What subsequently became more clear, however, is that whilst the remission question may have triggered off disorders, the public works prisons, which brought together in open spaces large numbers of convicts subject only to relatively light supervision, were possessed of serious control problems. In 1861 there was a major mutiny at Chatham, and another in 1864 at Portland, in the course of which the civil guard opened fire on the ringleaders.[38] By this time it was recognised that there was an endemic problem of control and the directors reported that 'The evils attendant on the massing together of such large bodies of convicts ... having become evident, we have taken steps ... for sub-dividing them so as to effect complete separation'.[39] It was not accurate to claim that the convicts had been completely separated,[40] since this would have been impossible on public works. But the various steps which were taken (which went far beyond merely physical alterations in the prisons) were apparently effective, and though there were some disturbances in later years, they took the form of attacks on individual staff rather than riots.[41]

Whilst these well publicised disturbances were going on,[42] Jebb and his colleagues grappled with staffing problems. The endless stream of dismissals and the generally high rate of staff turnover were familiar enough,[43] but there were also public accusations by former employees that the directors were inept and that they colluded with corrupt practices. In 1857 for example, Thwaites, a schoolmaster on the hulks (and later at Lewes invalid prison), made allegations about corruption, mismanagement and the maltreatment of prisoners. There may have been some substance in Thwaites's claims, but when he wrote to Jebb accusing him of striving to keep these irregularities from the light of

36 *Ibid.*

37 See, for example, the *RDCP*, PP, 1861, XXX, 237, 242-3.

38 *RDCP*, PP, 1865, XXV, 1, 87-8.

39 *RDCP*, PP, 1864, XXVI, 209, 9.

40 Essentially the authorities sought to sub-divide the convicts, and to prevent large congregations. At Portland and Chatham the halls, chapels and even parade grounds were partitioned (*RDCP*, PP, 1865, XXV, 1, 146).

41 See, for example, the description of events at Portland in the 1870 Report of the Directors (*RDCP*, PP, 1871, XXXI, 1, 118).

42 See, for example, *The Times*, 19 January 1861, 10a; 14 February 1861, 10d; 14 July 1864, 9d; 18 July 1864, 5f.

43 See pp. 464-6, below.

day, Jebb ordered his dismissal.[44] Thwaites would not be silenced, however, and in December 1858 warned Jebb, 'Your fame and honour are upon the point of being lost through the shameful manner in which you have prostituted your power in the Convict Service.'[45] Thwaites continued his campaign by means of articles and pamphlets for several years thereafter, and so vexatious did he become that Jebb was driven to consider an action for libel.[46] Thwaites's dismissal was supported by Jebb's close colleagues, one of whom, Captain Whitty, reminded Jebb how Thwaites had always been turning up at the Home Office 'in one unpleasant way or another like an evil spirit'.[47] The Civil Service Gazette made the dismissal an occasion on which to attack Jebb as the holder of 'irresponsible power' and whose recommendation 'has the admitted authority of a fiat to make and unmake'. The Gazette argued that this power 'should not be left in the hands of one individual unless it is really controlled by some independent superior tribunal'.[48]

Charles Measor, who had been deputy governor at Chatham during the riots, began to raise criticisms of a more measured kind at the beginning of the 1860s. At first his observations were sent privately to the directors, but after his resignation they were embodied in pamphlets on various aspects of penal policy and administration.[49] There also developed a protracted and heated debate on the comparative virtues of the Irish and English systems.[50]

Jebb took this last dispute to heart and went to considerable pains to keep in touch with Irish developments.[51] He was convinced that the

44 See the Jebb Papers (box 4), letters of 1 May and 25 December 1857, and those of 25 May and 15 December 1858.
45 Ibid., letter of 15 December 1858.
46 See letter from Park Nelson to Jebb, 28 December 1858 (Jebb Papers, box 4). Thwaites's pamphlet Our Convicts; Their Riots and Their Causes was supplemented by a similar publication by the Rev. T.K. Walpole dealing with the author's 'Excessive and Illegal Punishment' at Jebb's hands. Walpole had been an assistant chaplain at Portland in 1858. After a dispute with the chaplain he was transferred to Lewes, where he met up with Thwaites (see p. 449, below). Thwaites's allegations about the state of the Stirling Castle hulk were still being ventilated in the Civil Service Gazette in 1861 (4 April 1861, LX, no. 436, p. 281).
47 Jebb Papers, box 2, Whitty to Jebb, 1 January 1858.
48 Civil Service Gazette (4 April 1861), LX, no. 436, p. 281.
49 See the letters on Measor of 15 February and 15 April 1861 (Jebb Papers, box 4). Measor left the convict service for the Factory Inspectorate. His two best known pamphlets appeared after Jebb's death, Criminal Correction in 1864 and The Utilization of the Criminal in 1869.
50 This has been thoroughly discussed elsewhere and no useful purpose would be served by its recapitulation, but see, for example, Max Grünhut, Penal Reform, pp. 83-8.
51 He maintained regular correspondence with his friend and erstwhile colleague Captain Whitty, after the latter's move from the English directorate to the Irish Prisons Board, and also received lengthy reports from Mr Gibson at the convict station at Monkstown, Co. Cork.

apparently better results of the Irish system arose from the peculiar suitability of the rural Irish setting for the stage of 'intermediate imprisonment', which was the main distinguishing feature of the Irish system, and he doubted whether such a system would prove so successful in English towns and cities. No major penological figure took up the cudgels for Jebb, whilst on the other side were ranged Sir Walter Crofton (chairman of the Irish Prisons Board), Matthew Davenport Hill, Mary Carpenter, W.L. Clay and some of the Wakefield visiting justices.[52]

Although Jebb had anticipated, as early as 1858, that the Irish system would become a means of attacking the English convict service,[53] this foresight did not make the polemics any easier to bear. He wrote to the Yorkshire magistrates castigating the 'unfair' attack made on the English convict system by the Wakefield visiting justices and complaining of their failure to notify the home secretary of their intentions. The convict department, he wrote, had

> quite sufficient difficulties, but these difficulties are very greatly increased when the management of the Department is disparaged by statements from . . . Gentlemen connected with my own department . . . with whom I have been in the habit of acting on terms of mutual confidence and cooperation.[54]

In his *Times* reply to Thornton Smith (a supporter of the Irish system), Jebb showed the strength of his resentment:

> I do also protest against the deep injustice that is done to the whole of the officers who have for many years devoted their best energies to carrying out the views of the Government in regard to the proper

52 The literature on this debate is voluminous and includes the following on the Irish side: 'Four Visiting Justices of the West Riding Prison at Wakefield', *Observations on the Treatment of Convicts in Ireland*; M.D. Hill, *Suggestions for the Repression of Crime*; Thornton Smith, 'The Irish Convict System: Why it has Succeeded', *Cornhill Magazine* (April 1861), III, pp. 409-32, 'The English Convict System', *Cornhill Magazine* (June 1861), III, pp. 708-33; 'The Convict Out in the World', *Cornhill Magazine* (August 1861), IV, pp. 229-50; Mary Carpenter, *Our Convicts*; W.L. Clay, *Our Convict System*. Crofton himself published many articles including in 1860 *Success of the Irish Prison System and Supervision* and in 1864 *Recommendation for Extending Supervision to England*. Jebb himself opposed the claims of the Irish system in a reply to Thornton Smith in *The Times* (15 April 1877, 9d); 'Scrutator' argued against the Wakefield visiting justices in *Irish Fallacies and English Facts* (1863) as did John T. Burt in *Irish Facts and Wakefield Figures* of the same year.

53 Jebb Papers, box 2; Whitty to Jebb, 2 May 1858: 'I am very sorry to find from what you say . . . that there is almost a certainty of a clash between the English and Irish Convict systems.'

54 Jebb Papers, box 4, letter of July 1862.

mode of administering the law in connexion with the highest class of our secondary punishment.[55]

Even before the campaign on behalf of the Irish system reached its peak Jebb displayed considerable personal strain and anxiety. At the end of 1858 he had received a note of support from the home secretary; his fulsome reply is most revealing, and underlines his feelings of isolation and insecurity:

> I did not sufficiently express my sense of your kindness, or the value I attach to the expression of confidence with which you honoured me in your note; nor can I make you understand how greatly they have relieved my mind.
>
> I had feared you did not feel altogether satisfied with my Administration of the Convict Department, and this feeling, added to my other troubles was more than I could have borne.
>
> Having enjoyed the confidence of successive Secretaries of State, and, I may perhaps add, on the evidence of Committees, gained in some measure the confidence of Parliament and the country, by only advocating common sense principles and proving their soundness by their practical application, I confess that it has been a source of mortification and discouragement to find the late Lord Lieutenant of Ireland, at the great Liverpool meeting expressing his opinion . . . that the Irish Directors of Prisons under the inspirations derived from their Chief have practically solved the great problem which so long has perplexed our Government and legislature – namely, 'what should be done with our Convicts'.
>
> In this he sets aside, with an authority which remains unquestioned, all the system in building up which I have spent the last 20 years of my life and devoted my entire energies. . . .[56]

By the winter of 1862-3 Jebb had held office in the convict administration for twenty-three years, during fourteen of which he had been the country's most senior prison administrator and the most influential figure in penal policy. He was in his sixty-ninth year and on the verge of retirement. Reformers, such as Matthew Davenport Hill, may have been hoping that he would be succeeded by Crofton, but Jebb preferred his fellow sapper, Henderson, whom he considered to have done much sound practical work in the Western Australian convict settlement.[57] In those months a series of street

---

55 *The Times*, 15 April 1861, 9d.
56 Jebb to Walpole (home secretary, February 1858 until January 1859), 5 November 1858; Jebb Papers, box 4. (Walpole had also held the office of home secretary between February and December 1852.)
57 Du Cane, *op. cit.* (1897), p. 6.

robberies[58] occurred in London which brought to a head many of the criticisms of the prison system. It was widely suggested that the robberies were being committed by convicts released on licence under the 1857 Act. At the end of 1862 a Royal Commission on penal servitude was set up and two months later the Carnarvon Committee was established to inquire into the local prisons. Jebb gave evidence to both committees, but died shortly before they reported. There is no doubt that during this period he was under enormous pressure of work, exacerbated by the requirements of the two inquiries. One can only speculate on the unease with which he must have viewed the crisis of confidence in the country's penal system and the challenge to his own position.

Had Jebb lived to see the results of the inquiries he would have found that his policies and administration had largely been vindicated. The inquiries had been conducted in the midst of one of those political crises about crime and public order which erupt in most generations and which sweep opinion in a conservative, even reactionary, direction. But although the local prisons were roundly condemned by the Carnarvon Committee for their lack of uniformity in punishment, and brought under closer central government control by the 1865 Act, no major changes were recommended in the convict service by the Royal Commission. The commissioners held penal servitude to be insufficiently deterrent, yet blame for this was not attributed to the penal régime, but to the inadequate length of sentences.[59] Far from taking either the local or convict prisons in the direction desired by the penal reformers, the events of 1862-3 headed off and reversed their campaign. The directorate was put on a more secure political footing than ever before, and though Henderson presided over the tightening up of the disciplinary system, the changes were relatively minor and only 'more of the same'.

Governors

Convict service governors, in contrast with their local colleagues, dealt with long-term inmates and therefore prisons with a low turnover of population; this was particularly so in the public works prisons after the 1853 curtailment of transportation. Convict prison populations were, moreover, quite large and not subject to the same fluctuations as the local establishments; governors had no escort or court duties and

---

58 The 'garrotting' scare achieved major proportions following the robbery on his way home from the Commons of James Pilkington, the member for Blackburn, in the early hours of 16 July 1862.

59 Sentences were subsequently increased from a minimum of three to a minimum of five years, although the Royal Commission (para. 86.1) had recommended a minimum of seven years.

abundant assistance, and thus could concentrate on administration, staffing and the regulation and disciplining of inmates. Their establishments were of sufficient size to enable them easily to keep a social distance from the subordinate staff, whilst the employment of deputies from a similar background to their own relieved many of the pressures of responsibility.[60]

In the early years of the directorate many governors were appointed directly to the post, almost invariably following a naval or military career.[61] Later, appointments were, in the first instance, normally to deputy-governorships, an office always filled by direct appointment, and not by promotion from within the convict service.[62] Ostensibly a deputy governorship was not a stepping-stone to a governorship, but the Home Office acknowledged in 1874 that

> in practice it has been found convenient and desirable for many
> years past to fill the higher office by promotion from the lower
> ... the selection for both grades has always been made from
> men of the same class and age.[63]

As the convict service expanded, a pattern of transfers from one establishment to another came to be linked to promotions, with the intention of ensuring a wide and thorough knowledge of the service for those who achieved high rank. Captain Mark Gambier's career is a good illustration of such moves and promotions. Appointed first as deputy governor at Millbank, he became the first governor of the reopened Dartmoor in 1850, subsequently moving to Portsmouth and then back to Millbank as governor. In 1858 Gambier became a director, retaining that post until 1872. The number of directorships was limited, and only a few governors could be promoted to these top posts,[64] but movement from deputy to governor and from the less to the more important prisons was frequent. Immediately after the merging of the convict and local prisons in 1878, two convict governors were appointed

60 With only a few and occasional exceptions all convict prisons had deputy governors. The post was abolished at Parkhurst in 1862, when the prison was running down as a juvenile penitentiary (*RDCP*, PP, 1863, XXIV, 1, 97). On the other hand, Portland with its very large population merited (at least from 1864) two deputy governors (*RDCP*, PP, 1865, XXV. 1, 87).

61 In the 1850s and 1860s no person with a rank senior to captain or major appears to have entered the convict service, but by the 1870s the colonels began to make an appearance. See, for example, *Reports of the Officers of Convict Prisons*, PP, 1878-9, XXXV, 1.

62 Correspondence between the Home Office and Treasury, March 1874 (PRO HO 45/9358/31266A/4).

63 *Ibid*.

64 Captain J.S. Whitty, a friend of Jebb's, who eventually moved to the Irish convict service, was promoted from a governorship to a directorship. Captain W.J. Stopford, governor at Dartmoor from 1866 to 1868 and then briefly at Portsmouth, was similarly promoted in 1869.

to inspectorships, indicating the way in which career opportunities had been improved by the merging of the two administrations.

Another difference between convict and local governors was that the former were responsible not to a heterogeneous group of magistrates, but to a group of directors with backgrounds and opinions similar to their own, and to whose rank some, at least, of their number would some day be appointed. They worked within a unified and uniform disciplinary and administrative system in which diligence and ability could with greater clarity be measured and linked to promotion. Moreover, there was not in the convict service the same uncertainty over the question of pensioning as there was in the local prisons. Convict governors' pensions were linked by the 1859 Superannuation Act to years of service; the pensions of governors of local prisons remained in the hands of the magistrates, and a movement as governor from one locality to another remained a matter in which the exercise of much caution was advisable, even where a larger and more interesting prison, or more substantial salary, offered an initial inducement.

Chaplains

The relative decline in importance of religion in the régime of the convict prisons after 1848, which was outlined in the previous chapter, necessarily affected the standing and method of work of the chaplains. Extreme evangelical preaching, so prominent in the heyday of Pentonville, became increasingly less acceptable. By 1878, as Du Cane told the Royal Commission, it was thought that 'as the prisoners are a very mixed class, our desire is to get chaplains who do not have any extraordinary views of any kind, such as might cause bad feelings in the prison'.[65] Liturgical and pastoral duties did not change greatly over the years, except for a greater subordination of visitations, education and some religious services to the disciplinary arrangements of the prison,[66] which applied even to the separate prisons. The chaplain of Pentonville, the Reverend A. Sherwin, told the 1878 Royal Commission that 'The visiting is necessarily very irregular, because we are not allowed to interfere with the discipline in any way, so as to interrupt the hours of

---

65 1878 *RC*, q.632.
66 The rules stated that the chaplain 'shall be subject to no control in matters strictly within his department, but that of the Secretary of State, or of a Director'. This protection of the chaplain's position was more apparent than real, however, since the definition of his responsibilities changed considerably in the course of time. Moreover, the chaplain was by the same rule enjoined to 'take care not to interfere with the established rules and regulations of the prison, as to security or the routine of discipline and labour' (*Rules and Regulations for the Government of the Convict Prisons* (1858 ed.) (henceforth *RRGP*), p. 22).

labour or exercise or rest. . . .'[67]

The chaplain was required to visit every prisoner in the infirmary and those under punishment once a day (an indication that he still retained part of his original role of internal inspector);[68] he conducted two or three services on Sundays, various short services during the week, was responsible for the education department and (with the governor) for the censorship of prisoners' letters, and also helped to deal with petitions.[69] The Reverend G.B. de Renzi, chaplain of Millbank, told the 1878 Royal Commission that he liked to see all convicts as soon as possible after their reception, and that he gave the prisoners to understand that they could see him at any time thereafter by request. He pointed out that the visiting of prisoners was very fatiguing work and that he could not expect 'with satisfaction' to visit more than twelve or fourteen persons a day.[70] That visiting could only sparsely be undertaken is borne out by the report of a convict who had been in Millbank in the 1860s that during his thirteen months of confinement he was only once visited by a chaplain, and that for only three minutes.[71]

Until October 1863 the chaplains had an important role in licensing procedures. They were instructed to keep a journal and a character-book, wherein they should note their opinions on 'the character and moral and religious progress of every individual' so that they might 'be able with confidence to refer to this record, when called upon periodically to confer with the Governor on the necessary recommendation for the classification of the prisoners, or for their disposal on discharge'.[72] Chaplains also made inquiries as to a convicts' friends and possible employment on release, and until 1855 it is clear that the lack of reasonable prospects for resettlement prevented convicts being recommended to the home secretary for licence.[73] In 1863 it was decided to ignore resettlement prospects entirely in making a recommendation as to the grant of a licence,[74] and thereafter the chaplains' part in release procedures was restricted to helping convicts obtain accommodation and employment.[75]

67 1878 *RC*, q.5197.
68 *Ibid.*, q.2626; *RRGP*, 24.
69 1878 *RC*, qs. 634 and 5753-6; *RRGP*, 11, 24.
70 1878 *RC*, q.5857.
71 'One Who Has Endured It', *Five Years Penal Servitude*, pp. 48-9. He does mention that a scripture reader visited more regularly.
72 *RRGP*, 23-4.
73 Standing Order no. 31, 13 December 1855.
74 See p. 403, n. 97, above.
75 This, noted Henderson in a Standing Order, could best be accomplished 'by a private letter addressed . . . to the parochial clergyman, or to any person whom the prisoner may desire to be written to, in cases where he may think the step can safely be taken and will be attended with beneficial consequences' (Standing Order no. 101, October 1863).

From March 1864 Roman Catholic priests could be appointed to the convict prisons and payments made to them from public funds.[76] In order to allow the Roman Catholic chaplains most usefully to be deployed their flocks were concentrated at Millbank for the first stage of their sentence, and at Portsmouth for the public works stage. Jews and Nonconformists were visited by their own ministers, but the numbers involved were insufficient to warrant concentration.[77] Except for the different liturgy and sacraments and the censorship of convicts' letters, the duties of the Roman Catholic priests were similar to those of the Anglican clergy, and they undertook certain responsibilities for secular education.[78]

The introduction of Roman Catholic priests was a cause of some controversy, as there still existed a good deal of anti-popery among the Anglican chaplains;[79] indeed this may have been another reason for segregating the Roman Catholic convicts. Whilst the Prison Ministers Bill was going through Parliament in 1863 the Reverend J.H. Moran, chaplain of Brixton, wrote an indignant letter to Jebb, evidently under the impression that the measure was going to apply to the convict prisons. He complained that the bill was contrary to the spirit of 'our Protestant Constitution', and argued that hitherto the convict prison rules 'have secured full liberty of conscience to the Prisoners and have no way interfered with mine'. Obviously incensed by the prospect of Roman Catholic observances in the convict prisons Moran asked Jebb

76 Standing Order no. 125, 18 March 1864. The Prison Ministers Act (26 & 27 Vict., c.79) which had been passed the previous year and which authorised the appointment to local prisons of ministers not of the Established Church, and their payment from the rates, did not apply to convict prisons. Power to appoint such clergy lay with the home secretary, however, and Parliament voted funds for this purpose. In 1863 there were about 1,500 Roman Catholic convicts and 3,000-4,000 serving terms in the local prisons (*Hansard* (Third Series), CLXX, col. 402).

77 In its early days concentration had the unexpected consequence of inducing convicts to declare a change of religion in order to obtain a removal from one prison to another. This practice was stopped following the recommendation of the 1863 Royal Commission that convicts should not be allowed to change from the religion which they professed on reception (1863 *RC, op. cit.*, 49-50). Standing Order no. 104 of 14 October 1863 instructed governors to warn prisoners that they would not be allowed to change their declared religion 'except upon the gravest grounds, and after long and careful consideration of the authorities'. Henderson added, 'I need scarcely say that my object in framing this regulation is to put an end to the unseemly farce of convicts changing their nominal religion upon every idle whim and caprice.'

78 Standing Order no. 125, 18 March 1864, rule 12.

79 Joseph Kingsmill, the influential chaplain of Pentonville, had been particularly strident in his anti-popery; see p. 234, above. It is reasonable to assume that Anglican clergy of an evangelical persuasion, with a strong belief in the importance of personal salvation, would be attracted to work in the prisons, and among them dislike of Rome would be particularly likely.

on what grounds and by what authority all Roman Catholic Prisoners are to be handed over to a Roman Catholic Priest . . . contrary to the rule which allows them to see a Priest *if they wish it* and apply for this. On what grounds can I be excluded from visiting any prisoner *who does not* object to see me. On what grounds can Roman Catholic prisoners be prevented attending my ministrations in Chapel and attending school during the reading of scripture. All now attend school . . . are they to be compelled to absent themselves?[80]

An anti-popery row had also erupted between the chaplains at Portland in 1858. Holderness, the chaplain, was reported to Jebb by the assistant chaplain for speaking disrespectfully of the Prayer Book in a lecture to convicts. He was alleged to have said that 'it was defiled with Popery and was figuratively in the condition of a book that had been thrown down a chimney'.[81] To avoid the scandal of a public altercation between the two ministers, Sir George Grey decided that they should be posted to other establishments; Holderness was sent to Dartmoor and his assistant to the temporary invalid prison at Lewes.[82] A scandal of a different kind arose over the chaplain at Chatham in the summer of 1860. Captain Donatus O'Brien, the visiting director, reported to Jebb that the chaplain was behaving in a disreputable manner, and that he had been found drunk in his prison quarters. The problem in this case was that the chaplain had achieved a measure of notoriety throughout the convict service and it was difficult to get another prison to accept him.[83] Eventually it was decided that he would simply be excluded from Chatham prison.[84]

Such embarrassments were exceptional and the vast majority of chaplains carried out their duties loyally and unremarkably. It is clear,

---

80 Moran to Jebb, 9 August 1863, Jebb Papers, box 4. Similar language had been used during the debate on the bill. C.N. Newdegate, member for Warwickshire, saw the bill as a political concession which the government would lament, which forced 'into the cells of the unwilling prisoners the representatives of a priesthood whose success in moral instruction was illustrated by the enormous preponderance of Roman Catholic prisoners in our gaols' (*Hansard* (Third Series), CLXIX, col. 466). Another objector to the bill described Roman Catholic priests as the agents of a foreign power and a potential threat to Protestants (*ibid.*, col. 413).

81 Letter of 29 December 1858, Jebb Papers, box 4.

82 A transfer which Jebb was to regret, since at Lewes the assistant chaplain met and became an associate of Thwaites, the schoolmaster, who became a major thorn in Jebb's side (see pp. 440-1, above). In the 1863 debate on the Prison Ministers Bill it was alleged that 'at Dartmoor the Romish priest has cause the greatest confusion and disorder in the prison' (*Hansard* (Third Series), CLXX, col. 444), so Mr Holderness may have moved from one prison in religious turmoil to another.

83 O'Brien to Jebb, 7 August 1860 (Jebb Papers, box 4).

84 Letter of 18 August 1860 (Jebb Papers, box 4).

however, that the chaplains' subordination to secular authority in the prisons was as complete in policy as in administration. There was no Chaplain-General, nor was such a post contemplated by any of the committees of inquiry. Confined to the business of their own prisons, the chaplains could occasionally comment upon but in the end only accede to policy decisions taken elsewhere.

Medical officers

The quality of medical officers improved, so that by 1878 only candidates with both medical and surgical qualifications would be considered.[85] In convict prisons, long-term mental and physical illnesses, industrial injuries, and the general health of the convicts were at least as pressing as the process of reception and discharge, which dominated the working life of the local prison medical officer. The 1878 Royal Commission was told that two medical officers were appointed to each prison, but Du Cane agreed that sometimes (because of leave, illness and so forth) sole medical charge of as many as 1,500 convicts fell upon one medical officer. He defended existing staffing levels by pointing out that local medical assistance could always be obtained, and that staffing levels seemed appropriate if comparison were made with 'the proportion of medical officers to the free population'.[86] The latter claim is disingenuous, as the free population did not require as much routine inspection and attention as the convicts. In addition to attending to the sick and all receptions and discharges, medical officers were obliged to inspect every prisoner weekly and to see daily every prisoner under punishment.[87] With curious ambiguity Dr V.C. Clarke, chief surgeon at Pentonville, told the 1878 Royal Commission that he was not overworked, but that

> The pressure is very great, and some of the duty must be almost omitted. I am not speaking with reference to the duty in the prison but as to the duty without the prison; the officers and their families are visited by us, and with only one medical officer to perform the whole duty, it is almost impossible that the officers and their families can be attended to with so much regularity outside.[88]

Candidates were generally recommended by their hospitals and interviewed in London by the medical officer of Millbank. If he reported favourably the candidate's name was entered on a list, from which the

85 1878 *RC*, *op. cit.*, q.47.
86 *Ibid.*, q.628.
87 *Ibid.*, qs. 1616-21; *RRGP*, 33. A general inspection of the prison had to be made each month, and a report thereon submitted to the directors.
88 1878 *RC*, *op. cit.*, q. 2048.

directors made a selection when a vacancy arose.[89] In the first instance the appointment was as assistant surgeon, and a man could expect to serve for four or five years before being promoted to surgeon. Medical officers could not have a private practice, and some felt that this prohibition did not receive recognition in their salaries.[90] Although extra payment was given at the very large prisons, an assistant surgeon started at only £200 per year, rising by £5 per year to £250; surgeons had a maximum salary of £400.[91]

Bearing in mind the constant pressures arising from malingering,[92] medical and discipline staff seem to have clashed relatively infrequently. This may have been because the medical departments were reasonably self-contained, and there was little overlap between the duties of the governor and those of the surgeon; certainly at the invalid prisons, where duties could not so easily be separated, there was friction between the two grades of staff. At these prisons

> the medical man is literally the superintendent, and the governor
> is the first lieutenant to carry out his instructions, submitting all
> his acts to the approval of the medical superintendent. I think
> that there is apt to be a clashing in those cases, which you might
> not find in a prison were men are healthy, until they are taken
> into the infirmary, which is the province of the medical man.[93]

There were also occasional conflicts over punishments and diets. Dr William Guy of Millbank had strongly urged upon the Carnarvon Committee his view that medical staff should not have the power to

---

89 *Ibid.*, qs. 2979-80.
90 *Ibid.*, q. 8085 – evidence of Dr Roome of Parkhurst.
91 *Ibid.*, q. 2986.
92 John Campbell, *Thirty Years' Experience of a Medical Officer*, p. 67. Charles Measor observed in this regard that

> The position of the medical officer over convicts is not at all an enviable
> one and it requires strongly to be upheld and shielded by the discipline
> authorities of a prison. . . . The Surgeon has enough to do to guard the
> door of his infirmary against malingerers; and to do this effectually
> requires great firmness and determination. . . . There is no officer – not
> excepting the Governor, who exercises the power of punishment – who
> runs greater personal risks (*Criminal Correction*, p. 17).

93 1878 *RC*, *op. cit.*, q. 8082. According to John Campbell the converse applied in those prisons which contained both invalids and the healthy:

> The position of a medical officer intrusted with the charge of such men,
> located in a portion of a prison, is discouraging; for whilst his duties are
> arduous, responsible and dangerous, he is dependent on a local authority
> for the means of carrying on a work which from its nature requires
> great freedom of action (*ibid.*, 99).

order punishment,[94] but nevertheless medical sanction was necessary before dietary or corporal punishment could be inflicted. Disputes over diets arose because medical officers had power to vary the food provided they thought that health would otherwise be endangered. This could lead to a proliferation of different dietary scales, which was administratively inconvenient and which may have provided further encouragement to convicts to malinger and dissimulate. In the general tightening up of discipline which followed the Royal Commission of 1863, the medical officer's power to vary a diet was subjected to the authority of the visiting director. This procedure was altered only after 1878, when the Royal Commission recommended that the medical officer's dietary instructions should immediately be implemented, and considered by the director on his next visit.[95]

For some years the medical officer of Millbank was *de facto* senior prison medical officer,[96] but he had no responsibility for medical work or staff at other prisons. It was to assume this duty and to place the consultancy work on a more formal footing that the 1878 Royal Commission recommended the creation of the post of Superintending Medical Officer. They considered that the position should be filled by a 'physician or surgeon of high class and wide experience' whose duties would be to exercise a general superintendence; to visit each prison periodically 'at uncertain times' and to inspect the hospital and check on the manner in which medical duties were carried out; to consult with the resident MO in cases of alleged malingering; to make arrangements for the transfer of invalids and the mentally disordered; to investigate allegations of medical neglect, and to advise on the appointment of assistant surgeons.[97] These proposals in effect added a medical member to the Board of Directors, and were doubtless intended to

94 Guy's view was that a medical man should never inflict punishment as he was not a discipline officer

but he should so perform his functions as to promote the discipline of the prison. He ought not to interfere with it, but he ought never to inflict punishment. I venture to suggest that the right view to take of the functions of a medical man is that he should have the powers of restraint, not of punishment, in case of a prisoner doing that which greatly disturbs the other prisoners, or the officers of the establishment (*Select Committee of the House of Lords on Gaol Discipline* (Carnarvon Committee), PP, 1863, IX, 1, 399-400).

95 1878 *RC, op. cit.*, xxxvii-xxxviii. Measor held that changes in ordinary diet should not be made upon the unsupported recommendation of the surgeon, because of the pressures from convicts to which he would thereby be exposed (*Criminal Correction*, p. 17).

96 The practice of consulting with the Millbank MO on matters of general medical importance dated from the prison's penitentiary days, when a distinguished outside consultant physician had oversight of the medical arrangements.

97 1878 *RC, op. cit.*, xl-xli.

avoid those occasions on which a medical decision was subject to lay review. The recommendations were accepted, and the first superintending medical officer was appointed the following year.

The 1878 Royal Commission made a number of other proposals concerning convict medical services. They recommended that the appointment of assistant surgeons should be open to competition as vacancies occurred, rather than being based on private inquiry and interview. This change provided a greater measure of professional independence for medical officers, by making their selection less subject to the influence of the directors.[98] It was also proposed that assistant surgeons be subject to a period of probationary service during which they would be moved from prison to prison, substituting for or supplementing established staff during illness or leave. This, it was thought, would help to reduce the prisons' dependence upon outside staff and would provide a useful training for the probationers.[99]

Stewards

Since great importance was attached to productive labour, the steward was a key member of the senior staff. He was responsible for ordering, receiving and arranging payment for all supplies and stores, both domestic and industrial; and for such matters as the receipt and safe-keeping of convicts' money and property, the replacement of the prison's furniture and equipment and the maintenance of staff quarters.[100] The gardens and the produce thereof came under his charge, together with the general superintendence of the kitchens.[101] His overall duty was to promote economy, and to prevent wastage, misuse and theft of articles and supplies:

> As the saving of needless expense in the wear and tear and
> consumption of articles used in the Establishment, depends chiefly
> on the vigilance, intelligence and integrity of the Steward, he shall
> consider it his duty to watch carefully the demands which are
> made on him, and to bring to the knowledge of the Governor
> any circumstance which may demand notice with a view to check
> unnecessary or improvident expenditure and to promote the
> utmost economy in every branch of the Establishment.[102]

98 In 1880 the directors indicated that they were considering the establishment of an examination board for assistant surgeons (*RDCP*, PP, 1880, XXXVI, 1, xvi).

99 1878 *RC*, *op. cit.*, p. xli. This suggestion was not taken up because of the likely expense involved (*RDCP*, PP, 1880, XXXVI, 1, xvi).

100 *RRGP*, pp. 44-6.

101 *Ibid.*, pp. 45, 47.

102 *Ibid.*, p. 47.

The steward was resident at the prison, could follow no other occupation, and was required to provide sureties for the due performance of his duties.[103] He was forbidden to have any interest in any contract for the supply of the prison and could not accept 'under any pretence whatsoever' any fee or gratuity from any supplier or prisoner.[104] In an emergency the steward could be called upon by the governor to perform the duties of a discipline officer, but the practice followed at Millbank Penitentiary, where the steward had acted as deputy governor, was not continued.[105]

Staff management

Charges of militarism

It is not surprising that the directors, with their military background, sought to resolve some of the problems of staff selection by taking into employment a large proportion of men with army and navy backgrounds.[106] So consistent was this policy that by 1876 over two-thirds of subordinate officers had been in the army, marines or navy,[107] a pattern which appears to have been repeated among governors and deputy governors. This practice, which had been followed more moderately by earlier administrators, attracted both support and condemnation. The Howard Association, which emerged in the 1870s as a significant party in discussions of penal policy, was opposed to the employment of soldiers on the grounds that they had a tendency to impose an inappropriate type of discipline, and because of doubts about their moral character.[108] Soldiers and sailors continued to be stigmatised after the manner of Wellington's 'scum of the earth' remark, and this view was supported by a 'gentleman convict', who contended

103 *Ibid.*, p. 44: Standing Order no. 13, 30 March 1852 – £300 at all the prisons except the hulks and Fulham, where £200 was required. Governors were required to give even more substantial sureties: £1,200 at Dartmoor and Millbank, £1,000 at Parkhurst, Portland, Chatham, Woking and Portsmouth, £800 on the hulks and at Brixton, and £400 at Fulham. Most officials appear to have paid premiums to the Guarantee Society, rather than put up personal securities (see Standing Order no. 89, 8 January 1863).
104 *RRGP*, p. 44.
105 Charge of the prison during the governor's absence went first to the deputy governor, or should he not be available to the chief warder or senior principal warder (*RRGP*, p. 21).
106 W.L. Burn contends that the marked reliance upon naval and military officers at this time is an indication of the shortage of competent administrators and training facilities (*The Age of Equipoise*, p. 224).
107 1878 *RC, op. cit.*, Appendix A21, 1164.
108 Gordon Rose, *The Struggle for Penal Reform*, pp. 33-4; William Tallack, *Penological and Preventive Principles*, p. 218.

that since soldiers and sailors were recruited from 'the dregs of the population' their employment in prisons placed the first offender between two fires:

> It gives him as companions and tutors the habitual criminals . . . and it gives him as monitors and masters a set of beings whose morals are of the loosest, who have not the slightest respect for the truth or honour, and whose everyday language is almost as filthy as that of the filthiest whom they are paid to control.[109]

A strong but more measured attack was made by the *Civil Service Gazette*, which likened the convict service under Jebb to a section of the army:

> From the Directors down to the lowest Assistant-Warder, military men have been appointed by him almost exclusively — the very few civilians employed in this service barely numbering the exceptions requisite to prove the general rule. The several convict establishments under Sir Joshua Jebb's regime are in effect nothing more than so many barracks. The Visiting Director is the General; the Governor is the Colonel; the Deputy Governor is the Captain, the warders are the non-commissioned officers; and the convicts are the privates. The organization is military, the pervading spirit is military. Subordination is the aim and end — the sole practical result looked for.[110]

At the same time there were pressures from other quarters to employ even more former army and navy men in the civil service. During the army estimates debate in 1865 it was suggested that army recruitment would be improved if men who had completed eighteen years' satisfactory service were, *certeris paribus*, in competition for minor civil service posts, given preference to civilians.[111] Even among the convicts there were some who thought that military and navy men had an appropriate training:

> I am more than ever convinced that retired soldiers and sailors should be brought into this service to a greater extent than they do at present. Their former training fits them for the position. They themselves know how to obey, and that gives them a better knowledge of how to command.[112]

109 'A Ticket-of-Leave-Man', *op. cit.*, pp. 127-8.
110 *Civil Service Gazette* (18 May 1861), IX, no. 438, p. 313.
111 The minister replied that though he would be very pleased if other departments followed War Office practice in this regard, he did not think that it was a matter upon which pressure could be exercised (*The Times*, 21 March 1865, 9c).
112 'One Who Has Endured It', *op. cit.*, p. 170.

Very similar views were expressed by Du Cane. Whilst there was no rule restricting recruitment to former military men, many did apply and

> Their habits of order and discipline, of rendering and enforcing
> strict obedience, and their aptitude in dealing with large bodies of
> men, are unquestionably very valuable qualities for the office,
> and if not possessed by an officer on joining would have to be
> acquired more or less perfectly afterwards.[113]

By the early 1880s, when Du Cane wrote this, ministerial endorsement had been given to the recruitment of ex-servicemen for senior positions. On the day on which the commissioners took charge of the local prisons (1 April 1878), A.F.O. Liddell, on the instructions of the home secretary, wrote to Du Cane as follows:

> With regard to the superior appointments in Prisons, Mr. Cross
> would point out the advantage to the Public Service of
> recommendations for selection, whenever possible [of] Officers
> of the Army and Navy, with a view to facilitating retirement
> and promotion in those services. But this consideration should
> not be allowed to interfere in any way with the selection of
> the fittest, or to be held to exclude other candidates should
> they be better qualified.[114]

Pressures of patronage

Jebb and his successors had very extensive powers of patronage which made them the object of numerous applications and of special pleading. Although after the Northcote-Trevelyan report in 1853 the system of appointment to the civil service was extensively regulated, patronage and sponsorship still counted for much, and the higher appointments, in any event, remained unaffected by reform for many years.[115] In 1874, the home secretary indicated that he did not wish the post of deputy governor (which by then had become a stepping-stone to a governorship) to be thrown open to unrestricted competition,[116] and it was not until August 1880 that candidates for governorships and

---

113 Du Cane, *op. cit.* (1882), pp. 188-9.

114 Du Cane Papers, ref. c.650.94.

115   From 1855-1870 the duties [of the Civil Service Commission] were little
more than to test by written examination the basic qualifications of
candidates nominated for junior posts by the public departments; the
departments continued to do their own initial recruiting to junior posts,
and to make all appointments to higher posts, by the various methods of
patronage (Sir Laurence Helsby, 'Recruitment to the Civil Service', in
William A. Robson (ed.), *The Civil Service in Britain and France*, p. 35).

116 PRO HO 45/9358/31266A/4.

deputy governorships were required by the Civil Service Commission to take the qualifying examinations.[117] Indeed, the directors had been able to secure some exemption, first for subordinate staff at Broadmoor Asylum, and then for warders and prison staff generally, from the Order in Council of 21 May 1855 which stipulated that before even temporary appointment could be obtained a certificate of qualification had to be granted by the Civil Service Commission.[118]

The patronage of the directorate, and of the chairman in particular, was all the greater because, from the first establishment of the directorate, Sir George Grey excluded appointments in the convict service from political patronage. Du Cane applauded this decision:

> In introducing it – at a time when it was considered quite the right and natural thing for a Minister to use public appointments to provide berths for his friends and for their friends, and in enforcing it during all his tenure of office – Sir George Grey conferred a lasting benefit on the country, and gave a striking proof of his high mind and public spirit.[119]

Grey's approach had been strongly supported and extended by a notice issued by Palmerston in 1853:

> Whereas it has happened, in several instances, that officers in the convict service have attempted to obtain their promotion by means of applications from private friends, and whereas such practices are injurious to the good order and discipline of the service, notice is hereby given, that all officers in the convict service must understand that their prospects of promotion must depend on the report which their superiors may make, as to their qualifications for, and as to their conduct in, the performance of their duties.

117 PRO HO 45/9348/31266A/7-8.
118 Before issuing a certificate the commissioners were to ascertain that the candidate was within the prescribed age limits, that he was free from any physical defect or disease likely to affect the proper discharge of his duties, that his character was suitable for public employment and that he possessed the requisite knowledge and ability. The first instance of a dismissal from the convict service of a temporary officer for failure to obtain a civil service certificate was at Woking in 1864 (*RDCP*, PP, 1865, XXV, 1, 229). This followed a Treasury decision that the employment of unestablished officers was contrary to the Order in Council. By a Standing Order of 20 April 1864 such staff were required to sit the Civil Service Commission examination and all those who failed to obtain the certificate of qualification were obliged to leave the service (Standing Order no. 129). A concession was made in 1869, because of staff shortages, allowing Broadmoor subordinate staff to be provisionally employed for three months before taking the Civil Service Commission's examinations. In May 1874 this concession was extended to all situations in prisons and criminal lunatic asylums (PRO HO 45/9355/29813/1, 2, 5, 8, 9).
119 Du Cane, *op. cit.* (1882), p. 188.

Merit and not favour will thus be the ground for advancement, and any officer who may attempt to bring private interest to bear, for the purpose of influencing the directors to promote him, will be considered as having disqualified himself for the promotion he may thus have sought to obtain.[120]

Nevertheless private influence continued to be brought to bear to secure appointments. Several such approaches were made to Jebb by his brother-in-law, Lord Chichester,[121] and Du Cane was even subject to some pressure from Queen Victoria on behalf of the son-in-law of her physician, Dr Hoffmeister.[122] Even members of the government

120 Standing Order no. 17, 10 September 1853.
121 On 18 July 1857 Chichester recommended a man as 'a good officer and I know him to be a well educated intelligent man. . . . If you want a governor or a good deputy, I should think him quite worth further enquiry. He is a very gentlemanlike man in his manners' (Papers, box 2). In November of the same year he wrote about a man who he thought would make a suitable warder:

> I have this morning seen another man aged 32 who is very anxious to serve in a convict prison and who seems to me very eligible – just the sort of man I think you would like to have. He was 5 years in the 11th Hussars – discharged after the Crimea on account of his health – which however is restored. He has since been a police Constable at Lewes and is strongly recommended by one of the justices there, Capt. Dalbiac – an old Dragoon. His name is *Richard Davies* – he was a sergeant in the 11th . . . I have taken a fancy to the Hussar but perhaps his having been in the Balaclava charge prejudices me in his favour (*ibid.*).

122 The letter, dated 5 February 1870, was addressed to the home secretary, H.A. Bruce, who passed it to Du Cane with a note that he was 'to make inquiry as to Captain Malone's aptitude and fitness for the Post'. Having described Dr Hoffmeister's service to the queen the letter went on:

> Dr. Hoffmeister's Son in Law Captain Malone Royal Marine Light Infantry, has been for some time a candidate for an appointment as Governor or Dep' Governor of a Convict Prison and if he should not be an unfit person for such an employment it would be very satisfactory to The Queen to be able to confer a favour on Dr. Hoffmeister who has rendered Her Majesty considerable service.

Seven of Malone's testimonials were enclosed. At the bottom of his *curriculum vitae* there was the following note:

> In Addition to these services of Capt. Malone may be mentioned those of his Father, for a period of upwards of 50 years in H. Majesty's Navy. He was engaged at the taking of the Isle of France besides several minor actions, and died whilst serving as a Lieutenant in Royal Naval Hospital, Plymouth. Also those of his Uncle, Captn. Malone of 40th Regt. who was killed in the battle of the Pyrenees whilst leading his Company into Action (Du Cane Papers, ref. c.647.16).

Malone, however, did *not* obtain an appointment in a convict prison, despite his having such an illustrious patroness and gallant relatives.

sought to obtain favours in the matter of appointments. In October 1872 Henry Winterbotham, under-secretary at the Home Office, wrote,

My colleague in the representation of Stroud – Mr. Dickinson – writes me today on behalf of a relative of his, Captain Sebastian Rawlins 69th Regt. who he says is a candidate for the Deputy Governorship of Chatham. My excellent colleague is himself Deputy Chairman of Q Sessions and a very upright man. I am sure he would not recommend a man *he* did not believe to be thoroughly fit – but of course you will form your own opinion. If I can gratify my friend of course I shall be glad of the opportunity of doing so.

A week later, still awaiting his reply, Winterbotham wrote again: 'I see I am asked to sanction divers transfers – what answer am I to give my colleague as to Capt. Sebastian?'

Du Cane's response was tart and emphatic:

Capt. Rawlins is not up to the level of the men we want to get and succeed in getting into the Convict Service. We try to find men who have made a name and a position in their own profession, have been placed on special duties or have prepared themselves for them.

Capt. R. has done *nothing* but to marry Canon Tinling's daughter and if I had to select men of the pertinacity of their stepfathers I should certainly have spotted Capt. R. long ago for the venerable Gentleman certainly carries away the palm.

I did not know you wished an answer to your letter because Mr. Bruce [the home secretary] never requires one. I have this morning a letter referring to the same man in which he desires that I . . . carefully consider his claims – and he knows that I have done or will do so – and has already replied to his correspondence accordingly.

I am quite sure that 99 people out of 100 think that these things are all jobs and no doubt abuse me if I stand in the way of their friend's advancement – but I cannot help that. I believe the cynic was quite right when he said that for every appointment one makes 99 enemies and 1 lukewarm friend – –

I can truly say that I hate with an intensity known only to those who do similar duties – that part of my function which relates to appointments – and nothing wd. make me desire to continue that office – but the fact that it is of vital concern to the welfare of the Department that good men should be appointed.

In the face of such resolution Winterbotham beat a hasty retreat:

I am quite satisfied with your decision and you must not think I want to interfere with your discretion by passing on such applications as, coming from friends or colleagues, I am bound

to entertain and to answer. If the applications had come from
a stranger I should have sent it on to you without comment. I
don't care about this man myself one straw.[123]

Du Cane's insistence that staffing should be free from improper
personal considerations was simply a continuation of Jebb's practice of
accepting personal recommendations, but subjecting them to the same
scrutiny and testing as applications which arrived through normal
channels.[124] Moreover, promotion seems to have been kept free from
patronage,[125] although female basic grade staff could usually rise only
as far as the senior subordinate post of chief officer or chief matron (a
rank instituted at Millbank in the early 1860s). Above that level, the
posts of deputy superintendent and lady superintendent (female
governor), were 'filled from without by lady friends of the direction'.[126]
Since it had always been difficult to fill these posts with suitable
women because of the requirement that they should have the unusually
combined attributes of practicality, respectability and ability to command, Jebb must have welcomed recommendations,[127] and there seems
little reason to suppose that they led to the appointment of unsuitable
persons. Similar considerations applied to male staff.

Training

From an early point there was a recognition of the difficulties faced by
the convict service in training staff, particularly in the public works
prisons, where supervision was difficult and where the dispersal of the
convicts severely tested the abilities of individual officers:

> To form and bring into proper training an efficient and trustworthy
> staff of subordinate officers for a prison on public works is a task
> of considerable anxiety and difficulty, and the opportunities for
> an officer's early acquiring the requisite amount of discipline are

123 Du Cane Papers, refs c.647.116, 118, 122 and 120.
124 In the female convict prisons many personal recommendations were made,
but all recruits to the basic grades nevertheless underwent a period of
probationary testing:

> Lady friends of directors and superintendents will be ever prone to offer
> the services of their ladies' maids and upper servants; and though these
> may not pass the probationary stage yet their constant introduction . . .
> is a hindrance to the proper working of a complex machinery ('A Prison
> Matron', *op. cit.*, p. 322).

125 'A clever officer rises more rapidly than her contemporaries, promotion
going by merit in many cases, in lieu of seniority of service . . .' (*ibid.*,
pp. 19-20).
126 *Ibid.*
127 See pp. 456-8, above.

few, compared with those of a close prison, where discipline forms the first and principal teaching.[128]

Learning was by doing and watching in the post of assistant warder, but the existence of this probationary and training grade in itself caused problems:

> In this class, which must be considered the nursery or training school for the service, the character and qualifications of the men as a whole must be very fluctuating, and difficult of being reduced to a fixed standard of discipline and efficiency, arising from the constant changes which are occurring, either from the dismissal of newly admitted candidates, who upon trial are unfit, or from the resignation of others who have discovered that their duties demanded both moral and physical energies greater than they were able to bestow; time and continuous duty can alone fit a man for the varied and peculiar duties of a prison such as this, where invalids suffering severely, both bodily and mentally, are mixed up with other prisoners.[129]

Formal training of warders was first undertaken at the public works prisons in 1862. The chaplain of Portland reported that much effort was being put into training and somewhat defensively noted that the classes which had been instituted would increase the value of the officers as public servants. This venture did not prosper, however, and Sir William Crofton's proposal that there should be a training school for warders failed to win the endorsement of the 1878 Royal Commission. Indeed, the commissioners saw such initiatives as unnecessary since the newly nationalised local prisons could provide a range of 'look and learn' training opportunities for the convict prisons:

> as all prisons throughout the United Kingdom are now under the direct control of the Government, ample opportunity is afforded of testing officers in situations of comparatively small importance, before entrusting them with the more onerous duties of a convict prison.[130]

Remuneration and conditions of employment

Hours of work for subordinate staff were long, even at a time when a six-day week and ten-hour day were common in industry and shops. As late as 1865 there was compulsory messing in prisons and warders were

---

128 *RDCP*, PP, 1854-5, XXV, 33, 224.
129 *RDCP*, PP, 1856, XXXV, 1, 154; see also *RDCP*, PP, 1857-8, XXIX, 483, 668.
130 1878 *RC*, *op. cit.*, liv.

thus unable to take their meals with their families.[131] Until 1864 warders, obliged to work on Sunday, were allowed only half a day in lieu during the week; the regulation was then altered to permit them to take a day a fortnight.[132] The governor of Millbank described this allowance as 'a great boon ... without doubt it is a considerable set-off to the hard life of a prison officer'.[133] In 1875 Du Cane introduced alternate long and short day working in the public works prisons. Depending on the time of year, the long day was about thirteen and a half hours, and the 'short' day eleven and a half.[134] Women worked similar hours, which according to 'A Prison Matron' had pernicious effects:

> I have seen women off duty on the *twelve hour* nights fling themselves exhausted on their beds too tired to take advantage of the fresh air outside, which they are at liberty to seek. I have known young women enter full of health and strength, and depart from the service in a few years, aged and anxious-looking, with no strength left for any new employment; I have known others die.[135]

From October 1860, principal officers and those below them were given ten days' annual leave, whilst clerks, schoolmasters, chief warders, scripture readers, and foremen of works had three weeks.[136] In 1863 an extra day was granted to all ranks to mark the queen's birthday.[137] An attendance-book was kept, and every half day's absence on the part of subordinate officers was deducted from their annual leave, 'excepting under special circumstances'.[138]

131 Standing Order no. 220, 20 March 1865; *RDCP*, PP, 1866, XXXVIII, 1, 22. Messing at the prison had been required because officers were allowed rations as well as salaries. After the change £14 per year was added to officers' wages.

132 Standing Order no. 174, 9 November 1864 (also cited 'Report of the Committee Appointed to Inquire into the Position and Prospects of Convict Warders and Broadmoor Asylum Attendants' (Rosebery Committee), Appendix I, 75).

133 *RDCP*, PP, 1865, XXV, 1, 50.

134 Rosebery Committee, *op. cit.*, Appendix H, 74.

135 'A Prison Matron', *op. cit.*, pp. 20-1.

136 Standing Order no. 78, 24 October 1860. Superior officers were allowed six weeks' leave per year.

137 Standing Order no. 96, 8 June 1863.

138 Standing Order no. 78, 24 October 1860. Superior officers were allowed up to a day's absence before it began to count against annual leave. Rule 25 of the 'General Rules for Officers' provided that

> Any subordinate officer or servant who, in the course of one year, shall have been in the aggregate more than twenty days absent from duty, on account of sickness ... and others who are not in health to perform their duty properly, shall be examined and reported upon by the Medical

When the directorate was first established, different rates of pay operated in the various convict establishments which it took over, but in 1851 uniform scales of payment were introduced. Principal warders were paid £65, rising by annual increments of £1. 10s. 0d. to £80 per annum; warders received £55 rising to £67. 10s. 0d. and assistant warders £52 rising to £62.[139] The scales were changed in 1865 and in 1874 and the minimum annual net value of the appointments was increased as follows: principal warder £101.12s. 0d.; warder (London) £88. 8s. 0d., (country) £84. 10s. 0d.; assistant warder (London) £85. 8s. 0d., (country) £81. 10s. 0d.[140] These rates compared reasonably well with the £98. 16s. 0d. paid to a police sergeant, £104 maximum for a station inspector on the District Railway and £93. 12s. 0d. for engineers, machine-makers, iron-founders and pattern-makers.[141] Moreover, warders had security of employment, pensions and certain other advantages such as the cheap purchase of farm produce and supplies.[142] The Rosebery Committee estimated that in 1883 the value of pay and allowances of a convict service appointment for fifteen years was £1,380. 5s. 0d. and that of a metropolitan police officer £1,350. 13s. 0d.[143] The comparison was said to be even more favourable to the convict service than it appeared since the police had to contribute towards their superannuation whereas convict service pensions were non-contributory under the provisions of the 1859 Superannuation Act.[144]

Despite the favourable comparisons drawn by the Rosebery Committee, payments and emoluments were a source of much dissatisfaction. It was not simply a matter of hours; warders in the separate prisons were subject to the strains and tensions attendant on the 'close confinement' suffered by the prisoners, whilst on public works outdoor supervision of convicts in all kinds of inclement weather made demands of a different kind upon health and endurance.[145] In 1874 such

---

Officer, and the cases laid before a Director, and, unless there appear strong reasons for the contrary, they will be recommended to the Secretary of State for discharge (*RRGP*, p. 77).

---

139 All three grades were given rations, valued at £10. 13s. 0d. a year. Principal warders paid £3 per annum and warders and assistant warders £2. 8s. 0d. per annum for their uniforms, and those who lived in quarters paid between £2. 12s. 0d. and £10. 8s. 0d. rent. Warders at public works prisons received an additional allowance of £7. 16s. 0d. and £15. 12s. 0d. which was called 'exertion money' (Rosebery Committee, *op. cit.*, Statement no. 4, 119).

140 *Ibid.*, 120.

141 *Ibid.*, 119-20, 73 and 89.

142 Rosebery Committee, 73; Standing Order no. 220, 20 March 1865.

143 *Ibid.*, 88.

144 22 Vict., c.26.

145 At both separate and public works prisons staff were subject to a strict disciplinary code, supported by severe fines for lapses and violations. A table

considerations led Du Cane to suggest that convicts on public works should not labour on Saturday afternoons so that staff could have the half day free.[146] But at some of the isolated public works prisons free time was of only limited use, since there were so few recreational opportunities. In the early 1860s the chaplain of Dartmoor, William Holderness, made strenuous efforts to remedy this deficiency, arguing that the absence of suitable facilities for education and relaxation affected the officers' work with the convicts.[147] Progress in these matters was slow, and reading and recreation rooms were officially provided for staff at Portsmouth only in 1878.[148]

Families also suffered from a lack of suitable amenities. At Chatham, for example, the medical officer in 1860 drew attention to the damp and cold condition of the staff living quarters;[149] eight years later a different medical officer repeated those complaints and asserted that the high number of infantile disorders in officers' families was due to the inadequacy of their homes.[150] At Dartmoor in the early days the school for warders' children was most unsatisfactory, and in 1856 the governor drew the matter to the attention of the directors:

> I would venture to recommend for your favourable consideration
> the propriety of appointing more competent instructors for the
> children of the warders, and of appropriating to their use more
> commodious and better ventilated school buildings than exist at
> present. These officers have expressed themselves to me as most
> anxious to secure for their families a higher standard of education
> than they are at present receiving.[151]

The directors subsequently allowed the conversion of an old building, although the salaries of the master and mistress had to be met by a subscription from the warders and donations from the senior officers.[152]

Inability to recruit adequate numbers of satisfactory staff and a high number of resignations were the ways in which dissatisfaction over pay

approved by the home secretary and issued in 1865 set out fifty-six offences
for which staff could be fined sums of from 6*d*. (for being up to five minutes
late for duty) to three months' salary (for neglect or violation of duty, at the
discretion of the directors). Penalties were doubled and trebled for repeated
offences (Standing Order no. 230, 5 April 1865). The fines levied were of
sufficient volume to merit their being lodged in a special fund and disbursed
to officers or their families in cases of hardship (Standing Order no. 9, 22
January 1852; see also Standing Order no. 220, 20 March 1865).

146 PRO HO 45/9321/16982/27.
147 *RDCP*, PP, 1861, XXX, 237, 218.
148 *Reports of the Officers of Convict Prisons, op. cit.*, 420.
149 *RDCP*, PP, 1861, XXX, 237, 548.
150 *RDCP*, PP, 1868-9, XXX, 1, 237.
151 *RDCP*, PP, 1857, Sess. 2, XXIII, 65, 284.
152 *RDCP*, PP, 1857-8, XXIX, 483, 664.

and conditions had traditionally been manifested, just as the efficiency of recruitment was reflected by the number of discharges and dismissals which were necessary.[153] In the early 1870s, however, in contravention of the regulations, staff began to make collective representations to governors, to hold public meetings and to write to newspapers and members of Parliament.[154] Du Cane was seriously perturbed, and in June 1873 he submitted a memorandum to the Home Office, outlining the case for improved pay and allowances:

> Governors of the longest experience in the service . . . express themselves as decidedly of opinion that new subordinate officers, as a class, fall below the requirements of the service in physique, in attainment, and special fitness for the duties of their posts, and . . . can only account for this inferiority by supposing that the inducements offered are not sufficient to attract suitable men, in which I cannot but concur. . . . while 2,426 officers joined the service in the last ten years, 1,954 have left it. . . . The amount of change in the service indicated by these figures, not only shows that the service is not sufficiently attractive but it cannot in itself fail to be detrimental to the interests of the Department which has to

153 As was indicated by the governor of Millbank in 1863. Of the eighty-three staff who had joined Millbank during the year thirty had resigned because, said the governor,

> Close confinement upon prisoners necessarily entails close confinement upon officers. Young officers heretofore accustomed to a more active employment, feel the change, and leave without giving the place a more extended trial, some come without the remotest idea of the duties of a prison officer, and are at once discharged. . . . Again, a metropolitan prison officer is of course in charge of metropolitan prisoners, whose friends occasionally seek to allure officers from the path of duty, and, I regret to say, in some instances succeed in doing so (*RDCP*, PP, 1864, XXVI, 209, 256).

In January 1865 Henry Sutton, an assistant instructing warder at Portsmouth, was convicted of attempting to obtain money from a friend of a prisoner, and received a sentence of twelve months' imprisonment. Henderson drew the attention of governors to the case which was, he said, 'to be notified to all prisons as a warning to subordinate officers disposed to betray their trust by trafficking with prisoners or their friends' (Standing Order no. 195, 13 January 1865).

154 J.E. Thomas, *The English Prison Officer Since 1850*, pp. 68-9. Combinations among officers were prohibited by the home secretary in 1852:

> Any discussion or other proceedings with a view to, or tending to, or in the nature of a combination among officers or servants for any object connected with their duties or position in the prison, unless with the cognizance and sanction of the Governor, are strictly prohibited; and every officer or servant joining therein will be liable to dismissal or other punishment according to the degree of his offence (Standing Order no. 15, 24 September 1852).

depend on inexperienced or dissatisfied men for the performance of trying duties requiring a greater amount of tact, and, perhaps a stronger sense of duty, than almost any officer of similar grade in the Public Service.

TABLE 13.1   *Turnover of male subordinate officers in the convict service in the ten years ending 31 December 1877*

Year	Staff	Appointed	Resigned	Dismissed	Discharged	Died
1868	–	202	56	32	64	4
1869	1,189	361	64	53	76	7
1870	1,278	341	69	57	97	2
1871	1,266	284	120	59	73	4
1872	1,318	228	87	45	53	11
1873	1,323	154	59	35	47	5
1874	1,310	185	58	34	54	6
1875	1,343	164	49	30	58	14
1876	1,352	169	57	25	66	1
1877	1,352	179	56	21	89	6
Total		2,267	675	391	677	60

Source: Taken from *Report of the Commissioners Appointed to Inquire into the Working of the Penal Servitude Acts*, PP, 1878-9, XXXVII, Appendix A22, 1, 164.

Du Cane argued that the pay, conditions and prospects of a convict warder compared unfavourably with those of a sapper, and proposed an increase in pay and increments, simplified scales and a higher maximum in each scale. These changes, he suggested, would encourage good officers to stay in the service, whilst their cost could be offset to some extent by a reduction in the ratio of officers to prisoners.[155]

The Treasury at first suggested as an answer to the recruitment difficulties the establishment of 'some recognised and official channel of communication between the Directors and Military and Naval authorities, with the view of attracting to the Convict Service, good men who are taking their discharge'.[156] To this Du Cane responded that he had no doubt that

155 PRO HO 45/9321/16982/7.
156 PRO HO 45/9321/16982/8.

the advantages offered by the Convict Service are pretty well
known throughout the army on account of the number of
discharged soldiers now in it, but it may be advisable to send
from time to time notices on the subject to Commanding Officers
of regiments.[157]

Some four and a half months later, in December 1873, pay increases for
subordinate officers were authorised, on condition that the total
additional expenditure did not exceed £5,000, and that no opportunity should be missed for making reductions in staff. This improvement in pay did not meet the staff sense of grievance, and in March
1874 the Howard Association wrote to the home secretary, claiming
that there was dissatisfaction throughout the convict service because
the increases were thought to be inadequate. The letter also noted that
an increased rental allowance had been nullified by an equivalent rent
increase for quarters.[158] Although Du Cane challenged the accuracy of
their calculations, the Howard Association and the warders continued
to press their case. But apart from a reduction in the hours worked by
warders in the public works prisons[159] there was no conclusive settlement to these exchanges.

By 1878 there were 1,500 subordinate staff in the convict service. A
group of such a size would in time be bound to organise a collective
approach to their employer about their pay and conditions. It was only
in the 1860s that the convict service, having rid itself of the hulks and
transportation, and having acquired its basic stock of on-shore prisons,
settled down sufficiently for regular contacts between subordinate
staff to be made. The development of such links was hindered by the
dispersed location of the establishments, the high rate of staff turnover
and the severe penalties with which any attempt at combination could
be met. Despite these impediments, by the 1870s problems of staffing
were being taken up increasingly by staff themselves. Du Cane was
aware of the implications of this development and was anxious to head
it off by making changes and improvements as the necessity for them
became apparent, rather than leaving change to appear to result from
staff combination and public agitation.[160] Time was to show that
directorial intervention, whether benevolently or otherwise motivated,
could not be a substitute for, nor a means of averting the formation of
staff associations. The days when subordinate grades could be taken as
a fixed, if troublesome, part of the administrative equation were
passing.

157 PRO HO 45/9321/16982/9.
158 PRO HO 45/9321/16982/22.
159 PRO HO 45/9321/16982/27.
160 PRO HO 45/9321/16982/11.

Epilogue
The takeover of the local prisons

The decision to nationalise

With varying degrees of support and influence the case for greater uniformity in the discipline and administration of prisons, and for the centralisation of authority, had been constant features of nineteenth-century penological debate. The political opportunity and will to act, which had previously been absent, began to take shape in the early 1870s. This occurred because prison administration became an issue in fiscal and party policy, and the solid interests of finance and the maintenance of power gave weight and immediacy to a question which, if left in the ethereal realm of penological debate, would have waited on a crisis or scandal for further piecemeal resolution.

The redistribution of political power and wealth manifested in the 1867 extension of the franchise and in the unparalleled prosperity of industry demanded a fiscal realignment. In April 1872 Sir Massey Lopes, Liberal-Conservative member for South Devon, pressed for the removal or further reduction in the cost to the ratepayer of the administration of criminal justice, the maintenance of the police and the care of lunatics. In supporting his case Lopes resurrected and extended arguments about the relationship between taxpayer and rate-payer which had been a central element in the Corn Law disputes of the 1840s.[1] He drew attention to the fact that in 1870 the counties and boroughs had expended £667,000 on prisons, to which central government had added £118,000. In his opinion the 1865 Prison Act had

> placed the prisons of this country under the regulation of the Home Secretary, and the Right Hon. Gentleman obliged the prisons throughout the country to conform to all the regulations which he laid down. So arbitrary were these laws that the visiting justices

---

1 See pp. 256-9, above.

had scarcely any administrative power beyond determining the questions of salary with regard to a few of the warders. . . . Any deviation from the regulations laid down by the Home Secretary was attended with a threatened withdrawal of the Government grant for convicted prisoners, so that the magistrates had little, if any, control over the expenditure of the money, and the ratepayers by whom it was contributed still less.[2]

The suggestion that the localities should be freed from the injustice of being obliged to finance a national service was received not unsympathetically by the Liberal government. In September 1872 Sir Walter Crofton wrote to the home secretary, H.A. Bruce, pointing out that a change in the financing of prisons would provide an opportunity to secure a greater measure of uniformity in administration. Bruce passed the memorandum to Du Cane, informing him that he agreed with Crofton to the extent that should the government decide to increase its financial contribution to the local prisons 'the opportunity should not be lost in securing some increased hold on their management'.[3] No further Liberal action followed, however.

Gladstone's government was displaced by the Conservatives in January 1874, and although Disraeli's programme was cautious and lacking in new departures, it did include pledges to reduce central and local taxation. The prime minister, nearing his seventieth year, was 'a changed man, cautious and averse from innovation'.[4] The new home secretary, R.A. Cross, confirmed this view:

When the Cabinet came to discuss the Queen's Speech, I was, I confess, disappointed at the want of originality shown by the Prime Minister. From all his speeches, I had quite expected that his mind was full of legislative schemes, but such did not prove to be the case; on the contrary he had to entirely rely on the various suggestions of his colleagues, and as they themselves had only just come into office, and that suddenly there was some difficulty in framing the Queen's Speech.[5]

2 Lopes pointed out that of the £118,000 no less than £107,000 was for the maintenance of *convicted* prisoners; central government contributed nothing towards the maintenance of prisoners before conviction. He described this as 'a most galling anomaly' (*Hansard* (Third Series), CCX, cols 1343-4).

3 Bruce to Du Cane, 25 September 1872: Du Cane Papers, ref. c.647 111.

4 Paul Smith, *Disraelian Conservatism and Social Reform*, p. 198.

5 Richard Assheton Cross, *A Political History*, p. 25. Cross is described by Paul Smith as 'the only cabinet representative of what might be called the new Liberal-Conservatism of the industrial, commercial and professional middle-class, which had so much to do with the ministry's accession to office' (*op. cit.*, p. 194). He was a successful barrister and banker and received his appointment as home secretary without previously having achieved ministerial rank, but as a magistrate of some years' standing he was already familiar with

There was no attempt to construct an integrated or long-term social policy which would have led to an agreement on priorities: 'Each session's programme of legislation was drawn up *ad hoc*, by the simple process of writing round to ministers for whatever proposals they had in hand and collating the replies to form the Queen's Speech.'[6] It was very likely, therefore, that proposals which were already in the pipeline would be subject to somewhat closer than usual ministerial review. The notion of reorganising the finances and administration of local prisons was given further impetus by a deputation from the Social Science Association which waited on Cross shortly after his assumption of office and with whose representations he was favourably impressed.[7]

Because of his political beliefs and his experience as a magistrate, Cross was loath to carry any tightening of central government's grasp of local prisons to the point of nationalisation. In December 1874 when he wrote to Northcote, the chancellor of the exchequer, on the question of reallocating the costs of criminal prosecutions, he made clear his antipathy to any further extension of the powers of Whitehall.[8] For this reason he supported Crofton's proposal for an increase in the grant-in-aid to local prison authorities, rather than Du Cane's scheme for an administrative takeover. A greater defrayment of local costs, Cross held, 'would enable us to insist on more uniformity in carrying out hard labour and still leave the excellent institution of visiting justices untouched'.[9]

In the months which followed Cross continued to seek a redistribution of the burden of criminal justice expenditure between taxpayer and ratepayer. On 26 October 1875 he addressed a further letter to Northcote:

> I am not unmindful of the concessions the present Government have made. . . . But more remains to be done to satisfy the merits of the case, and I can see no reason why the waste and inefficiency due to the present divided authority over Police and Prisons should

---

many of the problems of prison administration (*Hansard* (Third Series), CCXXIX, cols 1536-7).

6 Smith, *op. cit.*, p. 200.

7 *Hansard* (Third Series), CCXXIX, col. 1536.

8   We shall have to take care that while fully protecting the Treasury we do not get too far in the way of centralization. I can clearly see that the traditions of my own office are [inclined] in that direction. My own inclinations are all the other way. Count Munster spoke to me the other day: 'How strange it is, you are all I can see in England moving in the direction of bureaucracy while in Germany we are going the other way' (Cross to Northcote, 26 December 1874, Iddesleigh Papers, vol. XXVIII, BM add. MSS 50,039).

9 *Ibid*.

be allowed to continue without an effort being made to improve
and consolidate the administration and thus relieve ratepayers from
the exceptional charges for objects of really national and not local
character, concerning which the Central Authority makes its control
felt in every direction save that of forbidding waste and needless
outlay. I rejoice that you have given us something like an assurance
in Parliament that the State will further relieve Localities of
charges for the administration of justice and I desire to urge on
Ministers the expediency in the first instance of making the cost
of Police and Prisons entirely national.[10]

Two months later, on a slightly different tack, he raised the issue
with Disraeli:

I am more and more convinced that we shall have troubled nights
in the HC unless we can do something to satisfy our farming
friends, in the way of local Taxations. Either by way of taking
the gaols from the local rates, or by way of giving some ratepaying
representation on the question of *finance* in counties. And so by
a small concession avert great and grievous disturbance of existing
wholesome arrangements when we go out of office.[11]

Cross's urgings were highly opportune. The economy was in a down-
ward phase and backbench Conservatives were vociferous in their
demand that action should be taken to relieve the ratepayers. Matters
reached such a pass that early in 1876 Lord Eustace Cecil warned Lord
Salisbury, a senior member of the Cabinet, that should nothing be done
about local taxation 'it does not require a prophet to foresee that the
coming Session will be the beginning of the end'.[12] On 19 January
1876, Cross submitted a memorandum on the local prisons to the
Cabinet. His proposals were agreed, and at the commencement of the
new session an undertaking was given in the Queen's Speech to shift the
cost of police and prisons to the Exchequer.[13]

From the proposals submitted to Cabinet it is clear that Cross had
completely revised his views on the form that government action on the
local prisons should take, and instead of Crofton's scheme for an
increase in the grant-in-aid, he now supported Du Cane's plan for a
complete administrative takeover. The need to produce substantial
savings in the rates and the arguments of Du Cane and the two inspectors, Folliott Powell and Briscoe, that wastage and inefficiency could
properly be curtailed only if many of the small local prisons were
closed, led Cross to conclude that

10 Cross Papers, vol. III, BM add. MSS 51265.
11 Hughenden (Disraeli) Papers, B/XX/CR/31 (27 December 1875).
12 *Cit.* Smith, *op. cit.*, pp. 207-8.
13 *Hansard* (Third Series), CCXXVII, col. 5.

The waste consequent upon the present system of small local prisons is so great that I could not advise the Cabinet to place the charge upon the Imperial Revenue unless the whole of the prisons were taken over absolutely into the hands of the Government.[14]

Nevertheless, Cross was convinced that there were objectives other than the purely financial to be sought. His plan, he informed his colleagues, would have

Among others, the following great advantages: economy, uniformity in labour, treatment and discipline and relief to local taxation. The only objection is the one of centralization: but if the maintenance of prisoners is an Imperial and not a local change, this seems to me to fall to the ground.[15]

Work on the bill commenced immediately Cabinet approval was given and, despite strong Treasury reservations, Du Cane and his colleagues were much involved at this stage.[16] Indeed, Du Cane's extensive memorandum on the matter, which Cross had laid before the Cabinet as an annexe to his own document, was to provide the basis for much of Cross's argument for his bill in the House.[17] The measure was of a complicated and comprehensive character and, despite reasonably speedy progress with the drafting, it was not until 1 June 1876 that it could be brought before the Commons.

The passage of the bill

Cross stressed that his intention was to ensure a greater measure of uniformity and to reduce costs, and he reminded the Commons of Lopes's contention that some charges were more fairly the responsibility of central government. These included the prisons:

14 Hughenden Papers, B/XX/CR/33. Memorandum prepared by Cross for Cabinet, 19 January 1876.

15 *Ibid*.

16 W.H. Smith, secretary to the Treasury, assured Cross on 21 January 1876:

Whatever additional professorial [?] assistance you find to be necessary to enable you to prepare your Bill, you must have, but don't mention Du Cane by name as he is a red rag to certain people here and it would be objected that he is not professorial [?] in the ordinary sense of the term (Cross Papers, *loc. cit*., 51268).

17 Use was also made of a memorandum sent to the home secretary within a few weeks of the Queen's Speech by Captain Wilson, governor of the county gaol at Maidstone, containing arguments and evidence supporting centralisation. This document was well received by Cross, Lushington (Home Office counsel) and Du Cane, and a number of the points on economy were developed in Cross's speech introducing the bill (PRO HO 45/9518/22208/43).

our prisons and our whole system of gaol discipline [are] kept up for the safety not only of real property, but of personal property, which did not pay its share, and not for the safety of property simply, but for the protection of life.[18]

He criticised the unequal and irrational distribution of local prisons pointing out, for example, that in Rutland there was one prison for 20,000 inhabitants, in Lancashire one for every 469,000 inhabitants and in Stafford one for 858,000.[19] In some localities substantial economies might be made by merging the town and county gaols, but these were not effected because of the inaction of the responsible authorities. Moreover, since daily average populations ranged from the tiny to the very large, there were considerable disparities in expenditure. Whereas in Salford prison the annual cost of upkeep of a prisoner was £15. 1s. 1d., in Oakham prison it was £150. 4s. 2d. Cross also expressed his concern over the great lack of uniformity in prison discipline, as shown in the very different amounts of hard labour required from the prisoners on the treadwheel, at stone-breaking and the crank. Similar criticisms could be made of the diet, the degree of separation and such important aspects of the régime as education, punishment and supervision. All these instances of waste and lack of uniformity he attributed to the local structure of administration. The solution, therefore, could not simply be an increase in the amount contributed by the Treasury to local revenues since this would 'in no way increase the efficiency of the gaols, although no doubt it would tend largely to increase the expenditure'. Instead, he urged, central government should 'take the whole expenses of all prisoners from the moment they are committed, and take the management of all the gaols into their own hands'.[20] By this means prisons could be located to maximum economic advantage, uniformity of discipline could be assured, and there would be saved 'a much larger sum than will be charged by the Government to the Treasury'.[21] It was intended that more than fifty of the existing 116 prisons should be closed, with a consequent reduction in staff and maintenance costs; a reduction in expense could also be achieved by the reintroduction of profitable industrial labour. All in all, Cross anticipated that local rates would be relieved by some £392,000, at a cost to the Exchequer of only £285,000 — a net saving of more than £100,000 per year.

Cross sought to set minds at rest about the important administrative arrangements set out in the bill. There was not to be direct Home Office management, but rather an indirect form of administration by a

18 *Hansard* (Third Series), CCXXIX, col. 1537.
19 *Ibid*., col. 1538.
20 *Ibid*., col. 1542.
21 *Ibid*.

small number of prison commissioners.[22] As for the sensitive matter of patronage, 'I have no wish to have the slightest amount of patronage more than I can help, for nothing more encumbers a Minister or gives him more trouble or anxiety'.[23] He therefore proposed that whilst the appointment of superior officers should rest with the home secretary, the appointment of subordinate staff would be entrusted to the commissioners. This would avoid the necessity of the home secretary exercising a vast amount of patronage and would also benefit staff:

> by being all together, there will be a much greater flow of promotion in the service, and a much greater inducement to officers to work well than there is at present, and practically you will get a much better staff of officers than you have had down to the present.[24]

It was intended that both the inspectors and the justices would be kept, but all would perform their duties in a modified form. The inspectors would become assistants to the commissioners, on whose behalf they would visit and report upon prisons, whilst the justices would henceforward act as local inspectors with appropriate changes being made to their mode of appointment and method of reporting, to reflect their new relationship to the home secretary.[25] Since the prisons and their equipment were not to be bought from the justices and boroughs, it was necessary to ensure a measure of equity between localities which had maintained a prison, and would therefore be transferring a valuable property to the state, and those who had contracted with another authority instead of maintaining their own prisons. In the latter case a calculation would be made of the accommodation which would have been needed during the previous five years; the locality would then have to pay an appropriate amount to the Exchequer, a loan being provided by the Public Works Loan

---

22 Cross maintained in his Cabinet memorandum that he was here simply following the model of the Directorate of Convict Prisons, in support of which course he drew the attention of his colleagues to the recommendations of the 1850 Grey Committee respecting a Central Board (Hughenden Papers, B/XX/Cr./33).

23 *Hansard* (Third Series), CCXXIX, col. 1545.

24 *Ibid.*

25 Cross had explained to the Cabinet:

> I should be very sorry to do away with Visiting Justices. I believe that their services would still, in a modified form, be most useful as a check upon the officers of the Prison, by reports to the Board, and as a satisfaction to the public that any ill-treatment or neglect of prisoners would be reported to the Board, and thence in turn to the Secretary of State (Hughenden Papers, B/XX/Cr. 33).

Commissioners for that purpose.[26]

In the long drawn out progress of the bill through its various stages virtually all the major issues in prison administration, together with certain principles of constitutional and legal theory, were touched upon. Securing its first and second readings by a large majority, the bill was sent to committee on 4 August 1876, only to be withdrawn five days later because of lack of time.[27] The intention had been to bring the measure into operation in April 1877, but its introduction at such a late point in the session and the consequent failure to get it through the various stages put this plan back by a year, since the whole process had to start again from the beginning in the new session. Altogether the Commons' debates occupy no fewer than 352 columns of *Hansard*, and *The Times* wrote of the local authorities fighting the bill 'inch by inch, as though it were imposing on them some new and unheard of grievance'.[28] The passage of the measure was obviously a major parliamentary and political task for Cross, accomplished in the face of considerable opposition and misgivings, both inside and outside Westminster.[29]

26 *Hansard* (Third Series), CCXXIX, cols 1546-7. The amount was £120 per cell. This provision was to be used as a means of wringing an important concession from the government for those localities which had provided accommodation in excess of what was required for their own prisoners. It was eventually conceded that whether or not such additional cells were required by the new national administration, and provided that the prison concerned was not closed within two years of the transfer of ownership, the local authorities were to receive compensation. According to Du Cane £127,478 was subsequently paid out for 1,376 cells, which were of little use to the new administration (*The Punishment and Prevention of Crime*, p. 69).
27 Disraeli made the most of the delay by commending the bill to the consideration of the country during the recess. The *Pall Mall Gazette* observed of this that 'unfortunately laws which appeal only to good sense seldom admit of being interesting', and that although magistrates would consider the Bill at their Autumn meetings 'it will rarely be discussed on its merits' (30 August 1876, XXIV, p. 781).
28 *The Times*, 2 March 1877, 9d.
29 It is difficult to see the basis for Blom-Cooper's claim that 'the legislation was passed with little fuss or bother' ('The Centralization of Governmental Control of National Prison Services, with Special Reference to the Prison Act, 1877', p. 65). When the bill was introduced again in 1877 *The Times* (12 February 1877, 9c) rather misleadingly observed that because of other matters of concern the bill had been subject to very little public debate. Whilst it is true that much parliamentary and political attention was being given to the 'Eastern Question' (the revolts against Turkish rule in Boznia and Herzegovina, Turkish atrocities and Russia's move towards war), *The Times* itself carried several reports of local authority opposition to the Prison Bill, besides the extensive debates in parliament. Strangely, Cross himself makes no mention of the Prison Bill in his political biography, *A Political History*, nor is it referred to in Paul Smith's *Disraelian Conservatism and Social Reform*, which deals exhaustively with other Conservative legislation at the time.

Parliamentary opposition came mainly from an odd mixture of Radicals, some backbench Conservatives and Liberals, and Irish members,[30] who variously questioned the claim that centralisation would be a cheaper form of administration, voiced fears about the constitutional significance of the proposals and about possible abuse of Whitehall's extensive new powers of patronage, and also entered into heated disputation concerning the implications of the change for the work and standing of the magistrates.

Considering the emphasis placed by the government upon the economies expected from the measure, not a great deal of attention was devoted to this matter. Peter Rylands, an Independent Radical, and one of the most steadfast opponents of the bill, accused the home secretary of exaggerating the cost of maintaining prisoners in small establishments, and insisted that the cost of appointing commissioners, assistant commissioners and the like would lead to 'the establishment . . . swelling up every year into large dimensions', with a consequent increase in expenditure.[31] Other members also questioned the government's ability to economise. The member for Chester noted that whilst in the matter of cost the local prisons compared adversely with the public

30 C.H. Hopwood, Liberal member for Stockport, for example, argued in the course of the second reading in 1877 that as taxpayers were mostly rich people the shift from local to central funding would take burdens from the poor and put them upon the wealthy and that this 'was as near an approach to Communism, taught by a Conservative Government, as any lapse in political economy they had ever committed' (*Hansard* (Third Series), CCXXXII, col. 400). Parnell condemned the treatment of the Irish treason-felony convicts, even though they were held in the convict rather than the local prisons (*ibid.*, CCXXXIII, col. 616). Dr Kenealy, who in 1873 had been leading counsel for the Tichborne Claimant (and was subsequently disbarred for his tempestuous handling of the case), raised the treatment and condition of his former client. Proprieties apart, this was hardly a relevant issue since the Claimant was in Dartmoor, a convict establishment (*ibid.*, col. 538). W. Forsyth, member for Marylebone, was successful in inserting an amendment to prevent prison industry from competing with free labour, citing as a supporting case the brush-makers of Bristol (*ibid.*, CCXXXII, cols 878-9).

31 *Hansard* (Third Series), CCXXX, cols 277, 282. Indeed, Rylands subsequently suggested that the desire of government officials to expand their career opportunities was one of the main reasons for the bill's introduction:

> These spending servants of the Crown formed a great army, and as was once remarked by the Hon. Gentleman the Member for Greenwich (Mr. Gladstone), they were always awake to their own interests; and whenever public opinion slept they took advantage of the opportunity of increasing the flow of promotion by the creation of new offices, and by advances in the rates of pay. They constituted, in fact, a great trades union, and every year were increasing in numbers and in influence (*ibid.*, CCXXXII, col. 395).

> Rylands went on to claim that the time was rapidly approaching when every householder would have 'a policeman at his front door, and an inspector in his backyard'.

works convict prisons, the comparison between local and separate system convict prisons such as Pentonville, Millbank and Woking was not unfavourable.[32] This point was developed by Sir Sydney Waterlow, who showed that at the more economical of the local prisons, akin to Salford and Preston, prisoners were maintained at less than half the cost than in the separate system convict establishments.[33] Sir Henry Selwin-Ibbetson, under-secretary at the Home Office, responded to these criticisms with the observation that had all the local authorities only followed the sound principles of economy of the efficient localities there would have been no need for the bill.[34] Others disputed the overall size of the savings which would be effected in the rates. In presenting a deputation of visiting justices to the home secretary in June 1876, for example, a member calculated that taking the prisons out of local control would make a saving of only three-sixteenths of a penny on the Lancashire rates.[35] Nevertheless, the government stuck firmly to its claim that nationalisation would promote a significant economy in administration, and Lord Beauchamp made this one of the central planks in his argument when introducing the bill in the Lords.[36]

Constitutional arguments against the measure were many and strongly expressed, prompting Cross, in replying to Charles Newdegate, the Conservative member for North Warwickshire, to observe that

> the popular Conservative idea of the Constitution is strictly
> limited by the old maxim that it includes everything 'whereof the
> memory of man runneth not to the contrary.' But the memory
> of man, as distinguished from the memory of books, is very
> short, and it seems exceptionally short in Warwickshire.[37]

Newdegate spoke of the home secretary taking 'unlimited discretionary power' over the administration of justice in the bill, which he condemned as a 'direct invasion of the Common Law of this country', and he proclaimed that he stood 'with the Radical Members of this House

---

32 *Hansard* (Third Series), CCXXX, col. 308.
33 *Ibid.*, CCXXXII, cols 421-2.
34 *Ibid.*, col. 434. He also reminded the House that convict prisons had a much larger staff than had local prisons, and that this was another reason for treating with some caution the comparisons which had been made.
35 *The Times*, 24 June 1876, 10a. The *Pall Mall Gazette* considered that the measure was justified mainly on the grounds of improved administrative efficiency and predicted that

> The lopping of a 'limb' of £100,000 or £200,000 a year will have no lasting effect upon the body of local expenditure and we shall look in a few years to find the ratepayer patient, or mutinous, as the case may be, under a burden of the same weight, or nearly so, as that with which he is at present laden (23 June 1876, XXIII, p. 2361).

36 *Hansard* (Third Series), CCCXXXV, col. 386.
37 *The Times*, 24 February 1877, 9c.

as firmly as any of them in protesting against the despotic tendencies of this measure'.[38] Newdegate was the most extreme Conservative opponent of the bill to participate in the debates, but some members, including Rylands, feared that the centralisation of the administration of the prisons would be followed by the centralisation of the police, on the similar premise that crime was a national rather than a local problem.[39] In the home secretary's view such fears were unjustified. He contended that there was little in the bill which would undermine the principle of local self-government,[40] and he expostulated that 'the looking after 18,000 miserable prisoners was necessary to preserve the dignity of local self-government, or the respect of local authorities, was really an insult to his common sense'.[41]

The constitutional objections to the bill were closely intertwined with anxieties about the extension of central government patronage. Rylands referred to the very large number of naval and military men who wished to work in prisons, and asserted that under central government administration such persons would have some political influence in the competition for posts.[42] Dr E.V. Kenealy feared that the result of the home secretary's likely appointment of army and navy men as commissioners would be unhappy since 'there was too much readiness among these gentlemen to resort to flogging'.[43] But some apparently grieved more for the loss of local patronage than for its exercise by

38 *Hansard* (Third Series), CCXXXII, cols 423-7, *passim*. During the committee stage he repeated these observations and accused the proponents of the measure of following the Code Napoléon (*ibid*., col. 859).

39 *Ibid*., CCXXXII, col. 399; see also CCXXX, cols 904, 912.

40 There was particularly strong Radical and Conservative opposition to centralisation of the police (see, for example, *Pall Mall Gazette* (24 February 1877), XXV, p. 762), but despite the financial relief given to the localities (see pp. 470-1, above) nationalisation of the police does not appear to have been considered by Cross as an acceptable means of pursuing rating and taxation economies.

41 *Hansard* (Third Series), CCXXX, col. 922.

42 *Ibid*., col. 281. J.W. Pease, member for South Durham, was of similar mind, claiming that one of the results of allowing the government to exercise patronage would be that 'the Home Secretary would be everlastingly troubled with hungry half-pay officers applying for gaol appointments' (*ibid*., col. 900). *The Times*, which firmly supported the bill, took the opposite view, observing that one advantage of the home secretary exercising patronage would be that

it will give him the opportunity of introducing a practice which has long been recommended in the interests of the Army. . . . There are few posts for which old soldiers would be more eligible. The work eminently requires the habits of discipline and temper which are specially cultivated in a soldier's life; and by appointing soldiers to such posts we should not merely be rewarding deserving men, but obtaining the best servants possible for such duties (24 March 1877, 12c).

43 *Hansard* (Third Series), CCXXXIII, col. 539.

Whitehall. According to the *Pall Mall Gazette* the lord mayor of London fell into this category:

> The Lord Mayor deserves the credit of having put into a single speech all the objections which the least intelligent section of the magistracy feel to the transfer of the control of prisons from the visiting magistrates to the Secretary of State.... he represented that when the magistrates give up time and attention to the management of prisons they expect to be paid, not in money, indeed, but in patronage.... The answer to this is that experience shows that if time and trouble are not to be had for nothing, it is very much better economy to pay for them in money than in patronage.[44]

Others saw the bill as a more general attack upon the magistracy. Thus, P.H. Muntz, Conservative member for Birmingham, in declaring his 'unqualified opposition', claimed that the measure 'cast a slur upon the magistrates'.[45] Sir Henry Jackson, member for Coventry, on the other hand, considered that while the bill might diminish the dignity of the magistrates and deprive them of patronage, it would not thereby prevent them from doing their duty.[46]

Lopes's view that the punishment of crime was an imperial rather than a local responsibility was not universally shared. The member for Hull maintained that the bill would 'diminish the inducement now felt by the magistrates to repress crime, and it would place sober localities on a level with drunken ones'.[47] Another Liberal claimed that the knowledge that 'a prisoner would be kept at the expense of the country generally instead of being a burden upon the county rate would tend to increase the number of persons sent to gaol'.[48] A variation of this view, held by some magistrates, was that uniformity in prison administration was not wholly desirable since crime had its local characteristics and the criminals of different localities therefore required different

44 *Pall Mall Gazette* (28 June 1876), XXIII, p. 2425.

45 *Hansard* (Third Series), CCXXX, col. 903.

46 Jackson also raised the interesting (if somewhat tenuous) historical argument that the gaoler had always been the officer of the sheriff and thus of the Crown, and that the passing of local prisons into the hands of the magistracy and the boroughs had been

> to a certain extent, an anomaly ... probably adopted by Parliament, with the consent of the Crown, merely for greater convenience and for facilitating the discharge of the administration of the law, which had always been the first duty of the Sovereign power (*ibid*., col. 908).

47 *Ibid*., col. 302.

48 *Ibid*., cols 899-900. This opinion was repeated the following year by yet another Liberal, C.H. Hopwood, who held that the measure would take away from the various localities all incentives to economy (*ibid*., CCXXXII, col. 400).

treatment.[49] Rylands drew attention to the petition from the corporation of Nottingham, which stated that £30,000 had been spent in the erection of a gaol, that the land upon which it was built was worth £20,000, and protesting that it was proposed to confiscate this property without compensation.[50] The member for East Gloucestershire spoke of the opposition in his own county from Barwick Baker, the penal reformer and eminent magistrate, who was of the opinion that the bill would put an end to voluntary efforts in the friend of prison reform since 'country gentlemen would be intruders where they were now lords and masters'.[51] J.W. Pease sounded a similar note, averring that none of the reforms of prisons had come from central government but had been 'commenced by a Howard, a Fry, a Buxton, a Gurney, and had been followed up and carried out by the visiting justices'.[52]

There was claim and counterclaim as to the extent of opposition or support for the bill among the magistrates. Samuel Whitbread, the

---

49 *Ibid.*, CCXXX, col. 902. The *Pall Mall Gazette* was characteristically scornful in its rebuttal of this argument, asserting that

> it seems to imply that there are local characteristics about crime which only magistrates bred in the district can properly appreciate. Thus when we hear of prisoners in one gaol being well fed and having nothing worse to do than to work at some trade, while prisoners in another gaol spend most of their days at the crank or on the treadmill, with no more food than is absolutely necessary to keep them in health, we are not to suppose that these are mere examples of the lamentable inequality which prevails in prison discipline. They are simply the distinctions which a sympathetic magistracy sees to be demanded by the different conditions of the counties in which the gaols are situated. Surrey, with its sandy heaths and miles of villas, may engender a class of crime which needs one sort of treatment. Leicester, with its rich pastures and hunting associations, may engender a class of crime which calls for a different sort of treatment. Only a magistrate of the county can divine the nature of the discipline suitable to each case (28 June 1876, XXXIII, p. 2425).

50 *Hansard* (Third Series), CCXXX, col. 279. To this the indefatigable *Pall Mall Gazette* replied that

> The State called upon each prison authority to provide a gaol. The authority was bound by this obligation; it could make no use of the property but as a gaol; it could not escape this obligation, and the gaol was very expensive to maintain; it was a *damnosa haereditas*, it was something of a white elephant, and all the State said was, so long as we pay for the prisoners we must have the use of this jail.

Since this was 'not only a fair way but the only reasonable way of putting the matter; the transaction thus described . . . has certainly no resemblance whatever to confiscation of property' (24 June 1876, XXIII, p. 2386).

51 *Hansard* (Third Series), CCXXX, cols 901-2. The member (J.R. Yorke) sought to placate both the county and the government by arguing that if every county were like Gloucestershire and every magistrate like Barwick Baker there would be no need for the measure.

52 *Ibid.*, col. 900.

Liberal member for Bedford (whose family had a long and honourable connection with prison administration and reform), declared that 'the localities would not easily agree to a proposal for grouping the small prisons' and that 'they would make a harder fight before giving up their gaols than in parting with one of their representatives'.[53] W.J.R. Cotton, who was a member for the City and lord mayor at the time, also claimed that the bill had been unfavourably received, but admitted that 'the indifference and apparently submissive manner of the magistrates was inexplicable to him'.[54] To this it was replied that the reason for the quietness of the magistrates was that they were satisfied with the measure: 'If they believed that a blow was thus struck at the weal of England he was sure that they would have made the country ring with their complaints.'[55]

Apparent differences between the attitudes to the bill of the town and county magistracies were seized upon to allege that some of the petitions from town councils against the measure were based 'on the interference which it would exercise with the purveying of meat and stores for these prisons'.[56] Whilst this accusation may with some justice have been made of certain localities, it was by no means a fair comment on the motives of all town justices. The considerable opposition from both Middlesex and the City, for example, was because of the transfer to central government of very valuable buildings and building land, the superannuation charges to which they would become liable after the transfer, and the substantial sum which would have to be paid to the Treasury in respect of the estimated shortfall in accommodation.[57] A special meeting of the Court of Common Council expressed sympathy with the objectives which had led the government to introduce the measure, but declared that

> they may be better secured without calling into existence the numerous . . . highly paid offices proposed to be created by the Bill, and which your Committee consider of even more importance, without destroying that local supervision and superintendence exercised by the unpaid magistrates throughout the country, with great advantage to the public.[58]

Moreover, the county magistrates had not entirely lost their tongues. The day after the bill received its second reading in 1876 a deputation of magistrates from several counties, described by *The Times* as 'one of the largest and most influential representative deputations received by

53 *Ibid*., CCXXIX, col. 1547.
54 *Ibid*., CCXXX, col. 887.
55 *Ibid*., col. 904.
56 *Ibid*., CCXXX, cols 907-8.
57 *The Times*, 15 June 1876, 10f.
58 *Ibid*., 21 June 1876, 12f.

any Minister during the present Session', waited upon the home secretary.[59] They complained that the bill would undermine the magistracy, would provide only small economies and would bring under government control much patronage 'likely to be used for political purposes'.[60]

The opposition inside and outside Parliament never seriously threatened the bill's passage. Modifications in the financial arrangements secured for the localities too great a financial boon to allow the Commons' majority in 1876 and 1877 to drop below one hundred.[61] The parliamentary opponents of the measure — Radicals, backbench Conservatives and the Irish — were too divided in their own objectives and broader allegiances to constitute an effective barrier. Besides the financial concessions there were few successful amendments and, apart from the withdrawal of a provision to allow the magistrates to appoint subordinate staff, they were of a minor nature or initiated by the government itself. On 9 July 1877 the bill received its final reading. The Royal Assent was given three days later and the Act came into operation on 1 April 1878, bringing to a close a long and involved chapter in the history of English prison administration.

59 The deputation, composed almost entirely of visiting justices, represented South-East Lancashire, Yorkshire, Kirkdale, Preston, Stafford, Kent, Gloucester, Hereford, Lincolnshire, Northampton, East Sussex, Nottingham, Leicestershire, Clifton, Surrey and Middlesex.
60 *The Times*, 24 June 1876, 10a.
61 See n. 26, p. 475, above. The financial concessions offered by the government prompted G.H. Walley, the member for Peterborough, to complain during the committee stage that Cross had undermined his earlier claims about the economies likely to be procured by centralisation since 'the bribe offered to the local prison authorities had been increased at each successive stage of the consideration of the provisions in Committee' (*Hansard* (Third Series), CCXXXII, col. 1240).

Bibliography

ORDER OF BIBLIOGRAPHY

Archives

Bedfordshire County Record Office
Cross Papers, British Library (Reference Division)
Du Cane Papers, Department of Western Manuscripts, Bodleian
    Library, Oxford
East Sussex County Record Office
Essex County Record Office
Gloucestershire County Record Office
Grey Papers, University of Durham
Hertfordshire County Record Office
Hughenden (Disraeli) Papers, Department of Western Manuscripts,
    Bodleian Library, Oxford
Huntingdonshire County Record Office
Iddesleigh Papers, British Library (Reference Division)
Jebb Papers, British Library of Political and Economic Science

Nottinghamshire County Record Office
Public Record Office
West Sussex County Record Office

Other unpublished material

i *Theses*

Bell, S. Peter, 'A Social History of Salford New Bailey Prison, 1823-1865', MSc, University of Salford, 1972

Condon, Richard Herrick, 'The Reform of English Prisons, 1773-1816', PhD, Brown University, Rhode Island, 1962

Cooper, Robert Alan, 'English Prison Reform 1773-1835: A Study in Administrative Change', PhD, University of North Carolina at Chapel Hill, 1975

Dobb, Clifford, 'Life and Conditions in London Prisons, 1553-1643, with Special Reference to Contemporary Literature', BLitt, University of Oxford, 1952

Donajgrodski, A.P., 'The Home Office 1820-48', DPhil, University of Oxford, 1973

Duffy, I.P.H., 'Bankruptcy and Insolvency in London in the Late Eighteenth and Early Nineteenth Century', DPhil, University of Oxford, 1973-4

Dwyer, F.J., 'The Rise of Richard Assheton Cross and His Work at the Home Office 1868-1880', BLitt, University of Oxford, 1955

Evans, Robin, 'Prison Design 1750-1842; A Study of the Relationship Between Fundamental Architecture and Penal Ideology', PhD, University of Essex, 1975

Macdonald, Norma Myra, 'The Presentation of Oppression in the English Novel from Goodwin to Dickens', PhD, University of Cambridge, 1976

Macnab, K.K., 'Aspects of the History of Crime in England and Wales Between 1805-1860', DPhil, University of Sussex, 1965

Mishra, R.C., 'A History of the Relieving Officer in England and Wales from 1834 to 1948', PhD, University of London, 1969

Moir, Esther, A.L., 'Local Government in Gloucestershire, 1775-1800: A Study of the Justices of the Peace and their Work', PhD, University of Cambridge, 1955

Oldham, Wilfred, 'The Administration of the System of Transportation of British Convicts 1763-1793', PhD, University of London (King's College), 1933

Orr, Richard Byron, 'In Durance Vile: Attitudes Towards Imprisonment in England during the Du Cane Régime, 1877-1895', PhD, University of Wisconsin, 1968

Passey, William E., 'Houses of Correction in England and Wales', MA, University of Liverpool, 1936

Pendry, E.D., 'Elizabethan Prisons and Prison Scenes', PhD, University of Birmingham, 1954

Raphael, Marios, 'The Origins of Public Superannuation Schemes in

England, 1684-1859', PhD, University of London (London School of Economics), 1957

Sheehan, Wayne Joseph, 'The London Prison System, 1666-1795', PhD, University of Maryland, 1975

ii *Manuscripts in Radzinowicz Library, University of Cambridge, Institute of Criminology*

Edis, John, 'Extracts from the Journal of John Edis, Governor of Cambridge Town Gaol, 1839-1865'

Hoskins, R. (ed.), 'Pentonville Prison, Governor's Journal, 1842-44'

iii *Documents in Prison Staff College Library, Wakefield*

Jebb, Lieutenant-Colonel Joshua, 'The Convict Question' (Confidential Report for the Cabinet, 17 November 1852)

[Lord Rosebery, Chairman] 'Report of the Committee Appointed to Inquire into the Position and Prospects of Convict Wardens and Broadmoor Asylum Attendants'

Statutes, parliamentary papers and official publications

i *Statutes*

Sheriff's Tourns Act, 1285: 13 Edw, I, c.13

Debtors Act, 1350: 25 Edw. III, St. V, c.17

Sheriff's Act, 1503: 19 Hen. VII, c.10

Gaol Act, 1531: 23 Hen. VIII, c.2

Vagabonds Act, 1535: 27 Hen. VIII, c.25

Poor Act, 1551: 5 & 6 Edw. VI, c.2

Poor Act, 1555: 2 & 3 Ph. & M., c.5

Vagabonds, etc., Act, 1572: 14 Eliz., c.5

Poor Act, 1575: 18 Eliz., c.3

Popish Recusants Act, 1592: 35 Eliz., c.2

Continuation of Acts Act, 1592: 35 Eliz., c.7

Poor Act, 1597: 39 Eliz., c.3

Vagabonds Act, 1597: 39 Eliz., c.4

Poor Relief Act, 1601: 43 Eliz., c.2

Vagabonds Act, 1609: 7 Jac. I, c.4

Gaols Act, 1698: 11 & 12 Will. III, c.19

Continuation of Acts Act, 1711: 10 Ann., c.14 (Ruffhead's edition), c.24 (Statutes of the Realm)

Deer-stealers Act, 1718: 5 Geo. I, c.15

Perpetuation of Acts, etc., Act, 1719: 6 Geo. I, c.19

Criminal Law Act, 1722: 9 Geo. I, c.22

Insolvent Debtors Relief Act, 1728: 2 Geo. II, c.22

Poor Prisoners Relief Act, 1737: 11 Geo. II, c.20

County Rates Act, 1738: 12 Geo. II, c.29

Justices Commitment Act, 1743: 17 Geo. II, c.5

Sale of Spirits Act, 1751: 24 Geo. II, c.40

Debtors Imprisonment Act, 1758: 32 Geo. II, c.28

Gaol Chaplains Act, 1773: 13 Geo. III, c.58

Discharged Prisoners Act, 1774: 14 Geo. III, c.20

Health of Prisoners Act, 1774: 14 Geo. III, c.59

Criminal Law Act, 1776: 16 Geo. III, c.43

Criminal Law Act, 1778: 18 Geo. III, c.62

Militia Pay Act, 1779: 19 Geo. III, c.54

Transportation, etc., Act, 1779: 19 Geo. III, c.74

Houses of Correction Act, 1782: 22 Geo. III, c.64 (Gilbert's Act)

Relief of the Poor Act, 1782: 22 Geo. III, c.83

Removal of Prisoners, etc., Act, 1783: 24 Geo. III, Sess. 1, c.12

Gaols Act, 1784: 24 Geo. III, Sess. 2, c.54

Houses of Correction Act, 1784: 24 Geo. III, Sess. 2, c.55

Transportation, etc., Act, 1784: 24 Geo. III, Sess. 2, c.56

Local (Gloucester Gaol) Act, 1785: 25 Geo. III, c.10

Shrewsbury Gaol Act, 1786: 26 Geo. III, c.24

Local (Middlesex Gaol) Act, 1786: 26 Geo. III, c.55

Local (Sussex Gaol) Act, 1787: 27 Geo. III, c.58

Local (Stafford Gaol) Act, 1787: 27 Geo. III, c.60

Local (Chester Improvement) Act, 1788: 28 Geo. III, c.82

Local (Surrey Gaol) Act, 1791: 31 Geo. III, c.22

Gaols Act, 1791: 31 Geo. III, c.46

Penitentiary for Convicts Act, 1794: 34 Geo. III, c.84

Removal of Offenders Act, 1806: 46 Geo. III, c.28

Penitentiary House, etc., Act, 1812: 52 Geo. III, c.44

Relief of Insolvent Debtors in England Act, 1813: 53 Geo. III, c.102

Poor Prisoners Relief Act, 1813: 53 Geo. III, c.113

Return of Persons Committed, etc., Act, 1815: 55 Geo. III, c.49

Gaol Fees Abolition Act, 1815: 55 Geo. III, c.50

Transportation Act, 1815: 55 Geo. III, c.156

Prisoner Act, 1816: 55 Geo. III, c.116

Male Convicts Act, 1823: 4 Geo. IV, c.47

Gaols, etc. (England), Act, 1823: 4 Geo. IV, c.64 (Peel's Gaol Act)

Vagrancy Act, 1824: 5 Geo. IV, c.83

Transportation Act, 1824: 5 Geo. IV, c.84

Gaols, etc. (England), Act, 1824: 5 Geo. IV, c.85

Criminal Justice Act, 1827: 7 & 8 Geo. IV, c.28

Millbank Penitentiary Act, 1827: 7 & 8 Geo. IV, c.33

Transportation Act, 1830: 11 Geo. IV & 1 Will. IV, c.39

Prisons Act, 1835: 5 & 6 Will. IV, c.38

Millbank Penitentiary Act, 1837: 7 Will. IV & 1 Vict., c.13

Parkhurst Prison Act, 1838: 1 & 2 Vict., c.82

Prisons Act, 1839: 2 & 3 Vict., c.56

Parliamentary Papers Act, 1840: 2 & 3 Vict., c.9

Bonded Corn Act, 1842: 5 Vict., c.92

Queen's Prison Act, 1842: 5 & 6 Vict., Sess. 2, c.22

Pentonville Prison Act, 1842: 5 & 6 Vict., c.29

Prisons Act, 1842: 5 & 6 Vict., c.98
Millbank Prison Act, 1843: 6 & 7 Vict., c.26
District Courts and Prisons Act, 1844: 7 & 8 Vict., c.50
Insolvency Act, 1844: 7 & 8 Vict., c.96
Lunatics Act, 1845: 8 & 9 Vict., c.100
Lunatics Act, 1845: 8 & 9 Vict., c.126
Small Debts Act, 1845: 8 & 9 Vict. c. 127
County Courts (England) Act, 1846: 9 & 10 Vict., c.95
Finance Act, 1846: 9 & 10 Vict., c.116
Mutiny Act, 1848: 11 & 12 Vict., c.11
Millbank Prison Act, 1848: 11 & 12 Vict., c.104
County Courts Act, 1849: 12 & 13 Vict., c.101
Convict Prisons Act, 1850: 13 & 14 Vict., c.39
County Courts Act, 1850: 13 & 14 Vict., c.61
Liberties Act, 1850: 13 & 14 Vict., c.105
Convicted Prisoners Removal Act, 1853: 16 & 17 Vict., c.43
Penal Servitude Act, 1853: 16 & 17 Vict., c.99
Youthful Offenders Act, 1854: 17 & 18 Vict., c.86
Removal of Prisoners in Custody Act, 1854: 17 & 18 Vict., c.115
Criminal Justice Act, 1856: 18 & 19 Vict., c.126
County Courts Act, 1856: 19 & 20 Vict., c.108
Penal Servitude Act, 1857: 20 & 21 Vict., c.3
Franchise Prisons Abolition Act, 1857: 21 & 22 Vict., c.22
Returns to Secretary of State Act, 1858: 21 & 22 Vict., c.67
Convict Prisons Abroad Act, 1859: 22 Vict., c.25
Public Service Superannuation Act, 1859: 22 Vict., c.26
County Court Judges Act, 1859: 22 & 23 Vict., c.57
Mutiny Act, 1860: 23 & 24 Vict., c.9
Debtors and Creditors Act, 1860: 23 & 24 Vict., c.147
Bankruptcy Act, 1861: 24 & 25 Vict., c.134
Discharged Prisoners' Aid Act, 1862: 25 & 26 Vict., c.44
Queen's Prison Discontinuance Act, 1862: 25 & 26 Vict., c.104
Prison Ministers Act, 1863: 26 & 27 Vict., c.79
Penal Servitude Act, 1864: 27 & 28 Vict., c.47
Prison Act, 1865: 28 & 29 Vict., c.126
Reformatory Schools Act, 1866: 29 & 30 Vict., c.117
Industrial Schools Act, 1866: 29 & 30 Vict., c.118
Prison Officers Compensation Act, 1868: 31 & 32 Vict., c.21
Capital Punishment Amendment Act, 1868: 31 & 32 Vict., c.24
Debtors Act, 1869: 32 & 33 Vict., c.62
Bankruptcy Act, 1869: 32 & 33 Vict., c.71
Bankruptcy Repeal and Insolvent Court Act, 1869: 32 & 33 Vict., c.83
Prevention of Crimes Act, 1871: 34 & 35 Vict., c.112
Convict Prisons Returns Act, 1876: 39 & 40 Vict., c.42
Prison Act, 1877: 40 & 41 Vict., c.21
Prison (Officers Superannuation) Act, 1878: 41 & 42 Vict., c.63
Summary Jurisdiction Act, 1879: 42 & 43 Vict., c.49

ii *Annual reports, etc.*

Annual Reports from the Commissioners of Pentonville Prison, 1843-50
Annual Reports of the Commissioners of Prisons, 1878-85
Annual Reports of the Committee of the General Penitentiary at Milbank, 1817-43
Annual Reports on the Convict Establishments at Bermuda and Gibraltar, 1859-63
Annual Reports on the Convict Establishment at Gibraltar, 1864-9
Annual Reports of the Directors of Convict Prisons, 1850-77
Annual Reports of the Inspectors of Prisons, 1835-77[1]
Judicial Statistics (England and Wales), 1856-80
Reports of J.H. Capper, Superintendent of the Ships and Vessels Employed for the Confinement of Offenders under Sentence of Transportation, 1816-47
Annual Reports Relating to Parkhurst Prison, 1839-50
Annual Report of the Poor Law Board, 1870
Reports of the Surveyor-General of Prisons, 1847-62[2]

iii *Reports of select committees and Royal Commissions*

Select Committee on Transportation of Offenders, 1785, JHC, XL, 954, 1161
Select Committee on Penitentiary Houses (Holford Committee). First Report, PP, 1810-11 (199), III, 567. Second Report, PP, 1810-11 (217), III, 691. Third Report, PP, 1812 (306), II, 363
Select Committee on Newgate, the Poultry Compter, Giltspur Street Compter, Ludgate Compter and Borough Compter, PP, 1813-14 (157), IV, 249
Royal Commission on State, Conduct and Management of the Fleet, Westminster Palace and Marshalsea, PP, 1819 (109), XI, 325
Select Committee on the State of Gaols, PP, 1819 (579), VII, 1
Select Committee on the Laws Relating to Prisons, PP, 1822 (300), IV, 67
Select Committee on the Penitentiary at Milbank (July 1823), PP, 1823 (533), V, 403
Select Committee on the Penitentiary at Milbank, PP, 1824 (408), V, 401
Select Committee on Criminal Commitments and Convictions, PP, 1826-7 (534), VI, 5
Select Committee on the Police of the Metropolis, PP, 1828 (533), VI, 1
Select Committee on the Best Mode of Giving Efficacy to Secondary Punishments, PP, 1831 (276), VII, 519; PP, 1831-2 (547), VII, 559

---

1 Initially there were four districts: Home; Southern and Western; Northern and Eastern; and Scotland, Northumberland and Durham. In 1857 these were reduced to three: Northern, Southern and Midland; and in 1863 to Northern and Southern only.
2 These reports by Jebb are variously numbered, as shown in the text.

Select Committee on the Present State of Agriculture, and of Persons Employed in Agriculture, in the United Kingdom, and to Whom Several Petitions on the Subject Were Referred, PP, 1833 (612), V, 1

Royal Commission on Municipal Corporations in England and Wales, PP, 1835 (116), XXIII, 1

Royal Commission Appointed to Inquire Respecting County Rates (Preliminary Report), PP, 1835, XXXVI, 17

Select Committee of the House of Lords on Gaols and Houses of Correction in England and Wales. First Report, PP, 1835 (438), XI, 1. Second Report, PP, 1835 (439), XI, 495. Third Report, PP, 1835 (440), XII, 1. Fourth and Fifth Reports, PP, 1835 (441), XII, 157

Select Committee on the Laws Relating to Prisons, PP, 1836 (454), XXI, 301

Royal Commission Appointed to Inquire Respecting County Rates, PP, 1836 (58), XXVII, 1

Select Committee on Transportation, PP, 1837 (518), XIX, 1; PP, 1837-8 (669), XXII, 1

Royal Commission on Constabulary Force, PP, 1839, XIX, 1

Select Committee of the House of Lords Appointed to Inquire into the Execution of the Criminal Laws, Especially Respecting Juvenile Offenders and Transportation (Brougham Committee). First Report, PP, 1847 (447), VII, 1. Second Report, PP, 1847 (534), VII, 637

Royal Commission on the Management of Millbank Prison, PP, 1847 (760), XXX, 1

Select Committee on Expenditure for Miscellaneous Services, PP, 1847-8 (543), XVIII, 1

Select Committee on Prison Discipline (Grey Committee), PP, 1850 (632), XVII, 1

Report on the Discipline and Management of Convict Prisons, PP, 1851 (1638), XXVII, 213

Select Committee on Criminal and Destitute Children, PP, 1852-3 (448), XXIII, 1

Royal Commission Appointed to Inquire into the Condition and Treatment of the Prisoners Confined to Birmingham Borough Prison, PP, 1854 (1809), XXXI, 1

Royal Commission on the Condition and Treatment of Prisoners Confined in Leicester County Gaol and House of Correction, PP, 1854 (1808), XXXIV, 197

Report of the Select Committee of the House of Lords Appointed to Inquire into the Provisions and Operation of the Act 16 & 17 Vict., c.99, PP, 1856 (244), XVII, 1

Reports of the Commissioners of Lunacy, PP, 1857 (157), Sess. 2, XVI, 351; PP, 1867 (366), XVIII, 201; PP, 1877 (200), XLI, 1; PP, 1882 (357), XXXII, 1

Royal Commission on the Purchase and Sale of Commissions in the Army, PP, 1857 (2267), Sess. 2, XVIII, 1; PP, 1857-8 (2292), XIX, 233

Royal Commission on the State of Popular Education in England, PP, 1861 (2794-1), XXI, Part 1

BIBLIOGRAPHY

Report of the Commissioners Appointed to Inquire into the Operation of the Acts Relating to Transportation and Penal Servitude, PP, 1863 (3190), XXI, 1

Select Committee of the House of Lords on Gaol Discipline (Carnarvon Committee), PP, 1863 (499), IX, 1

Select Committee on the Working of the Bankruptcy Act, 1861, PP, 1864 (512), V, 1; PP, 1865 (144), XII, 589

Report of a Committee Appointed by the Home Office to Inquire into the Dietaries of County and Borough Gaols, PP, 1864 (467), XLIX, 9

Select Committee on the Prisons Bill, PP, 1865 (3880), XII, 425

Report of the Commissioners Appointed by the Home Department to Inquire into the Treatment of Certain Treason-Felony Convicts in English Convict Prisons, PP, 1867 (3880), XXXV, 673

Commission of Inquiry into the Treatment of Treason-Felony Convicts, PP, 1871 (c.319), XXXII, 1

Report of the Commissioners Appointed to Inquire into the Working of the Penal Servitude Acts, PP, 1878-9 (c.2368), XXXVII, 1

Royal Commission on Reformatories and Industrial Schools, PP, 1884 (c. 3876), XLV, 1

Royal Commission on Local Taxation. First Report, PP, 1899 (c.9141), XXXV, 733. Second Report, PP, 1899 (c.9142), XXXV, 795

House of Commons, *Fifteenth Report from the Expenditure Committee* (3 vols), HCP 662, I-III, HMSO, 1977-8

iv *Returns and estimates*

An Account of All the Gaols, Houses of Correction and Penitentiaries in the United Kingdom, PP, 1819 (135), XVII, 371

Account of the Number of Convicts Transported to the British Colonies, PP, 1824 (144), XIX, 181

Reports and Schedules Transmitted to the Secretary of State from the Several Counties, Cities and Towns in England and Wales under the Provisions of 4 Geo. IV, c.64, PP, 1824 (104), XIX, 181

A Return of the Expense for the Convicts in the Hulks at Bermuda, PP, 8130 (in 52), XXIII, 17

Estimate of the Sum that will Probably be Required to Defray the Charge of the Establishment of the Penitentiary at Milbank, PP, 1831-2 (158), XXVIII, 638; PP, 1836 (157), XXXVIII, 378

Return of the Salary Paid to the Chaplain of Every Prison in England and Wales, PP, 1831-2 (622), XXXIII, 533

Return of the Establishment of Officers and Servants Employed in Each County Gaol and House of Correction in England and Wales, PP, 1833 (493), XXVIII, 391; PP, 1835 (441), XII, 435

Return of All the Gaols and Houses of Correction in England and Wales, Including those under Corporate Jurisdiction, PP, 1833 (484), XXVIII, 549

Abstract of Answers to Queries Sent by Order of the House of Lords to the Governors of Gaols, PP, 1835 (in 438), XI, 393

Return of Salaries Paid to Chaplains in Gaols, Hours of Attendance, Emoluments from Other Sources, PP, 1835 (200), XLV, 187

Estimates etc., Miscellaneous Services, PP, 1835 (481), XXXVII, 537

Tables Showing the Number of Criminal Offenders Committed for Trial or Bailed for Appearance at the Assizes and Sessions in Each County in the Year and the Result of the Proceedings, PP, 1836 (61), XLI, 11; PP, 1846 (701), XXXIV, 1

Estimates to Defray the Salaries and Expenses of Inspectors of Prisons, PP, 1836 (157), XXXVIII, 387; PP, 1837 (146), XL, 336; PP, 1843 (91-111), XXXI, 424; PP, 1850 (256-111), XXXIV, 356

Abstract Return of the Establishment of, and Persons Confined in, and Expenditure of Each Gaol and House of Correction in England and Wales, PP, 1840 (438), XXXVIII, 241

Returns Relating to Prisoners in the Penitentiary, and of Attendances of the Superintending Committee at the Respective Meetings, PP, 1840 (372), XXXVIII, 689

Tables Showing the Number of Criminal Offenders in the Year 1840, PP, 1841 (318), XVIII, 255

Returns of the Number of Prisoners Sent to the Penitentiary in Each of the Last Five Years – of Prisoners Removed on the Ground of Insanity, etc., etc., PP, 1841 (249), XVII, 655

Returns Relating to Prisoners in the General Penitentiary at Milbank, and of Attendances of the Superintending Committee at Respective Meetings During the Last Five Years, PP, 1841 (250), XVIII, 655

Reports and Schedules Transmitted to the Secretary of State, Pursuant to s.24 of 4 Geo. IV, c.64 and s.14, 5 Geo. IV, c.12, PP, 1843 (48), XLIII, 1

Return of an Address to the Honourable The House of Commons, dated 19th March 1847 for Copies of Any Circular Letter Addressed by Her Majesty's Secretary of State to the Justices in Quarter Sessions, Relative to the Confinement of Convicts After Sentence, and of the Replies Received Thereto, PP, 1847 (256), XLVIII, 5

Return of Salaries Paid to Each of the Governors or Keepers of the Common Gaols and Houses of Correction in England, PP, 1843 (315), XLIII, 257

Estimates etc. Miscellaneous Services, PP, 1847-8 (327-11), XL, 349; PP, 1849 (268-111), 347; PP, 1850 (256-1), XXXIV, 356 and 364

Abstract of Return of the Number of Convicts under Sentence of Transportation Confined in Prisons or Hulks in England, Scotland and Ireland, on the 1st day of January in Each Year, 1839 to 1848, PP, 1847-8 (292), LII, 1

Digest and Summary of Information Respecting Prisons in the Colonies in Answer to Circular Despatches of the Secretary of State for the Colonies, PP, 1867-8 (3961, 3961-1), LVII, 557, 675

Return Giving the Names of the Persons who have been Appointed to be Unpaid Inspectors of Convict Prisons in England, with the Instructions Issued to Them, PP, 1880 (346), LIX, 527

v *Miscellaneous*

Rules and Regulations of the General Penitentiary at Milbank, PP, 1817 (85), XVI, 333; PP, 1819 (134), XVII, 339

Report of William Crawford, Esq., on the Penitentiaries of the United States; Addressed to His Majesty's Principal Secretary of State for the Home Department, PP, 1834 (593), XLVI, 349

Letter Written by Direction of the Secretary of State for the Home Department to the Committee for the Management of the Penitentiary, with the Report of the Committee in Answer Thereto, PP, 1837-8 (205), XLII, 317

First Report of the Constabulary Force Inspectors, PP, 1839 (169), XIX, 1

Papers Relative to the Transportation and Assignment of Convicts, PP, 1839 (582), XXXVIII, 749

Penitentiary (Milbank) Return to an Address of the Honourable the House of Commons, PP, 1840 (301), XXXVIII, 689

Regulations for Prisons in England and Wales, PP, 1843 (in 457), XXV and XXVI, 15

Correspondence on Convict Discipline and Transportation, PP, 1843 (158, 159), XLII, 353, 451

Report and Evidence on the Inquiry into the Conduct of the Governor of the County Gaol of Carnarvon, PP, 1843 (422, 477), XLIII, 261

Report of the Inspectors of Millbank Prison, PP, 1844 (586), XXVIII, 1

Report of the Surveyor-General of Prisons, on the Construction, Ventilation, and Details of Pentonville Prison, with Various Plans, PP, 1844 (594), XXVIII, 197

Report of an Inquiry into the General Treatment and Condition of the Convicts in the Hulks, at Woolwich, PP, 1847 (831, 831-11), XVIII, 1, 547

Correspondence Relating to the Recall of Sir Eardley Wilmot from Van Diemen's Land, PP, 1847 (262, 400), XXXVIII, 513, 527

Report by the Superintendent Respecting the Treatment of Convicts in the Hulks at Woolwich, PP, 1847 (149), XLVIII, 63

Correspondence on the Subject of Convict Discipline in Van Diemen's Land, PP, 1847 (785, 800, 811), XLVIII, 93, 297, 313

Report of the Manager of the Convict Hulk Establishment, for the Years 1848 and 1849, PP, 1850 (1177, 1178), XXIX, 1, 13

Report of the Directors of Convict Prisons on the Discipline and Management of Millbank Prison for the Year 1850, PP, 1851 (1409), XXVIII, 113

Report of the Directors of Convict Prisons on the Discipline and Management of Portland Prison for the Year 1850, PP, 1851 (1409), XXVIII, 141

Report of the Directors of Convict Prisons on the Discipline and Management of the Hulks for the Year 1851, PP, 1852 (1524), XXIV, 197

Report of the Directors of Convict Prisons on the Discipline and Management of Pentonville Prison for the Year 1851, PP, 1852 (1524), XXIV, 197

Correspondence on the Subject of Convict Discipline and Transportation, Despatches from Governor Fitzgerald, PP, 1849 (809), XLIII, 603 and PP, 1852 (961), XLI, 341

Correspondence on the Subject of Convict Discipline and Transportation, PP, 1852-3 (1601, 1677), LXXXII, 11, 267; PP, 1854 (1795), LIV, 303; PP, 1863 (3224), XXXIX, 513; PP, 1863 (492), XXXIX, 263

Papers Relative to the Convict Establishment at Bermuda, PP, 1860 (581), XLV, 269

Report of a Committee Appointed by the Home Office to Inquire into the Dietaries of Convict Prisons, PP, 1864 (467), XLIX, 9

Letters from Gentlemen Connected with the Colony of Western Australia to the Secretary of State for the Colonies, on the Discontinuance of Transportation, PP, 1864 (247), XXXVII, 367

Correspondence between Government and the Governments of the Australian Colonies Relating to the Discontinuance of Transportation, PP, 1865 (3424), XXXVII, 911

Digest and Summary of Information Respecting Prisons in the Colonies Supplied by the Governors of Her Majesty's Colonial Possessions in Answer to Mr. Secretary Cardwell's Circular Despatches at 16th and 17th January 1865, PP, 1867-8 (2026-4), LVII, 557

Twenty-Second Annual Report of the Poor Law Board, PP, 1870 (c.123), XXXV, 1

Reports of the Officers of Convict Prisons, PP, 1878 (c.2175), XLIII, 1; 1878-9 (c.2446), XXXV, 1

Reports of the Commissioners of Prisons, PP, 1878 (c.2174), XLII, 1; PP, 1878-9 (c.2442), XXXIV, 1

Report from the Departmental Committee on Prisons, PP, 1895 (c.7702), LVI, 1 (Gladstone Committee)

vi *Official Publications*

Routines Carried Out at Pentonville Prison, HMSO, 1848

Regulations for Prisons in England and Wales, Shaw & Sons (for the Secretary of State), 1849

Rules and Regulations for the Government of the Convict Prisons, HMSO, 1858

Rules and Regulations for Military Prisons, HMSO, 1863

Standing Orders for Convict Prisons, HMSO, 1865

'Royal Warrant for the Pay and Promotion, Non-effective Pay and Allowances of Her Majesty's British Forces Serving Elsewhere than in India, 3rd February 1866, Part 1', in *Revised Army Regulations*, Vol. 1, HMSO, 1866

Rules and Regulations for the Government of the Convict Prisons, HMSO, 1872

Rules for the Government of Convict Prisons, HMSO, 1886

Home Office Advisory Council on the Penal System, *Sentences of Imprisonment: Review of Maximum Penalties*, HMSO, 1978

Books, essays and journal articles

Publishers' names have been omitted from works published before 1900; unless otherwise stated the place of publication is London.

Abell, Francis, *Prisoners of War in Britain, 1756 to 1815: A Record of their Lives, their Romance and their Sufferings*, Oxford University Press, 1914

Adshead, Joseph, *Prisons and Prisoners*, 1845

Adye, Steven Payne, *A Treatise on Courts Martial* (8th edn), 1810

Albery, William, *A Millennium of Facts in the History of Horsham and Sussex*, Horsham, Horsham Museum Society, 1947

Anon. (attrib. Thomas Wontner), *Old Bailey Experience, Criminal Jurisprudence and the Actual Working of our Penal Code of Laws. Also, an Essay on Prison Discipline, to which is added a History of the Crimes Committed by Offenders in the Present Day*, 1833

Arnell, J.C., 'Bermuda as a Naval Base', *Bermuda Historical Quarterly*, XXXV (Winter 1978), 4

Ashton, Thomas Southcliffe, *An Economic History of England: The Eighteenth Century*, Methuen, 1955

Aydelotte, Frank, *Elizabethan Rogues and Vagabonds*, Oxford University Press, 1913; reprinted Frank Cass, 1967

Babington, Anthony, *The English Bastille: A History of Newgate Gaol and Prison Conditions in Britain 1188-1902*, Macdonald, 1971

Bassett, Margery, 'Newgate Prison in the Middle Ages', *Speculum* (1943), XVIII, 233

Bassett, Margery, 'The Fleet Prison in the Middle Ages', *University of Toronto Law Journal* (1944), V, no. 2

Beales, Hugh Lancelot, 'Travel and Communication', in A.S. Turberville (ed.), *Johnson's England*, Oxford University Press, 1952

Beattie, John M., 'The Pattern of Crime in England 1660-1800', *Past and Present* (February 1974), no. 66, p. 47

Beaumont, Gustave de, and Tocqueville, Alexis de, *On the Penitentiary System in the United States and its Application in France*, Philadelphia, 1833; reprinted Southern Illinois University Press, 1964

Beccaria, Cesare, *An Essay on Crimes and Punishments*, 5th revised English translation, 1801

Becher, Rev. John Thomas, *A Report Concerning the House of Correction at Southwell*, Newark, Notts., 1806

Becher, Rev. John Thomas, *Observations on the Punishment of Offenders and the Preservation of the Peace*, Newark, Notts., 1812

Becher, Rev. John Thomas, *The Antipauper System*, 1828

Bellamy, John, *Crime and Public Order in England in the Later Middle Ages*, Routledge & Kegan Paul, 1973

Bennet, Hon. Henry Grey, 'A Letter to the Common Council and Livery of the City of London, on the Abuses Existing in Newgate; Showing the Necessity of an Immediate Reform in the Management of that Prison', *Pamphleteer* (1818), XI, no. 277, p. 15

Bennet, Hon. Henry Grey, *A Letter to Viscount Sidmouth, Secretary of*

State for the Home Department on the Transportation Laws, the State of the Hulks, and of the Colonies in New South Wales, 1819

Bentham, Jeremy, *The Rationale of Punishment*, 1830

Bentham, Jeremy, *Works*, ed. John Bowring, Edinburgh, 1843

Bentham, Jeremy, *Correspondence*, ed. T.L.S. Sprigge, 1968

Best, Geoffrey Francis Andrew, *Mid-Victorian Britain 1851-75*, Panther, 1973

Best, Geoffrey Francis Andrew, *Shaftesbury*, Mentor, 1975

Bindoff, Stanley Thomas, *Tudor England*, Harmondsworth, Penguin, 1950

Blackstone, Sir William, *Commentaries on the Laws of England* (15th edn), 1809

Bleakley, Horace, *The Hangmen of England*, Chapman & Hall, 1929

Blom-Cooper, Louis (ed.), *Progress in Penal Reform*, Oxford University Press, 1974

Blom-Cooper, Louis, 'The Centralization of Governmental Control of National Prison Services, with Special Reference to the Prison Act, 1877' in John C. Freeman (ed.), *Prisons, Past and Future*, Heinemann, 1978

Bochel, Dorothy, *Probation and Aftercare: Its Development in England and Wales*, Edinburgh, Scottish Academic Press, 1976

Boswell, James, *Boswell's Life of Johnson, Together with Boswell's Journal of a Tour to the Hebrides, and Johnson's Diary of a Journey into North Wales*, ed. George Birkbeck Hill, revised and enlarged edition by Lawrence Fitzroy Powell (6 vols), Oxford, Clarendon Press, 1934

Bowen, Thomas, *Extracts from the Records and Court Books of Bridewell Hospital and Remarks upon the Report of a Select Committee of Governors of Bridewell Hospital*, 1798

Boyd, Derek, *The Royal Engineers*, Leo Cooper, 1975

Bradley, Ian, *The Call to Seriousness*, Jonathan Cape, 1976

Briggs, Asa, *The Age of Improvement*, Longmans, 1959

Burford, Ephraim John, *In the Clink*, New English Library, 1977

Burn, William Laurence, *The Age of Equipoise*, Allen & Unwin, 1964

Burt, John Thomas, *Results of the System of Separate Confinement as Administered at Pentonville Prison*, 1852

Burt, John Thomas, *Irish Facts and Wakefield Figures in Relation to Convict Discipline in Ireland*, 1863

Butler, Bishop Joseph, *Sermon Preached Before the Lord Mayor, Aldermen, Sheriffs, and Governors of Several Hospitals of London at the Parish Church of St. Bridget on Monday in Easter Week 1740*, 1740

Butterfield, Herbert, *The Whig Interpretation of History*, Harmondsworth, Penguin, 1973

Buxton, Thomas Fowell, *An Enquiry Whether Crime and Misery are Produced or Prevented by Our Present System of Prison Discipline*, 1818

Camden Society, The, *Economy of the Fleete, or an Apologeticall Answeare of Alexander Harris unto 19 Articles sett forth Against Him by the Prisoners*, ed. Augustus Jessop, XXV, 1879

Campbell, John, *Thirty Years' Experience of a Medical Officer in the English Convict Service*, 1884

Cannan, Edwin, *The History of Local Rates in England*, King, 1912

Carlebach, Julius, 'Major-General Sir Joshua Jebb, K.C.B., 1793-1863', *Prison Service Journal* (April 1965), IV, no. 15, p. 26

Carlebach, Julius, *Caring for Children in Trouble*, Routledge & Kegan Paul, 1970

Carlyle, Thomas, 'Model Prisons', *Latter Day Pamphlets*, 1858

Carpenter, Mary, *Our Convicts* (2 vols), 1864

Checkland, Sydney George, and Checkland, Edith Olive Anthony (eds), *The Poor Law Report of 1834*, Harmondsworth, Penguin, 1974

Chesterton, George Laval, *Peace, War and Adventure: An Autobiographical Memoir* (2 vols), 1853

Chesterton, George Laval, *Revelations of Prison Life; with an Enquiry into Prison Discipline and Secondary Punishments* (2 vols), 1856

Chichester, the Earl of (ed.), *Reports and Observations on the Discipline and Management of Convict Prisons by the Late Major General Sir Joshua Jebb, K.C.B.*, 1863

Clark, George Kitson, *The Making of Victorian England*, Methuen, 1962

Clay, Charles Travis, 'The Keepership of the Old Palace of Westminster', *English Historical Review*, LIX (January 1944), p. 1

Clay, Rev. Walter Lowe, *The Prison Chaplain: A Memoir of the Rev. John Clay, B.D.*, 1861

Clay, Rev. Walter Lowe, *Our Convict System*, Cambridge, 1862

Cobbett, William, *Rural Rides in Southern, Western and Eastern Counties of England, Together with Tours in Scotland and in the Northern and Midland Counties of England, and Letters from Ireland*, ed. George Douglas Howard and Margaret Cole (3 vols), Davies, 1930

Cohen, Emmeline W., *The Growth of the British Civil Service 1780-1939*, Allen & Unwin, 1941; reprinted Frank Cass, 1965

Coke, Edward, *Institutes of the Laws of England*, 1877

Cole, George Douglas Howard, 'Town-Life in the Provinces', in A.S. Turberville (ed.), *Johnson's England*, Oxford University Press, 1952

Cole, George Douglas Howard, and Postgate, Raymond William, *The Common People, 1746-1938*, Methuen, 1938

Collins, Philip Arthur William, 'Dickens and the Prison Governor, George Laval Chesterton', *Dickensian* (1961), LVII, p. 11

Collins, Philip Arthur William, *Dickens and Crime*, Macmillan, 1962

Cragg, Gerald Robertson, *The Church and the Age of Reason 1648-1789*, Harmondsworth, Penguin, 1976

Critchley, Thomas Alan, *The Conquest of Violence*, Constable, 1970

Crofton, Sir Walter, *Success of the Irish Prison System and Supervision*, 1860

Crofton, Sir Walter, *Recommendation for Extending Supervision to England*, 1864

Crofton, Sir Walter, *The Criminal Classes and Their Control. Prison*

Treatment and its Principles (addresses to Social Science Congress, Birmingham, October 1868), 1868

Cross, Sir Richard Assheton, *A Political History* (privately printed), 1903

Deane, Phyllis, and Cole, William Alan, *British Economic Growth, 1688-1959*, Cambridge University Press, 1967

Dickens, Charles, *American Notes*, 1896

Dixon, William Hepworth, *The London Prisons*, 1850

Dobb, Clifford, 'London's Prisons', in A. Nicoll (ed.), *Shakespeare in His Own Age* (Shakespeare Survey, XVII), Cambridge University Press, 1965

Donajgrodski, A.P., 'New Roles for Old: The Northcote-Trevelyan Report and the Clerks of the Home Office 1822-48', in Gillian Sutherland (ed.), *Studies in the Growth of Nineteenth-Century Government*, Routledge & Kegan Paul, 1972

Du Cane, Major Edmund Frederick, RE, *An Account of the Manner in which Sentences of Penal Servitude are Carried Out in England*, 1872

Du Cane, Col. Sir Edmund Frederick, KCB, RE, *The Punishment and Prevention of Crime*, 1882 and 1885

Du Cane, Col. Sir Edmund Frederick, KCB, RE, *A Description of the Prison of Wormwood Scrubs with an Account of the Circumstances Attending its Erection*, 1887

Du Cane, Major-General Sir Edmund Frederick, KCB, RE, 'The Unavoidable Uselessness of Prison Labour', *Nineteenth Century*, XL (July-December 1896), 632

Du Cane, Major-General Sir Edmund Frederick, KCB, RE, 'Lieutenant-Colonel Sir Edmund Yeomans Walcot Henderson', *Royal Engineers Journal* (1 February 1897), p. 4

Du Cane, Major-General Sir Edmund Frederick, KCB, RE, 'Early Days in Westralia', *Cornhill Magazine* (May 1897), LXXV (no. 2, third series), p. 617

Du Cane, Major-General Sir Edmund Frederick, KCB, RE, 'The Civil Service and Reform', *Monthly Review* (April 1900)

Dyos, Harold James, and Aldcroft, Derek Howard, *British Transport — An Economic Survey from the Seventeenth Century to the Twentieth*, Leicester, Leicester University Press, 1969

Eden, Sir Frederick Morton, *The State of the Poor*, 1797; facsimile reprint, Frank Cass, 1966

Edington, Robert, *A Descriptive Plan for Erecting a Penitentiary House for the Employment of Convicts; to Which are Added, Plans for the Prevention of Frauds and Thefts so far as Respects his Majesty's Dockyards, Public Works, and Stores, etc.*, n.d. (1803?)

Emblem, Donald Lewis, *Peter Mark Roget: The Word and the Man*, Longmans, 1970

Elton, Geoffrey Rudolph, *The Tudor Revolution in Government*, Cambridge University Press, 1966

Fairn, Richard Duncan, 'Prisons 1866-1966', in Hugh John Klare (ed.), *Changing Concepts of Crime and its Treatment*, Oxford University

Press, 1966

Fairweather, Leslie, 'The Evolution of the Prison', in United Nations Social Defence Research Institute, *Prison Architecture*, The Architectural Press, 1975

Field, Rev. John, *The Advantages of the Separate System of Imprisonment as Established in the New County Gaol of Reading with a Description of the Former Prisons and a Detailed Account of the Discipline Now Pursued*, 1846

Fielding, Henry, *An Enquiry into the Causes of the Late Increase of Robbers*, 1751

Finberg, Herbert Patrick Reginald, *The Formation of England 550-1042*, Granada Publishing, 1976

Finer, Samuel Edward, 'The Transmission of Benthamite Ideas 1825-50', in Gillian Sutherland (ed.), *Studies in the Growth of Nineteenth Century Government*, Routledge & Kegan Paul, 1972

Fortescue, Hon. Sir John, 'The Army', in A.S. Turberville (ed.), *Johnson's England*, Oxford University Press, 1952

Foucault, Michel, *Discipline and Punish*, Allen Lane, Harmondsworth, Penguin, 1977

'Four Visiting Justices of the West Riding Prison at Wakefield', *Observations on the Treatment of Convicts in Ireland with Some Remarks on the Same in England*, 1863

Fox, Sir Lionel Wray, *The English Prison and Borstal Systems: An Account of the Prison and Borstal Systems in England and Wales after the Criminal Justice Act 1948, with a Historical Introduction and an Examination of the Principles of Imprisonment as a Legal Punishment*, Routledge & Kegan Paul, 1952

Fry, Rev. Henry Phibbs, *A System of Penal Discipline, with a Report on the Treatment of Prisoners in Great Britain and Van Diemen's Land*, 1850

Goldthorpe, John, and Hope, Keith, *The Social Grading of Occupations; a New Approach and Scale*, Oxford, Clarendon Press, 1974

Griffiths, Major Arthur George Frederick, *Memorials of Millbank and Chapters in Prison History* (2 vols), 1875

Griffiths, Major Arthur George Frederick, *Fifty Years of Public Service, etc.*, Cassell, 1904

Grünhut, Max, *Penal Reform*, Oxford University Press, 1948

Gurr, Ted Robert, Grabowsky, Peter N., and Hula, Richard C., *The Politics of Crime and Conflict*, Beverly Hills, Calif., Sage, 1977

Guy, William Augustus, 'Address on John Howard', *Journal of the Statistical Society* (1875), XXXVIII, p. 430.

Halévy, Elie, *A History of the English People in the Nineteenth Century*, Ernest Benn, 1961

Hammond, John Lawrence, and Hammond, Barbara, 'Poverty, Crime and Philanthropy', in A.S. Turberville (ed.), *Johnson's England*, Oxford University Press, 1952

Hanway, Jonas, *Solitude in Imprisonment, with Proper Profitable Labour, and a Spare Diet, the Most Humane and Effectual Means of Bringing Malefactors who have Forfeited their Lives, or are Subject to Transportation, to a Right Sense of their Condition*, 1776

Harris, John Sharp, *British Government Inspection*, Stevens & Sons, 1955

Harrison, John Fletcher Clews, *The Early Victorians 1832-51*, Panther, 1973

Hart, Sir William Ogden, and Garner, Professor John Francis, *Hart's Introduction to the Law of Local Government* (9th edn), Butterworth, 1973

Hartshorne, Albert, *Hanging in Chains*, 1891

Hasluck, Eugene Lewis, *Local Government in England*, Cambridge University Press, 1936

Headlam, John, *A Letter to the Rt. Hon. Robert Peel on ... Prison Labour*, 1823

Heath, James, *Eighteenth Century Penal Theory*, Oxford University Press, 1963

Helsby, Sir Laurence, 'Recruitment in the Civil Service', in William Alexander Robson (ed.), *The Civil Service in Britain and France*, Hogarth, 1956

Henriques, Ursula Ruth Quixano, 'The Rise and Decline of the Separate System of Prison Discipline', *Past and Present*, 54 (February 1972), 61

Hibbert, Christopher, *The Road to Tyburn*, Longmans Green, 1957

Hill, Christopher, *Society and Puritanism in Pre-revolutionary England*, Panther, 1969

Hill, Frederic, *Crime: Its Amount, Causes and Remedies*, 1853

Hill, Frederic, *Frederic Hill: An Autobiography of Fifty Years in Times of Reform*, ed. Mary Constance Hill, 1893

Hill, Matthew Davenport, *Suggestions for the Repression of Crime*, 1857

Hinde, Richard Standish Elphinstone, *The British Penal System 1773-1950*, Duckworth, 1951

Historical Manuscripts Commission, *Huntingdonshire Quarter Sessions*, 1958

Holdsworth, Sir William, *A History of English Law*, Methuen, 1938

Holford, George, *Substance of a Speech in Support of an Amendment to Withhold from the Visiting Justices of Prisons the Power of Authorising the Employment, without their Own Consent of Prisoners Committed for Trial*, 1824

Holford, George, *The Convict's Complaint in 1815, and the Thanks of the Convict in 1825; or, Sketches in Verse of a Hulk in the Former Year, and of the Millbank Penitentiary in the Latter, ... with a few Prefatory Statements and Remarks*, 1825

Holford, George, *Third Vindication of the General Penitentiary; ... being an Answer to Some Observations Contained in a Work, Published by P.M. Latham, M.D., Entitled: 'An Account of the Disease Lately Prevalent at the General Penitentiary'*, 1825

Holford, George, *Statements and Observations Concerning the Hulks*, 1826

Holford, George, *Letter to the Editor of the Quarterly Review on a*

Misstatement Contained in the 42nd Volume of that Work Page 155, Relative to the Supposed Ill-success of the General Penitentiary at Millbank, 1830

Howard, Derek Lionel, *John Howard: Prison Reformer*, Christopher Johnson, 1958

Howard, Derek Lionel, *The English Prisons: Their Past and Future*, Methuen, 1960

Howard, John, *The State of the Prisons in England and Wales with Preliminary Observations, and an Account of some Foreign Prisons and Hospitals* (3rd and 4th edns), Warrington, 1784 and 1792

Hume, L.J., 'Bentham's Panopticon: An Administrative History', *Historical Studies* (October 1973), 61, 703; and (April 1974), 62, 36

Ignatieff, Michael, *A Just Measure of Pain*, Macmillan, 1978

Ives, E.W., 'The Law and the Lawyers', in A. Nicoll (ed.), *Shakespeare in His Own Age*, Cambridge University Press, 1965

Jackson, William Eric, *Local Government in England and Wales*, Harmondsworth, Penguin, 1951

Jebb, Major Joshua, RE, *Modern Prisons: Their Construction and Ventilation*, 1844

Johnson, William Branch, *The English Prison Hulks*, Chichester, Phillimore, 1970

Jones, Kathleen, *Mental Health and Social Policy 1845-1959*, Routledge & Kegan Paul, 1960

Jones, Kathleen, *A History of the Mental Health Services*, Routledge & Kegan Paul, 1972

Judges, Arthur Valentine, *The Elizabethan Underworld*, Routledge & Kegan Paul, 1965

Kingsmill, Rev. Joseph, *Chapters on Prisons and Prisoners and the Prevention of Crime* (3rd edn), 1854

Latham, Peter Mere, *An Account of the Disease Lately Prevalent at the General Penitentiary*, 1825

Laurence, John, *A History of Capital Punishment*, Sampson Low, 1932

Le Breton, Thomas, *Thoughts on the Defective State of Prisons and Suggestions for their Improvement*, 1822

Lecky, William Edward Hartpole, *A History of England in the Eighteenth Century*, 1892

Leonard, E.M., *The Early History of Poor Relief*, Cambridge University Press, 1900

Loades, David Michael, *Politics and the Nation 1450-1660*, Fontana/Collins, 1974

Longmate, Norman, *The Workhouse*, Temple Smith, 1974

McLachlan, Noel, 'Penal Reform and Penal History: Some Reflections', in Louis Blom-Cooper (ed.), *Progress in Penal Reform*, Oxford University Press, 1974

Makus, Thomas A., 'Pattern of the Law', *Architectural Review* (October 1954), 694, 251

Mandeville, Bernard de, *An Enquiry into the Causes of the Frequent Executions at Tyburn: and a Proposal for Some Regulations*

Concerning Felons in Prison. . . . To which is Added a Discourse on Transportation; and a Method to Render that Punishment more Effectual, 1725

Mannheim, Hermann, *The Dilemma of Penal Reform*, Allen & Unwin, 1939

Marshall, Dorothy, *The English Poor in the Eighteenth Century*, George Routledge & Sons, 1926

Marshall, Dorothy, 'Manners, Meals and Domestic Pastimes', in A.S. Turberville (ed.), *Johnson's England*, Oxford University Press, 1952

Mayhew, Henry, and Binny, John, *The Criminal Prisons of London and Scenes of London Life*, 1862; reprinted Frank Cass, 1968

Measor, Charles Pennell, *Criminal Correction*, 1864

Measor, Charles Pennell, *The Utilization of the Criminal*, 1869

Mill, James, *Essays on Government, Jurisprudence, Liberty of the Press, Prisons and Prison Discipline, Colonies, Law of Nations and Education, Reprinted from the Supplement to the Encyclopaedia Britannica*, 1828

Milton, Frank, *The English Magistracy*, Oxford University Press, 1967

Mitchell, Brian Redman, *Abstract of British Historical Statistics*, Cambridge University Press, 1962

Mynshul, Geffray, *Essayes and Characters of a Prison and Prisoners*, 1618; republished Edinburgh, 1831

Neild, James, *The State of the Prisons in England, Scotland and Wales*, 1812

Nihill, Rev. David, *Prison Discipline in its Relation to Society and Individuals*, 1839

O'Donoghue, Edward Geoffrey, *Bridewell Hospital: Palace, Prison, Schools: I, from the Earliest Times to the Reign of Elizabeth*, John Lane, The Bodley Head, 1923

O'Donoghue, Edward Geoffrey, *Bridewell Hospital: Palace, Prison, Schools: II, from the Death of Elizabeth to Modern Times*, John Lane, The Bodley Head, 1929

Olson, Alison Gilbert, *The Radical Duke*, Oxford University Press, 1961

'One Who Has Endured It', *Five Years Penal Servitude*, 1878

'One Who Has Tried Them', *Her Majesty's Prisons: Their Effects and Defects*, 1883

Paley, William, *The Principals of Moral and Political Philosophy* (17th ed.), 1809

Parker, Charles Stuart (ed.), *Sir Robert Peel* (3 vols), 1891

Paul, Sir George Onesiphorus, *A State of Proceedings on the Subject of a Reform of Prisons Within the County of Gloucester*, Gloucester, 1783

Paul, Sir George Onesiphorus, *Address Delivered at a General Meeting of the Nobility, Gentry, Clergy and Others, Assessed to the County Rate for the County of Gloucester, Convened by the High Sheriff, for the Purpose of Receiving a Statement of the Proceedings of the Committee Appointed to Carry into Execution the Resolutions of the Said County to Rebuild the Gaols and Bridewells thereof: and held on Monday the 9th July, 1792*, Gloucester, 1792

Paul, Sir George Onesiphorus, *Address to His Majesty's Justices of the Peace for the County of Gloucester, On the Administration and Practical Effects of the System of Prison Regulation Established in that County*, Gloucester, 1809

Paulson, Ronald, *Hogarth: His Life, Art, and Times* (2 vols), New Haven, Conn., Yale University Press, 1971

Phillips, Sir Richard, *A Letter to the Livery of London Relative to the Views of the Writer in Executing the Office of Sheriff*, 1808

Playfair, Giles, *The Punitive Obsession: An Unvarnished History of the English Prison System*, Gollancz, 1971

Plumb, John Harold, *England in the Eighteenth Century*, Harmondsworth, Penguin, 1950

Porter, Whitworth, *History of the Corps of Royal Engineers*, Chatham, The Institution of Royal Engineers, 1951

'Prison Matron, A' (attrib. to Robinson, Frederick W.), *Female Life in Prison*, 1864

Pugh, Ralph Bernard, *Imprisonment in Medieval England*, Cambridge University Press, 1968

Radzinowicz, Leon, *A History of English Criminal Law and its Administration from 1750* (4 vols), Stevens & Sons, 1948-

Radzinowicz, Leon, *Ideology and Crime*, Heinemann Educational, 1966

Ranken, William Bayne, *English Convicts Before and After their Discharge*, 1863

Reade, Charles, *It's Never Too Late to Mend*, Leipzig, Tauchnitz, 1856

Religious Tract Society, *Sarah Martin: The Prison Visitor of Yarmouth*, 1872

Rhodes, Gerald, *Public Sector Pensions*, Allen & Unwin, 1965

Roberts, David, *Victorian Origins of the Welfare State*, New Haven, Conn., Yale University Press, 1960

Rose, Gordon, *The Struggle for Penal Reform: The Howard League and its Predecessors*, Stevens & Sons, 1961

Rose, Gordon, *Schools for Young Offenders*, Tavistock, 1967

Rosenau, Helen, *Social Purpose in Architecture*, Studio Vista, 1970

Rothman, David Jay, *The Discovery of the Asylum*, Boston and Toronto, Little, Brown, 1971

Ruggles, Thomas, *The History of the Poor: Their Rights, Duties and the Laws Respecting Them. In a Series of Letters* (2 vols), 1793-4

Rumbelow, Donald, *I Spy Blue*, Macmillan, 1971

Russell, Rev. Whitworth, 'Abstracts of the "Statistics of Crime in England and Wales, from 1839 to 1843" ', *Journal of the Statistical Society of London* (1847), X, 38

Salgado, Gamini, *The Elizabethan Underworld*, Dent, 1977

Salt, Henry Stephens, *The Flogging Craze*, Allen & Unwin, 1916

Schulz, Maureen, 'The Development of the Grant System', in C.H. Wilson (ed.), *Essays on Local Government*, Oxford, Blackwell, 1948

Scott, Sir Walter, *Journal*, ed. J.G. Tait, Oliver & Boyd, 1941

'Scrutator', *Irish Fallacies and English Facts: Being an Appeal to the Common Sense of the British Public on the Subject of the Irish Convict System*, 1863

Scull, Andrew T., *Museums of Madness*, Allen Lane, 1979

Shaw, Alan George Lewers, *Convicts and the Colonies: A Study of Penal Transportation from Great Britain and Ireland to Australia and Other Parts of the British Empire*, Faber & Faber, 1966

Slice, Austin van der, 'Elizabethan Houses of Correction', *Journal of Criminal Law and Criminology* (1937), XXVII, p. 45

Smith, Ann Dorothea, *Women in Prison: A Study in Penal Methods*, Stevens & Sons, 1962

Smith, Paul, *Disraelian Conservatism and Social Reform*, Routledge & Kegan Paul, 1967

Smith, Thornton, 'The Irish Convict System: Why it has Succeeded', *Cornhill Magazine* (April 1861), III, pp. 409-32

Smith, Thornton, 'The English Convict System', *Cornhill Magazine* (June 1861), III, pp. 708-33

Smith, Thornton, 'The Convict Out in the World', *Cornhill Magazine* (August 1861), IV, pp. 229-50

Smith, William, MD, *State of the Gaols in London, Westminster and Borough of Southwark*, 1776

Society for the Improvement of Prison Discipline, *Third Report*, 1821

Southerton, Peter, *The Story of a Prison*, Reading, Osprey, 1975

Stanhope, Philip Henry, 5th Earl, *Notes of Conversations with the Duke of Wellington, 1831-51*, 1889

Stockdale, Eric, 'The Bedford Gaol that John Howard Knew', *Bedfordshire Magazine* (Summer 1973)

Stockdale, Eric, 'The Rise of Joshua Jebb, 1837-1850', *British Journal of Criminology* (1976), XVI, p. 164

Stockdale, Eric, *A Study of Bedford Prison, 1660-1877*, London and Chichester, Phillimore, 1977

Such, Augustus, *Remarks on Prison Discipline, and the Model Prison*, 1841

Sykes, Rev. N., 'The Church', in A.S. Turberville (ed.), *Johnson's England*, Oxford University Press, 1952

Tallack, William, *Penological and Preventive Principles*, Wertheimer, Lea & Co., 1889

Tawney, Richard Henry, *Religion and the Rise of Capitalism*, Harmondsworth, Penguin, 1966

Tawney, Richard Henry, and Power, Eileen, *Tudor Economic Documents*, Vol. II, Longmans, Green, 1924

Taylor, John, 'The Praise and Vertue of a Jayle and Jaylers', in *All the Workes of John Taylor the Water-Poet*, 1630

Thomas, James Edward, *The English Prison Officer Since 1850; A Study in Conflict* (International Library of Social Policy), Routledge & Kegan Paul, 1972

Thompson, Edward Palmer, *The Making of the English Working Class*, Harmondsworth, Penguin, 1968

Thompson, Edward Palmer, *Whigs and Hunters*, Allen Lane, 1975

Thomson, David, *England in the Nineteenth Century*, Harmondsworth, Penguin, 1950

Thwaites, William, *A Blue Book, Our Convicts; Their Riots and Their*

Causes, 1861

'Ticket-of-Leave-Man, A', *Convict Life; or Revelations Concerning Convicts and Convict Prisons*, 1879

Tobias, John Jacob, *Crime and Industrial Society in the Nineteenth Century*, Harmondsworth, Penguin, 1972

Tobias, John Jacob, *Nineteenth Century Crime: Prevention and Punishment*, Newton Abbot, David & Charles, 1972

Tobias, John Jacob, *Prince of Fences*, Valentine, Mitchell, 1974

Tomlinson, Margaret Heather, ' "Not an Instrument of Punishment": Prison Diet in the Mid-Nineteenth Century', *Journal of Consumer Studies and Home Economics* (1978), 2, pp. 15-26

Trevelyan, George Macauley, *English Social History*, Longmans, Green, 1944

Turner, Joseph Horsfall, *The Annals of Wakefield House of Correction*, Bradford, Harrison & Sons, 1904

Unwin, George, *Studies in Economic History: The Collected Papers of George Unwin*, Macmillan, 1927

Waddington, William, *Considerations on the Proper and Original Objects of the Royal Hospital of Bridewell: Addressed to the Governors*, 1798

Wakefield, Edward Gibbon, *Facts Relating to the Punishment of Death in the Metropolis*, 1832

Walker, Nigel, and McCabe, Sarah, *Crime and Insanity in England*, Edinburgh, University Press, 1968

Ward, Ned, *The London Spy, Compleat in Eighteen Parts*, 1700; Casanova Society, 1929 (Folio Society Edition, 1966)

Watson, John Steven, *The Reign of George III, 1760-1815*, Oxford University Press, 1960

Webb, Sidney, and Webb, Beatrice, *English Prisons Under Local Government*, Longmans, Green, 1932

Webb, Sidney, and Webb, Beatrice, *Methods of Social Study*, Longmans, Green, 1932

Webb, Sidney, and Webb, Beatrice, *English Poor Law History: The Old Poor Law*, Frank Cass, 1963

Webb, Sidney, and Webb, Beatrice, *The Parish and the County*, Frank Cass, 1963

Wedderburn, Alexander, *Observations on the State of the English Prisons, and the Means of Improving Them: Communicated to the Reverend Henry Zouch, a Justice of the Peace by the Rt. Hon. Lord Loughborough, New Lord High Chancellor of Great Britain*, 1793

Wesley, Rev. John, *The Journal of the Rev. John Wesley* . . . Edited by Nehemiah Curnock, assisted by Experts (8 vols), Robert Culley, 1909-16

Western, Charles Callis, *Remarks Upon Prison Discipline*, 1821

Whately, Richard, *Substance of a Speech on Transportation Delivered in the House of Lords, May 19th, 1840*, 1840

Whateley, Richard, *Thoughts on Secondary Punishment in a Letter to Earl Grey . . . to Which are Appended Two Articles on Transportation to New South Wales and on Secondary Punishments; and Some*

Observations on Colonization, 1832

Whiting, John Roger Scott, *Prison Reform in Gloucestershire 1776-1820*, Chichester, Phillimore, 1975

Williams, Basil, *The Whig Supremacy, 1714-1760*, Oxford University Press, 1962

Williams, Geraint L. (ed.), *John Stuart Mill on Politics and Society*, Fontana, 1976

Williams, Montague, *Leaves of a Life*, 1890

Woodward, Sir Ernest Llewellyn, *The Age of Reform 1815-1870*, Oxford University Press, 1962

Young, Agnes Freda, and Ashton, Elwyn Thomas, *British Social Work in the Nineteenth Century*, Routledge & Kegan Paul, 1956

Young, George Malcolm, *Victorian England: Portrait of an Age*, Oxford University Press, 1936

Journals, newspapers and works of reference

Annual Register
Bermuda Historical Quarterly
Civil Service Gazette
Cobbett's Parliamentary Register
Dictionary of National Biography
Encyclopaedia Britannica (1911 edition)
Fortnightly Review
English Reports
Gentleman's Magazine
Hansard
Illustrated London News
Journals of the House of Commons
Journal of the Statistical Society of London
Nineteenth Century
Pall Mall Gazette
Prison Service Journal
Quarterly Review
Reports of the Society for the Improvement of Prison Discipline
Statutes of the Realm (1810; reprinted 1963)
Sussex Advertiser
The Times
Victoria County History
Wellesley Index to Victorian Periodicals

Index

384, 425; his unpopularity in Treasury, 472 n. 16; mentioned, 189, 376, 396, 464, 470-1

Ducie, Lord, 112 n. 31

Duffy, I. P. H., 341 n. 46

Dunscombe, T. S. (MP for Finsbury): alleges ill-treatment on hulks, 200

Durham gaol, 322, 358-9

Eagle House Refuge (for female convicts), 427

Eccleshall debtors' gaol, see Staffordshire

Eden, Sir Frederick, 25 n. 10, 117 n. 43

Eden, William (later Lord Auckland): opposed to imprisonment, 84; and Penitentiary Act (19 Geo. III, c.74), 132 n. 96; mentioned, 83

Edinburgh prison, 270-1 n. 20

Edis, John (governor, Cambridge town gaol), 266 nn. 11, 13, 280 n. 50

education: chaplains' responsibility for, 409, 447; as crime preventative, 329-30 passim, 409-10; at Millbank Penitentiary, 148, 164 bis; and penal servitude, 409-11; trade training, 397 bis; mentioned, 473

Edward VI, 30

Elliot, Sir Gilbert (penitentiary supervisor), 108

emoluments (see also pensioning; salaries): of convict service, 461-7 passim; in local prisons, 290-2; of Millbank Penitentiary governor, 147 n. 46

enslavement, 26, 82 n. 18

escapes: consequences of, 263-4; from local prisons, 336

escort duties, see court duties

Essex: attempt to dismiss Springfield governor, 286-7 n. 72; books kept at Ilford gaol, 278; duties of governor of Ilford gaol, 268, 277 n. 39; Harwich franchise gaol, 292; new county gaol at Springfield (Chelmsford), 185 n. 51; pensioning of keeper of Halstead house of correction, 297; rebuilding at Springfield gaol, 254-5 n. 116; sexual misbehaviour at Springfield, 231-2 n. 46; Springfield governor defends emoluments, 291-2;

Springfield governor's complaints, 280-1 bis; Springfield governor's salary, 292; Springfield régime criticised, 208-9 n. 140; welfare work at Ilford gaol, 278 bis

Euryalus (hulk), 199

Evangelicals: influence of declines, 259; influence on social and penal policy, 78-80, 219-20

Evans, R.: on Pentonville, 186-7 n. 52, 239 n. 70; on 'tell-tale' clocks, 212 n. 147

Everest, G. (principal criminal clerk, Home Office), 378 bis

executions: and work of prisons, 274-5; mentioned, 143, 237, 274 n. 31, 321 n. 80, 336

executive discretion (see also remission): and allocation to Gloucester penitentiary, 101, 103; and allocation to Millbank Penitentiary, 139-40; Home Office view of, 392 n. 44; and penal servitude, 383-4; in prison management, 246; and release on licence, 419 n. 180; in separate and silent systems, 247; and transportation, 386; and whipping, 273 bis; mentioned, 390-2 passim

Eyles, John (warden of the Fleet), 295 bis

Falmouth town gaol, see Cornwall

Farnborough, Lord, 135 n. 2

fee-taking (see also finance): expands in eighteenth century, 52; incompatible with reformatory régime, 92; prohibited in gaols, 247-8; in public administration, 8-9; mentioned, 68 n. 69, 69, 86-7, 224, 233

Fennor, W.: on gaolers, 10 n. 45, 20

Field, Rev. John (chaplain, Reading gaol): on régime for debtors, 342; on workhouse offences, 239

Fielding, Henry: on difficulty of reforming prisons, 62; on maximum general deterrence, 60; on weakness of prison law, 66 n. 63; mentioned, 49, 55

finance (see also costs; fee-taking): Bentham's Panopticon proposals, 124-6; of Bridewell, 31-8 passim; of Bury St Edmunds house of correction, 40; case for national

INDEX

Hulme, George (governor, Appleby gaol): his career, 314

Huntingdon county gaol: attempted escape from, 284 n. 63; dispute concerning appointment of governor, 320-1; escape from, 263-4 n. 2; fluctuation in population of, 283; governor's pension at, 298 *bis*; resignation of governor, 310; staff leave granted at, 281-2; mentioned, 263-4 n. 2, 265 n. 6, 276 n. 37, 279 n. 47, 280 n. 51, 314 *bis*

hypocrisy: among prisoners, 164, 166 *bis*, 361 n. 156; and release on licence, 419 n. 180; among staff, 166

identification (of prisoners), 276, 327-8, 422-3

Ilchester gaol, *see* Somerset

Ilford gaol, *see* Essex

improvement commissions, 89

industrial schools, 333-8 *passim*

Ingram, William (governor, Devonport borough gaol), 314

insanity, *see* health

insolvency, *see* debtors

inspection: Bentham's scheme deficient in, 134 n. 99; at Bridewell, 35; chaplain's role in, 357; of convict prisons, 343-7; at Gloucester penitentiary, 126; independent internal inspection urged, 133; infrequent on Gibraltar, 395; of London prisons, 19; at Millbank Penitentiary, 146, 156-9; by public proposed, 124-5; by visiting justice, **285-7**

inspectorate (of prisons): its campaigns for closures, 367-74; and the Carnarvon Committee, 348 n. 86; clashes with Jebb, 181-7; convict governors appointed to, 445-6; differs over separate system, 175-6; duties of, 174-5; establishment of, 250-4; Home District primacy within, 171-2; and prison labour, 350-1; recommended qualities for, 170-1; salaries of, 171-2 n. 7; mentioned, **170-6**

Inspector-General of Military Prisons, 431-2

Ipswich house of correction (Christ's Hospital), 39-40

Irish convict system, 420, 441-3 *passim*

irons (*see also* 'scavenger's daughter'): as a means of extortion, 9-11; as precaution against escapes, 284 n. 63; as punishment, 361-2, 411; mentioned, 51

Ives, E. W.: on 'benefit of clergy', 3 n. 11

Ives, James (keeper, Southwark county gaol): on staff, 153; mentioned, 127 n. 80

Jackson, Sir Henry (MP for Coventry): on justices and sheriffs, 479 n. 46; on 1876 Prison Bill, 479

Jebb, Major-General Sir Joshua: appointed to Directorate of Convict Prisons, 216; appointed surveyor-general of prisons, 177-8; attacked by *Civil Service Gazette*, 435-6, 441; awarded KCB, 431; and Broadmoor Criminal Lunatic Asylum, 340; on prison building programme, 254-5 n. 116; clashes with inspectors of prisons, 181-7; on combining reformatory and punitive objectives, 347-8; Commissioner of Pentonville, 177; on convict labour, 396-7; on convict station, 388 n. 34; criticises ticket-of-leave system, 422 *ter*; is criticised, 438-58 *passim*; his death, 444; and discharged prisoners' aid societies, 424 *bis*; and Directorate of Convict Prisons, 431; draws on his Royal Engineers experience, 195; duties and influence of, 178, 318 n. 74; and English *versus* Irish convict system dispute, 441-3; and home discharge of convicts, 390-1; on hulks, 393; inspector-general of military prisons, 177; on intermediate sentences, 388 n. 29; on outcry against ticket-of-leave men, 420 n. 187; his patronage, 318; his penal philosophy and policy, 179-81; and pressure of inquiries, 444; on prison labour, 350; and the progressive-stage system, 361; and recommendations for posts, 460; on reformation as release criterion, 419 n. 180; on remission, 401; his refusal to appoint Du Cane to Directorate,

518

servitude, 384, 390-2, 400-3; and transportation, 195; mentioned, 336

Renzi, Rev. G. B. de (chaplain, Millbank convict prison): on chaplains' duties, 447

residence, staff, *see* housing

restraint harness, *see* strait-jacket

Retribution (hulk), 313 n. 64

revenue prisoners, 256

Reynolds, Sir Joshua, 72 n. 82

Rhodes, Gerald: on public pension schemes, 295 n. 12

Richmond, 3rd Duke of, 89-94

Richmond, 5th Duke of: corresponds with Jebb, 178 n. 32; on inspectorate of prisons, 171; resigns as Pentonville commissioner, 213-14 *bis*

Ridley, Bishop Nicholas, 28-9

Roberts, D.: on inspectorate of prisons, 171 *bis*

Roget, Peter Mark, 145 n. 38

Romilly, Sir Samuel: commends Paul and Becher, 112; and lunacy reform, 339; and penitentiaries, 111 *bis*; on policy during French wars, 110 n. 23; sponsors Bennet's Act, 247 n. 91

Romney Marsh liberty prison, *see* Kent

Rosebery Committee, 463

Rotch, Benjamin (Middlesex justice), 285 n. 67

Rothman, D.: on the history of the asylum, 23

Rowan, Sir Charles: on migration of criminals, 376

Royal Engineers: and Directorate of Convict Prisons, 431-2 *passim*; and the use of convict labour, 195; mentioned, 177 *bis*, 382

Royal Military Academy, 177

Ruggles, Thomas: on poor-law administration, 70

Ruggles-Brise, Sir Evelyn, 70 n. 75

rules and regulations: and 1865 Act, 379-80; Bentham rejects as method of administrative control, 124; code issued for local prisons, 255; for debtors, 342 *bis*; at Gloucester penitentiary, 101, 123; home secretary's powers over, 377-8; at Horsham county gaol, 90-1; at Norwich house of correction, 39-40; provided by Gilbert's Act,

93; at Southwell house of correction, 123

Russell, Sir Henry, 172 n. 10

Russell, Lord John (home secretary 1835-9): appoints nephew a prison inspector, 172 *bis*; proposes changes in transportation, 189-90; reluctantly approves Millbank Penitentiary appointment, 165-6; mentioned, 188

Russell, Rev. Whitworth (chaplain, Millbank Penitentiary, then inspector of prisons): appointed inspector, 171; his background, 172-3; clashes with Jebb, 181-7 *passim*; on criminal statistics, 264 n. 5; criticises employment of military, 315-16; his duties, 175; on governors, 267, 304; his inquiries at Carnarvon gaol, 171-2 n. 7, 252-3; his objections to public works, 196 *bis*; and pensioning of subordinate staff, 296-7 n. 16; and Pentonville, 176 n. 24; and 1839 Prisons Act, 245 n. 85; on religion at Reading gaol, 243 n. 82; and silent system, 246; on subordinate staff, 301; his suicide, 216-17 n. 166; on transportation, 194; urges demolition of Millbank, 210 *bis*; mentioned, 94, 164 *bis*, 165, 168, 171, 217, 228 n. 38, 252-4 *passim*, 269, 287, 318 n. 74, 353, 354, 374, 399-400 *passim*, 405, 407, 408

Rust, Benjamin, 314

Rust, James (visiting justice, Huntingdon county gaol): in dispute over appointment of governor, 320-1

Rutland, 473

Ryde, Henry (governor, Millbank Penitentiary): on 'talebearing', 159 n. 85

Ryder, Richard (home secretary 1809-12), 111 n. 29

Rylands, Peter (MP for Burnley): fears centralisation of police, 478; on civil influence of naval and military men, 478; on Nottingham corporation's petition, 480; queries savings of nationalisation, 476 *bis*

St Albans gaol, 368 n. 183

St Augustine's house of correction,